CONTENDING WITH ANTISEMITISM IN A RAPIDLY CHANGING POLITICAL CLIMATE

STUDIES IN ANTISEMITISM
Alvin H. Rosenfeld, editor

Edited by **Alvin H. Rosenfeld**

CONTENDING WITH ANTISEMITISM IN A RAPIDLY CHANGING POLITICAL CLIMATE

INDIANA UNIVERSITY PRESS

This book is a publication of

Indiana University Press
Office of Scholarly Publishing
Herman B Wells Library 350
1320 East 10th Street
Bloomington, Indiana 47405 USA

iupress.org

© 2021 by Indiana University Press
All rights reserved

No part of this book may be reproduced or utilized in any form or by any means, electronic or mechanical, including photocopying and recording, or by any information storage and retrieval system, without permission in writing from the publisher. The paper used in this publication meets the minimum requirements of the American National Standard for Information Sciences—Permanence of Paper for Printed Library Materials, ANSI Z39.48-1992.

Manufactured in the United States of America

Cataloging information is available from the Library of Congress.

ISBN 978-0-253-05811-9 (hardback)
ISBN 978-0-253-05812-6 (paperback)
ISBN 978-0-253-05814-0 (ebook)

First printing 2021

This book is dedicated, with gratitude and appreciation,
to

Dr. David Pfenninger,
who keenly understands the lethal character of antisemitism
and the threats it poses,
and also to the memory of
Louis Mervis
and
Gerald Paul,
cherished friends
and longtime supporters of the work
of Indiana University's
Borns Jewish Studies Program and
the Institute for the Study of Contemporary Antisemitism

CONTENTS

Foreword / *Dina Porat* — ix
Introduction / *Alvin H. Rosenfeld* — 1

I. The IHRA Definition of Antisemitism and Its Ramifications

1. The IHRA Definition and Its Critics / *Bernard Harrison and Lesley Klaff* — 9

2. Applying the IHRA Working Definition to the UN and Human Rights NGOs / *Gerald M. Steinberg* — 44

II. Intellectual and Ideological Currents of Antisemitism

3. Israel as a White Colonial-Settler State in Activist Social Science / *Balázs Berkovits* — 75

4. Traditionalism or the Perennial Philosophy: Religionism, Politics, and the New Right / *Mark Weitzman* — 96

5. Antisemitism on the Left: The Case of Jewish Voice for Peace / *Miriam F. Elman* — 113

III. Antisemitism on College and University Campuses

6. Contending with Antisemitism in Its Many Forms on American Campuses / *Kenneth Waltzer* — 137

7. In the Context of a Coarsened Climate: Campus Antisemitism and the Alt-Right, Alt-Lite, and Far Left / *Linda Maizels* — 158

8. Rethinking Campus Antisemitism in America and How to Address It / *Tammi Rossman-Benjamin* — 185

IV. The Global Reach of Antisemitism

9. Orchestrating Public Blindness in Contemporary France / *Daniel Dayan* — 211

10. Legislating and Distorting the History of the Holocaust:
The Polish Case / *Jan Grabowski*   231

11. The Changing Faces of European Antisemitism—the Hungarian Case:
Attitudes toward Jews in Viktor Orbán's Semiauthoritarian Regime /
János Gadó   249

12. Contradiction as Program: The German AfD between the Rejection
of the Memory of the Holocaust and a Self-Proclaimed Political
Home for Jews / *Marc Grimm*   267

13. A "Serious Attack on Jewish Life": Antisemitic Stereotypes in the
Public Debate about Ritual Male Circumcision in Germany in 2012 /
Dana Ionescu   287

14. What Role Does Antisemitism Play in Jeremy Corbyn's
Labour Party? / *Dave Rich*   313

15. Antisemitism and the Left in the UK and the Global Significance of
the Return of the "Jewish Question" / *Philip Spencer*   325

16. Rethinking the Role of Religion in the Arab-Israeli Conflict and Its
Reflection on Arab Antisemitic Discourse / *Esther Webman*   344

17. Can the European Institutions Combat Antisemitism Effectively? /
Michael Whine   367

Index   383

FOREWORD

Dina Porat

IN MARCH 2016, THE PRESIDENT OF INDIANA UNIVERSITY, Professor Michael McRobbie, received a letter from Juli Edelstein, the Speaker of the Israeli Knesset, or Parliament. It referred to a conference, "Anti-Zionism, Antisemitism, and the Dynamics of Delegitimization," which was about to take place on Indiana University's Bloomington campus.[1] "As the Speaker of the Israeli Knesset," Edelstein remarked, "I write to express my deep appreciation of your principled stand on these matters. . . . Your courageous position . . . is highly appreciated. . . . I would also like to express my appreciation to Indiana University for nurturing one of the world's leading research institutes for the study of antisemitism," referring to the Institute for the Study of Contemporary Antisemitism, founded and led by Professor Alvin H. Rosenfeld.

More words of appreciation were included in an additional letter, this one from Professor Judea Pearl, the father of Daniel Pearl. Addressed to the organizers of the conference and to the "distinguished scholars from across the globe" who would be participating in it, the letter acknowledged that "this conference is noble, timely and crucial" and concluded with this wish: "May the spirit of Daniel strengthen yours."[2] Daniel Pearl, a talented young Jewish journalist, was brutally murdered in 2002 in Pakistan.

President McRobbie also addressed the participants of the conference, emphasizing that antisemitic incidents of all kinds were on the rise around the world, including hate speech, the spread of neo-Nazi graffiti and other forms of verbal and written threats, the defacement of synagogues and Jewish cemeteries, and even acts of murderous terror. During the previous year, for instance, Jews were killed in Paris and Copenhagen. Referring pointedly to aggressive rhetoric spreading on American campuses, President McRobbie warned that "dangerous rhetoric often is the precursor of tragedy and must be unconditionally condemned before it can take root and spread."[3]

Among North American universities, in some of which anti-Zionism and antisemitic utterances and behavior have become a notable and disturbing presence, the Institute for the Study of Contemporary Antisemitism at Indiana University and the overall tolerant atmosphere of this university are a welcome oasis. The institute is the only one of its kind in the United

States (except for the Yale Program for the Study of Antisemitism, which works in a different way) and is seriously engaged in teaching and ongoing research on antisemitism. In addition, it stands out for the numerous high-level conferences it organizes, as well as for its many important publications brought out by Indiana University Press, including the leading scholarly journal in the field, *Studies in Antisemitism*.

The abovementioned 2016 conference was part of a large-scale and unique scholarly enterprise: over the last decade, the Institute for the Study of Contemporary Antisemitism has organized and hosted four major conferences at Indiana University. As its title indicated, the first of these, in 2011, was dedicated to examining "Resurgent Antisemitism—a Global Perspective." Then came "Deciphering the New Antisemitism" in 2014, followed by "Anti-Zionism, Antisemitism, and the Dynamics of Delegitimization" in 2016, and "Contending with Antisemitism in a Rapidly Changing Political Climate" in 2019. Each of these conferences was international in scope, bringing together over two hundred scholars from sixteen or seventeen countries. Each conference has also resulted in the publication of a major collection of carefully edited scholarly essays. All of these books have appeared with Indiana University Press and close to the dates of the conferences themselves: in 2013, 2015, and 2019, and, now, the present volume.

Remarkably, during this same time frame, the Indiana University institute has also helped organize and cohost with German colleagues three additional conferences on antisemitism in Berlin. Indiana scholars have also presented lectures on today's anti-Jewish animus on campuses and in communities throughout North America as well as in India, Israel, Austria, Belgium, France, Germany, Russia, and other places in Europe.

For all these scholars' expertise, dedication, and commitment, much remains to be done. Today's anti-Jewish hostility takes many forms and is not easy for any one group of scholars to address in a comprehensive way. Professor Rosenfeld's institute, for instance, leaves it to others to monitor daily events and focuses its work on clarifying the revival of emotionally charged accusations against Judaism and the Jews that date back centuries and have been newly reenergized in our own day. The Indiana scholars acknowledge that these myths are too deep-seated to be eradicated, "but by analyzing their origins and exposing them as myths, it may be possible to help people recognize this pathology for what it is and thereby mitigate some of its harmful effects."[4] In other words, the goals that the institute sets for itself and that shape its conferences, lectures, and publications are both scholarly (analyzing the origins of anti-Jewish myths and exposing them as such) and practical (opening people's eyes to seeing these myths for what they really are, and—hopefully—working with others to devise ways to restrain them).

Of course, each of the conferences has had its specific goals, as defined by its particular topic. The first aimed to offer a global perspective on resurgent antisemitism as it looked in 2011, ten years after the infamous Durban conference, which set the tone and prepared the ground for a new era of virulent and violent antisemitism. The second sought to decipher the "new antisemitism," a term that encompasses the changes in anti-Jewish thinking and behavior made manifest at Durban and that were present in 2014: more violence, extensive use of social media, new expressions of Muslim anti-Jewish propaganda and a flow of funds to activate the scene, and the emergence of western Europe as the center of aggressively hostile events. The third Indiana University conference, in 2016, was dedicated to the relationship between antisemitism and anti-Zionism—an issue that has often taken center stage worldwide—and to defining the fine line between these two as well as understanding the academic theories and political trends that nourish anti-Zionism within a wider context. The fourth and most recent conference, in 2019, was anchored in the rapidly changing political climate: the triangle made up of the strengthening far right due in large part to responses to the immigration problem and also to the rise of fanatical white nationalist and white supremacist groups; the far left and anti-Zionist left and their impact on both domestic and international arenas, as exemplified by the Labour Party in the United Kingdom; and, on occasion, positions acquired by extreme Muslim activists in domestic and international institutes.

Participants in the Indiana conferences have come from numerous countries, ranging from India to Canada and from eastern Europe to Latin America. Some have participated in two or even three of the conferences, creating a new and important fraternity of scholars. The unusually hospitable setting and generous handling of these events by the conference organizers have unfailingly offered fertile ground for serious discussion among experts, for sharing knowledge, and for establishing future contacts and defining goals for common work.

The keynote speakers of the four conferences also deserve mention. Hannah Rosenthal and Ira Forman, who served as the first and the second State Department special envoys to monitor and combat antisemitism (appointed during President Obama's term), brought to the conferences their perspectives on the state of the matter worldwide during their period

xii | Foreword

of service. Professor Irwin Cotler, a world-renowned scholar of international law, former Canadian minister of justice, and a staunch fighter against any kind of discrimination and bigotry, came third, speaking about the use of universal public values by anti-Zionist and anti-Jewish activists to launder the delegitimization of the Jewish people and its state. And then came Katharina von Schnurbein, appointed in 2015 as the first European Commission coordinator on combating antisemitism, now acclaimed for her diligent and persistent work in the field. She spoke about the European Union and the fight against antisemitism, a fight in which she has led a number of battles, such as the struggle for the adoption of the working definition of antisemitism and the blocking of antisemitic expressions by social media servers.

All four keynote speakers were and are top figures in the field. The fact that they traveled to Bloomington in the midst of their many commitments attests to the importance they attributed to these scholarly gatherings.

These impressive conferences and the volumes published in their wake are to the credit of Professor Rosenfeld, who founded the Borns Jewish Studies Program at Indiana University in 1973. After having served as its director for thirty years, he then founded the Institute for the Study of Contemporary Antisemitism in 2009 and serves as its director to this day. He has written prolifically on American poetry, Jewish literature, and the Holocaust and its cultural impact, and in recent years he has published a number of incisive articles on contemporary antisemitism, some of which have evoked intense debate. A member of many national and international committees and the recipient of numerous prestigious awards, he has made the Institute for the Study of Contemporary Antisemitism an active focal point since its inception for publishing, teaching, research, and the convening of scholars in all related fields.

With a mind toward the future continuation of the enterprise, Professor Rosenfeld has encouraged an excellent young German scholar, Dr. Guenther Jikeli, to locate his own work in the field in Bloomington. Dr. Jikeli now holds the Erna B. Rosenfeld Professorship at the Institute for the Study of Contemporary Antisemitism.

* * *

The present volume originates in the March 2019 conference, "Contending with Antisemitism in a Rapidly Changing Political Climate." Some sixty scholars from more than fifteen countries came to Bloomington for this conference, presented papers, and participated in the lively discussions.

These numbers attest to the sense of urgency felt by many people, Jews and non-Jews alike, in 2018 and the first quarter of 2019.

Let us outline the main developments in 2018 in order to lay the background for that sense of common concern for the well-being of Jews everywhere that brought together so many scholars for almost a full week of serious reflection on the growing threats of antisemitism. "*Ça suffit!*" ("That's enough!"), called French Jews, whose monitoring agency confirmed the findings of their Ministry of the Interior, which indicated that not a day has gone by without an antisemitic manifestation. These incidents increased in number and intensity worldwide as former taboos were broken and ugly slogans such as "Jews to the gas!" and "Death to the Zionists!" were heard more and more often. These unrestrained verbal assaults seemed to reflect the notion that it is the very existence of Jews, Jewish communities, and a Jewish state that arouses hostility. The number of major violent cases during this period increased by 13 percent, and the uncountable number of nonviolent incidents, most notably on social media sites, resulted in the uneasy feeling that antisemitism is becoming normalized, mainstreaming into everyday life. In the face of this reality, Jews have started to question their association with places and societies they have lived in for a long time, sometimes centuries. Many worried that they were gradually turning into outsiders, no longer welcome in their own countries. Several large-scope surveys corroborated and highlighted the perceptions expressed by Jews, warning that the real situation is much worse, with as many as 75 percent of cases not even reported.

The reasons for this situation vary and include growing ignorance, especially among younger generations, regarding World War II and its consequences. Many know little, if anything, about Nazi ideology and the Holocaust or about the complex reality in the Middle East. In addition, classical antisemitism, deeply rooted in European Christian culture, reappears in times of crisis. As a result, the term *Jew* has turned or returned into a pejorative epithet in many countries, and in some places, contemporary rhetoric has readily accommodated post-Holocaust images of the Jew as greedy (for financial compensation), foreign, guilty of double loyalty, ego centered, tribalistic, power seeking, and money thirsty. Add to this an intensification of anti-Zionism, often drawing on antisemitic motifs. Despite the absence of serious military confrontations between Israel and its neighbors in Gaza and elsewhere for almost five years, the "stereotypes of classical Judeophobia are projected onto the Jewish state . . . and Israel-related hate is becoming a politically correct form of antisemitism."[5]

These explanations are rooted in history and culture, yet the contemporary political arena is no less fertile a ground for the growth of antisemitism, as Indiana University's fourth conference stressed. Scholars gathered there recognized and analyzed the crisis of democracies, the traditional bastion of human and minority rights, which intensified in 2018 and the beginning of 2019; the strengthening of right-wing political parties; newly assertive national postcommunist identity quests in eastern Europe; tensions created by the influx of large numbers of immigrants in the countries of central and western Europe, where the far right feeds on fears and economic worries; the political turmoil in the United Kingdom owing to Brexit, which has polarized British society and politics; the deepening social and economic crisis in France, coupled with a strong Muslim presence there and a vocal right-wing party; the growing rift between the two major political parties in the United States; and open opposition to Angela Merkel's immigration policy—all of these developments are closely connected to the rise of antisemitism.[6]

In this generally gloomy picture, there have also been some positive developments. First and foremost is the growing awareness among governmental agencies that they are responsible for the well-being and security of their Jewish citizens and for confronting the situation in order to prevent further deterioration. Leaders in various countries have been approached and urged to act decisively. Consequently, workshops and conferences, together with individual and media appeals, have become the order of the day, sometimes concluding with serious and hopefully effective declarations and promises. The adoption of the working definition of antisemitism has gained significant ground, and a catalog of clearly stated policies and the means to fight antisemitism was published and distributed worldwide.[7] Some legal steps, especially against the boycotts, divestment, and sanctions (BDS) movements and for regulations aimed at limiting the proliferation of antisemitic expressions on social media, have proved successful.

Thus, Indiana University's 2019 conference took a hard look at the roots of today's antisemitism and documented and analyzed the many worrying and few comforting political developments that were apparent during the period it covered. Neither the scholarly participants nor the conference organizers fostered the illusion that their efforts would quickly or radically change the situation. At the same, the publication of the conference's deliberations is bound to bring greater knowledge of contemporary antisemitism to more people. And with knowledge, there is hope for the kind of preventative action necessary to put checks on today's growing hostility. May that be our reward.

Notes

1. Institute for the Study of Contemporary Antisemitism (ISCA), *Anti-Zionism, Antisemitism, and the Dynamics of Delegitimization: An International Scholars Conference, April 2-6, 2016*, (Bloomington: Indiana University, 2016), 4–5, https://isca.indiana.edu/documents/isca-conference-programs/2016-full-conference-booklet-updated-2017.pdf.
2. ISCA, *Anti-Zionism, Antisemitism*, 6.
3. ISCA, 3.
4. ISCA, 3.
5. Monika Schwartz-Friesel, "The Persistence of European Antisemitism," BESA Center Perspective Paper no. 1067, January 18, 2019.
6. For a full picture of data, reasons, and Jewish perceptions by country, see Kantor Center for the Study of Contemporary European Jewry, *Antisemitism Worldwide—2018—General Analysis*, ed. Esther Webman and Talia Naamat (Tel Aviv: Tel Aviv University, published with the European Jewish Congress, 2018), 150.
7. A. Lange, A. Muzicant, D. Porat, L. H. Schiffman, and M. Weitzman, *An End to Antisemitism! A Catalogue of Policies to Combat Antisemitism* (Vienna: European Jewish Congress, 2018), 146.

DINA PORAT is head of the Kantor Center for the Study of Contemporary European Jewry at Tel Aviv University and chief historian of Yad Vashem. She was awarded prizes for some of her many publications, including the National Jewish Book Award for her biography of Abba Kovner and the Bahat Prize for her new book on postwar attempts to take revenge on the Germans. She is also the recipient of Tel Aviv University's Faculty of Humanities award for best teacher (2004) and the Raoul Wallenberg Medal (2012) and is on *Marker* magazine's list of the fifty leading Israeli scholars (2013) as well as the *Forbes* 2018 list of the fifty leading women in Israel. Professor Porat served as an expert on the Israeli Foreign Ministry delegations to UN world conferences and as the academic advisor of the International Task Force on Holocaust Education, Remembrance, and Research (now IHRA). A Festschrift in her honor, *Holocaust and Antisemitism: Research and Published Discourse*, was published in 2015.

CONTENDING WITH ANTISEMITISM IN A RAPIDLY CHANGING POLITICAL CLIMATE

Introduction

Alvin H. Rosenfeld

> Europe is in the grip of a rage that threatens to destroy everything it stands for, but which it does not understand. That rage comes from the far Left and the far Right, from Muslims and Christians, from town and country. It is a ghost from the past and a harbinger of the future. It is antisemitism. . . . Unless it is exorcized, it will destroy us.[1]

DANIEL JOHNSON, THE BRITISH HISTORIAN QUOTED ABOVE, ISSUED his warning about the return of ghosts from the past in February 2019, and he had Europe chiefly in mind. He had every reason to speak out as he did, for anti-Jewish incidents on the continent have been increasing in both number and lethal effect since the turn of the millennium. In Belgium, France, Germany, Italy, the Netherlands, Poland, the United Kingdom, and other countries, assaults on Jews have now become common. This is a distressing but not surprising fact, for reputable surveys of public opinion in European countries, including the Anti-Defamation League's Global 100 survey,[2] reveal that one-quarter of Europeans hold attitudes hostile to Jews. In some of these countries, Poland and Ukraine in particular, the figures are closer to 50 percent of the population.

Attitudes in the United States are better than in Europe, but murderous attacks on Jews in synagogues in Pittsburgh, Pennsylvania, and Poway, California, in 2018 and 2019, plus ongoing assaults on Jews and Jewish institutions in New York City and elsewhere, show that America is hardly immune to the violent expression of today's anti-Jewish passions. The country has never been altogether free of antisemitic incidents, but the latter seem to be increasing. The FBI's November 2019 report on hate crimes in the United States points to 1,617 victims of such crimes in America in 2018, of which some 57 percent were motivated by anti-Jewish bias. In Brooklyn alone, there were at least ninety-three incidents of anti-Jewish violence in 2018. And most informed observers believe that these figures are probably low, for many of these crimes are unreported or underreported.

The worrisome fact is that antisemitism, quiescent for a time after the persecution and mass murder of the Jews during the Nazi period, has reawakened energetically in our own day and now exists on a global scale. Moreover, it shows no signs of abating. It is therefore imperative that we understand its most serious contemporary manifestations and devise ways to contend with the threats they pose currently and are likely to present in the immediate future. The chapters of this book have been written in pursuit of these goals, focusing particularly on the rise of hostility toward Jews in a rapidly changing political climate.

The democratic values that took hold in many countries in the decades after the end of World War II are under threat today from extreme movements within the political right, the political left, and political Islam (or Islamism). The rise of populism, nativism, nationalism, authoritarianism, theocratic extremism, and historical revisionism suggests that we have entered a new and highly fraught historical moment. Far from being firmly and permanently established, the acclaimed virtues of life in the free and open societies of the democratic West and other parts of the world now face serious challenges.

At such a time, and often in the name of high ideals, ideological movements of various kinds seek to win a new and more prominent place in intellectual, political, and social life. Some of these movements shape aggressively hostile attitudes toward people considered alien, suspicious, undesirable, and unwanted. Jews have historically been targeted in such a way, and, with the resurgence of antisemitism in recent years, they are so once again.

A major aim of this book is to examine today's antisemitism against a backdrop of rising nationalism and illiberalism on the right, new forms of intolerance and anti-liberal movements on the left, and militant deeds and demands on the part of political Islam. In addition to clarifying the role that antisemitism plays within the framework of these developments, this book seeks to formulate ways to effectively contend with the most threatening manifestations of anti-Jewish hostility in our day and in the period ahead.

The authors represented in the following pages were part of a group of sixty-five scholars from fifteen countries who met at Indiana University for four days of intensive discussion on the social, political, and ideological forces that advance present-day anti-Jewish hatreds at their most widespread and intense. Under the auspices of Indiana University's Institute for the Study of Contemporary Antisemitism, they participated in a major international scholars' conference, "Contending with Antisemitism in a Rapidly Changing Political Climate," convened on the university's

Bloomington campus from March 23 to 27, 2019. It was the institute's fourth major conference in eight years and brought fresh and rigorous thinking to some of the most pressing issues of our day. These issues included the ramifications of defining antisemitism, the intellectual and ideological currents of present-day anti-Jewish hostility, the growing presence of such animosity on university campuses, and the international reach of contemporary Jew hatred.

These and related questions are explored in depth in the chapters of this book. All are revised and edited versions of a selection of the more than forty papers presented at the March 2019 conference.

I thank the conference participants for their dedication to thoughtfully and energetically engaging with the difficult subject matter before us. Their insights and ideas, developed over the course of our deliberations and now presented in the pages of this book, should help readers better understand the multifaceted character of today's antisemitism and the urgency of finding ways to effectively counter it.

Special thanks go to Katharina von Schnurbein, the European Commission coordinator on combating antisemitism, who came to Bloomington from Belgium to offer the conference's keynote address, "The European Union and the Fight against Antisemitism." Her well-attended public presentation set the tone and direction for much of what followed.

I also wish to thank Doron Ben-Atar, Bruno Chaouat, Günther Jikeli, and Elhanan Yakira for serving on the conference's academic advisory committee. Their contributions were crucial to the conceptualization of the conference's theme and the selection of speakers.

I am particularly grateful to Bethany Braley-Romashov, who assisted me in organizing the conference and looked after its many logistical details. To host an international gathering of this size, length, and complexity is a large undertaking, and Bethany carried it out successfully from start to finish. She did so in the most collegial of ways and was a pleasure to work with. The same can be said for Melissa Deckard, Melissa Hunt, Tracy Richardson, and Günther Jikeli, all of whom likewise proved to be of substantial assistance.

Janet Rabinowitch read and carefully edited many of the book's chapters in her typically gracious and cooperative spirit. Her editorial skills, honed over many years, are of the highest order, and I am enormously grateful for her contribution to this volume's clarity and coherence. I likewise am grateful to Bethany Braley-Romashov, who also had a major hand in editing the papers that became the chapters of this book and prepared the manuscript for publication. Her work as my research assistant over the course of an especially busy year was invaluable.

My deepest gratitude goes to the following friends, colleagues, and benefactors, without whose support this book and the conference that preceded it would not have been possible: the Bodman Foundation, Robert and Sandra Borns, Glick Philanthropies, Ted Cohn, David and Suzanne Pfenninger, Jay and Marsha Glazer, Leslie and Kate Lenkowsky, the Office of the Provost of Indiana University, Dorit and Gerald Paul, Reid and Laurie Klion, Stephen and Marlene Calderon, Sheldon and Jody Hirst, Tom Kramer, and Mary Hunter.

I also thank the following Indiana University departments, programs, and offices, which, as conference cosponsors, offered their encouragement and support: Borns Jewish Studies Program, College of Arts and Sciences, Indiana University European Gateway, Institute for European Studies, Office of the Provost, Polish Studies Center, Indiana University Press, Hutton Honors College, Islamic Studies Program, Near Eastern Languages and Cultures, Office of the Vice President for International Affairs, Russian and East European Institute, and the Hamilton Lugar School of Global and International Studies.

Thanks go to Kenneth Waltzer and the Academic Engagement Network as well for the award of a microgrant for the publication of this volume.

The study of antisemitism can be a disheartening endeavor, and we were fortunate at the end of a long and demanding conference to have our spirits lifted by a lively concert of Jewish music and dance given by Svetla Vladeva, Lauren Bernovsky, Tomas Lozano, and Leah Savion. It is a pleasure to thank them for their rich and most welcome contribution to our work.

Finally, I am most grateful to President Michael McRobbie and Provost Lauren Robel for their ongoing support of the work of the Institute for the Study of Contemporary Antisemitism. Indiana University is one of only two institutions of higher learning in the United States that house a research institute of this kind. It is a privilege to be a faculty member at a university whose administrative leadership is as principled and supportive of the initiatives that the Institute for the Study of Contemporary Antisemitism undertakes as these distinguished colleagues are. I feel immensely fortunate to have worked with them over these many years.

* * *

Shortly before this book went to press, news reached us that one of our contributors, Esther Webman, of Tel Aviv University, had suddenly died. An esteemed scholar and an exceptionally warm and caring person, she was a treasured colleague and added greatly to our understanding of the sources of antisemitism in parts of the Muslim world. Her chapter in this volume is one of her last contributions to scholarship on this subject. We are honored to include it in these pages.

May her memory be a blessing.

Notes

1. Daniel Johnson, "The Spectre of Anti-Semitism Threatens to Destroy Europe," *TheArticle*, February 18, 2019, https://www.thearticle.com/the-spectre-of-anti-semitism-threatens-to-destroy-europe/.

2. Survey results, ADL/Global 100, accessed January 19, 2021, https://global100.adl.org/map.

ALVIN H. ROSENFELD holds the Irving M. Glazer Chair in Jewish Studies at Indiana University and serves as Founding Director of the university's Institute for the Study of Contemporary Antisemitism. Previously, he created and for thirty years directed Indiana University's Borns Jewish Studies Program. He is author of numerous books and articles on the Holocaust, antisemitism, and Jewish literature, including *A Double Dying: Reflections on Holocaust Literature*, *Imagining Hitler*, and *The End of the Holocaust*. He is editor of *Resurgent Antisemitism: Global Perspectives*, *Deciphering the New Antisemitism*, and *Anti-Zionism and Antisemitism: The Dynamics of Delegitimization*, among other works. In 2018, Indiana University awarded him the President's Medal, the university's highest award, in recognition of his many distinguished contributions to scholarship and leadership.

I. THE IHRA DEFINITION OF ANTISEMITISM AND ITS RAMIFICATIONS

1

The IHRA Definition and Its Critics

Bernard Harrison | Lesley Klaff

Introduction

In May 2016, the International Holocaust Remembrance Alliance (IHRA) adopted a "non-legally binding working definition" of antisemitism. In October of that year, the British House of Commons Select Committee on Home Affairs published a report entitled "Anti-Semitism in the UK." This report recommended the adoption of the IHRA definition, subject to two caveats that the committee considered necessary in the interests of free speech:

> C_1: It is not anti-Semitic to criticise the government of Israel, without additional evidence to suggest anti-Semitic intent.
>
> C_2: It is not anti-Semitic to hold the Israeli government to the same standards as other liberal democracies, or to take a particular interest in the Israeli government's policies or actions, without additional evidence to suggest anti-Semitic intent.

In a published response, the government of the day adopted the definition but considered the exclusion of "criticism of Israel similar to that levelled against any other country," already stated in the definition itself, to provide a sufficient safeguard for freedom of speech. According to a statement from the prime minister's office at the time, the intention of adopting the definition was to "ensure that culprits will not be able to get away with being anti-semitic because the term is ill-defined, or because different organizations or bodies have different interpretations of it."[1]

In 2017 and 2018, the opposition Labour Party, under its new hard-left leader Jeremy Corbyn, found itself widely accused of antisemitism and was placed under considerable pressure to adopt the definition. The National Executive Committee finally did this in September 2018 but only subject to a caveat that its adoption would in no way constrain criticism of Israel.[2]

The years 2017 and 2018 also saw the publication of a series of critical articles attacking the definition as obscure, unfair, and harmful in the practical effects to be feared from its wide adoption. These included two extended, carefully argued opinions sought by Palestinian-supporting nongovernmental organizations from two senior British lawyers specializing in human rights law Hugh Tomlinson, QC,[3] and Geoffrey Robertson, QC.[4] The conclusions of both are supported in an article by a third distinguished legal authority, Sir Stephen Sedley, a former Court of Appeal judge (1999–2011) and currently a visiting professor at the University of Oxford,[5] and finally (for the moment) in a full-dress scholarly study by Rebecca Ruth Gould, a professor of Islamic and comparative literature at the University of Birmingham.[6]

In general, these criticisms focus on two alleged defects of the IHRA definition: first, that it fails to provide any legally effective definition of antisemitism and, among other things, fails to show that several of the examples it offers are actually examples of antisemitism; and second, that, in consequence of that alleged failure, any attempt to apply the definition as a means of restraining supposedly antisemitic speech or action must pose grave dangers to freedom of speech.

The object of the present paper—whose authors are, respectively, a non-Jewish philosopher and a Jewish academic lawyer—is to examine the validity of these two claims. Our conclusions are as follows:

1. The first of these charges rests wholly on the presence of minor flaws of drafting in the wording of the IHRA definition; these flaws would be easily rectified by, for instance, the addition of supplementary elucidation.
2. All of the examples offered by the IHRA definition correctly identify types or instances of antisemitism.
3. Provided one is careful to distinguish, as a matter both of moral common sense and of common equity, between criticism and defamation, and in the latter case, between defaming Israel and by so doing defaming Jews or the Jewish community, the IHRA definition, suitably accompanied by an explanatory note, can easily be shown to offer no obstacle whatsoever, either to the exercise of freedom of speech or to criticism of Israel.

The Definition

The IHRA definition is a version of the international working definition, or the EUMC definition. This was originally published in January 2005 by the Fundamental Rights Agency (FRA) of the European Union, then known as the European Union Monitoring Centre on Racism and Xenophobia (EUMC). It differed from the multitude of previous definitions, for the most part formulated by individual scholars and writers, by having emerged from lengthy discussion by teams of scholars, government officials, and representatives of community and civil rights organizations. No doubt because of this, the definition broke new ground in recognizing for the first time that antisemitism "could also target the State of Israel, conceived as a Jewish collectivity."[7]

In 2013, the FRA quietly removed the working definition from its website during a remodeling of the site. Under pressure from Jewish organizations, the FRA's spokesperson at the time, Blanca Tapia, dodged the issue, emphasizing that the working definition had never been sanctioned within the European Union. With questionable logic and contrary to earlier declarations by the FRA of the urgent practical need for such a definition, her statement maintained that "the agency does not need to develop its own definition of anti-Semitism in order to research these issues."[8]

Despite this, the working definition has been enormously influential. Versions of it have been adopted by the US Department of State, the US Commission on Civil Rights, the Organization for Security and Co-operation in Europe, and other agencies. At its conference in Ottawa on November 7–9, 2010, the Inter-parliamentary Coalition for Combating Antisemitism (an international body composed of parliamentarians of many countries) urged universities to "use the EUMC Working Definition of Antisemitism as a basis for education, training and orientation."[9] In November 2016, Senators Bob Casey and Tim Scott introduced and the Senate passed the Anti-Semitism Awareness Act, a bipartisan bill aimed specifically at combating campus antisemitism, whose effective clauses are also based closely on the international working definition.

All versions of the international definition share the same format. Each begins with a formula, essentially unchanged from the EUMC version, intended to establish the nature of antisemitism—to say what antisemitism is. In the IHRA version, this reads, "Antisemitism is a certain perception of Jews, which may be expressed as hatred toward Jews. Rhetorical and physical manifestations of antisemitism are directed toward Jewish or non-Jewish individuals and/or their property, toward Jewish community institutions and religious facilities." The importance attached to the above statement is often indicated by enclosing it on the page in a printed box. This is followed by a brief elucidation of the above and by a series of examples, which, it is proposed, "may serve as illustrations." The elucidation reads,

> Manifestations might include the targeting of the state of Israel conceived as a Jewish collectivity. However, criticism of Israel similar to that levelled against any other country cannot be regarded as antisemitic. Antisemitism frequently charges Jews with conspiring to harm humanity, and it is often used to blame Jews for "why things go wrong." It is expressed in speech, writing, visual forms and action, and employs sinister stereotypes and negative character traits. Contemporary examples of antisemitism in public life, the media, schools, the workplace and in the religious sphere could, taking into account the overall context, include, but are not limited to:

The list of "contemporary examples" then follows. It includes the following (numbers added):

1. Calling for, aiding, or justifying the killing or harming of Jews in the name of a radical ideology, or an extremist view of religion.
2. Making mendacious, dehumanising, demonizing, or stereotypical allegations about Jews as such, or the power of Jews as collective—such as, especially but not exclusively, the myth about a world Jewish conspiracy or of Jews controlling the media, economy, government or other societal institutions.
3. Accusing Jews as a people of being responsible for real or imagined wrongdoing committed by a single Jewish person or group, or even for acts committed by non-Jews.
4. Denying the fact, scope, mechanisms (e.g. gas chambers) or intentionality of the genocide of the Jewish people at the hands of national socialist Germany and its supporters and accomplices during World War II (the Holocaust).
5. Accusing the Jews as a people, or Israel as a state, of inventing or exaggerating the Holocaust.
6. Accusing Jewish citizens of being more loyal to Israel, or to the alleged priorities of Jews worldwide, than to the interests of their own nations.
7. Denying the Jewish people their right to self-determination, e.g., by claiming that the existence of a State of Israel is a racist endeavor.
8. Applying double standards by requiring of it [Israel] a behavior not expected or demanded of any other democratic nation.
9. Using the symbols and images associated with classical antisemitism (e.g., claims of Jews killing Jesus or blood libel) to characterise Israel or Israelis.
10. Drawing comparisons of contemporary Israeli policy to that of the Nazis.
11. Holding Jews collectively responsible for actions of the state of Israel.

Objections to the IHRA Definition

Objection 1: The Definition as a Legal Tool

Tomlinson, in his advice to Free Speech on Israel, Independent Jewish Voices, Jews for Justice for Palestine, and the Palestine Solidarity Campaign, is primarily concerned with exposing the shortcomings, as he sees it, of the IHRA definition as a "legal tool," a project in which he is joined in part by Robertson in his advice to the Palestine Return Centre. It perhaps therefore deserves emphasis that the definition is not a part of any law or in any way legally binding. Nor does it even pretend to offer a rigorous definition of the term *antisemitism* or *antisemitic*. The definition was designed merely to provide guidelines for judging whether, in a given context, an act or utterance is antisemitic—hence the name "*working* definition." A decision still has to be made, on any given set of facts, whether something is antisemitic or not. The definition is intended to provide a guide to that decision, not a means of evading it.

No doubt the reply of both Tomlinson and Robertson to these objections would be that although the definition neither constitutes in itself a legal instrument nor is legally enforceable, its adoption by government agencies and others might have legal consequences in which the wording of the definition might play a decisive role. It is perhaps for such reasons that both stress the obscurity and imprecision, as they see it, of the opening formula of the IHRA definition. Tomlinson finds the language of the definition "vague and unclear" in ways that make it "very difficult to use as a [presumably legal] 'tool.'... These problems of language come to a head in the definition's fundamental characterisation of the *nature* of antisemitism, as '*a certain perception of Jews, which may be expressed as hatred towards Jews*'" [our italics]. The word *may*, he suggests, is confusing, since if understood in its usual sense of possibility it suggests that while it is possible that the "perception of Jews" that supposedly constitutes antisemitism may be expressed as hatred of Jews, it is also possible that it may be expressed in other ways that the IHRA definition leaves entirely unspecified.

The very least that is needed to clarify matters, Tomlinson continues, is to reformulate the first sentence to read, "Antisemitism is a particular attitude towards Jews, which is expressed as hatred toward Jews." But even thus amended, Tomlinson argues, the definition remains obviously unsatisfactory in general terms: "The apparent confining of antisemitism to an attitude which is 'expressed' as a hatred of Jews seems too narrow and not to capture conduct which, though not *expressed* as hatred of Jews is clearly a manifestation of antisemitism. It does not, for instance, include discriminatory social and institutional practices."[10] This last point is echoed by Robertson, who points out that "hatred is a very strong word" that "falls short of capturing those who express only hostility or prejudice, or who practice discrimination":

> "I don't like Jews and never employ them, but I don't hate them."—this speaker is anti-Semitic, but it does not seem included in this definition. Similarly, "I am prejudiced against Jews because they are not 'one of us' and their religious practices are ridiculous, but I don't hate them." Or "I think we should deport all Jews to Israel, because they would be happy there. It would be in their own interests—I certainly don't hate them, I just think they don't fit in here in England." Under the IHRA definition, these anti-Semitic comments would not be deemed "anti-Semitic." This consideration, above all others, convinces me that the definition is not fit for purpose, or any purpose that relies upon it to identify anti-Semitism accurately.[11]

According to both Tomlinson and Robertson, the obscurity of the opening clauses of the IHRA definition extends to the identification as antisemitic of at least some of the eleven examples offered—but not, it must be said, to all eleven. Robertson finds examples 1, 3, 4, 5, 9, and 11 "unexceptionable," or virtually so, as offering instances of antisemitism. But as far as the remaining five examples are concerned, including all those explicitly mentioning Israel, Robertson's view is that while conduct covered by any of them could amount to antisemitism, it need not necessarily do so.

Tomlinson, similarly, argues that a number of types of act widely criticized as antisemitic could not be properly described as antisemitic by the criteria established by the international definition. He opines that if a university or public authority were to ban an event on such grounds, justifying it by appeal to the IHRA definition but without providing such further evidence, the ban would be unlawful. The examples he suggests include the following:

- Describing Israel as a state enacting policies of apartheid.
- Describing Israel as a state practising settler colonialism.
- Describing the establishment of the State of Israel, and the actions associated with it, as illegal or illegitimate.
- Campaigning for policies of boycott, divestment or sanctions against Israel, Israeli companies or international companies complicit in violation of Palestinian human rights (unless the campaigner was also calling for similar actions against other states).
- Stating that the State of Israel and its defenders "use" the Holocaust to chill debate on Israel's own behaviour towards Palestinians.[12]

The chief difficulty identified by Tomlinson as obstructing appeals to the IHRA definition to justify describing this or that kind of conduct as antisemitic is that the initial identification of antisemitism as a form of hatred necessarily constrains the legal interpretation of the examples offered in the remainder of the definition: "These examples must be read in the light of the definition itself, and cannot either expand or restrict its scope. All of them must be regarded as examples of activity which can properly be regarded as manifesting 'hatred of Jews.'"[13] Thus, an accusation of the type cited in example 6—that Jews are more loyal to Israel than to their nation of citizenship—could be classed as antisemitic, according to the terms of the definition, only if it could be shown to be motivated by hatred of Jews. If motivated by "a reasonable belief" that the actions of a particular Jewish citizen or group had indicated such a shift of loyalties, the accusation would not be antisemitic.

Robertson makes essentially the same point: "It must be said that all eleven examples are of conduct that 'could' amount to anti-Semitism, so long as the core definition is applied, namely that they express hatred toward Jewish people *as a race* [our italics]. . . . If the extended definition (i.e. core definition plus examples) were ever put to law, a court would doubtless find that the core definition must control each example."[14] Hence, he argues, it cannot be established by appeal to the IHRA definition that, in the words of example 10, "drawing comparisons of contemporary Israeli policy to that of the Nazis" is necessarily antisemitic:

> It will usually be an exaggeration, or else inappropriate, and will inevitably give offense to many Jewish people, but that does not make it anti-Semitic unless the Nazi comparison was intended to show contempt for Jews in general. In the early years of Hitler governance, Nazi anti-Semitic policy took the form of discrimination which made it more difficult for Jews to find employment or enter the professions: it would not be anti-Semitic to liken current Israeli policy to these measures (however inappropriately) unless it displays hatred to all Jews or the intention was to manifest hostility to all Jews, and not just the present Government.[15]

A preliminary comment is appropriate here. The requirement to prove antisemitic intent not only renders the IHRA definition useless with respect to the examples identified by Tomlinson and Robertson. It renders it extremely difficult to devise effective legal restraints on racist speech and action of any kind. It was for this reason that the Macpherson Report of 1999 emphasized "outcomes" rather than "intention." We see in a later section ("The Coherence of the IHRA Definition") that exactly the same choice is available in respect to antisemitic speech and action.

Objection 2: Alleged Consequences for Freedom of Speech

Tomlinson's treatment of the IHRA definition should perhaps be seen as mainly designed to expose its shortcomings as a tool for singling out antisemitic speech and action for legal purposes. The three remaining critics,

Robertson, Sedley, and Gould, are also concerned with exposing what they see as the dangers to free speech posed by the adoption of the definition, both by government and by such nongovernmental institutions as universities, trade unions, and political parties. Robertson takes it upon himself to define the present state of the law on these matters as follows:

> Anti-Semitic utterances, unless intended or likely to foment hatred against Jewish people, do not amount to an offence under English law. But this discreditable and indeed contemptible behaviour may result in disciplinary action, expulsion from organizations, and a loss of the right to practise certain employments or professions. To accuse someone wrongly of anti-Semitism is defamatory and would incur damages in a civil action.
>
> The position taken by British law differs from that in certain European countries with historic experience of Nazi repression, which have stricter laws against racism and genocide denial. Even so, all European countries are subject to the Convention, Article 10 of which lays down:
>
>> "Everyone has the right to freedom of expression. This right shall include freedom to hold opinions and to receive and impart information and ideas without interference by public authority and regardless of frontiers."
>
> This principle may only be overborne a) by a precise law, which is b) necessary in a democratic society either in the interests of national security, the prevention of disorder or the protection of the reputation and rights of others, and c) counts as a proportionate measure to achieve these legitimate aims. But the need for restrictions must be established convincingly and they must be "clear, certain and predictable"—i.e. formulated with sufficient precision to enable citizens to regulate their conduct. The European Court of Human Rights has also held that they must be a proportionate response to a pressing social need. The right may be availed of by those whose utterances "offend, shock or disturb." The scope for criticism of states and statesmen is wider than for private individuals because of the need for free and open discussion of politics.[16]

The above account is as it stands incomplete. Robertson's opening sentence presumably refers to section 18(1) of the Public Order Act 1986, which deals with intention to stir up racial hatred or the likelihood of stirring up racial hatred. But he has neglected to refer to section 5 of the same act, which makes it an offense to "display, with hostility towards a racial or religious group, any writing, sign or other visible representation which is threatening, abusive, or insulting, within the sight of a person who is likely to be caused harassment, alarm or distress by it."[17] He also fails to mention other relevant laws—for example, antisemitic hostile environment harassment under section 26 of the Equality Act 2010, which is a civil claim but renders antisemitism actionable in other respects also; and section 13 of the Equality Act, which allows a claim for direct or indirect discrimination, including "antisemitic expression," on the basis of a protected characteristic (religious beliefs or ethnicity in respect to Jews). We return to these issues later.

Leaving these wider questions of law aside for the moment, the problem created by widespread governmental and nongovernmental adoption of the IHRA definition, as Robertson sees it, is that the costs of invoking Article 10 in defense of freedom of speech may be such as to render such a defense nugatory:

> While it is true that the European Convention protects free speech that is a protection offered by the courts in what is termed "judicial review" of the actions of public authorities. Like all cases that end in court, this can be very expensive even if you win—costs only cover part of your legal expenses. For cash-strapped NGOs and student organisations, this is obviously a deterrent when faced with threats of legal action which require an expensive legal defence to protect their fundamental right to criticise Israel when it is unjustifiably limited by the application of the IHRA definition and its examples.[18]

The question naturally arises: To what extent does, or might, the IHRA definition "unjustifiably" limit the right to criticize Israel? Over the past twenty years, voices from sections of the left sympathetic to the boycotts, divestment, and sanctions (BDS) movement have consistently argued that any and all accusations of antisemitism on their part, even when addressed to quite specific and limited claims concerning Israel, are to be dismissed out of hand as politically disingenuous attempts to silence all criticism of Israel. Except Tomlinson, all of our critics appear prepared to give credence to this non sequitur. Robertson notes "suggestions in the media" to the effect that "the definition and its examples were drafted with the 'hidden agenda' that they could be used to ban criticism of Israeli policy and to label the nascent BDS movement as 'anti-Semitic.'"[19] And while he wisely scouts the damaging suggestion that the definition was actually drafted with such ends in mind, he does observe darkly that "there have been attempts to use it in this way."[20]

Sedley goes further:

> Shorn of philosophical and political refinements, anti-Semitism is hostility towards Jews as Jews. Where it manifests itself in discriminatory acts or inflammatory speech it is generally illegal, lying beyond the bound of freedom of speech and of action. By contrast, criticism (and equally defence) of Israel or of Zionism is not only generally lawful: it is affirmatively protected by law. Endeavours to conflate the two by characterising anything other than anodyne criticism of Israel as anti-Semitic are not new. What is new is the adoption by the UK government (and the Labour Party) of a definition of anti-Semitism which endorses the conflation.[21]

Gould, for her part, goes all the way. For her, the IHRA definition threatens legitimacy not just of harmful criticism of Israel but of (her term) "Israel-critical speech" per se, which means, presumably, any criticism of Israel whatsoever: "The very possibility of the document's legal ratification within a legal regime that would formally sanction Israel-critical speech ought to be cause for concern among scholars and activists concerned with safeguarding freedom of speech."[22] None of these increasingly radical claims concerning the supposed power of the definition to silence criticism of Israel appear to be supported by the terms of the IHRA definition itself. The range of specific criticisms of Israel identified as antisemitic by examples 2, 6, 7, 8, and 10 appears to be remarkably narrow. These criticisms include (1) denying the right of the Jewish people to political autonomy, (2) taking concern for the welfare of Israel on the part of non-Israeli Jews to be tantamount to a demonstration of lack of concern for the welfare of their nations of citizenship, (3) describing Israel as an essentially racist state, (4) describing it as a Nazi state, (5) asserting the existence of a Jewish conspiracy, and (6) singling out Israel alone for condemnation in respect to conduct that would be condoned on the part of any other nation.

Nonantisemitic Criticism of Israel

And that's it. *Pace* Sedley, the list seems lean enough to leave room for a wide range of far-from-anodyne criticisms of Israel. Take, for example, the following accusations: (7) Israel engages in targeted assassinations of leading figures in groups such as Hamas or Hizballah; (8) it committed a war crime by using white phosphorus in the first of the recent campaigns in Gaza; and (9) its housing policies in the West Bank proceed in defiance of international law.

Such criticisms open a range of issues that are very usefully argued back and forth by critics and defenders of Israel. Criticism 8, for instance, figured as a major element in the report by the UN Human Rights Council on the Gaza campaign of 2008–9. That report was chaired by Richard Goldstone, a former South African supreme court judge and hero of the struggle against apartheid, and it accused both Hamas and Israel of war crimes, in Israel's case involving the military use of white phosphorus in populated areas. In 2011, however, Goldstone published a personal retreat from some of the conclusions of the report, asserting that "if I had known what I now know, the Goldstone Report would have been a different document." His reasons are in part those contained in the following paragraphs:

> Our main recommendation was for each party to investigate, transparently and in good faith, the incidents referred to in our report. McGowan Davis has found that Israel has done this to a significant degree; Hamas has done nothing.

Our report has led to numerous "lessons learned" and policy changes, including the adoption of new Israel Defence Forces procedures for protecting civilians in cases of urban warfare and limiting the use of white phosphorus in civilian areas. The Palestinian Authority established an independent inquiry into our allegations of human rights abuses—assassinations, torture and illegal detentions—perpetrated by Fatah in the West Bank, especially against members of Hamas. Most of these allegations were confirmed by this inquiry. Regrettably, there has been no effort by Hamas in Gaza to investigate the allegations of its war crimes and possible crimes against humanity.[23]

Leaving these conclusions and the arguments surrounding them aside, however, what seems clear is that none of criticisms 7–9 could seriously be classed as "anodyne" and that, equally, none of them could be silenced as "antisemitic" either by appeal to anything to be found in the IHRA definition of antisemitism or by appeal to the somewhat different, though closely related, account of the nature and functions of antisemitism presented in the remainder of the present chapter.

Conceptual Shortcomings

A further question now arises. Why exactly are criticisms 1–6, as listed in the previous paragraphs, antisemitic, while criticisms 7–9 are not? The IHRA definition appears to offer little in the way of a plausible answer. And that shows it to be defective in a way unnoticed and unexplored by our four critics: defective not merely as a source of definitions adequate to legal purposes but on a deeper, conceptual level. It is defective as a proposed characterization of the content of a concept—the concept in question, of course, being antisemitism.

The international definition conforms in its general structure to a pattern of definition common in medicine and the more descriptive parts of the natural sciences. The pattern of definition to which it belongs works by first characterizing the nature of a given condition and then offering a series of symptoms or manifestations of that condition by which its presence can be recognized. It is essential to the intelligibility of such a definition that the nature of the condition should be characterized in such a way as to make it clear why the listed symptoms are to be regarded as symptoms of that condition. In the case of the medical condition known as angina, for instance, the symptoms (breathlessness, nausea, weakness, and chest pain) can be readily explained by reference to the nature of the condition, to what it consists in—namely, the narrowing and hardening of the main blood vessels going to the heart, which limits the blood and therefore oxygen supply to it.

This conceptual requirement, that the singling out of some state of affairs as a manifestation of a condition be explicable by appeal to the nature of that condition, is clearly not (or at least not consistently) met by the IHRA definition. All it offers by way of elucidating the nature of antisemitism is the statement that antisemitism is a "certain perception of Jews." The nature of that "perception" is then elucidated as possibly (and therefore, presumably, not necessarily) consisting in "hatred toward Jews." While it is certainly clear that some of the appended examples (example 1, for instance, or 2, insofar as the "allegations" that the latter invokes are "dehumanizing" or "demonizing") intrinsically involve hatred toward Jews, it remains quite unclear why most of the others need, in every imaginable circumstance, involve anything of the kind. In their case, that is to say, the statement that they manifest antisemitism remains, as Tomlinson in effect points out, on the level of bare or ex cathedra assertion.

Two Types of Antisemitism

The opening sentence of the IHRA definition is, in fact, profoundly ambiguous, particularly regarding two very different ways in which antisemitism may manifest itself. It reads, "Antisemitism is a certain perception of Jews, which may be expressed as hatred toward Jews." A perception, in ordinary as well as philosophical English, is a belief state. To perceive something, X, in a certain manner is to entertain a specific collection of beliefs concerning X. Hatred, on the other hand, is an emotional disposition toward X. Such dispositions may contain an element of belief; but equally, they may not. Thus, Peter may hate spinach because, absurdly, he believes it to lower sexual energy. Or he may just hate it, period.

In the same way, a belief state may be causally linked to an emotional disposition, but it need not be. And even if it is, such linkages, as David Hume taught us, are never necessary. Peter hates spinach because of worries about his sexual powers. Paul, on the other hand, an ascetic Christian, who has read the same nonsense about spinach on the web, eats it (though he hates the taste) precisely because he too believes in its presumed power to control his carnal appetites. James, as it happens, also believes the same rubbish about spinach but believes it without any accompanying emotional disposition toward spinach. For him, it is simply an exotic vegetable eaten in another part of the world; the markets he uses never carry it.

With these thoughts in mind, the opening move in a conceptual (as distinct from a legal) critique of the IHRA definition should be, "Which is it to be, then? Are you identifying antisemitism as a belief state (a 'perception') or as an emotional disposition?" An astute defender of the definition would be well advised to reply—and now, as we shall see, we are getting somewhere—"Both." Antisemitism can indeed manifest itself in either of these conceptually distinct forms: as an emotional state, with Jews as its object, or as a collection or system of beliefs about Jews.

In the first of these guises, social antisemitism, it is a version of what sociologists and social psychologists like to call *ethnic prejudice*. In the second, political antisemitism, it is a delusive explanatory theory concerning the supposedly central role played not by this or that individual Jew but by a supposedly all-powerful and malign Jewish collectivity in controlling non-Jewish life and history.[24]

The theory in question purports to explain why some current turn of events is—as perceived by the antisemite—going badly for non-Jews. The purported explanation is that the non-Jewish institutions that appear to be in charge of events have ceased to discharge their proper functions. They have ceased to do so because they have been hollowed out and taken over by agents of a vast Jewish conspiracy and perverted to the service of Jewish ends. In the face of the Jewish threat, there is little that can be done by the simple and deluded non-Jew, unless and until he or she has been sufficiently roused to the urgency of that threat to take action against it, action that can only consist in expelling the Jews wholesale from their secret positions of power—at which point the world will, if the job has been done properly, inevitably return to the state of normality from which the Jewish conspiracy alone has perverted it.

This version of antisemitism—antisemitism as a body of doctrine rather than a mere emotional disposition—was common enough in Europe before World War II. It is, for instance, what Sartre is talking about in the following passage from *Antisemite and Jew*: "Anti-Semitism is thus seen to be at bottom a form of Manichaeism. It explains the course of the world by the struggle of the principle of Good with the principle of Evil. . . . Look at Céline: his vision of the universe is catastrophic. The Jew is everywhere, the earth is lost, it is up to the Aryan not to compromise, never to make peace."[25] While the specific accusations leveled against Jews by this or that version of political antisemitism may change, the main tenets of the theory remain, in all its versions, roughly as follows:

> PA_1. The Jewish community is organized to pursue goals of its own at whatever cost to the lives and interests of non-Jewish groups. In consequence, it is directly and solely responsible for human suffering on a scale far exceeding anything that can be alleged against any other human group.

PA$_2$. The Jewish community is conspiratorially organized in the pursuit of its self-seeking and heinous goals to an extent that endows it with demonic powers not to be suspected from the weak and harmless appearance of its individual members.

PA$_3$. Through the efficacy of its conspiratorial organization and through its quasi-miraculous ability to acquire and manage money, the Jewish community has been able to acquire secret control over most of the main social, commercial, political, and governmental institutions of non-Jewish society.

PA$_4$. Given the secret control exercised by world Jewry over (only apparently) non-Jewish institutions and given the obsessive concern of the Jewish community with its own interests to the exclusion of those of non-Jews, it is simply not feasible to remedy the evils occasioned by the presence of the Jews in non-Jewish society by any means short of the total elimination of the Jews.

PA$_5$. Since the evils that the Jews do in the world owe their existence solely to Jewish wickedness, the elimination of the Jews will cause those evils to cease, without the need for any further action on the part of non-Jews, whose world will, in the nature of things, return forthwith to the perfect state of order natural to it, from which it would never have lapsed had it not been for the mischievous interventions of the Jews.

Two leading and connected features of the theory are its exceptionalism and its eliminationism with respect to the Jews. On the one hand, it holds that the Jewish community is exceptional, in the sense of being radically unlike any other human group. On the other, it sees this supposed exceptionalism as posing insurmountable difficulties to assimilation. The Jewish community, in short, is so radically Other that it cannot be lived with; it can only be got rid of—eliminated in one way or another.

Finally, it goes without saying that the entire theory is delusive. The problem is not just that the Jewish community is too small, too divided, and too much at odds with itself to be capable of secretly taking over the world (though it manifestly is all of those things). It is, rather, that no community could possibly play the role envisaged for the Jews by the political antisemite. Political antisemitism, in short, requires no refutation—it refutes itself by its own internal absurdities.

Political Antisemitism and Israel

The fundamental absurdity of a pseudoexplanatory theory presents no more solid an obstacle to credulity in the case of political antisemitism than it has over the centuries in the case of, say, phrenology or astrology, or for that matter in those of the innumerable conspiracy theories now flourishing on the internet. In general, whatever people feel a strong temptation to believe, many of them actually will believe. At the present time, there exists a strong temptation, felt by many on the left, to articulate opposition to Israel in terms of a refurbished version of political antisemitism.

That temptation arises in the following way. An enduring vein of opposition to Israel, one represented by Iran, Hamas, and Hizballah, among others, and one with which a substantial section of the Western left sympathizes, is essentially revanchist in character. It wishes to see the result of the 1947–48 war reversed. It wishes to see Israel abolished as a Jewish-majority state and replaced by a Muslim-Arab-majority state, from which Jews would be expelled or in which they would remain as a minority. It is essential to the business of promoting this program, particularly in the West, to have some good reason for claiming that the state of Israel is "illegitimate," should never have been allowed to come into existence in the first place, and should not be allowed to continue in existence now. That is the position advanced, for instance, by the BDS movement, whose whole raison d'être is to rally a sufficiently wide and articulate body of Western opinion behind a policy of boycott, divestment, and sanctions to reduce Israel to the status of a "pariah state."

The object of BDS, in short, is to spread the message that Israel is and always was an illegitimate state. It is in fact unclear, as the philosopher Elhanan Yakira notes, what could even be meant by describing a state—as such—as "illegitimate." There is a long tradition of legal and philosophical theory (Bodin, Hobbes, Locke, Rousseau, Weber, and others) concerning the legitimacy of political authority, but that tradition deals with the relationship between the state and the citizen. This vast web of learned discussion, as Yakira points out,[26] proposes criteria of many kinds for assessing the legitimacy of a government or a regime but can offer no guidance on the legitimacy of a state as such, since it simply presumes the existence of the state as a given. Matters are made worse by the fact that Israel is the only state against whose legitimacy as a state anyone is prepared to mount a campaign.

One obvious way of cutting through these philosophical cobwebs is to claim that a state can reasonably be regarded as illegitimate and ripe for abolition when it embraces, as a condition of its very existence, policies so harmful to human rights that its existence can no longer be tolerated. This is the line of argument behind which the BDS-supporting left has, broadly speaking, chosen to place itself. A state makes itself illegitimate by committing evil—by the gravity of its crimes. And if the only Jewish state in the world is also the only state in the world whose legitimacy as a state anyone is prepared to question, that is because (so goes the argument) the crimes of the Jewish state far exceed in gravity those of any other state in the world.

It is not hard to find examples of eminent public intellectuals of "anti-Zionist" tendency prepared to take up this suggestion and run with it. Jacqueline Rose, professor of English at Queen Mary College, University of London, catches the general spirit of this line of anti-Zionist rhetoric: "How did one of the most persecuted peoples of the world come to embody some of the worst cruelties of the modern nation-state?"[27] In the same vein, the late Edward Said was prepared to describe Israel's occupation of the West Bank and (at that time) of Gaza as "in severity and outright cruelty more than rivaling any other military occupation in modern history."[28] Such claims are, of course, not easy to expand and drive home in detail. Events from 1914 to the present day have set the bar of atrocity far too high for it to be easily surmounted by a nation as small and civilized as Israel. Where are the Israeli atrocities capable of standing comparison to those committed by, to name a few, the Pol Pot regime in Cambodia, the Assad regime in Syria, Isil in Iraq and Syria, or the Nazis, first in Germany and later throughout Europe between 1933 and 1945? And to name these few, after all, is to offer a very short extract indeed from the crowded roll of potential twentieth- and twenty-first-century competitors.

To create a body of opinion prepared to see Israel as a "pariah state," however, it is hardly necessary to make out a detailed case against Israel. All that is necessary is to find some means of associating Israel, in suitably receptive minds, with things already widely considered to represent the nadir of evil. Such things include Nazism, racism, the apartheid regime in South Africa, colonialism, and war. And such associations, as Joseph Goebbels taught us long ago, can be implanted in receptive minds at the cost of very little argument or appeal to verifiable fact. All that is necessary is to repeat them as frequently as possible in the context of any current news item that can be "spun" in such a way as to give them some degree of anecdotal foothold. In this way it has become, over the past twenty years, axiomatic in certain sectors of Western opinion that Israel is a "Nazi" state, that it is a "racist" or "apartheid" state, that it is a "colonial-settler state," that it is the "main threat to peace" in the Middle East and perhaps in the world itself, and so on.

Unfortunately, these more specific claims turn out on closer examination to be no more consonant with the facts than the more general claim—that Israel's "crimes" exceed in gravity those of all other nations—that they pretend to explicate in detail. Regarding the idea that Israel is the main threat to peace in the region, events have shown the issue of war and peace in the Middle East to turn far more on such issues as the rise of Islamism, the Arab Spring and its consequences, and the rivalry between Shia and Sunni regional powers than on anything having to do with Israel. Nor can Israel reasonably be described as a "racist" state. Only about 70 percent of its population is Jewish, and this includes Jews of every race, including African Jews from Ethiopia and elsewhere. The remainder of the population consists of Muslim and Christian Arabs, Druse, Circassians, and various other groups. Israel is, in fact, an extraordinarily diverse, multicultural society. Freedom to practice religion is guaranteed, including to minority groups such as the Baha'i subject to severe persecution elsewhere in the Middle East. In the context of the persecution suffered by Copts and other Christian denominations elsewhere in the region, it is also significant that Israel is the only country in the region in which the number of Christians is actually increasing. Nor does anything remotely resembling the apartheid system once practiced in South Africa obtain in Israel. Every citizen of Israel, of whatever race or religion, has full access to all public institutions. Girls wearing hijabs are a familiar sight in Israeli universities. There are Arab members of the Knesset and, for that matter, Arab ministers of state and Arab judges, including a former justice of the Israel Supreme Court. Druse, Circassians, and even a few Muslim Arab Israelis serve in the IDF. Nor is it reasonable to describe Israel as a "colonial-settler" state. The impression this charge attempts to give is that the Jewish population of Israel is wholly European in origin, was implanted in the country by armed aggression with the connivance of the European powers, and confronts a subject population of equally wholly Middle Eastern descent. In fact, the increase in the original Jewish element of the (very small) historical population of Palestine after 1880 remained for several decades a continuation of the long antecedent tradition of immigration into the Ottoman Empire by Jewish individuals and groups. Over half a million Jews of Arab and African descent also flooded into the country after 1948 to escape persecution in their own countries. The foundation of the state of Israel resulted not from colonialist aggression by the Jews but from the fact that the forces of the *Yishuv* happened to win a war, against overwhelming odds, begun by the (Palestinian) Arab Higher Committee and continued by the armies of the surrounding Arab powers, with the stated objective of driving the Jews into the sea.[29]

In short, what we are dealing with in the anti-Zionist propaganda put about by BDS, and the elements of the Western left that support it, is not criticism of Israel but rather politically motivated defamation. Moreover, it follows a pattern made familiar by earlier versions, including the prewar Nazi version, of political antisemitism. That is to say, it offers an "explanation" of certain disturbing features of modern life—in the present case, the ever-renewed turmoil in the Near East and the Maghreb, along with the ongoing problems for European societies caused by that turmoil—in terms of the putative centrality to these disquieting events of "the Jew," as represented for present purposes by the state of Israel. The explanation offered is that the upheavals in the region over the past half century, along with the (putatively) otherwise inexplicable hostility of many in the Islamic world toward Europe, are entirely to be explained by the natural resentment felt by the indigenous inhabitants of the region for the implantation among them by the European powers—in (it is said) a misguided attempt to "compensate" the Jews for the Holocaust—of a Jewish polity, Israel, whose crimes exceed those of all other nations in modern history, including those of the Third Reich. Given the extraordinary gravity of these crimes—the argument continues—the only way of addressing the situation is to work, by every means possible, toward the overthrow of Jewish political autonomy in Israel. Once that goal is achieved, the argument concludes—displaying at this point a degree of blindness to the actual savagery of Middle Eastern politics that will surprise only those unfamiliar with the intellectual left—Palestine will become, as it should always have been, a Muslim-majority state in which Jews may continue to live perfectly happily as a minority, while the region, relieved at last of the poisonous and disruptive presence of organized Jewry, will also return to a state of peace and prosperity in which its affairs will cease to trouble the nations of Europe.

Such a view shares the exceptionalism and the eliminationism characteristic of political antisemitism in all its versions. They are, indeed, built into the fundamental claim of BDS that the crimes of Israel are far in excess of those of any other nation (exceptionalism) and that the Jewish state, again unlike any other, hence lacks legitimacy (eliminationism).

The problem with this version of political antisemitism, as with earlier versions, is merely that its main doctrines (the extensive influence of the Jews in world affairs; the vast scope of the evils they are able to work at the expense of the non-Jewish world; the immense, quasi-demonic capacity for financial and conspiratorial organization that gives Jews the power to work these evils to the ruin of the simple and trusting goy; and [saddest of all] the belief that the world will automatically return to normality [however that elusive condition may appear to this or that generation of antisemites] once the "Jewish threat" has been definitively dealt with) compose a tissue of delusions so bizarre that no subordinate argument could possibly succeed in rooting them in reality. One is reminded of something the novelist Henry Fielding said long ago about a very different matter—namely, the proposition, common among the philosophers and divines of his day, that the practice of virtue is the certain road to happiness (and vice to misery) in this world: "A very wholesome and comfortable doctrine, and to which we have but one objection, namely, that it is not true."[30]

The Coherence of the IHRA Definition

Depressing as these reflections are, they at least offer us an answer to a question we raised earlier: why the examples of antisemitism offered by the IHRA definition stigmatize certain types of observation concerning Israel as antisemitic while excluding, or at least failing to mention in that capacity, others (including those mentioned earlier) that might be considered equally or more politically damaging. The list of observations there stigmatized as antisemitic comprises denying the right of the Jewish people to exercise political autonomy, describing Israel as an essentially racist or Nazi state, asserting the existence of a Jewish conspiracy in relation to Israel, asserting that concern for the welfare of Israel among non-Israeli Jews argues a lack of concern for the welfare of their nations of citizenship, and singling out Israel for condemnation in respect to conduct passed over or condoned in other nations.

The answer suggested by the above reflections is that the examples chosen involve not criticism of Israel but defamation of Israel. More specifically, the examples single out types of defamatory falsehood characteristic of political antisemitism. It is, after all, intelligible to deny the right of the Jewish people, alone among the nations of the world, to exercise political autonomy only if there is some good reason why they should be denied it. That reason can rest only in the alleged commitment of the Jews to harming, on an altogether overwhelming scale, the interests of others. This allegation forms the central plank of antisemitism considered as a delusive explanatory theory. Other claims stigmatized as antisemitic by the examples, specifically the claim that Israel is a Nazi or racist state, form part of current efforts to persuade people of the central claim of political antisemitism with respect to Israel: that Israel is the epitome of evil.

As we have already argued, none of these claims can be defended by the sober recitation of facts. Hence, the goal of "delegitimating" Israel can be pursued only by means of the remaining two elements in Natan Sharansky's famous "3D" test for distinguishing legitimate criticism of Israel from antisemitic defamation.[31] Delegitimation, that is to say, can be achieved only by way of demonization and double standards. Similarly, belief in the existence of a Jewish conspiracy, lately rehashed as the claim that the activities of the Israel lobby in the United States are conspiratorial and opposed to the national interest of the United States, is a familiar element in any version of political antisemitism, as is the closely related belief that Jews by their nature operate, in effect, as agents of a foreign power.

To make clear, in this way, the legitimacy of examples 2, 6, 7, 8, and 10 as examples of antisemitism certainly requires us to distinguish between antisemitism as an emotional state (essentially, hatred of Jews as Jews) and antisemitism as a body of delusive beliefs about Jews. And certainly, the IHRA definition is unclear on this issue as it stands. That may, of course, be because the distinction between antisemitism as an emotional disposition and antisemitism as a delusive, pseudoexplanatory theory was felt by the authors of the distinction to be too obvious to need belaboring. Be that as it may, the wording of its opening definition not only allows but invites clarification in this direction, possibly by the circulation of some further explanatory guide to its intended meaning.

Free Speech versus Defamation

Does the wide adoption of the IHRA definition pose, as our four critics contend, a serious threat, actual or potential, to freedom of speech? The argument to that effect pursued by both Tomlinson and Robertson rests fundamentally on the idea that, as Sedley puts it, "anti-Semitism is hostility to Jews as Jews."[32] He, like Tomlinson and Robertson, interprets the opening sentence of the IHRA definition as strengthening this interpretation of the meaning of the term to require not merely hostility but "hatred" as the criterion. Both Tomlinson and Robertson see this interpretation as yielding two successive conclusions. The first is that an act or utterance can be considered antisemitic only if it can be shown to express or manifest hatred toward Jews as Jews. The second is that, since no current expression of political hostility toward Israel or Zionism (including those stigmatized as antisemitic in the examples section of the IHRA definition) can be shown to meet this criterion, and since, therefore, the IHRA definition offers no plausible ground for distinguishing between legitimate and antisemitic criticism of Israel, we have no option but to class all criticism of Israel as legitimate political discourse, in which case it stands protected by law—in particular, as Robertson reminds us, by the European Convention on Human Rights, Article 10 of which states, "Everyone has the right to freedom of expression. This right shall include freedom to hold opinions and to receive and impart information and ideas without interference by public authority and regardless of frontiers."[33] This argument displays two points of weakness:

1. It shows only that the IHRA definition as presently formulated offers no basis for a distinction between antisemitic and nonantisemitic criticism of Israel. It in no way excludes the possibility that a revised version of the definition might succeed in adequately grounding that distinction.
2. It assumes the factual adequacy of a certain account of the nature of antisemitism—of what sort of phenomenon antisemitism is. The favored account says, in effect, that antisemitism is a species of emotional disposition—namely, a disposition to hate Jews qua Jews.

No serious supplementary argument for point 2 is offered by either Robertson or Tomlinson or, for that matter, Sedley; worse still, the arguments that are offered are seriously unimpressive. Robertson cites in support the OED and "Wikipedia, with reference to Encyclopaedia Britannica, Paul Johnson and Bernard Lewis,"[34] but reference to such authorities, while useful enough for the limited purposes served by dictionaries and encyclopedias, can hardly be regarded as sufficient to close a question of this degree of complexity, and one, moreover, central to the argument. Sedley, for his part, simply assumes, ex cathedra as it were, that antisemitism just is "hostility towards Jews as Jews" and that there, in effect, as Dr. Johnson put it in another context, "is an end on't."

None of this will quite do. Even if we consider the nature of antisemitic activity only over the past century or two, it seems evident that it has not consisted solely in rancorous or frothing railing against any Jew whatsoever qua Jew. It has consisted also, and much more dangerously, in a sustained attempt to propagate and popularize a range of extraordinary beliefs concerning not Jews taken one by one ("distributively," as the logicians say) but rather the Jewish community, conceived as a conspiratorially organized entity, secretly dominating a range of institutions central to the welfare of non-Jewish societies and hence posing a permanent and terrible threat to the stability and welfare of the non-Jewish world. Nazi antisemitism—the kind of antisemitism sedulously disseminated, for instance, by the Nazi weekly tabloid newspaper *Der Stürmer*—was of exactly this type. And it is because it was of this type that the Nazis were foolish enough, as well as wicked enough, to divert German manpower, trains, and other materiel to the imaginary "war against the Jews" that they might have been wiser to devote to the real war against the Allied Powers. One does not seriously impede the war effort in this way merely to get rid of people whom one happens to dislike and despise. One does so only because one imagines the people in question to present a serious threat to the welfare of the nation. It is no doubt for this reason that the Nazis relied heavily on the blood libel to convince their enemies to be receptive to antisemitism. They successfully spread the belief in the reality of Jewish ritual murder as "proof" of a more general Jewish murder plot against non-Jewish humanity.

In the light of these facts, it seems reasonable to conclude, as we have done here, that antisemitism manifests itself not in one but in two fundamental forms. It indeed manifests as an emotional disposition. But it also manifests as a body of doctrine—specifically, as a delusive explanatory theory concerning the supposed centrality to world events of a Jewish conspiracy.

We have argued, as have many others, that a version of that body of doctrine has in recent years attached itself to the state of Israel. Its central thesis is that the crimes of Israel outweigh those of any other nation and that Israel should therefore be regarded as an illegitimate state, one that should never have been allowed to come into existence in the first place. In defense of that thesis, its proponents advance a range of subordinate supporting claims, all of them hyperbolic in the highest degree and all at the same time manifestly false—for example, that Israel is a Nazi state, an apartheid state, a racist state, and so on. The hyperbole and falsehood of these claims, along with their evident roots in the long tradition of antisemitism as a body of essentially delusive doctrine, is sufficient to allow a clear distinction to be drawn between plainly antisemitic claims such as these and a vast range of perfectly legitimate criticisms of Israel that are in no sense hyperbolic or indefensible by appeal to the facts and that are, for those reasons, also in no sense antisemitic.

Another relevant point is that in order to convict of antisemitic intent, say, the material propagated each week by *Der Stürmer*, it is not necessary to show that its authors were animated by "hatred of Jews qua Jews," or as Robertson occasionally puts it, "hatred of Jews as a race." They may have been, and given the atmosphere of Nazi politics, they very likely were. But it is at least logically possible that one or more of them might not have been. It is possible to imagine someone entirely persuaded by Nazi propaganda concerning the overwhelming threat to the nation posed by the Jewish conspiracy, but who nevertheless does not believe that individual Jews of his acquaintance are personally connected with that conspiracy. Such a person believes a great deal of antisemitic rubbish but is not himself an antisemite, at least in the specific sense of someone who entertains hatred toward Jews qua Jews. And in the same way, of course, someone who nowadays both entertains and sedulously propagates a great deal of antisemitic rubbish concerning Israel may nevertheless be able to claim with reason that he or she is not an antisemite, if we mean by that a hater of Jews qua Jews. But equally, of course, the fact that someone is not an antisemite in that sense does not imply or entail that he or she is not an antisemite in the sense of one who habitually propagates and disseminates antisemitic material. The requirement to demonstrate intent, in line with the findings of the Macpherson Report, as we noted earlier, is irrelevant to most cases where antisemitism is at issue (*pace* both Tomlinson and Robertson).

All four of our legal critics of the IHRA definition display a strong commitment to the principle of freedom of speech (most radical in the case of Gould, who appears to imply, quite mistakenly in law, that the right to free speech is an absolute rather than a qualified right), and more specifically to that principle as embodied in Article 10 of the European Convention of Human Rights. It seems unclear, given the strength of their expressed commitments in this respect, whether any of them would even support the suppression of *Der Stürmer*, were that weekly still in existence today.

Might this not, though, be a nettle that should be grasped? It is surely reasonable, at least in principle, to hold that the conduct of politics in a democratic state requires the fullest possible freedom of all parties to the debate to express their opinions without fear of legal restraint. But it is also reasonable to retort that no guarantee of rights in a democratic state can altogether dispense with marginal restrictions designed to meet competing demands. For that matter, the right of free expression under Article 10 of the European Convention, as Sedley puts it, "is not absolute or unqualified: it can be abrogated or restricted where to do so is lawful, proportionate and necessary for (among other things) public safety, the prevention of disorder or the protection of the rights of others. [Though] these qualifications do not include a right not to be offended."[35] Do such reasons obtain in the case of the (as we have seen, rather short and limited) list of specific lines of attack on Israel qualified as antisemitic by the IHRA definition? They do, we suggest; and they are of two types. The first are straightforwardly legal in character and have to do with the protection of the rights of others as prescribed by law. The second concern relates to issues of public safety, including the need to restrain the power of radical politics to threaten the coherence of society.

We discuss the legal grounds first. While there is no specific law prohibiting antisemitism, antisemitic activity might be covered by legislation on hate crime, online abuse, and equalities. There are three different ways that legislation deals with hate crime motivated on the grounds of race or religion. These are offenses of stirring up hatred, aggravated forms of certain "basic" criminal offenses, and enhanced sentencing for offenses motivated by hate. The Crown Prosecution Service guidance suggests that antisemitic hate crime can be dealt with as either racist or religious hate crime.

Part III of the Public Order Act 1986 criminalizes certain acts that are intended to stir up racial hatred, defined as "hatred against a group of persons defined by reference to colour, race, nationality (including citizenship), or ethnic or national origin." A Part III offense can also be committed where "it is likely, having regard to all the circumstances, that racial hatred will be stirred up." To constitute the crime, the acts, which include "words," "behaviour," or "material," must be "threatening, abusive or insulting." There is no freedom of expression defense to racial hatred.

How does this section impact the IHRA's examples of antisemitism that have been rejected by our three critics? Let us take the "Nazification of Israel," which has been described as the principal signifier or reference point of contemporary anti-Zionist discourse.[36] The 2009 Report of the European Institute for the Study of Contemporary Antisemitism (EISCA), *Understanding the "Nazi Card": Intervening against Antisemitic Discourse*,[37] stated that the "Nazification of Israel" has the potential to incite violence against British Jews, as it is the biggest component of racial hatred against them. Indeed, the late distinguished historian Professor Robert Wistrich referred to the Israel/Nazi trope as "in practice . . . the most potent form of contemporary antisemitism," because those who engage in it "exploit the reality that Nazism in the post-war world has become the defining metaphor of absolute evil."[38]

It is also interesting to note that the Israel/Nazi trope is not far removed from Holocaust denial, which Robertson does accept as antisemitic. Acclaimed historian Deborah Lipstadt, author of the 1993 book *Denying the Holocaust: The Growing Assault on Truth and Memory* and the 2019 book *Antisemitism: Here and Now*, coined the neologism "soft-core denial" to explain the Nazi/Israel equivalence. This is because the false comparison between Israel and the Nazis "lessens by a factor of a zillion what the Germans did," thus whitewashing the crimes of the Nazis and trivializing the Holocaust.[39] It is reasonable to assume that if Robertson accepts that Holocaust denial is antisemitic, then he should accept that Holocaust equivalence is also antisemitic. In fact, Lipstadt says that its deployment is "a very convenient way of engaging in antisemitism," because it involves "accusing Jews of atrocities."[40]

Judging by the annual and biannual antisemitic incidents reports produced by the Community Security Trust, it appears that all the examples that Robertson and Tomlinson reject as antisemitic without specific proof of intent incite attacks on Jews, whether these be verbal, physical, or property damage. Furthermore, spikes in antisemitic attacks have been shown to occur during clashes between Israel and Hamas.[41] This is presumably because of the increase in media attention given to Israel and the attendant awakening among Israel's detractors of examples 2, 6, 7, 8, and 10 in the IHRA definition. This is why the police force's *Hate Crime Operational Guidance* has incorporated the IHRA definition with all eleven examples.

Note that Part 3A of the Public Order Act 1986 makes a similar provision for acts intended to stir up religious hatred, defined as "hatred of a group of persons defined by reference to religious belief or lack of religious belief." It criminalizes only acts *intended* to stir up religious hatred, and there is a freedom of expression defense to allow for "discussion, criticism, or expressions of antipathy, dislike, ridicule, insult or abuse of particular religions or the beliefs or practices of their adherents, or of any other belief system or the beliefs or practices of its adherents, or proselytising or urging adherents of a different religion or belief system to cease practicing their religion or belief system."[42] Part 3A was specifically enacted in 2007 to protect Muslims, who, unlike Jews and Sikhs, are not classed as a racial group on the grounds that they cannot be "defined by reference to their ethnic origins."

Under the Crime and Disorder Act 1998, perpetrators of specified "basic" criminal offenses can be charged with an aggravated form of the offense (carrying a longer maximum sentence) if they demonstrated or were motivated by hostility on the basis of race or religion. The specified offenses covered by the 1998 act include assault, criminal damage, public order offenses, harassment, and stalking. The Crown Prosecution Service says that "monitoring had indicated that these were the most common types of crime experienced by the victims of racially and religiously aggravated violence or harassment."[43]

Section 145 of the Criminal Justice Act 2003 applies when the court is sentencing an offender for an offense other than one of the aggravated offenses under the 1998 act. The section requires the court to consider whether the offense was racially or religiously aggravated. If so, the court must treat that as an aggravating factor for sentencing purposes and must state in open court that the offense was so aggravated.

There are several general criminal offenses that can be used to prosecute online antisemitism, the most relevant of which are as follows. Section 1 of the Malicious Communications Act 1988 makes it an offense to send indecent, grossly offensive, threatening, or false electronic communications if the purpose (or one of the purposes) of the sender is to cause the recipient distress or anxiety. Section 127 of the Communications Act 2003 makes it an offense to use a public electronic communications network to send a message (or other matter) that is grossly offensive or of an indecent, obscene, or menacing character; or to send a false message "for the purpose of causing annoyance, inconvenience or needless anxiety to another." Harassment or stalking offenses may be prosecuted under section 2, 2A, 4, or 4A of the Protection from Harassment Act 1997, which deals with behavior that alarms or distresses the victim and may include racial and religious harassment.

In May 2018, section 127 of the Communications Act 2003 was used to convict a Holocaust revisionist of Holocaust denial online. Alison Chabloz was convicted of two counts of causing obscene material to be sent and one of sending obscene material. She performed two songs, titled "Nemo's Antisemitic Universe" and "I Like It How It Is," at the right-wing London Forum in 2016, and she uploaded a third onto YouTube titled "(((survivors)))." In the latter, Chabloz mocked Jewish figures, including Elie Wiesel and Anne and Otto Frank, to the tune of "Hava Nagila." The judge said that he was "entirely satisfied" that the material was "grossly offensive" and that it was "intended to insult Jewish people."[44] Chabloz lost her appeal against the conviction in February 2019.[45] While the Chabloz case does not relate directly to Israel, it does illustrate that freedom of speech may be severely curtailed by the law and that Holocaust trivialization, which is essentially what the Israel/Nazi equivalence is, may be held to be against the law even in the absence of specific laws criminalizing Holocaust denial.

The Equality Act 2010 prohibits discrimination in relation to "protected characteristics," which include both race and religion. Antisemitism is likely to be prohibited on both grounds. As Employment Judge Snelson observed in *Fraser v. University and College Union* (2013), "Jewishness is a characteristic which attracts protection under the race and religion or belief provisions of the 2010 Act."[46]

In *R (E) v. Governing Body of JFS* [2009] UKSC 15, Lord Phillips explained how Jews possess both characteristics: "One of the difficulties in this case lies in distinguishing between religious and ethnic status. One of the criteria of ethnicity . . . is a shared religion. In the case of Jews, this is the dominant criterion. In their case it is almost impossible to distinguish between ethnic status and religious status. The two are virtually co-extensive. A woman who converts to Judaism thereby acquires both Jewish religious status and Jewish ethnic status."[47] The effect of this is that antisemitism is likely to constitute both race and religious discrimination. Consequently, the Equality Act 2010 would protect Jews from discrimination, harassment (including hostile environment harassment), and victimization in the fields to which the act applies, such as employment, services, education, and housing.

To illustrate how criticism of Israel as identified in two of the examples rejected by Robertson could be actionable under the Equality Act 2010, let us consider the following scenario. Section 26 of the act, which recognizes that "Jewish" is a "protected characteristic" as it refers to "a 'race,' a 'religion' or 'a belief,'" provides that "a person A harasses another B if a) he engages in unwanted conduct related to a *relevant* protected characteristic, and b) the conduct has the purpose or effect of (i) violating B's dignity, or (ii) creating an intimidating, hostile, degrading, humiliating or offensive environment for B." A hostile environment for a Jewish student or lecturer could conceivably be created in the university setting by the display of a poster showing a swastika, an equal sign, and the Star of David; a poster showing Netanyahu morphing into a jackbooted storm trooper; and a poster stating that "Israel is a racist endeavour." Such posters are commonly seen on some British campuses during Israeli Apartheid Week. Note that section 26 does not require antisemitic "intent."

The display of these posters could be grounds for a Jewish individual to claim hostile environment harassment because successive reports of the Institute for Jewish Policy Research have indicated that a majority of Jews in Britain support Israel and self-identify as Zionists.[48] That fact alone is enough to make Israel an essential aspect of contemporary Jewish identity, as that is perceived not only by many Jews but also by many of their non-Jewish neighbors, and hence enough to make Israel relevant to the "protected characteristic" of being Jewish in the terms of section 26. Although the Employment Tribunal in *Fraser v. The University and College Union* (2013) unanimously held to the contrary, stating that Israel is not an aspect of Jewish identity[49] because not all Jews are Zionists and not all Zionists are Jews, it must be noted that the decision was one of first instance only and therefore did not set a precedent, and *pace* Employment Judge Snelson and the two lay decision-makers, the decision and reasoning on that point are open to serious criticism.

It is entirely possible to advance factually well-grounded criticisms of the policies of the government of Israel in a manner that avoids abusing or wrongfully defaming Israel and, by association, the majority of British Jews. But reasoned and factually well-grounded criticism of Israel is in no way threatened by the IHRA definition. What the IHRA definition singles out as antisemitic is, rather, the violent and belligerent repetition of a small range of entirely factually ungrounded but profoundly defamatory slogans, to the effect that Israel is a "racist," "apartheid," or "Nazi" state whose "crimes" outweigh those of any other modern political entity. As a result, Jews are harassed and ostracized with accusations of "Zio-Nazi," "Nazi," "apologist for apartheid," and so on. This results from the Jewish self-identification with Israel and the connection non-Jews make between Jews and Israel. It is also because of the fact that the majority of Jews support Israel, although not necessarily the policies of the government of Israel. Rather, they support Israel in the sense of wanting it to exist as a Jewish state because it was their ancestral homeland and acknowledging its role as a psychological and physical refuge from antisemitism.

Nor can the resulting harassment be regarded as an unfortunate side effect of the overriding need to protect free political speech. While, as Robertson points out in his opinion, political speech is given a particularly strong degree of legal protection "because of the need for free and open discussion in politics,"[50] it has been defined by the European Court of Human Rights as "speech on matters of general public concern."[51] Moreover, the justification for according political speech privileged status—and this also has explicit recognition in UK domestic law—is that it allows citizens to participate fully in a democracy and to make informed decisions about who to vote for. It also ensures that citizens are provided with enough information to hold the government to account. When one considers its legal definition and the reasons for its high degree of legal protection, it is clear that "political speech" so understood can hardly include the expressions of hostility to Israel identified as antisemitic by the IHRA definition.

What is morally and legally wrong with the type of sloganizing identified as antisemitic by the IHRA definition may be but need not *only* be that it "expresses hatred toward Jews as a race" or stirs up hatred toward Jews as a race, whether intentionally or not. It may not do so, and in any case, it is always possible to whitewash the sloganizing by means of caveats (e.g., that it is not antisemitic but merely "anti-Zionist"). But so what? What is morally and legally wrong with the mindless defamation that such sloganizing articulates is simply that it is defamatory—that it is libel and slander. Whether it defames all Jews or merely those—in the majority—who happen to support Israel is entirely irrelevant to the fundamental character of such discourse as politically motivated collective defamation.

Robertson correctly notes, in the published opinion we have been discussing, that "it is defamatory to wrongly accuse a person of being antisemitic." So it is; but in that case, why is it not also defamatory to wrongly accuse a Jewish supporter of Israel of being, solely by virtue of that support, a racist, a friend of apartheid, and a Nazi? And if such accusations are made daily in certain workplaces (frequently ones connected with universities where the pro-BDS narrative is prevalent), as one element in an effectively inescapable atmosphere of heated political rhetoric, why would this not constitute conduct that in effect, if not in intent, creates a hostile, degrading, humiliating, or offensive environment for Jews? In the university setting, antiharassment codes that effectively operate as "hate speech codes" expressly prohibit expression that degrades, humiliates, threatens, or offends minority students. This is to protect the students' right to equal educational opportunity, which can be jeopardized because of the documented harms of hate speech. These consist of a range of psychological and physiological harms, which can result in missed lectures, lower grades, poorer job prospects, and consequent economic losses.[52]

If the legality of allowing the dissemination of material concerning Israel of the kinds stipulated as antisemitic by the IHRA examples is dubious, the wisdom of allowing it to claim the protection of Article 10 is even more so. "Public safety" justifications for restricting the application of Article 10 have so far generally concerned the politics of the far right. These include the criminalizing of Holocaust denial in certain European countries and the recent unprecedented banning of the neo-Nazi group National Action in Britain. Talk of Israel as a "criminal," "Nazi," "apartheid," or "racist" state, the carrying of banners showing the swastika and the Star of David connected by an equal sign, and so on are currently overwhelmingly associated with the extreme or "hard" left. But organizations of the extreme right, on social media and in other ways, constantly take the opportunity to express their support of left-wing organizations that, in their terms, have finally won through to the insight that all the evils besetting the world are Jewish in origin. Thus, former BNP leader Nick Griffin supported Jeremy Corbyn's claim in August 2018 that British Zionists do not understand English irony.[53]

To such unwanted expressions of support, the left, naturally enough, tend to reply that their quarrel is not with Jews but with Israel. But if that were really the case, then surely the very large numbers of non-Jews who publicly support Israel, including the non-Jewish coauthor of this chapter, could expect to find themselves vociferously attacked and pilloried by the left. But that is not what happens. In fact, the only supporters of Israel who find themselves vociferously attacked and pilloried by the various organizations providing active support for BDS are Jewish supporters of Israel, or supporters of Israel who they think are Jewish. In America these are chiefly Jewish university students, but in Britain they include Jewish university faculty, Jewish members of Parliament, and other politically salient members of the Jewish community. Moreover, these attacks are often violent to a degree that in Britain has, on a number of occasions fully reported by the press, required police protection for the Jewish students, MPs, or others involved. For instance, Jewish MP Luciana Berger served as a Labour MP for Liverpool Wavertree from 2010 until February 2019, when she left the party to form the Independent Group (TIG) with seven other MPs. She claimed that she was driven out of the party by antisemitic bullying. While this took the form mostly of verbal abuse, such were the threats against her that in September 2018, she had to have a police escort to the Labour Party Annual Conference.[54]

Public safety concerns have not always involved the politics of the far right or the hard left. The concern to prevent incitement to racial and religious hatred, for example, is also underpinned by the perceived need to prevent public disorder, hence the name given to the relevant legislation—the Public Order Act. In 2016, the High Court upheld an appeal against a decision by the University of Southampton to cancel a conference organized by two of its professors. The conference, entitled "Public Law and the State of Israel: Legitimacy, Responsibility and Exceptionalism," was to be held on the university's premises in April 2015. The conference was canceled amid concerns that the safety of staff, students, and visitors could not be guaranteed. The judge observed that "the Defendant (University of Southampton) made what appears on the face of it to be a perfectly rational and lawful decision on appeal against its refusal of permission for a conference to be held on its premises on 17–19 April 2015 because of concerns about security." This was because some of the planned conference speakers were controversial, the conference would promote only one point of view, and there was a high risk of large demonstrations. The judge added that the decision had been made by the university in good faith with conscientious application of the duty to protect free speech. There were no arguable grounds to challenge it.[55]

As we pointed out earlier, the more extreme and factually unfounded lines of current defamation of the Jewish state—as "criminal" to a supposedly altogether operatic degree; as supported by conspiratorially organized Jewish groups supposedly able to effortlessly control such organizations as the US State Department and presidency; as "Nazi," "racist," and so on—display strong structural similarities to the traditional and recurrent lines of defamation of Jews in general that make up the content of what we have here and elsewhere called *political antisemitism*—antisemitism as a delusive, pseudoexplanatory political theory. The connection may be obscure to eminent human rights lawyers, but it is as evident to a great many Jews as it is to both the authors of this chapter. Moreover, the specific slurs against Israel and the Jews characterized as antisemitic by the IHRA definition are also, as we have seen, easy enough to link back to the traditional vocabulary of political antisemitism, including its (genuinely) Nazi version. It is for that reason deeply disquieting to British Jews that the British Labour Party (which since the accession of Jeremy Corbyn to its leadership has become deeply embroiled in repeated controversies over its alleged antisemitism), though it has been reported in the press as having accepted the IHRA definition, has accepted it only subject to caveats. As David Conway describes this situation,

> While Corbyn has vociferously denied charges that he is an anti-Semite, he was eventually led to acknowledge the presence of anti-Semitism in certain pockets of his party and vow to do something about it. This he notionally did by appointing a special commission to look into the problem under his Shadow Attorney General Shami Chakrabati. Her report was published in June 2016. Besides that report, which on the whole exonerated the party, little action appeared to address the problem, much to the mounting consternation of many of party members and the general public, especially Jews.
>
> Their mounting frustration erupted at the end of March this year into a hastily convened demonstration on the steps of Parliament. Under the banner "Enough is Enough," protestors voiced frustration after reading press reports that five years earlier Jeremy Corbyn had lent his support on Facebook to an artists' display in London's East End of a large street mural depicting several distinctly Jewish-looking financiers playing Monopoly on the backs of several crouching naked people.
>
> Matters came to a head in July, after Labour's governing National Executive Committee endorsed a definition of anti-Semitism drawn up in 2016 by the International Holocaust Remembrance Alliance (IHRA), which has since become widely adopted elsewhere in Britain and other liberal democracies. The rub was that Labour accepted the IHRA definition but declined to embrace several illustrative examples the IHRA had given as part of the definition. Most notable among the illustrative examples of anti-Semitism that Labour's NEC declined to accept were the following: accusing Jewish people

of being more loyal to Israel than their home country; claiming that Israel's existence as a state is a racist endeavour; and likening contemporary Israeli polices to those of the Nazis.[56]

In effect, the National Executive Committee of the British Labour Party has reserved the right to accuse Jews, simply by virtue of supporting Israel, of caring nothing for the welfare of any race other than their own, of being potential traitors to their nations of citizenship, and of being fellow travelers of Nazism. The first two are standard components of previous versions of political antisemitism, including the Nazi version; the third offers an interesting new twist on the old delusions. In a political climate in which things like this can happen, it is not surprising that, as Conway notes, "reportedly, as many as 40 percent of Britain's 300,000 Jewish population have intimated that they would seriously consider moving to Israel if Jeremy Corbyn becomes PM."

Conclusion

We conclude that, *pace* our four critics, there is not a great deal wrong with the IHRA definition as a guide to current antisemitism. If it has a defect, it is merely that the ambiguity of its opening general characterization of the nature of antisemitism needlessly allows critics to read it as stressing the identity of antisemitism as a form of emotional disposition while ignoring its other identity as a form of pseudoexplanatory delusion. But that, as we have seen, is a defect very easily remedied.

Notes

1. Peter Walker, "UK Adopts Antisemitism Definition to Combat Hate Crime against Jews," *Guardian*, December 12, 2016.
2. "This does not in any way undermine the freedom of expression on Israel and the Palestinians"; see "Labour Adopts Antisemitism Definition, but Guarantees Free Speech on Israel," BICOM, September 5, 2018, http://www.bicom.org.uk/news/labour-adopts-antisemitism-definition-but-guarantees-free-speech-on-israel.
3. Hugh Tomlinson, "In the Matter of the Adoption and Potential Application of the International Holocaust Remembrance Alliance Working Definition of Anti-Semitism," Free Speech on Israel, March 8, 2017, https://freespeechonisrael.org.uk/ihra-opinion/#sthash.BfwCEkhE.dpbs.
4. Geoffrey Robertson, "Anti-Semitism: The IHRA Definition and Its Consequences for Freedom of Expression," Doughty Street Chambers, August 31, 2018, https://www.doughtystreet.co.uk/news/ihra-definition-antisemitism-not-fit-purpose.
5. Stephen Sedley, "Defining Anti-Semitism," *London Review of Books*, May 4, 2017.
6. Rebecca Ruth Gould, "Legal Form and Legal Legitimacy: The IHRA Definition of Antisemitism as a Case Study in Censored Speech," *Law, Culture and the Humanities* 14 (August 2018): 1–34.

7. Kenneth L. Marcus, *The Definition of Anti-Semitism* (Oxford: Oxford University Press, 2015), 18.
8. Marcus, *Definition of Anti-Semitism*, 22–23.
9. Marcus, 20.
10. Tomlinson, "In the Matter," n.p.
11. Robertson, "Anti-Semitism," 7.
12. Tomlinson, "In the Matter," n.p.
13. Tomlinson, n.p.
14. Robertson, 18.
15. Robertson, 17–18.
16. Robertson, 1–2.
17. Public Order Act 1986, s. 5.
18. Robertson, 23.
19. Robertson, 7.
20. Robertson, 7.
21. Sedley, "Defining Anti-Semitism," 8.
22. Gould, "Legal Form and Legal Legitimacy," 9.
23. Richard Goldstone, "Reconsidering the Goldstone Report on Israel and War Crimes," *Washington Post*, April 1, 2011, https://www.washingtonpost.com/opinions/reconsidering-the-goldstone-report-on-israel-and-war-crimes/2011/04/01/AFg111JC_story.html.
24. For the origins of this distinction and the associated terminology, see Bernard Harrison, *The Resurgence of Anti-Semitism: Jews, Israel and Liberal Opinion* (New York: Rowman and Littlefield, 2006), 12–13. For a more developed account, see Bernard Harrison, *Blaming the Jews: The Persistence of a Delusion* (Bloomington: Indiana University Press, 2020).
25. Jean-Paul Sartre, *Antisemite and Jew* (New York: Grove, 1962), 41.
26. Elhanan Yakira, "Antisemitism and Anti-Zionism as a Moral Question," in *Resurgent Antisemitism: Global Perspectives*, ed. Alvin H. Rosenfeld (Bloomington: Indiana University Press, 2013), 56.
27. Jacqueline Rose, *The Question of Zion* (Princeton, NJ: Princeton University Press, 2005), 115–16.
28. "An Exchange on Edward Said and Difference," *Critical Inquiry* 15 (Spring 1989): 641.
29. This account of the origins of Israel is in no way controversial but follows the account given by Benny Morris in *1948: The First Arab-Israeli War* (New Haven, CT: Yale University Press, 2008) and many other historians.
30. Henry Fielding, *The History of Tom Jones* (London: Folio Press, 1959), book XV, chapter 1, 495.
31. Natan Sharansky, "Antisemitism in 3D," *Jerusalem Post*, February 23, 2004.
32. Sedley, "Defining Anti-Semitism," 8.
33. Robertson, "Anti-Semitism," 2.
34. Robertson, 3.
35. Sedley, "Defining Anti-Semitism," 9.
36. Alan Johnson, "Antisemitism in the Guise of Anti-Nazism: Holocaust Inversion in the UK during Operation Protective Edge" (paper presented at the Anti-Zionism, Antisemitism and the Dynamics of Delegitimization conference, Institute for the Study of Contemporary Antisemitism, Indiana University, Bloomington, April 2–6, 2016).
37. Paul Iganski and Abe Sweiry, "Playing the Nazi Card: Israel, Jews, and Antisemitism" in *Politics and Resentment: Antisemitism and Counter-Cosmopolitanism in the European Union*, ed. Lars Rensmann and Julius H. Schoeps (Leiden, Neth.: Brill, 2010), 183–96.

38. Robert S. Wistrich, "Anti-Zionism and Antisemitism," *Jewish Political Studies Review* 16, nos. 3–4 (Fall 2004): 29.

39. Amy Klein, "Denying the Deniers: Q & A with Deborah Lipstadt," *JTA News*, April 19, 2009.

40. Klein, "Denying the Deniers."

41. The Community Security Trust's "Antisemitic Incidents Report 2018" suggested that the highest monthly total of antisemitic incidents (182) in May was likely to be caused in part by reactions to the surge in violence on the border between Israel and Gaza during that month. "CST Antisemitic Incidents Report 2018," Community Security Trust, February 7, 2019, https://cst.org.uk/news/blog/2019/02/07/antisemitic-incidents-report-2018.

42. Part 3A Public Order Act 1986, inserted (1.10. 2007) by Racial and Religious Hatred Act 2006 (c. 1), ss. 1, 3(2), Sch.; S. I. 2007/2490 {art. 2}.

43. Crown Prosecution Service, *Hate Crime: What It Is and How to Support Victims and Witnesses*, October 2016, https://www.cps.gov.uk/sites/default/files/documents/publications/Hate-Crime-what-it-is-and-how-to-support-victims-and-witnesses.pdf.

44. Ben Welch, "Alison Chabloz Convicted over Antisemitic Songs in Landmark Case," *Jewish Chronicle*, May 25, 2018, https://www.thejc.com/news/uk-news/alison-chabloz-antisemitic-songs-blogger-1.464612.

45. R v. Alison Chabloz, [2019] Southwark Crown Court, February 13.

46. Mr R. Fraser v. University & College Union, (2013), https://www.judiciary.uk/judgments/fraser-uni-college-union/.

47. R (E) v. Governing Body of JFS, [2009] UKSC 15, para. 39.

48. David Graham and Jonathan Boyd, "Committed, Concerned and Conciliatory: The Attitudes of Jews in Britain towards Israel," JPR/Institute for Jewish Policy Research, July 15, 2010, https://archive.jpr.org.uk/download?id=1509.

49. Lesley Klaff, "Anti-Zionist Expressions on the UK Campus: Free Speech or Hate Speech?," *Jewish Political Studies Review* 22, nos. 3–4 (Fall 2010): 87–109.

50. Robertson, "Anti-Semitism," 1–2

51. Lingens v. Austria, 8 E.H.R.R. 407 ECtHR (1986) at 42.

52. Mari J. Matsuda, "Public Response to Racist Speech: Considering the Victim's Story," *Michigan Law Review* 87, no. 8 (1989): 2320–81. Richard Delgado and Jean Stefancic, *Understanding Words That Wound* (Boulder, CO: Westview, 2004).

53. Harry Yorke, "Jeremy Corbyn Praised by Nick Griffin and Former KKK Leader after 'British Zionists Don't Understand English Irony' Comments," *Telegraph*, August 21, 2018, https://www.telegraph.co.uk/politics/2018/08/24/jeremy-corbyn-praised-nick-griffin-former-kkk-leaderafter-video/.

54. Oliver Milne, "Jewish MP Luciana Berger Flanked by Police Protection at Labour Conference after Months of Antisemitic Threats," *Mirror Online*, September 24, 2018, https://www.mirror.co.uk/news/politics/jewish-mp-luciana-berger-flanked-13298354.

55. Ben-Dor & Ors, R (on the application of) v. University of Southampton, [2016] EWHC 953.

56. David Conway, "Is Jeremy Corbyn's Labour Party a Home for Anti-Semitism?," Law/Liberty.org, September 10, 2018, https://lawliberty.org/jeremy-corbyn-labour-anti-semitism/.

BERNARD HARRISON holds emeritus chairs in philosophy at the University of Utah and the University of Sussex, UK. He is author of *The Resurgence of Antisemitism: Jews, Israel and Liberal Opinion*

(Rowman and Littlefield, 2006) and *Blaming the Jews: Politics and Delusion* (Indiana University Press, 2020). Other books include *What Is Fiction For? Literary Humanism Restored* (Indiana University Press, 2015) and—with Patricia Hanna—*Word and World: Practice and the Foundations of Language* (Cambridge University Press, 2004). A wide selection of journal articles and other shorter pieces, including much recent work on antisemitism, can be downloaded from his website at http://bernardharrison1.academia.edu.

LESLEY KLAFF is Senior Lecturer in Law at the Helena Kennedy Centre for International Justice, Sheffield Hallam University, and provides pro bono legal assistance on behalf of UK Lawyers for Israel (UKLFI). She is editor in chief of the *Journal of Contemporary Antisemitism* and is a member of the editorial board of the International Journal of the Social Science Research Foundation. She is also a member of the advisory board of the Louis D. Brandeis Center for Human Rights under Law. She has published widely on contemporary antisemitism, and in 2015 and 2016 she organized (with Jonathan Campbell) two Bristol-Sheffield Hallam Colloquia on Contemporary Antisemitism. Her most recent work, *Unity and Diversity in Contemporary Antisemitism: The Bristol-Sheffield Hallam Colloquium on Contemporary Antisemitism* (edited with Jonathan G. Campbell), was published by Academic Studies Press in October 2019. In 2018, she was named by the *Algemeiner* newspaper as one of the top one hundred people positively influencing Jewish life.

2

Applying the IHRA Working Definition to the UN and Human Rights NGOs

Gerald M. Steinberg

A GROWING BODY OF RESEARCH HAS EMERGED IN recent years on the topic of the "new antisemitism," in contrast to the "old" far-right and theological version. The new form focuses specifically on Israel, shifting the focus of hostility from Jews as individuals or as a foreign religious and cultural collective to Jewish political power through the state of Israel and its citizens.[1] As noted British solicitor and academic Anthony Julius wrote, anti-Zionism is "predicated on the illegitimacy of the Zionist enterprise."[2] In recent years, the radius and intensity of this visceral hostility have increased significantly, from the British Labour Party under Corbyn to university campuses in Britain, Europe, and North America; to United Nations frameworks; and to other institutions.[3]

While anti-Zionist antisemitism targeting the Jewish political collective is indeed "new," research and analysis have shown that it shares a number of properties and expressions that are characteristic of the "old" theological and nationalistic version. In particular, symbols and images of Jews appear in both, in the form of conspiracy theories (spiderwebs, octopuses, etc.) that emphasize vengeance, blood lust, avarice, and similar characteristics.[4] Some anti-Israel frameworks, particularly linked to radical Palestinian church-based NGOs (such as the Sabeel Ecumenical Liberation Theology Center), repeat the classical antisemitic formulation known as supersessionism (also called replacement theology) and the delegitimization of the Jewish religion. Sabeel and similar groups also promote the 2009 Kairos Palestine document.[5]

The violence that has accompanied the spread of the new antisemitism adds to the urgency of this analysis. Data show the close correlation between the intensity of Israel-focused "modern antisemitism" and the incidence of violent attacks against Jews and Jewish institutions around the world. Attacks are linked to a public atmosphere in Europe that paints Israel as a monster that is responsible for terrible violations of human rights, thus adding to the underlying antisemitism.[6] Accusations couched in the language of human rights and international law and made in venues such as the United Nations Human Rights Council and the International Criminal Court add to this hostility.[7]

The new antisemitism is not simply "criticism of Israel" or of Israeli policies, as is sometimes claimed. Rather, it denies the Jewish people the status of a nation with national rights and rejects the legitimacy of the Jewish state, regardless of borders, often through the prism of postcolonial ideology.[8] As Kenneth L. Marcus notes, "The ideology of the new antisemitism consists of negative stereotypes describing the Jewish state and its members, supporters, and coreligionists as immoral, threatening, and categorically different than other people, and it favors the use of exclusion, restriction, and suppression in solving the 'Israel problem.'"[9] Similarly, according to Irwin Cotler, "The new anti-Semitism involves the discrimination against, denial of, or assault upon, the right of the Jewish people to live as an equal member of the family of nations masked through the language of universal public values and, under the protective cover of the UN, the authority of international law, the culture of human rights, and the struggle against racism."[10]

The IHRA Working Definition: Background

In seeking to accurately describe, analyze, and respond effectively to the return of antisemitism, both old and new, to the world stage, it is important to clearly and consistently identify its salient manifestations. In recent years, a consensus has developed around the working definition promulgated by the International Holocaust Remembrance Alliance (IHRA).

The IHRA framework was launched in 2000 at the Stockholm International Forum on the Holocaust, and, as of June 2019, had thirty-five state members,[11] eleven observers, and a number of permanent international partners, including the Claims Conference, the European Union's Agency for Fundamental Rights (FRA), the OSCE Office for Democratic Institutions and Human Rights (OSCE/ODIHR), UNESCO, the UN, and the Council of Europe.¹² In 2016, the members of IHRA adopted a working definition of antisemitism, based on a 2005 document prepared by the EU Monitoring Centre on Racism and Xenophobia (EUMC)[13] and its successor, the FRA.[14] As of July 2019, the IHRA definition has been adopted by seventeen countries, including the UK and Canada, and supported in resolutions of national legislatures in Austria, Bulgaria, Germany, Lithuania, Romania, and North Macedonia.[15] A very similar version is used by the United States Department of State and Civil Service Commission.[16] A number of legislative bodies, including the European Parliament, have also adopted resolutions endorsing the IHRA working definition.[17]

The terms and examples in the IHRA working definition encompass both the old and the new antisemitism. The former include "making mendacious, dehumanizing, demonizing, or stereotypical allegations about Jews as such or the power of Jews as collective—such as, especially but not exclusively, the myth about a world Jewish conspiracy or of Jews controlling the media, economy, government or other societal institutions."

The latter, as presented in the document, include the following:

i. Denying the Jewish people their right to self-determination, e.g., by claiming that the existence of a State of Israel is a racist endeavor.
ii. Applying double standards by requiring of it a behavior not expected or demanded of any other democratic nation.
iii. Using the symbols and images associated with classic antisemitism (e.g., claims of Jews killing Jesus or blood libel) to characterize Israel or Israelis.
iv. Drawing comparisons of contemporary Israeli policy to that of the Nazis.
v. Holding Jews collectively responsible for actions of the state of Israel.[18]

The IHRA document has become the primary reference in determining whether a particular statement or action is indeed antisemitic and is a widely used analytical framework in relevant research and policy contexts. The specific implementation of the definition varies from state to state—in some cases, the working definition is largely declaratory, while in other situations, it is embodied into legal frameworks.[19] Several British church frameworks have also adopted the IHRA definition, including the bishops of the Church of England,[20] the general assembly of the Church of Scotland,[21] and the Church of Wales.[22]

However, there are significant international frameworks where the IHRA working definition remains unrecognized, such as the United Nations and affiliated agencies.[23] Robert Wistrich referred to "the systematic manner in which Israel is harassed at international forums such as the

United Nations, where the Arab states have for decades pursued a policy of isolating the Jewish state and turning it into a pariah."[24] The infamous 1975 "Zionism is racism" resolution (rescinded in 1991) and the 2001 UN Durban Conference (see below) highlighted the ease with which this body is exploited for singling out Israel, and there are numerous and ongoing manifestations.

An academic systematic study of UN General Assembly resolutions between 1990 and 2013 showed that "65% of instances in which a country is criticized in a resolution, the country is Israel, with no other country criticized in more than 10% of resolutions."[25] Similarly, the activities and agendas of UN agencies such as the Department of Palestinian Affairs (DPA), the Committee on the Exercise of the Inalienable Rights of the Palestinian People (CEIRPP), the UN Relief and Works Agency (UNRWA), the Palestine office of UNICEF, and the Human Rights Council (UNHRC) often exhibit the traits that the working definition cites as illustrations of antisemitism.[26]

A number of prominent NGOs claiming normative agendas on human rights, international law, promoting peace, and similar topics, who are frequent participants and partners in these UN frameworks, are also among the leaders in using double standards to single out Israel for condemnation, applying double standards, denying the Jewish people the right to self-determination, and comparing Nazi actions with those of Israel.

Applying the IHRA Definition to the BDS Movement

In applying the IHRA working definition to political groups, including NGOs that promote political and ideological positions in the Israeli-Palestinian conflict, the recognition of the BDS (boycotts, divestment, and sanctions) movement as a form of antisemitism is of increasing importance. BDS arose in the context of the 2001 NGO Forum of the Durban Conference, which launched the anti-Israel boycott and lawfare campaigns, applying the tools that were used during the antiapartheid struggle in South Africa.[27] As the boycott campaigns gained visibility, this process was accompanied by the assertion that this activity was a form of antisemitism.

With the publication of the IHRA working definition in 2016, the debate was clarified and became more intense. Although the text does not mention BDS per se, the linkages, according to the document, were made in a number of cases. In particular, these claims argued that BDS undermines the fundamental Jewish right to self-determination, citing statements at the First Palestinian Conference for the Boycott of Israel "that the

BDS campaign does not only target Israel's economy, but challenges Israel's legitimacy, being a colonial and apartheid state, as part of the international community." Such statements fall under the IHRA category of "denying the Jewish people their right to self-determination, e.g., by claiming that the existence of a State of Israel is a racist endeavor."

Other aspects of this campaign exemplify the IHRA category of "applying double standards by requiring of it a behavior not expected or demanded of any other democratic nation." In particular, justifications of BDS are based on repeated allegations of Israeli "war crimes" and violations of international law, when no or few parallel claims are made in other contexts of violent and asymmetric ethno-national or religious conflicts.[28] The fact that no BDS campaigns exist in any other contexts highlights the double-standards dimension.

On this basis, and citing the IHRA working definition, a number of institutions have officially endorsed this linkage. For example, in Germany, on May 17, 2019, the Bundestag approved the governing coalition's resolution condemning BDS as antisemitism, which quoted and was based on the IHRA definition.[29] Germany's resolution inspired other European leaders, including British Secretary of State for Foreign and Commonwealth Affairs Jeremy Hunt, who tweeted on May 18, 2019, "Boycotting Israel—the world's only Jewish state—is antisemitic. I salute Germany for taking a stand."[30]

Criticism of the IHRA Definition

The acknowledgment that ideological anti-Zionism and the obsessive singling out of Israel are indeed expressions of antisemitism has been a gradual and evolutionary process, accompanied by efforts to block and reverse this recognition. In parallel to the increasing acceptance of the IHRA working definition, the actors that have been promoting the very behavior and activities that made it necessary to codify and apply expressions of the "new antisemitism" have sought to delegitimize this process.

The most common denunciation embodies the claim that the real objective in the expansion of the definition in this way is to "silence all criticism of Israel" and to "mobilize Jewish victim power against the Palestinians." (David Hirsh refers to this as the Livingstone formulation, named after the former London mayor.[31]) Similarly, in their comprehensive analysis of this issue, Bernard Harrison and Lesley Klaff quote the accusation that "the definition and its examples were drafted with the 'hidden agenda' that they could be used to ban criticism of Israeli policy and to label the nascent BDS movement as 'anti-Semitic.'"[32] (To the degree that the reference to a "hidden agenda" is an echo of Jewish conspiracy theories, it is itself an example of antisemitism, in which classical antisemitic themes are attributed to Jewish and non-Jewish supporters of Israel.) The same holds for clearly politicized analyses that reject the IHRA working definition as an attempt to "conflate" the issues "by characterising anything other than anodyne criticism of Israel as anti-Semitic."[33]

In addition, the IHRA working definition and its application to BDS, among other campaigns, is attacked as "inhibiting freedom of speech." In recognition of these counterarguments, when the British government adopted the definition in 2016, it reiterated the comparative dimension in the IHRA formulation, noting that "criticism of Israel similar to that levelled against any other country" is clearly not antisemitic.[34]

The numerous responses and counters to these claims emphasize the differences between criticism of Israel and defamation, and the use of double standards singling out Israel as the nation-state of the Jewish people in contrast to criticism of the actions of other democratic societies. As per Harrison and Klaff, none of the criticisms "concerning the supposed power of the definition to silence criticism of Israel appear to be supported by the terms of the IHRA definition itself."[35] The language in the document is very specific, and most of the accusations against Israel, including many false claims that are far from "anodyne," would not meet the criteria of antisemitism. And at the same time, the space for intense criticism remains very wide, without needing to cross the line into flagrant double standards, Nazi comparisons, and the other specific parameters in the working definition.[36]

Case Study: Human Rights Watch

When Human Rights Watch (HRW; originally called Helsinki Watch) was founded by Robert Bernstein in the 1970s, its mandate and actions were clearly defined and consistently pursued, based on promoting the Universal Declaration of Human Rights, particularly in closed societies and on behalf of political prisoners.[37] HRW grew rapidly in budget, scope, and influence, and by the 1990s, it was (along with Amnesty International) the most powerful and significant human rights NGO in the world. Officials from the organization testified in the US Congress and other parliaments, addressed UN bodies, were invited to address academic conferences, and were featured frequently in a wide range of media platforms.[38]

With the end of the Cold War and the collapse of the Soviet Union, the organization's emphasis shifted to advocacy campaigns centered on claims regarding international law, the laws of armed conflict, and responses to terrorism. In parallel, under the leadership of Kenneth Roth, who has been the executive director since 1993, the activities of HRW and particularly the Middle East and North Africa (MENA) Division increasingly highlighted Israel, with repeated condemnations, denunciations, and calls for sanctions. Roth hired activists such as Joel Stork and Sarah Leah Whitson who had previously been involved in anti-Israel campaigns, and they, in turn, hired others with similar records. In assessing the overall approach, Jonathan Foreman concludes that "it often feels as if Roth has a religious sense of mission regarding Israel; it's his crusade. In general, Roth never admits to being wrong and consistently represents HRW and its staff as infallible.... But he responds with particular, extraordinary ferocity to any and all skeptical questioning of himself and the organization concerning Israel. HRW is of course not alone in subjecting Israel to disproportionate attention and particularly hostile scrutiny."[39]

Double Standards Requiring Behavior Not Expected or Demanded of Any Other Democratic Nation

In assessing HRW's record on Israel in light of the IHRA working definition, the first criterion refers to "applying double standards by requiring of it a behavior not expected or demanded of any other democratic nation." Beyond the IHRA, it should be noted that double standards and nondiscrimination are also fundamentally incompatible with the principle of universality in human rights, as highlighted in studies by Robert Blitt and others.[40]

A number of previously published analyses of HRW and Israel, including the study by Pascal Vennesson and Nikolas M. Rajkovic, have suggested a record of double standards, discriminatory behavior, and disproportionate criticism. In several examples, they examine HRW's efforts to use the organization's perceived moral authority against the Israel Defense Forces (IDF), citing bias and contradictory HRW "fact finding" in making accusations.[41]

Similarly, Catherine Fitzpatrick, research director at HRW during the 1980s and 1990s, has noted, "The chief problem of Human Rights Watch in this and other matters related to the Middle East is that it sees itself as the sole honest arbiter of what constitutes compliance with human rights. Yet it does so in a highly politicized manner, not recognizing the essential 'political' act of picking and choosing cases and priorities, and engaging with or rejecting this or that regime ... human rights groups would do better to 'go where the violations are' instead of 'endlessly balancing the saddle bags.'"[42] Making a similar but more generalized point, Foreman argues that "the overall amount of material put out on Israel, measured by words and pages, is strikingly out of balance and because HRW's reports on Israel are uniquely accompanied in almost every case by high-profile press releases and press conferences. As its executive director, Roth has devoted much of his letter writing and public work to alleged Israeli crimes, to the exclusion of other matters."[43]

These observations are supported by a detailed quantitative comparative analysis of all HRW reports, press releases, letters, and commentaries between 2005 and 2010 on the MENA region. The 259 press releases on Israel and the 20 large-scale reports (1,903 pages) published in this period were the highest among the countries in the MENA region and far exceeded HRW's output on Syria (4 reports, 217 pages, and 85 press releases) and Saudi Arabia (9 reports, 616 pages, and 142 press releases), for example. As shown in this research, the number of reports and pages devoted by HRW to the countries of the Middle East stands in inverse correlation to the openness of the different societies, as measured by Freedom House. From 2005 to 2008, while maintaining a continuous flow of reports and media activities targeting Israel, HRW did not publish a single report on Saudi Arabia.[44] This record highlights the disproportionality in the focus on Israel.

Other comparative studies of HRW's agenda also note the inherent bias and double standards, which are particularly evident during periods of violence and when media attention is heightened beyond the already elevated background level regarding Israel. During the July–August 2014 Gaza war, the double standards were reflected through analysis of HRW output on the violent conflicts in Yemen and Ukraine taking place during this period, compared to Gaza. In this study as well, the evidence of disproportionality and singling out was clear.[45] And in contrast to Roth's casual claim that HRW devotes 1 percent of its budget to Israel (this in response to questions about disproportionality), the actual amount appears significantly higher.[46] Among other indicators, the number of personnel in the organization focusing on Israel and the involvement of senior officials, in comparison to other countries (particularly in the MENA division), reinforces the evidence of significant disproportionality.

The excessive focus on Israel is also evident in HRW's social media activity. An analysis based on NGO Monitor's catalog of more than four hundred tweets from Ken Roth during and around the 2014 Gaza war (July 5–September 2, 2014) noted that these constituted one-quarter of his posts. In some weeks, this number approached 50–60 percent.[47] As Foreman notes, Roth's tweets were dominated to an extraordinary degree by one specific country: Israel and its conduct of the war with Hamas. No other subject received half or even a third of the attention. On some days up to half of Roth's tweets (and he can tweet up to 40 times in a day, including retweets) were devoted to Gaza.... On July 23, out of 28 tweets by Roth, 12 were critical of Israel.... Other things happened in the world.... The last week in July was the worst in Syria's civil war for some three years—with 1,700 deaths.... Meanwhile, the terrorist group Islamic State in Iraq and Syria (ISIS) persecuted and drove out the Christians of Mosul. Roth did tweet about the crises in both places ... but with nothing remotely like the obsessive energy he brought to the Israel issue.[48]

Based on evidence of HRW's double standards, founder Robert Bernstein made a sharp break with the organization, denouncing HRW in an opinion column he published in the *New York Times*.[49] He accused HRW of using its resources and influence to lead the campaign seeking to "turn Israel into a pariah state." In subsequent speeches at the University of Nebraska[50] (2010) and Hebrew Union College in New York[51] (2013), he went into further detail in accusing the leaders of the organization he had founded of abusing their positions.

In addition to the quantitative evidence based on HRW's overall output regarding Israel compared to other countries, an analysis of many specific campaigns between 2001 and 2019 reinforces the evidence of double standards and disproportionality.[52] Similarly, the use of language largely applied to Israel alone also constitutes a form of double standard in the context of the IHRA working definition.[53]

For this analysis, HRW's prominent participation in the antisemitic 2001 NGO Forum of the Durban Conference is a useful starting point. Copies of antisemitic literature, such as the *Protocols of the Elders of Zion* and cartoons of hook-nosed Jews with "pots of money surrounding their victims," were distributed, and Jewish and Israeli delegates were subject to physical intimidation,[54] including incidents in which the head of the HRW delegation, Reed Brody, participated.[55] The Forum's Final Declaration included a number of demonizing statements, such as, "targeted victims of Israel's brand of apartheid and ethnic cleansing methods have been in particular children, women and refugees" (Article 164). Similarly, Article 425 advocated "a policy of complete and total isolation of Israel as an apartheid state ... the imposition of mandatory and comprehensive sanctions and embargoes, [and] the full cessation of all links."[56] In terms of the IHRA antisemitism criteria, the Durban Conference was a very clear example of "double standards ... requiring of [Israel] a behavior not expected or demanded of any other democratic nation."

Following Durban, HRW continued to be centrally involved in double standards and a disproportionate focus designed to uniquely delegitimize Israeli responses to Palestinian mass terror attacks. From the IDF antiterror operation in Jenin in 2002, the 2006 Lebanon war, and more than a decade of Gaza conflicts to the most recent border clashes in 2019, HRW's record reflects a systematic bias. While the organization published sporadic criticism and made allegations of war crimes in many other cases of armed conflict, including the involvement of US-led coalitions in Iran and Afghanistan and Russian forces in Georgia and Ukraine, the intensity of the focus of criticism against Israel, using terms such as *war crimes*, reflects a major and systematic bias. Additional unique aspects of HRW responses on Israel are the repeated calls for investigations by the inherently biased United Nations Human Rights Council in order to impose sanctions, and prosecutions by the International Criminal Court.[57]

In the time frame under consideration in this study (2001–2018), HRW issued an almost continuous stream of condemnations related to military clashes involving Israeli responses to terrorism and armed attacks. A complete and detailed analysis of each of the instances is beyond the scope of this research, but a few examples demonstrate a pattern that applies to many other cases.

For example, in April 2002, after Palestinian officials claimed that the IDF had committed a "massacre" in an antiterror operation at the Jenin refugee camp, HRW issued fifteen press releases and reports in a four-week period accusing Israel of "indiscriminate" attacks, "disproportionate" use of force, "murder," "willful killing," and "war crimes" and demanding the appointment of an "independent investigative committee." HRW's campaign, which was echoed in the international media, was instrumental in triggering UN Secretary-General Kofi Annan's decision to appoint a "fact-finding team" to "investigate" the allegations; the report generally followed HRW's narrative.[58] In this time frame, and despite ongoing armed conflicts in other regions, there were no other instances of UN investigations, thereby reflecting the impact of the double standard applied to Israel.

A second example is the June 2006 "Gaza Beach incident," in which eight Palestinian civilians were reportedly killed in an Israeli attack. Though the details were and remain confused, HRW initiated a major campaign condemning Israel, led by Marc Garlasco, the "senior military analyst." In a series of highly publicized statements and a press conference in Gaza, the purported details of the explosives and technical information, which relied on dubious sources such as a "forensics" facility in Gaza, changed rapidly.

HRW repeatedly accused the IDF of being "incapable of uncovering the truth" and repeated the call for an "independent, international investigation."[59] (Garlasco's "military expertise" has been widely questioned, and HRW terminated his employment after he was revealed to be an obsessive collector of Nazi memorabilia.[60]) HRW issued three condemnations over six days—the first less than twenty-four hours after the event.

One month later, in July 2006, HRW again launched a major campaign in the context of the Second Lebanon War (triggered by a Hizballah missile attack and cross-border raid in which eight Israelis were killed and two kidnapped). HRW issued over fifty documents, including letters, op-eds, and long reports claiming that the IDF had "deliberately indiscriminately" bombed civilian targets, used "indiscriminate force," and showed a "disregard" toward international law. (HRW mentioned the Hizballah attacks briefly, and its only report on Hizballah's indiscriminate rocket fire into Israel was published a full year after the war ended.[61]) As in the past, HRW called for UN investigations and "war crimes" prosecutions of the "Israeli Commanders who . . . ordered such attacks."[62] An examination of HRW's agenda in the case of many other armed conflicts around the world shows the unique intensity of the effort surrounding the Lebanon war—there are no comparable examples in terms of the number of documents and their contents.

A very similar campaign took place around the three-week Israeli military operation in Gaza that began on December 28, 2008. HRW again played a leading role, issuing six reports on this conflict. Roth again pressed UN Secretary-General Ban Ki-Moon to "lean on all actors, protect civilians, and ensure accountability. Only an impartial international investigation can achieve that."[63] As in the past, the UNHRC established the framework for a "fact-finding investigation" focused exclusively on Israel and led by Richard Goldstone.[64]

HRW was deeply involved in the nomination of Goldstone, who was a member of HRW's board. Between Goldstone's appointment in April 2009 and the publication of the final report, HRW issued more than fifteen calls praising the inquiry, promoting Goldstone's "eminent" character, demanding that Israel cooperate despite the inherent bias, and pressuring the newly elected Obama administration and others to use leverage to force Israel to cooperate and accept the legitimacy of this one-sided effort.

The 452-page Goldstone Report, presented on September 29, 2009, purported to document thirty-six incidents of alleged war crimes, primarily citing unverified NGO claims. Echoing HRW's language, the terms *crimes* and *war crimes* appear seventy times in Goldstone's text, as well as accusations of "indiscriminate attacks," discrimination against Palestinians (forty citations), and "intentional" targeting of civilians (nineteen citations).⁶⁵

In the month immediately after the publication of the report, HRW released twelve statements in support of Goldstone, and HRW officials were widely quoted in the media.⁶⁶ Many repeated the central accusation that Israel had been guilty of "willfully" killing civilians. HRW's campaign continued in 2010, with fourteen publications alleging the "inadequacy" of Israeli investigations into the Gaza War.⁶⁷ (On April 2, 2011, Goldstone published an op-ed article in the *Washington Post* acknowledging that "our fact-finding mission had no evidence" for the claims and conclusions of the report.⁶⁸)

Between 2010 and 2019, there were many more examples following the same pattern, in which HRW's activities reflected double standards and the singling out of Israel through allegations of "war crimes" and "intentional killing of civilians."⁶⁹ HRW's campaign during the 2014 Gaza confrontation followed the overall pattern in the previous cases, in particular from the 2008–9 conflict. Once again, the contrast between the frequency and intensity of the condemnations of Israel (for which HRW had no verifiable information) and the organization's far less extensive activities in other areas is striking. During the height of the Gaza conflict, a civilian airliner (Malaysian Airlines flight MH17) was shot down in Ukraine, killing 298 people, including 80 children. This was undoubtedly a massive war crime, but HRW issued only one short statement after a three-day delay.⁷⁰

The most recent illustration focused on the violence that took place in confrontations along the border fence separating Israel from Hamas-controlled Gaza (the "Great March of Return"). As in the past, HRW published dozens of condemnations of Israel, in the form of reports, letters, news releases, and other documents, which were largely aimed at influencing media coverage and again pressing for a UNHRC "investigation," which would again find Israel uniquely guilty and lead to sanctions. The report of the Committee of Investigation was published in March 2019 and included a number of references to and quotes from HRW.⁷¹

Singling Out Israel: HRW as a Leader in the BDS Movement

As noted, the campaign to boycott Israel, which is institutionalized in the BDS movement, has been widely defined as a form of antisemitism reflecting the "double standards" identified in the IHRA working definition. The

2019 resolution backed by the German government coalition and approved by the Bundestag explicitly linked BDS, antisemitism, and the IHRA document.[72] Although Roth claims that "no one representing Human Rights Watch . . . has advocated a boycott of Israel or of any Israeli entity. . . . we do not promote BDS, we do not promote boycotts," the evidence clearly shows otherwise.[73]

HRW involvement in and support of BDS campaigns began in the 2001 Durban NGO Forum. Roth and many of the employees in HRW's MENA division, including Whitson and Stork, as well as Lucy Meir (hired in 2005 as a researcher and previously affiliated with the Electronic Intifada website), Nadia Barhoum (a Palestinian campus BDS activist, added in 2008), Sari Bashi, and Omar S. Shakir (BDS and "one-state" advocate, hired in late 2015), have been centrally involved in these efforts. HRW reports, press releases, social media posts, and videos repeatedly link allegations of Israeli "war crimes" with calls for "sanctions."[74] Among recent examples, in June 2018 HRW again accused Israel of "apparent war crimes in Gaza" and demanded that "third countries should impose targeted sanctions" against Israelis.[75]

In the United States, HRW played a central role in the initial boycott efforts in 2004 targeting Caterpillar, including emails and letters, as well as demonstrations in Chicago during the company's annual shareholders' meeting.[76] (Caterpillar was ostensibly targeted for selling the IDF its D-9 bulldozers, which, according to HRW's contentious 135-page publication entitled "Razing Rafah," launched by executive director Ken Roth at a press conference in Jerusalem, were used to destroy structures along the border with Gaza.[77] These structures were located above openings to tunnels that were used for terror attacks against Israel.) In a CNN interview, Roth called for "conditioning" or cutting US aid funds to Israel.[78]

Throughout the following decade, HRW reports and allegations were among the main sources used by the BDS movement, while individual staff members continued to promote the campaign. In 2010 and 2011, HRW officials appeared in a video ("Occupation 101") shown at Israel Apartheid Week events held at university campuses in North America, and a prominent Palestinian BDS organization listed HRW among the resources in its "Handbook for Student Divestment Campaigns."[79] The organization is also actively involved in European "product labeling" campaigns, which are designed to prepare the ground for more intense BDS policies.[80]

In recent years, HRW's role in the BDS movement has intensified, including playing a central role in pressing the United Nations Human

Rights Council to publish a blacklist ("database") of Israeli and non-Israeli businesses that are falsely accused of violating international law. This resolution (31/36) was adopted in March 2016. Whitson, Roth, and Shakir have focused significant resources and time in promoting this effort, in coordination with Palestinian organizations and BDS-dedicated NGOs such as Who Profits. Between March 2016 and July 2019, HRW published sixteen reports, UN statements, public letters, commentaries, and news releases promoting this effort, as well as dozens of Twitter posts. The UN database of businesses, published in February 2020, marked a major victory for the BDS movement and perhaps the most significant development since the campaign was initiated.

However, as of July 2019, the publication has been delayed by approximately two years, reflecting the reluctance of the high commissioner for human rights to proceed with this BDS measure. In March 2019, after another decision to delay, Whitson tweeted, "Each delay further entrenches their support of systematic rights abuses of Palestinians tied to illegal settlements."[81]

The scale of HRW's effort is reflected in a number of highly publicized moves. For example, in January 2016 the organization published "Occupation Inc.," a 162-page report pressuring businesses to cease operations in the West Bank.[82] In November 2016, Sari Bashi, HRW Israel/Palestine advocacy director at the time, sent a public letter to the UN's high commissioner for human rights, Zeid Ra'ad Al Hussein, praising the blacklist resolution and specifying two non-Israeli companies (as well as Israeli soccer teams) to be included.[83] In November 2017, HRW issued a press release applauding the UNHRC database project for its role in "build[ing] pressure on businesses."

Banks were central targets of HRW's BDS efforts during this period, as reflected in the September 2017 publication "Israeli Law and Banking in West Bank Settlements." In an Associated Press interview, Bashi declared, "There are many, many steps banks can and should take. . . . If they choose not to take steps, institutional investors who care about their own human rights activity should take action."[84] The campaign was amplified in a May 2018 publication, "Bankrolling Abuse: Israeli Banks in West Bank Settlements," with a companion video and infographics.[85]

The high-tech accommodation and tourism firm Airbnb was another central HRW BDS target. For two years, Omar Shakir, hired by HRW in 2016, was the lead staffer for this campaign, directly lobbying the company's executives as well as coordinating outside pressure including demonstrations outside Airbnb's headquarters and extensive social media efforts.⁸⁶ In November 2018, Airbnb announced a policy of delisting properties owned by Jews in the West Bank, although claiming (without credibility) that this was not a form of BDS. Shakir, Whitson, Roth, and other HRW officials celebrated their success in social media posts. (The day after the Airbnb announcement, HRW and Kerem Navot—a small Israeli NGO also involved in BDS campaigns—published "Bed and Breakfast on Stolen Land: Tourist Rental Listings in West Bank Settlements."⁸⁷) However, their celebration was short-lived; a few months later, Airbnb reversed its policy, thereby acknowledging that despite the disclaimer, the action constituted participation in the anti-Israel boycott campaign.

Shakir also led HRW's campaign pressuring the international football (soccer) federation FIFA to expel, boycott, or sanction Israel.⁸⁸ (The original published version falsely claimed that one of the two fields had "illegally" usurped private land.) The campaign included letters, reports, extensive social media posts, and lobbying, accusing Israel of various "abuses." As in the Airbnb campaign, HRW's attempt to pressure FIFA into participating in the organization's BDS efforts failed.

In parallel to promoting BDS, HRW in general and Roth in particular also campaigned vigorously against the decision of the German Bundestag acknowledging BDS to be a form of antisemitism.⁸⁹ A representative of the American Jewish Committee responded sharply to Roth, stating, "Your research on this issue is as biased and incomplete as your Israel reports."⁹⁰ Similarly, when an official of the Jewish Museum in Berlin was criticized for appearing to endorse BDS, Roth tweeted that the head (Peter Schaefer) was being attacked "for not adhering slavishly to the Netanyahu view on Jerusalem and BDS. He included the Palestinian point of view in an exhibit and tweeted an article against equating BDS with anti-Semitism."⁹¹

"Denying the Jewish People Their Right to Self-Determination, e.g., by Claiming That the Existence of a State of Israel Is a Racist Endeavor"

The repeated use of terms such as *racism*, *apartheid*, and *colonialist* to describe Israel is a central element of the demonization process, as reflected in the 1975 UNGA Resolution (equating Zionism with racism) and the Durban NGO Forum Final Declaration.⁹² This aspect of the IHRA working definition of antisemitism is also relevant when parallel terms are invoked, such as *apartheid*, or "inherently discriminatory" terms that have the effect of "denying the Jewish people their right to self-determination."

In examining the record of HRW and its officials, the use of such language to refer to Israel is frequent and extends over the past two decades. In media appearances during the 2001 Durban Conference, Roth defended the event, referring to "Israeli racist practices" as "an appropriate topic."[93] In another form of "denying the Jewish people their right of self-determination," Roth and HRW endorsed the Palestinian claim to a "right of return" for millions of descendants of refugees from the 1948 war.[94] This position is interpreted as equivalent to calling for "the demise of Israel as a Jewish state."[95] In the context of BDS and the IHRA working definition, the leading scholar of antisemitism Yehuda Bauer has written,

> The meaning of the clause in the BDS platform that calls for the Palestinian "right of return," which if realized would put an end to the existence of the State of Israel as the state of the Jewish people, is very clear. Such an objective can be achieved only by war, since the vast majority of Israeli Jews—and not just them—will fight for their homes, and only their annihilation will accomplish a "right of return." Supporting the right of return clause is therefore a clear case of anti-Semitism; moreover, it is anti-Semitism that could lead to the genocide of Jews.[96]

These themes, as well as campaigns to delegitimize Israel as the national state of the Jewish people through analogies with racial segregation in the US ("Jim Crow laws of the American South"), are highlighted in HRW's condemnations of policies with respect to the Arab minority within Israel[97] and Palestinians in the West Bank and Gaza, such as in a 2010 publication headlined "Separate and Unequal."[98] This report includes 133 references to "discrimination" (or "discriminatory") and 11 references to "racism" (or "racial" and "racist").

Sarah Leah Whitson, HRW's director for the Middle East and North Africa since 2004, has frequently used these themes, including "racism" and "apartheid," to describe Israel.[99] In a 2011 op-ed headlined "A Matter of Civil Rights," Whitson wrote, "In a week when the U.S. paused to recall the assassination of Dr. Martin Luther King, President Peres might have considered King's message—an end to segregation—and why such a system of racial inequality remains in place in the Occupied Palestinian Territories." Her article contains twenty-three such references, including accusations of "laws and policies [that] strictly segregate Jews from Palestinians," "blatant racial inequality," and "racial discrimination and segregation."[100]

HRW's condemnations of Israeli democracy also emphasize these demonizing allegations. For example, a post on the April 2019 elections by Khulood Badawi (an HRW consultant) used the term *bigotry* in the headline and included references to "racial discrimination" and "entrenched discrimination and systematic rights abuses" as if these were inherent and self-evident in the mere existence of Israel.[101] (The subtitle read, "Israel's two leading parties spent the campaign jostling over who can carry out war crimes against Palestinians more aggressively.")

These terms are also prominent in the social media posts of HRW officials, including many by Whitson, Shakir, and Roth. In June 2019, Shakir tweeted, "As @hrw Israel Director, I can tell you that Israel is built on a two-tiered discriminatory regime & systematically violates the rights of millions."[102] On the Israeli elections, Whitson promoted Badawi's post, writing, "@KhuloodBadawi reveals more ugly bits and pieces of the racism machinery in #Israel." In another tweet responding to the head of the Zionist Organization of America, she asked, "Why is a racist ethno-nationalist state bad in US but ok in #Israel?" In a May 2018 tweet, in the context of violent clashes at the Gaza border, Whitson referred to the IDF as "ghouls."[103] A search of the tweets posted by these HRW officials as well as the retweets yields hundreds of examples where these terms are used in reference to Israel.[104]

In a July 2019 radio interview, Roth was asked directly and repeatedly to address the legitimacy of Israel as "a Jewish state." His response was long and circuitous and avoided a clear answer, asserting that "every state has a right to exist. But every state also has a duty to apply international human rights principles. . . . As a democracy . . . Israel can define itself any way it wants. I mean, lots of governments define themselves in nationalist terms. But that's not an excuse . . . because there are many Palestinians who live in Israel too who are citizens who deserve full rights."[105] While Roth did not deny the Jewish people their right to self-determination, he also refused repeatedly to affirm this right, and his language repeats HRW's characterization of Israel as "a racist endeavor."

"Using the Symbols and Images Associated with Classic Antisemitism (e.g., Claims of Jews Killing Jesus or Blood Libel) to Characterize Israel or Israelis"

The classic antisemitic themes of vengeance and avarice ("stolen land") are frequently used in HRW references to Israel. One of the most blatant examples is included in Roth's response to criticism of HRW's barrage of accusations during the 2006 Lebanon war: "An eye for an eye—or, more accurately in this case, twenty eyes for an eye—may have been the morality of some more primitive moment. But it is not the morality of international humanitarian law."[106] The *New York Sun* decried this statement as "a slur on the Jewish religion itself that is breathtaking in its ignorance.... To suggest that Judaism is a 'primitive' religion incompatible with contemporary morality is to engage in supersessionism, the de-legitimization of Judaism, the basis of much antisemitism."[107] Presumably chastened, Roth and other NGO staffers did not return to the theme of "an eye for an eye" or use other references to the Hebrew Bible in referring to Israel or Jews.

The intense HRW campaign that accompanied and followed the Gaza combat at the end of December 2008 and in early 2009 (known in Israel as Operation Cast Lead) featured repeated accusations against the IDF and the Israeli political leadership of deliberate and intentional killing. These were the main themes of over thirty HRW publications (reports, public letters, statements, and press releases), including six major publications with headlines such as "White Flag Deaths: Killings of Palestinian Civilians during Operation Cast Lead" during this period.[108]

Amplifying the direct impact of HRW's allegations of "vengeance" and "deliberate killing" in media reports, they were repeated and incorporated, without independent verification, in the highly publicized report of the UN Commission of Investigation (COI) headed by Goldstone. Goldstone had been a member of HRW's international advisory board and was close to Roth. Although Goldstone subsequently acknowledged that the COI lacked the factual basis for such conclusions, thereby implicitly repudiating HRW's accusations, by the time this was published (more than eighteen months after the initial report), the image linking Israel to intentional killing of civilians was widely disseminated.[109]

The images of deliberate killing and bloodlust continue to be a staple of HRW's agenda regarding Israel and were prominent during the later periods of combat in Gaza. One illustration is Roth's tweet after the reported deaths of Palestinians in a strike aimed at missiles and terror sites: "Cheap excuse. There were no 'human shields' when Israel targeted boys on beach, attacked hospital, killed 25 in house."[110] Foreman's analysis of Roth's tweets during this period notes that "the clear sense one gets from this tweet is that he *knew*, knew in his marrow, that the IDF was out for Gazan blood. He might never have fired an artillery piece or sent or received coordinates or been under fire, but there are some things you just know. Like the fact that the IDF is driven by vengeance and is looking for reasons to kill Arab kids."[111]

The themes of Jews as thieves and poisoners of wells and other antisemitic libels are featured in many of HRW's activities related to BDS and campaigns regarding land disputes, both inside pre-1967 Israel and in the occupied (or disputed) territories. The reference to "stolen land" in the headline and frequently in the text of the November 2018 publication "Bed and Breakfast on Stolen Land: Tourist Rental Listings in West Bank Settlements" is a case in point.[112] And on occasion, HRW staffers have also invoked the classic antisemitic themes of Jewish power and conspiracies, as highlighted in the *Protocols of the Elders of Zion*. In February 2019, referring to a tweet on antisemitism from the UK Labour party, Whitson tweeted, "Why is this #Israel interference in domestic UK politics acceptable? Is it only a problem when Russia does this?"[113]

"Drawing Comparisons of Contemporary Israeli Policy to That of the Nazis"

On numerous occasions, HRW officials have made statements and social media posts that were antisemitic in content and tone while turning a blind eye to the waves of violent antisemitism that should be a primary focus of any group claiming to promote a human rights agenda. A search of HRW's website for "anti-Semitism" covering the period from 2002 to 2019 yields only ninety-nine items and no reports dedicated to the topic.[114] None of the murderous antisemitic attacks of recent years in Europe and in the United States (including the synagogue shootings in Pittsburgh and Poway) led to a significant HRW focus on this issue.

In contrast, HRW has been actively engaged with the increase in "comparisons of contemporary Israeli policy to that of the Nazis." For example, in August 2014, Roth, HRW European media director Andrew Stroehlein, HRW EU director Lotte Leicht, and others promoted an advertisement in the *New York Times* and the *Guardian* placed by a fringe group, the International Jewish Anti-Zionist Network, equating "Nazi genocide" with "the massacre of Palestinians in Gaza." In their tweet, they added the text, "'Never again' must mean NEVER AGAIN FOR ANYONE!'"[115] (This post received approximately twenty-seven hundred retweets and thirteen hundred likes.) As noted by scholar Deborah Lipstadt, such comparisons constitute "softcore Holocaust denial," which is thriving "in phrases like 'Gaza is genocide' or that the Hamas tunnels are like the ones of the Warsaw Ghetto."[116] Making the same comparison in January 2015, Whitson commented on a US Holocaust Museum's display of "death and torture in Syria," declaring that the museum should "also show pics of death and destruction in #Gaza."[117]

In another example (September 2017), Roth tweeted, "Many rights activists condemn Israeli abuse & anti-Semitism. Some white supremacists embrace Israel & anti-Semitism."[118] The tweet was linked to an article, "Birds of a Feather," by Nada Elia on the theme of "similarities between fascism and Zionism" and referred to Israel as a "model for ethnic exclusion."[119] Daniel Kohn observed the degree to which this maliciously alludes "to 1930s Germany in order to besmirch the Jewish-majority state and its supporters. Roth, a trained attorney and son to a German Jew who fled Germany in 1938, knows this."[120]

Conclusion

The IHRA working definition of antisemitism can provide a useful template for analyzing the activities and agendas of institutions that go beyond governmental boundaries, including the United Nations and influential NGOs. Based on a research framework that uses the Israel-as-the-nation-state-of-the-Jewish-people dimensions of the IHRA document (in this example, four out of the five criteria), we have presented a detailed case study of Human Rights Watch, which is one of the most significant NGOs claiming a human rights agenda and is deeply involved in the relevant issues. The analysis expands and helps focus previously published criticism of Human Rights Watch in addition to providing additional examples and perspectives.

While a single case study, even when focused on a major actor and archetype, is limited in terms of the overall conclusions that can be drawn, the use of this analytical framework for additional relevant case studies is essential to formulating generalizable principles and conclusions. In the important and emerging academic field of antisemitism studies, generalizable results based on consistent definitions add to the critical mass. In parallel, debate and criticism of the model and template can lead to improvements and an evolving research approach. As additional research-rich case studies are undertaken, published, critiqued, and revised, the implementation of this approach will result in a significant contribution.

Notes

1. Bernard Harrison, *The Resurgence of Anti-Semitism: Jews, Israel and Liberal Opinion* (New York: Rowman and Littlefield, 2006); Bernard Lewis, "The New Anti-Semitism," *New York Review of Books*, April 1986.

2. Anthony Julius, *Trials of the Diaspora: A History of Anti-Semitism in England* (London: Oxford University Press, 2010), 456.

3. See, for example, David Hirsh, *Contemporary Left Antisemitism* (London: Routledge, 2018); Dave Rich, *The Left's Jewish Problem: Jeremy Corbyn, Israel and Anti-Semitism* (London: Biteback, 2016).

4. International Holocaust Remembrance Alliance, *Fact Sheet: Working Definition of Antisemitism*, October 24, 2017, https://holocaustremembrance.com/sites/default/files/fcat_sheet_working_definition_of_antisemitism.pdf.

5. The Kairos Palestine Document calls for churches to "stand against injustice and apartheid . . . [and] revisit theologies that justify crimes perpetrated against our people and the dispossession of the land." It has been denounced by many Jewish and Christian organizations, including the Central Conference of American Rabbis ("CCAR Resolution on the 2009 Kairos Document," April 15, 2010, https://www.ccarnet.org/ccar-resolutions/ccar-resolution-2009-kairos-document/) and the Simon Wiesenthal Center ("SWC Extremely Concerned by Flawed Presbyterian Palestinian 'Kairos' Study Guide," June 24, 2011, https://web.archive.org/web/20151225115557if_/https://www.wiesenthal.com/site/apps/nlnet/content2.aspx?c=lsKWLbPJLnF&b=6478433&ct=10887407#.Vn0uo537RhE).

6. See, for example, "CST Antisemitic Incidents Report 2018," Community Security Trust, February 7, 2019, https://cst.org.uk/news/blog/2019/02/07/antisemitic-incidents-report-2018.

7. Gerald M. Steinberg and Anne Herzberg, "The Role of International Legal Justice Discourse in Promoting the New Antisemitism," in *Anti-Zionism and Anti-Semitism: The Dynamics of Delegitimization*, ed. Alvin H. Rosenfeld (Bloomington: Indiana University Press, 2019), 117.

8. Robert S. Wistrich, "Anti-Zionism and Anti-Semitism," *Jewish Political Studies Review* 16, no. 3 (2004): 27–31; Robert S. Wistrich, *From Ambivalence to Betrayal* (Lincoln: University of Nebraska Press, 2012). See also Alvin H. Rosenfeld, "Introduction," in *Anti-Zionism and Anti-Semitism: The Dynamics of Delegitimization*, ed. Alvin H. Rosenfeld (Bloomington: Indiana University Press, 2019), xi; Gerald M. Steinberg, "Post-colonial Theory and the Ideology of Peace Studies," *Israel Affairs* 13, no. 4 (2007): 786–96.

9. Kenneth Marcus, "Jurisprudence of the New Anti-Semitism," *Wake Forest Law Review* 44 (April 2009): 101–60, https://papers.ssrn.com/sol3/Delivery.cfm/SSRN_ID1376592_code791913.pdf?abstractid=1376592&mirid=1.

10. Irwin Cotler, "Anti-Semitism, Old and New," *Algemeiner*, January 27, 2015, https://www.algemeiner.com/2015/01/27/anti-semitism-old-and-new/.

11. "Countries and Membership," International Holocaust Remembrance Alliance, 2019, https://www.holocaustremembrance.com/countries-and-membership.

12. "Permanent International Partners," International Holocaust Remembrance Alliance, 2018, https://www.holocaustremembrance.com/membership/permanent-international-partners.

13. IHRA, *Fact Sheet*.

14. R. Amy Elman, *The European Union, Antisemitism, and the Politics of Denial* (Lincoln: University of Nebraska Press, 2015); Kenneth L. Marcus, *The Definition of Anti-Semitism* (New York: Oxford University Press, 2015), 166–67; Michael Whine, "Applying the Working Definition of Antisemitism," *Justice*, no. 61 (Fall 2018): 9–16, http://intjewishlawyers.org/justice/no61/#14/z.

15. "Applying the Working Definition." See also "Policy Brief: International Holocaust Remembrance Alliance (IHRA) Definition of Antisemitism," CIJA, March 18, 2019, https://cija.ca/policy-brief-ihra-defining-antisemitism/.

16. "Defining Antisemitism," US Department of State, June 8, 2010, https://2009-2017.state.gov/j/drl/rls/fs/2010/122352.htm.

17. "Policies," European Commission, accessed January 25, 2021, https://ec.europa.eu/info/policies/justice-and-fundamental-rights/combatting-discrim.

18. "Working Definition of Antisemitism," International Holocaust Remembrance Alliance, May 26, 2016, https://www.holocaustremembrance.com/working-definition-antisemitism.

19. "EU Adopts Measures against Antisemitism, World Jewish Congress Cheers," *Jerusalem Post*, December 6, 2018, https://www.jpost.com/Diaspora/EU-adopts-measures-against-antisemitism-World-Jewish-congress-cheers-573646.

20. "Bishops Adopt International Definition of Antisemitism," Church of England, September 11, 2018, https://www.churchofengland.org/more/media-centre/news/bishops-adopt-international-definition-antisemitism.

21. "Seeking to Challenge Rising Antisemitism in UK, Church of Scotland Adopts IHRA Definition of Jew-Hatred," *The Algemeiner*, May 24, 2019, https://www.algemeiner.com/2019/05/24/seeking-to-challenge-rising-antisemitism-in-uk-church-of-scotland-adopts-ihra-definition-of-jew-hatred/.

22. "Bishops Adopt Anti-Semitism Definition," Church in Wales, June 17, 2019, https://web.archive.org/web/20190830024332/https://www.churchinwales.org.uk/news/2019/06/bishops-adopt-anti-semitism-definition/.

23. In September 2019, the UN Office of the High Commissioner of Human Rights published a report on religious freedom focusing on antisemitism. This document ("Report of the Special Rapporteur on Freedom of Religion or Belief," https://undocs.org/A/74/358) included detailed references to and discussion of the dissemination of antisemitic propaganda, negative stereotyping of Jews, and the singling out of Israel, citing the language of the IHRA's working definition of antisemitism. Whether this report will provide a foundation for action by the UN remains to be seen.

24. Wistrich, "Anti-Zionism and Anti-Semitism," 28.

25. Raphael N. Becker, Arye L. Hillman, Niklas Potrafke, and Alexander H. Schwemmer, "The Preoccupation of the United Nations with Israel: Evidence and Theory," *Review of International Organizations* 10, no. 4 (December 2015): 413–37.

26. Anti-Defamation League, *The United Nations Committee on the Exercise of the Inalienable Rights of the Palestinian People: 35 Years of Demonizing Israel*, 2009, https://www.adl.org/sites/default/files/documents/israel-international/un-international-organizations/c/CEIRPP-FINAL-REPORT-2009.pdf. See also "The United Nations and BDS (Boycott, Divestment and Sanctions): Modern Antisemitism," Human Rights Voices, 2018, http://www.humanrightsvoices.org/EYEontheUN/antisemitism/?l=69&p=3639.

27. Gerald Steinberg and Naftali Balanson, *NGOs and the Durban Review Conference: History Repeating Itself*, World Jewish Congress Research Institute, Policy Study No. 32, 2008, https://www.ngo-monitor.org/data/images/File/Durban-WorldJewishCongress.pdf.

28. Elman, *European Union*, 2.

29. "Der BDS-Bewegung entschlossen entgegentreten—Antisemitismus bekämpfen," Deutscher Bundestag Drucksache 19/10191 19, Wahlperiode Antrag, der Fraktionen CDU/CSU, SPD, FDP und BÜNDNIS 90/DIE GRÜNEN, May 15, 2019, http://dipbt.bundestag.de/doc/btd/19/101/1910191.pdf.

30. Jeremy Hunt, "Tremors, turbulence & terror in Mid East remind us of urgent need for peace: two-state solution. But the foundations for peace are respect & coexistence," Twitter, May 18, 2019, https://twitter.com/Jeremy_Hunt/status/1129736648890159109?s=03.

31. David Hirsh, "The Livingstone Formulation Fails to Rescue Livingstone," Engage, April 28, 2016, https://engageonline.wordpress.com/2016/04/28/the-livingstone-formulation-david-hirsh/.

32. Bernard Harrison and Lesley Klaff, "The IHRA Definition and Its Critics," in this volume, *Contending with Antisemitism in a Rapidly Changing Political Climate*, ed. Alvin H. Rosenfeld (Bloomington: Indiana University Press, 2021), citing Geoffrey Robertson, "Anti-Semitism: The IHRA Definition and Its Consequences for Freedom of Expression," Palestine Return Center, August 31, 2018, https://freespeechonisrael.org.uk/wp-content/uploads/2018/08/Geofrey-Robinson-QC-opinion-on-IHRA.pdf.

33. Harrison and Klaff, "IHRA Definition and Its Critics," in this volume *Contending with Antisemitism in a Rapidly Changing Political Climate*, ed. Alvin H. Rosenfeld (Bloomington: Indiana University Press, 2021), citing Stephen Sedley, "Defining Anti-Semitism," *London Review of Books*, May 4, 2017.

34. Harrison and Klaff, "IHRA Definition and Its Critics."

35. Harrison and Klaff.

36. Yehuda Bauer, "Daniel Blatman's Anti-Semitic Attack," *Haaretz*, August 1, 2019, https://www.haaretz.com/world-news/europe/.premium-daniel-blatman-s-anti-semitic-attack-1.7613216.

37. This case study is based on the application of four out of the five dimensions related to Israel and new antisemitism provided in the IHRA working definition. While there is some evidence on HRW activities with respect to the remaining dimension, "Holding Jews collectively responsible for actions of the state of Israel," this evidence appears to be isolated, in contrast to the evidence regarding the other four categories.

38. Robert L. Bernstein, *Speaking Freely* (New York: New Press, 2016).

39. Jonathan Foreman, "The Twitter Hypocrisy of Kenneth Roth," *Commentary*, September 1, 2014.

40. Robert Blitt, "Who Will Watch the Watchdogs? International Human Rights Nongovernmental Organizations and the Case for Regulation," *Buffalo Human Rights Law Review* 10 (2007): 261, 288.

41. Pascal Vennesson and Nikolas M. Rajkovic, "The Transnational Politics of Warfare Accountability: Human Rights Watch versus the Israel Defense Forces," *International Relations* 26, no. 4 (2012): 409–29.

42. Catherine Fitzpatrick, "What Happened in Luganskaya Stanitsa? Human Rights Watch Tells Only a Partial Story," *Minding Russia*, July 6, 2014, http://3dblogger.typepad.com/minding_russia/2014/07/what-happened-in-luganskaya-stanitsa-human-rights-watch-tells-only-a-partial-story.html. See also Michael Rubin, "Should Human Rights Watch Be Trusted?," *Commentary*, September 3, 2014.

43. Foreman, "Twitter Hypocrisy of Kenneth Roth."

44. Gerald M. Steinberg, "International NGOs, the Arab Upheaval, and Human Rights: Examining NGO Resource Allocation," *Journal of International Human Rights* (Northwestern University School of Law) 11 (2012): 1.

45. Gerald M. Steinberg and Anne Herzberg, "NGO Fact-Finding for IHL Enforcement: In Search of a New Model," *Israel Law Review* 51, no. 2 (2018): 261–99.

46. "Transcriptions of Kann Radio Interview by Eran Cicorel with Kenneth Roth and Omar Shakir," NGO Monitor, August 5, 2019, https://www.ngo-monitor.org/in-the-media/transcriptions-of-kann-radio-interviews-by-eran-cicorel-with-kenneth-roth-and-omar-shakir/.

47. "Kenneth Roth Twitter Activity on Israel & Pal Authority," NGO Monitor, accessed January 25, 2021, https://docs.google.com/document/d/1Iie7Hp5zpQTHpPbqA3hbGCvmlq5-x5YHxf1pc2k1a8k/pub.

48. Foreman, "Twitter Hypocrisy of Kenneth Roth."

49. Robert L. Bernstein, "Rights Watchdog Lost in the Middle East," *New York Times*, October 20, 2009, https://www.nytimes.com/2009/10/20/opinion/20bernstein.html.

50. Robert L. Bernstein, "Human Rights in the Middle East" (Shirley and Leonard Goldstein Lecture on Human Rights, University of Nebraska at Omaha, November 10, 2010), https://www.ngo-monitor.org/nm/wp-content/uploads/2019/06/bernstein_nebraska_speech_2010.pdf.

51. Robert Bernstein, "Remarks upon Receiving Dr. Bernard Heller Prize" (speech, Hebrew Union College, New York, NY, May 2, 2013), https://www.ngo-monitor.org/remarks_upon_receiving_dr_bernard_heller_prize.

52. Blitt, "Who Will Watch the Watchdogs?"

53. On the use of specific terminology such as *apartheid* and *colonialist* to single out Israel, see "Word Crimes: Reclaiming the Language of the Israeli-Palestinian Conflict," ed. Donna Robinson Divine, Miriam Elman, and Asaf Romirowsky, special issue, *Israel Studies* 24, no. 2 (2019): 1–16.

54. William Korey, *Taking on the World's Repressive Regimes: The Ford Foundation's International Human Rights Policies and Practices* (New York: Palgrave Macmillan, 2007), 249–51; Irwin Cotler, "Durban's Troubling Legacy One Year Later: Twisting the Cause of International Human Rights against the Jewish People," *Jerusalem Issue Brief* 2, no. 5, Institute for Contemporary Affairs/Jerusalem Center for Public Affairs, August 20, 2002, http://www.jcpa.org/brief/brief2-5.htm; Tom Lantos, "The Durban Debacle: An Insider's View of the World Racism Conference at Durban," *Fletcher Forum of World Affairs* 26, no. 1 (Winter/Spring 2002): 31–52; Gerald M. Steinberg, "From Durban to the Goldstone Report: The Centrality of Human Rights NGOs in the Political Dimension of the Arab-Israeli Conflict," *Israel Affairs* 18, no. 3 (2012): 372–88.

55. Anne Bayefsky, "Human Rights Watch Coverup," *Jerusalem Post*, April 13, 2004.

56. "NGO Forum Declaration and Programme of Action," World Conference against Racism, Racial Discrimination, Xenophobia, and Related Intolerance, Durban, South Africa, September 3, 2001, https://academic.udayton.edu/race/06hrights/WCAR2001/NGOFORUM/.

57. In 2006, HRW campaigned in support of a minimal reform agenda for the UN Human Rights Council (formerly Commission), in opposition to efforts from the US and Israel to remove Permanent Agenda Item 7, which singles out Israel uniquely—no other country is the subject of a permanent agenda item. This is significant because both allegations made by HRW are consistently amplified by the UN human rights mechanisms, particularly through reports of biased commissions of investigation. For analyses of the role of the Organization of Islamic Cooperation in campaigns to delegitimize Israel, see Theresa Squatrito, Magnus Lundgren, and Thomas Sommerer, "Shaming by International Organizations: Mapping Condemnatory Speech Acts across 27 International Organizations, 1980–2015," *Cooperation and Conflict* 54, no. 3 (2019): 356–77; Hillel C. Neuer, "The Struggle against Anti-Israel Bias at the UN Commission on Human Rights," Jerusalem Center for Public Affairs, January 2006, http://www.jcpa.org/phas/phas-040-neuer.htm.

58. Martin Sieff, "Analysis: Why Europeans Bought Jenin Myth," UPI, May 20, 2002, http://www.upi.com/Business_News/Security-Industry/2002/05/21/Analysis-Why-Europeans-bought-Jenin-myth/UPI-34731022008462/.

59. See "Gaza Beach Incident: Timeline of HRW Involvement and Activities June 9–21 2006," NGO Monitor, June 21, 2006, http://www.ngo-monitor.org/article/gaza_beach_incident_timeline_of_hrw_involvement_and_activities_june_.

60. Jonathan Foreman, "Nazi Scandal Engulfs Human Rights Watch," *Sunday Times* (London), March 28, 2010, https://web.archive.org/web/20110718192222/http://www.timesonline.co.uk/tol/news/world/us_and_americas/article7076462.ece.

61. "Civilians under Assault: Hezbollah's Rocket Attacks on Israel in the 2006 War," HRW, August 28, 2007, https://www.hrw.org/reports/2007/iopt0807/.

62. "Why They Died: Civilian Casualties in Lebanon during the 2006 War," HRW, September 5, 2007, https://www.hrw.org/reports/2007/lebanon0907/.

63. "Israel: End Gaza's Humanitarian Crisis at Once," HRW, January 13, 2009, http://www.hrw.org/en/news/2009/01/12/israel-end-gaza-s-humanitarian-crisis-once.

64. "Res. S-9/1: The Grave Violations of Human Rights in the Occupied Palestinian Territory, Particularly Due to the Recent Israeli Military Attacks against the Occupied Gaza Strip," UNHRC, January 12, 2009, https://web.archive.org/web/20110609190043/http://domino.un.org/unispal.nsf/0/404e93e166533f828525754e00559e30.

65. UNOHCHR, *Report of the United Nations Fact-Finding Mission on the Gaza Conflict*, September 25, 2009, http://www2.ohchr.org/english/bodies/hrcouncil/docs/12session/A-HRC-12-48.pdf.

66. "Human Rights Watch: Selling Goldstone's Indictment," NGO Monitor, October 15, 2009, http://www.ngo-monitor.org/article/human_rights_watch_selling_goldstone_s_indictmento.

67. "HRW in 2010: More Bias, Even Less Credibility," NGO Monitor, January 6, 2011, http://www.ngo-monitor.org/article/hrw_in_more_bias_even_less_credibility.

68. Richard Goldstone, "Reconsidering the Goldstone Report on Israel and War Crimes," *Washington Post*, April 2, 2011, http://www.washingtonpost.com/opinions/reconsidering-the-goldstone-report-on-israel-and-war-crimes/2011/04/01/AFg111JC_story.html.

69. "Israel: Apparent War Crimes in Gaza: Accountability Needed for Officials Who Authorized Lethal Force," HRW, June 13, 2018, https://www.hrw.org/news/2018/06/13/israel-apparent-war-crimes-gaza.

70. Rachel Denber, "Dispatches: Urgent Need for Ukraine Crash Site Access," HRW, July 20, 2014, https://www.hrw.org/news/2014/07/20/dispatches-urgent-need-ukraine-crash-site-access.

71. "Report of the Independent International Commission of Inquiry on the Protests in the Occupied Palestinian Territory—A/HRC/40/74," UN Human Rights Council, February 28, 2019, https://www.ohchr.org/EN/HRBodies/HRC/CoIOPT/Pages/Report2018OPT.aspx.

72. "Der BDS-Bewegung entschlossen entgegentreten—Antisemitismus bekämpfen," Deutscher Bundestag Drucksache 19/10191 19, Wahlperiode Antrag, der Fraktionen CDU/CSU, SPD, FDP und BÜNDNIS 90/DIE GRÜNEN, May 15, 2019, http://dipbt.bundestag.de/doc/btd/19/101/1910191.pdf.

73. "Transcriptions of Kann Radio Interviews."

74. In addition to the sources in this text, see the Dutch article "Human Rights Watch vliegt uit de bocht" [HRW flies off the road], *Nieuw Israëlietisch Weekblad*, February 15, 2019.

75. "Israel: Apparent War Crimes in Gaza."

76. "Speakers for Press Conference in Chicago: Biographies and Contact Information," Stop Caterpillar, accessed March 12, 2021, https://web.archive.org/web/2009/www.catdestroyshomes.org/article.php?id=298;"Israel: Caterpillar Should Suspend Bulldozer Sales," HRW, November 21, 2004, www.hrw.org/en/news/2004/11/21/israel-caterpillar-should-suspend-bulldozer-sales.

77. "Razing Rafah: Mass Home Demolitions in the Gaza Strip," HRW, October 2004, www.hrw.org/reports/2004/rafah1004/.

78. Kenneth Roth, CNN, December 10, 2002.

79. US Campaign to End the Israeli Occupation, *Divest Now! A Handbook for Student Divestment Campaigns*, September 16, 2010, https://bdsmovement.net/files/2011/02/divestguide.pdf.

80. Sarah Leah Whitson, "A Matter of Civil Rights," *Huffington Post*, April 15, 2011, https://www.huffpost.com/entry/a-matter-of-civil-rights_b_848067.

81. Sarah Leah Whitson, Twitter, "Disappointed that @mbachelet has punted—as did her predecessor—on publishing UN database on businesses complicit in settlement expansion," March 5, 2019, https://twitter.com/sarahleah1/status/1102961105628995584.

82. "Occupation, Inc.: How Settlement Businesses Contribute to Israel's Violations of Palestinian Rights," HRW, January 19, 2016, https://www.hrw.org/news/2016/01/19/occupation-inc-how-settlement-businesses-contribute-israels-violations-palestinian.

83. "Human Rights Watch Recommendations on the Implementation of Human Rights Council Resolution 31/36 Business Activities in Israeli Settlements," HRW, November 21,

2016, https://www.un.org/unispal/document/auto-insert-196447/. In 2018, after his term as head of the UNHRC, Zeid Ra'ad Al Hussein joined HRW's board of directors.

84. Associated Press, "Rights Group Blasts Israeli Banks for Settlement Expansion," *The National*, September 13, 2011, https://www.thenational.ae/world/mena/rights-group-blasts-israeli-banks-for-settlement-expansion-1.628144.

85. HRW, *Bankrolling Abuse: Israeli Banks in West Bank Settlements*, May 2018, https://www.hrw.org/sites/default/files/report_pdf/israel0518_web.pdf.

86. Omar Shakir, "Breaking: after 2 yrs of engagement & day ahead of release of 65pg @hrw/@KNavot report, @Airbnb says it'll stop brokering rentals in illegal Israeli settlements," Twitter, November 19, 2018, https://twitter.com/OmarSShakir/status/1064570267962351617.

87. "Bed and Breakfast on Stolen Land: Tourist Rental Listings in West Bank Settlements," HRW, November 20, 2018, https://www.hrw.org/report/2018/11/20/bed-and-breakfast-stolen-land/tourist-rental-listings-west-bank-settlements.

88. "Israel/Palestine: FIFA Sponsoring Games on Seized Land," HRW, September 25, 2016, https://www.hrw.org/news/2016/09/25/israel/palestine-fifa-sponsoring-games-seized-land.

89. Human Rights Watch, "Few know better than @hrw's Germany Dir @WenzelMichalski that antiSemitism is on the rise, but antiBDS laws restrict speech, punish rights activists," Twitter, May 28, 2019, https://twitter.com/hrw/status/1133453474027495425.

90. Daniel Schwammenthal, "Your research on this issue is as biased and incomplete as your Israel reports. This was only the last of many faux pas over many years," Twitter, June 17, 2019, https://twitter.com/DSchwammenthal/status/1140631273553244161.

91. Kenneth Roth, "The director of the Jewish Museum in Berlin is forced to resign for not adhering slavishly to the Netanyahu view on Jerusalem and BDS," Twitter, June 15, 2019, https://twitter.com/KenRoth/status/1139953738985168897?s=03.

92. "Word Crimes," Divine, Elman, and Romirowsky, eds.

93. Bayefsky, "Human Rights Watch Coverup."

94. In 2000, Roth sent letters to Clinton, Arafat, and Barak arguing (falsely) that a "right of return . . . is a right that persists even when sovereignty over the territory is contested or has changed hands." "Human Rights Watch Urges Attention to Future of Palestinian Refugees," HRW, December 21, 2000, https://www.hrw.org/news/2000/12/21/human-rights-watch-urges-attention-future-palestinian-refugees.
See also Birnbaum, "Minority Report."

95. Yosef Kuperwaser, "The 'Peaceful' Movement to Destroy Israel," *Tablet Magazine*, May 1, 2019, https://www.tabletmag.com/jewish-news-and-politics/283307/in-thrall-to-bad-ideas.

96. Bauer, "Daniel Blatman's Anti-Semitic Attack."

97. Lucy Mair, "Equal Citizens?," HRW, March 30, 2008, https://www.hrw.org/news/2008/03/30/equal-citizens; "For Israel's Palestinian Citizens, an Issue Unsettled," HRW, March 30, 2012, https://www.hrw.org/news/2012/03/30/israels-palestinian-citizens-issue-unsettled.

98. "Separate and Unequal: Israel's Discriminatory Treatment of Palestinians in the Occupied Palestinian Territories," HRW, December 19, 2010, https://www.hrw.org/report/2010/12/19/separate-and-unequal/israels-discriminatory-treatment-palestinians-occupied.

99. David Bernstein, "Daniel Levy's Defense of Human Rights Watch," *Volokh Conspiracy*, July 20, 2009, http://www.volokh.com/posts/1248146595.html.

100. Whitson, "Matter of Civil Rights."

101. Khulood Badawi, "The Israeli Election Put the Bigotry of Its Political Class Front and Center," Foreign Policy in Focus, April 11, 2019, https://fpif.org/the-israeli-election-put-the-bigotry-of-its-political-class-front-and-center/. Badawi was previously employed by UN OCHA and was fired for "a bogus post on Twitter alleging that a pictured Palestinian girl had been killed by the IDF during the 2012 shelling of Gaza." Alex Margolin, "Khulood

Badawi Finally Fired from UN," Honest Reporting, February 7, 2013, https://honestreporting.com/khalood-badawi-finally-fired-from-un/. Continuing her Palestinian propaganda role, Badawi moved to the PLO's Negotiations Support Unit / Negotiations Affairs Department. There, she prepared materials for "Israeli target audiences."

102. Omar Shakir, Twitter, June 19, 2019, https://twitter.com/OmarSShakir/status/1141348912827121669?s=20.

103. Sarah Leah Whitson, "Even @NYDailyNews gets it. The whole word gets it. Israel and The US are the ghouls in #Gaza," Twitter, May 15, 2018, https://twitter.com/sarahleah1/status/996272337384337410.

104. Advanced Twitter search, accessed August 6, 2019, https://twitter.com/search?q=Israel%20(racism%20OR%20racist%20OR%20discriminatory%20OR%20discrimination)%20(from%3Akenroth%20OR%20from%3Aomarsshakir%20OR%20from%3Ahrw%20OR%20from%3Asarahleah1)&src=typed_query.

105. "Transcriptions of Kann Radio Interviews."

106. Kenneth Roth, "Getting It Straight," Letters to the Editor, *New York Sun*, July 31, 2006, https://www.nysun.com/opinion/letters-to-the-editor-2006-07-31/36984/.

107. "Roth's Supersessionism," editorial, *New York Sun*, July 31, 2006, https://www.nysun.com/editorials/roths-supersessionism/36993/.

108. "White Flag Deaths: Killings of Palestinian Civilians during Operation Cast Lead," HRW, August 13, 2009, https://www.hrw.org/report/2009/08/13/white-flag-deaths/killings-palestinian-civilians-during-operation-cast-lead.

109. Goldstone, "Reconsidering the Goldstone Report."

110. "Ken Roth's Twitter War with Hillel Neuer," UN Watch, September 1, 2017, https://unwatch.org/hillel-neuer-vs-ken-roth/.

111. Foreman, "Twitter Hypocrisy of Kenneth Roth."

112. "Bed and Breakfast."

113. Herb Keinon, "Human Rights Watch Head Claims Israel Interfering in UK Politics," *Jerusalem Post*, February 9, 2019, https://www.jpost.com/Israel-News/Human-Rights-Watch-head-claims-Israel-is-interfering-in-UK-politics-580216.

114. Search results, accessed August 9, 2019, hrw.org.

115. Andrew Stroehlein, "'"Never again" must mean NEVER AGAIN FOR ANYONE!'—Holocaust survivors slam #Israel on #Gaza bit.ly/1wltkna," Twitter, August 23, 2014, https://twitter.com/astroehlein/status/503236540399906817.

116. "Deborah Lipstadt on the Rise of 'Softcore' Holocaust Denial," *Jewish News* (UK), August 26, 2014, https://jewishnews.timesofisrael.com/special-report-will-remember-holocaust-survivors-gone/.

117. Sarah Leah Whitson, "@BBCKimGhattas @DRovera @HolocaustMuseum @BBCNewsUS should also show pics of death and destruction in #Gaza," Twitter, January 29, 2015, https://twitter.com/sarahleah1/status/560700886805389312.

118. Kenneth Roth, Twitter, August 27, 2017, https://twitter.com/KenRoth/status/901898833201954818.

119. Nada Elia, "Birds of a Feather: White Supremacy and Zionism," Middle East Eye, August 24, 2017, https://www.middleeasteye.net/opinion/birds-feather-white-supremacy-and-zionism.

120. Daniel Kohn, "Human Rights Watch Tweet Exposes Decades-Old Anti Israel Bias," *Forward*, September 8, 2018.

GERALD M. STEINBERG, Professor Emeritus of Political Science at Bar Ilan University, is president of the Institute for NGO Research. He focuses his research on diplomacy and international relations, hard and soft power, and the politics of human rights NGOs, including the new antisemitism. Publications include "NGOs, Human Rights, and Political Warfare in the Arab-Israel Conflict" (*Israel Studies*), "The Role of International Legal and Justice Discourse in Promoting the New Antisemitism" (authored with Anne Herzberg), and *Menachem Begin and the Israel-Egypt Peace Process: Between Ideology and Political Realism* (authored with Ziv Rubinovitz, Indiana University Press, 2019). He is a recipient of the prestigious Bonei Zion and Menachem Begin prizes.

II. INTELLECTUAL AND IDEOLOGICAL CURRENTS OF ANTISEMITISM

3

Israel as a White Colonial-Settler State in Activist Social Science

Balázs Berkovits

WITH EVER-INCREASING INTENSITY, THE LAST SEVERAL DECADES HAVE borne witness to a large-scale production of texts that might be grouped under the common heading "academic anti-Zionism." These texts represent the output of certain disciplines that belong to a kind of "activist" social science: "critical whiteness studies," "critical race studies," "colonial-settler studies," and so on. This phenomenon raises the following questions: How do these disciplines construe "Jewish whiteness" and imagine "Israeli settler colonialism?" How and why does the "Jewish problem" reemerge in these critical works, and what are the methodological and discursive means by which they strive to achieve their critique?

Social science becomes activist when critical and political interest supersedes cognitive interest in the formation of concepts, rendering interpretation and empirical description subordinate to criticism, and when the explicit or implicit call for political action supplants theoretical reflection to a large degree. As Theodor W. Adorno, writing about the relationship between theory and practice, has put it, "Where experience is blocked or altogether absent, praxis is damaged and therefore longed for, distorted, and desperately overvalued. Thus what is called the problem of praxis is interwoven with the problem of knowledge."[1]

Undoubtedly, a reflexive science of society is necessarily related to criticism and therefore cannot and should not be a completely neutral enterprise, striving solely to describe or explain (and Adorno would be the last to advocate a science that did). However, when social scientific analysis displays the tendency or ambition to become exclusively critical and practice-oriented, it is more susceptible to ignoring its scientific tasks of explanation and description. This is why, as I try to show, the politics of such social scientific analysis regulates its methodology and predetermines its empirical findings to a large degree. "Overvalued praxis" and the call for immediate action hinder the understanding of social and historical realities. More precisely, researcher-ideologues are convinced ahead of time that they know what the reality looks like and are only looking for a theoretical framework that can help them adequately express their preexisting knowledge in a manner concordant with academic standards. However, in the end, their unquestioned political vision and stance come to define this framework, which turns out to be just as rigid and essentialized as their politics.

Due to their academic prestige and scientific aura, and because they are widely taught in academic institutions, the abovementioned branches of study supply major sources on which more overt expressions of anti-Zionism in the public sphere can rely today—they do so by providing theoretical justification, philosophical underpinnings, and political legitimation for raising the "Jewish problem" in the form of contemporary anti-Zionist discourse, which is increasingly linked to antisemitism or is at least prone to fueling antisemitism. It is also important to note that because of their academic-institutional background, these activist fields of study are more immune to criticism than are outright political statements coming from politicians, which garner much media attention but are also more easily countered in public debates.

Critical Whiteness Studies and the Jews

Critical whiteness studies has been established as an academic discipline with an activist agenda aiming to question whiteness as the default color, as "neutral" in contrast to people of color.[2] Whiteness remained unexamined and unquestioned for a long time, even in critical analyses of racism; however, it is also a socio-historical product that, according to the program advanced by critical whiteness studies, needs to be de-essentialized.[3] The means of this de-essentialization is conceived as the writing of the social history of various minorities that appeared in the United States in different periods.[4] But how did different, initially nonwhite minorities (including Jews) achieve the status of whiteness? Karen Brodkin's *How Jews Became White Folks*,[5] the pioneering work on the "whitening" of Jews, interprets Jewish acculturation and assimilation in the United States in terms of color.

According to a narrative that assumes a social-historical framework, Jews were not always considered to be "white" as they suffered discrimination, but they gradually became white in a process spanning several decades and concluding, by and large, by the end of World War II. So "whiteness" as an interpretive concept describes the successful integration of certain minority groups, including Jews, as discrimination against them gradually ceases or attenuates.

But whiteness in critical whiteness studies is also meant to express a position of domination and privilege, thereby becoming a critical rather than merely an interpretive concept. "White" is not a natural or essential category, as it is the product of a historical process; but neither it is neutral, as it is constituted against the backdrop of those Black and colored populations who are still discriminated against. It is neither a descriptive nor simply an interpretive but rather a critical concept. This means that due to embedded racialized structures in society, white people as a collectivity benefit from their dominant position and are complicit in oppression. It is an interesting and important perspective, although it raises numerous doubts regarding the targets of its criticism in general; it becomes even more problematic when it tries to erase every other source of discrimination and persecution not related to the color line. For example, in this conceptual framework the particular traits of antisemitism—that is, everything that renders it different from racism—become insignificant. In fact, one of the main methodological principles of whiteness studies dealing with Jews and Jewish assimilation (even if it remains implicit or unstated) is the interpretation of antisemitism as just another form of racism, having to do with "color" conceived of not solely as a perceptual quality but as a historically changing marker of the level of discrimination.[6]

However, this tacitly applied methodological principle is taken to be an empirical finding—as if the history of Jews in the United States followed the pattern of assimilation of every other "whitened" ethnic group, becoming flawlessly integrated into the dominant white majority. Therefore, Jews, because they are now considered white, supposedly will not experience racism anymore, for they are now placed on the safe and dominant side of the color divide. Jews are not the target of racism, or if they still sometimes are, it cannot be considered a "systemic" type of racism. Hence, within this discursive framework, Jews are excluded from the multicultural space of other dominated ethnic groups[7] and by the same token, following a totalized binary logic, become part of the dominant and oppressive majority. However, this slippage into the moral-critical meaning of "whiteness" with regard to Jews can be achieved only by intentionally overlooking Jewish history and experience. Therefore, whiteness as a critical concept applied to Jews is the result of a theoretical overdetermination, and as the interpretive content gradually fades away, it gives way to a crude criticism. It is fairly clear that the objective of Brodkin's book is to eclipse or even erase the interpretive content in order to achieve a critical binary or literally black-and-white divide.

Without a doubt, it is highly problematic to talk about Jewish whiteness when this concept is meant to assert that Jews are part of the oppressive majority, for the contention is not only that Jews cannot experience racism but also that they are to be counted among those who enjoy some kind of racial privilege and take part in oppressing the population of color. This approach to addressing the role of Jews in American society can be viewed as a new way of posing the "Jewish question."

To consider Jews as white and part of the majority is a discursive situation to which certain academic disciplines—not only critical whiteness studies but also postcolonial studies, colonial-settler studies, and other related fields—contribute greatly. Therefore, within these disciplines, the minority experience of Jews cannot even be taken into account.[8] As Bryan Cheyette, a literary theorist who is receptive to mainstream postcolonialism while also being critical of it, has put it in reference to an article by Willi Goetschel and Ato Quayson, the Jewish experience of modernity, by proposing some "fertile templates," could contribute fruitfully to the interpretation of many themes which are highly important for postcolonial studies.[9] These themes range from various minority, diaspora, racial, ethnic, and colonial conditions to all kinds of experiences of cultural difference and hybridity. The problem of course is that "postcolonial studies has not yet been informed by the commonalities with Jewish studies" and, more importantly, that these "'fertile templates' are even negated by supersessionist thinking."[10]

Supersessionist thinking is another formulation of the phenomenon identified by the French sociologist Danny Trom in his book *The Promise and the Obstacle, the Radical Left and the Jewish Problem*. Trom tries to establish that many critical approaches regard the memory of the Holocaust as an obstacle to criticism: the Holocaust is perceived as belittling the suffering of other people, as if there is only a limited amount of suffering to be distributed.[11] From there follow manifold strategies of relativization and de-Judaization, as well as instrumentalization of the Holocaust by critical thinkers (which accompanies the posing of the Jewish question/problem).

It is not only the Holocaust that supersessionist and activist scholarship is trying to combat; as we have seen, it is also trying to belittle the antisemitic phenomenon, and there is a growing tendency to place the history of the Israeli state within the theoretical framework of settler colonialism.

Israel as a White Colony

The theoretically and politically overdetermined conception of Jewish whiteness is undoubtedly gaining in popularity and thus has an even greater career whenever racism scholars take Israel as their object of analysis. I interrogate the way in which this kind of activist scholarship interprets the supposed linkage between colonialism and whiteness with regard to Israel. The critique of whiteness in relation to Israel can be developed in two different directions, both of which already inhere in the concept (as it has been conceived by whiteness scholars). One way to pursue the critique is taking issue with "Jews as white dominators" (by their social position and international standing), while the other is to highlight "Jews as white racists." In these perspectives, it is supposedly Israel that demonstrates most convincingly that Jews are really white, or that they have been whitened by Zionism or by the creation of a genuine settler state on the European model.

Either the position of the state in the Middle East or its position in the world demonstrates what was already obvious to whiteness scholars dealing with Jewish assimilation, namely that Jews are dominators—that is, white. As the eminent racism scholar David Theo Goldberg put it, Israelis, as Western imperialists, "occupy the structural position of whiteness in the Middle-East."[12] Zionism is a European white movement operating with the intent to colonize and civilize the aboriginals of the Middle East: "The Zionist vision for Israel . . . represents the modernizing imperative in a region seen as still marked by the biblical backwardness of its Arab inhabitants."[13] This demonstrates the first sense of whiteness defined in this framework. The second sense comes to the fore when Goldberg states that Jews have become white as a result of their treatment of the Palestinians, who, in this imagery, occupy the position of Black people. This means that the Jewish name is totally eclipsed by the white designator: Israelis are only white and nothing else, while Palestinians are only Black; or, the Israelis are Nazis, while Palestinians are the real Jews, as for Goldberg these two binary oppositions seem to be equivalent: "Palestinians in particular, and Arabs more generically, are treated as a subjugated race, directly. Beaten in the name of devaluating stereotypes, concentrated in camps in the name of generalized security, displaced in the name of biblical right ... killed in the name of retributive justice."[14] The catchwords of these citations—"subjugated race," "concentrated in camps," "displaced," "killed"—clearly raise the Nazi analogy without the author providing any empirical analysis or even examples. This kind of criticism is nothing other than the imaginary development of whiteness, a free association based on the critical concept and applied to the case of Israel.

Canadian racism scholar Abigail Bakan[15] goes even further than Goldberg, at least in her theoretical recklessness, constructing a link between Jews becoming white in the United States (taken from Brodkin) and "Jewish-Zionist hegemony": "I argue that a transnational historical turning point occurred after World War II, marking the failure of earlier promises of Jewish emancipation and the simultaneous ascendance of Zionism to a position of hegemony, coinciding with changes in the class and racial configuration of 'Jewishness'. The close association of Zionism with Jewish whiteness in the United States ascribed these claims specifically with Ashkenazi (European) Jewish populations and intersected with the idea of Israel as an abstract 'Jewish' space."[16]

Not surprisingly, Bakan does not offer details concerning this supposed relationship, for if she had, she would have had to acknowledge that Zionist ideologies and settlement had been on their way long before Jews in the US "became white" (should we temporarily accept this framework just for the sake of the argument). But even if we consider the aftermath of World War II at least until the founding of the state and somewhat further, it is not the case that American Jews and especially the US as a superpower (which was even hesitant about whether to recognize it[17]) played a determining role in the life of the new state.

In other parts of her paper, Bakan maintains that it is by the act of the foundation of the state that Jews became white—leaving the diaspora through the creation of Israel had a whitening effect on Jews. In turn, "this transition to whiteness enabled diasporic Jews to access a level of influence and status previously unknown, contrasting sharply with the historic normalization of Jewish oppression, and modern anti-Semitism, in the Western world."[18] So, in this rendering, Jews are either oppressed victims of antisemitism or hegemonic dominators when they found their own state and expand Western "global geopolitical interests" associated with a "specific type of 'Jewish' whiteness" that Bakan terms "whiteness by permission."[19] Bakan is close to being nostalgic about good old European antisemitism, which maintained Jews in their oppressed minority positions. But more importantly, we find here the same absolute binary as in Brodkin, this time without even the slightest intention of providing historical evidence.

Bakan thus uses whiteness less as a critical concept than as an outright accusation, even with antisemitic overtones, all the more so because the perspective has gained, as we see, a world-historical outlook and because Jews are described as being subservient to Western interests in exchange for their new, higher status ("whiteness by permission"). It is also telling that Bakan talks about the necessity of reformulating the "Jewish question," which she takes to be something objective. According to her, the "Jewish question" today is linked "to specific configurations at the intersection of race, class, and colonialism," by which she refers to Israel.[20] In this description, the "Jewish question" has migrated to Israel/Palestine, where Jews oppress and colonize Palestinians on a racial basis (this would be whiteness in the second sense) by reintroducing the scheme of the white-black divide: "Whiteness is a relational category that involves the racialization of the non-white 'other.' In the Middle East, the 'other' was clearly the Orientalized Palestinian. However, in the West this 'other' was commonly resident racialized peoples, specifically the Black population of the United States."[21]

But if the "Jewish question," when viewed as something objective, needs to be resolved in our epoch by tackling Israel, then it is also susceptible to gaining retrospective historical legitimacy. This framework suggests that with the existence of Israel, the "Jewish question" (or rather, "problem") merely reappears in a different guise, and that it is only now becoming obvious what has always characterized the Jews: they are dominators and exploiters, unless they are maintained in a minority position. Therefore, the persistence of the "eternal Jewish question" can be inferred from Bakan's ideas even if her initial intention was merely to pose the Jewish question with regard to Israel and Zionism. Presumably, the solution to the Jewish question posed in this way would be the de-Judaization of Palestine. Bakan is more radical in her linguistic formulations than others, as she, perhaps unintentionally, retroactively legitimizes past antisemitic discourse; however, the substance of her ideas can be found in the texts of most anti-Zionist critics in academia.

Zionism and Colonialism

Goldberg and Bakan maintain a more theoretical focus on questions of racism and whiteness in relationship to Israel without actually conducting empirical research, but there is also the vast field of colonial and settler-colonial studies, supposedly built on historical findings, in which the activist agenda and the theoretical and political overdetermination are less evident at first sight. However, on closer examination, it becomes clear that these overdeterminations equally characterize these more "historical" disciplines, which make them activist to the same degree. As Zeev Sternhell formulated it in a very polite way in his polemic on Gabriel Piterberg's book,[22] "the extreme politicization of anti-Zionist discourse and its considerable exposure in the media have not benefited research."[23] In fact, not only has it not benefited research, but now it seems that research, or rather a certain academic production of texts, frequently serves only the anti-Zionist political struggle.

The weaponization of certain concepts (such as apartheid, colonialism, Zionism, indigeneity, and settlements) was also the subject of an issue of *Israel Studies* entitled "Word Crimes."[24] It elicited a heated polemic (hosted by the *Fathom Journal*), as some anti-Zionist critics felt that the articles published there questioned free speech by stifling and even criminalizing criticism. As Gershon Shafir has put it, "By excluding other interpretations and analyses of these words, the editors and contributors threaten the freedom of scholars to engage in unrestricted and uncensored debate; they pose a threat to the academic enterprise and academic freedom itself."[25] However, this counterargument, by misleadingly (not to say hypocritically) invoking the principle of freedom of speech and by encouraging extreme politicization of the debate, not only begs the question but also projects its own type of approach onto its adversary. Furthermore, it is not surprising that Shafir does not want to engage with the real issue at hand, which can be described as the exclusively normative and delegitimizing use of once-analytical concepts (which he seems to think have preserved their analytical content). Simply put, under the cloak of analysis and interpretation, a political agenda is being pursued that is certainly bad for research and equally bad for politics. As John Strawson formulated it in his response to Shafir with regard to the concept of colonialism, "The description of Israel as a 'colonial-settler state' is now in frequent usage. It is used not merely as a scholarly nomenclature but has political implications. Many draw the conclusion that if Israel is a colonial-settler state, it is illegitimate, should not have been created, and perhaps should therefore cease to exist."[26] This is precisely the crux of the issue: much academic research on Israel has gradually lost scientific ambition by adopting a solely political objective—the designation of a state as a colony is instrumental in this theoretical-political warfare, as it inherently comprises that state's illegitimacy and calls for its termination.

This tendency is well illustrated by the positions taken up by Piterberg in a debate with Sternhell on the colonial nature of Zionism. Sternhell, in his critique of Piterberg's book,[27] asserts the following: "If Mandate-era Jewish Palestine was not based on any of the characteristic features of a colonial society—the exploitation of a native work-force; the confiscation of the natural riches of the country; a monopoly of political power that created two different classes of inhabitants, citizens and others who had no rights—it could not have been a colonial society. The truth was rather the opposite: in order to build a nation, the Jews of Palestine formed themselves into a self-sufficient and closed society."[28] Piterberg replies at first by reasserting those characteristics that people usually associate with colonialism: "From the moment Zionism's goal became the resettlement of European Jews in a land controlled by a colonial European power, in order to create a sovereign political entity, it could no longer be understood as 'just' a central or east European nationalism; it was also, inevitably, a white-settler colonialism."[29]

Furthermore, this colonial settlement, according to him, was realized not only on a territory "controlled by a colonial power" but also "under the bayonets of a metropole colonial power,"[30] which hints at Great Britain as the mother country of the Jewish state. It is well known that this was not the case, as even Piterberg tacitly acknowledges later on in his article when he introduces a conceptual distinction between "metropole colonialism" and "settler colonialism" (which is not his own invention but borrowed from settler-colonial studies; see below). It is this latter term that would come to characterize Zionist colonization, whereas Sternhell's arguments could be considered valid only with regard to the former. But instead of countering Sternhell's arguments, this formulation only begs the question. Certainly, in settler colonization, settlements tended to gradually become independent from the metropole and thereafter were no longer managed from an imperial center. Undoubtedly, the "European settlers ... with the passage of time, sought to make the colony their national patrimony,"[31] but, contrary to what Piterberg wants to imply, this says nothing about Zionist settlement, as in this case there never was a metropole colonial power behind the enterprise.

After this tactical move, Piterberg tries to develop other aspects of settler colonialism, making special reference to the works of Shafir, who, according to him, renewed the colonial paradigm by introducing new subcategories; and he also mentions the "comparative settler colonialism" paradigm, which today is attracting more and more attention. Finally, Piterberg equally proposes a political solution that, according to him, seeks not the violent annihilation of the Jewish state but rather only its "peaceful" termination by ending what he calls "Judeo-supremacy": "What I would argue for is the de-Zionization of the single state that has now de facto existed between the Jordan River and the Mediterranean for 43 years—more than twice the duration of Israel within the Green Line—so that it may become a modern state based on something resembling universal suffrage, rather than one predicated upon Judaeo-supremacy."[32]

So what new insights can we learn from Shafir with regard to Zionism as colonialism? In his article, which can be considered a late summary of his 1989 book, Shafir at first duly enumerates the unique traits of Zionist "colonization," which show it to be a very improbable candidate for the qualification of colony: the lack of a colonial metropole that would have encouraged emigration, the fact that Zionists were not guided by economic interests, the fact that they did not occupy but rather purchased land, the fact that a large part of them were refugees and lacking economic means, and the fact that they did not employ indentured or slave labor but did in the first stages of settlement employ cheap local labor.[33] Shafir further acknowledges that "Zionists rejected the rigid ethnic or racial hierarchy typical of the plantation and ethnic plantation colony"; however, he argues that not all colonial models were informed by this distinction. Then he goes on to identify the "real" colonial trait characterizing Zionism: the "conquest of labor," which in his model means the exclusion of Palestinians from the labor force.[34] This exclusion was meant to create a society free of Palestinians through the creation of an ethnically homogenous society.

This diagnosis allows us to make sense of one of Shafir's initial statements: "The question faced by Jewish immigrants in Palestine was whether they wanted to exclude Palestinians from their society or make them into a lower economic caste."[35] This is the dichotomy on which he intends to build his entire subsequent argument. However, as his argument unfolds, this dichotomy collapses both conceptually and empirically.

Which side of the dichotomy has been realized? According to Shafir, Zionists finally opted for the first solution: they did not subject Palestinians to exploitative work conditions but decided that they should work themselves and preferred separation between themselves and the Palestinians. Shafir thinks that this further explains why Zionists were rather moderate in their acquisition of territory—they were willing to limit their territorial ambitions in the face of demographic concerns for the sake of Jewish exclusivity, which is why they accepted the partition plan for Palestine: "In order to increase the ratio of Jewish population to unit of land, the leaders of the Labor Movement recognized that the territory taken possession of by Jews would have to be limited."³⁶ Is this not, however, a curious type of colonization? Instead, the Zionists could have opted for more conquest, the subjugation of the Palestinian population, or even for its displacement or expulsion (especially in light of the later settler-colonial paradigm, which asserts that ethnic cleansing and the displacement of the native population are inherent to Zionist colonization).

However, continues Shafir, after 1967, this conception of self-restraint with regard to territory was totally transformed. After this point land acquisition happened not by purchase but by conquest; in combination with this, the labor market was equally extended to Palestinians from the West Bank. Obviously, as Shafir also acknowledges, after its actual foundation, Israel as a "universalist state" (Shafir's term) already extended the labor market to include Israeli Arabs. "Economic separatism" was no more. (Naturally, Shafir never mentions the fact that the 1967 war resulting in conquest was not initiated by Israel.)

Assuredly, it is rather curious to assert that limited territorial claims and enhanced territorial ambitions are both traits of colonialism, furthermore of the very same colonial movement, and, by the same token, to claim that exploitation of the local labor force and its contrary, the nonexploitation resulting in the separation of the two peoples, are both colonial features that unequivocally qualify an entity as colonial. And although Shafir is keen on distinguishing several different periods of "Israeli settler colonialism," which is probably meant to be a meticulous empirical description, all these ultimately point in the same direction: the intention to prove that Zionism is colonialism through and through and that it essentially does not differ from other enterprises that we generally term as colonial.

Therefore, colonialism is one, possessing everlasting essential traits, and Zionism is one, while the two are also one and the same, regardless of the manifold differences showcased by Zionism. If, in the specific case of Zionist colonialism, it is understood to be one thing and also its contrary, then it is hardly surprising that all these phenomena relating to the history of Zionism should be interpreted within a "single theoretical framework": "My intention in this chapter was to do away with the customary frameworks that analyzed Israeli society, dividing up its history between two airtightly sealed and separated periods: the pre- and post-1967 eras. To that end, I propose to use a single theoretical framework, based on the colonial dimensions of Israeli society and now on its ongoing, though still very partial, decolonization."³⁷

However, this "single theoretical framework" is not established as a result of theoretical reflection; rather, it is simply asserted. How and why could one extend the scope of the category of the colonial to the Zionist case? And why is the category itself not substantially modified by this inclusion? Is "colony" a Wittgensteinian prototype, useful for perceiving family resemblances between cases? Or is it a Weberian ideal-type, instrumental for historical comparisons? Certainly neither, since prototypes and ideal-types are not essentialized categories—they are methodological tools for making comparisons among diverse phenomena of empirical reality, while the category is neither methodologically nor politically fetishized. Shafir continues, "I offer . . . a theoretical and conceptual perspective that highlights the continuous centrality of colonization in Zionism and at the same time gives appropriate weight to the changes that have taken place, under new circumstances, within the framework of settlement."[38]

What we have here in Shafir's case is a curious methodology: heterogeneity is not denied but seemingly revealed; however, it is subsumed under the totalizing concept of the colonial, which itself remains unchanged and thereby conveys the usual moral and political connotations. Does any interpretive value remain in such an extended category, while its critical intention and political meaning seem to be unaffected or even reasserted? It is more than doubtful.

Israel in "Settler-Colonial Studies"

The fast-developing academic field of settler-colonial studies is the latest academic enterprise to single out Israel, in the words of Ilan Pappé, as "the last remaining active settler-colonialist movement or project."[39] The interpretation of Israel as a colony is nothing new; Palestinian and Marxist authors (such as Faez Sayegh, Maxime Rodinson, and Edward Said) from the sixties on have written about dispossession and colonization. The discourse on Israel as a colony was continued in the writings of the Israeli new historians (such as Benny Morris and Pappé) and critical sociologists (such as Baruch Kimmerling and Shafir). A large part of academic writing on Israel has taken up the vocation of proving that Zionism is a white settler movement resulting first in a colonial and now in an "apartheid" state.

However, settler-colonial studies differs somewhat from previous approaches working with the concept of colony, since it imagines itself as a separate paradigm operating with large-scale comparisons and applying a theoretical framework with clear-cut definitions. Various comparative projects have been conceived following this paradigm "seeking to explore the dynamics of settler domination and indigenous subjugation in various contexts, most commonly Australia, Canada, the United States and New Zealand,"[40] and so in reality dealing almost exclusively with white settler states. Also, it has now asserted itself as a separate academic discipline with its own academic review: *Settler Colonial Studies*. Israel has been added to the countries mentioned, and its treatment as a settler colony has been celebrated as a theoretical revolution in the interpretation of Zionism by adepts of the paradigm.

This so-called paradigm change is often presented as a great victory over Jewish and Israeli "exceptionality," as the breaking of an age-old taboo, a discursive liberation, which is supposed to be the precursor of a liberation on the ground in Palestine. At long last, in public perception as well as in academic imagery, Israel joins the series of white colonial oppressor regimes; although whiteness is not much emphasized in this framework, as this aspect is taken as self-evident and represents only the starting point, emphasis falls instead on the "logic of elimination of the natives" practiced by Israelis. According to this view, Israel was not treated as a colony or as an apartheid state because of the special status of the Holocaust and Jewish exceptionality, or because of Jews' general standing in the world and also due to their status either as eternal victims or as whitened colonizers.

The number of works on Israel as a settler colony has grown significantly over the last fifteen to twenty years. The academic review *Settler Colonial Studies*, founded by Lorenzo Veracini in 2010, has already published three special issues on Israel; generally speaking, almost one-third of the articles from these ten years deal exclusively with Israel, and certainly many more at least mention it in a so-called comparative perspective.

It seems that treating Israel as a settler-colonial state is supposed to provide the ultimate justification for singling it out for criticism and also to legitimize the Palestinian struggle in all its forms as an anticolonial movement. This presentation of Israel is to accentuate that the struggle is not between competitive nationalisms but between the conqueror, on the one hand, and the conquered, the displaced, the occupied, on the other.[41] It is the colonial framework that creates a necessary binary opposition, the absolute inequality of power relations, and the image of settlers as illegitimate invaders striving to eliminate the natives. In this regard, we can speak of some fairly general postulates, not to say axioms, adopted by such analyses, which seem to constitute an unchangeable and essentialized scheme.

The settler-colonial paradigm starts out with what its adepts call a "key distinction between colonialism and settler colonialism . . . the former is organized around a logic of *exploitation* while the latter is characterized by a logic of *elimination*. In contrast to the colonizer who seeks the labour of the colonized, the *settler* colonizer instead seeks their land, with the elimination of the native part and parcel of the settler's attempt to replace them."[42] According to Patrick Wolfe, who alongside Veracini is considered a founder of the paradigm, this eliminatory logic is inherent and absolutely primary in settler colonialism. In his many articles, Wolfe emphasizes that settler colonialism is a "structure"—that is, it is permanent in space and time—and remains unchanged until decolonization happens: in the "systematic understanding of settler colonialism as a historical programme of elimination, not only does the necessity for violence emerge as intrinsic to the project. . . . The violence does not go away. Indeed, it remains ever-present and manifest in post-frontier symptoms such as disproportionate Indigenous incarceration rates, zonal police deployments."[43] In an introduction to one of the special issues on Israel of *Settler Colonial Studies*, we can read, "Viewed through the lens of settler colonialism, the *Nakba* in 1948 is not simply a precondition for the creation of Israel or the outcome of early Zionist ambitions; the *Nakba* is not a singular event but is manifested today in the continuing subjection of Palestinians by Israelis."[44] According to Lorenzo Veracini, the settler-colonial paradigm perceives Israelis and Palestinians not as simple adversaries but as natives confronting settlers. It is supposed to achieve a "discursive overturning of presumed power relations"[45]; however, it seems that this ambition is not limited to the discursive field. Wolfe states that what we have here is a "zero-sum logic whereby settler societies, for all their internal complexities, uniformly require the elimination of Native alternatives,"[46] and when referring to critiques of this conception, he maintains that the repudiation of this binary logic is nothing short of a settler's distorted perspective. Similar formulations abound. Pappé, for example, who apparently does not want to be surpassed in radicality, catches up by using the exact same terms found in Wolfe and Veracini: "I see the whole project of Zionism as a structure, not just as one event. . . . As long as the colonisation is not complete and the indigenous population resists through a national liberation movement, each such period that I'm looking at is just a phase within the same structure. . . . So I suggest talking about decolonization, not peace. I suggest talking about changing the legal regime that governs the life of Israelis and Palestinians."[47]

Thus, in Pappé's view, one should talk about inherent eliminatory logic as of a lasting, unchanged structure of dispossession and oppression while breaking away from the framework of competing nationalisms and taking the whole history of Zionism (both as program and as practice) from its beginnings, regardless of conflicts, wars, territorial changes, religions, and fundamentalisms (these latter are never even mentioned), as a colonial project. And most importantly, it has to be maintained that the Six-Day War brought nothing new—the creation of the state in 1948 and the territories acquired in 1967 obeyed the same logic, both being products of the same underlying structure. These approaches practically never talk about the Palestinians, either—they are absent from the analysis and when present are pictured only as passive victims.

However, there have been some attempts at empirical verification. Veracini has authored a whole book entitled *Israel and Settler Society*, in which he compares Israel to apartheid South Africa, French Algeria, and Australia. And although he does not hide the differences between these countries and Israel, he still tries to treat these divergences as unessential in order to preserve the concept of "settler colony" unchanged by emphasizing presumed structural continuities. Wherever he is unable to find factual evidence, he either turns to impressions or cites Israeli fringe political opinion. For example, while he acknowledges that the respective conditions of Israeli Arabs and the Palestinians of the occupied territories differ to a large degree, he nevertheless maintains that the two situations can be brought closer, as there is a "growing feeling of political disenfranchisement."[48] Or, to cite another example, even if it is true that Israeli Arabs have political representation, it is also true that in apartheid South Africa the Black population had some kind of political representation as well (Veracini asserts this without describing what it was). Also, he talks about "recurring calls" for the "transfer" of Palestinians and proposals for withdrawing their citizenship, without mentioning that these are minority positions that never had any chance of being realized.[49] This same strategy is highlighted by David Hirsh with regard to Joseph Massad. For example, Massad takes the translation of an article from an obscure Russian-language newspaper, which calls for the expulsion of all the Arabs. Hirsh calls this strategy the assumption of "Zionist unity": one example stands for the whole and represents it without remainder. "The assumption of Zionist unity," he writes, "means that one opinion piece in one newspaper can be understood to illustrate the nature of Zionism as a whole."[50]

Therefore, even the tentative collection of empirical evidence does nothing to change the global picture—namely, that the whole history of Zionism and Israel can flawlessly be inserted into the conceptual framework of settler-colonial studies. To the contrary, this conceptual novelty is presented as a genuine Copernican revolution, as a total transformation of interpretation and even of perception—at long last, it asserts, as the unveiling of its real nature has become possible, we can understand why Israel is such a deranging phenomenon. Consequently, previous research is criticized for being too empirical and not "structuralist" enough: "In many ways scholarly production accurately mirrors the dynamics of incoherent contemporary Palestinian politics."[51]

In order to characterize settler colonialism but also to broaden its theoretical and even moral significance, Wolfe uses the term *structural genocide*, which includes not only mass killing but also removal and assimilation: "I suggest that the term 'structural genocide' avoids the questions of degree—and, therefore, of hierarchy among victims—that are entailed in qualified genocides, while retaining settler colonialism's structural induration."[52] In this respect he also talks about "genocide in abeyance," which means that even when there is no actual genocidal practice, there is certainly more to come because the structure itself doesn't go away.[53] No empirical finding could refute the potentiality (which is, here, taken to be equivalent with the actuality) of genocide understood in this extremely flexible yet essentialized manner. Wolfe is relativizing genocide (a concept forged by reference to the Holocaust) while at the same time using the powerful imagery associated with it and turning it against Israel. In fact, this is Holocaust relativization, instrumentalization, and inversion all in one move, very similar to Giorgio Agamben's treatment of the "camp" when he forges a universalized, structural concept on the basis of the Nazi camps but uses its dramatic force to criticize completely different social and political phenomena.[54] (Although, it must be said, Agamben is much more tacit with respect to Israel.)

The previously cited programmatic article "Past Is Present" clearly states that research should be motivated by the need for political action: "In order to move forward and create a transformative, liberatory research agenda, it is necessary to analyse Zionism's structural continuities and the ideology that informs Israeli policies and practices in Israel and toward Palestinians everywhere. In other words, while Israel's tactics have often been described as settler colonial, the settler colonial structure underpinning them must be a central object of analysis."[55] This means that it is necessary to view Israel/Palestine as the outcome of the structural continuities of settler colonialism and that doing so should, furthermore, awake us to the necessity of a "liberatory research agenda." But of course, liberation and decolonization make sense only if we have already accepted that Israel can be described as a settler colony, which has not been demonstrated. Therefore, this would be a most evident case of circular argument were it not for the belief that the framework vows for itself and that it is ultimately much more a political than a scientific issue.

Thus, Rachel Busbridge, who is a sympathetic critic of the settler-colonial paradigm, offered a telling characterization of it, saying that it "offers a radically different framing of the conflict than what has come to be fairly standard in the international arena." "Framing," continues Busbridge, is understood here as the generation of collective beliefs and action by presenting the issue at hand from a certain angle.[56] However, such a definition casts this scientific-interpretive paradigm as something possessing outright propagandistic-political goals—to talk about "framing" in the sense of packaging of the message means we have jumped from scientific interpretation to propaganda and strategies for collective action. In fact, these kinds of formulations abound in *Settler Colonial Studies*—for example, "The central question for committed scholarship and liberatory movements should be how to develop a praxis that brings back decolonisation and liberation as the imperative goal. . . . Otherwise, settler colonialism remains a descriptive category that does not move beyond sentiment and into strategy."[57] Now it seems that applying the settler-colonial paradigm is insufficient, as it constitutes only the first step; and in fact, the academic discipline of settler-colonial studies imagines itself as an enterprise akin to a social-political movement. Further proof of this extreme politicization is that a kind of "intersectionality" is equally proposed, first with "the Arab struggle for self-determination" and then with the whole of "indigenous struggles" waged in North and South America as well as Oceania and elsewhere.[58]

How can all this be judged with regard to scientific methodology? In one of his articles on scientific objectivity, Max Weber states, "The basic idea of modern epistemology, which goes back to Kant, is that concepts are, and can only be, theoretical means for the purpose of intellectual mastery of the empirically given."[59] Therefore, theoretical means should never be confounded with the ends of the analysis: "Concepts, in other words, are tools, and not the end point of the analysis."[60] Weber's method of ideal-types is a perfect illustration of what he means by conceptual tools, which have to be constantly modified as they are being measured against empirical reality. However, one does not have to be a Weberian to value this fundamental distinction and to repudiate the reification of concepts, the binaries and the false analogies in use within critical whiteness studies, settler-colonial studies, and other fields of activist social science. But fallacious methodology has a clear function in these analyses—namely, a certain symbolic usage of the terms *whiteness*, *colony*, and *settler colony*, which inherently comprises an unequivocal moral judgment. Thus, here, it is in fact the concept that constitutes the absolute end point of the analysis, after which action should follow, and this an action entirely informed by the concept. As Cheyette puts it, "The slippage into the crudest forms of analogical thinking . . . is illustrative of precisely what is lost when critical thinking is replaced by actionism."[61] "Liberatory action" will find the theory that suits it the best, and vice versa—a "liberatory research agenda" will inform political action in an unequivocal way.

Notes

1. Theodor W. Adorno, *Critical Models and Catchwords* (New York: Columbia University Press, 2005), 260.

2. A more detailed critical account on critical whiteness studies can be found in Balázs Berkovits, "Critical Whiteness Studies and the 'Jewish Problem,'" *Zeitschrift für kritische Sozialtheorie und Philosophie* 5, no. 1 (April 2018): 86–102.

3. See, for example, Ruth Frankenberg, *White Women, Race Matters: The Social Construction of Whiteness* (Minneapolis: University of Minnesota Press, 1993).

4. For example, see the following works: Noel Ignatiev, *How the Irish Became White* (New York: Routledge, 1994); David Roediger, *The Wages of Whiteness* (London: Verso, 1999); Eric L. Goldstein, *The Price of Whiteness: Jews, Race and American Identity* (Woodstock, UK: Princeton University Press, 2006).

5. Karen Brodkin, *How Jews Became White Folks and What That Says about Race in America* (New Brunswick, NJ: Rutgers University Press, 1999).

6. On the conceptual contradictions relative to "whiteness" and "color" conceived in such a way, see Peter Kolchin, "Whiteness Studies: The New History of Race in America," *Journal of American History* 89, no. 1 (2002): 154–73; Ladelle McWhorter, "Where Do White People Come From? A Foucaultian Critique of Whiteness Studies," *Philosophy and Social Criticism* 31, nos. 5–6 (2005): 533–56; Berkovits, "Critical Whiteness Studies."

7. See Sander L. Gilman, *Multiculturalism and the Jews* (New York: Taylor and Francis, 2006).

8. Derek Penslar is one of the few authors (though not mentioned by Cheyette) who tried to link European Jewish experience with postcolonialism and argued against treating Zionism as "colonial," for which he was severely criticized by some postcolonial theorists. See "Is Zionism a Colonial Movement?," in *Israel in History* (London: Routledge, 2007), republished in *Colonialism and the Jews*, ed. Ethan B. Katz, Lisa Moses Leff, and Maud S. Mandel (Bloomington: Indiana University Press, 2017), 275–300, along with critiques written by Joshua Cole and Elizabeth F. Thompson, and a reply from Penslar.

9. Willi Goetschel and Ato Quayson, "Introduction: Jewish Studies and Postcolonialism," *Cambridge Journal of Postcolonial Literary Inquiry* 3. no. 1 (Winter 2015): 1–9.

10. Bryan Cheyette, "Against Supersessionist Thinking: Old and New, Jews and Postcolonialism, the Ghetto and Diaspora," *Cambridge Journal of Postcolonial Literary Inquiry* 4, no. 3 (2017): 427.

11. Danny Trom, *La promesse et l'obstacle: La gauche radicale et le problème juif* (Paris: Edition du Cerf, 2007).
12. David Theo Goldberg, *The Threat of Race: Reflections on Racial Neoliberalism* (Malden, MA: Blackwell, 2009), 117.
13. Goldberg, *Threat of Race*, 108.
14. Goldberg, 141.
15. Although one could find Bakan's ideas to be idiosyncratic and extreme, she is a legitimate scholar who has worked in major Canadian academic institutions.
16. Abigail B. Bakan, "Race, Class, and Colonialism: Reconsidering the 'Jewish Question,'" in *Theorizing Anti-racism: Linkages in Marxism and Critical Race Theories*, ed. Abigail B. Bakan and Enakshi Dua (Toronto: University of Toronto Press, 2014), 254.
17. See Michael B. Oren, *Power, Faith and Fantasy: America in the Middle East, 1776 to the Present* (New York: W. W. Norton, 2007).
18. Bakan, "Race, Class, and Colonialism," 261.
19. Bakan, 258–62.
20. Bakan, 253.
21. Bakan, 260.
22. Gabriel Piterberg, *The Returns of Zionism: Myths, Politics and Scholarship in Israel* (London: Verso, 2008).
23. Zeev Sternhell, "In Defence of Liberal Zionism," *New Left Review*, no. 62 (2010): 99.
24. "Word Crimes: Reclaiming the Language of the Israeli-Palestinian Conflict," ed. Donna Robinson Divine, Miriam F. Elman, and Asaf Romirowsky, special issue, *Israel Studies* 24, no. 2 (2019), 1–16.
25. Gershon Shafir, "The Word Crimes Controversy (2): Gershon Shafir Responds to Cary Nelson," *Fathom*, July 2019, http://fathomjournal.org/the-word-crimes-controversy-2-gershon-shafir-responds-to-cary-nelson/.
26. John Strawson, "The Word Crimes Controversy (6): A Personal Reflection by John Strawson," *Fathom*, July 2019, http://fathomjournal.org/the-word-crimes-controversy-6-a-personal-reflection-by-john-strawson/.
27. Piterberg, *Returns of Zionism*.
28. Sternhell, "In Defence of Liberal Zionism," 110.
29. Gabriel Piterberg, "Settlers and Their State. A Reply to Zeev Sternhell," *New Left Review*, no. 62 (2010): 116.
30. Piterberg, "Settlers and Their State," 117.
31. Piterberg, 118.
32. Piterberg, 123.
33. Gershon Shafir, "Zionism and Colonialism: A Comparative Approach," in *Israel in Comparative Perspective: Challenging the Conventional Wisdom*, ed. Michael N. Barnett (Albany: State University of New York Press, 1996), 230–31.
34. Shafir, "Zionism and Colonialism," 233–34.
35. Shafir, 231.
36. Shafir, 235.
37. Shafir, 241.
38. Shafir, 228.
39. Eli Massey, "Ilan Pappe: Israel Is the Last Remaining, Active Settler-Colonialist Project," *In These Times*, May 5, 2016, https://inthesetimes.com/article/19107/ilan-pappe-Bernie-Sanders-Noam-Chomsky-BDS-Israel-Palestine.
40. Rachel Busbridge, "Israel-Palestine and the Settler Colonial 'Turn': From Interpretation to Decolonization," *Theory, Culture and Society* 35, no. 1 (2018): 92.

41. Lorenzo Veracini, "What Can Settler Colonial Studies Offer to an Interpretation of the Conflict in Israel–Palestine?," *Settler Colonial Studies* 5, no. 3 (2015): 268.
42. Busbridge, "Israel-Palestine," 92, italics in the original.
43. Patrick Wolfe, "Recuperating Binarism: A Heretical Introduction," *Settler Colonial Studies* 3, nos. 3–4 (2013): 270.
44. Omar Jabary Salamanca, Mezna Qato, Kareem Rabie, and Sobhi Samour, "Past Is Present: Settler Colonialism in Palestine," *Settler Colonial Studies* 2, no. 1 (2012): 2.
45. See Busbridge, "Israel-Palestine," 99.
46. Wolfe, "Recuperating Binarism," 257.
47. Mustafa Abu Sneineh, "Interview: Ilan Pappé—How Israel Turned Palestine into the Biggest Prison on Earth," Portside, November 28, 2017, https://portside.org/2017-11-28/interview-ilan-pappe-how-israel-turned-palestine-biggest-prison-earth.
48. Lorenzo Veracini, *Israel and Settler Society* (London: Pluto, 2006), 23.
49. Veracini, *Israel and Settler Society*, 28.
50. David Hirsh, *Contemporary Left Antisemitism* (London: Routledge, 2018), 190.
51. Salamanca et al., "Past Is Present," 3.
52. Patrick Wolfe, "Settler Colonialism and the Elimination of the Native," *Journal of Genocide Research* 8, no. 4 (2006): 403.
53. Wolfe, "Settler Colonialism," 403.
54. Balázs Berkovits, "Social Criticism and the 'Jewish Problem,'" in *Anti-Zionism and Antisemitism: The Dynamics of Delegitimization*, ed. Alvin Rosenfeld (Bloomington: Indiana University Press, 2019), 53–83.
55. Salamanca et al., "Past Is Present," 2.
56. Busbridge, "Israel-Palestine," 98.
57. Salamanca et al., "Past Is Present," 4.
58. Salamanca et al., 5.
59. Max Weber, "The 'Objectivity' of Knowledge in Social Science and Social Policy," in *Collected Methodological Essays*, ed. H. H. Bruun and S. Whimster (London: Routledge, 2012), 134–35.
60. Richard Swedberg, "How to Use Max Weber's Ideal Type in Sociological Analysis," *Journal of Classical Sociology* 18, no. 3 (2017): 3.
61. Cheyette, "Against Supersessionist Thinking," 426.

BALÁZS BERKOVITS is a sociologist and philosopher pursuing postdoctoral research at the Bucerius Institute and the Herzl Institute, University of Haifa. Previously, he was a researcher at the Psychological Institute of the Hungarian Academy of Sciences, assistant professor at the Department of Philosophy at the University of Miskolc, Hungary, visiting scholar at Indiana University, and postdoctoral fellow at EHESS, Paris. He also works as a translator of social scientific works and a journalist. He is currently working on a book on the reemergence of the "Jewish problem" in contemporary works of philosophical, social, and political criticism, understood in the framework of the crisis of social critique. His publications on the topic include "Critical Whiteness Studies and the Jewish

Problem," *Zeitschrift für kritische Sozialtheorie und Philosophie* 5, no. 1 (April 2018), and "Social Criticism and the 'Jewish Problem,'" in *Anti-Zionism and Antisemitism: The Dynamics of Delegitimization*, ed. Alvin Rosenfeld (Bloomington, Indiana University Press, 2019). Previously, he published widely on topics related to the sociology of education, social theory, the epistemology of the social sciences, critical sociology, and social constructivism.

4

Traditionalism or the Perennial Philosophy
Religionism, Politics, and the New Right

Mark Weitzman

ALTHOUGH HE HAS NOT BEEN SPOTLIGHTED AS MUCH since he left the Trump White House, Steve Bannon's efforts during Donald Trump's successful run for the presidency carved out his reputation as the man who created an "intellectual basis for Trumpism"[1] and even caused a *New York Times* political correspondent to tweet, "Whether u [sic] respect him or not Bannon is a deep if narrow reader who is trying to create an ideological/intellectual foundation for Trumpism" (@GlennThrush, April 15, 2017).[2] Part of Bannon's reputation rested on a talk he gave (electronically) at the Vatican in 2014, which referenced what one writer described as "nationalist thinkers of an earlier age."[3] These "thinkers of an earlier age" included such figures as René Guénon and Julius Evola, and Bannon also referred to the current Russian political theorist Aleksandr Dugin. They can all be described as belonging to the Traditionalist school of esoteric thought. Bannon also referred directly to Traditionalism, saying, "We the Judeo-Christian West really have to look at what he's [Vladimir Putin] talking about as far as traditionalism goes—particularly the sense of where it supports the underpinnings of nationalism . . . —and I happen to think that the individual sovereignty of a country is a good thing and a strong thing." And while he was running Breitbart News, Bannon told a contributor, "I do appreciate any piece that mentions Evola."[4]

Although there has been a great deal of recent writing about Traditionalism, especially in connection to its politics, there is still much to uncover, particularly regarding the current nexus among Traditionalism, politics, and antisemitism. To begin with, we need to define what we mean by the term *Traditionalism*. Also known as the perennial philosophy, it has been outlined by the scholar Mark Sedgwick as "belief and practice that should have been transmitted but was lost to the West during the last half of the second millennium a.d. According to the Traditionalists, the modern West is in crisis as a result of this loss of transmission of tradition."[5] Sedgwick explains that Guénon's 1927 book, *The Crisis of the Modern World*, highlighted this predicament, while his 1939 book, *Oriental Metaphysics*, along with Evola's 1934 book, *Revolt against the Modern World*, posed ways out of this dilemma. But who were these thinkers with whom Bannon claimed familiarity?

René Guénon (November 15, 1886–January 7, 1951) was born into a Catholic family in France. In his student years, he was already drawn into the world of esoteric and occult seekers, but his career actually began in the Catholic circles that opposed "atheistic" Freemasonry, materialism, and secularism. Closely connected in his youth to the ultramontane Action Française movement,[6] Guénon appears to have also been influenced by the reactionary thinker Joseph de Maistre.[7] After studying Hinduism and publishing his first book on the topic in 1921, Guénon was drawn to Islam. (The book was originally a thesis that was rejected by Sylvain Levi, the great Sorbonne orientalist. It was, however, supported by the Catholic philosopher Jacques Maritain, who at that point was a friend and supporter of Guénon.) Guénon evidently converted to Islam, becoming a Sufi in 1910 under the name ʿAbd al-Wāḥid Yaḥyā. By 1930, he had moved to Cairo, where he lived as a pious Muslim for the rest of his life.[8]

Guénon's thought has been described by Sedgwick as "not especially original. It was composed of a number of elements, most of which had been part of Western thought for centuries. His achievement was to form an entirely new synthesis out of these ideas, and then to promote his synthesis to the point where it could be taken further by others."[9] These ideas include elements such as "inversion," or the sense that we are not progressing but are rather in decline, that wisdom came from the East and later migrated to the Middle East (from Hindu to Tao to Islam), and that this tradition is hidden to the masses and available only through initiation to a select few who form an elite of philosopher-priests. Guénon's commitment to Islamic practice later added another element of ritual practice to his system. After his association with the Action Française ended around 1926, Guénon shunned direct and overt political activism, but traces of political perspectives, such as his critique of modernity and his vison of rulers and the ruled, remained intact and would later inform other Traditionalist thinkers.

Guénon's attacks on Freud and other modern Jewish thinkers were explicit in their antisemitism and reflected the milieu that helped shape his thinking. In his 1945 book, *The Reign of Quantity and the Signs of the Times*, which was written as a reaction to World War II, Guénon could not refrain from writing, "Why is it that the principal representatives of the new tendencies, like Einstein in physics, Bergson in philosophy, Freud in psychology, and many others . . . are almost all of Jewish origin, unless it be because there is something involved that is closely bound up with the 'malefic' and dissolving aspect of nomadism when it is deviated, and because that aspect must inevitably predominate in Jews detached from their tradition?"[10] Despite this and some similar statements, antisemitism was not seen as a primary factor in Guénon's thinking, at least not in the overt sense that it appeared in the wrings of Julius Evola, a prominent Italian Traditionalist.

The major practical political application of Traditionalism began in the writings of Evola (May 19, 1898–June 11, 1974), an Italian philosopher and artist. Evola's stream of writing and his international network of personal connections made him a figure of significance. Born into a minor aristocratic family (he was a baron), Evola was a prolific writer throughout his career, publishing on various topics including art, politics, gender, and mysticism.

In the early 1920s, Evola had begun to immerse himself in esotericism, and by 1928 he was publishing on politics, beginning with an attempt to push fascism into restoring the principles of ancient Rome, even in opposition to the values of the Catholic Church. These themes would remain consistent throughout his long career. However, while the look backward at an ancient golden age and the downward descent into the terrible modern situation are hallmarks of Traditionalist thought and certainly are present in Guénon's writings, there were significant differences between the two thinkers.[11]

Near contemporaries, Evola and Guénon corresponded with each other, although they never met. In a 1925 letter written to another party, Guénon stated that Evola's point of view "appeared to me too philosophical" and that it "prove[s] that he did not understand very much about what I expounded."[12] In another letter from 1926, he wrote that "Evola doesn't lack any pretentions, as you see; but, for my part, I continue to think that he does not understand at all what we mean by 'intellectuality,' 'knowledge,' 'contemplation,' etc., and that he doesn't even know how to make the distinction between the 'initiatic' point of view and the 'profane' point of view."[13] By 1930 they were corresponding directly, and Guénon made no hesitation in telling Evola, "Obviously, the point of view you are assuming is quite distinctive and certainly cannot be mine."[14] Their correspondence continued in this vein until at least 1949, shortly before Guénon's death. The disagreements between the two were not only on philosophical or esoteric issues; more germane for our purposes was the split between them over politics and activism. This came through clearly in their respective views on the description of the elite level of society. For Guénon's mature thought, the West can be preserved only through the efforts of an intellectual elite, which Sedgwick clarifies as "spiritual, metaphysical" and which transmits the hidden teachings of the Orient.[15] However, Evola's description of the elite involved a unity of spiritual and secular power, of warrior-kings and philosophers based on, for example, Indo-Aryan sources that demonstrated how the priests actually served in supportive roles to the ruler.[16] In other words, this difference in approaches was described by Sedgwick as reflecting that "Evolian Traditionalism pointed toward the political right, separating it definitively from Guénonian Traditionalism, which was essentially apolitical."[17]

Evola was associated with fascism from the late 1920s on and traveled in fascist circles in Europe in the 1930s. His friendship with the Romanian scholar Mircea Eliade, who later became the world's most prominent historian of religion in the late twentieth century, dates from that period. Although their correspondence goes back to the 1920s, when Eliade was still a university student in Bucharest, they apparently did not meet until Evola visited Bucharest in 1937.[18] It was during that visit that Eliade took Evola to visit Cornelius Codreanu, the virulently antisemitic leader of the fascist Iron Guard. Evola's account of this meeting, published in 1937, has been translated and is available on right-wing sites online.[19] In this account, Evola fawned over Codreanu, describing him as a "a young, tall, slender man, with an uncommon expression of nobleness, frankness and energy imprinted on his face" and as one who is "challenging Israel, and the forces which are more or less in cahoots with it, at work in the Romanian national life." Evola adds that "Codreanu's movement has sought to fight in every sector this Jewish offensive launched in Romania by the two and a half million Israelites there and by the forces affiliated to or financed by Israel." The account concludes with the killing of Codreanu on orders of King Carol in November 1938, a murder mourned by both by Evola and Eliade.[20] Eliade even published an extremely laudatory review of Evola's *Revolt against the*

Modern World in 1935. In addition to saying that "Evola's work is situated in the cultural lines of Gobineau, Chamberlain, Spengler," Eliade notes "the rigour of his philosophical analysis, his critical spirit, and the courage that he has."[21] Although he never wanted it publicly known and was rebuked by Evola for hiding his Traditionalist leanings, it has been suggested that Eliade responded by saying that his intent was to "to introduce [a] Trojan horse [Traditionalism] into the university citadel."[22] (Eliade's complicity with fascism and antisemitism has been much discussed, and a vast literature has grown up around it.[23])

While Evola rejected the "crude" *volkisch* antisemitism of the Nazis, he espoused a deep-seated antisemitism based on the identification of Jews with modernity (similar to that of Guénon). However, Evola went beyond Guénon by devoting both word and action to furthering his antisemitism—for instance, publishing the foreword to the second Italian edition (1938) of the *Protocols of the Elders of Zion*, which he claimed "contained the plan for an occult war, whose objective is the utter destruction in the non-Jewish peoples, of all tradition, class and hierarchy and of all moral, religious or supra-material values."[24]

Evola tried to establish himself with the Italian fascists, meeting with Mussolini after he published his 1941 book *Synthesis of the Doctrine of Race*, only to eventually break with him.[25] His efforts to establish a base with the SS ended in failure when an evaluation commissioned by Heinrich Himmler reported that "Evola works from a basic Aryan concept but is quite ignorant of prehistoric Germanic institutions and their meaning" and recommended that Evola not be supported by the SS. Himmler accepted the recommendation. However, even without any official base, Evola still was able to maintain his contacts in the fascist and Nazi hierarchy.[26] When Mussolini was rescued by Otto Skorzeny in 1943, Evola was among those invited to Hitler's Wolf's Lair mountain retreat for the meeting between Hitler and Mussolini.

Codreanu, Hitler, and Mussolini were only some of the many personalities associated with extreme right-wing politics whom Evola knew and who, together with his writings, helped raise him over the course of his eventful life to iconic stature in the post–World War II movement. His status is apparent in many corners of today's alt-right or extreme right-wing circles. According to Richard Spencer, widely considered the founder of the alt-right movement in the United States, "Evola is one of the most fascinating men of the 20th century."[27] Evola's books have been translated and published by the Arktos publishing house of Budapest, which has been called "the world's largest distributor of far- and alt-right literature."[28] A recent search of Evola on Arktos's website turned up about sixty-five entries.[29] Arktos is not the only source of writings by Evola online. John Morgan, a former editor at Arktos who was forced out in a power struggle, started another site called Counter-Currents that also features a great deal of material on Evola.[30] A recent count on this site showed approximately one hundred articles featuring Evola, with titles including "What Would Evola Do"[31] "Julius Evola: The World's Most Right Wing Thinker,"[32] and "Julius Evola: Racism and Antisemitism."[33]

Evola also influenced many leading figures in today's extremist world. In Italy he and Guénon were important influences on Claudio Mutti, a former university lecturer who followed Guénon's path to Islam. Mutti's Islamic name is Omar Amin, chosen to honor the SS officer Johann Amin von Leers who became an aide to Egypt's Gamel Abdel Nasser after World War II and who specialized in antisemitic propaganda (von Leers was another convert to Islam).[34] Mutti also is a radical antisemite and a follower of Libya's former leader Muammar Gaddafi. His efforts include collaborating with Iran's government, participating in at least one government-organized conference in Teheran, and founding his own publishing house (Edizioni All'insegna Del Veltro) with a roster of authors and topics that include such notorious figures as Hitler, Codreanu, and the French collaborators and antisemites Drieu La Rochelle and Robert Brassilach, along with the recently deceased French Holocaust denier Robert Faurisson. While he has embraced radical Islam, Mutti is still engaged with Traditionalism, including writing studies on Guénon, Evola, and Eliade. Mutti, who from his young days was engaged in radical politics, has significant relationships with far-right European circles as well as with Russian extremists (more on that below).[35]

The English New Right activist Troy Southgate published an eight-part series on Evola on the English version of a Russian propaganda and sensationalist website.[36] Southgate has been associated with the radical Catholic Traditionalist Society of Saint Pius X movement (SSPX) as well as with the National Front and International Third Position groups.[37] By the late 1990s, perhaps influenced by Evola's writings, he abandoned his Catholicism and shifted to Traditionalism. One of Southgate's core assertions is that Evola's distinction between classes, between "superior" and "inferior" stations, is essential. As Southgate writes, "The fact that Evola so openly acknowledges that there are various stations in life will outrage liberals, Marxists and advocates of democracy alike. But he is, nevertheless, absolutely correct.

Forcing people to accord with a societal conglomeration which has been enshrined in law by a coterie of dogmatists and architectural levellers is simply not allowing people to discover and thus accomplish their true destinies. Evola believes that historical events have often been determined by the manner in which 'the inferior'—which is not used in a derogatory sense—regard their 'superior' counterparts."[38]

Another important figure who has acknowledged his debt to Evola is the Frenchman Alain de Benoist. With a career as a far-right extremist that extends back to the early 1970s,[39] de Benoist is perhaps the single most important intellectual figure in European far-right circles today (his English publisher, Arktos, describes him as "the leading thinker of the European 'New Right' movement" or ND[40]), but his influence extends beyond those circles and has impacted mainstream politics.[41] As one scholar wrote, the ND "has . . . shaped a decidedly more right-wing political culture in Europe in a transnational spirit."[42] De Benoist is explicit about his admiration for Evola. In an article entitled "Julius Evola, Radical Reactionary and Committed Metaphysician: A Critical Analysis of the Political Thought of Julius Evola," de Benoist concluded his discussion of Evola's *Men among the Ruins* with the following words: "As much by its contents as by the influence that this book has exercised, *Men Among the Ruins* indisputably constitutes an important work from the point of view of the historiography of the ideas of the Right. For our part, there are above all certain critiques formulated by Evola that seem to us likely to inspire a reflection—a timely one, moreover—on the evolution to the present world."[43]

De Benoist and Mutti shared a connection with the third of the figures mentioned by Bannon in his Vatican talk, the Russian theorist Aleksandr Dugin. The fifty-seven-year-old Dugin was recognized by Bannon as being an important Russian ideologue. In Bannon's words, "Vladimir Putin, when you really look at some of the underpinnings of some of his beliefs today, a lot of those come from what I call Eurasianism; he's got an adviser who harkens back to Julius Evola and different writers of the early 20th century who are really the supporters of what's called the traditionalist movement."[44] Dugin has been described as "the main ideologue of neo-Eurasianism," but his range of influence and contacts is much wider.[45] The Eurasianist theory is considered to be one of the primary ideological drivers of Vladimir Putin's Russia today. It has been defined by the scholar Marlene Laruelle as encompassing four major points:

> (1) A rejection of Europe, the West, and capitalism through criticism of "Atlanticist" domination, considered disastrous for the rest of mankind; (2) an

assertion of the cultural unity and common historical destiny of Russians and non-Russian peoples of Russia, the former Soviet Union, and parts of Asia; (3) the idea that the central geographical position of this Eurasian space naturally and inevitably entails an imperial form of political organization, and that any secession is destined to fail, leaving newly independent states no choice but to revert to a unified political entity; and (4) a belief in the existence of cultural constants that explain the deeper meaning of contemporary political events.[46]

Dugin began his career flirting with Pamyat, the Russian antisemitic and fascist party of the 1980s, and then moving around various permutations of the extreme-right nationalist political scene in Russia. His international connections go back to that period as well.[47] He first met de Benoist in the late 1980s, and they became collaborators, with Dugin becoming known as the "Russian Proponent of the New Right" (ND).[48] Dugin's efforts and connections soon reached the Russian political elites, and he was invited to teach at the Academy of the General Staff and the Institute for Strategic Research in Moscow. His book *The Foundations of Geopolitics: Russia's Geopolitical Future* became a best seller and went through four printings. Dugin then became an advisor to the Duma's spokesman, and in 1999 he was named to chair the geopolitical section of the Duma's National Advisory Council on National Security. He continued his upward trajectory, and by 2014, *Foreign Affairs*, the journal of the Council on Foreign Relations, was calling Dugin "Putin's Brain."[49] While these claims of direct influence on Putin might be somewhat overblown, there is no question that Dugin has had a significant impact on Russian intellectual and political thinking.[50] He was a major propagandist behind Russia's invasion and annexation of Ukraine whose initiatives included blaming the US as part of his virulent anti-American stance. In 2015, he said, "America wishes to wage the war against Russia not by its own hands but by the hands of the Ukrainians. . . . The United States carried out the coup d'état during the maidan for the purpose of this war. The United States raised neo-Nazi Russophobes to the power for the purpose of this war."[51]

These actions resulted in Dugin being named in 2015 to the sanctions list of the US Treasury Department's Specially Designated Nationals List Update.[52] At the same time, Russian rightists (including Dugin) were attempting to knit together European far-right parties from Britain, France, Germany, Greece, Italy, and other countries in a network that included support for Russia's aggression in the Ukraine.[53] Dugin was a prolific writer; his other important work, *The Fourth Political Theory*, was published by Arktos in English in 2012. Dugin's claim is that liberalism, fascism, and communism (the prior three theories) have been proved to be failures, so what is now necessary is a new theory that blends elements of the previous three into a new nationalistic brew highlighted by opposition to the US and its materialist focus and by its threatened global hegemony. In his words, "I strongly believe that Modernity is absolutely wrong and the Sacred Tradition is absolutely right. USA is the manifestation of all I hate—Modernity, westernization, unipolarity, racism, imperialism, technocracy, individualism, capitalism. It is in my eyes the society of Antichrist."[54] Dugin was not the first Russian thinker to stress this approach, as he has followed in the footsteps of Lev Gumilev, the Russian theorist who Dugin acknowledged "has given two thousand years of our fate back to us."[55]

Dugin's attraction seems not only to rest in his political theory but also to be augmented by his deeply held religious beliefs, which include a strange brew of Traditionalism and Russian Old Orthodox beliefs. Dugin has self-identified as a Traditionalist thinker, acknowledging debts to Guénon and Evola, affirming that "first of all in my early youth I was deeply inspired by Traditionalism of Rene Guénon and Julius Evola" and acknowledging that "Traditionalism was and rests central as the philosophic focus of all my later developments."[56] While appreciating Guénon, Dugin has expressed his allegiance to the Orthodox Church; thus, a significant difference between the two thinkers is that Dugin views Orthodoxy as the esoteric exception to Guénon's paradigm of exoteric Christianity. With Evola, Dugin shared an affinity for political theory, rejection of Western Christianity, restoration of elements of paganism, a complex antisemitism, and hatred of modernity and its results. In an interview in 2012, Dugin acknowledged his debt, saying, "I consider Evola to be a master and a symbolic figure of the final revolt and the great revival."[57] However, it should be pointed out that some scholars question Dugin's attribution as a Traditionalist.[58]

Although Dugin's attitude toward Jews and Judaism has been described as "complex,"[59] most scholars agree that it reflects some deeply held antisemitic views. His perspective combines positive thoughts about certain aspects of Israeli right-wing politics (Israel is "the only state that has partly succeeded in putting into practice certain aspects of the conservative revolution") with an appreciation of elements of kabbalah, even to the extent of speaking alongside Orthodox rabbis and kabbalists at a conference in France in 2011.[60] In a letter posted online in 1999, Dugin even claimed that from a young age he was "reading the precious books of Professor Gershom Scholem, whom I consider to be the greatest traditionalist thinker."[61] Nonetheless, Dugin's problematic attitude toward Judaism can be seen in his distinction between "exoteric" Rabbinic Judaism, which he views negatively, and esoteric, mystical Judaism, which Dugin sees in a more positive light, a distinction that reflects traditional Christian antisemitic tropes.[62] Another traditional antisemitic trope employed by Dugin is the myth of an international Jewish conspiracy. For Dugin, the myth of the "international Jewish conspiracy" is the explanation for the "Judaization" of the world, which has caused the disastrous results of modern civilization.[63] In Dugin's words, "Jews['] ... aspiration [is] to introduce the 'New World Order.' ... That is, a 'Jewish dictatorship over the Goyim peoples.'"[64]

Dugin's influence on today's far-right scene is immense. His prolific writings, interviews, and reviews of his work proliferate online in different languages. Pseudointellectual movement venues such as the Occidental Observer and Counter-Currents as well as figures such as the academically credentialed Australian Kerry Bolton discuss his theories, and Arktos publishes him. Prominent movement leaders such as David Duke and Richard Spencer have hailed Dugin (Spencer's ex-wife was Dugin's English translator). In congressional testimony, former neo-Nazi Christian Picciolini traced this Russian connection back to the "kinship between David Duke and Aleksandr Dugin."[65] Most recently, in June 2018, two far-right figures (including one of the Pizzagate conspiracy theorists), Lauren Southern and Brittany Pettibone, visited Dugin in Moscow and described themselves as "enthralled" with him.[66]

Spencer, who became notorious as the alleged founder of the alt-right and the organizer of the infamous "Unite the Right" rally in Charlottesville, Virginia, in 2017 that featured Nazi chants and led to the murder of one counterprotestor, not only was close to Dugin but also was an admirer of Evola. In a 2017 *New York Times* story on Bannon's intellectual sources, Spencer stated that "Julius Evola is one of the most fascinating men of the 20th century" and that "it means a tremendous amount" that Mr. Bannon was aware of Evola.[67] Although Spencer, a former Duke PhD student (in European intellectual history) has at times tried to present himself as a respectable political leader, a recent leaked recording exposed his violent antisemitism and racism.[68]

Another figure prominently associated with the Charlottesville rally was Matthew Heimbach, who was once called "potentially the new face of American racism."[69] Heimbach, a college graduate, acknowledged Evola (and Guénon) among his seminal influences and even called the short-lived group that he founded the Traditionalist Workers Party.[70] In a speech he gave that was posted to but subsequently deleted from YouTube, Heimbach focused on Evola and even displayed a large picture of Evola to emphasize his intellectual debt to the Italian thinker.[71] Heimbach's propensity for violence is well documented. He pleaded guilty to disorderly conduct for attacking a protestor at a Trump rally in 2017, and in 2018 he was arrested for two counts of battery that led to his pleading guilty.[72] Immediately after his guilty plea, Heimbach joined forces with the overtly neo-Nazi National Socialist Movement.[73]

Since he left the White House, Bannon has attempted to position himself, with varying success, as the keeper of the faith of the authentic right-wing revolution that Trump claims to reflect. Bannon's efforts in the US appeared to flame out when he was forced out of Breitbart News and lost his major financial donor, Rebekah Mercer, in January 2018.[74] Bannon has been only slightly more successful in traveling around Europe, meeting with various far-right leaders and trying to stitch together some sort of international right-wing front.[75] His most recent effort is the announced creation of a "modern gladiator school" in an ancient monastery in Italy to teach activists how to defend "the Judeo-Christian West."[76] While it is questionable how much of a practical impact Bannon has had recently, with major failures in the US and no great enthusiasm in Europe,[77] he has at least managed to bring mainstream attention to three previously generally marginalized thinkers. Yet these thinkers, Guénon, Evola, and Dugin, despite being on the fringe of modern thought, have managed to plant ideas that have served as the underpinning for a significant assault on Western and liberal traditions. While Guénon did not necessarily embrace the overt antisemitism of Evola and Dugin, nonetheless his work and the thought of Evola and Dugin have served to nourish far-right-wing extremists in their antisemitism and in their attempt to subvert and overthrow US and Western society.

The affinities between Traditionalism and fascism stem from some basic shared assumptions. If we follow Roger Griffith's definition of fascism as "a revolutionary species of political modernism . . . whose mission is to combat the allegedly degenerative forces of contemporary history (decadence) by bringing about an alternative modernity and temporality (a 'new order' and a 'new era') based on the rebirth, or palingenesis, of the nation,"[78] then we see the similarities to Traditionalism as Sedgwick defined it above. Both schools of thought look back to a perceived golden era instead of visualizing a progressive march to a future utopia. Although we can say that at least Guénon's version of Traditionalism seems to reflect a more interior vision, there is no question that the version of Traditionalism that follows Evola and Dugin's model of political engagement while incorporating elements of retrogressive idealism has become a representative philosophy that undergirds significant elements of extreme right-wing activism today.

The allure of Traditionalism for today's right-wing movement is multifold. It provides the movement with coherence and belief. It links to ideas of enlightened elites that in theory should govern the unenlightened masses. It allows for conspiracy theories to be legitimized, and it situates our world as being in crisis that can only be reversed if modernity and liberalism are rejected. The answer is hidden and lies in the past, in secrets handed down through the ages by those who abandoned Western thought and found the answer in Oriental teachings and remnants of pagan lore. And by making liberalism and modernity into the prime enemies of humanity, it allows for those most identified with originating and profiting from those movements, namely Jews, to be cast as the enemy who stands behind all that is evil. Even Christianity is tainted by its birth from Judaism, which is another reason why Oriental and pagan thought, free from the Jewish stain, are elevated. While Traditionalism is not necessarily absolutely antisemitic, it is clear that most any attempt to marry it with politics (à la Evola and Dugin) invariably includes or rests on a deep-seated base of antisemitism. And in today's world, the increasing legitimacy and political potency of Traditionalist politics presents still another challenge in the fight against antisemitism.

Notes

1. Joshua Green, *Devil's Bargain* (New York: Penguin, 2017), 208.
2. Glenn Thrush, "Whether u respect him or not Bannon is a deep if narrow reader who is trying to create an ideological/intellectual foundation for Trumpism," Twitter, April 15, 2017, https://twitter.com/GlennThrush/status/853308417942982656.
3. Green, *Devil's Bargain*. The talk itself can be found at J. Lester Feder, "This Is How Steve Bannon Sees the Entire World," BuzzFeed News, November 16, 2016, https://www.buzzfeed.com/lesterfeder/this-is-how-steve-bannon-sees-the-entire-world?utm_term=.fk1dR9n78#.piwwaQgNP.
4. Joseph Bernstein, "Here's How Breitbart and Milo Smuggled White Nationalism into the Mainstream," BuzzFeed News, October 5, 2017, https://www.buzzfeednews.com/article/josephbernstein/heres-how-breitbart-and-milo-smuggled-white-nationalism.
5. Mark Sedgwick, *Against the Modern World* (Oxford: Oxford University Press, 2009), 21.
6. Paul Chacornac, *The Simple Life of René Guénon* (Hillsdale, NY: Sophia Perennis, 2005), 70. Chacornac points out that Guénon's positive relationship was with Leon Daudet in contrast to the "less sympathy" that existed between Guénon and Charles Maurras.
7. Jean-Yves Pranchere, "The Persistence of Maistrian Thought," in *Joseph de Maistre's Life, Thought, and Influence: Selected Studies*, ed. Richard Lebrun (Montreal: McGill-Queen's University Press, 2001), 294.
8. For an overview of Guénon's life and work, see Sedgwick, *Against the Modern World*, 21–131; Harry Oldmeadow, "René Guénon's Life and Work," World Wisdom, 2008, http://www.worldwisdom.com/public/authors/Rene-Guenon.aspx.
9. Sedgwick, *Against the Modern World*, 264.

10. René Guénon, *The Reign of Quantity and the Signs of the Times* (Hillsdale, NY: Sophia Perennis, 2004), 227.

11. For a more detailed look at various facets of Evola's life and thought, see Sedgwick, *Against the Modern World*, 98–109, 179–87; H. T. Hanson, "A Short Introduction to Julius Evola," in *Revolt against the Modern World*, by Julius Evola (Rochester, VT: Inner Traditions, 1995); H. T. Hanson, "Julius Evola's Political Endeavors," in *Men among the Ruins*, by Julius Evola (Rochester, VT: Inner Traditions, 2002), 1–104; Kevin Coogan, *Dreamer of the Day: Francis Parker Yockey and the Postwar Fascist International* (New York: Autonomedia, 1998).

12. Guénon to Guido de Giorgio, November 20, 1925, Gornahoor, https://www.gornahoor.net/?p=4308. This is a Traditionalist site.

13. Guénon to de Giorgio, November 20, 1925.

14. Guénon to Evola, August 24, 1930, Gornahoor, http://www.gornahoor.net/?p=4489.

15. René Guénon, *Orient et Occident*, 169–87, cited in Sedgwick, *Against the Modern World*, 26.

16. Evola, *Revolt against the Modern World*, 69.

17. Sedgwick, *Against the Modern World*, 267.

18. Sedgwick, 109–10, 114.

19. Julius Evola, "The Tragedy of the Romanian 'Iron Guard,'" Counter-Currents, September 13, 2013, https://www.counter-currents.com/2013/09/the-tragedy-of-the-romanian-iron-guard-2/.

20. Eliade, in his mid-July 1974 journal entry upon hearing of Evola's death, recalled how Evola had been "dazzled" by Codreanu at their meeting thirty-seven years earlier. The fullest English version of Evola's account I could find can be accessed at https://archive.org/details/TheTragedyOfTheIronGuardCodreanu. A shorter version (Evola, "Tragedy") mirrors the text as it appears in Julius Evola, "Legionary Asceticism: Colloquium with the Head of the Iron Guard," in *A Traditionalist Confronts Fascism* (Budapest: Arktos, 2015), 71–76.

21. Cologero, "Eliade on Evola's Revolt," Gornahoor, May 30, 2012, https://www.gornahoor.net/?p=4303. Gornahoor is a Traditionalist website, apparently based in the US, with a focus on Evola.

22. While Evola's response is extant and can be found in translation online at https://www.gornahoor.net/?p=4949, Eliade's original letter has been lost. See also Moshe Idel, *Mircea Eliade, From Magic to Myth* (New York: Peter Lang, 2014), 254.

23. Steven Wasserstrom's *Religion after Religion* (Princeton, NJ: Princeton University Press, 1999) is generally credited with highlighting the controversy, although there had been many earlier exposures. In his late novel *Ravelstein* (New York: Viking, 2000), Saul Bellow gave a fictional portrayal of Eliade and had another character succinctly saying about Eliade's alter ego, "The man was a Hitlerite." One of the more recent and valuable discussions is in Idel, *Mircea Eliade*.

24. Horst Junginger, "From Buddha to Adolf Hitler: Walther Wust and the Aryan Tradition," in *The Study of Religion under Fascism*, ed. Horst Junginger (Leiden: Brill, 2008), 136.

25. Evola's account of the meeting with Mussolini can be found at https://www.counter-currents.com/2015/07/mussolini-and-racism/.

26. Sedgwick, *Against the Modern World*, 107.

27. Jason Horowitz, "Steve Bannon Cited Italian Thinker Who Inspired Fascists," *New York Times*, February 10, 2017, https://www.nytimes.com/2017/02/10/world/europe/bannon-vatican-julius-evola-fascism.html.

28. Thomas Chatterton Williams, "The French Origins of 'You Will Not Replace Us,'" *New Yorker*, November 27, 2017, https://www.newyorker.com/magazine/2017/12/04/the-french-origins-of-you-will-not-replace-us.

29. Search results for "evola," Arktos, accessed January 27, 2021, https://arktos.com/page/1/?s=evola.

30. For one insider perspective on this power struggle, see Matt Forney, "Statement on Greg Johnson, *Counter-Currents*, and My Disassociation with the Alt-Right," MattForney.com, June 19, 2017, https://mattforney.com/statement-greg-johnson/.

31. John Morgan, "What Would Evola Do?," Counter-Currents, May 23, 2017, https://www.counter-currents.com/2017/05/what-would-evola-do/.

32. Jonathan Bowden, "Julius Evola: The World's Most Right-Wing Thinker," Counter-Currents, October 17, 2014, https://counter-currents.com/2014/10/julius-evolathe-worlds-most-right-wing-thinker/. This is a transcription of a 2010 lecture that can be viewed at https://www.youtube.com/watch?v=wqGIz6cCRJc.

33. Julius Evola, "Racism and Anti-Semitism," Counter-Currents, July 16, 2015, https://counter-currents.com/2015/07/racism-and-anti-semitism/.

34. For an overview of Mutti's career, see Giovanni Savino, "From Evola to Dugin: The Neo-fascist Connection in Italy," in *Eurasianism and the European Far Right*, ed. Marlene Laruelle (Lanham, MD: Lexington Books, 2015), especially 104–17. On Von Leers's Nazi past, see Robert Wistrich, *Who's Who in Nazi Germany* (London: Routledge, 2002), 152–53; Jeffrey Herf, *The Jewish Enemy* (Cambridge, MA: Harvard University Press, 2006), 180–81.

35. For more on Mutti, see Savino, "From Evola to Dugin," 260.

36. Unfortunately, the work by Troy Southgate, *Julius Evola: A Radical Traditionalist*, can no longer be accessed online; however, a short summary can be found on the pravda.ru website: "Julius Evola: A Radical Traditionalist," pravda.ru, November 5, 2002, https://english.pravda.ru/news/opinion/42464-n/.

37. On the SSPX and the radical Traditionalist Catholic movement, see Mark Weitzman, "'Every Sane Thinker Must Be an Anti-Semite': Antisemitism and Holocaust Denial in the Theology of Radical Catholic Traditionalists," in *Antisemitism before and since the Holocaust: Altered Contexts and Recent Perspectives*, ed. Anthony McElligott and Jeffrey Herf (Cham, Switzerland: Palgrave Macmillan, 2017), 83–113; Mark Weitzman, "Antisemitism and the Radical Catholic Traditionalist Movement," in *Deciphering the "New" Antisemitism*, ed. Alvin Rosenfeld (Bloomington: Indiana University Press, 2015), 242–86.

38. "Julius Evola: A Radical Traditionalist," pravda.ru. See also note 37 above.

39. By 1975, de Benoist was already an established figure and was corresponding with extremists such as Wills Carto, an American Holocaust denier and supporter of neo-Nazi efforts. See the letters between de Benoist and Carto at "Alain de Benoist," Willis A. Carto Library, June 26, 2017, http://willisacartolibrary.com/2017/06/26/alain-de-benoist/.

40. "Alain de Benoist: The Leading Thinker of the European New Right," Arktos, accessed January 27, 2021, https://arktos.com/people/alain-de-benoist/.

41. See, for example, the series of essays de Benoist began publishing in the 1990s in the prestigious American journal *Telos*.

42. Tamir Bar-On, *Rethinking the French New Right: Alternatives to Modernity* (London: Routledge, 2013), 31.

43. Alain de Benoist, "Julius Evola, Radical Reactionary and Committed Metaphysician," Academia, accessed December 19, 2018, https://www.academia.edu/11654515/_Julius_Evola_Radical_Reactionary_and_Committed_Metaphysician. This is the authorized English translation of an article by de Benoist originally published in Italian in 2002.

44. J. Lester Feder, "This Is How Steve Bannon Sees the Entire World," BuzzFeed News, November 16, 2016, https://www.buzzfeed.com/lesterfeder/this-is-how-steve-bannon-sees-the-entire-world?utm_term=.fk1dR9n78#.piwwaQgNP).

45. Marlene Laruelle, ed., *Eurasianism and the European Far Right* (Lanham, MD: Lexington Books, 2015), xi. See also Laruelle's essay "The Eurasianist Ideology and the Eurasian History: Empire as the *Natural* Solution for the Post-Soviet Space," an unpublished paper given at the Sixth Annual International Young Researchers Conference, "Orienting the Russian Empire," Havighurst Center, Oxford-Miami University, Ohio, October 26–28, 2006. The full text of this essay can be found at http://miamioh.edu/cas/_files/documents/havighurst/orienting/laruelle.pdf.

46. For an excellent introduction to the concept of Eurasianism, see Marlene Laruelle, "The Eurasianist Ideology" (see also note 45 above).

47. Marlene Laruelle, *Russian Eurasianism* (Baltimore: Johns Hopkins University Press, 2012), 126–27.

48. Laruelle, *Russian Eurasianism*, 109. See also Laruelle, *Eurasianism and the European Far Right*; Anton Shekhovtsov, "Aleksandr Dugin's Neo-Eurasianism: The New Right à la Russe," *Religion Compass: Political Religions* 3, no. 4 (2009): 697–716, https://www.academia.edu/197900/Aleksandr_Dugins_Neo-Eurasianism_The_New_Right_à_la_Russe.

49. Anton Barbashin and Hannah Thoburn, "Putin's Brain: Alexander Dugin and the Philosophy behind Putin's Invasion of Crimea," *Foreign Affairs,* March 31, 2014, https://www.foreignaffairs.com/articles/russia-fsu/2014-03-31/putins-brain.

50. As with so many of Bannon's references, it appears that the mention of Dugin was more name-dropping than a statement based on any deep knowledge.

51. Cited in Suzanne Loftus, *Insecurity and the Rise of Nationalism in Putin's Russia: Keeper of Traditional Values* (Cham, Switzerland: Palgrave Macmillan, 2018), 145.

52. "Treasury Announces New Designations of Ukrainian Separatists and Their Russian Supporters," US Department of the Treasury, Press Center, March 11, 2015, https://www.treasury.gov/press-center/press-releases/Pages/jl9993.aspx.

53. Gabrielle Tetrault-Farber, "Russian, European Far-Right Parties Converge in St. Petersburg," *Moscow Times,* March 22, 2015, https://www.themoscowtimes.com/2015/03/22/russian-european-far-right-parties-converge-in-st-petersburg-a45010. Some of the participants included such well-known figures as Udo Voight, Nick Griffith, and Roberto Fiore. Dugin was reported to have sent a letter of support to Greece's Nikos Michaloliakos.

54. Alexandr Dugin, "Maoism Is Too Modern for Me," Fourth Political Theory, March 2015, http://4pt.su/en/content/maoism-too-modern-me.

55. Mark Bassin, *The Gumilev Mystique* (Ithaca, NY: Cornell University Press, 2016), 220. Although the son of two of Russia's greatest poets and victims of Stalinism, Nikolai Gumilev and Anna Akhmatova, Gumilev become infamous for his rabid antisemitism, anti-liberalism, and Russian-centric Eurasianism, which caused his mother great distress.

56. "The Long Path: An Interview with Alexander Dugin," cited in Jafe Arnold, *Guénon in Russia: The Traditionalism of Alexander Dugin,* forthcoming in French in *Politica Hermetica* 34 (2021). Arnold's essay can be previewed at acadmia.edu: https://www.academia.edu/44845633/Gu%C3%A9non_in_Russia_The_Traditionalism_of_Alexander_Dugin. Charles Clover points out that Dugin devoted two books, published in 1990, to the works of Guénon and Evola. Clover, *Black Wind, White Snow: The Rise of Russia's New Nationalism* (New Haven, CT: Yale University Press, 2016), 173.

57. Alexander Dugin, "Interview with Alexander Dugin," Counter-Currents, July 27, 2012, https://www.counter-currents.com/2012/07/interview-with-alexander-dugin/.

58. Anton Shekhnovtsov and Andreas Umland, "Is Aleksandr Dugin a Traditionalist?," *Russian Review* 68, no. 4 (October 2009): 662–78, https://www.academia.edu/197910/Is_Aleksandr_Dugin_a_Traditionalist_Neo-Eurasianism_and_Perennial_Philosophy.

59. Laruelle, *Russian Eurasianism,* 135.

60. On Dugin's philo-Zionism, see Marlene Laruelle, "Aleksandr Dugin: A Russian Version of the European Radical Right?" (Occasional Paper No. 294, Kennan Institute, Woodrow Wilson International Center for Scholars, 2006), https://www.wilsoncenter.org/sites/default/files/media/documents/publication/OP294_aleksandr_drugin_laruelle_2006.pdf; Jean-Yves Camus, "A Long-Lasting Friendship," in Laruelle, *Eurasianism and the European Far Right*, 89.

61. Alexander Dugin, "Exoteric and Esoteric Judaism: Isaac Luria and Sabbatai Zevi in Russian Orthodoxy," Kheper, accessed October 23, 2018, https://web.archive.org/web/20140814071318/http:/www.kheper.net:80/topics/Kabbalah/Exoteric_vs_Mystical.html.

62. Boaz Huss, "Prof. Dugin on 'Exoteric' vs. 'Mystical' Judaism," Kheper, accessed October 23, 2018, https://web.archive.org/web/20150102152938/http:/www.kheper.net/topics/Kabbalah/Exoteric_vs_Mystical-BHH.html.

63. Vladim Rossman, *Russian Intellectual Antisemitism in the Post-Communist Era* (Lincoln: University of Nebraska Press, 2002), 54–57.

64. Aleksandr Dugin, *Konspirologia (nauka o zagovorakh, sekretnykh obshchestvakh i tainoi voine)*, cited and translated in Viktor Shnirelman, "Building a Bridge between Eschatology and Conspiracy," in *The Handbook of Conspiracy Theories and Contemporary Religion*, ed. Asbjørn Dyrendal, David G. Robertson, and Egil Asprem (Leiden: Brill, 2018), 452.

65. Christian Picciolini, *Meeting the Challenge of White Nationalist Terrorism at Home and Abroad*, Free Radicals Project, September 18, 2019, https://homeland.house.gov/imo/media/doc/Picciolini%20-%20Testimony%20REVISED.pdf.

66. Casey Michel, "Why Is This Pizzagate Truther Meeting with a Russian Neo-fascist?," ThinkProgress, June 10, 2018, https://archive.thinkprogress.org/why-is-this-pizzagate-truther-meeting-with-a-russian-neo-fascist-b84eb73aa549/.

67. Horowitz, "Steve Bannon Cited Italian Thinker."

68. Jane Coaston, "Audio Tape Reveals Richard Spencer Is, as Everyone Knew, a Racist," Vox, November 4, 2019, https://www.vox.com/identities/2019/11/4/20947833/richard-spencer-white-nationalism-audio-milo-alt-right.

69. Brett Barrouquere, "Days after Guilty Plea, Matthew Heimbach Re-emerges in New Alliance with National Socialist Movement," Southern Poverty Law Center, September 24, 2018, https://www.splcenter.org/hatewatch/2018/09/24/days-after-guilty-plea-matthew-heimbach-re-emerges-new-alliance-national-socialist-movement.

70. Robert King, "Indiana White Nationalist Called 'the Next David Duke' Isn't Stopping with Charlottesville," *IndyStar*, August 27, 2017, https://www.indystar.com/story/news/2017/08/27/indiana-white-nationalist-called-the-next-david-duke-isnt-stopping-charlottesville/573817001/.

71. Clement Pulaski's critique of Heimbach's talk from an extreme right-wing perspective, "Contra Heimbach: Long Live America!" (True Sons of Abraham, December 23, 2014) is no longer available online; however, a critical view of Pulaski's critique by Russell James, a self-described "Calvinist who believes in ethnic nationalism and monarchy," can be found at http://praxis-mag.blogspot.com/2015/08/hail-to-king.html.

72. For a redacted copy of the state's filing, see County of Orange, State of Indiana v. Matthew W. Heimbach, 59D01-1803-F6-000300 (Orange Superior Ct., 2018), https://www.splcenter.org/sites/default/files/59d01-1803-f6-000300_redacted.pdf.

73. Barrouquere, "Days after Guilty Plea."

74. Kenneth P. Vogel, Jonathan Martin, and Jeremy W. Peters, "Led by the Mercers, Bannon's Allies Abandon Him," *New York Times*, January 4, 2018, https://www.nytimes.com/2018/01/04/us/politics/bannon-mercer-trump.html.

75. Matthew Karnitschnig, "Steve Bannon Populist Roadshow Hits Europe," Politico, March 6, 2018, https://www.politico.eu/article/steve-bannon-populism-donald-trump-i-still

-love-the-guy/; Maïa de La Baume and Silvia Sciorilli Borrelli, "Welcome to Europe's 'Club' for Populists," Politico, October 2, 2018, https://www.politico.eu/article/euroskeptics-steven-bannon-mischael-modrikamenwelcome-to-europes-first-populist-club/.

76. Haley Ott, "Steve Bannon Backs 'Gladiator School' to Bolster Europe's Right Wing," CBS News, March 3, 2019, https://www.cbsnews.com/news/steve-bannon-trisulti-italy-benjamin-harnwell-school-bolster-europe-right-wing/.

77. On Bannon's public embrace of Roy Moore, the failed and disgraced Republican senatorial candidate in Alabama, and his other US political setbacks, see Tom McCarthy, "Steve Bannon's Year: Ex-Strategist Clings to Controversy after White House Firing," *Guardian*, September 5, 2018, https://www.theguardian.com/us-news/2018/sep/05/steve-bannon-fired-one-year-later. For the problems with Bannon's European efforts, see Daniel DePetris, "How Steve Bannon Tried—and Failed—to Crack Europe," *Spectator*, March 6, 2019, https://spectator.us/steve-bannon-failed-crack-europe/; Maïa de La Baume and Silvia Sciorilli Borrelli, "Steve Bannon's Stuttering European Adventure," Politico, March 5, 2019, https://www.politico.eu/article/steve-bannon-european-parliament-the-movement-stuttering-european-adventure/.

78. Roger Griffin, *Modernism and Fascism: The Sense of a Beginning under Mussolini and Hitler* (Basingstoke: Palgrave Macmillan, 2007), 181.

MARK WEITZMAN is Director of Government Affairs for the Simon Wiesenthal Center, Chief Representative of the Center to the United Nations in New York, and member of the US delegation to the International Holocaust Remembrance Authority (IHRA). He spearheaded the IHRA's adoption of the working definition of Antisemitism. He is a participant in the program on Religion and Foreign Policy of the Council on Foreign Relations, served as a member of the advisory panel of Experts on Freedom of Religion or Belief of the Organization for Security and Co-operation in Europe (OSCE), and is Vice President of the Association of Holocaust Organizations. Mr. Weitzman is currently coediting the *Routledge History of Antisemitism*, scheduled for publication in 2021. He was a winner of the 2007 National Jewish Book Award for best anthology for *Antisemitism, the Generic Hatred: Essays in Memory of Simon Wiesenthal*, which he coedited. Other publications include *Jews and Judaism in the Political Theology of Radical Catholic Traditionalists* (2015) and *Dismantling the Big Lie: The Protocols of the Elders of Zion* (authored with Steven L. Jacobs), the first full refutation of the infamous *Protocols* (2003).

5

Antisemitism on the Left
The Case of Jewish Voice for Peace

Miriam F. Elman

AFTER OPERATING IN RELATIVE OBSCURITY FOR OVER TWO decades, the California-based organization Jewish Voice for Peace (JVP) has today become one of the most active agents in the United States normalizing a virulent form of anti-Israel discourse and activism. According to the Anti-Defamation League (ADL), JVP is a radical fringe group within American Jewry, but it is also now among the top US-based anti-Israel organizations.[1] Through its national campaigns, media engagement, and other forms of activism, JVP has become a major source of anti-Israel programming on university and college campuses, in progressive mainline churches, and in municipal and city-level politics. In these arenas, JVP activists routinely cast Zionism as a racist ideology and Israel as a fundamentally tyrannical and illegitimate state. Furthermore, Israel's supporters are depicted as intolerant bigots, even malevolent for failing to support the boycott, divestment, and sanctions (BDS) movement arrayed against the Jewish state.

Appropriating the language of human rights and social justice, JVP presents itself as committed to advancing these goals through nonviolent means. But the reality is that JVP often glorifies terrorists and partners with extremist individuals and groups who demonize and delegitimize Israel, while propagating negative stereotypes of Jews. Its increasingly radical rhetoric and activism have opened up a dangerous space for antisemitism among progressives. There is now an astonishing amount of evidence to suggest that JVP is not just another progressive Jewish activist organization but is in fact a radical and reactionary movement that directly puts Jews at risk.[2]

This chapter considers JVP's rhetoric and activism as an example of antisemitism on the left. It focuses on the sources of JVP's appeal in left-wing circles in the United States and highlights how the group has taken an even more radical turn in recent years. While JVP has long advanced an antisemitic form of anti-Zionism, the organization now not only provides cover and legitimacy "as Jews" for antisemitic coalition partners; it has also begun to actively traffic in classical antisemitic tropes and canards. JVP's activism is also becoming more aggressive toward American Zionists and mainstream national Jewish organizations, with far-reaching negative implications for a resurgent antisemitism on the left in the United States.[3] The chapter's concluding section considers several possible strategies for combating this new form of intolerance on the left and JVP's brand of antisemitic anti-Israelism.

Anti-Zionism and Antisemitism in Jewish Voice for Peace's Rhetoric

JVP views itself as the "Jewish wing" of the Palestinian solidarity movement. The ADL has long designated JVP to be the "largest and most influential" Jewish anti-Zionist group in the US and lists it among the top ten organizations "fixated with delegitimizing Israel."[4] JVP's influence is negligible among America's Jews, but anti-Zionists have long gravitated to the organization because it serves the useful purpose of deflecting accusations of anti-Jewish bias and hostility inherent to the BDS movement. Dexter Van Zile, the Christian media analyst for the Committee for Accuracy in Middle East Reporting in America (CAMERA), rightly notes that "anti-Zionists will invoke their alliance with Jewish Voice for Peace and say in effect, 'We're not antisemites! Heaven forbid! Some of our best friends are Jews! And guess what? They agree with *us*!'"[5]

It is important to note that JVP's rhetoric moves well beyond legitimate criticism of Israeli policies. In fact, the organization routinely engages in antisemitic forms of anti-Israel expression.[6] Taken as a whole, via its online materials and publications, social media feeds, and public speaking, JVP maintains that Zionism has no place in America's liberal antiracist movement because it is a "white supremacist" ideology that uses the history of Jewish persecution to justify contemporary injustices and state violence. As former JVP deputy director Cecilie Surasky writes, "It is important that we situate what is happening in Israel and Palestine today, and the work we must do in the US for justice, as part of a lengthy historical cascade of impacts rooted in European colonialism, white racism, US Empire, anti-Muslim and anti-Jewish oppression, corporate greed, and so on . . . what is absolutely clear is that Early Zionist leaders were simultaneously both the victims of, and willing agents of white supremacists' colonialism. . . . Virtually every colonized or oppressed group internalizes the eyes, in some way, of their oppressors."[7]

JVP's former executive director Rebecca Vilkomerson has argued that liberals who go "out into the streets" to oppose white supremacy in the United States should consistently apply their political principles to Israel: "It's high time to get out into the streets with us to oppose similar policies in Israel."[8] Similarly, JVP's media manager, Naomi Dann, has argued that white supremacist Richard Spencer "might be right about Israel" when he drew spurious comparisons between Zionism and his desire for a white ethno-state. Dann's remarks underscore JVP's view of Zionism as a form of white supremacy, reflecting the group's ignorance of the role that antisemitism plays in white supremacist ideology and the ways in which Jews are in fact its primary victims.[9]

In JVP's perspective, Zionism itself is something uniquely detestable. It is not a liberation movement for a persecuted people but a manifestation of everything the left must abhor: imperialism, racism, colonialism, and apartheid. Furthermore, JVP presents Zionism as a morally indefensible project sustained by well-connected, politically powerful, and wealthy Jews. Ironically, these antisemitic tropes, common in left-wing antisemitism, are presented as antiracist and as evidence of JVP's devotion to social justice.[10]

Andrew Mark Bennett, a lawyer and doctoral fellow at the Freie Universität Berlin, correctly notes that while anti-Israel activism makes up the lion's share of JVP messaging, its underlying worldview is even more problematic.[11] JVP's rhetoric is "obsessed with Jewish wrongdoing." It identifies Jews with state power and accuses them of working against progressive social justice movements. JVP activists thus position themselves as the "good Jews" of the left—admitted and championed in progressive circles as the Jews who oppose other Jews.[12]

In staking out this position, JVP's leaders and activists repeatedly insist that anti-Zionism is not antisemitism. Furthermore, they situate themselves as victims of baseless charges of antisemitism, seeing themselves and their pro-BDS allies as "accused and targeted more than the growing far-right" in order to silence criticism of Israel and "suppress the conversation about Palestinian rights."[13] JVP's latest book, *On Antisemitism*, fails to include authors who have actual expertise in the study of anti-Jewish prejudice; instead, the book aims to give voice to those who "are marginalized" by allegedly false allegations of bias in "mainstream discussions of anti-Semitism"—such as activist Linda Sarsour and BDS spokesperson Omar Barghouti.[14] Rather than attempting to understand contemporary antisemitism, the volume's contributors are concerned with the "fraudulent use" of anti-Jewish hostility to shut down pro-Palestinian voices. Yet, as reviewer Alvin Rosenfeld rightly points out, nowhere in the book do any of the authors provide evidence of this censorship or repression of substantive discussion of Israel.[15] In fact, the exact opposite is true—in many cases, those who attempt to challenge the received wisdom regarding Zionism's wickedness and Israel's malevolence are deplatformed, silenced, and smeared.[16]

JVP's understanding of antisemitism amounts to justifying it whenever it is connected to Israel. Emily Shire notes that "according to the logic of JVP, Jews must denounce openly their support for Jewish sovereignty if they are to be welcomed [in progressive circles]. If they don't disavow their Zionism, then it's perfectly okay to slander, attack and exclude them without such behavior having the taint of anti-Semitism."[17]

In sum, JVP is a key player in the anti-Israeli movement because it serves to discredit Jewish concerns about antisemitism, casting them instead as a deceitful conspiracy to censor legitimate discourse and debate. According to JVP, it is not merely that Jews are mistaken when they raise the issue of antisemitism on the left or that they are oversensitive—they are actually lying.[18]

Jewish Voice for Peace's Activism and Key Campaigns

JVP presents itself as committed to social justice, civil liberties, and human rights and to advancing these causes through nonviolent methods. But the reality is that, both on and off campus, JVP frequently platforms terrorists and advances the work of organizational allies with ties to violent extremism. JVP's decision to stand in solidarity with convicted Popular Front for the Liberation of Palestine (PFLP) supermarket bomber Rasmea Odeh received national and international media coverage.[19] Less well known is JVP's ongoing promotion of the group Defense for Children International-Palestine, which has documented links to the PFLP.[20] JVP is also one of the lead sponsors of the US Academic and Cultural Boycott of Israel's campaign to boycott study-abroad programs in Israel. Among the other cosponsors of the campaign is Samidoun, a group that also has ties to terror organizations.[21]

JVP activists are a visible presence in many campus anti-Israel BDS campaigns, at mainline Protestant church general assemblies and conventions where anti-Israel resolutions are in play, and in progressive activist circles where Jews who connect and identify with Israel are ostracized and even bullied, harassed, and defamed. In these forums, they deflect allegations of antisemitism, as noted earlier, by standing up "as Jews" in support of their allies.[22]

For example, several years ago, JVP's Chicago chapter rushed in to excuse the bigotry of the city's Dyke March activists who forced a group of queer Jewish women out of its parade because they were carrying rainbow pride flags adorned with the Jewish Star of David.[23] JVP also took the side of a Black Lives Matter group in St. Louis that slandered a highly regarded progressive rabbi there because she had visited Israel on a tour sponsored by the American Israel Public Affairs Committee (AIPAC).[24] On campuses, JVP students defended Oberlin College professor Joy Karega after her virulently antisemitic social media posts were exposed. JVP's Advisory Academic Council also urged followers to reject "false accusations" of antisemitism directed toward Rutgers University professor Jasbir Puar, who has peddled modern-day blood libels.[25]

JVP has promoted the BDS agenda in America's progressive Protestant churches for over a decade.[26] For example, its activism at the general assemblies and synods of the Presbyterian Church (USA) and at the United Church of Christ (UCC) has demonstrated the "outsize role" that JVP plays in these forums as staffers make themselves available to delegates at general assemblies and synods.[27]

At the UCC conference in 2015, Reverend Mitri Raheb, a Christian Palestinian and pastor of the Evangelical Lutheran Church in Jordan and the Holy Land, sanitized his keynote speech by acknowledging JVP. In his keynote address, Raheb received a standing ovation for attacking the legitimacy of the Jewish people, denying Jews' biblical history, erasing the Jewish roots of Christianity, and portraying modern-day Israel as the source of all Palestinian suffering. He also referenced the thoroughly debunked racist claim that modern-day Jews are descended not from the ancient Hebrews of the Middle East but from the eastern European Khazar tribe.[28] Plenary speakers continually referenced JVP support for the resolutions. One even said that the General Synod should pass the divestment resolution "in order to stand with Jewish Voice for Peace."[29] Reverend Graylan S. Hagler, senior minister of the Plymouth Congregational UCC of Washington, DC, who has in the past opened his pulpit to the notorious antisemite Gilad Atzmon, noted with satisfaction how "instrumental" JVP was for the plenary vote.[30]

JVP has become an important ally in US church anti-Israel activity precisely because it is one of the few Jewish lobbies that anti-Israel Christian activists will embrace. Over the past decade, JVP has established a strong alliance with Sabeel/Friends of Sabeel North America (FOSNA), with which it has cosponsored over two dozen events. JVP's Rabbinical Council issued a statement of support for Sabeel/FOSNA, a notoriously anti-Israel self-identified Christian group, that declared, "As rabbis and people of faith, we stand in solidarity with the work of FOSNA." JVP and Sabeel/FOSNA also cosponsored the National Rasmea Defense Committee, which lobbied the US government to discontinue its proceedings against Rasmea Odeh.[31]

Leaders in JVP are also top FOSNA activists. David Glick, a prominent JVP member, is also a member of the NorCal Friends of Sabeel chapter and has written for Sabeel publications. For the spring 2012 edition of Sabeel's quarterly publication, *Cornerstone*, Glick authored a poem titled "Hear O Israel" that claims Israel is inherently racist and compares Israeli policies to those of Nazi Germany. The Ithaca-based anti-Israel activist Ariel Gold was also a leader in JVP and a professional organizer for FOSNA for some years before moving on to CODEPINK. She also was a key activist for the NY Committee for Justice in Palestine, which once posted on its website a grotesque photoshopped image of Jewish concentration camp victims holding signs to "Free Gaza."[32] Several years ago, JVP's Shelley Cohen Fudge spoke at the Sixth Presbyterian Church in Washington, DC, for a spring program hosted by Sabeel/FOSNA's DC Metro affiliate. There, according to journalist Shiri Moshe, Fudge sat on a panel where one speaker after another depicted Jews as "genocidal racists, foreigners, and oppressors who are engaged in a colonialist project and control the American government."[33] According to Moshe, JVP's representative made no objections to these attacks.

JVP activists operate in multiple arenas to exploit Jewish culture, traditions, celebrations, and life-cycle events. In doing this, JVP claims that its anti-Israel positions are not merely consistent with Jewish values but actually based on them. Toward this end, JVP usurps Jewish religious holidays by incorporating anti-Israel themes into them. For example, JVP's High Holiday resources replace the primary themes of the Days of Awe—God's sovereignty and mercy and the longing for the day when his mastery will be acknowledged by all human beings—with a narrative that both denigrates the centrality of Zion to Judaism and subverts one of the key themes of the High Holidays: God's plan for the Jewish people's freedom, nationhood, and acceptance of the Torah in the land of Israel.[34]

JVP's materials for Rosh Hashanah and Yom Kippur attack the very core of the Jewish High Holidays and the basic concepts of Judaism. In 2016, JVP released a fourteen-page guidebook to be used at the holiday dinner that ushers in the Jewish New Year. Users are encouraged to fight for Palestinian liberation via the BDS strategy, also presented as consistent with Jewish values. In various holiday blessings and traditions, participants are repeatedly reminded of the many alleged crimes that Israel perpetrates against the defenseless Palestinians and are invited to celebrate BDS victories.[35]

The "table blessing ritual" also reinforces the anti-Israel message in the recent manifesto of the Black Lives Matter (BLM) movement, which it also aims to connect to Jewish values. Users of the guide are supposed to view Israel as complicit in America's racial tensions and the policing problems in its inner cities. A "special reading for 2016" links "Ferguson to Palestine" in an intersecting system of oppression. One passage notes the "ever-increasing profits" of arms manufacturers, which "display their products on the streets in Black neighborhoods and the skies above Gaza." Another passage conjoins the "sounds of the shofar [ram's horn]" to the "BLM cry: I Can't Breathe."[36] Thus, the guide seeks to legitimize JVP's position as a central ally of the anti-Israel activists who infiltrate the BLM movement—such as the Dream Defenders.[37]

JVP's identity theft of Jewish heritage has been particularly visible during Passover, when its annually released Haggadah promotes BDS and it stages "liberation seders," appropriating the holiday's rituals and texts for an anti-Israel narrative.[38] JVP's Haggadah twists the Jewish text used during the Passover seder—for example, by dedicating the third cup of wine to the BDS movement and featuring a section on the "Ten Plagues of the Israeli Occupation" (including the "plague" of the "denial of the right of return").

JVP has also usurped Chanukah for anti-Israel messaging. In 2017, it organized "actions" in twenty-five cities across the country to coincide with the holiday.[39] The community events mainly involved people coming together in outdoor vigils to protest Islamophobia and racism and were highly politicized anti-Trump rallies. Many participants spoke of the vigils sending a "message of togetherness" and unity in the wake of the presidential election. That is not surprising given how JVP rolled out this Chanukah campaign, specifically conveying a sense of urgency to "Shine a Light" on President-elect Trump and the "Netanyahu-Trump alliance" forged after the elections.

Based on the many images of these "Chanukah actions" shared online, in media reports, and in several videos, there appeared to be very little actual telling of the holiday story going on at them. Participants waxed eloquent for a "return of the light" in American politics and society but failed to impart that the Festival of Lights is about the Jewish people vanquishing their enemies, emerging victorious as a people, and regaining control of their faith, land, and holy temple. There was no effort to sing any traditional songs. When blessings on the candles were included, they were doctored to reflect various social justice issues. Basically, the underlying message at these JVP Chanukah vigils was that, according to Jewish values themselves, to be an antiracist progressive you must treat Israel as a malevolent oppressor and see its policies as driven by false accusations of Muslim and Arab threats. That these threats may in fact be very real, or that the policies may not be "repressive" but necessary counterterror measures, were dismissed out of hand.[40]

Over the centuries, traditional antisemites sought to convert Jews. By contrast, JVP seeks to convert Judaism to a religion of anti-Israelism. As Joshua Muravchik recently noted, "[Its] lingo suggests that JVP's interpretation of Jewish tradition is elastic, if not idiosyncratic. Apart from commemorating the escape from bondage in Egypt, Judaism's focus is on self-demand and self-discipline (10 commandments, 613 mitzvot), not self-liberation. The roots of JVP's thought on 'liberation' can be traced more readily to Marxism and 1960s New Leftism than to Judaism. . . . JVP constantly invokes Jewish words and symbols, while freighting these with contemporary political import."[41]

JVP's Campaign Targeting Birthright

In addition to the activism noted above, JVP fields multiyear national campaigns. One of its recent initiatives takes aim at Taglit-Birthright Israel, by far the most successful and largest Jewish educational endeavor in the world, which since 1999 has sponsored free ten-day trips to Israel for young diaspora Jews (ages eighteen to twenty-six) aimed at strengthening their Jewish identity and connection to Israel, its people, and the Jewish heritage. Political viewpoints are not reviewed for eligibility purposes, and Jews from all recognized denominations are welcome. In nearly twenty years, it has brought over six hundred thousand Jewish young adults to Israel, from sixty-seven countries (including fifty US states) and from nearly one thousand colleges. While they have been in Israel, some eighty thousand Israeli peers have connected with them during the visits.

Birthright is funded through a public-private partnership between the Israeli government, Jewish Federations of North America, and American donors. Original funders included Michael Steinhardt and Charles Bronfman; in recent years, Sheldon Adelson—the casino billionaire, GOP megadonor, and PM Benjamin Netanyahu supporter—has become its largest benefactor. To hear JVP tell it, young people who go on Birthright come out of it with the "politics of Adelson." But scholarly studies disprove this.[42] Research conducted by the Cohen Center for Modern Jewish Studies at Brandeis University shows that Birthright does positively alter the future trajectory that participants have with regard to engagement in Jewish life and their connection to Israel, and their support for Israel rises across the board. But Birthright participants do not come away with right-wing political viewpoints about the Israeli-Palestinian conflict. For example, the trips have no effect on participant attitudes regarding West Bank settlement—participants are no more likely to oppose dismantling settlements than are applicants to the program who ultimately did not participate. Birthright, for its part, views itself as an apolitical Zionist program that is on neither the right nor the left and that aims merely to foster homeland attachment without promoting any narrowly construed political narrative.

In its new "Return the Birthright" national campaign, JVP proudly states that "Israel is not our birthright" and calls on young Jews to reject the "tempting offer" to participate in the "racist Birthright tour of Israel." According to Ben Lorber, JVP's campus coordinator, the new campaign grew out of several anti-Birthright initiatives on individual campuses that "inspired" JVP's leadership to take the initiative to "campuses across the country."[43] Separate pages on its website invite people to hold workshops and teach-ins challenging Birthright on campuses and offer "templates and resources." JVP has also produced a list of dozens of "alternative tours" to Israel and the West Bank. They include outfits with innocuous-sounding names, such as the International Solidarity Movement and Green Olive Tours, but that deliver anti-Israel propaganda while encouraging tourists to clash with Israel's police and security forces at checkpoints and at Palestinian protests.

In this campaign, JVP and its allies, such as the left-wing group IfNotNow, aim to stop American Jewish students from participating in a rewarding educational opportunity that enables them to engage with students and their peers overseas. But in trying to undermine this program, they are not merely opposing certain policies that they may legitimately disagree with—they are opposing the very idea of young American Jews developing an attachment to the Jewish people, Jewish history, and Jewish rights. That is, they are standing against the promotion of Jewish identity—a clear expression of antisemitism.[44]

JVP's Deadly Exchange Campaign

In the summer of 2017, JVP rolled out a new "Deadly Exchange" campaign alleging that five of the leading organizations of American Jewish life—the ADL, the AIPAC, the Jewish Institute for National Security Affairs (JINSA), the American Jewish Committee (AJC), and Taglit Birthright Israel—were deliberately conspiring to harm innocent Americans by helping organize and fund training programs for US law enforcement officials in Israel.

According to JVP, these trainings are "deadly exchanges" where American and Israeli security officials and experts "trade tips" and share "worst practices" that "promote and extend discriminatory and repressive policing that already exist in both countries," including fatal police shootings of African Americans and the "extrajudicial killings" of Palestinians in the West Bank.[45] Initially, the campaign focused primarily on blaming Israel and its alleged mistreatment of Palestinians for the oppression of American minorities. The campaign highlighted the "Ferguson to Palestine" meme, positing a fictitious "intersectional equivalence" between the situation facing the Palestinians and the problems of policing in America's inner cities.[46] For years, anti-Israel activists have been blaming Israel for US police shootings. But the notion that Israeli counterterror trainings are responsible for a complex and multifaceted phenomenon like militarized policing in the US is an absurd accusation for which there is not a shred of evidence.[47]

Deadly Exchange conceives of Israel as a malevolent part of a wider Jewish conspiracy. The Jewish state thus serves the role that the Jews historically have served in international conspiracy theories.[48] JVP's more recent campaign materials double down on this foundational antisemitic trope by alleging that mainstay organizations of American Jewry are coconspirators in this nefarious mission to oppress their fellow citizens, including people of color and immigrant groups. Deadly Exchange essentially defames American Jewish organizations as a "hidden and moneyed force" behind the degradation of societies and the manipulation of governments—a claim right out of the infamous antisemitic forgery, *The Protocols of the Elders of Zion*.[49]

JVP is thus now at the forefront of an effort to stoke racial tension and hatred of Jews by portraying Israel and its American supporters as oppressors (and even murderers) of minorities.[50] It is important to realize that JVP is consequently no longer merely condoning or excusing anti-Jewish hatred but is in fact now producing and disseminating it. As one astute observer of the campaign recently put it, JVP has now itself become "nothing other than an antisemitic organization."[51]

Since its launch several years ago, the Deadly Exchange campaign has been widely condemned. The ADL released a blistering statement charging JVP with "taking increasingly radical positions and . . . questionable tactics in pursuit of its mission to diminish support for Israel."[52] The criticism has come from the Jewish left too, by some who are often otherwise sympathetic to JVP and even to BDS. For example, Rabbi Jill Jacobs slammed the campaign for veering uncomfortably close to antisemitism.[53] Commenting in *Haaretz*, another prominent left-leaning Canadian scholar also condemned JVP for its unsubstantiated insinuation of a Jewish cabal out to harm America's minority communities: "Saying that Jewish groups are the primary drivers of US aid to Israel and for the scourge of institutionalized racism in America makes me queasy in that the causal logic is so deeply implied but so empirically thin as to imply a secret conspiracy."[54] JVP promised to take this "critical feedback" into account but in fact has failed to do so.[55] In reaction to the ADL statement, JVP took pride in its campaign having hit a nerve and questioned the civil rights organization's liberal credentials. It then opened an online petition that calls on the ADL to end its funding of the US-Israel training programs.[56]

JVP's Deadly Exchange campaign has continued to resonate in far-left progressive circles. In 2019, Tamika Mallory, one of the co-organizers of the Women's March and a defender of the notorious antisemite Louis Farrakhan, specifically referred to the campaign's central claims in castigating Starbucks for hiring the ADL to conduct antibias training for its employees, claiming that the "ADL is CONSTANTLY attacking black and brown people."[57] By the end of 2018, JVP could proudly proclaim its campaign's first successes, as several local government entities—Durham, North Carolina; Northampton, Massachusetts; and the Vermont state police—announced their disengagement from US-Israel police exchange programs.[58] In spring 2019, the campaign also started to make its way onto university and college campuses.[59]

Case Study: Jewish Voice for Peace's Collaboration with Conspiracist Alison Weir

JVP's relationship with the notorious antisemitic conspiracist Alison Weir offers a useful lens into the group's ideology and the way in which it is today mainstreaming anti-Jewish hatred on the left. This section recounts the internal fault lines that emerged within JVP when the organization attempted to sever its ties with Weir in 2015.[60]

On November 22, 2015, Al-Awda—the Palestine Right to Return Coalition—announced on its social media feeds that it was cohosting the notorious antisemitic conspiracy theorist Weir at an event in Cleveland, in partnership with JVP. It is not surprising that Al-Awda would take the lead in promoting Weir and her group, If Americans Knew (IAK), as the two organizations are basically cut from the same cloth. According to the ADL, Al-Awda is an anti-Israel campaigner that views Zionism as "inherently racist" and is unwilling to accept Israel's right to exist. Meanwhile, Weir's criticism of Israel and Zionism over the last fifteen years so consistently "crosses the line into distortions customarily found in the literature of anti-Semites" that the ADL has issued a ten-page report on her work. The highlights include a nasty habit of modernizing anti-Jewish blood libels and characterizing Jews as conspiratorial groups of people who control America and the world.

The fact that JVP's Cleveland chapter cohosted Weir tells us a lot about JVP. First, it is an example of JVP's primary function noted above, which is to provide cover "as Jews" for antisemitic allies and partners. JVP has catapulted its way into a leading role in the US anti-Israel movement precisely because it serves this very useful role as the "Jewish sword and shield" of BDS, using its position as Jews to help safeguard its partners from allegations of antisemitism and providing it with a veneer of legitimacy.[61] Second, it highlights the nature of JVP as a grassroots movement in which the activism of local chapters and key activists at the local level matter as much—and often even more—than the work of its executive director and others in leadership positions.

Indeed, that the Cleveland JVP chapter sponsored Weir along with Al-Awda is telling because only a few months before, JVP's then executive director, Rebecca Vilkomerson, had decided to no longer work with her. JVP officially disassociated itself from Weir in a May 2015 letter, which subsequently went viral, and in a widely publicized June statement.[62] The letter sheds considerable light on JVP's understanding of antisemitism because, in rebuffing Weir, JVP avoided speaking out against its ex-ally's Jew-hating rhetoric even as it sought to distance JVP from her. Thus, the decision to cut ties can plausibly be interpreted to have been solely a strategic move—a marketing ploy to protect JVP's brand. JVP appears to have been less interested in condemning Weir's antisemitism than in protecting JVP's image as a champion of progressive causes and as an organization committed to "love, justice, and equality for all people." It is reasonable to draw this conclusion since nowhere in JVP's initial letter or in its subsequent released statement is Weir herself identified as antisemitic.

JVP's beef with Weir can be read as solely associational—namely, that Weir spends too much time giving interviews to neo-Nazis and white supremacists. Basically, from JVP's perspective, it was acceptable for Weir to demonize Israel, even by resorting to antisemitic tropes and canards. But since she is not also willing to despise America's "racist and white supremacist" power structures, Weir had likely become a liability and bad for business. That is, for JVP, the main problem with Weir seems to be that she is not willing to play ball and lump the United States into the same "fundamental political frame" as Israel—one in which both countries are seen as dominated by structures of white privilege and white settler colonialism. Like the BDS movement as a whole, JVP is all about othering and isolating Jews as white, privileged, and unworthy of the kind of restorative justice that a persecuted minority deserves—a worldview that perfectly accounts for the nature of the group's renunciation of Weir.

Despite JVP's national leadership cutting ties with Weir, however, JVP activists at the local level refused to support Vilkomerson's move, soon launching a campaign on Weir's behalf. An open letter was posted for signature.[63] It admonished JVP's Vilkomerson for her "recent unfounded attacks on one of the top organizations" working in the "struggle for justice for Palestinians" and its "dedicated leader, Alison Weir." Among the initial signatories was JVP activist Hedy Epstein, an elderly Holocaust survivor, founder of JVP's St. Louis branch, and a member of the Free Gaza movement, a radical group that has over the years organized flotillas to directly challenge Israel's siege by initiating confrontations with its navy.[64] In August 2014, she was arrested in downtown St. Louis during the unrest after Michael Brown's death, giving an interview about it to DemocracyNow! in which she compared the situation on "the streets of Ferguson, Missouri," to the "Israeli assault on Gaza." The remainder of the original signatories to the open letter were vehemently anti-Israel campaigners who have also consistently attacked Jews and Judaism. The pile-on no doubt blindsided JVP's steering committee and board, who probably did not see it coming. There is nothing to suggest that JVP's national leadership anticipated the fast and furious backlash or expected so many of JVP's rank and file to rally around Weir.

But the fact that JVP's non-Jewish allies would turn on it with a vengeance was in fact entirely predictable. It highlights the fundamentally untenable position that JVP finds itself in whenever it disagrees with its non-Jewish ideological cohorts. JVP as a self-declared "Jewish" group is generally accepted by its non-Jewish allies, but only as far as it remains in agreement with them and no further. JVP is trotted out as being the rare Jews you can trust; indeed, their status as Jews-who-criticize-other-Jews gives them enhanced credibility. As David Schraub noted in a thoughtful blog post on this incident, "Superstanding is a fickle thing—it lasts only as long as the critic remains critical. Superstanding . . . does not come with any general grant of authority or deference. It is unsurprising that once the JVP tried to draw upon the 'credibility' they earned as ideological fellow-travelers to take a position not favored by their non-Jewish allies, they'd find that the well of goodwill suddenly went dry."[65] This example of the mutiny in the ranks of JVP tells us that for many JVP activists, stamping out antisemitism matters less than "galvanizing our collective political power" and protecting the "integrity" of the larger BDS movement. In the words of self-described non-Zionist Jew and member of JVP Susan Landau, "As activists, public shaming is a time honored and effective toolkit of choice employed against our external enemies: war criminals, racist cops, greedy corporate bosses, and other unsavory characters. What culture do we create when we use similar tactics on each other? Is there another way? . . . It doesn't bode well . . . when groups doing solidarity work can't get along." By my count, 126 JVP members affiliated with twenty-five local JVP chapters eventually signed on to the open letter in defense of Weir. Many of them self-identified as serving in leadership roles in their chapters, and more than a few noted that they had resigned their positions in protest "since the vilification of Alison Weir." In a two-hundred-plus-page report on American anti-Israel activist groups who have associated with anti-Jewish haters on- and offline, British-based researcher David Collier exposes how JVP activists are still cavorting with Weir and other notorious antisemites.[66]

Conclusion: Resisting Jewish Voice for Peace

Today's left antisemitism is often termed a "new" form of anti-Jewish animus, but it in fact has had a long pedigree. Its roots can be traced to Soviet anti-Western propaganda in the decades after World War II, which cast Israel as a reactionary state.[67] From this perspective, Israel is condemned as an outpost of the Western imperialist bloc. Kenneth Waltzer puts it well: "What the Jew was to racial anti-Semites historically, an ally of the devil, the Jewish state now becomes as a Western ally in the global Left power perspective. The Jews were once hated because they were thought of individually as alien and other; they are now hated for being linked with and supportive of a sovereign Jewish state."[68] Jewish Voice for Peace aids and abets this vilification of Israel and American Zionists. Specifically, it legitimizes and mainstreams opposition to Israel by providing it with a facade and veneer of Jewish legitimacy. In the past, JVP's main utility for the anti-Israel movement was to shield its non-Jewish allies and the global BDS movement as a whole from accusations of antisemitism. JVP still plays that role, but it's also important to understand that JVP is itself now trafficking in antisemitism.

Now that JVP has taken this radical turn, combating it will require a concerted effort to expose it and then peel it away from the left. It will be crucial to uncouple JVP from its intersectional allies by emphasizing that it does not in fact speak for people of color or other minorities and instead is cynically hijacking their causes for its virulent anti-Israel agenda. One example of such an effort occurred in 2019 in Georgia, where an organization representing the state's Native Americans released a statement condemning JVP's Deadly Exchange campaign.[69] A 2019 statement, "Sephardic and Mizrahi Communal Response to Jewish Voice for Peace," also offers a scathing critique—all the more impactful because it speaks for people of color. Spearheaded by Jews Indigenous to the Middle East and North Africa (JIMENA) and signed by dozens of organizations, the statement deeply undercuts JVP's narrative that it is an ally to marginalized minorities.[70]

In addressing JVP, voices that are critical of it need to be heard at both the national and local levels of organizational leadership, Jewish and otherwise, so that JVP will find it more difficult to present itself as a progressive organization committed to universal justice. Consider that the *New York Times* on December 7, 2017, depicted JVP as "a liberal group . . . critical of the right-wing Israeli government of Benjamin Netanyahu" and that on August 7, 2015, the *Boston Globe* described JVP as "an anti-discrimination group." JVP activists often allow these fabrications to stand, allowing the organization to be cast as merely critical of the Israeli government and its policies. By trying to pass as merely antioccupation, JVP activists have managed to muscle their way into Jewish leadership positions. There, they can maintain that they speak for the Jewish community. In Durham, North Carolina, several JVP activists held these kinds of Jewish community leadership positions.[71] When they advocated on behalf of JVP's antisemitic Deadly Exchange campaign, their words carried more weight than they ever should have. Moving forward, mainstream Jewish organizations—Hillel, the Jewish Federations of North America, and the Jewish Community Relations Council, for example—need to be unequivocal and consistent in explaining to the non-Jewish world that JVP's fringe and radical positions are not representative of the American Jewish community.

Notes

1. "Jewish Voice for Peace: Increasing Anti-Israel Radicalism," Anti-Defamation League, July 19, 2017, www.adl.org/blog/jewish-voice-for-peace-increasing-anti-israel-radicalism.

2. Yitzhak Santis, *"Driving a Wedge": JVP Strategy to Weaken U.S. Support for Israel by Dividing the Jewish Community*, NGO Monitor, July 8, 2013, https://www.ngo-monitor.org/data/images/File/NGO_Monitor_Report-JVP_DRIVING_A_WEDGE.pdf. See also Jonathan S. Tobin, "Call Out Jewish Voice for Peace for What They Are: Anti-Peace Extremists," *Haaretz*, September 6, 2017, https://www.haaretz.com/opinion/.premium-call-out-jewish-voice-for-peace-for-what-they-are-anti-peace-extremists-1.5448695; Hen Mazzig, "JVP's Summer of Discontent: It's Time for Rebecca Vilkomerson to Step Down," *Jerusalem Post*, October 31, 2017, https://www.jpost.com/Opinion/JVPs-summer-of-discontent-Its-time-for-Rebecca-Vilkomerson-to-step-down-510972; Jarrod Tanny, "Jewish Voice for Peace Is Spreading Hate on Campus. It's Time for Jewish Academics to Speak Up," *Tablet*, July 5, 2017, www.tabletmag.com/jewish-news-and-politics/239913/jewish-voice-for-peace-campus; John-Paul Pagano, "How Anti-Semitism's True Origin Makes It Invisible to the Left," *The Forward*, January 29, 2018, https://forward.com/opinion/393107/how-anti-semitisms-true-origin-makes-it-invisible-to-the-left/.

3. Andrew Bennett, "The Antisemitism of the So-Called Jewish Voice for Peace," Medium, June 29, 2017, https://medium.com/@acandidworld/the-antisemitism-of-the-so-called-jewish-voice-for-peace-12e42f595cbf.

4. "News: Ranking the Top 10 Anti-Israel Groups in 2013," Anti-Defamation League, October 21, 2013, https://www.adl.org/news/press-releases/news-ranking-the-top-10-anti-israel-groups-in-2013-adl.

5. Dexter Van Zile, "JVP an Accessory to the Spread of Antisemitism in the U.S.," *Times of Israel*, July 16, 2014, http://blogs.timesofisrael.com/jvp-an-accessory-to-the-spread-of-antisemitism-in-u-s/.

6. For discussions of antisemitic forms of anti-Zionism, see Shany Mor, "On Three Anti-Zionisms," in "Word Crimes: Reclaiming the Language of the Israeli-Palestinian Conflict," ed. Donna Robinson Divine, Miriam F. Elman, and Asaf Romirowsky, special issue, *Israel Studies* 24, no. 2 (Summer 2019): 206–16; Jamie Palmer, "The Left and the Israeli-Palestinian Conflict: The Path to Righteous Hatred," *Fathom*, Summer 2017, http://fathomjournal.org/the-left-and-the-israeli-palestinian-conflict-the-path-to-righteous-hatred-2/; Ruth R. Wisse, "The Functions of Anti-Semitism," *National Affairs*, Fall 2017, https://www.nationalaffairs.com/publications/detail/the-functions-of-anti-semitism.

7. Cecilie Surasky, "Settler Colonialism, White Supremacy, and the 'Special Relationship' Between the U.S. and Israel," Jewish Voice for Peace, March 10, 2015, https://jewishvoiceforpeace.org/settler-colonialism-white-supremacy-and-the-special-relationship-between-the-u-s-and-israel/.

8. Rebecca Vilkomerson, "Why Jews Shouldn't Be Scared of the Palestinian Right of Return," *Haaretz*, September 17, 2017, www.haaretz.com/opinion/.premium-why-jews-shouldn-t-be-scared-of-the-palestinian-right-of-return-1.5451361.

9. Andrew Bennett, "JVP's Anti-Semitic Obsession with Jewish Power," *The Forward*, January 9, 2018, https://forward.com/opinion/391783/jvps-anti-semitic-obsession-with-jewish-power/.

10. Joshua Muravchik, "Not So Jewish, Not for Peace," *Commentary*, March 2019, https://www.commentarymagazine.com/articles/not-so-jewish-not-for-peace/; Palmer, "Left and Israeli-Palestinian Conflict."

11. Bennett, "JVP's Anti-Semitic Obsession."

12. The far left's view of state power as inherently oppressive and corrupt provides insight into why Zionism and the Jewish state are treated as anathema. For an extended discussion, see Sharon Goldman, "Jews Must Not Embrace Powerlessness: The Danger of Intersectionality," *Commentary*, February 19, 2019, https://www.commentarymagazine.com/articles/jews-must-not-embrace-powerlessness/.

13. Rebecca Vilkomerson, "Antisemitism and Support for Israel Are Not Incompatible: We Must Confront Both," Truthout, April 13, 2017, https://truthout.org/articles/antisemitism-and-support-for-israel-are-not-incompatible-we-must-confront-both/.

14. Jewish Voice for Peace, *On Antisemitism: Solidarity and the Struggle for Justice* (Chicago: Haymarket Books, 2017).

15. Alvin H. Rosenfeld, "Book Review: On Antisemitism: Solidarity and the Struggle for Justice; Industry of Lies: Media, Academia, and the Israeli-Arab Conflict," *Antisemitism Studies* 3, no. 1 (Spring 2019): 133–34.

16. Jonathan S. Tobin, "Is There Room in the Academy for Honest Scholarship on Israel?," *Commentary*, May 17, 2019, www.jns.org/opinion/is-there-room-in-the-academy-for-honest-scholarship-on-israel/. Rosenfeld ("Book Review," 137–38) points to one essay in JVP's book that explicitly engages in conspiracy thinking about Jews. He correctly notes that it is more than simply offensive or lamentable to find tropes about Jewish power in a book called *On Antisemitism*: "It is outrageous, for it reproduces the very malady that such a book ostensibly sets out to clarify and combat."

17. Emily Shire, "The Absurdity of Linda Sarsour and JVP Discussing Anti-Semitism," *The Forward*, November 15, 2017, https://forward.com/opinion/387684/the-absurdity-of-linda-sarsour-and-jvp-discussing-anti-semitism/.

18. For a discussion of how the UK equivalent of JVP—Jewish Voice for Labour—plays the analogous role in Britain, see Stephen Daisley, "The British Labour Party's 'Kosher Stamp' for Anti-Semitism," *Tablet*, October 16, 2017, www.tabletmag.com/jewish-news-and-politics/247057/british-labour-corbyn-anti-semitism. For more on the leftist strategy of deflecting accusations of antisemitism as a "dirtier trick than antisemitism itself," see David Hirsh, "How Raising the Issue of Antisemitism Puts You Outside the Community of the Progressive: The Livingstone Formulation," in *From Antisemitism to Anti-Zionism: The Past and Present of a Lethal Ideology*, ed. Eunice G. Pollack (Boston: Academic Studies Press, 2017), 2–28.

19. Josefin Dolsten, "Jewish Voice for Peace to Host Convicted Terrorist at Confab," *Times of Israel*, March 22, 2017, https://www.timesofisrael.com/jewish-voice-for-peace-to-host-convicted-terrorist-at-confab/. See also William A. Jacobson, "Memorial Service Held for Victims of Rasmea Odeh, as Jewish Voice for Peace Celebrates Her," *Legal Insurrection*, April 2, 2017, https://legalinsurrection.com/2017/04/memorial-service-held-for-victims-of-rasmea-odeh-as-jewish-voice-for-peace-celebrates-her/.

20. NGO Monitor, *Defense for Children International-Palestine's Ties to the PFLP Terrorist Organization*, January 27, 2020, http://ngo-monitor.org/pdf/DCIP_0120.pdf.

21. Peter Hasson, "Inside the Ties between Anti-Israel BDS Groups and Palestinian Terror Orgs," Daily Caller, May 8, 2019, https://dailycaller.com/2019/05/08/anti-israel-bds

-palestinian-terrorist-pflp-hamas/. Reports released in 2014 by the ADL and in 2013 by NGO Monitor also document JVP's willingness to collaborate with extremists, including cosponsoring fundraisers with the International Solidarity Movement (ISM), an organization whose founders have endorsed violence as a form of Palestinian resistance and whose members have collaborated with Palestinian hard-line organizations.

22. Miriam Elman, "Jewish Voice for Peace—'Jew Washing' the Anti-Israel Movement," *Legal Insurrection*, July 12, 2015, https://legalinsurrection.com/2015/07/jewish-voice-for-peace-jew-washing-the-anti-israel-movement/. For a detailed analysis of "Jew-washing," see Andrew Pessin, "The Indelible Stain of Antisemitism: The Failed Practice of 'Jew-Washing,'" *Times of Israel*, June 24, 2017, https://blogs.timesofisrael.com/the-indelible-stain-of-antisemitism-the-failed-practice-of-jew-washing/.

23. Muravchik, "Not So Jewish"; William A. Jacobson, "Jewish Voice for Peace-Chicago Sides with 'Dyke March' Anti-Semites," *Legal Insurrection*, June 26, 2017, https://legalinsurrection.com/2017/06/jewish-voice-for-peace-chicago-sides-with-dyke-march-anti-semites/.

24. Miriam Elman, "Anti-Israel Activists Attack Progressive St. Louis Rabbi Who Supports #BlackLivesMatter," *Legal Insurrection*, December 8, 2015, https://legalinsurrection.com/2015/12/anti-israel-activists-attack-progressive-st-louis-rabbi-who-supports-blacklivesmatter/.

25. Cary Nelson, *Israel Denial: Anti-Zionism, Anti-Semitism, and the Faculty Campaign against the Jewish State* (Bloomington: Indiana University Press and the Academic Engagement Network, 2019); David Mikics, "Ivory Tower Bigots," *Tablet*, October 16, 2018, https://www.tabletmag.com/jewish-arts-and-culture/272512/ivory-tower-bigots; Petra Marquardt-Bigman, "Jewish Voice for Peace Defends Anti-Semitism," *Times of Israel*, March 16, 2016, http://blogs.timesofisrael.com/jewish-voice-for-peace-defends-anti-semitism/.

26. Miriam Elman, "ALERT: Three U.S. Churches to Vote on Anti-Israel Resolutions This Spring," *Legal Insurrection*, February 21, 2016, https://legalinsurrection.com/2016/02/alert-three-u-s-churches-to-vote-on-anti-israel-resolutions-this-spring/.

27. Dexter Van Zile, "An Exodus of Members Doesn't Stop the UCC from Attacking Israel," *Philos Project*, June 25, 2015, http://www.swuarchive.com/news/article.asp?id=4035.

28. Dexter Van Zile, "A Word about Mitri Raheb's Sermon at the UCC's Synod," CAMERA Snapshots (blog), July 2, 2015, http://blog.camera.org/archives/2015/07/a_word_about_mitri_rahebs_serm.html.

29. William A. Jacobson, "United Church of Christ Divests from Israel," *Legal Insurrection*, June 30, 2015, https://legalinsurrection.com/2015/06/united-church-of-christ-divests-from-israel/.

30. Elman, "JVP—'Jew Washing' the anti-Israel movement."

31. For more on the antisemitism of Sabeel/Fosna, see Miriam Elman, "Sabeel—the Anti-Israel Christian Activists You Never Heard Of," *Legal Insurrection*, June 28, 2015, https://legalinsurrection.com/2015/06/sabeel-the-anti-israel-christian-activists-you-never-heard-of/.

32. William A. Jacobson, "Sick: BDS Groups Spread Photoshop of Concentration Camp Inmates Holding Anti-Israel Signs," *Legal Insurrection*, November 28, 2014, https://legalinsurrection.com/2014/11/sick-bds-groups-spreads-photoshop-of-concentration-camp-inmates-holding-anti-israel-signs/.

33. Shiri Moshe, "A Sermon of Hate in the District of Columbia," *The Tower*, June 2015, http://www.thetower.org/article/a-sermon-of-hate-in-the-district-of-columbia/.

34. Miriam Elman, "Jewish Voice for Peace Hijacks High Holidays for Anti-Israel Messaging," *Legal Insurrection*, October 5, 2016, https://legalinsurrection.com/2016/10/jewish-voice-for-peace-hijacks-high-holidays-for-anti-israel-messaging/.

35. Elman, "JVP Hijacks High Holidays."

36. Elman, "JVP Hijacks High Holidays."

37. Occam's Razor, "Dream Defenders: Defending the Dream of Anti-Israel Activism," *Legal Insurrection*, October 1, 2016, https://legalinsurrection.com/2016/10/dream-defenders-defending-the-dream-of-anti-israel-activism/.

38. Miriam Elman, "Jewish Voice for Peace Passover Haggadah: 'Next Year in al-Quds!,'" *Legal Insurrection*, April 9, 2017, https://legalinsurrection.com/2017/04/jewish-voice-for-peace-passover-haggadah-next-year-in-al-quds/.

39. Miriam Elman, "'Jewish Voice for Peace' Hijacks Chanukah for Anti-Israel Messaging," *Legal Insurrection*, January 1, 2017, https://legalinsurrection.com/2017/01/jewish-voice-for-peace-hijacks-chanukah-for-anti-israel-messaging/.

40. Elman, "'JVP' Hijacks Chanukah."

41. Muravchik, "Not So Jewish."

42. Theodore Sasson et al., "Does Taglit-Birthright Israel Foster Long Distance Nationalism?," *Nationalism and Ethnic Politics* 20, no. 4 (November 2014): 438–54.

43. Allison Kaplan Sommer, "Jewish Voice for Peace Urges Young Jews to Boycott Birthright Israel," *Haaretz*, September 2, 2017, https://www.haaretz.com/us-news/jewish-voice-for-peace-urges-young-jews-to-boycott-birthright-1.5447614.

44. Founded in 2014 to protest Israel's counterterror operations against Hamas, IfNotNow (INN) is similar to JVP in that it also attempts to appeal to young American Jews. Branding itself as an organization merely opposed to Israel's occupation and "neutral" regarding BDS, Zionism, and the two-state solution to the Israeli-Palestinian conflict, INN has sought in recent years to position itself within the leftist mainstream and has had some measure of success in doing so. Abraham Riesman, "The Jewish Revolt," *New York*, July 12, 2018, http://nymag.com/intelligencer/2018/07/ifnotnow-birthright-ramah-bds-israel.html. But while some still consider INN to be a legitimate voice, its recent collaborative work with JVP and the fact that most of its leading activists are today also members of JVP underscore INN's radical turn and a growing relationship between the two groups. For example, in tandem with JVP, it has appropriated Passover themes and holiday rituals to promote anti-Israel "liberation" seders on college campuses. Aiden Pink and Helen Chernikoff, "Harvard Students Walk a Careful Line to Host Anti-Occupation 'Liberation' Seder," *The Forward*, March 30, 2018, https://forward.com/news/national/397771/harvard-students-walk-a-careful-line-to-host-anti-occupation-liberation/. INN has also joined JVP's campaign against Birthright, most notably by orchestrating a number of walkouts from its trips while participants were already in Israel. Jeremy Sharon, "IfNotNow Gatecrash New Birthright Group, Go on East Jerusalem Tour," *Jerusalem Post*, July 15, 2018, www.jpost.com/Diaspora/IfNotNow-gatecrash-new-Birthright-group-go-on-east-Jerusalem-tour-562567. It is also now actively promoting JVP's Deadly Exchange initiative. Perhaps most indicative of INN's increasing radicalization was its recent anti-Israel "street actions" that involved reciting Kaddish, the Jewish mourners' prayer, for Hamas militants who were killed in the course of attempted terrorist infiltrations at the Israel-Gaza border. Tzvi Lev, "'Kaddish' for Dead Gazans?," Israel National News, April 12, 2018, www.israelnationalnews.com/News/News.aspx/244319.

45. "About Deadly Exchange," Jewish Voice for Peace, accessed April 12, 2021, https://deadlyexchange.org/about-deadly-exchange/; and "Deadly Exchange: The Dangerous Consequences of American Law Enforcement Trainings in Israel," Researching the American-Israeli Alliance and Jewish Voice for Peace, September 2018, https://deadlyexchange.org/wp-content/uploads/2019/07/Deadly-Exchange-Report.pdf.

46. Yoav Fromer, "How Israel Is Being Framed: Why Palestine Is Not Ferguson," *Tablet*, December 3, 2015, http://www.tabletmag.com/jewish-news-and-politics/195487/how-israel-is-being-framed.

47. William A. Jacobson, "Exposed: Years-Long Effort to Blame Israel for U.S. Police Shootings of Blacks," *Legal Insurrection*, July 18, 2016, https://legalinsurrection.com/2016/07/exposed-years-long-effort-to-blame-israel-for-u-s-police-shootings-of-blacks/; Alan Dershowitz, "Alan Dershowitz: Whom Do Bigots Blame for Police Shootings in the U.S.? Israel, of Course!," *Algemeiner*, July 13, 2016, www.algemeiner.com/2016/07/13/alan-dershowitz-whom-do-bigots-blame-for-police-shootings-in-america-israel-of-course/.

48. Jacobson, "Exposed."
49. Bennett, "Antisemitism of Jewish Voice for Peace."
50. Jacobson, "Exposed."
51. Bennett, "Antisemitism of Jewish Voice for Peace."
52. ADL, "Jewish Voice for Peace."
53. Miriam Elman, "Jewish Voice for Peace Doubles-Down on Antisemitic 'Deadly Exchange' Campaign," *Legal Insurrection*, August 10, 2017, https://legalinsurrection.com/2017/08/jewish-voice-for-peace-doubles-down-on-antisemitic-deadly-exchange-campaign/.
54. Mira Sucharov, "Jews Drive U.S. Police Brutality against People of Color? JVP Crosses Over into Anti-Semitism," *Haaretz*, July 10, 2017, www.haaretz.com/opinion/has-jewish-voice-for-peace-crossed-the-line-into-anti-semitism-1.5492843.
55. Rebecca Vilkomerson, "Own It to Fight It: Yes, We Jews Are Complicit in Violence against Palestinians and People of Color," *Haaretz*, July 19, 2017, www.haaretz.com/opinion/u-s-jews-complicit-in-violence-against-palestinians-people-of-color-1.5431275.
56. "Breaking: Hundreds of JVP Activists across U.S. Demonstrating against ADL's Role in U.S.-Israel Deadly Exchange Programs," Jewish Voice for Peace, November 8, 2017, https://jewishvoiceforpeace.org/breaking-hundreds-jvp-activists-across-u-s-demonstrating-adls-role-u-s-israel-deadly-exchange-programs/.
57. Ben Sales, "How a Jewish Civil Rights Group Became a Villain on the Far Left," Jewish Telegraphic Agency, April 19, 2018, www.jta.org/2018/04/19/news-opinion/jewish-civil-rights-group-became-villain-far-left-2. Starbucks subsequently complied and demoted the ADL.
58. Miriam Elman, "Anti-Semitic 'Deadly Exchange' Campaign Can Be Defeated when Local Pro-Israel Groups Respond Quickly," *Legal Insurrection*, December 9, 2018, https://legalinsurrection.com/2018/12/anti-semitic-deadly-exchange-campaign-can-be-defeated-when-local-pro-israel-groups-respond-quickly/; Miriam Elman, "Demonization: Durham NC City Council Bans Police Exchanges with Israel," *Legal Insurrection*, April 22, 2018, https://legalinsurrection.com/2018/04/demonization-durham-nc-city-council-bans-police-exchanges-with-israel/; Jonathan S. Tobin, "The BDS Fifth Column," Jewish News Syndicate, May 7, 2018, https://www.jns.org/opinion/the-bds-fifth-column/; Carolyn Glick, "Column One: Time to Cut JVP Down to Size," *Jerusalem Post*, April 20, 2018, https://www.jpost.com/Opinion/Column-One-Time-to-cut-JVP-down-to-size-551291.
59. Miriam Elman, "The Intersectional, Antisemitic 'Deadly Exchange' Comes to Campus," *Algemeiner*, April 8, 2019, www.algemeiner.com/2019/04/08/the-intersectional-antisemitic-deadly-exchange-campaign-comes-to-campus/.
60. Miriam Elman, "Jewish Voice for Peace Can't Seem to Stay Away from Alison Weir," *Legal Insurrection*, December 1, 2015, https://legalinsurrection.com/2015/12/jewish-voice-for-peace-cant-seem-to-stay-away-from-alison-weir/.
61. Elman, "'Jew Washing' the Anti-Israel Movement."
62. "Letter to Alison Weir," Jewish Voice for Peace, June 14, 2015, https://jewishvoiceforpeace.org/letter-to-alison-weir/; "Jewish Voice for Peace Statement on Our Relationship with Alison Weir," June 15, 2015, https://jewishvoiceforpeace.org/jewish-voice-for-peace-statement-on-our-relationship-with-alison-weir/. See also Miriam Elman, "Jewish

Voice for Peace? Not really," *Legal Insurrection*, June 11, 2015, https://legalinsurrection.com/2015/06/jewish-voice-for-peace-not-really/.

63. Elman, "JVP Can't Seem to Stay Away from Alison Weir."

64. In 2011, Epstein participated in the Gaza Freedom Flotilla as a passenger on the US-flagged ship *The Audacity of Hope*.

65. David Schraub, "JVP Disassociates from Alison Weir," *Debate Link*, May 31, 2015, http://dsadevil.blogspot.com/2015/05/jvp-disassociates-from-alison-weir.html.

66. David Collier, "Americans Inside Palestine Live," Beyond the Great Divide (blog), March 2019, https://david-collier.com/wp-content/uploads/2019/03/190319_americanlivereport_finalv2.pdf.

67. John Strawson, "Colonialism," in "Word Crimes: Reclaiming the Language of the Israeli-Palestinian Conflict," ed. Donna Robinson Divine, Miriam F. Elman, and Asaf Romirowsky, special issue, *Israel Studies* 24, no. 2 (Summer 2019): 33–44; Izabella Tabarovsky, "Understanding the Real Origin of That New York Times Cartoon: How Anti-Semitic Soviet Propaganda Informs Contemporary Left Anti-Zionism," *Tablet*, June 6, 2019, https://www.tabletmag.com/jewish-arts-and-culture/285781/soviet-anti-semitic-cartoons.

68. Kenneth Waltzer, "Antisemitisms of the Left and Right (with Mark G. Yudof)," *Times of Israel*, October 21, 2017, http://blogs.timesofisrael.com/antisemitisms-of-the-left-and-right-with-mark-g-yudof/.

69. Miriam Elman, "National Black Law Enforcement Group Backs Georgia-Israel Police Exchange Program," *Legal Insurrection*, February 24, 2019, https://legalinsurrection.com/2019/02/black-law-enforcement-group-backs-georgia-israel-police-exchange-program/.

70. JIMENA, "Sephardic and Mizrahi Communal Response to Jewish Voice for Peace," *The Tower*, January 23, 2019, www.thetower.org/7095-sephardi-mizrahi-jewish-groups-reject-jvp-statement-accuse-it-of-racist-exclusion/.

71. Tobin, "BDS Fifth Column."

MIRIAM F. ELMAN is Executive Director of the Academic Engagement Network, an educational nonprofit that promotes academic freedom and free expression, combats antisemitism, and works to improve Israel literacy on American campuses. She is Associate Professor of Political Science and Inaugural Robert D. McClure Professor of Teaching Excellence at the Maxwell School of Citizenship and Public Affairs, Syracuse University, where she has served as research director in the Program for the Advancement of Research on Conflict and Collaboration (PARCC) for nearly a decade. An award-winning scholar and teacher, Elman is editor and coeditor of five books and author and coauthor of over sixty-five journal articles and book chapters. Recently, she coedited "Word Crimes: Reclaiming the Language of the Israeli-Palestinian Conflict," a special issue of the journal *Israel Studies*.

III. ANTISEMITISM ON COLLEGE AND UNIVERSITY CAMPUSES

6

Contending with Antisemitism in Its Many Forms on American Campuses

Kenneth Waltzer

IN THE EARLY NINETIES, A BLACK MAN BEATEN by police in Los Angeles asked, "Can't we all get along?" In subsequent decades, the question has continued to resonate. America is more divided today by race and racial ideology than in the past, despite the growth of a Black middle class whose offspring are college-going. We are divided on the philosophy of America First, as in 1939–41 when such modern xenophobic American nationalism first appeared. We are divided over key aspects of our democratic republic—the Fourteenth Amendment, equal rights, birthright citizenship, national citizenship, the Fifteenth Amendment, voting rights, legal and illegal immigration, hard or soft control of the border, diversity, gun control, an expansive welfare state, and unchecked executive power. Antisemitism is demonstrably rising amid such broadening divisions, and American Jews as well as African Americans know the fear of possibly being violently targeted in their communities and places of worship. In August 2017, the unthinkable (but not unprecedented) in America happened—neo-Nazis and white supremacists marched openly in Charlottesville, Virginia, and at the University of Virginia, wielding lit torches, holding guns, and carrying signs warning "The Jews Will Not Replace Us." In October 2018, a white supremacist, Robert Bowers, killed eleven people in the Tree of Life Synagogue in Pittsburgh, his deepest fears stoked by white supremacist posters indicating that Jews were the catalysts behind global changes, rising migration by peoples of color and Muslims, and efforts at investigation in Washington to preserve the rule of law.[1]

American universities are institutions mostly set apart from and governed independently of the flux in national currents; yet they exist in society and the polity, and many in these institutions are deeply impacted by such currents and divisions. American universities also form a locus for a discrete set of issues as they host a distinctive field of conflict for movements seeking to legitimize their causes or attract supporters and recruits. The boycott, divestment, and sanctions (BDS) movement, with activist faculty and aggressive students, as part of a highly ideological, global movement committed to exposing and tagging Israel as a pariah state, has specifically targeted American campuses for political work. Alongside a decade of vigorous anti-Zionist, anti-Israel campaigning, discourses and behaviors easily identifiable as antisemitic have become more audible and visible on campuses, and social divisions marking and setting off Jews, especially those supporting Israel (Zios), have grown more open and substantial. So have forays by white identity groups onto campuses urging students to help preserve an endangered white America, and these groups have posted and distributed materials identifying Jews as key elements shaping a world hostile to white racial primacy.

Contending with antisemitism in its many forms on campus has thus been a growth industry in recent years and, in a new development, has meant contending with antisemitism both on the left and on the right. These two forms of antisemitism have different roots and contents, reflecting and serving different political agendas; but together, they have worked cumulatively to transform campus life for many Jewish-identifying faculty and students. Most college and university leaders confirm that antisemitism is increasing on their and on other campuses. In a 2019 survey, some 65 percent of university leaders thought antisemitism was increasing on campuses, as did some 80 percent of university leaders in public doctoral institutions.[2]

This chapter characterizes the swirling currents of antisemitism on contemporary American campuses, explores some differences in the form and content of left and right antisemitism, and probes some of the impacts of hate and intolerance. Such forms, identifying Jews as a key problem that traces back to differing historical roots and precedents and is shaped by and reflects different politics, have strongly impacted campus climates (especially in leading universities and smaller liberal arts institutions), influenced how Jewish students feel about and experience work and life in these institutions, and posed real challenges for university leaders charged with enforcing codes of conduct and establishing moral clarity about speech and behavior.

The chapter also considers some of the patterns of leadership and institutional response visible on the campuses. University leaders have been relatively slow to respond to expressed concerns about antisemitism, reflecting their preoccupation with competing priorities, including the high salience of racial insult and assault, their lack of comprehension about antisemitism, and perhaps even a sense that Jews have power and influence to deal with these matters on their own. In recent years, university leaders have responded more quickly and forcefully and have sought to integrate active responses to antisemitism with responses to other forms of hate and intolerance. A model policy initiative since 2016 has been the University of California Regents working report and statement, "Principles against Intolerance," which has called on chancellors to speak out against antisemitism wherever encountered. However, after two years and despite earnest efforts on several campuses (some better than others), this promising initiative has still not stemmed the worst excesses. Consequently, Jews on contemporary campuses inhabit environments that are suffused with numerous anti-Israel and anti-Jewish currents, and Jewish students are vulnerable targets for shunning, separation, and social isolation. In turn, such students must wrestle with special issues of self-effacement and denial in the face of challenge and insult.

Antisemitism Today

Although a misnomer, a term invented in the 1870s to indicate a modern form of Judeophobia, we continue to use the label *antisemitism* today to identify a serious animus against Jews. Antisemitism has an extraordinarily long history and includes numerous themes and tropes by which antisemites have classically characterized their enemy, real or imagined. Contrary to others in the contemporary policy landscape, in my view, there is no need for new definitions imported or new standards borrowed from contemporary European monitoring organizations or the International Holocaust Remembrance Alliance (IHRA) to better identify antisemitic currents today on American campuses.[3] When contemporary expressions about Jews are accompanied by classic canards against Jewish power and influence or charges about Jewish money, when classic references to conspiracy, clannishness, or double loyalty start appearing openly in the discourse, we should realize in what moral universe we are standing.

When anti-Zionist expressions, for instance, especially those claimed to be merely anti-Israel, are accompanied by obsessive claims about Jewish global power and influence or Jewish conspiracy and manipulation, we ought to suspect that we are in the presence of what has been dubbed the new antisemitism. As numerous scholars have argued for nearly two decades, the new antisemitism consists of the attribution of all features historically assigned to the pariah Jew to the existing Jewish state. If the focus of classic antisemitism was the Jewish being, the focus of the new antisemitism is the being of the Jewish state. Similarly, the circulation of posters on campuses blaming Jews as the unseen power shaping American immigration and multiculturalism and threatening an imaginary white Christian America or seeing Jews as interfering with the march of originalist jurists on the US Supreme Court indicates the presence of an identitarian racial or right antisemitism.

It is worth stating here that antisemitism is above all a hatred rooted in an idea or portrait of the Jew as a negative being, an extraordinarily malevolent and powerful being, a threat, or a danger. Antisemitic thought at its core is shaped by conspiratorial presumptions; is accompanied by related beliefs about the Jews as powerful, influential, and dangerous; and is Manichean—drawing a world sharply divided between good and evil, in which the Jew is the opposite of the good and constitutes the malevolent, deformed, and threatening Other.

We must also understand several points about antisemitism—namely, that it

- is changeable and malleable, lives in history, and changes in history (it mutates like a virus);
- rises and falls in intensity;
- shifts in the content of the idea of the Jew (religious, racial, political, or cultural being);
- is part of a narrative in which the Jew is a negative presence or problem;
- involves an agenda or action program to remedy the problem and improve the world

At bottom, that is, antisemitism rests on a belief that the world would be improved if Jews were superseded or replaced or if their influence were limited or made to disappear.[4] For antisemites, Jews are the devil's people, a brood of swine and vipers, a people barred from grace, the untrue Israel now surpassed by a newer and truer Israel. Or they are an economic threat and a danger to public well-being, a selfish and conniving people, who manipulate currencies, spread plagues, poison wells, or—in insult to God's loving mercy—seek a pound of flesh. Or Jews are a racial enemy and a danger, a people who masquerade behind a mask of acculturation, taking on the accents and demeanor of host nations, yet always somehow remaining alien and apart. It is in their blood or genetic heritage that Jews are a threat, a bacillus, an infection. Jews are cultural defilers, sprinkled into the cracks and crevices of the national abode, or they are politically subversive, part of an international conspiracy to dominate the world and subvert the nation.

Writing over fifty years ago, the Tunisian-born French Jew and student of Sartre Albert Memmi, in his remarkable *Portrait of a Jew*, insisted that the Jew is a figure of misfortune. He remarked, What is Jewish history but "a continual alert, punctuated by ghastly catastrophes"? Jews face a "hostility," he observed, which keeps them apart, separates them, and crucially shapes their relations with others. Antisemitism marks the Jew as different. The Jew is someone who stands accused. He is a defendant. He cannot ever fully be sure of his innocence. Memmi talked about a constant ambiguous feeling that scarcely ever left him, a feeling of "being both of this world and not of it."[5] Rereading Memmi's *Portrait of a Jew* offers significant insight into the cumulative impact of hostile BDS campaigns and charges and of antisemitic claims, depictions, and social media outbursts on many Jewish students on activist campuses. Rebekah Katz (an undergraduate at Swarthmore) and numerous other students have written powerfully about how, where BDS has been a strong presence, it has acted in ways to create a persistent affront to and denial of their existence. Others have written about having to hide their personal identities and to mask their conversations and social loyalties to conform to dominant opinion or otherwise risk social isolation.[6] Jews at campuses where BDS and Students for Justice in Palestine (SJP) dominate continually stand accused of aligning with evil, being okay with apartheid, approving and serving as apologists for racism, and being unable in their alleged white privilege to even imagine oppression. The charges create a cumulative impact on the campus discourse and importantly shape the experience of being a Jew on campus.

The Study of Antisemitism on American Campuses

In a July 1915 report, "Antisemitism on the College Campus: Perceptions and Reality,"[7] researchers Leonard Saxe, Theodore Sasson, and others of the Cohen Center for Modern Jewish Studies at Brandeis University surveyed a large sample of Jewish students on American and Canadian campuses and found that one-quarter (25%) of the respondents described hostility toward Israel on campus by their peers to be "fairly" or "very" problematic. Nearly one-sixth (15%) perceived the same level of hostility toward Jews generally. The respondents in the study were eligible 2015 Taglit-Birthright trip students (students who identified as Jews). In several Canadian universities, some California state campuses, and a few Big Ten universities, hostility to Israel and to Jews was even higher. Nearly one-quarter of the student respondents reported having been blamed during the year for Israel's actions because they were Jewish. Remarkably, about one-third of the undergraduate respondents reported having been verbally harassed because they were Jewish. Nearly three-quarters said they had been exposed during the year to antisemitic statements, including claims that Jews have too much power.

The Anti-Defamation League (ADL) issued a report in 2017[8] noting that antisemitic incidents on college campuses had nearly doubled during the year and that violence against Jews was rising. According to the ADL, ninety anti-Jewish incidents were reported at sixty schools, whereas forty-seven incidents were reported on forty-three campuses a year earlier. Such incidents included a spate of swastika-spraying events on campuses on commemorative dates such as the anniversary of the liberation of Auschwitz and usually coincided with local BDS campaigns. ADL head Jonathan Greenblatt noted that most Jewish students felt safe on their campuses and that when incidents occurred, administrators were generally responsive; yet Greenblatt also observed that a significant minority of students reported they encountered expanded hostility because they support Israel or were assumed to do so because they were Jews.

In particular, the number of incidents involving conduct aimed to suppress freedom of speech and assembly for Jewish students on campuses doubled in 2015–16 and then doubled again in 2016–17. Consideration by student governments of anti-Israel divestment resolutions, the activist group AMCHA insisted, was strongly correlated with surges in campus antisemitic incidents. AMCHA thought that the injection of the anti-Zionist movement onto campus was fueling a significant resurgence in antisemitism.[9] Jewish students reported that anti-Zionist activists singled out, harassed, intimidated, and even assaulted them, regardless of their personal feelings on Israel. Anti-Zionist expression was also increasingly laced with centuries-old stereotypes. After a divestment resolution passed in the Undergraduate Students Association Council at UCLA in November 2014, prodivestment senators attempted to deny a Jewish student a position on the student government judicial board based on her Jewish identity and leadership in the local Jewish community. After a divestment resolution passed at UC Davis in 2015, a pro-BDS student senator celebrated by writing "Israel will fall" on social media, and vandals defaced the Alpha Epsilon Pi fraternity house with a swastika. That same year, after a BDS campaign at UC Santa Cruz, a Jewish student senator was instructed to abstain from voting because of his leadership in the Jewish community and his supposed identification with a "Jewish agenda." Amid the 2015 divestment debate at UC Santa Barbara, pro-BDS students made blatantly racist and conspiratorial comments, including that the US government is controlled by Jews. At UC Berkeley, graffiti proclaimed, "Zionists should be sent to the gas chamber."[10]

At that time, there were no guns, lit torches, or signs proclaiming that "Jews will not replace us." But at San Diego State University, numerous racist posts appeared on social media platforms such as Yik Yak, including "SDSU Divest so we can get rid of the Jews." At Stanford in 2015, a student group interviewed a Jewish student candidate for student government, Rachel Beyda, and questioned her as a Jew about how she would vote on divestment. At Hunter College of the City University of New York in November 2015, students protesting college tuition mounted a raucous demonstration, demanding "Zios out of CUNY," and threatened Jewish students standing nearby.

At the beginning of the new academic year in 2016, reports openly warned newly matriculating Jewish students what they might now expect to confront on American campuses; Jewish organizations echoed similar sentiments. One hopeful countertrend was that, between 2015 and 2017, twelve student governments passed resolutions condemning antisemitism on campus, signaling the issue's growing salience. Also, responsive to the evidence of rising antisemitism on California campuses and after extensive discussion, the University of California Board of Regents unanimously adopted a revised working report and "Statement of Principles against Intolerance" on March 24, 2016, identifying "antisemitism" and "anti-Semitic forms of anti-Zionism" as forms of bigotry and discrimination demanding attention along with other forms of intolerance. The regents called on university leaders to speak out against antisemitism and other hatreds by offering instructive speech to counter bad speech. The regents' principles also called on university leaders to challenge antisemitism and other discrimination wherever they appeared.[11]

Good responses to antisemitism on campuses, in this writer's view, ought to include forthright identification of antisemitism as a form of bigotry, just like racism, sexism, homophobia, Islamophobia, and other forms of intolerance. Leadership responses that affirm principles of free speech but at the same time distance university leaders and the institution from the specific antisemitic speech or action are inadequate. Constructive responses should include outspoken condemnation, should approach these events as teachable moments, and ought to tie condemnation of antisemitism with enduring principles of democratic thought and tolerance. Appropriate follow-through should also lead to serious training and education of relevant university administrators and staff as well as key leaders of student groups and resident advisors in the dorms. Over a longer term, they should also include, if possible, university hiring initiatives and academic changes to include, where possible, expanded faculty attention to Israel and to Jewish experience and antisemitism in the curriculum as well as additional visiting speaker initiatives to augment whatever limitations of personnel shape the curriculum. Above all, they should include follow-through on the appropriate review, upgrading, and enforcement of student conduct codes and prosecution of those who disrupt others' rights.

A recent opinion survey of a sample of Jewish students on five California campuses offers an alternative, revisionist view of the situation, suggesting that some heightened concern about antisemitism has been overheated, the phenomenon being less worrisome than Jewish organizations claim, and emphasizing that in general Jewish college students feel largely positive about their campuses. This portrait of Jewish student life offered by Ari Y. Kelman at Stanford University is a more stable and positive one than that in earlier reports from Brandeis.[12] But Kelman, it should be noted, draws on a very narrow sample of Jewish students and colleges to find such differing results. To some extent, Kelman is right—most students find ways to sidestep, ignore, and, like Memmi earlier, live with the hostility privately, although not without burden—but Kelman is also wrongheaded in thinking that his limited sample, excluding those on campus most identified as Jewish or linked with Jewish organizations, stands well for Jewish student opinion and experience overall. After all, these are campuses where anti-Israel themes have been sounded in classes and in a surprisingly large number of cocurricular programs, and where Israel has been regularly and demonstratively portrayed as a villain in a human rights framework annually on the campus quad. My belief is that there is more to be concerned about in terms of how Jewish students feel than Kelman credits.

Antisemitism of the Left and the Right on Campuses Today

Today there is both a new antisemitism on the hard left and a newly revitalizing antisemitism on the right. One form finds support among some faculty and programs in the humanities and soft social sciences, in select area studies programs, and in sections of student activism. We make a mistake to think it is either powerful or overwhelming generally—the truth is that most opinion on campus does not care about or even engage it. Nonetheless, it is a persistent background noise and has important effects. The other form of antisemitism invades from off campus, doing hit-and-run poster placement, media manipulation, threat graffiti, and property defacement.

Most scholars, if not all, identify the left antisemitism with the label "the new antisemitism." This antisemitism includes new content different from the old, and especially a set of nonracist or antiracist assumptions that are suitable for a postracial age. The distinctive feature is that it focuses on Israel, representing the collective Jew (the Jewish state) as the pariah Jew was represented earlier. Other nations are celebrated for asserting themselves to achieve national liberation and sovereignty; the Jewish state is criticized. The national liberation of the Jews is a cause of dismay. Jewish state building is represented as a crime. Some even go so far as to attack the idea that Jews are a nation at all. In all this, Israel is conceived as an extraordinarily powerful and evil entity and a global problem—it is a threat to peace and to world order, a violator of human rights, a state unlike any other. If it would be eliminated, replaced, transformed, or decolonized, a better world would ensue.

Scholars have a range of views on how closely anti-Zionism and antisemitism overlap and interact. Some, like French philosopher Bernard-Henri Lévy, think anti-Zionism functions basically as a mask for antisemitism. Lévy said at a New York City gathering two years ago, "Anti-Zionism is the new dressing for the old passion of antisemitism." The late Rabbi Jonathan Sacks of Great Britain also called anti-Zionism "the antisemitism of our time." He said, "Antisemitism means denying the right of Jews to exist collectively as Jews with the same rights as everyone else."[13]

The late Robert Wistrich, a prolific historian and writer on antisemitism, understood well that antisemitism and anti-Zionism had separate, independent origins but came to think the two phenomena had converged. In an essay in 2004, Wistrich argued that "anti-Zionism and anti-Semitism are two distinct ideologies that over time (especially since 1948) have tended to converge, generally without undergoing a full merger."[14] Moreover, Wistrich insisted, "Anti-Zionism has become the most dangerous and effective form of anti-Semitism in our time, through its systematic delegitimization, defamation, and demonization of Israel." Anti-Zionism seemed "an old-new version of anti-Semitism in which Jews are rapacious, bloodsucking colonialists." The Jews are rootless imperial invaders, conquerors aiming to cleanse the land and dispossess its inhabitants; they are strangers coming from outside to displace the indigenes.

More compelling in my view, though, is the view of others, such as political theorist Alan Johnson, who see and trace the development of an antisemitic anti-Zionism as a distinctive tendency on the hard left in England and America. For Johnson, "antisemitic anti-Zionism bends the meaning of Israel and Zionism out of shape until both become fit receptacles for the tropes, images and ideas of classical antisemitism. In short, that which the demonological Jew once was, demonological Israel now is: uniquely malevolent, full of blood lust, all-controlling, the hidden hand, tricksy, always acting in bad faith, the obstacle to a better, purer, more spiritual world, uniquely deserving of punishment."[15]

Antisemitism on the right differs from the left's new antisemitism. First, it is not Ziono-centric but rather Americano-centric. Second, its roots extend back to early twentieth-century racial antisemitism and to America Firstism, and there are elements of contemporary identity politics also in the mix. The ADL says many in the alt-right define themselves as identitarians, a term from France and the founding of the Bloc Identitaire movement with its youth section, Generation Identitaire. Others say they are neoreactionaries, neo-Nazis, like the National Socialist Legion, or "race realists." Third, the main premise is that "white identity" is under attack in the US just as Christian identity is in Europe and that Jews are to blame. As posters placed all over the University of Minnesota campus three years ago (with accompanying swastikas) screamed, "White Man, Are You Sick and Tired of the Jews Destroying Your Country Through Mass Immigration and Degeneracy?" The threats are immigrants and refugees—Mexican and Central American immigrants and Muslim refugees—as well as African Americans; the motor forces are the multifold displacements and anxieties accompanying transformative economic and cultural change. But it is the Jews who catalyze all into motion and are key opponents of a white republic. Eric K. Ward, formerly a senior fellow with the Southern Poverty Law Center, says that "American White nationalism . . . is a revolutionary social movement committed to building a Whites-only nation, and antisemitism forms its theoretical core."[16] Indeed, most such right antisemites consider Jews not as white but as having an identity neither white nor European.

Older themes familiar in our history—Henry Ford–type claims from the *Dearborn Independent* about international Jewish power, Father Charles Coughlin themes about Jews and financial conspiracy, and Charles

Lindbergh-type demands opposed to the Jewish desire to push the nation into a needless World War II—reappear in new guises, offering a sharp counterpoint to left antisemitism. Screeds against immigrants and immigration and appeals to stock themes about grasping Jews mark flyers placed on the campuses. "Every time some Anti-White, Anti-American, Anti-Freedom Event Takes Place, You Look at It, and It's Jews Behind It," announced a flyer on campuses after Justice Kavanaugh's Supreme Court appointment was contested. Another proclaimed the "Right of Revolution" with a man aiming a gun at a hook-nosed Jew shaped like an octopus with tentacles. The late Philip Roth's novel *The Plot against America*, a fictive history of the early 1940s, appears increasingly prescient. Antisemitism on the right is accusatory and angry, and it seeks to restore a world that never was.

Identifying Antisemitism

Today, the language of the old racial antisemitism, even updated, works poorly on campus, as war, the Holocaust, and the broad sweep of postwar decolonization have delegitimized such racialist thinking. So left antisemitism now contains a newer system of concepts and justifications suitable to a post-Holocaust, postnational, postimperialist, and antiracist age. The new antisemitism constructs Zionism as a monolithic racial ideology in an antiracist age and as a settler-colonial movement in a postimperial age. Supporters of Israel are evil, because Israel is evil. The new antisemitism depicts Israel as diabolical and genocidal, and most Jews are thought to be part of a conspiracy of support. Good Jews are those who opt out, support Palestinian national liberation, and steer clear of the Israel lobby. Israel is also accused of using the memory of Jewish dead as justification for contemporary racist actions. Exaggerated and obsessive anti-Zionism, Holocaust inversion and denial, and over-the-top efforts to liken Israel and Israelis to Nazis are all parts of an agenda to delegitimize Israel and isolate its supporters. So prevalent is this on many campuses that commercial guides are now available about where Jewish students should attend to avoid the sharply isolating effects of such currents.[17]

Anti-Zionism on campus need not be antisemitic; BDS is committed to the elimination of the state of Israel, but some supporters may embrace a purely political view opposed to nationalism and affirming universalist principles. Or they may think that Israel should not have been created at the expense of the Palestinians. Yet anti-Zionism on many campuses often crosses a line to become antisemitic anti-Zionism, recycling old themes in recognizable ways.

When anti-Zionism continuously treats Israel as a caricature of extreme evil, offering cartoon versions of Zionism as inherently racist and colonialist, removed from real history, this is antisemitic anti-Zionism. When adherents of anti-Zionism insist that, even though all other nations enjoy a right to self-determination and sovereignty, Jews are not similarly eligible, this is antisemitic anti-Zionism.

When anti-Zionism absorbs mystical claims or tropes about Jewish evil and power into discussion of the Jewish state and attributes claims made about Jews as part of the long history of antisemitism to the Jewish collective today, this too is antisemitic anti-Zionism. When anti-Zionism absorbs representations, images, and depictions of the physical Jew clearly derived from the long history of antisemitism into its standard discourse, we are witnessing antisemitic anti-Zionism. Such representations picture the Jew as an insect, a hook-nosed devilish figure, a figure with horns, deformed, ugly, and grasping. When magical powers able to hypnotize the world are attributed to Jews, this is antisemitic anti-Zionism.

When anti-Zionists raise questions about the fitness for student office of students of Jewish background or affiliated with Jewish community institutions, because they will not be able to act objectively in representing other students, this is also antisemitic anti-Zionism. When anti-Zionists accuse Jews who call out antisemitism of raising the issue in bad faith in order to silence anti-Zionism, this too is antisemitic anti-Zionism. They accuse those who cry antisemitism of engaging in a swindle or a lie and acting in bad faith.

Finally, when anti-Zionists argue that European or American Jews far removed from Israel or Palestine (such as the Jews in the Paris kosher grocery Hypercacher, shot after the Charlie Hebdo attack) are fair game for attack as part of the broad anticolonial "resistance" because all Jews everywhere are allies of Israel, this too is antisemitic anti-Zionism. The presumption is that there are no such things as individual Jews, people of independent mind and action; there are only members and loyalists of the Zionist collective.

The evidence suggests that the weight of antisemitic influence in campus life today continues to be heavily shaped by BDS aggression and ongoing campaigns to win university divestment from American corporations selling to Israel. There were twenty BDS campaigns in 2017–18, down from a peak of forty-four in 2015–16, but such efforts remain a campus fixture. In 2018–19, there were fifteen divestment campaigns, including new ones at NYU, Brown, Cornell, Swarthmore, UC Santa Barbara, and elsewhere. This also flows from the determination on the left to use the vogueish theme of "intersectionality," emphasizing the alleged connectedness of oppressions to help create cross-group alliances among minorities while labeling Jewish students as privileged whites without minority experience or familiarity with oppression. The intersectionality approach emphasizes spurious linkages in particular among minority causes and Palestinian rights and leads progressive alliances on campuses, for example at NYU, to exclude Jews and Jewish groups.[18] At the same time, numerous faculty members aligned with the BDS movement openly refuse to write letters of recommendation for Jewish and other students seeking to study in Israel (the US Committee on the Academic and Cultural Boycott of Israel's guidelines prohibit faculty writing such letters); the same organization asks faculty to get institutions to end study-in-Israel programs.

Right antisemitism is mostly an off-campus phenomenon. Right antisemitic groups mostly communicate via social media, but reports have appeared that white supremacist groups have pushed to recruit students on campuses in some states, and some frictions in residence halls indicate a modest influence. A rise in Holocaust jokes, the reappearance of references to Jews as "kikes" in popular parlance, and similar new usages departing from norms that have prevailed for several decades reflect a shift in the moral compass shaping events in the university's private spaces, including residence halls, fraternities, and sororities. Groups such as Identity Evropa, Vanguard America, the Iron Guard, and the National Socialist Legion are engaged in serious efforts to recruit members on campus.

What Are the Consequences?

What has this meant for campus climates, students, faculty, and administrators? Wherever antisemitism is influential, Jewish students may be called to account (stand accused) for their support of Israel; Jewish students who identify as Jewish, wish to be liberal like their parents, and join progressive social organizations on campuses are increasingly likely to discover themselves pronounced guilty of racism and white privilege and barred from participation. It means that in the discourse of campus arguments, Jewish students are often linked with powerful collectives allegedly controlling banks and the media in the minds of some fellow students or with a lobby that supposedly has the power to shape American action in the Middle East. Jewish students are rebuked and told without any historical understanding that they cannot know what real oppression is—even when they are the grandchildren of Holocaust survivors.

At San Francisco State University, Jewish students faced open calls in late spring 2017 that Jews supporting Israel should get off the campus. A lawsuit against the university that has been settled claims, "Jewish students who are open about their Jewish identities . . . feel vulnerable, intimidated, and threatened on their own campus."[19] At the University of Illinois, SJP equated fascism, white supremacy, and Zionism in a divestment resolution: "If you support Israel, you're a racist and a fascist."[20] Nearly as disconcerting, at New York University, where there have been several successful BDS campaigns, fifty-three student groups last spring declared support for BDS and agreed to boycott and quarantine two Jewish groups supporting Israel. Despite a mild statement from university leaders saying this violates NYU's values, a discriminatory ghetto appears, defining who can join in progressive activities and who is excluded.[21]

The challenge in dealing with left antisemitism is to openly identify and point out the hate, especially to antiracists (much like those in the British Labour Party) who think that they are not antisemitic and that no hate exists. Supporters of Jewish students must aggressively call it out when it appears, work to help students comprehend it, and press administrators to follow up and enforce codes of faculty and student conduct when students engage in open disruption of Jewish-sponsored events. Hate directed at Jewish students deserves no less response than hate directed at other minority students. Disruption of free speech violates the idea of a university. British sociologist David Hirsh argues that we must see antisemitism on campus as a social phenomenon, not just as a social attitude of hostility or hatred. Like other forms of racism, it is embodied in patterns of thinking and behaving, supported in discursive and institutional forms, propagated in narratives spoken to others and to oneself, and expressed in purposive actions and restatements of classic themes.[22] It is also reinforced in open exclusions. What are the consequences of the mainstreaming on campus of classic canards about Jews, the return of exclusionary behavior toward Jews and Jewish organizations, and the renewed sense that Jews are a problem?

Reports in 2018 indicated that the antisemitic targeting of students on campus increased after the Squirrel Hill shootings in Pittsburgh in October and that, in the face of this, university leaders initially failed to speak out quickly or specifically enough.[23] Statements at Columbia and Dartmouth, for instance, failed to satisfy and needed to be reissued. Such failures left students, supportive faculty, and parents dissatisfied. The demand was to message current and prospective students, families, and community members that such hate and intolerance will not be tolerated.[24] Talia Katz, the daughter of an Israeli immigrant, in a statement like many others in the recent period, recounted the accumulating difficulties at the University of Michigan a year earlier—seeing swastikas on bathroom walls, walking past apartheid walls at the center of campus, watching out for reprimands from professors and teaching assistants for being Jewish and supporting Israel, and hearing frequent statements about Jewish power, influence, and privilege. And if that were not enough, the place of Black nationalist thought in some current Black protests on campus pressures Jews to respond to claims that Jews are white and that the Israeli-Palestinian conflict is a conflict between whites with power and people of color who lack power, a misleading analogy and ignorant flight of fantasy.

University leaders have gotten better recently at responding more vigorously to antisemitic speech and incidents, although it appears that responses are quickest and strongest to incidents of right antisemitism. In reaction to antisemitic flyers found at UC Davis, Chancellor Gary May, who had been under pressure for not speaking out, spoke quickly to denounce these in mid-October 2018, asserting, "I won't stand for intolerance of any kind."[25] Duke president Vincent E. Price sent a letter to the Duke community on November 19, 2018, when a tribute on campus to those killed at the Tree of Life Synagogue in Pittsburgh was defaced by a large red swastika. He planned to join with public officials and community leaders to develop a program of education and activism to confront antisemitism on campus and in Durham. University leaders at Cornell, the University of Tennessee Knoxville, and elsewhere offered firm statements and gathered besieged Jewish students together. But Jewish students wanted the universities, they said, to educate students more actively about antisemitism, put together workshop initiatives, and sponsor appropriate training. At about the same time, President Melvin Oliver of tiny Pitzer College reacted forcefully to a faculty advisory vote to close down the study-abroad program at Haifa University in the Jewish state, saying forthrightly that such action was out of step with core values of the university and opposed to the academic freedom of students. So strong was Oliver's fine statement that the ten chancellors of the University of California followed suit in mid-December, declaring their continued opposition to the academic boycott.[26]

A Promising Policy Initiative: The University of California Principles against Intolerance

Antisemitic themes in political discourse, antisemitic markings on buildings, antisemitic clashes during apartheid week, and BDS-related efforts to disrupt events or isolate Jewish student groups are problems with which university leaders must now regularly deal. The most constructive initiative has been the creation by the University of California Board of Regents of a set of Principles against Intolerance, which forthrightly condemned "anti-Semitism, anti-semitic forms of Zionism, and other forms of discrimination."[27] The report and principles emerged from several years of turmoil on California public campuses accompanied by outright antisemitic narratives and claims.

The principles that the regents adopted were applicable to students and faculty at all UC campuses immediately, but purposive action awaited subsequent implementation. The principles steered clear of recommending disciplinary punishments or imposing hard-and-fast guidelines. The writers envisioned a process in which each campus would define the concepts related to local experience and context and find distinctive ways to integrate policy into local practice. Remarkably, this was the first time an American public university had gone on record about the need to respond actively to antisemitism as well as to other forms of hatred and discrimination and to condemn related actions such as disruption and harassment.

The principles called on university leaders to confront intolerance by speaking out against hatred. In the face of disagreement about how to define antisemitism and particularly its relation to anti-Zionism, and amid worry by some faculty that university action would cramp teaching, debate, and scholarship, the regents courageously called on university leaders to apply the Principles against Intolerance and other university antidiscrimination policies to the full extent permissible under law. Orders from the Office of the President to campus chancellors demanded that they have processes in place to respond promptly, at the highest levels, when intolerant or discriminatory acts occur.[28]

The University of California at Irvine (UCI) was the first to make progress and offer leadership and example to other UC campuses, especially after a student disruption in mid-May 2016. Pro-Palestinian students chanted, "Long live the Intifada," and physically intimidated Jewish students gathered to watch a film until UCI campus police were called and escorted the targeted students to safety. The principles had promised an end to harassment, threat, assaults, and vandalism. Activist Jewish groups now demanded of UCI chancellor Howard Gillman, "What Is Your Plan for Implementing the Regents Principles against Intolerance?"[29] Patience also wore thin as the postincident investigation dragged on into summer and when SJP, the offending group, received only a written warning.

In this context, "to ensure alignment with the Regents' statement," Chancellor Gillman asked historian Douglas E. Haynes, vice provost for academic equity, diversity, and inclusion, to lead a comprehensive assessment of UCI's policies, procedures, and practices. Haynes consulted with community partners, students, the Advisory Council on Campus Climate, Culture, and Inclusion, the Faculty Academic Senate, and others and produced a report, titled *Higher Ground: The Alignment of UCI's Policies, Principles, and Programs with the UC Regents' Principles against Intolerance*. The report made nineteen recommendations about integrating the principles into UCI practice and improving the climate for Jewish students as part of the effort to create "inclusive excellence."[30] It acknowledged the importance of doing more and better for Jewish students, who reported high levels of satisfaction with UCI but stated that they experienced "implicit and explicit bias, and perhaps more disturbing, fear." They were subjected to demeaning stereotypes and disruptive actions. Much was due to a schedule of invited speakers or sponsored exhibitions that made outrageous comparisons of Israeli policies and actions to those of Nazi Germany during the liquidation of European Jewry. The report also acknowledged "a sense of situational social isolation" due to a reluctance by non-Jewish organizations to include Jews supporting Israel in social justice projects.

The *Higher Ground* report highlighted a commitment to regular annual programming on the challenge of antisemitism in the US and globally, including "the circumstance under which legitimate anti-Zionism protesting crosses the line of acceptability and becomes a form of antisemitism"; it also committed to creating university-sponsored programming aimed at educating student government leaders and social justice student groups about the concerns of Jewish students. UCI promised to publicly and specifically name acts of bias and bigotry, including antisemitism, with other forms of hate, and to upgrade campus police training. The report also committed UCI to engage in extensive education and training initiatives, including new freshman seminars, general education courses, and capstone projects, as well as to explore adding faculty resources in Israel studies and Jewish studies.

University leaders affirmed the principles and acknowledged antisemitism as a threat to inclusive community. When antisemitism reared its head, administrators committed to identify it as such; they would speak out against bigotry and point it out as threatening to community. In matters of speech, administrators would speak out. In matters of conduct, they would condemn acts of antisemitism violating the rights of others to free speech and assembly, institute investigative and judicial proceedings, and fairly enforce codes of behavior.

By the end of 2018, actions were also underway on several other UC campuses to develop initiatives, including at UCLA, UC Davis, and UC Riverside, for which UCI's actions were instructive. To date, building on the *Higher Ground* recommendations, UC Irvine has moved more quickly and further than other campuses to develop a coherent response. The effort has sponsored significant academic change on campus, including the development of a new Center for Jewish Studies with courses on antisemitism and on Israel. It has also involved creating a UCI Academy for Inclusion involving new courses, research opportunities, and cocurricular and public-affairs programming to promote dialogue and engagement. Yet, disappointingly, nothing has thus far stemmed the commitment by SJP and pro-Palestinian students at UCI—or at the other campuses—to mount an annual anti-Zionism week coinciding with Holocaust commemoration or to soften SJP's desire in the name of BDS to continue disrupting Jewish student events. On March 10, 2017, SJP students repeated the disruption carried out the year before, shouting down an IDF Reservists panel and forcing program organizers to take attendees (accompanied by police) out the side of the building.[31] In August 2017, after a substantial investigation, UCI put SJP on academic probation for two years.

Adopting the principles was a significant step forward in highlighting the problem of antisemitism on California campuses, but the model did not stem the tide of pro-Palestinian disruption of Jewish student events and activities. In summer 2018, the Office of the President of the University of California was organizing campus leaders to push implementation further.[32] More needed to be done to deal with continued disruptions of Jewish-sponsored events and to address the continued isolation felt by Jewish students at many campuses.

Notes

1. Joe Heim, "Recounting a Day of Rage, Hate, Violence, and Death," *Washington Post*, August 17, 2017, https://www.washingtonpost.com/graphics/2017/local/charlottesville-timeline/?utm_term=.2067df7fc235; Jonathan D. Sarna, "The Future of the Pittsburg Synagogue Massacre," *Tablet*, November, 5, 2018, https://www.tabletmag.com/jewish-news-and-politics/274291/future-pittsburgh-synagogue-massacre; Lila Corwin Berman, "American Jews Always Believed the U.S. Was Exceptional. We Were Wrong," *Washington Post*, November 1, 2018, https://www.washingtonpost.com/outlook/american-jews-always-believed-the-us-was-exceptional-we-were-wrong/2018/11/01/43be2f62-dd7c-11e8-b3f0-62607289efee_story.html?utm_term=.6760937b44ba.

2. "Survey of College and University Presidents 2019," discussed in Doug Lederman, "The Mood Brightens: A Survey of Presidents," Inside Higher Education, March 8, 2019, https://www.insidehighered.com/news/survey/2019-survey-college-and-university-presidents.

3. For a different view, see Kenneth Marcus, *The Definition of Antisemitism* (New York: Oxford University Press, 2015).

4. Useful background reading is available in Walter Laqueur, *The Changing Face of Antisemitism: From Ancient Times to the Present Day* (New York: Oxford University Press, 2008); David Nirenberg, *Anti-Judaism: The Western Tradition* (New York: W. W. Norton and Sons, 2014).

5. Albert Memmi, *Portrait of a Jew* (New York: Orion, 1962), 21–22, 25–26, 36–38, 56–57, 82ff.

6. Rebekah Katz, "BDS Is a Denial of My Existence," *The Phoenix*, October 25, 2018, https://swarthmorephoenix.com/2018/10/25/bds-is-a-denial-of-my-existence/. See also personal stories of Arielle Mokhtarzadeh and Ben Rosenberg at UCLA, Brennan Thorpe at Portland State, and David Bernstein at Santa Cruz in Anthony Berteaux, "In the Safe Spaces on Campus, No Jews Allowed," *The Tower*, February 2016, http://www.thetower.org/article/in-the-safe-spaces-on-campus-no-jews-allowed/. Bernstein observed, "Anti-Semitism is still very much a problem that each and every one of us are faced with every single day."

7. Leonard Saxe, Theodor Sasson, Graham Wright, and Shahar Hecht, *Antisemitism and the College Campus: Perception and Reality* (Waltham, MA: Cohen Center for Modern Jewish Studies, 2015).

8. Corky Siemaszko, "Anti-Semitic Incidents on College Campuses on the Rise: ADL," NBC News, June 22, 2016, https://www.nbcnews.com/news/us-news/anti-semitic-incidents-college-campuses-rise-adl-n596966. Antisemitic incidents on university and college campuses doubled further in 2016–17, said ADL, from 108 to 204 (89 percent). "2017 Audit of Anti-Semitic Incidents," ADL, https://www.adl.org/resources/reports/2017-audit-of-anti-semitic-incidents.

9. AMCHA Initiative, *Report on Antisemitic Activity during the First Half of 2016 at U.S. Colleges and Universities with the Largest Jewish Undergraduate Populations*, 2016, https://www.amchainitiative.org/wp-content/uploads/2016/07/Report-on-Antisemitic-Activity-During-the-First-Half-of-2016.pdf.

10. Sam Sokol, "University of California Forms Panel to Probe Antisemitism on Campus," *Jerusalem Post*, September 20, 2015, https://www.jpost.com/Diaspora/University-of-California-forms-panel-to-probe-anti-Semitism-on-campus-416743?.

11. Josh Logue, "Anti-Semitism vs. Anti-Zionism," Inside Higher Education, March 24, 2016, https://www.insidehighered.com/news/2016/03/24/u-california-draft-policy-intolerance-modified-and-moves-forward.

12. Ari Y. Kelman et al., *Safe and on the Sidelines: Jewish Students and the Israel-Palestine Conflict on Campus* (Palo Alto, CA: Stanford Graduate School of Education, 2017). Kelman et al. suggests that there are lower levels of antisemitism on campus than Jewish organizations think. This interesting but flawed study draws on data from only a few campuses and relies on a nonrepresentative sample of participants excluding Jews openly identified as Jews and active in Hillel. Kelman et al. surveys just five campuses in California and sixty-six undergraduates.

13. See Bernard-Henri Lévy, "Anti-Zionism Is the New Dressing for the Old Passion of Antisemitism" (conversation with Charlie Rose, New York, January 11, 2017); see also Bernard-Henri Lévy, "Fighting Back against the New Antisemitism" (speech, Jewish Community Center of San Francisco, June 16, 2015). See Jonathan Sacks, "The Mutating Virus: Understanding Antisemitism," September 27, 2016, http://rabbisacks.org/mutating-virus-understanding-antisemitism/.

14. Robert Wistrich, "Anti-Zionism and Anti-Semitism," *Jewish Political Studies Review* 16 (2004): 3–4, http://www.jcpa.org/phas/phas-wistrich-f04.htm.

15. Alan Johnson, "The Left and the Jews: Time for a Rethink," *Fathom*, Autumn 2015, http://fathomjournal.org/the-left-and-the-jews-time-for-a-rethink/. See also David Hirsh, *Contemporary Left Antisemitism*. (London: Routledge, 2017).

16. Eric K. Ward, "Skin in the Game: How Antisemitism Animates White Nationalism," Political Research Associates, June 29, 2017, https://www.politicalresearch.org/2017/06/29/skin-in-the-game-how-antisemitism-animates-white-nationalism/.

17. See Jerome Ostrov, *Finding the Right School in the Era of BDS and Intersectionality: A Jewish Parents' Guide to Colleges in the 2018–19 Academic Year* (n.p.: independent publisher, 2018).

18. Kenneth Waltzer, "From 'Intersectionality' to the Exclusion of Jewish Students: BDS Makes a Worrying Turn on US Campuses," *Fathom*, July 2018, http://fathomjournal.org/from-intersectionality-to-the-exclusion-of-jewish-students-bds-makes-a-worrying-turn-on-us-campuses/; Kenneth Waltzer (with Mark G. Yudof), "Antisemitisms of the Left and Right," *Times of Israel*, October 21, 2017; Kenneth Waltzer, "Some Notes on Antisemitism in the U.S. Today," *Times of Israel*, March 8, 2017.

19. Alexander Nazaryan, "Middle East Conflict Comes to US Campuses as Jewish Students File Antisemitism Suit," June 25, 2017, https://www.newsweek.com/anti-semitism-alleged-san-fran-state-628469.

20. See Tamara Zieve, "After 'Anti-Fascist' Rally Targets Zionists, U. of Illinois 'Welcomes' Jews," *Jerusalem Post*, September 27, 2017, https://www.jpost.com/Diaspora/After-anti-fascist-rally-targets-Zionists-U-of-Illinois-welcomes-Jews-506069.

21. Shiri Moshe, "Advocates Urge NYU to Take Action against Student Clubs That Pledged to Boycott Pro-Israel Peers," *Algemeiner*, April 26, 2018, https://www.algemeiner.com/2018/04/26/advocates-urge-nyu-to-take-action-against-student-clubs-that-pledged-to-boycott-pro-israel-peers/; Kenneth Waltzer, "Illiberalism on Campus: Boycotting Jewish Students at NYU," *Times of Israel*, April 17, 2018.

22. Hirsh, *Contemporary Left Antisemitism*.

23. Jeremy Bauer-Wolf, "A Surge of Anti-Semitism," Inside Higher Education, December 5, 2018, https://www.insidehighered.com/news/2018/12/05/anti-semitic-incidents-surge-college-campuses-after-pittsburgh-synagogue-shooting.

24. Bauer-Wolf, "Surge of Anti-Semitism"; Talia Katz, "Anti-Semitism, Run Amok on Campus: A University of Michigan Student Says It's Time to Say 'Enough,'" *Daily News*, October 13, 2018, https://www.nydailynews.com/opinion/ny-oped-anti-semitism-run-amok-on-campus-20181012-story.html.

25. Gary S. May, "Statement on Community Principles," UC Davis Leadership, October 8, 2018, https://leadership.ucdavis.edu/news/message-uc-davis-community-0.

26. "UC Chancellors Issue Statement Opposing Israel Boycotts," *Jewish News of Northern California*, December 13, 2018, https://www.jweekly.com/2018/12/13/uc-chancellors-join-to-oppose-israel-boycotts/.

27. University of California Regents Working Group, *Final Report of the Regents Working Group on Principles against Intolerance*, January 22, 2016, https://regents.universityofcalifornia.edu/policies/4403.pdf.

28. "Regents Policy: Principles against Intolerance," UCI Office of Academic Integrity and Student Conduct, accessed January 28, 2021, https://aisc.uci.edu/policies/pacaos/principles-against-intolerance.php.

29. "Letter to UC Irvine Chancellor Gillman: 53 Groups Urge Immediate Response to SJP Disruption in Framework of Principles against Intolerance," AMCHA Initiative, June 10, 2017, https://amchainitiative.org/letter-to-uc-irvine-chancellor-gillman-June-2017-2

30. Douglas M. Haynes, *Higher Ground: The Alignment of UCI's Policies, Principles and Programs with the UC Regents' Principles against Intolerance*, October 2016, http://ucioie.wpengine.com/wp-content/uploads/2016/10/Higher_Ground.pdf.

31. "Letter to UC Irvine Chancellor Gillman," AMCHA Initiative; Rachel Frommer, "Pro-Israel Groups Claim Criminal Action at UC-Irvine Protest Call on School to Hold Perpetrators Accountable," *Algemeiner*, July 10, 2017.

32. Conversation with UC Vice Provost Yvette Gullatt by phone with Ken Waltzer, July 27, 2018. Disruption of Jewish students took place again at UCI in 2018 and at UCLA in 2018 despite the implementation of the principles.

KENNETH WALTZER is Professor Emeritus of History at Michigan State University and former Director of Jewish Studies. He was a Graduate Prize Fellow at Harvard and came to MSU in the early 1970s to help build James Madison College, the university's highly reputed residential college in public affairs. He later was dean and associate dean of the college. During a productive forty-three-year career at MSU teaching and researching urban and immigrant history and the Holocaust and antisemitism, he also helped build the field of Jewish studies. His most recent research has focused on the rescue of children and youths at Buchenwald and on patterns of social solidarity under extreme conditions in the camps. Professor Waltzer served from 2015 to 2019 as the founding executive director of the Academic Engagement Network, a national faculty association created to counter the BDS movement on American campuses.

7

In the Context of a Coarsened Climate
Campus Antisemitism and the Alt-Right, Alt-Lite, and Far Left

Linda Maizels

IN RECENT YEARS, A RISE IN ANTISEMITISM ON both the left and the right has led many who once thought otherwise to question the long-regnant narrative of American exceptionalism.[1] This chapter analyzes a particular segment of society, American college and university campuses, to provide a deeper understanding of contemporary antisemitism from both ends of the political spectrum. Specifically, this research asks whether and where there is confluence or disparity in the animosity expressed toward Jews or Israel by partisans of both the left and the right. The chapter concludes by speculating about what this might tell us about effectively combating antisemitism on campus, regardless of its provenance.

To answer the questions of what attributes, if any, the far right shares with the progressive left on American campuses and how such confluence or disparity affects expressions of campus antisemitism, this chapter examines five salient categories. The first two, Transgression and Trump, demonstrate that although the underlying ideologies of the two political extremes are at odds with one another on these topics, their interaction negatively influences the overall atmosphere of the campus for Jews and Israel supporters. The next three, Transmission, Truth, and purity, suggest that the far right and extreme left display some level of confluence in their methods or the ways in which they express hostility to Jews and to Israel. In order to keep the alliterative consistency of this rubric, this chapter defaults to explaining purity through the Hebrew translation *Taharanut*, thus prompting the (hopefully) helpful mnemonic device of the "five Ts" of campus antisemitism. Before discussion of the five Ts, a brief background section comprises a thumbnail sketch of antisemitism on campus and defines some essential terms.

Background: Charting Antisemitism on Campus

There were no significant national-level studies of attitudinal American antisemitism that looked specifically at campus antisemitism until the beginning of the twenty-first century.[2] However, after sponsoring similar surveys in 1992 and 1998, the Anti-Defamation League's (ADL's) 2002 national survey to measure public attitudes and opinions about Jews included information particular to American campuses. Unlike the previous surveys in the series, the 2002 version, conducted by the Marttila Communications Group and SWR Worldwide and entitled "Anti-Semitism in America," included two additional sections comprising survey responses from eight hundred college students and five hundred faculty members.

The 2002 survey was one of the first to show that anti-Israel attitudes were linked conclusively to some antisemitic tendencies. For those parsing the conclusions, this suggested that students and faculty might show greater propensities toward antisemitic attitudes because anti-Israel attitudes were more pronounced on campus. However, survey data also indicated that those with higher levels of education—including students and faculty—were shown to have lower levels of attitudinal antisemitism than other Americans.[3] Nevertheless, the perception of many in the American Jewish community, as well as scholars of the phenomenon, was that antisemitism was a growing issue on some American campuses because of its connection to anti-Israel and anti-Zionist activities.

Scholars and Jewish organizations now routinely study campus antisemitism as a specific and separate subset of antisemitism in the United States, but they still have difficulty agreeing about the scope and the severity of the problem. One of the most contentious issues is that of finding a broadly acceptable definition of antisemitism.[4] Supporters say that a definition is necessary to offer guidelines for university administrators on the difference between legitimate criticism of Israel and antisemitism. Critics, even those who are sympathetic to Israel, are quick to point out that the danger of enshrining a definition of antisemitism that is too rigid on the subject of criticism of Israel may lead to unwanted limitations on politically protected freedom of speech.[5]

It is no coincidence that the campus discourse influences and is influenced by a similarly heated dialogue on Israel and antisemitism currently taking place within the Democratic Party between centrist liberals and an increasingly vocal progressive wing. Two junior Democratic congresswomen, Rashida Tlaib and Ilhan Omar, the first two Muslim women elected to the US Congress, have unnerved centrist Democrats with comments that are openly anti-Israel and, in some cases, antisemitic. Republicans have also inserted themselves into the fray, prompting the allegation that conservatives hope to use antisemitism, particularly that associated with anti-Israel or anti-Zionist sentiments, as a wedge issue to split the Democratic Party.[6]

Definitions

The Alt-Right

The organized Jewish community has followed the waxing and waning of right-wing antisemitism in the United States in general for decades and has taken a hard look in recent years at similar manifestations on campus. ADL's Center on Extremism continues to track a growing number of white supremacist propaganda efforts targeting college campuses, including the distribution of racist, antisemitic, and Islamophobic fliers, stickers, banners, and posters. The 2017–18 data show a 77 percent increase in incidents from the previous academic year, with 292 cases reported, up from 165 in 2016–17.[7]

Since the 2016 election, the far right has reinvented itself as the alternative or "alt-right," a term coined and popularized by avowed white nationalist Richard Spencer.[8] Despite their attempts at some degree of unity, the alt-right is a fractious coalition of white supremacist, white nationalist, and white identity groups, some of which have been around for decades: neo-Nazis, the Ku Klux Klan, Christian identity, Patriot and militia groups, and others.[9] They espouse misogyny, homophobia, and racism, and while not all are Trump supporters, many approve of what they assume is his worldview.[10] Alt-right groups position themselves as hip and edgy, in part through their adherents' adept use of social media to appeal to a younger and more sophisticated urban audience and also to act as a contemporary rejoinder to the identity politics of the left.

The alt-right is thoroughly and unapologetically antisemitic. Civil rights strategist Eric Ward pointed out in a 2017 essay that "American White nationalism, which emerged in the wake of the 1960s civil rights struggle and descends from White supremacism, is a revolutionary social movement committed to building a Whites-only nation, and antisemitism forms its theoretical core." He also stressed that even more than racism, antisemitism is the "the lynchpin of the White nationalist belief system."[11] The far right imagines Jews as an alien, nonwhite group that has learned how to assimilate successfully into white America while simultaneously conspiring to bring about its downfall; this is a contrast with the campus left that asserts that Jews are white and privileged.

Campus manifestations of the alt-right usually originate outside of academia. The Unite the Right rally at the University of Virginia in Charlottesville on August 12, 2017, was originally publicized as a reaction to the decision by the city of Charlottesville to take down Confederate monuments and statues. The actual rally, however, was less about defending Confederate honor than it was a show of force by white supremacist and white nationalist individuals and groups. The blatant racism and antisemitism that ensued, including chants of "Jews will not replace us" and threatening behavior outside of a local synagogue, made a clear statement that the right-wing antisemitism of the outside world could easily encroach on American campuses.[12]

The Alt-Lite

The alt-lite shares some of the traits of the alt-right, such as its misogyny, its gleeful puncturing of leftist campus culture, its interest in transgression, sarcasm, and irony, and its disdain for what it sees as the effete, ineffectual politics of the mainstream right, which it refers to as "cuckservative," indicating that it has been cuckolded by liberal American culture. The ranks of the alt-lite include strident champions of bucking what its adherents see as the stifling political correctness dictated by campus progressivism, as well as ardent supporters of free speech; in this context, free speech usually means the right to freely offend others, including (or especially) those groups most supported by progressives: people of color, the LGBTQ community, and other marginalized groups.[13]

Still, most of the supporters of the alt-lite do not openly express white supremacy or white nationalism—although they do push back against the alleged privileging of the voices of women and people of color on campus and argue for the ability to openly express pride in their white, male, heterosexual identity. While some of the individuals identified as alt-lite may use antisemitic rhetoric, the alt-lite does not seem to have a specific Jewish problem at this time. The question is whether the alt-lite might be a metaphorical gateway to the hardcore white supremacy and antisemitism of the alt-right.[14]

The Progressive Left

Many of the scholars interested in twenty-first-century American antisemitism have busied themselves largely with manifestations of this phenomenon on the left, especially as they have seen it develop on American college and university campuses.[15] The American Jewish community has also invested much of its time, energy, and resources in combating antisemitism associated with the reflexive anti-Israelism and anti-Zionism characteristic of the contemporary progressive left, usually on campuses but sometimes in other localities congenial to left-of-center politics, such as mainstream Protestant churches and labor unions.[16]

Explicit in the progressive critique is that Israel is a settler-colonial state that is almost solely culpable for the Israeli-Arab conflict and the plight of the Palestinians. Israel, despite the fact that the majority of its population emigrated from countries in the Middle East and North Africa, is described as a nation filled with descendants of Europeans, while the Palestinians are seen as people of color and analogies are made between their plight and that of African Americans.[17]

The boycott, divestment, and sanctions (BDS) movement uses this critique to portray Israel as a racist and malevolent actor and to buoy its claims that Israel alone among the nations deserves to be isolated, marginalized, and punished for its actions. Student supporters of the BDS movement have had some success at passing student government resolutions condemning Israel and demanding that their schools divest all funds invested in Israeli companies or companies that students designate as assisting in the occupation of Palestinian lands. While none of these resolutions have had any effect on university or college investment portfolios, and such resolutions are routinely opposed by university and college presidents and their administrations, the BDS movement declares moral victory over the process, even when it loses the vote. Similarly, on the faculty level, a handful of academic associations have passed or attempted to pass resolutions that would lead to the boycott of Israeli academic institutions and, ultimately, Israeli faculty. While the resolutions themselves may not employ openly antisemitic rhetoric or tropes, a number of the leaders of the BDS movement have expressed their desire for a "one-state solution," and the conversations surrounding such efforts have included allegations about Jewish power and economic success that borrow liberally from traditional antisemitism.[18]

At the same time, American Jewish students are understood to be "white" and "privileged," which often translates in practical terms to exclusion from meaningful participation in the larger campus discourse on issues of identity. Jewish students, especially if they hope to enter into this discourse with an awareness of the long history of antisemitism or if they choose to identify as Zionists or supporters of Israel, may find that they are unwelcome because their Jewishness is seen a synonym for white oppression. One student, Isabel Storch Sherrell, described her experience at Oberlin College:

> Because at oberlin, and indeed in the US overall, Jews are viewed as white and privileged (sometimes even above the avg white privilege, since yaknow, we're all superrich and stuff) therefore our struggle does not intersect with other forms of racism and bigotry and ignorance that are so tenaciously fought against on campus. As a part of my processing and letting go of the pain I experienced, I will list a few memorable antisemitic moments/incidents here—
> 1. The multiple times the Holocaust was referred to as "white on white crime" by my POC peers and hip white Jewish peers . . . 2. That time a Jewish person made a comment on fb [Facebook] saying "the only reason people care about the Holocaust is because it happened to white people" and got tons of likes from white and POC friends alike . . . 5. That time I was told I should be ashamed for what my people are doing to the Palestinians, by someone I didn't even know, upon learning I was Jewish . . . 6. That time my African Studies professor had an antizionist jewish south african man come in to talk to the class about jazz and resistance. During Q&A she praised a Jewish student for their anti Israel comments relating Israel to South African apartheid. The prof then made funny faces and funny eyes when I spoke up and tried to make the point that we should try to understand the Israeli-Palestinian conflict within its OWN historical context and that its unfair to both Israelis and Palestinians to rely only on shaky comparisons. It was clear, in that classroom, who was the good Jew and who was the bad Jew, in that professors' eyes. I was bad . . . 7. Those times antiblack and antisemitic incidents occurred simultaneously, and then the uproar followed but the antisemitism was essentially ignored by the campus at large. And if I brought that up I was told "dont derail the real issue here." . . . 10. The fact that so many Jewish students are bullied into silence, whether its about their own ethnic identity . . . their relationship to Israel, or their concern about antisemitism in general/ on campus. 11. The intense and unrelenting vilification of Israel out of proportion to any other nation on the planet where terrible shit happens // People literally refusing to talk to me because I identify as a Zionist . . . 15. Generally antisemitic ideas floating around such as Jews are milking the Holocaust for their own gain// everything is as bad as the Holocaust except for the actual Holocaust which wasnt as bad as people say it was// Jews only care about themselves (another AAST professor told me, "your people really take care of each other" at first i thought it was a compliment but when i told my mother about it she explained that it was not) . . . 18. Having my own ethnic identity policed. Being told I was

simply European and Judaism is a religion not an ethnicity/ or that I am a descendent of Khazarian converts to Judaism and therefore have no right to claim any sort of indigenousness in the Levant.[19]

Contemporary identity politics are also intertwined with the concept of "intersectionality," a term coined by Kimberlé Crenshaw as a helpful legal concept to describe the "overlapping discriminations" experienced by Black women because the solutions to gender and racial discrimination assume that a woman is white and an African American is male. In a seminal article, Crenshaw explained, "Because the intersectional experience is greater than the sum of racism and sexism, any analysis that does not take intersectionality into account cannot sufficiently address the particular manner in which Black women are subordinated."[20]

The meaning of the term has morphed over the years since Crenshaw's essay was published and is now employed as an all-encompassing theory that links various marginalized groups and demands that their overlapping oppressions be recognized and opposed. Critics of intersectionality contend that it has become a dogma of sorts that demands allegiance to and support for a virtual party line of approved reactions to various oppressions experienced by identity groups. Intersectionality can also cause particular problems for Jews because support for Israel and Zionism is often defined as inherently oppressive to Palestinians and others.

For instance, in the violent aftermath of a white policeman shooting an African American teenager in Ferguson, Missouri, the slogan "From Ferguson to Palestine" grew in popularity to indicate that the issues of racism and discrimination faced by Black people in the United States were the same as the plight of the Palestinians under Israeli rule. In the political platform of the Movement for Black Lives, words such as *apartheid* and *genocide* were liberally applied as descriptors of Israel and its culpability for the Israeli-Palestinian conflict. Progressive Jews who are also pro-Israel were torn between their desire to support the Black community and their abhorrence for this segment of the platform.[21]

Under the umbrella of intersectionality, right-wing antisemitism is acknowledged as an issue, but antisemitism is almost never mentioned on its own and is usually paired with another oppression, such as racism or Islamophobia, probably because of the issue of perceived Jewish "whiteness." Sometimes, however, instances of right-wing antisemitism are ignored or overlooked. In the aftermath of Charlottesville, the National Women's Studies Association (NWSA) issued a statement condemning the racism and violence of the event. It was immediately called to the association's attention, however, that the blatant antisemitism expressed by the marchers had been completely ignored. The board hastened to make amends, but it was clear that the writers were so used to ignoring antisemitism that they could not see it even when it was right in front of their eyes. The amended statement reads as follows, with the additions in bolded italics:

> The National Women's Studies Association denounces the actions of white supremacists in Charlottesville, Virginia last weekend that terrorized that community and shocked the entire country. We further condemn the actions of James Alex Fields, Jr., who drove into a crowd of counter-protesters killing 32-year old Heather Heyer and injuring at least 19 others, and the stick-wielding vigilantes that viciously attacked and beat a young Black man, De'Andre Harris, in a nearby parking structure. ***We also condemn threats made against local synagogues, and the use of Nazi-era slogans such as "blood and soil" and "Jews will not replace us" at these protests.***
>
> White supremacy and fascism have always been intricately connected with misogyny, patriarchy, transphobia, homophobia, ableism, ***anti-Semitism***, and settler-colonial logics. This fact is evidenced both by the makeup of those who rallied last weekend—primarily young, white, able-bodied, cisgender men—and the messages promoted at the rally and by those supporting it, which included anti-woman and anti-LGBT slogans and statements. The NWSA believes that ending white supremacy is a primary feminist political objective.[22]

The political left's blind spot in dealing with antisemitism and Jewish issues brings up the related paradox of its recurring alliance with reactionary elements of Islam. One example of this type of cognitive dissonance is the support offered by the four main organizers of the 2017 Women's March for the Nation of Islam, specifically one of its leaders, Louis Farrakhan, who is notorious for decades of antisemitic, antiwhite, misogynist, and homophobic rhetoric.[23] The backlash to the organizers' intransigence on this issue, coupled with their hostility to confronting antisemitism in their ranks and allegations that they privileged issues of race and religion over core feminist topics, led to a precipitous drop in support for the march and the simultaneous growth of unaffiliated marches organized at the local level.[24]

In academia, the tenets of freedom of speech and academic freedom, particularly at a state university that receives federal funding, assert that the rights of speakers, even those with a message offensive to a segment of the campus population, should be protected.[25] Thus, speakers from the Nation of Islam have been a fixture on American campuses for decades, usually sponsored by Black student groups that are attracted by the speakers' calls for Black pride and achievement. Despite protests from Jewish students and other affected groups, the speakers' antiwhite and antisemitic messages are often either actively supported or dismissed as irrelevant by both Black student groups and progressives.[26] Similarly, when the Muslim Student Union (MSU) at the University of California Irvine hosted Sheikh Osman Umarji for a spring 2019 speech, he spoke without serious interruption, even when he accused US Jews of dual loyalty in their support of Israel and leveled unsubstantiated allegations about the Israeli military purposely destroying Palestinian crops.[27]

However, the courtesy afforded to a speaker who may have offended the sensibilities of Jewish or pro-Israel students was not accorded to former Israeli ambassador to the US Michael Oren, who was shouted down and prevented from speaking in 2010 on the Irvine campus; ten members of MSU were later found guilty of disrupting his speech.[28] Oren is certainly not alone in this distinction; attempts by progressive groups to disrupt and silence the public appearances of speakers supportive of Israel have been well documented. Even progressive speakers who are critical of Israel are opposed, particularly if they support engagement and dialogue rather than outright condemnation.[29]

Progressive groups also judge speakers on their previous statements when they decide whom to protest. This can include some highly offensive alt-right provocateurs but also includes those like feminist Ayaan Hirsi Ali, born into the Muslim faith in her native Somalia, where she was a victim of genital cutting. Brandeis University rescinded the honorary degree it had planned to award her and disinvited her from a planned speaking engagement after receiving pressure from a student-generated petition. Hirsi Ali criticizes Islam in general (not just its radical variant), contends that Islam must be "defeated," and voices her fears about the encroachment of political Islam in Europe and North America. She is also an outspoken supporter of Western values and make positive statements about Israel.[30] However, Linda Sarsour, one of the leaders of the Women's March who was hailed in a *New York Times* piece as a "Brooklyn homegirl in a hijab,"[31] was the commencement speaker at the City University of New York (CUNY) School of Public Health, despite her earlier dismissal of the oppression of women in Saudi Arabia and her support for some of the more repressive elements of sharia law; her only caveat concerning the treatment of women in the Middle East is that Zionism is incompatible with feminism. When Jewish groups protested her inclusion, they were supported by conservatives but opposed by progressives.[32] As one writer explained, "Linda Sarsour is a religiously conservative veiled Muslim woman, embracing a fundamentalist worldview requiring women to 'modestly' cover themselves, a view which has little to do with female equality and much more of a connection with the ideology of political Islam than feminism. Could we imagine a wig-wearing Orthodox woman emerging from a similar 'purity'-focused culture predicated on sexual segregation and covering women, headlining such an event? No, because she is rightly assumed to be intensely conservative, not progressive on issues surrounding women's roles and their bodies."[33]

The reactionary tactic of restricting freedom of speech on campus is no longer associated primarily with conservative politics as it may have been in previous decades. Instead, leftist groups, including Students for Justice in Palestine (SJP) and Jewish Voice for Peace (JVP), engage in "deplatforming" or silencing speakers who diverge from the progressive agenda. As the example of Sarsour suggests, this agenda is not always logically consistent, but it does seem to have one constant: opposition to Israel and sometimes to Jews. The examples given above consequently provide a natural segue into the next section, which examines the confluence or disparity between the ideology and tactics of the political right and those of the political left and how this affects expressions of antisemitism on campus.

The Five Ts

Transgression

For the first category in this rubric, it is clear that the campus right and the campus left are on entirely different trajectories. In simple terms, the contemporary campus right embraces transgression, while the contemporary left eschews it. But how might this affect their relationship to Jews and Israel, and how might this result in expressions of antisemitism?

Embracing transgression was once one of the defining features of the progressive movement in America. The bohemian left of the 1950s, followed by the political New Left of the 1960s and 1970s and the concurrent rise of the youth counterculture, shattered what remained of the postwar cultural consensus on a number of controversial and transgressive topics, including political expression, sexual and gender norms, drug use, and freedom of speech. Supporters of the Berkeley Free Speech Movement demanded the political freedom to criticize the government, while comedians such as Mort Sahl, Lenny Bruce, and others labeled "sick comics" led the way in promoting a style of humor that purported to make Americans laugh by insulting everyone, regardless of race, gender, religion, or personal creed.[34]

Many or most of the supporters of the contemporary campus left, in contrast, now support the curtailment of at least some of the speech that they find offensive.[35] Despite the fact that the left achieved at worst partial victories in certain aspects of the culture wars—for example, passing the Civil Rights and Voting Rights Acts, legalizing gay marriage, and normalizing and supporting women's increased participation in the work force—these triumphs have led to a less permissive attitude in the area of expression. Leftists' often rigid devotion to viewpoint orthodoxy on subjects such as gender and race frequently translates to callout culture and public shaming if individuals stray from preapproved political stances. What this can mean in practice is that those who do not follow these dictates—including opposition to Israel and Zionism—are condemned, and this condemnation may also include anti-Jewish or antisemitic rhetoric or actions.[36]

The silencing of pro-Israel speech is a notable example of where transgression is assumed even before a speaker has the chance to say anything provocative. The list of speakers who have been shouted down and kept from addressing campus audiences since 2000 includes former Israeli prime minister Ehud Olmert, Israeli army reservists, Jerusalem mayor Nir Barkat, and Israel's former ambassador to the United States Michael Oren.[37] The dictates of the campus left call for the suppression of speech that is deemed offensive, and any positive information about Israel or Zionism can be deemed oppressive to progressive sensibilities. Zionists, in some cases, are automatically seen as equivalent to racists, neo-Nazis, and other undesirable groups.[38]

However, there is a long history of speakers who are offensive to Jewish or pro-Israel sensibilities but are passionately defended by the campus left, especially if they bring a message of empowerment to students who are a part of minority identity groups.[39] Similarly, speakers who make unfounded accusations about Israel are defended by university administrations on the basis of free speech and academic freedom, even when their accusations resonate with classic antisemitic tropes.[40]

In contrast to the left, the denizens of the right, as detailed above, have become passionate supporters of freedom of expression, which often translates to the freedom to offend. The alt-right champions freedom of speech to gain legitimacy in voicing white supremacist viewpoints denigrating other identity groups that they dislike, including Jews. However, as this chapter explores further, the alt-right's presence on campus is limited and usually comes from off campus.

The alt-lite is somewhat more complex in its support for freedom of speech. Angela Nagle, in her book *Kill All Normies,* underlines the impulse toward transgression as one of the motivating factors behind the alt-lite. Nagle alleges that its proponents lifted the idea of transgression from the radical left and the counterculture of the 1960s and its supporters' reaction to conservative orthodoxies. Consequently, the alt-lite positions itself as a radical and transgressive force against leftist or progressive orthodoxies and has a more pronounced on-campus presence.[41]

This penchant for transgression is ably personified by Milo Yiannopoulos, a British media personality and provocateur whom the ADL labels "an alt-right apologist" rather than part of the alt-right. His "Dangerous Faggot" tour in 2016, in which he spouted views such as "Feminism is Cancer," was an attempt to inflame progressives at campuses around the country.[42] Yiannopoulos understood that transgression was at the heart of the rise of this new incarnation of the right. In "An Establishment Conservative's Guide to the Alt-Right," published by Breitbart, he explained, "Today's youth are drawn to the alt-right for the same reason that young Baby Boomers were drawn to the New Left in the 1960s: because it promises fun, transgression, and a challenge to social norms they don't understand."[43]

Despite his inflammatory and offensive rhetoric, Yiannopoulos is often classified as alt-lite rather than alt-right, in part because he is openly gay, has been romantically and sexually linked to men of color, and claims freely that he is of Jewish descent.[44] However, one might ask if his continuing quest for spotlight and notoriety after his earlier fall from grace may pull Yiannopoulos into a more overtly alt-right sphere. Recently, he was caught trying to troll a Jewish journalist by sending her $14.88: 14 to represent the infamous "Fourteen Words" (a mantra about securing "a future for white children") and 88 to represent the eighth letter of the alphabet and "Heil Hitler." Although payment platforms PayPal and Venmo barred him from using their services after this action, Yiannopoulos received more of the publicity that he clearly craves.[45] Thus, Yiannopoulos may foreshadow the trajectory of some of the transgressive alt-lite denizens on campus and the way that they might be receptive to more overt antisemitism in the future.[46]

The opposing approaches to transgressing cultural norms demonstrated by both the alt-right and the progressive left can lead to challenges for Jews and Israel supporters on campus. The alt-right has no problem with attacking Jews or Jewish interests; the progressive left chooses when transgression is acceptable, which can be damaging to both Jews and Israel supporters; and the alt-lite is, at this point, agnostic on the question of Jews and Israel. This brings up several questions. First, does the progressive left's animosity toward Jews and Israel contribute to a campus culture that is more accepting of antisemitism from the far right? Second, is the alt-lite willing to accommodate Jews, Israel, and other Jewish issues because its sympathizers see Jews—and their support of Israel—as similarly beleaguered by the campus left? Third, will this implied recognition that Jews and Israel are allies of the right exacerbate the problems of antisemitism that Jews and Israel supporters may face on campus? The next section looks more closely at the problems caused by a perceived alliance between Jews, Israel, and the contemporary right.

Trump

Clearly, the reactions of the campus left and right to former president Trump and his administration is another area where there is almost no confluence of opinion. The question remains the same as it was above: how might the two sides' divergent views on the Trump presidency affect their respective relationships to Jews and Israel, and how might this result in expressions of antisemitism?

It is not the purpose of this chapter to argue whether former president Donald Trump is personally anti-Jewish or antisemitic. However, there is widespread consensus that the president's flouting of established social and political conventions, indulgence in vulgar and offensive language, and penchant for amplifying far-right conspiracy theories contributes to a less civil, more coarsened climate that implies greater latitude for hateful speech. Critics also maintain that he has both explicitly and implicitly encouraged racism, misogyny, homophobia, and antisemitism. All of these phenomena feed into the needs of the alt-right and alt-lite, which then clash, sometimes violently, with campus progressives' ideals.

Although the majority of American Jews register and vote Democratic, Israel is increasingly identified both on- and off-campus as a right-wing or conservative concern. This is in part because of the close relationship between former president Trump and Israeli prime minister Benjamin Netanyahu, which is a stark contrast with what was understood to be a more antagonistic relationship between the Israeli prime minister and former president Barack Obama. However, another explanation for this shift is that young people no longer see Israel as a country that shares their progressive values. Consequently, while the majority of Jews still support Israel, the strength of this relationship appears to be waning for younger generations.[47]

These trends may have been exacerbated by Richard Spencer's grotesque tribute to Israel, in which he stated that he was a "white Zionist" who hoped to create an ethnic enclave for whites that mimicked the Jewish state. Spencer's disingenuous statement may have fooled some on the left into proclaiming that this rhetorical support was sufficient evidence to prove that Israel is inextricably tied to the racist right. However, even a cursory examination of right-wing websites demonstrates that the alt-right in general is not supportive of Zionism or the national self-determination of the Jewish people.[48]

There is an argument to be made that the right's support for Israel, including the close ties between the Trump and Netanyahu administrations, exacerbates the anti-Israel tendencies of the left, on campus and elsewhere. In a sense, the Trump presidency placed Jews and Israel supporters in double jeopardy. The coarsened climate on campus leaves Jews vulnerable to antisemitic attacks from the right, while the perception that Jews and Israel were allies of the Trump presidency invites acrimony from the left against Zionism, Israel, and sometimes Jews. As a result, young progressive Jews who want to support Israel may feel isolated, vulnerable, and subject to antisemitism from both sides of the political spectrum.[49]

Transmission

Transmission, the third category, refers to the ways that campus political actors and organizers transmit their overall message to their peers. This is an area of confluence because both the right and the left make effective use of social media and internet technologies to transmit and propagate their messages. Whether it is the political right using Facebook to trumpet its transgressive message and inviting others to join them in flouting established convention, or the political left wielding social media as a means of appropriating the moral high ground and shaming others into ideological conformity, both sides have clearly mastered the integration of technology into their methods of operation and messaging transmission. How might this affect their respective relationships to Jews and Israel and result in expressions of antisemitism?

In 1999, long before the internet had become the ubiquitous global presence that it is today, Kenneth S. Stern recognized that technology could create a virtual connection between otherwise disparate groups through their mutual animosity toward Jews and their support for Holocaust denial: "Once someone finds one site, he or she will be advised of, and with one mouse-click transported to, other like-minded groups through 'links.' Each hate group no longer communicates in isolation: it uses the Internet to advertise and to create the illusion that hate is not practiced in isolation at the fringes, but is part of a strong worldwide movement. The irony is that a black hate group that dehumanizes whites and a white hate group that dehumanizes blacks frequently are two mouse-clicks from each other, the connective tissue being antisemitism in general, and Holocaust denial in particular."⁵⁰ The salient shared factor between disparate groups is that both sides of the political spectrum not only oppose each other but also assume that Jews and Israel are allied in some way with their opponent. The method for transmitting this information is often electronic, but other, more primitive, technologies are no less effective. Cartoons, symbols, and slogans can be transmitted through print media, murals, and fliers.

The neo-Nazis behind the *Daily Stormer* under Andrew Anglin have orchestrated several campaigns to transmit their message by blanketing campuses with antisemitic fliers. In 2016 and 2017, fliers proclaiming "WHITE MAN ARE YOU SICK AND TIRED OF THE JEWS DESTROYING YOUR COUNTRY THROUGH MASS IMMIGRATION AND DEGENERACY?" were automatically printed when campus systems were hacked at more than a dozen campuses.⁵¹ In 2018, fliers blaming Jews for sexual assault allegations against Supreme Court Justice Brett Kavanaugh read "EVERY TIME SOME ANTI-WHITE, ANTI-AMERICAN, ANTI-FREEDOM EVENT TAKES PLACE, YOU LOOK AT IT AND IT'S JEWS BEHIND IT," while cartoonish pictures of prominent Jews such as Senators Chuck Schumer and Dianne Feinstein, their foreheads marked with Jewish stars, stared threateningly at a picture of a hapless Kavanaugh.⁵² White supremacist propaganda on campuses, usually produced by off-campus groups, increased by 7 percent during the 2018–19 academic year.⁵³

The left does not in any way have a similarly orchestrated campus campaign. In 2019, however, at Tufts University, a flyer with imagery borrowed from a cartoon created by the Black Panthers in the 1960s was placed at the Hillel at Tufts University. In the original, three pigs carrying rifles and wearing flak jackets labeled "Local Police," "National Guard," and "Marines" stand below the headline "It's all the same." The newer version posted at Tufts accompanies the graphic with the words "DESTROY ISRAELI APARTHEID FORCES AND AMERIKKAN PIGS WHICH FUND IT. FREE PALESTINE." As of this writing, there is no indication of whether the flier was produced by an on- or off-campus group.⁵⁴

This type of message transmission is not a new phenomenon for leftist groups. In the 1990s, for instance, there was a long-running conflict over a mural of Malcolm X created by a member of the Pan-Afrikan Student Union, commissioned by the Student Union Governing Board, and paid for by student activity funds that included images of "Stars of David superimposed with dollar signs, pentagrams and skulls and crossbones, and the words 'African Blood' painted prominently."[55]

While remaining true to their respective ideologies, both the alt-right and the left use Jews, Jewish issues, and Israel symbolically to communicate their very different larger political agendas. But a swastika employed by the far right as a vehicle to demonstrate admiration for the Nazi program of genocide and a swastika used by the left to equate Israel with the Third Reich are both used to denigrate and intimidate Jewish students and Israel supporters. The confluence in transmission of two ideologically different messages produces an effect that is essentially the same.

Truth

The fourth category in this rubric, truth, demonstrates confluence between the two extremes of campus politics. Both sides show willingness to bend and twist information to fulfill their immediate and long-term political needs. How might this affect their relationship to Jews and Israel, and how might this result in expressions of antisemitism?

There is historical precedent to demonstrate how politically motivated untruths are used by both the political left and right in an academic context. In the 1990s, the Committee for Open Debate on the Holocaust made a splash by attempting to place ads in campus newspapers denying the Holocaust; some student editors, swayed by specious arguments about "free speech," consented to run the ads, while others refused.[56] At roughly the same time, faculty members in African and African American studies such as Leonard Jeffries of City College of New York and Tony Martin of Wellesley College began to assign readings to their students such as *The Secret Relationship between Blacks and Jews*, a book rife with antisemitic content and Holocaust denial that assigns almost sole culpability for the transatlantic slave trade to Jews. While leftists would not, for the most part, get on board with right-wing Holocaust deniers, there were those on both the student and faculty levels willing to excuse faculty and students of color for their support of false history because they were from oppressed minority groups.[57]

The contemporary right is increasingly open to a world of "alternative facts."[58] This is not a new phenomenon; Holocaust deniers have long had a similar relationship to evidence-based truths. What may be new, however, is the appeal that a wide variety of dubious conspiracy theories have to provide simple explanations for complex problems for an ever-broadening slice of the general population. In this worldview, the massacre of grade school children in Sandy Hook, Connecticut, was a "false flag" operation meant to discredit gun owners; the September 11 attacks were orchestrated by the American government or the Mossad; and Jews are the shadowy puppet masters behind ZOG, the Zionist Occupied Government that controls the United States and various international multilateral organizations. While some experts have speculated about the permeability between the alt-lite and the alt-right, others, such as Leonard Zeskind and David Neiwert, posit that this blurring of boundaries also pertains to the contemporary mainstream conservative movement and its alternatives on the far right.[59]

But the political left also has a history of playing fast and loose with facts, especially when there is a political point to be made about Israel, and, in some cases, their tactics do not differ substantially from right-wing efforts. For instance, Jasbir Puar alleged in her book *The Right to Maim* that Israel harvests organs from Palestinians killed in the conflict. Cary Nelson, who has painstakingly detailed what he calls Puar's "obsessive demonology as a research agenda," contends that Puar predetermined the outcome of her research because of her implacable anti-Zionism, which presented speculation as well-documented fact. Nelson contends, "Puar's dedicated, impassioned ideology, and the resulting weaknesses in her method, were reinforced by a Duke University Press process that apparently left them unchallenged and thus effectively endorsed them."[60]

Critics contend that Puar's unsubstantiated allegations are reminiscent of the medieval blood libel, but they might also be compared to the similarly undocumented ravings of right-wing conspiracy theorist Alex Jones, who told his supporters that the American Jewish mafia "run[s] the health care, they're going to scam you, they're going to hurt you."[61] The difference is that Puar is championed by some of the same people who would call Jones a right-wing lunatic.

Joy Karega, who advocated for social justice as an assistant professor of rhetoric and composition at Oberlin College, simultaneously used her social media presence to spread conspiracy theories worthy of the alt-right when she opined that the Israeli Mossad and the CIA created ISIS; the 9/11 attacks were perpetrated by Zionists and Jews; and the Rothschilds control banks, government, and the media and "financed both sides of every war since Napoleon." After an investigation, Oberlin dismissed her in 2016 for "failing to meet the academic standards that Oberlin requires of its faculty and failing to demonstrate intellectual honesty," but there were students and faculty who spoke out on her behalf, alleging that her dismissal was predicated not on her antisemitic worldview but on discrimination because of her race and gender.[62]

There is also a growing body of evidence documenting untruths wielded against scholars who support Israel, sometimes to the detriment of their careers. In a few instances, students who alleged that pro-Israel faculty had physically assaulted them were discredited when video that they posted to social media as proof of their mistreatment was found to be doctored or selectively edited.[63]

The examples above demonstrate that both the extreme left and the far right are not averse to blurring the line between fact and fiction, and their allegations about Jews and Israel, while motivated by opposing ideologies, are often surprisingly similar. What is not surprising is that this can lead to an overall campus climate that is hostile to Jews and Israel while simultaneously lowering the integrity of the humanities and academia in general.

Purity/Taharanut

The concept of purity is an area of confluence because it is a reference to the absolute ideological purity demanded by both sides. An individual who transgresses the narrowly defined agenda of either political extreme risks public shaming or even expulsion from the larger group. How might this affect the relationship of the political right and left toward Jews and Israel, and how might this result in expressions of antisemitism?

The political far right is predicated on the exclusion of those deemed inferior or unworthy—eligibility is reserved for those who are deemed racially or ethnically pure. Having passed this test, individuals are then indoctrinated into the associated worldview, usually rife with paranoid assumptions and conspiracy theories. Those who are drawn to alt-right groups for one specific reason, such as racism or misogyny, may be exposed to new ideas, such as antisemitism, leading to increased ideological cohesion with the larger group. However, one characteristic of this quest for purity is the inevitable disappointment when an individual fails to live up to the exacting standards of the group. The history of the political right is also littered with intra-and intergroup squabbles that can devolve into name-calling, shaming, and excommunication.[64]

The marginalization of the alt-right on campus seems to mute the effect of its acolytes' quest for ideological purity in that setting. In some cases, conservative students have split between those who support bringing intentionally provocative speakers like Milo Yiannopoulos to campus and those who oppose such efforts, but the result is often dialogue rather than excommunication. As one UCLA student opined, "The question goes to the issue of why the Bruin Republicans exist. Is the club's mission simply to provoke people? If so, Yiannopoulos would make perfect sense as a speaker. But then, so would Richard Spencer. Or Chris Cantwell. Or Ward Churchill. Provocation has an absolute value sign around it and once you make that your guidestar, there is no logical way to differentiate between provocateurs. I would argue that while the Bruin Republicans might provoke people with the speakers we host, that's tangential to our true mission: To promote conservative ideas in the public square."[65] The contemporary progressive left, in contrast, seems to share traits with the alt-right in its demands for ideological purity. While leftist or liberal politics is comparatively expansive because it is predicated on embracing the most marginalized, its animosity toward Israel can lead to attempts to shun or exclude Jews and Israel supporters from campus activities. It can also lead to ideological inconsistency as the needs of one marginalized group are prioritized over the needs of another.

For instance, at Stony Brook University, statements by SJP called for the expulsion of the Jewish student organization Hillel from campus because of its support for Israel. As one member explained, "We want Zionism off this campus, so we want Hillel off this campus. What we want is a proper Jewish organization that allows Jews to express their faith, have sabbath—everything like that, that are not Zionists, that doesn't support Israel." In this example, non-Jewish students are empowered to tell Jewish students that there are acceptable and unacceptable ways for them to express their Jewish identity and that, in the case of Hillel, any positive or acceptable actions—such as providing kosher food and convening Shabbat services—are negated by the organization's Zionism. Additionally, anyone calling for reasoned discourse in such a situation was a candidate for expulsion and excommunication. Thus, when a Muslim chaplain joined the Stony Brook Interfaith Center in condemning such ideas as intolerant, SJP students called for her to lose her job.[66]

Similarly, when former first daughter Chelsea Clinton tweeted critically about anti-Israel comments made by US congresswoman Ilhan Omar that many construed as antisemitic, she was quickly called out by New York University students Leen Dweik and Rose Asaf. The two students confronted Clinton at a vigil all three were attending at the NYU Islamic Center for the victims of the New Zealand mosque massacre, maintaining not only that Clinton's tweet was anti-Muslim but also that her rhetoric helped create the conditions that led to the horrific massacre of Muslims at a New Zealand mosque. The inevitable video of the encounter posted online went viral and spawned a cascading chain of attacks and counterattacks.[67]

The irony of the confrontation taking place at a vigil where everyone was present to mourn the loss of forty-nine Muslim worshippers appeared to escape Dweik and Asaf. Additionally, to label Clinton's admonishment of Omar, whether ill-constructed or not, as anti-Muslim was an example par excellence of putative allies falling out over issues of ideological purity. Perhaps unsurprisingly, Dweik and Asaf, both SJP members, were the coauthors of a 2018 BDS resolution that passed at NYU.[68]

The intolerance of both the left and the right in their quest for ideological purity can have deleterious effects on the larger campus atmosphere and on Jews and Israel supporters. While the internecine arguments of the left may have a greater effect on campus than those of the largely off-campus squabbles of the alt-right, the similarities between the two political extremes on issues of ideological purity offer an explanation of the polarization of the contemporary campus atmosphere and how this affects expressions of anti-Jewish and anti-Israel animosity.

Conclusion

In relation to the campus, the progressive left, it can be argued, has a much deeper and more substantial impact than either the alt-lite or alt-right. But the Five Ts outlined above demonstrate that even in areas where the progressive left and alt-right show wide differences in ideology, there are similarities in effect when both groups deal with issues related to Jews and Israel. In the context of the coarsened climate that is apparent not just on campuses but also in America in general, the antisemitism of both groups looks surprisingly similar.

In a perfect world, the anti-Jewish and anti-Israel extremes expressed by both sides of the political spectrum would be marginalized by a more active and engaged center that chooses the more difficult option of robust discussion and debate over name-calling, demonization, shunning, and simplistic, Manichean solutions to complex problems. Because of the increased polarization of our contemporary political climate, though, this idea is unfortunately more aspirational than actual. Continuing radicalization of the center, including the possibility discussed above of a further radicalization of the transgressive alt-lite, will certainly not help remedy the situation.

What may help is for those who are not situated on the outer fringes of political reason to begin with introspection. In the case of antisemitism directed at Jews and at Israel, all of us must identify our own blind spots. If we can rationalize or excuse the antisemitism of our own political tribe while condemning that of the tribe we oppose, then we are not going to be part of a productive solution.

At the same time, we need to study these movements in tandem and not in a way that reinforces the partisanship that helped produce them. Perhaps a viable selling point for increased rationality in our political discourse is to do the work to show that the two extreme sides of the political spectrum have more in common than either of them would care to admit. A center that is appalled by the excesses of these extremes—even if individuals lean closer to one end or another on the political spectrum—is one that will be less likely to be swayed by bad ideas and specious arguments, including (but not limited to) antisemitism.

Notes

1. Leonard Dinnerstein, in his classic work *Anti-Semitism in America* (Oxford: Oxford University Press, 1994), acknowledged that antisemitism would never disappear but described a more hopeful trajectory. More recently, scholars such as Jonathan G. Sarna ("The Future of the Pittsburgh Synagogue Massacre," *Tablet*, November 5, 2018, https://www.tabletmag.com/jewish-news-and-politics/274291/future-pittsburgh-synagogue-massacre) and Lila Corwin Berwin ("American Jews Always Believed the U.S. Was Exceptional. We Were Wrong," *Washington Post*, November 1, 2018, https://www.washingtonpost.com/outlook/american-jews-always-believed-the-us-was-exceptional-we-were-wrong/2018/11/01/43be2f62-dd7c-11e8-b3f0-62607289efee_story.html?utm_term=.4e743e427d66) have questioned this optimism.

2. ADL professionals Arnold Forster and Benjamin R. Epstein devoted a chapter of their book *The New Anti-Semitism* (New York: McGraw Hill, 1974) to campus antisemitism. In the late 1970s through the 1990s, Jewish organizations were also starting to take a closer look at trends in behavioral and attitudinal antisemitism specific to American colleges and universities. The ADL issued "Anti-Semitism on the Campus: A Preliminary Survey," in September 1979, and the National Jewish Community Relations Advisory Council (NJCRAC) issued "Anti-Semitism on the Campus: A Report" in November 1990.

3. A contemporary article from the period summarizes the conclusions of the survey: Lisa Anderson, "Anti-Israel Views Stoke Anti-Semitism, ADL Survey Says," *Chicago Tribune*, June 12, 2002, https://www.chicagotribune.com/news/ct-xpm-2002-06-12-0206120272-story.html.

4. Linda Maizels, "ADL Says Anti-Semitism Is Rising. Students Disagree," *The Forward*, March 5, 2018, https://forward.com/opinion/395655/adl-says-anti-semitism-is-rising-students-disagree/.

5. Kenneth L. Marcus, *The Definition of Anti-Semitism* (Oxford: Oxford University Press, 2015); Ron Kampeas, "It's Jew vs. Jew as Congress Weighs a New Definition for

Antisemitism," *Jerusalem Post*, November 10, 2017, https://www.jpost.com/Diaspora/Its-Jew-vs-Jew-as-Congress-weighs-a-new-definition-for-antisemitism-513941. For testimony on the subject, see "Examining Anti-Semitism on College Campuses," House Committee on the Judiciary, accessed June 21, 2019, https://judiciary.house.gov/legislation/hearings/examining-anti-semitism-college-campuses. Similar debates occurred when the University of California Board of Regents adopted the "Principles against Intolerance": Jordana Narin, "University of California Regents Approve Anti-Semitism Statement," *Tablet*, March 25, 2016, https://www.tabletmag.com/scroll/198928/university-of-california-regents-approve-anti-semitism-statement.

6. Nahal Toosi and Marc Caputo, "Dems Gunning for Trump Fear 2020 Split over Israel," Politico, February 12, 2019, https://www.politico.com/story/2019/02/12/democrats-israel-2020-1166291; Sheryl Gay Stolberg, "From Celebrated to Vilified, House's Muslim Women Absorb Blows over Israel," *New York Times*, February 1, 2019, https://www.nytimes.com/2019/02/01/us/politics/ilhan-omar-rashida-tlaib-israel.html?module=inline.

7. Jonathan Greenblatt, "It's Time to Call Out Campus Anti-Semitism by Both the Left and the Right," *Washington Post*, October 26, 2018, https://www.washingtonpost.com/opinions/its-time-to-call-out-campus-anti-semitism-by-both-the-left-and-the-right/2018/10/26/344f0de8-d89b-11e8-a10f-b51546b10756_story.html?utm_term=.78d50cb72396.

8. Graeme Wood, "His Kampf," *The Atlantic*, June 2017, https://www.theatlantic.com/magazine/archive/2017/06/his-kampf/524505/.

9. "Alt Right: A Primer about the New White Supremacy," ADL, accessed June 25, 2019, https://www.adl.org/resources/backgrounders/alt-right-a-primer-about-the-new-white-supremacy.

10. David Neiwert, *Alt-America: The Rise of the Radical Right in the Age of Trump* (New York: Penguin Random House, 2018); Craig Timberg and Drew Harwell, "Racism and Anti-Semitism Surged in Corners of the Web after Trump's Election, Analysis Shows," *Washington Post*, September 6, 2018.

11. Eric Ward, "Skin in the Game: How Antisemitism Animates White Nationalism," Political Research Associates, June 29, 2017, https://www.politicalresearch.org/2017/06/29/skin-in-the-game-how-antisemitism-animates-white-nationalism/.

12. Jane Coaston, "Trump's New Defense of His Charlottesville Comments Is Incredibly False," Vox, April 26, 2019, https://www.vox.com/2019/4/26/18517980/trump-unite-the-right-racism-defense-charlottesville; Abigail Levin and Lisa Guenther, "White 'Power' and the Fear of Replacement," *New York Times*, August 28, 2017, https://www.nytimes.com/2017/08/28/opinion/white-power-and-the-fear-of-replacement.html; Emma Green, "Why the Charlottesville Marchers Were Obsessed with Jews," *The Atlantic*, August 15, 2017, https://www.theatlantic.com/politics/archive/2017/08/nazis-racism-charlottesville/536928/.

13. "From Alt Right to Alt Lite: Naming the Hate," ADL, accessed June 27, 2019, https://www.adl.org/resources/backgrounders/from-alt-right-to-alt-lite-naming-the-hate.

14. Angela Nagle makes the case that the alt-lite can be a gateway to the harder alt-right in *Kill All Normies: Online Culture Wars from 4Chan and Tumblr to Trump and the Alt-Right* (Alresford, UK: Zero Books, 2017). Similarly, misogyny expressed by "incels" (involuntary celibates) can also act as a gateway to hardcore antisemitic and racist beliefs. Steve Hendrix, "How Male Supremacy Fueled Scott Paul Beierle's Incel Attack on Florida Yoga Studio," *Washington Post*, June 7, 2019, https://www.washingtonpost.com/graphics/2019/local/yoga-shooting-incel-attack-fueled-by-male-supremacy/?utm_term=.cf5d402057ab.

15. Phyllis Chesler, *The New Antisemitism: The Current Crisis and What We Must Do about It* (San Francisco: Jossey-Bass, 2003); Abraham H. Foxman, *Never Again? The Threat of the New Anti-Semitism* (San Francisco: Harper, 2003); Gabriel Schoenfeld, *The Return of*

Anti-Semitism (San Francisco: Encounter Books, 2004); Ron Rosenbaum, ed., *Those Who Forget the Past: The Question of Anti-Semitism* (New York: Random House, 2004); Alvin Rosenfeld, ed., *Resurgent Antisemitism: Global Perspectives* (Bloomington: Indiana University Press, 2013); Alvin Rosenfeld, ed., *Deciphering the New Antisemitism* (Bloomington: Indiana University Press, 2015); Alvin Rosenfeld, ed., *Anti-Zionism and Anti-Semitism: The Dynamics of Delegitimization* (Bloomington: Indiana University Press, 2019).

16. Some of the groups formed include the Israel Action Network, a product of the Jewish Council for Public Affairs (JCPA) and the Jewish Federations of North America (JFNA); the David Project (now absorbed into Hillel); Stand with Us; the Israel on Campus Coalition; Scholars for Peace in the Middle East (SPME); AMCHA; and the Academic Engagement Network.

17. For an article that accuses Israel of settler colonialism, see Patrick Wolfe, "Purchase by Other Means: Dispossessing the Natives in Palestine," in *Traces of History: Elementary Structures of Race* (New York: Verso Books, 2016), 203–38. Disputing this argument are essays by S. Ilan Troen, "Zionist Settlement in the Land of Israel," in *Essential Israel: Essays for the 21st Century*, ed. S. Ilan Troen and Rachel Fish (Bloomington: Indiana University Press, 2017), 62–88; and John Strawson, "Colonialism," *Israel Studies* 24, no. 2 (Summer 2019): 33–44.

18. For more on the BDS movement, see Cary Nelson and Gabriel Noah Brahm, eds., *The Case against Academic Boycotts of Israel* (New York: MLA Members for Scholars' Rights, distributed by Wayne State University Press, 2014); Rachel S. Harris and Martin B. Shichtman, "BDS, Credibility, and the Challenge to the Academy," *Shofar* 36, no. 1 (Spring 2018): 161–82; Linda Maizels and Ken Waltzer, *Academic Freedom, Freedom of Expression, and the BDS Challenge: A Guide and Resource Book for Faculty* (n.p.: Academic Engagement Network, September 2017).

19. David Bernstein, "The Holocaust as 'White on White Crime' and Other Signs of Intellectual Decay," *Washington Post*, February 5, 2016, https://www.washingtonpost.com/news/volokh-conspiracy/wp/2016/02/05/the-holocaust-as-white-on-white-crime-and-other-signs-of-intellectual-decay/?utm_term=.1e0a48dcc719. Misspellings and grammatical errors in this quote are intentional.

20. Kimberlé Crenshaw, "Demarginalizing the Intersection of Race and Sex: A Black Feminist Critique of Antidiscrimination Doctrine, Feminist Theory and Antiracist Politics," *University of Chicago Legal Forum* 1, no. 8 (1989): 139–67; "A Primer on Intersectionality," African American Policy Forum, January 17, 2013, https://44bbdc6e-01a4-4a9a-88bc-731c6524888e.filesusr.com/ugd/62e126_19f84b6cbf6f4660bac198ace49b9287.pdf; Kimberlé Crenshaw, "Why Intersectionality Can't Wait," *Washington Post*, September 24, 2015, https://www.washingtonpost.com/news/in-theory/wp/2015/09/24/why-intersectionality-cant-wait/?utm_term=.63e0639ea44e; Jane Coaston, "The Intersectionality Wars," Vox, May 28, 2018, https://www.vox.com/the-highlight/2019/5/20/18542843/intersectionality-conservatism-law-race-gender-discrimination.

21. Emma Green, "Why Do Black Activists Care about Palestine?," *The Atlantic*, August 18, 2016, https://www.theatlantic.com/politics/archive/2016/08/why-did-black-american-activists-start-caring-about-palestine/496088/.

22. The amended version is here: National Women's Studies Association, "NWSA EC Letter on Charlottesville," University of Kentucky, Department of Gender and Women's Studies, August 18, 2017, https://gws.as.uky.edu/nwsa-ec-letter-charlottesville.

23. Some members of the Nation of Islam (NOI) claim not to support Farrakhan's radical views or those of NOI founder Elijah Muhammad. For more information on this shift in NOI ideology, see Raquel Ukeles, "The Evolving Muslim Community in America: The Impact of 9/11," *Mosaica—Research Center for Religion State and Society*, Winter 2003–4. Nevertheless, a quick perusal of the NOI website features Farrakhan prominently (https://www.noi.org/,

accessed September 10, 2019), and the online bookstore is still selling three volumes of the antisemitic publication *The Secret Relationship between Blacks and Jews* (https://store.finalcall.com/collections/the-secret-relationship-between-blacks-and-jews).

24. Leah McSweeney and Jacob Siegel, "Is the Women's March Melting Down?," *Tablet*, December 10, 2018, https://www.tabletmag.com/jewish-news-and-politics/276694/is-the-womens-march-melting-down; Farah Stockman, "Women's March Roiled by Accusations of Anti-Semitism," *New York Times*, December 23, 2018, https://www.nytimes.com/2018/12/23/us/womens-march-anti-semitism.html; Phyllis Chesler, "The Women's March Is a Con Job," *Times of Israel*, January 18, 2019, https://blogs.timesofisrael.com/the-womens-issues-that-the-womens-march-refuses-to-address-and-the-jewish-question/; Bari Weiss, "When Progressives Embrace Hate," *New York Times*, August 1, 2017, https://www.nytimes.com/2017/08/01/opinion/womens-march-progressives-hate.html.

25. Mark G. Yudof and Kenneth Waltzer, "Free Speech, Campus Safety, or Both," *Chronicle of Higher Education*, September 15, 2017, https://www.chronicle.com/article/Free-Speech-Campus-Safety-or/241220.

26. Linda Maizels, "On Whiteness and the Jews," *Journal for the Study of Antisemitism* 3, no. 2 (2011): 463–88; Linda Maizels, "Black Nationalist Antisemitism on Campus Requires Jews to Be 'White,'" *Jerusalem Post*, April 30, 2018, https://www.jpost.com/Opinion/Black-nationalist-antisemitism-on-campus-requires-Jews-to-be-white-553160.

27. Steven Emerson, "US-Based Sheikh Calls on University Students to 'Fight Zionism,'" *Algemeiner*, May 8, 2019, https://www.algemeiner.com/2019/05/08/us-based-sheikh-calls-on-university-students-to-fight-zionism/.

28. Justin Davidoff, "Irvine 11 Students Were Not Practicing Free Speech," *Daily Trojan*, September 21, 2011, http://dailytrojan.com/2011/09/21/irvine-11-students-were-not-practicing-free-speech/.

29. Scott Jaschik, "Who Gets Shouted Down on Campus?," Inside Higher Ed, February 26, 2018, https://www.insidehighered.com/news/2018/02/26/event-sponsored-jewish-and-pro-israel-groups-university-virginia-disrupted-and; Cary Nelson and David Greenberg, "Students Are Shouting Down Pro-Israel Speakers—and Silencing Free Speech," *Washington Post*, December 7, 2016, https://www.washingtonpost.com/opinions/students-are-shouting-down-pro-israel-speakers--and-silencing-free-speech/2016/12/07/9211c3b8-bbd7-11e6-91ee-1adddfe36cbe_story.html.

30. Richard Pérez-Peña and Tanzina Vega, "Brandeis Cancels Plan to Give Honorary Degree to Ayaan Hirsi Ali, a Critic of Islam," *New York Times*, April 8, 2014, https://www.nytimes.com/2014/04/09/us/brandeis-cancels-plan-to-give-honorary-degree-to-ayaan-hirsi-ali-a-critic-of-islam.html?_r=0; William A. Jacobson, "Linda Sarsour's Little Lie about Her Vile Attack on Ayaan Hirsi Ali Is a Big Deal," *Legal Insurrection*, May 24, 2017, https://legalinsurrection.com/2017/05/linda-sarsours-little-lie-about-her-vile-attack-on-ayaan-hirsi-ali-is-a-big-deal/.

31. Alan Feuer, "Linda Sarsour Is a Brooklyn Homegirl in a Hijab," *New York Times*, August 7, 2015, https://www.nytimes.com/2015/08/09/nyregion/linda-sarsour-is-a-brooklyn-homegirl-in-a-hijab.html.

32. Collier Meyerson, "Can You Be a Zionist Feminist? Linda Sarsour Says No," *The Nation*, March 13, 2017, https://www.thenation.com/article/can-you-be-a-zionist-feminist-linda-sarsour-says-no/; Malhar Mali, "The Trouble with Linda Sarsour," *Aero*, January 27, 2017, https://areomagazine.com/2017/01/27/the-trouble-with-linda-sarsour/ (site discontinued).

33. Emma-Kate Symons, "Agenda for Women's March Has Been Hijacked by Organizers Bent on Highlighting Women's Differences," Women in the World, January 19, 2017, http://worldviraltrend.blogspot.com/2017/01/agenda-for-womens-march-has-been.html.

34. Judith Clavir Albert and Stewart Edward Albert, *The Sixties Papers: Documents of a Rebellious Decade* (New York: Praeger, 1984).

35. Caitlin Flanagan, "That's Not Funny!" *The Atlantic*, September 2015, https://www.theatlantic.com/magazine/archive/2015/09/thats-not-funny/399335/.

36. Nagle, *Kill All Normies*.

37. "Disruptions," AMCHA Initiative, accessed June 30, 2019, https://amchainitiative.org/sjp-disruption-of-jewish-events/#disruption-of-jewish-events/display-by-date3/.

38. Doron Ben-Atar and Andrew Pessin, "The Silencing of Pro-Israel Students on Campus," *Tablet*, March 20, 2018, https://www.tabletmag.com/scroll/257840/the-silencing-of-pro-israel-students-on-campus.

39. Maizels, "Black Nationalist Antisemitism."

40. Mark G. Yudof and Ken Waltzer, "Majoring in Anti-Semitism at Vassar," *Wall Street Journal*, February 17, 2016, https://www.wsj.com/articles/majoring-in-anti-semitism-at-vassar-1455751940.

41. Nagle, *Kill All Normies*.

42. "Milo Yiannopoulos: Five Things to Know," ADL, accessed June 20, 2019, https://www.adl.org/resources/backgrounders/milo-yiannopoulos-five-things-to-know.

43. Allum Bokhari and Milo Yiannopoulos, "An Establishment Conservative's Guide to the Alt-Right," Breitbart, March 29, 2016, https://www.breitbart.com/tech/2016/03/29/an-establishment-conservatives-guide-to-the-alt-right/.

44. VICE, "'I'm a gay Jew immigrant Brit with a black fiancé.' We questioned Milo Yiannopoulos on the rise of the Alt Right," Facebook video, January 27, 2018, https://facebook.com/story.php?story_fbid=1726301347391448&id=167115176655082&refsrc=http%3A%2F%2Fwww.google.com%2F&_rdr.

45. "PayPal Suspends Milo Yiannopoulos over Nazi-Based Trolling of Jewish Journalist," *Times of Israel*, June 29, 2018, https://www.timesofisrael.com/paypal-suspends-milo-yiannopoulos-over-nazi-based-trolling-of-jewish-journalist/.

46. See note 14 above.

47. Danielle Ziri, "'Massive Drop in US Jewish College Students' Support for Israel,'" *Jerusalem Post*, June 22, 2017, https://www.jpost.com/American-Politics/Israel-dramatically-losing-support-among-Jewish-college-students-in-US-497605; Ben Sales, "Israel Is Losing Support among Minorities and Millennials, Study Finds," Jewish Telegraphic Agency, June 30, 2017, https://www.jta.org/2017/06/30/united-states/israel-is-losing-support-among-democrats-minorities-and-millennials-study-finds.

48. Yair Rosenberg, "Richard Spencer Says He Just Wants 'White Zionism.' Here's Why That's Malicious Nonsense," *Tablet*, August 18, 2017, https://www.tabletmag.com/scroll/243556/richard-spencer-says-he-just-wants-white-zionism-heres-why-thats-malicious-nonsense.

49. Brianna Goodlin and Daniel B. Jeydel, "300 Millennial Jewish Leaders to Netanyahu: You're Making It Hard for Us to Defend Israel," Jewish Telegraphic Agency, March 22, 2019, https://www.jta.org/2019/03/22/opinion/300-millennial-jewish-leaders-to-netanyahu-youre-making-it-hard-for-us-to-defend-israel.

50. Kenneth S. Stern, *Hate and the Internet*, American Jewish Committee, 1999, http://kennethsstern.com/wp-content/uploads/2018/12/Hate-and-the-Internet.pdf.

51. Scott Jaschik, "After Hack by Neo-Nazi Group, Anti-Semitic Fliers Appear on Campus Printers," Inside Higher Ed, March 28, 2016, https://www.insidehighered.com/quicktakes/2016/03/28/after-hack-neo-nazi-group-anti-semitic-fliers-appear-campus-printers; Carl Straumsheim, "More Anti-Semitic Fliers Printed at Universities," Inside Higher Ed, January

27, 2017, https://www.insidehighered.com/quicktakes/2017/01/27/more-anti-semitic-fliers
-printed-universities.

52. "Fliers on 4 College Campuses Blame Jews for Kavanaugh Assault Allegations," Jewish Telegraphic Agency, October 9, 2018, https://www.jta.org/2018/10/09/politics/flyers-uc-davis
-campus-blame-jews-kavanaugh-assault-allegations.

53. Josefin Dolsten, "College Campuses Saw a 7 Percent Increase in White Supremacist Fliers This Year," Jewish Telegraphic Agency, June 27, 2019, https://www.jta.org/quick-reads
/college-campuses-saw-a-7-percent-increase-in-white-supremacist-fliers-this-year.

54. Jeremy C. Fox, "Anti-Israel Posters Found at Tufts Hillel," *Boston Globe*, February 13, 2019, https://www.bostonglobe.com/metro/2019/02/13/anti-israel-posters-found-tufts-jewish
-center/KbgClPbAHgwyUoL4iU9XXP/story.html.

55. Asher Miller, "In the Crossfire of the Mural War," *New Voices*, September/October 1994.

56. Deborah Lipstadt, *Denying the Holocaust: The Growing Assault on Truth and Memory* (New York: Free Press, 1993). See especially chap. 10, "The Battle for the Campus." See also Kenneth S. Stern, *Holocaust Denial* (New York: American Jewish Committee, 1993).

57. Henry Louis Gates Jr., "Black Demagogues and Pseudo-scholars," *New York Times*, July 20, 1992; Maizels, "On Whiteness and the Jews."

58. The term *alternative facts* was coined by Kellyanne Conway, senior advisor to President Trump, to rationalize false claims made by White House press secretary Sean Spicer about the size of the crowd at the president's 2017 inauguration.

59. Neiwert, *Alt-America*; Leonard Zeskind, *Blood and Politics: The History of the White Nationalist Movement from the Margins to the Mainstream* (New York: Farrar, Straus and Giroux, 2009).

60. Cary Nelson, *Israel Denial: Anti-Zionism, Anti-Semitism, and the Faculty Campaign against the Jewish State* (Bloomington: Indiana University Press, 2019), 205.

61. Zack Beauchamp, "Trump Booster Alex Jones: I'm Not Anti-Semitic, but Jews Run an Evil Conspiracy," Vox, October 26, 2016, https://www.vox.com/policy-and-politics/2016/10/26
/13418304/alex-jones-jewish-mafia.

62. Coleen Flaherty, "Unacademic Freedom?," Inside Higher Ed, March 1, 2016, https://
www.insidehighered.com/news/2016/03/01/does-academic-freedom-protect-falsehoods; Coleen Flaherty, "Oberlin Ousts Professor," Inside Higher Ed, November 16, 2016, https://
www.insidehighered.com/news/2016/11/16/oberlin-fires-joy-karega-following-investigation
-her-anti-semitic-statements-social.

63. See Andrew Pessin and Doron Ben-Atar, eds., *Anti-Zionism on Campus: The University, Free Speech, and BDS* (Bloomington: Indiana University Press, 2018). Chap. 6 ("On Radio Silence and the Video That Saved the Day: The Attack against Professor Dubnov at the University of California San Diego, 2012," by Shlomo Dubnov) and chap. 17 ("Friday, November 13, 2015, at the University of Texas, Austin: Anti-Zionists on the Attack," by Ami Pedahzur and Andrew Pessin) discuss incidents involving video.

64. See Zeskind, *Blood and Politics*; Andrew Marantz, "The Alt-Right Branding War Has Torn the Movement in Two," *New Yorker*, July 6, 2017, https://www.newyorker.com
/news/news-desk/the-alt-right-branding-war-has-torn-the-movement-in-two; Kelly Weill, "Satanism Drama Is Tearing Apart the Murderous Neo-Nazi Group Atomwaffen," *Daily Beast*, March 21, 2018, https://www.thedailybeast.com/satanism-drama-is-tearing-apart-the
-murderous-neo-nazi-group-atomwaffen?ref=home; Erin Keane, "Infighting Tears Apart a Modern Hate Group, Just as It Did for the Klan," *Salon*, March 14, 2018, https://www.salon
.com/2018/03/14/infighting-tears-apart-a-modern-hate-group-just-like-it-did-for-the-klan/;

Linda Maizels, "The Universal Nature of Hatred: Keith Stimely and the Culture of Holocaust Denial" (unpublished MA thesis, Portland State University, 1999).

65. Mariela Muro, "I Helped Get Milo Yiannopoulos Disinvited from UCLA. Here's Why," *Weekly Standard*, February 21, 2018, https://www.weeklystandard.com/mariela-muro/i-helped-get-milo-yiannopoulos-disinvited-from-ucla-heres-why.

66. Rebecca Liebson, "SJP Issues Critique of Interfaith Center and SBU Muslim Chaplain," *The Statesman*, May 5, 2018, https://www.sbstatesman.com/2018/05/05/sjp-issues-critique-of-interfaith-center-and-sbu-muslim-chaplain/; Kenneth Waltzer, "From 'Intersectionality' to the Exclusion of Jewish Students: BDS Makes a Worrying Turn on US Campuses," *Fathom*, July 2018, http://fathomjournal.org/from-intersectionality-to-the-exclusion-of-jewish-students-bds-makes-a-worrying-turn-on-us-campuses/.

67. Colby Itkowitz, "Students at Center of Viral Chelsea Clinton Video at New Zealand Vigil Speak Out," *Washington Post*, March 17, 2019, https://www.washingtonpost.com/politics/2019/03/16/new-zealand-vigil-chelsea-clinton-confronted-over-her-criticism-rep-ilhan-omar/?utm_term=.56b71bbed2ef.

68. "Israeli Co-authors NYU Resolution to Divest from Companies with Israel Ties," *Times of Israel*, December 8, 2018, https://www.timesofisrael.com/israeli-co-authors-nyu-resolution-to-divest-from-companies-with-israel-ties/.

LINDA MAIZELS is currently writing a new book, *What Is Anti-Semitism? A Contemporary Introduction*, to be published by Routledge as part of their book series What Is This Thing Called Religion? She wrote her dissertation, "'Charter Members of the Fourth World': Jewish Student Identity and the 'New Antisemitism' on American Campuses, 1967–1994," at the Avraham Harmon Institute of Contemporary Jewry at the Hebrew University of Jerusalem. Most recently, she was a Franklin Fellow in the Security Affairs Office of the Bureau of African Affairs at the US Department of State. She also was a Faculty Fellow teaching in the departments of Jewish Studies and Religious Studies at Colby College, and she taught in the History and Judaic Studies departments at Portland State University.

8

Rethinking Campus Antisemitism in America and How to Address It

Tammi Rossman-Benjamin

THE GROWING POLARIZATION OF AMERICAN SOCIETY HAS LED to more hatred, and more virulent expressions of that hatred, on college and university campuses across the country. This is especially true of antisemitism, which has itself become a deeply politicized and polarizing issue. As a result, Jewish students have increasingly become the targets of antisemitic behavior, much of it Israel related, that comes from the political left and right and from a variety of religiously motivated Muslim and Christian activists.

Protecting Jewish Students Using Title VI of the 1964 Civil Rights Act

In order to provide some measure of protection for Jewish students, many Jewish communal organizations have directed their efforts to ensuring that federal antidiscrimination law, particularly Title VI of the 1964 Civil Rights Act,[1] extends to Jewish students. This has been an uphill struggle fraught with considerable controversy, largely because Title VI, established to eradicate racial inequality in federally funded schools, prohibits discrimination on the basis of race, color, and national origin; religion is notably omitted from the list of protected characteristics, and for decades Jewish students were not deemed eligible for Title VI protection by the US Department of Education's Office of Civil Rights (OCR), the agency tasked with enforcing Title VI.

However, in response to rising levels of campus antisemitism and pressure from concerned Jewish organizations, in 2004[2] and 2010[3] OCR's directors issued formal statements announcing that Jews were eligible for Title VI protection as a national-origin group. Nevertheless, several complaints filed on behalf of Jewish university students were dismissed by OCR,[4] in large part because the complainants' allegations of anti-Zionist-motivated harassment were not considered actionable, even when the degree of harassment met OCR's stringent standards. In other words, although Jewish students were now considered eligible for protection from antisemitic harassment under Title VI, they were still not afforded the protection they needed because OCR did not deem conduct motivated by anti-Zionism to be antisemitic.

In an effort to remedy this discrepancy, in late 2016, the Anti-Semitism Awareness Act (AAA) was introduced into Congress.[5] The AAA required that OCR use the US State Department's definition of antisemitism set forth by the Special Envoy to Monitor and Combat Anti-Semitism in a fact sheet issued in 2010,[6] including its identification of anti-Zionism as a form of antisemitism, in adjudicating Title VI cases. The bill failed in two successive Congresses. A third version of the bill, this one requiring OCR to use a nearly identical definition of antisemitism adopted by the International Holocaust Remembrance Alliance (IHRA) in 2016 and the US State Department in 2018,[7] was considered by the 116th Congress but also failed to pass.

The IHRA Definition and Its Critics

Meanwhile, in fall 2018, another effort with similar intent, this one from the current OCR director, Kenneth Marcus, was more successful. Shortly after he was appointed, Marcus announced in a letter sent to a Jewish organization that OCR would be investigating a complaint involving the anti-Zionist harassment of students, using the IHRA definition of antisemitism in determining "whether students face discrimination on the basis of actual or perceived Jewish ancestry."[8] The full IHRA definition was reproduced verbatim in the body of Marcus's letter as follows:

> Antisemitism is a certain perception of Jews, which may be expressed as hatred toward Jews. Rhetorical and physical manifestations of antisemitism are directed toward Jewish or non-Jewish individuals and/or their property, toward Jewish community institutions and religious facilities.
> Contemporary examples of antisemitism in public life, the media, schools, the workplace, and in the religious sphere could, taking into account the overall context, include, but are not limited to:
> - Calling for, aiding, or justifying the killing or harming of Jews in the name of a radical ideology or an extremist view of religion.
> - Making mendacious, dehumanizing, demonizing, or stereotypical allegations about Jews as such or the power of Jews as collective—such as,

especially but not exclusively, the myth about a world Jewish conspiracy or of Jews controlling the media, economy, government or other societal institutions.
- Accusing Jews as a people of being responsible for real or imagined wrongdoing committed by a single Jewish person or group, or even for acts committed by non-Jews.
- Denying the fact, scope, mechanisms (e.g. gas chambers) or intentionality of the genocide of the Jewish people at the hands of National Socialist Germany and its supporters and accomplices during World War II (the Holocaust).
- Accusing the Jews as a people, or Israel as a state, of inventing or exaggerating the Holocaust.
- Accusing Jewish citizens of being more loyal to Israel, or to the alleged priorities of Jews worldwide, than to the interests of their own nations.
- Denying the Jewish people their right to self-determination, e.g., by claiming that the existence of a State of Israel is a racist endeavor.
- Applying double standards by requiring of it a behavior not expected or demanded of any other democratic nation.
- Using the symbols and images associated with classic antisemitism (e.g., claims of Jews killing Jesus or blood libel) to characterize Israel or Israelis.
- Drawing comparisons of contemporary Israeli policy to that of the Nazis.
- Holding Jews collectively responsible for actions of the state of Israel.

Both the AAA and Marcus's announcement have been met with fierce opposition from groups associated with pro-Palestinian advocacy as well as from First Amendment watchdog groups. Claiming that animus toward Israel is not antisemitic, pro-Palestinian advocates reject the definition's assertion that its examples of Israel-related language and imagery are motivated by "a certain perception of Jews, which may be expressed as hatred toward Jews," and they accuse the supporters of the bill and policy of simply wanting to shut down and even penalize pro-Palestinian student advocacy.[9] Free speech advocates claim that the definition's Israel-related examples are overbroad and describe language or imagery that, depending on context, may not necessarily be motivated by hatred at all but rather by the desire to express political dissent.[10] Both groups agree that requiring OCR to use the IHRA definition in its Title VI adjudications will lead to the agency's greatly overidentifying cases of antisemitic harassment, which in turn would lead to the unfair and potentially unlawful suppression of protected speech.

Why the Critics Have Succeeded

The critics' arguments have been vigorously challenged by supporters of the AAA and new OCR policy.[11] But given that these arguments have thus far succeeded in derailing efforts to turn the AAA into law and have called into question the viability of the new OCR policy, it is important to consider what makes them so compelling.

First, the IHRA definition's formulation itself allows critics to challenge its accuracy and question the motivation of its drafters and those who advocate for its use in federal antidiscrimination law and OCR policy. Although the definition's core statement, that antisemitism is "a certain perception of Jews, which may be expressed as hatred toward Jews," is relatively uncontroversial, the contemporary examples of antisemitism that follow are problematic in a number of ways. Except the first two examples ("calling for, aiding, or justifying the killing or harming of Jews" and "making mendacious, dehumanizing, demonizing, or stereotypical allegations about Jews"), which seem to encompass the totality of behaviors intended to physically and verbally harm Jews, there is no explicit organizing principle or logic that would allow someone to easily understand why certain examples have been chosen and not others, how the examples relate to one another, or how they exemplify the core definition of antisemitism. This is especially so for the six Israel-related examples.

Second, despite the claims of supporters of the legislation and policy that OCR's use of the IHRA definition to determine antisemitic motivation would not infringe on First Amendment rights,[12] the bill's enactment would almost inevitably lead to the suppression of free speech. This is not because of the legislation or policy per se but rather a consequence of how *any* speech is treated when it is deemed discriminatory toward a group protected under federal antidiscrimination law. According to Erwin Chemerinsky and Howard Gillman in their book *Free Speech on Campus*, "Freedom of speech does not protect a right to harass an individual on account of his or her race, sex, religion or sexual orientation."[13] Consequently, when speech is considered to be a form of harassment directed at individuals because of their membership in a group protected under Title VI, that speech is not protected under the First Amendment to the same extent as similar speech directed at individuals who are not members of groups protected under Title VI.

For instance, in 2010, OCR itself lodged a Title VI complaint and launched an investigation after four instances of speech and symbolic expression allegedly directed against African American students at the University of California San Diego.[14] These expressive behaviors were not seen as free speech by either OCR or the university, which considered[15] or took[16] disciplinary measures against the actors in two of these incidents and allowed the student government to carry out punitive measures in response to the other two incidents.[17] The Title VI charges not only resulted in the punishment of what in other contexts would have been deemed protected speech, they led to initiatives that would further erode free speech on that campus, including the university establishing training programs to avoid "verbal, written and visual" harassment[18] and initiatives that would "prevent experiences of microaggressions such as insensitive or disparaging remarks [and] offensive visual images."[19] Even if these measures did not explicitly restrict free speech, they could not help but create a hypersensitivity to certain kinds of expression that would, at the very least, lead to self-censorship and the chilling of protected speech. In a similar way, if the Israel-related examples of the IHRA definition were used to determine whether harassment against Jewish students was motivated by antisemitism and a violation of Title VI, campus free speech would undoubtedly be affected in both the short and long term.

The impact of federal antidiscrimination law on free speech, demonstrated above, highlights one final challenge to the enactment of legislation or policy requiring OCR to use the IHRA definition in determining the antisemitic motivation of behavior, which is revealed not in what the critics argue but in their silence. While loudly and vigorously challenging the restriction of speech resulting from Title VI enforcement in the case of Jewish students facing anti-Zionist harassment, the pro-Palestinian advocates and First Amendment watchdogs say little or nothing in the face of the same free speech restrictions resulting from the application of Title VI in the case of other protected groups.[20] This double standard suggests that in the eyes of these critics, Jewish students facing even severe anti-Zionist-motivated harassment may never be worthy of Title VI protection. More ominously, it raises the question of whether Jews, often construed as socioeconomically "privileged" and "white," should be protected at all under Title VI, which was established in 1964 to combat discrimination against underprivileged students of color.

These issues must be forthrightly addressed before Jewish students can be adequately protected from all forms of antisemitic harassment. The remainder of this chapter presents a new way of conceptualizing campus antisemitism that not only accurately models the anti-Jewish hostility found on many campuses today but also leads directly to a new approach for overcoming the above obstacles and ensuring adequate protection for Jewish students.

Rethinking the Definition of Antisemitism

In his book *The Definition of Anti-Semitism*, Kenneth Marcus surveys several different approaches to defining antisemitism and suggests that the best definitions will reflect that antisemitism consists of "negative attitudes toward the Jewish people, individually or collectively; conduct that reflects these attitudes; and ideologies that sustain them."[21] At the same time, however, Marcus recognizes that different definitions serve different purposes and, as such, will stress one component—attitude, conduct, or ideology—over or even to the exclusion of the other components in order to address specific needs.[22] Such is the case with the IHRA definition. While it begins with a statement about negative attitudes toward the Jewish people individually and collectively—"Antisemitism is a certain perception of Jews, which may be expressed as hatred toward Jews"—it is considered a praxeological, or conduct-centered, definition because of its inclusion of multiple examples of contemporary manifestations of antisemitism and the absence of an ideological component. This focus makes sense, given that the definition's drafters intended it to help governments and nongovernmental organizations "to monitor, catalogue, quantify and compare anti-Semitic incidents within and among different countries,"[23] as well as "to develop guidelines for determining which actions could be deemed anti-Semitic and which not."[24]

Despite the widespread acceptance and use of this praxeological definition in countries around the world, its proposed use by OCR has been hotly contested, in large part due to the missing ideological framework that could justify the definition's choice of examples and their relationship to one another and to the attitudes they reflect. In the next section, I closely examine the IHRA definition in an effort to discover its organizing principles and internal logic.

Internal Structure and Logic of the IHRA Definition

Let us begin the analysis using Marcus's three desiderata for a definition of antisemitism, which will help clarify what we are looking for. Logically, the three definitional components fit together in the following way: an antisemitic ideology or set of beliefs about Jews generates negative attitudes and feelings about Jews that may be expressed in conduct that negatively affects Jews.

Here is the progression of antisemitic components for the IHRA definition: Some unspecified antisemitic ideology gives rise to "a certain perception of Jews, which may be expressed as hatred toward Jews." This hatred may in turn be expressed as "rhetorical and physical manifestations of antisemitism [that] are directed toward Jewish or non-Jewish individuals and/or their property, toward Jewish community institutions and religious facilities." These rhetorical and physical manifestations, which can target individual Jews, the Jewish people, or the state of Israel, "conceived as a Jewish collectivity," are then illustrated with eleven examples.

A closer look at the definition's examples, which are each intended to demonstrate one or more harms that can be inflicted on Jews individually or collectively, reveals that they can be divided into two broad categories: rhetorical harm (speech and imagery) and physical harm (action). Except a portion of the first example—"aiding . . . the killing or harming of Jews," which is the sole example of physical harm in the definition—the remaining examples illustrate harm conveyed by means of language (including the symbolic language of imagery). Presumably, this imbalance reflects the fact that antisemitic actions are much more easily identified than antisemitic language and therefore do not require multiple examples.

The IHRA definition's examples of rhetorical harm can be further divided into language intended to malign Jews and language intended to condone or incite violence against Jews. Here, too, only part of the first example—"Calling for . . . or justifying the killing or harming of Jews"—fits into the category of language condoning or inciting violence, with the remaining ten examples illustrating language that seeks to malign Jews.

It is important to note that these three categories of harm—language that maligns Jews, language that condones or incites violence against Jews, and violence against Jews—form a logical progression of antisemitic conduct. First, Jews are maligned in order to portray them as worthy of harm. Then, harm against Jews is justified and incited. Finally, harm is inflicted on Jews.[25]

Now let us turn to the ten examples in the IHRA definition that fit into the category of language that maligns Jews. Although they are the most problematic part of the definition and at the heart of the controversy over it, on closer analysis these examples turn out to be the key that not only unlocks the definition's logic but also reveals the unique nature of antisemitism.

One of the major contributors to the definition's lack of transparency is the fact that these ten examples are presented in one undifferentiated list, with the implication that they are illustrating discrete phenomena on the same hierarchical level and of the same general kind. But in fact, they are not. For instance, the first of the rhetorical manifestations, "Making mendacious, dehumanizing, demonizing, or stereotypical allegations about Jews as such or the power of Jews as collective," does not illustrate a specific antisemitic expression but rather gives a category of expressions that includes most of the bulleted examples that follow. And accusing Israel of "inventing or exaggerating the Holocaust" is quite different from "applying double standards" to Israel; the former illustrates rhetoric that is antisemitic because of *what* is said, while the latter illustrates rhetoric that is antisemitic because of *how* it is said (i.e., the type of argumentation).

A careful analysis of the first rhetorical example reveals that it not only encompasses all but one of the bulleted examples that follow but also contains a concise, nearly complete definition of antisemitic expression. Specifically, the example identifies as antisemitic those allegations about Jews, as individuals or as a collective, that are "mendacious, dehumanizing, demonizing, or stereotypical." On first blush, these four adjectives seem to describe similar negative qualities. But on closer inspection, they can be seen to describe three different but related features of antisemitic expression that can help make sense of the remaining rhetorical examples:

1. Mendacious argumentation—One feature of antisemitic expression is that it typically employs one or more types of mendacious argumentation to present falsehoods about Jews. Three of the definition's examples focus specifically on illustrating the process of false argumentation involved in antisemitism: "accusing Jews as a people of being responsible for real or imagined wrongdoing committed by a single Jewish person or group" and "holding Jews collectively responsible for actions of the state of Israel" are both examples of faulty generalizations, in which the behavior or characteristics of a single case or subgroup is falsely applied to the whole group, and "applying double standards by requiring of [Israel] a behavior not expected or demanded of any other democratic nation" illustrates moral hypocrisy, where someone condemns a type of act or policy on the part of one agent while ignoring or condoning it on the part of others.

    Other kinds of mendacious argumentation implicit in the definition's examples include lying (e.g., Holocaust denial or accusing Jews or Israel of inventing the Holocaust), false analogy (e.g., comparing Israeli policy to that of the Nazis), and false premise (e.g., accusations that Jews are more loyal to the interests of Israel than of the country where they live, which is based on the false premise that it is impossible to simultaneously hold multiple political allegiances).

2. Dehumanizing or demonizing content—A second feature of antisemitic expression is that it maligns Jews in one of two ways: either by dehumanizing them or demonizing them. Dehumanizing language portrays Jews individually or collectively as lacking positive human qualities or being less than human, often equating them with animals, vermin, insects, or diseases. No specific examples of dehumanization were included in the

IHRA definition, perhaps because the ubiquity of such expression during the Nazi era has made it so easy to recognize as antisemitism that it does not need illustration. However, contemporary examples include the dehumanizing comment of Nation of Islam leader Louis Farrakhan, "I'm not anti-Semitic, I'm anti-Termite,"[26] and a tweet from Iran's supreme leader calling Israel "a malignant cancerous tumor."[27]

Demonizing rhetoric attributes to Jews, individually or as a conspiratorial collective, malevolent demonic or Satanic powers that give them an unnatural ability to control human affairs for self-serving purposes. Explicit examples of demonizing expression in the IHRA definition include allegations of "a world Jewish conspiracy or of Jews controlling the media, economy, government or other societal institutions" as well as "claims of Jews killing Jesus or blood libel" that are used "to characterize Israel or Israelis." Demonizing expression is also an implicit feature of accusations that Jews or Israel invented the Holocaust, allegations that they are more loyal to "the alleged priorities of Jews worldwide, than to the interests of their own nations," and comparisons of Israelis to Nazis.

It is important to note that both dehumanizing and demonizing antisemitic language marks Jews as Other not just relative to a specific societal norm or a particular reference group but in an absolute sense. Both kinds of language cast Jews as Other to the rest of humanity, portraying them as either subhuman in the case of dehumanization or suprahuman in the case of demonization.

3. Stereotypical themes—The third feature of antisemitic expression mentioned in the IHRA definition is more accurately seen as an essential component of the dehumanizing or demonizing portrayal of Jews that provides these depictions with historical continuity. The definition itself cites accusations of a Jewish conspiracy to malevolently control human affairs and "blood libel" (i.e., the accusation that Jews murder non-Jews, especially children, for ritual purposes) as examples of antisemitic stereotypes that have existed for centuries. Even language and imagery that draw on modern-day concepts to malign Jews or Israel, such as by equating Jews to white supremacists or calling Israel an "apartheid," "racist," "settler-colonial," or "genocidal" state, can be demonstrably linked to age-old antisemitic stereotypes that portray Jews as "sinister, greedy, criminal, conspiratorial, treacherous, power-hungry, and diabolical."[28]

Although the IHRA definition focuses primarily on observable manifestations of antisemitism and says little about antisemitic attitudes and nothing at all about antisemitic ideology, the dehumanizing and demonizing depictions of Jews and the stereotypical themes that comprise them could serve as core symbols or beliefs of an antisemitic ideology capable of engendering antisemitic attitudes and actions. For example, the belief that Jews are less than human would lead naturally to an attitude of disgust toward Jews and the desire to rid one's environment of them, not unlike a desire to rid one's home of insects or one's body of disease. And the belief that Jews have malevolent, supernatural powers would lead naturally to an attitude of existential fear and the desire to defend oneself and one's group from the demonic Jews by any means necessary.

Thus far, we have managed to incorporate all but one of the IHRA definition's examples into a model of antisemitism. One example, however, does not yet fit: "Denying the Jewish people their right to self-determination." This example is neither language nor action but can be viewed as the precursor of both. The denial of Jewish self-determination describes the intent of both rhetoric that attacks the legitimacy and therefore the existence of a Jewish polity, and actions that seek to eliminate it. The inclusion of this example suggests that we should expand our model to include an additional component that serves as a bridge between antisemitic attitude and action, namely, the antisemitic desire or intent to suppress or eliminate the expression of Jewishness or Jewish collectivity, up to and including genocide.

A New Conceptualization of Antisemitism

My analysis has yielded not only a much deeper understanding of the IHRA definition's internal structure and logic but also a new way of conceptualizing antisemitism that can be summarized as follows. An antisemitic ideology that includes dehumanizing and demonizing beliefs about the absolute otherness and inhumanity of Jews gives rise to a hatred of Jews that can be described as disgust and fear, which fosters the desire to suppress or eliminate all expressions of Jewishness and Jewish peoplehood. Antisemitic intention gives rise to antisemitic rhetoric, consisting of language that maligns Jews as worthy of suppression or elimination and that condones or incites harm against them, as well as antisemitic actions. Language that maligns Jews can be further characterized by its mendacious argumentation, its inclusion of dehumanizing or demonizing portrayals of Jews, and its use of stereotypical themes linking these portrayals to those in previous generations. While antisemitic intention can lead directly to actual harm, there is often a natural progression from antisemitic language that portrays Jews as worthy of harm to language that condones or calls for their harm to actual physical harm against Jews.

This conceptual model can be visualized in the following way:

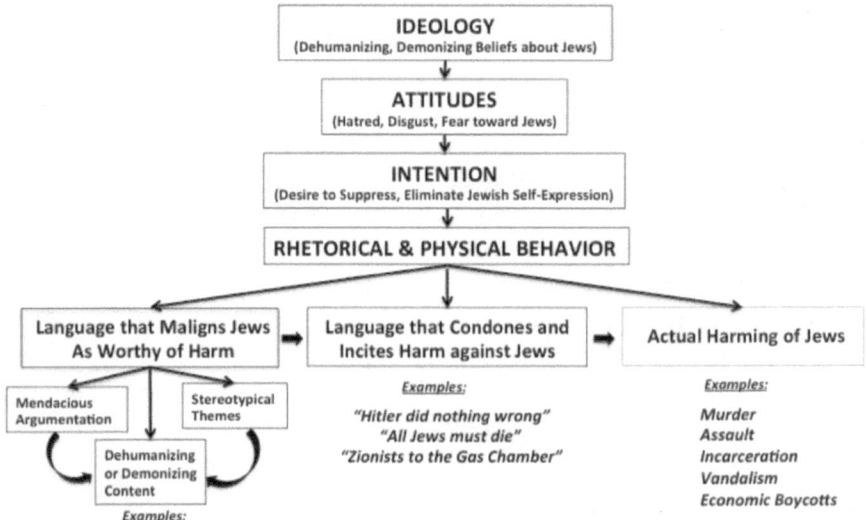

Figure 8.1. Conceptual model of antisemitism.

Although based on the IHRA definition, this conceptualization overcomes the definition's difficulties by making transparent its organizing principles and logic. This is accomplished by fitting the definition's core statement of antisemitism "as a certain perception of Jews, which may be expressed as hatred toward Jews" and its eleven examples of rhetorical and physical manifestations of antisemitism into a conceptual framework that characterizes the hierarchical relationships and processes that relate them. In particular, the model highlights how the same ideology, attitudes, and intentionality engender similar rhetorical and physical behavior directed toward Jewish individuals, the Jewish people, and the Jewish state.

The Inadequacy of Using Title VI to Protect Jewish Students

Given that this new model of antisemitism is not burdened with many of the weaknesses of the IHRA definition that have made its adoption by OCR so controversial, it would seem a more fitting tool for use in identifying antisemitic motivation in Title VI cases. However, careful consideration of the model raises serious doubts not only about the model's usefulness in adjudicating Title VI cases but also about whether federal antidiscrimination law is the right way to combat campus antisemitism at all.

The first problem is that the model's conceptualization of antisemitism—the dehumanizing and demonizing beliefs about Jews that cast them as the absolute Other to all of humanity, the extreme disgust and existential fear those beliefs engender, the eliminationist intentions aroused by those attitudes, and the observable rhetorical and physical manifestations of those eliminationist intentions—sets antisemitism apart from racism and other forms of social prejudice and their expression as they are framed by the Civil Rights Act of 1964. For example, racial discrimination, the primary expression of social prejudice addressed by the act, is conceived of as the behavioral manifestation of negative perceptions of members of a particular racial or ethnic group, based on the belief that one's own racial or ethnic group is superior to theirs. Within this conceptual framework, racial discrimination is seen not as a set of rhetorical and physical behaviors that cause specific intentional harms to their victims but rather as behaviors that promote racial inequality by disadvantaging one racial or ethnic group over another.

The reason for this conceptual difference traces back to the origins of the Civil Rights Act. Established in response to race riots and escalating racial tensions, the overarching goal of the act was not to eradicate antisocial behaviors per se but rather to eradicate the social inequality underlying these behaviors. This may seem like an irrelevant distinction, but it turns out to be consequential when considering whether and to what extent antisemitism can be addressed by antidiscrimination law.

While all antisemitic behaviors clearly disadvantage their Jewish victims and are, to that extent, discriminatory, according to the conceptual model we have developed, these behaviors are not manifestations of feelings of ethnic superiority, as racial discrimination is conceived to be, but manifestations of ethnic hatred and the concomitant desire to suppress or eliminate the source of that hatred—namely, Jews. The difference between these two frameworks for understanding behavior highlights several challenges of protecting Jewish students under Title VI.

First, if antisemitic behavior is simply viewed as a form of discrimination that itself is useful only as an indicator of ethnic inequality, the true nature of the threat posed to Jewish students from antisemitic behavior—including its eliminationist intent, its incorporation of age-old dehumanizing and demonizing tropes, and its natural progression from language that maligns Jews to language that condones and incites violence against Jews to actual violence against Jews—will be ignored or underestimated by OCR officials. As a result, Jewish students will not receive adequate protection against behavior that intends them significant harm.

Second, according to the model of antisemitism offered here, while one effect of antisemitic behavior may be that it discriminates against Jewish students, that discrimination does not reflect social inequality in the same way that racist, sexist, or homophobic behavior does. As such, OCR officials tasked with enforcing a law whose goal is to eliminate racial and other forms of social inequity may not see antisemitism as a civil rights issue at all and may be prejudiced against pursuing Title VI cases with allegations of antisemitic harassment. This is especially true of cases involving anti-Zionist rhetoric and action, which are even less likely to be viewed as forms of discrimination based on ethnic inequality than are cases of classic antisemitic harassment.

Finally, while the new model of antisemitism offers a principled argument for why certain forms of Israel-related rhetoric are antisemitic, even if the model were to be adopted by OCR for use in adjudicating Title VI cases, it would do little to quell the free speech critics' arguments, since speech related to Israel would be no more protected using this model than using the IHRA definition that is currently being used by OCR. Once again, however, it is important to point out that suppression of free speech is not specific to the case of antisemitic anti-Zionism but is rather a consequence of how all speech is treated when it is deemed discriminatory toward any group protected under Title VI. Therefore, criticism that focuses on the suppression of speech only when it comes to Title VI enforcement regarding antisemitism, but not when it comes to other protected groups, is disingenuous at best and antisemitic at worst.

In sum, a more robust model of antisemitism does little to increase protection for Jewish students under Title VI or to address the concerns of free speech critics. In addition, it raises serious doubts about whether federal antidiscrimination law will ever be able to provide adequate and reliable protection for Jewish students from antisemitic harassment, and it begs the question: is there a better alternative?

A New Approach to Combating Campus Antisemitism

Searching for a new approach to addressing campus antisemitism requires taking a bird's-eye view of the approach we are currently pursuing. American civil rights law affords protection to certain individuals based on their group identity, though this protection has generally been afforded only to individuals from groups that have faced historical and continuing discrimination and inequality in America. Since at least 2004, advocates for Jewish college and university students have tried to ensure that Jews are one of the groups protected under this law, but, as we have seen, there has been considerable resistance to this notion from many quarters.

Moreover, the conceptual model of antisemitism we have developed suggests that even if Jews were to be unambiguously accepted as a full-fledged protected group under federal antidiscrimination law, the behaviors targeting Jews for harm would not be adequately addressed by a law whose primary focus is on the group identity of the victim rather than on the specific behaviors that caused the victim harm. Instead, the model encourages us to look in a different direction for the legal protection of Jewish students, one that focuses primarily on behavior rather than group identity. More than that, it urges us to turn our current approach inside out: instead of seeking protection for individual Jewish students through their membership in a federally protected group, we are urged to seek protection for Jewish students as individuals, with the same rights as all other individuals to be free from behaviors that seek to suppress or deny their expression of (Jewish) belief or (Jewish) group identity.

Framed in this way, it is apparent that the most appropriate law for protecting these rights is the First Amendment of the US Constitution, which guarantees basic liberties, including the freedom of speech, religion, and assembly, in conjunction with the Equal Protection Clause of the Fourteenth Amendment ensuring that every individual is guaranteed equal protection of these basic liberties. Before these laws can be applied in a way that will help Jewish students, however, two things must be established: first, that Jews are indeed denied these basic liberties as a direct result of antisemitic behaviors, and second, that any individual would be denied these liberties as a result of being targeted by similar behaviors.

The conceptual model of antisemitism that I have developed can be used to establish both these preconditions. First, within this model the link between antisemitic attitudes and behavior is "eliminationist intent," which is understood as the desire to suppress or eliminate all expression of Jewishness, whether religious, ethnic, or nationalistic. That intention is conveyed rhetorically in dehumanizing and demonizing language that portrays individual Jews, the Jewish people, or the Jewish state as worthy of suppression and elimination, as well as language that condones or incites such acts. These rhetorical manifestations lead naturally to actions whose goal is to suppress or eliminate Jewish self-expression, causing various degrees

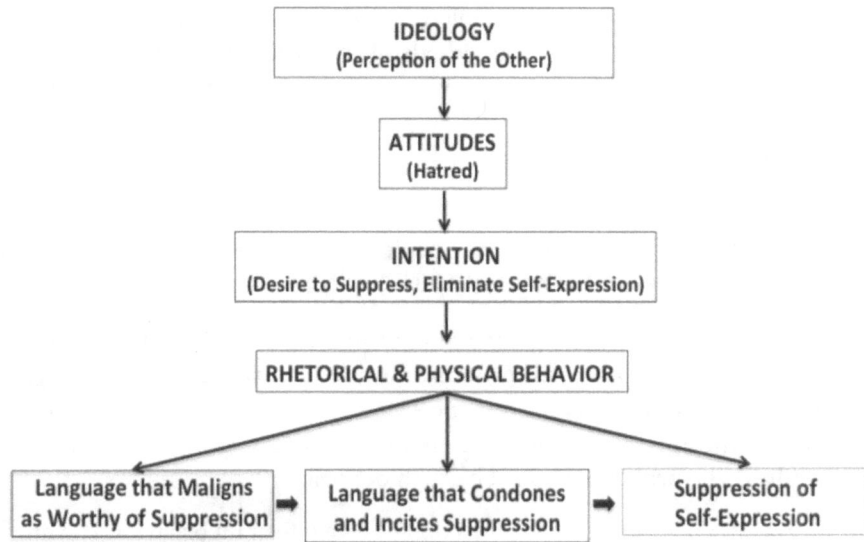

Figure 8.2. Universal model of intolerance.

of harm to individual Jews, up to and including loss of life. While some of these behaviors may be illegal (e.g., defamation, incitement to violence, vandalism, and murder), according to this model *all* antisemitic behaviors can be characterized by some degree of additional harm that results from the suppression of a Jewish individual's freedom to express his or her religious, ethnic, or national identity.

A compelling case for the second precondition of this approach—that similar behaviors would result in a similar suppression of the basic liberties of any individual or group—can also be made using my model of antisemitism, if one considers its general characteristics. Indeed, the model's primary categories and relationships can easily be reformulated as a universal model of intolerance, which can be described as follows: A set of negative beliefs about others fosters intolerant attitudes toward them and a desire or intention to prevent them from expressing opinions, beliefs, or identities that are deemed intolerable. Intolerant attitudes and intentions lead naturally to rhetorical and physical behavior that includes language portraying the targeted individuals or groups as unworthy of the right to self-expression, language calling for or condoning actions that suppress self-expression, and finally, actions that deny self-expression. Such a universal model of intolerance can be diagrammed as pictured in figure 8.2.

In contrast to a Title VI framework that recognizes antisemitism as a variant of racism, the proposed intolerance model considers antisemitism, racism, and all other forms of intolerance as separate varieties of hatred, whose end goal is to deprive individuals of their basic liberties. Nevertheless, antisemitism's intensity, complexity, ubiquity, and longevity set it apart quantitatively and qualitatively and suggest that it may serve as the prototype of all other forms of intolerance.[29]

Advantages of the Intolerance Model in Combating Campus Antisemitism

Looking at behaviors through the lens of intolerance rather than of discrimination against protected groups affords important advantages to the student victims of these behaviors, both Jewish and non-Jewish, as well as to school administrators and government officials seeking to adjudicate and address the problems caused by such behaviors:

- Provides all students protection—Since intolerant behaviors can affect any student and not just those in protected groups, this model makes the case that all students should be afforded equal protection and equal redress from behaviors that deny their right to self-expression, regardless of the motivation of the perpetrator or the identity of the victim. For Jewish students, this would be a significant step forward. As opposed to the uncertainty of Title VI protection, particularly when it comes to anti-Zionist-motivated harassment, Jewish students would be guaranteed protection and redress from behavior that is determined to impede their ability to express their religious, ethnic, national, or even political identity, whether the perpetrator was motivated by classic antisemitism, anti-Zionism, or neither. In fact, such an approach renders a definition linking anti-Zionism and antisemitism—or any definition of antisemitism—unnecessary for determining whether Jewish students merit protection or can seek redress from a denial of their basic liberties. Nor can Jewish students be accused of special pleading for protection they do not deserve, since according to the intolerance model, all students are equally deserving of protection. In addition, non-Jewish students who are not members of groups protected under federal law (e.g., white heterosexual men) as well as protected students who are harassed for reasons other than their protected characteristics (e.g., an African American student harassed for her conservative views) would also be protected with this approach.
- Uses a single standard of behavior—In order for all students to be equally protected from behavior that impedes their self-expression, colleges and universities must have a single standard by which

behavior is judged; language and actions deemed unacceptable when directed at students from one group must be deemed unacceptable when directed at any student, irrespective of the motivation of the perpetrator or the identity of the victim. While any behavioral standard that is equitably applied could be suitable, the standard for harassment currently used by OCR in adjudicating Title VI cases and by many schools in their antidiscrimination policies is particularly appropriate to our new approach. Based on the definition provided by the US Supreme Court in *Davis v. Monroe County Board of Education*,[30] OCR defines harassment as behavior that is "sufficiently severe, pervasive or persistent so as to interfere with or limit the ability of an individual to participate in or benefit from the services, activities or privileges provided by any recipient [of federal funds]."[31] Although OCR and most school policies apply this definition only in cases where the harassment is directed at individuals because of their race, color, national origin, and so on, the definition is nevertheless consistent with the effects of intolerant behavior that can target any student. It is therefore reasonable that this definition be used as the single standard for determining when intolerant behavior is unacceptable.

- Protects free speech—Based on First Amendment principles, the goal of the proposed approach is to protect speech and other forms of expression from rhetorical and physical behaviors that seek their suppression. In contrast to federal antidiscrimination law, whose enforcement can easily lead to the suppression of speech directed at members of protected groups, the proposed approach would limit speech and other forms of expressive behavior only in those cases where the behavior itself limits the expression of others to some undesirable degree. In addition, by distinguishing among three kinds of intolerant behaviors—language that denigrates, language that condones or incites harm, and actions that harm—the intolerance model can help school administrators evaluate which behaviors are protected by the First Amendment and which are not. For example, except in rare cases, denigrating language, including dehumanizing and demonizing antisemitic statements, are constitutionally protected, as is most language that condones violence. Threats of imminent harm are not constitutionally protected, nor are expressive behaviors that inflict substantial harm to the basic liberties of others, such as physical assault, destruction of property, and severe disruption of speech or assembly.
- Creates a healthier campus climate—In contrast to the current approach of protecting students by virtue of their membership in legally protected groups, which can easily lead to the exacerbation of

group differences and an unhealthy competition for group rights, the proposed approach focusing on individual rights and their equal protection under the Constitution offers the possibility of a healthier campus climate. This is not only because group differences become irrelevant when ensuring the protection of individual students but also because the notion of individual rights itself exists within the framework of a set of shared values concerning the equality and dignity of every person, values that can serve to inspire and unite the campus community if properly communicated.

Recommendations for Implementation of the Intolerance Approach

University Practice

How could this approach be incorporated into university practice? One possibility is that its implementation could be modeled after the infrastructure that currently exists on most campuses to ensure compliance with federal antidiscrimination law. This generally includes antidiscrimination and harassment policies, a complaint procedure, administrative offices that enforce these policies and resolve complaints, and educational and training programs for students, faculty, and staff.

Creating a similar infrastructure around a model of intolerance would start with a review of all existing campus policies and procedures regarding the protection of freedom of expression and the prohibition of harmful conduct, including policies pertaining to general student behavior, harassment, bias, discrimination, tolerance, respect, civility, bullying, protest, and demonstration. These would be revised as necessary to ensure that all students' freedom of expression and right to full participation in campus life are equally protected and that disciplinary measures are applied strictly on the basis of behavioral considerations, without respect to the identity, opinion, or legally protected status of victim or perpetrator.

Protocols would also be developed to handle expression that is intolerant but constitutionally protected. Whether the school decides to handle such expression by loudly condemning it or by taking a more hands-off approach, it must be addressed in an equal manner for all students, without regard to the identity or legally protected status of those responsible for the objectionable speech or those who are affected by it.

Educational and training programs would be an important component of this approach. These would encourage the expression of a wide range of views, beliefs, and identities in a productive and respectful manner; instill an appreciation for individual dignity and communal responsibility; and foster an understanding of and appreciation for the First Amendment and its critical role in supporting the academic mission of the university.

State and Federal Law

Based on First Amendment principles, the intolerance approach is also consistent with and could piggyback on recent efforts at the state level to guarantee the free speech rights of college and university students. These efforts are in large measure a response to a rash of protests against campus speakers that resulted in disinvitations and event disruptions, as well as a growing number of examples of college and university administrators over-constraining student speech.

Several state legislatures have considered bills to establish campus free speech guidelines, and at least nine have already adopted them.[32] In general, these bills prohibit state-supported universities and colleges from impeding students' constitutionally protected expression such as by imposing restrictive speech codes, establishing free speech zones, or disinviting speakers based on anticipated reaction or opposition to the speech content. Some of the bills also require the university to impose strict disciplinary measures on individuals who violate the free speech rights of others, but within the context of these bills the disciplinary measures are apparently directed at those who engage in event disruptions and protests. The broader category of intolerant behavior that deprives students of their rights to freedom of expression and full participation in campus life is not addressed by the bills that have been adopted, with one notable exception. In addition to the measures found in similar state bills, the Tennessee legislature's Campus Free Speech Protection Act, approved in May 2017, calls for all public institutions of higher education in the state to adopt a policy on "student-on-student harassment" that can be used in "disciplining students for their speech, expression or assemblies."[33] While the Tennessee law recognizes the harmful impact of conduct "that is so severe, pervasive, and objectively offensive that it effectively bars the victim's access to an educational opportunity or benefit," such conduct is prohibited only when it is "discriminatory on a basis prohibited by federal, state or local law," leaving students who are not members of a legally recognized group unprotected from such conduct.

Future state legislation on campus free speech could incorporate provisions that acknowledge the harmful impact of conduct that deprives any student of his or her right to self-expression and that prohibit such conduct when it reaches the behavioral standard for harassment as defined by the US Supreme Court. Unlike the Tennessee bill, however, future legislation must afford protection from "student-on-student harassment" to all students equally.

At the federal level, one solution could be the establishment of new federal legislation that, like Title VI of the Civil Rights Act, would make a school's federal funding dependent on its ability to ensure adequate protections for students. Unlike Title VI, however, legislation focusing on intolerant behavior and its impact on self-expression would require federally funded schools to ensure that all students are equally protected from behavior that meets the US Supreme Court's definition of harassment.

Conclusions

In politically challenging times like these, there is an understandable desire to circle the Jewish wagons and focus squarely on Jews and how the threat of antisemitism must be fought by any means necessary. On American campuses, that has included the demand for more and better legal protections for Jewish students as a group. But, as I have tried to argue, that may well be a strategic mistake, since antisemitism is fundamentally different from racism and other forms of group bigotry treated under antidiscrimination law. Even if Jewish students were to be fully recognized as a protected group, it is unlikely that the protection afforded by Title VI would be adequate. At the same time, I have argued that antisemitism is fundamentally the same as other forms of intolerance whose intent is to deny the constitutionally protected self-expression of others, and I have suggested that an approach to campus antisemitism that incorporates a model of intolerance based on First Amendment principles would be most beneficial not only to Jewish students but to all students.

This approach could not be more timely on college campuses, where intolerant conduct, whose goal is to prevent some students from expressing their opinions, beliefs, or identity, is rampant. When students are demonized, threatened, harassed, and bullied into silence, it not only negatively impacts their own educational experience but undermines the entire academic endeavor; the whole campus community suffers. Jewish students are best protected when all students are equally protected from the intolerant behavior that violates their freedom of expression and denies them full participation in campus life.

Notes

1. "Title VI of the Civil Rights Act of 1964," US Department of Justice, accessed January 29, 2021, https://www.justice.gov/crt/fcs/TitleVI.

2. Kenneth L. Marcus, "Title VI and Title IX Religious Discrimination in Schools and Colleges," US Department of Education, September 13, 2004, https://www2.ed.gov/about/offices/list/ocr/religious-rights2004.html.

3. Russlynn Ali, "Dear Colleague Letter," US Department of Education, October 26, 2010, https://www2.ed.gov/about/offices/list/ocr/letters/colleague-201010.html.

4. For example, Title VI complaints filed on behalf of Jewish students against University of California (UC) Irvine, UC Santa Cruz, and UC Berkeley in 2008, 2009, and 2012, respectively, were dismissed by OCR in 2013, and a complaint filed on behalf of Jewish students at Rutgers University in 2011 was dismissed in 2014.

5. "S.10—Anti-Semitism Awareness Act of 2016," Congress.gov, December 2, 2016, https://www.congress.gov/bill/114th-congress/senate-bill/10/text.

6. Antisemitism fact sheet, US Department of State, June 8, 2010, https://2009-2017.state.gov/documents/organization/156684.pdf.

7. "Defining Anti-Semitism," US Department of State, accessed January 29, 2021, https://www.state.gov/defining-anti-semitism/.

8. Kenneth L. Marcus to Susan B. Tuchman, August 27, 2018, https://www.politico.com/f/?id=00000165-ce21-df3d-a177-cee9649e0000.

9. See, for example, this letter from nine pro-Palestinian advocacy organizations to the congressional committee tasked with reviewing the AAA in 2016: Dima Khalidi et al. to Bob Goodlatte and John Conyers Jr., December 5, 2016, https://static1.squarespace.com/static/548748b1e4b083fc03ebf70e/t/584eca8ee6f2e17fd89fa3ca/1481558672194/AntiSemitism+Awareness+Act+Opposition+Letter+final.pdf.

10. See, for example, this letter from PEN America White Paper analyzing the AAA and its potential impact on campus free speech: PEN America, *Wrong Answer: How Good Faith Attempts to Address Free Speech and Anti-Semitism on Campus Could Backfire*, November 7, 2017, https://pen.org/wp-content/uploads/2017/11/2017-Wrong-Answer.pdf.

11. See, for example, Shannon Gilreath, "Freedom of Speech and the Anti-Semitism Awareness Act on College Campuses," *The Hill*, January 20, 2017, https://thehill.com/blogs/congress-blog/politics/315195-freedom-of-speech-and-the-anti-semitism-awareness-act-on-college; "What Is the Anti-Semitism Awareness Act Really All About?," ADL, December 11, 2019, https://www.adl.org/blog/what-is-the-anti-semitism-awareness-act-really-all-about; Morton A. Klein and Susan B. Tuchman, "Jewish Leaders Must Urge Students: Use Title VI to Fight Anti-Semitism," *New Jersey Jewish News*, November 19, 2018, https://njjewishnews.timesofisrael.com/jewish-leaders-must-urge-students-use-title-vi-to-fight-anti-semitism/.

12. See, for instance, Jackson Richman, "Bill to Fight Rising Anti-Semitism on Campus Introduced in Congress," *Washington Examiner*, May 30, 2018, https://www.scott.senate.gov/media-center/in-the-news/bill-to-fight-rising-anti-semitism-on-campus-introduced-in-congress; L. Rachel Lerman, "The Anti-Semitism Awareness Act Doesn't Restrict Free Speech—It Helps Prevent Bullying," *Newsweek*, May 31, 2018, https://www.newsweek.com/anti-semitism-awareness-act-doesnt-restrict-free-speech-helps-prevent-bullying-951190; ADL, "What Is the Anti-Semitism Awareness Act About?"; Gilreath, "Freedom of Speech."

13. Erwin Chemerinsky and Howard Gillman, *Free Speech on Campus* (New Haven, CT: Yale University Press, 2017), 118.

14. Correspondence between US Department of Justice and UC San Diego, AMCHA Initiative, August 3, 2012, https://amchainitiative.org/wp-content/uploads/2019/01/DOJ-initiatl-letter-to-UCSD.pdf.

15. Larry Gordon, "UC San Diego Condemns Student Party Mocking Black History Month," *Los Angeles Times*, February 18, 2010, http://articles.latimes.com/2010/feb/18/local/la-me-ucsd18-2010feb18.

16. Ana Tintocalis, "UCSD Student Suspended for Hanging Noose," KPBS, February 26, 2010, https://www.kpbs.org/news/2010/feb/26/ucsd-student-suspended-hanging-noose/.

17. "Show's Racial Slur Prompts Hold on UCSD Student Media," *San Diego Union-Tribune*, February 23, 2010, https://www.sandiegouniontribune.com/sdut-ucsd-media-outlets-see-funds-frozen-2010feb23-htmlstory.html.

18. "Resolution Agreement," Office for Civil Rights, last modified January 15, 2020, https://www2.ed.gov/about/offices/list/ocr/docs/investigations/09116901-b.html.

19. *Student Life: 2012–13 Campus Climate Initiatives*, UC San Diego, March 4, 2013, https://students.ucsd.edu/_files/student-life/StudentLife_campus-climate-initiatives.pdf.

20. For instance, the Foundation for Individual Rights in Education (FIRE), an organization that has vociferously challenged the use of the State Department definition of antisemitism on university campuses on First Amendment grounds, acknowledges that "speech constituting harassment in violation of these statutes [Title IX of the Education Amendments of 1972 (sexual harassment) and Title VI of the Civil Rights Act of 1964] is not protected by the First Amendment, subject to an exacting legal standard." Nevertheless, FIRE challenges cases in which the university ignores an "exacting legal standard" and restricts speech that these statutes do not intend to be restricted. See Samantha K. Harris to Velma Montoya, August 1, 2009, https://d28htnjz2elwuj.cloudfront.net/pdfs/6b056cc0a8700d31f7f8c0fe63518ab8.pdf.

21. Kenneth Marcus, *The Definition of Anti-Semitism* (Oxford: Oxford University Press, 2015), 192.

22. Marcus, *Definition of Anti-Semitism*, 30.

23. Marcus, 41.

24. Marcus, 155.

25. This progression is consistent with the historical record. According to Robert Wistrich, as soon as Hitler came to power in 1933, "the whole apparatus of an increasingly totalitarian German state was now devoted to creating a hallucinatory demonic image of the Jews in order to justify their isolation, segregation, defamation, persecution, and eventual expulsion." Antisemitic propaganda was followed in short order by "an avalanche of legal measures" that provided the legal justification for actions that harmed Jews by excluding them from "the civil service, the army, the judiciary, the universities, the free professions, and arts and sciences." Within a few years, "the steady barrage of anti-Semitic propaganda and laws led the mass of Germans to unquestioningly accept the transformation of Jews into social pariahs, as if it were something normal and inevitable. By the time of the 'Crystal Night' nationwide pogrom of November 9–10, 1938 (an unprecedented orgy of anti-Jewish violence), the German public was either numbed or, in certain cases, willing to participate in the brutalities." Robert Wistrich, *A Lethal Obsession* (New York: Random House, 2010), 244–45.

26. Jeremy Sharon, "Farrakhan Compares Jews to Termites, Says Jews Are 'Stupid,'" *Jerusalem Post*, October 17, 2018, https://www.jpost.com/Diaspora/Farrakhan-compares-Jews-to-termites-says-Jews-are-stupid-569627.

27. Tamar Pileggi, "Khamenei: Israel a 'Cancerous Tumor' That 'Must Be Eradicated,'" *Times of Israel*, June 4, 2018, https://www.timesofisrael.com/khamenei-israel-a-cancerous-tumor-that-must-be-eradicated/.

28. Marcus, *Definition of Anti-Semitism*, 67.

29. The archbishop of Canterbury, Justin Welby, recently expressed a similar idea. Noting that the Jewish people has been "hated more specifically, more violently, more determinedly and more systematically, than any other group," he called antisemitism "a tap root, for all racism, all discrimination, all cruelty, because of the nature of the human being in our culture." "Archbishop of Canterbury and Chief Rabbi Visit Yad Vashem," Archbishop of Canterbury, March 5, 2017, https://www.archbishopofcanterbury.org/speaking-and-writing/latest-news/archbishop-canterbury-and-chief-rabbi-visit-yad-vashem.

30. Davis v. Monroe County Bd. of Ed. (97-843) 526 U.S. 629 (1999), https://www.law.cornell.edu/supct/html/97-843.ZS.html.

31. "Racial Incidents and Harassment against Students," US Department of Education, March 10, 1994, https://www2.ed.gov/about/offices/list/ocr/docs/race394.html.

32. "Campus Free-Speech Legislation: History, Progress, and Problems," American Association of University Professors, accessed January 29, 2021, https://www.aaup.org/report/campus-free-speech-legislation-history-progress-and-problems.

33. Amendment No. 1 to SB0723, http://www.capitol.tn.gov/Bills/110/Amend/SA0333.pdf, passed in May 2017.

TAMMI ROSSMAN-BENJAMIN is cofounder and Director of AMCHA Initiative, a nonprofit organization that investigates, documents, and combats antisemitism at institutions of higher education in America. She was a faculty member in Hebrew and Jewish studies at the University of California Santa Cruz from 1996 to 2016. For the last several years, she has been involved in efforts to study and combat the rise of campus antisemitism. She has written articles about academic anti-Zionism and antisemitism and has lectured widely on these developments and the growing threat they pose to the safety of Jewish students on university campuses.

IV. THE GLOBAL REACH OF ANTISEMITISM

9

Orchestrating Public Blindness in Contemporary France

Daniel Dayan

Qualifying Something as Antisemitic

This chapter is about battles for identification and aims to find out whether certain forms of violence against Jews (including in some cases torture, murder, or both) involve any antisemitism at all or whether they should be considered mere accidents or episodes of temporary insanity whose authors should by no means be held responsible. It considers battles for identification and aims to find out whether certain speeches, plays, and operas, as well as their authors, are antisemitic or on the contrary virtuous and above suspicion. Finally, this chapter identifies what is meant by "antisemitism" today. Does this notion still have any meaning, and is this meaning relevant to the life of contemporary societies?

Affirmative Antisemitism, Defensive Antisemitism

France is experiencing an overlap of two antisemitisms. The first is archaic, affirmative, and accusatory. It relies on canonical stereotypes whose wording is episodically updated. It is a serene antisemitism. The second is contemporary and defensive. It consists basically in denying the antisemitism of the speaker himself yet also suggests that situations in which Jews are under attack should not be considered antisemitic. Among the actors of this contemporary antisemitism, we find perpetrators in search of justifications as well as those whom we are invited to view as clear-sighted spectators, enlightened observers, or impartial witnesses.

Four Pillars of Blindness

Proceeding to an orchestration of public blindness in a context characterized by the inertia of political authorities, judiciary authorities, and the media, antisemitism in France has developed four distinct registers. These registers tend to blend into each other, yet analytically, they may be seen as distinct. Two of these registers are versions of what I would call defensive antisemitism. Denied antisemitism takes the form of denying or disclaiming one's own antisemitism. Equivocal antisemitism consists of playing hide-and-seek with those who might accuse or denounce you. A third type, magisterial (or spectatorial) antisemitism, stresses the irrelevance of antisemitism to certain situations or actions in which Jews are deliberately harmed. Magisterial antisemitism purports to assess the antisemitism of others and claims to submit it to a neutral assessment. It does so from a position of authority conferred by status or by supposed knowledge. The fourth and last type, which I call virtuous antisemitism, is an antisemitism perpetrated in the name of altruism. Claiming to be guiltless, this form of antisemitism is practiced in the name of ethics itself.

Contemporary antisemitism, with the various forms of denial it practices, is certainly not worse than its violent alternative. In fact, it often joins forces with that alternative and serves as its defensive shield, one that is very much needed in a culture that has been shaped by a long tradition of enlightenment, that stigmatizes those who are considered "racist," and that creates a cult around those who can claim the status of "victims."

Four Explorations

The discussion I propose in the current chapter opens with a brief account of the intellectual and social-political context of the resurgence of antisemitism in France and then explores several of the registers evoked above: denied antisemitism, equivocal antisemitism, and magisterial antisemitism. The second part of this chapter looks at the epistemological stance frequently adopted by those who practice a magisterial form of antisemitism. Thus, it asks the question, "How does one identify antisemitism?" as well as, conversely, the question, "How can one manage not to identify it?" Is there, in other terms, a method in this blindness? The chapter's conclusion addresses the issue of virtuous antisemitism and poses the question of an ethics without perplexity, an ethics that is based on a deliberate confusion of the two meanings of the adjective *wrong*. It furthermore discusses the reliance of virtuous antisemitism on theories of otherness meant to hierarchize Others into those who deserve regard and those who do not.

Sketching the French Context

Coordinating Antisemitisms

Today's France harbors antisemitisms of various origins. Antisemitic factions are competing with each other; they are also making attempts at coordination, which often means reciprocal co-optation and instrumentalization of their respective claims. Coordination among various antisemitisms can also be achieved by the social media, whose algorithms—like some invisible hand—prove capable of matching certain contents to certain user profiles. Hate groups are thus introduced to one another and familiarized with distinct but potentially convergent traditions.

Islamist Antisemitism and Its Traveling Companions

When it comes to explosions of violence against Jews, two main groups are in competition. The first group is trying to perpetuate the antisemitic traditions of the French far right. The second group is mostly Muslim and includes migrants or descendants of migrants either from the Maghreb or from former French African colonies dominated by Islam. For a long time, a Muslim antisemitism was claimed not to exist. The only conceivable antisemitism had to come from the French far right. Today, the existence of a militant antisemitism among some Islamist groups in France is no longer questioned. Simultaneously, the far right has become less visible, less active, and less eloquent; the "Front National" has adopted a low profile, and those who claim to perpetuate neo-Nazi traditions seem often engaged in mere nostalgic exercises. Antisemitic inventiveness seems to be elsewhere.[1]

In the present day, the existence of Islamism is no longer challenged. While posing a challenge to the far right, Islamist antisemitism often joins forces with the far left under the banner of their common "anti-Zionism." Based on countless misunderstandings, this alliance is embarrassing to both sides. Yet a modus vivendi has been found. Most violent actions against Jews have been committed by radical Islamists. At the same time, most intellectual elaborations meant to retrospectively excuse or justify already committed crimes have been provided by the far left.[2] Such retrospective justifications can easily be read as marks of approval, if not as prospective incitations.

Visibility

One of the effects of the attacks emanating from Islamist militants was to confer on Jews a visibility they had largely lost after World War II. Attacks on Jews had the explicit ambition to harm. But they also had a serendipitous effect: they made Jews visible and isolated them for display as a special group within the nation. This secondary effect may have been fortuitously discovered, but it became part of a consistent strategy that I would call "dissimilation" (as opposed to assimilation) or "extegration" (as opposed to integration). This strategy consisted in making Jews Other, of returning Jews to the status of aliens. Notwithstanding their contribution to the construction of the French language (Rachi) and to French culture (from Michel de Montaigne to Marcel Proust), Jews were said to be incompatible with France, and the existence of Israel became instrumental in challenging their self-definition as French citizens.

The role accorded to Israel and Zionism in this scenario is crucial. No matter how politically incoherent and no matter how inconsistent with the ideals of the left, left-wing anti-Zionism has been instrumental in waking up a largely dormant antisemitism.[3] Like some Prince Charming, anti-Zionism may have shaken French antisemitism out of the long inertia that had turned it into a Sleeping Beauty.

Orphaned Jews: Losing Confidence in the State

As pointed out by Danny Trom, there was a time when "Jews who could no longer count on the various royal alliances that used to offer them shelter and protection . . . enthusiastically endorsed the republican order as a substitute."[4] Today, "the weakening of European sovereign states" makes Jews skeptical as to the degree of protection they should expect. Theirs is not only a memory of past treasons. It is an awareness of growing impotence."[5]

In fact, the antisemitism that has flourished in France during recent years has been accompanied by various forms of impotence. Terrorism has often been directed at political elites and representatives of the French state. And this terrorism itself is only the culminating form of a "French intifada" of sorts—a series of civilian attacks against bus drivers, teachers, firemen, and policemen, which finally succeeded in forcing entire neighborhoods to live outside the rule of French law and making them known as "les Territoires Perdus de la République."[6] On top of all this, the social movement of the "yellow vests," while originally expressing economic concerns, has escalated into violent rioting and challenged for many months, week after week, the authority of a democratically elected government. "Yellow-vest" populism has coincided with the return of an explicit, unabashed antisemitism, which we see manifested in graveyard desecrations, verbal aggressions, physical attacks, conspiracy theories, and even musings about the execution of a president described as an emblem of Jewish power.

Listen to Jean Claude Milner pointing to the impotence that afflicts the old continent now that it sees itself as a space without borders, destined to a peace without end: "Such a chimaera," he notes, "involves at least two heavily consequential blind spots. Having hastily declared that nations are over, federal Europe is unable to address its violent return in Eastern Europe. Having no less hastily denied its own crimes, Europe is incapable of providing a credible protection against hatred."[7]

This situation, for Trom, might prefigure the end of French Jewry and foreshadow the future of European Jews in general: "Jews have started leaving certain cities and neighborhoods where daily life has become impossible. They are taking their children out of public schools they perceive as too dangerous. They start settling abroad." France is thus turning into "a country of emigration."[8]

Betrayed Jews: Antisemitism Goes Progressive

Besides losing confidence in the power of state institutions to protect them, French Jews also feel betrayed. An unexpected metamorphosis is turning the progressive left against itself and against them. Of course, progressive intellectuals are not the only ones involved in such an about-face. Yet their defection hurts more. We are now dealing with the thinking elite whose members have been on the forefront of all battles against antisemitism throughout the two last centuries. That antisemitic formulations would emanate from some of those whom French Jews always saw as their natural friends and allies is particularly painful for Jewish intellectuals.[9] It is as if Émile Zola, taking back his "J'accuse," announced he was no longer on Captain Dreyfus's side. How could French Jews not feel betrayed? And how would European Jews not feel betrayed when progressive intellectuals not only stop combating antisemitism but seem on their way to drafting the next forms it will take? As Milner puts it, "One may then wonder whether Europe is not about to become the world's champion of guiltless antisemitism."[10]

Guiltless antisemitism is the subject of this chapter. The actions I discuss are not about harming bodies but about impairing common sense, reason, and the very possibility of ethical thinking. They are generally conducted in the cultural sphere and in the name of virtue. Let me start with denied antisemitism.

Denied Antisemitism

Antisemitism is not the same when the sun shines and when it rains. Depending on the political climate, antisemites may be blunt (triumphalist, ostensible, vociferous, frontal, and blatant) or defensive (oblique, indirect, circuitous, and circumspect). Both antisemitisms exist, not only in contemporary France but in a number of advanced democracies as well. Hence, the examples I offer below are mostly but not exclusively French.

These examples predominantly concern the antisemitism of rainy days—a defensive, cautious antisemitism whose rhetorical strategies combine emphatic disclaimers with an expert reliance on the art of ambiguity (double entendre, double binds, and duplicitous polysemy). In short, defensive antisemitism includes both a denial register and an equivocal register.

Disclaiming One's Own

Denied antisemitism consists in disclaiming one's antisemitism. Disclaimers of this sort may seem grotesque or caricatural. Curiously, they may succeed in looking quite reasonable when they occur. A major example of disclaimed antisemitism and of the use of anti-Zionism as a smoke screen involves the story of a hostage-taking on the Italian liner *Achille Lauro* in 1984. Palestinian terrorists boarded the ship and captured a small group of Jewish passengers. They chose one of them, an American pensioner named Leon Klinghoffer, who was paralyzed and got around in a wheelchair. Klinghoffer was shot in the head and thrown overboard, together with his wheelchair.

Director Peter Sellars, librettist Alice Goodman, and composer John Adams then decided to compose an opera on the basis of this incident. Entitled *The Death of Klinghoffer*, this opera, they said, was supposed to account for the Middle East conflict by respecting the "points of view of both parties." The opera was intended to be "impartial and balanced."[11] It was created, and the authors further insisted that it contained "absolutely no bias" (Adams) and that it was "talking about man in general, beyond all political differences" (Sellars).[12] Goodman was the only one to express regrets. She regretted her own naivete in imagining that Palestinians would be granted a place in an opera. When the opera was given on a Brooklyn stage, members of the Jewish community issued a protest. This protest was rebuked by the authors, who issued outraged statements, and by most progressive newspapers, whose theater critics refused to speak of antisemitism. Yet one may wonder whether this opera was simply about granting a place to the Palestinians. What was it that the authors found "balanced" about a paralyzed man shot at close range in the head and thrown into the water in his wheelchair? In what way were the "points of view of both parties" accounted for? Let us take a brief look at the opera's opening.

As soon as the choir concludes a heroic evocation of Palestinian suffering, the action moves to a Jewish family in an American living room. While the paterfamilias is playing with his remote control, a recitative from his wife reminds us that he spends far too much time in the toilet. Klinghoffer himself is not better served. The only aria the paralyzed man is allowed to sing concludes with the profound remark, "I should have worn my hat." Of course, there is no crime in juxtaposing a tragedy and a gallery of grotesque characters, *The Trojan Women* and a soap opera. But why treat the death of Klinghoffer like an episode of *I Love Lucy*? Some pensioners do have bad taste. But is this bad taste their own? Or is it a convenient way of dehumanizing them? And if they have indeed had bad taste, is it a reason for executing them?

All this leads to a rather simple question: What is Leon Klinghoffer doing in this opera? The authors spoke of respecting "the points of view of both parties." But who are these two parties? The balanced symmetry announced by the authors could have led to a casting of Palestinians and Israelis. But Klinghoffer was not an Israeli. He had only one thing in common with the Israelis: he was a Jew. In other words, this "balanced" opera celebrates the killing of Jews at random in the name of Palestinian suffering. How do you then distinguish this highbrow, virtuous anti-Zionism from your usual brand of lowbrow, vulgar antisemitism? Should we consider it normal that neither the authors of the opera nor many of the major progressive newspapers in the world (except the *New York Times* and the *Wall Street Journal*) found it useful to listen to those who protested? This is precisely the sort of public blindness that is at issue in cases of denied antisemitism.

Massacre at Vincennes

The following example is even more telling. While his Jewish victims were lying on the floor, the savvy perpetrator of a massacre in a Paris kosher supermarket informed surviving clients that they should avoid jumping to conclusions. Below is the testimony of a survivor filmed on a news channel, his face hidden.[13] This senior civil servant recalls the moment during which he was submitted to the equivalent of a Nazi "selection" by hostage-taker Amedy Coulibaly, who asked him about his identity:

—Your origin? asks Coulibaly.

—French.

—What religion?

—Catholic, answers the hostage after a short hesitation due to the embarrassment he feels in offering an answer which, although true, may mean survival by distinguishing him from the other hostages.

Coulibaly seemed to be guessing the hostage's thoughts. In a calm, almost friendly voice, he told him,

—You know, I have nothing against Jews. I'm not antisemitic.

As he spoke, two customers, Philippe Braham and François Michel Saada, were lying dead on the floor. An employee, Yohan Cohen, seriously injured in the face, was bleeding to death. When the store manager tried to offer some help, Coulibaly shot him in the hand. Coulibaly, who was systematically killing the Jewish customers of a kosher supermarket, asserted, "I have nothing against Jews. I'm not antisemitic." If Coulibaly's action was not antisemitic, is there anything that could be?

But then, why would Coulibaly make such a statement? Was it a tactical move? A lie intended to gain favors? But what favors could the killer expect after such a rampage? It would be tempting to dismiss his statement. Yet it remains to be seen whether Coulibaly is not sincere. Such a sincerity would only make things worse—by revealing, for example, the emergence of a new zeitgeist in which antisemitism would no longer be a relevant notion. But let us address another possibility: Was Coulibaly playing games?

Equivocal Antisemitism

Equivocal antisemitism is a form of defensive antisemitism that specializes in ambiguous statements, statements that lend themselves to a double entendre and are therefore easy to disclaim. But equivocal antisemitism is not merely defensive. It also belongs in the realm of perverse pleasures—the pleasure of playing cat and mouse, the pleasure of adding insult to injury, and the pleasure of hurting one's victims twice.

The French stand-up comedian Dieudonné is a master at this game. After the collective slaughter of the journalists at *Charlie Hebdo*, and while all of France was holding posters reading "I am Charlie" in solidarity with the victims, Dieudonné offered a slightly different formulation. He announced, "I am Charlie-Coulibaly." Dieudonné's solidarity with the victims is also solidarity with the killers.

One of the identifying features of equivocal antisemitism consists in turning compassion into a vehicle of sarcasm. Think of the British Labour leader Jeremy Corbyn, whose party decided not to publish a statement about the Pittsburgh shootings because this would give undue attention to antisemitism. When British Jews protested, Corbyn retorted that they were taking some of his statements too literally. He further mocked them by noting that they "clearly have two problems. One is that they don't want to study history, and secondly, having lived in this country for a very long time, probably all their lives, they don't understand English irony, either."[14]

Corbyn's apparent apology ended up as an insult. Inserting antisemitic attacks into the very statements that ostensibly repudiate antisemitism or confirming one's attacks in the very act of disclaiming them is of course infuriating to the victims. Instead of being entitled to protest, these victims are caught in a language game meant to silence them. They are confronted with the impossibility of seeking redress, for the language in which they would do so is controlled by the perpetrator.[15] As a spokesman for Corbyn has put it, "He does not have an anti-Semitic bone in his body."[16]

Equivocal antisemitism is an obvious source of perverse pleasures, one that is akin to the molestation of children as described by British psychoanalyst Jonathan Sklar, in reference to the work of Sandor Ferenczi.[17] Both equivocal antisemitism and child molestation tend to occur in two steps. In the case of equivocal antisemitism, step one consists of antisemitic attacks. In step two, the victim is told that the attack was just a joke, which this victim was too silly to understand. In the case of child abuse, step one is the moment of traumatic seduction. Step two consists in silencing the abused children by telling them they misunderstood what took place or even invented the whole thing.

As opposed to the games played by those who practice equivocal antisemitism, most who would rather disclaim their own antisemitism tend to adopt a didactic, pedagogic pose. They step back, look at themselves, and proffer "objective" conclusions regarding their own behavior and regarding what antisemitism "really" is. Yet there are cases in which the disclaiming does not directly come from the perpetrators themselves.

Magisterial Antisemitism

What or Who Qualifies as Antisemitic?

There exists an antisemitism of signs, statements, and accusations. There also exists an antisemitism expressed in outbursts of pure violence. Reliance on signs leaves little doubt as to the antisemitic character of a situation. Outbursts of violence are more problematic. Take the case of a physical attack on a person who happens to be Jewish. Unless it is framed by explicit statements or insults and unless such statements are publicly uttered, such an attack can easily be dismissed as not antisemitic at all. Thus, and quite ironically, the assassination of one Jewish person—for example, Mireille Knoll—might be deemed less antisemitic than public insults aimed at another (for instance, Alain Finkielkraut). Controversies about antisemitism often take the form of battles for identification. Are certain texts or cultural works antisemitic, or are they unjustifiably slandered? Are certain cases of violence against Jews, including sometimes assassination, really something more than mere accidents, or are they instances of banal delinquency?

Magisterial antisemitism feeds on these questions. Answers typically emanate from individuals vested with an intellectual or moral authority: experts, pundits, public intellectuals, judges, magistrates, police officers, and last but not least, journalists. These individuals usually represent monitoring institutions. They are in charge of validating—or invalidating—realities, of performatively producing what we call "social facts." As opposed to what takes place in denied antisemitism, these "priests of factuality" are not in the business of justifying themselves. Rather, they are assessing the antisemitism of others. Magisterial antisemitism occurs when, in the name of their intellectual or jurisdictional "magisterium," such privileged spectators refuse to accept as antisemitic certain actions or behaviors that common sense would consider so.

Of course, common sense may be wrong, and those who deny the role of antisemitism in a particular situation are sometimes justified. Yet other times they are not, and the reticence of those who practice magisterial antisemitism may amount to a form of complacency toward the perpetrators.

In a little-noticed section of his book *Qui Est Charlie?*, demographer Emmanuel Todd wonders why the January 2015 attacks on *Charlie Hebdo* completely overshadowed the simultaneous massacre of the clients of a kosher supermarket in Vincennes.[18] Todd speaks of "the astonishing underestimation of the antisemitic dimension of the whole event."[19] This type of underestimation is what magisterial antisemitism is all about.

Requalifying Crimes

Antisemitic crimes are often requalified. They turn into ordinary crimes, common misdemeanors, and forms of temporary madness. Their victims are dismissed as exaggeration prone if not altogether delusional. Let me quote Françoise Cotta and Gilles Antonowicz, the lawyers of the gang that kidnapped Ilan Halimi, tortured him for weeks, and finally dumped the body of the young man, whom they left to die. Writing after the conclusion of the trial of the so-called gang of Barbarians and its leader, Yousouf Fofana, Cotta and Antonowicz are speaking no longer as lawyers but as enlightened citizens offering their guidance to the public:

> Mr. Fofana did not kill Ilan Halimi because the latter was Jewish. Mr. Fofana may have entertained antisemitic beliefs, but these beliefs are irrelevant. The only motive of Fofana's action was greed.... For political reasons some would like public opinion to believe that antisemitism is rampant in our society. Yet this scourge has never been historically lower.... Those who systematically and unthinkingly exploit every incident that might possibly carry an antisemitic connotation, whether it actually occurred or not, run the risk of creating a rift between communities and of feeding the very evil they are endlessly denouncing.[20]

Let me stress four of the points made in this typical op-ed, which appeared in *Le Monde* on July 12, 2009. (All italics that follow here are mine.) First, besides mentioning incidents that "actually occurred *or not*," the lawyers speak of the kidnapping of Ilan Halimi, who was targeted because "Jews are rich," as an incident *"that might possibly carry antisemitic connotations."* Second, the lawyers insist that mere *"greed"* was Fofana's unique concern (leading us to wonder what the gang leader's economic interest was in damaging—torturing, in fact—his only potential asset). Third, the op-ed describes the "scourge" of antisemitism as having *"never been historically lower."* In fact, and starting with the early 2000s, it was at its highest level since the period of Nazi occupation. Fourth, the last sentence in the piece speaks of the danger for French Jews of "feeding the very evil they are endlessly denouncing." Bluntly put, the message is as follows: "Either Jews stop complaining of antisemitism, or else." This is in fact a beautifully worded threat.[21]

Seeing Nothing, Seeing Something Else

When practiced by the media, magisterial antisemitism can take two forms. The first consists in seeing nothing, in turning events into nonevents. Acts of antisemitic violence are suppressed and treated as if they had never happened. In the second case, something is indeed acknowledged as having taken place, but this something has nothing to do with antisemitism. The killing of Sarah Halimi illustrates both strategies. It was originally considered a nonevent and buried amid statistics. Only in retrospect was the old lady's death acknowledged as having held some significance.

In his powerful book *Un temps pour Haïr*, writer Marc Weitzmann discusses antisemitic aggressions committed in 2017 and 2018, the most traumatic of which were, first, the killing of Sarah Halimi, who was beaten up and thrown out of a window by a neighbor, Kobili Traore, on April 4, 2017;

and then, a year later, the stabbing of eighty-five-year-old Mireille Knoll, who died of eleven knife wounds and was subsequently set on fire by a young man named Yacine Mihoub, who was her neighbor and protégé.[22] Weitzmann stresses two important points.

In the first place, throughout the seven months following the murder of Mrs. Halimi, her family and the Jewish media were the only ones to describe her killing as antisemitic violence. The major media took a different stand. Since both Halimi and Knoll were killed by isolated individuals and not in the course of a concerted rampage, their killers were declared not to be antisemitic. Lending credit to the obviously incorrect accusations proffered by Jews would mean surrendering objectivity, giving in to emotion, and running the risk of igniting "Islamophobia." This had to be avoided at all costs.

Secondly, unlike the death of Sarah Halimi, the assassination of Mireille Knoll did trigger public emotion. The fact that Knoll was a survivor of the Vel' d'Hiv Roundup conferred on her killing a dimension of continuity with sinister doings in the past. That Knoll had taken care of her future executioner throughout his childhood turned her story into a grim replay of the famous novel by Romain Gary in which a Shoah survivor—Madame Rosa—adopts a Muslim boy. Finally, the second murder, Weitzmann observes, shed a retrospective light on the first one, leading to the embarrassment of those who had chosen to ignore it.

Despite this public emotion, monitoring instances remained skeptical as to the antisemitic nature of the murder. Judges, journalists, talk-show guests, and lawyers kept pondering: Is this really antisemitism? Shouldn't we rather speak of a crisis of temporary madness? Controversies blossomed. One had to choose. Tricking the public into such dilemmas was, in a certain way, the point, since nothing in fact prevented the assassin of Knoll from being both antisemitic and paranoid. Sticking to a naive "either-or-ism" and to a linear conception of causality merely allowed further distillation of doubt. Despite an appearance of scientific rigor, the notion that an attack on Jews had to be either antisemitic or caused by insanity was just a way of making antisemitism invisible until some new event would emerge and monopolize public attention. In this excellent example of magisterial blindness, epistemological concerns offered a lofty alibi.

Blindness by Methodology: Toward "Inexistentialism"

But there exists another form of magisterial blindness that also wraps itself in a mantle of methodological rigor. It concerns all the cases in which antisemitic or terrorist violence is perpetrated by former victims of colonization.

Such a production of blindness often emanates from militant social scientists who, specializing in the "sociology of domination," reject the possibility that the dominated might profess an antisemitism of their own.

Take the case of Mickael Harpon, a convert to Islam and employee of the Paris police intelligence department. In October 2019, Harpon managed to stab four police officers to death and seriously injured a fifth before being himself shot. Activists almost immediately dismissed the terrorist dimension of this rampage by claiming that Harpon was not a terrorist guided by religious convictions but a man who acted in response to discrimination. In other terms, Harpon's massacre was not an action at all but only a reaction (caused by his deafness). That this reaction should have taken the form of attacks directed against French officers is deemed irrelevant.

In the same vein, many self-proclaimed "experts" argue that discussing the motivations behind antisemitic actions is a simple waste of time. Reasons for perpetrating antisemitic violence have to be sought out in objective factors rather than ideological motives. No matter what the perpetrators might themselves indicate, their actions are in fact dictated by circumstances that the expert observer has the privilege of defining. Within such a framework, contextual causes are considered sufficient to explain actual episodes of violence with no need for motivations that would connect such causes to given courses of action. The fact that the very same situations of domination may trigger extremely different responses ranging from terror to ordinary crimes to antisemitic violence, to no response at all, is considered inconsequential. Thus, perpetrators who insist that their attacks were specifically targeted at Jews do not deserve to be listened to. They are nothing but examples of "false consciousness."

In a brilliant paper, Paul Zawadzki contrasts this quasi-Pavlovian approach to that of "sociologists of comprehension."[23] Not only is this approach uninterested in the perpetrators' motives, but, giving little credit to the existence of their free will, it turns these perpetrators into mindless automatons. Such a reductionism offers the advantage of preempting any moral judgment. Who would be silly enough to condemn a mechanical process?

But this methodological approach offers further benefits. Replacing deliberate gestures with automatisms allows turning symbolic actions into meaningless occurrences. Acts of antisemitic violence are indissociable from certain representations. If the motivations and ideologies of violent actors are not to be accounted for, antisemitic violence then ceases to be antisemitic. It becomes just violence. Erasing the why of an antisemitic action amounts to suppressing the what of that action. Ruling out motivation means dissolving antisemitism itself.

This type of hocus-pocus is typical of an attitude for which philosopher Marcel Gauchet forged an interesting term: *inexistentialism*. Inexistentialism is a drastic way of disencumbering sociological inquiry by disposing of embarrassing objects, especially those one is purporting to explain. Thus, thinkers in charge of accounting for given social situations put themselves in the strange position of dismissing the main features of their objects of study. They are willingly condemning themselves to a form of cognitive blindness. Why should they do so? The answer is rather simple. Such a blindness is precisely what they wish to achieve.

Virtuous Antisemitism

Moishe Postone once noted that today we are facing a form of antisemitism that is apparently progressive and "anti-imperialistic" and that there is a true danger in trusting its supposedly emancipatory dimension. What I call "virtuous antisemitism" corresponds to that type of antisemitism. Conducted in the name of noble causes, antisemitic actions or statements are committed or proffered out of respect for suffering others. The list of such others does not include Jews. Here is an example.

Mrs. Goldberg and the Two Rabbis

At the end of 2012, twenty-five students at the University of La Rochelle staged a play. Written under the guidance of a woman director and a young Canadian visiting professor by the name of Eric Noel, the play concerns Jewish financiers who invest in newborn babies in order to put them in debt for life and to turn future generations into mortgaged assets. The play is a comedy. Its title is *The Role of Your Children in the World's Economic Recovery*.[24]

Among the play's main characters, we find a shrill, ugly, greedy woman named Martha Goldberg who keeps shouting, "I am everywhere at home!" We also meet two characters dressed as religious Jews. These two "rabbis" are called Cohen One and Cohen Two. Both are Nazi hunters but are ready to grant the Nazis forgiveness in exchange for cash—to stop their hunt and shake Nazi hands as soon as they are offered a large bundle of banknotes.[25]

A professor at the University of La Rochelle happened to attend a performance of this play. This professor—incidentally named Michel Goldberg—complained to the university president about the actual content of "theater" classes. He was met by cries of outrage and cast as "an enemy of freedom and creative talent."[26]

"I first thought," writes Goldberg, "that the president of the university, my local union, and the league for human rights, would support my decision to protest the play.... I was amazed to find out that all three institutions were in fact among the play's most fervent supporters, and that I was the enemy of secularism and freedom of speech." At the same time, the Canadian dramaturg who had coordinated the writing of the play was officially reinvited for the following year. "His work must have been a source of pride," continues Goldberg, since "this was the first antisemitic play to be financed by a French university."[27]

Offended Virtue

The most telling aspect of this event is the reaction of the Canadian dramaturg. Noel demonstrates that the constancy of his antiracist commitments is simply incompatible with any antisemitism on his part.[28] Here is what he writes:

> I am 29 years old and a professional theatre writer, a graduate of the National Theatre School of Canada, a member of the "Centre des auteurs Dramatiques" and of the "Association Québecoise des auteurs dramatiques" ... For 3 years, I participated in setting up the fundraising programs of the Quebec AIDS Foundation. I now devote more than 35 hours a week to working for several organizations: the Canadian Red Cross, Médecins sans frontières, etc., etc. I am a member of a left-wing political party ("Québec Solidaire") and a fervent spokesperson for minorities. I am an activist, an advocate for humanitarian causes.

Yet, despite all this, "My work has been belittled. I was attacked and even suspected of being anti-Semitic."[29]

The self-justification of the playwright from Quebec seems grotesque. Is this young Canadian unaware of the violence of the accusations his play is circulating? But how can anyone who teaches in a university be so abysmally ignorant as to have never heard of the blood libel or of *The Protocols of the Elders of Zion*? The very irrelevance of the young man's list of good deeds and qualifications poses a disturbing question: Is the condemnation of antisemitism no longer part of his ethical world? May he, in good faith, affirm that he is not antisemitic simply because antisemitism has vanished from the moral landscape? Is antisemitism on the way to becoming an obsolescent construct, not because its reality has disappeared but because it seems inconsequential and unworthy of ethical attention?

Super-Other, Subaltern, and Anti-Other

In a way, Noel's plea justifies Deborah Baum's critique of a "political correctness" that, though meant to respond to ethical concerns, only offers a prepackaged ethics, one that protects the ethical subject from many uncomfortable dilemmas by pronouncing a hierarchy between the various situations that call for moral judgment and by privileging some of them in view of a selective engagement.[30] Thus, some victims are worthy of your guilt. Some are less so. Some do not deserve it at all.[31] At the heart of this selectivity is the question of the Other.

Since ethics necessarily involves otherness, one often hears invocations of "the Other." But who is this Other? And why is there only one, as if the use of capitals subsumed every possible otherness? Why indeed put otherness in the singular in the first place? What about the claims of many Others to be recognized? What about the faces of many Others demanding to be seen and the voices of many Others asking to be listened to? What about the fact that there are simultaneously many ways of being not me?

Abolishing some of the Others in our moral world certainly simplifies it. A map of victimization is thus provided to anyone who would like to become an ethical subject. It offers the list of those who deserve our guilt, regard, or compassion—a list of all those who are established as "validated Others." And it excludes of course those whose otherness is perceived as lacking and whose suffering is deemed inadequate. Validated victims are those who are worthy of recognition.[32] The remaining Others are invited to keep quiet. They should avoid cluttering an already busy moral scene.[33]

Preformatted ethics thus leads to a kind of moral fetishism; it dedicates a cult to those I would define as the "super-Others" and simultaneously neglects the "deficient" Others, treating them as "sub-Others," or, in the literal sense of an already existing word, "subalterns." On this ethical scale, Jews have become subaltern. Their suffering is no longer significant. The fact that Jews are themselves Others and that Judeophobia precisely aims at making them so is not only dismissed, but there is furthermore a special concern for groups whom Jews (and their rhetorical substitutes, the Zionists) are accused of disregarding, offending, or persecuting. Far from being just subaltern, Jews are also on the wrong side of domination. They are detestable, and their detestability takes an apparently original form. They are enemies of the super-Other, of the validated Other. They are guilty of the crime of "Lèse-otherness." This is why, when anti-Zionists condemn the existence of a Jewish state, it is never for egoistical reasons (such as harm done to themselves). It is for altruistic reasons (such as harm done to the Palestinian super-Other and to ethical ideals in general).[34]

In the theatrics of heterophilia, virtuous antisemitism haughtily begrudges recognition of Jewish suffering—such a recognition is not to be wasted on subalterns. Virtuous antisemitism also pronounces Jews detestable and does so out of compassion for the true Other. One can safely, virtuously, comfortably hate Jews as soon as one sees them as tormentors of the suffering Other, the validated Other, or the super-Other.

A Brief Conclusion

"Blood-baths did not stop when the war ended," Levinas writes. "Racism, imperialism, and exploitation are still with us. . . . But violence no longer dares assert itself. Think of the loneliness of those who died in a world shaped by Hitler's triumphs, a world in which evil perceived itself as excellent and in which lying about it was not even necessary."[35]

Are we now reentering the type of world in which lying is no longer necessary? How long will antisemitism continue to rely on the chiaroscuro strategies this paper has described? On the denials of perpetrators? On the blindness of observers? On the tactics that make it possible to be antisemitic and feel virtuous? To enjoy your antisemitism and dismiss it, too?[36]

Notes

1. Let me take the example of an antisemitic discourse produced by the far right, a discourse whose cautious, defensive nature says a lot about power relations in the field of antisemitism. Published in 2014, *Le Vrai Visage de Manuel Valls* (The true face of Manuel Valls) is a book devoted to former French prime minister Manuel Valls. Multiplying conspiracy tropes, it insists that Valls is not what he seems to be, exposes the foreign origins of this "umbrageous Catalan," promises "120 pages of explosive revelations," and stresses Valls's presence in various power networks. The cover page mentions Valls's "eternal ties to the Jewish community and Israel." A chapter links the Valls family to a Rabbi Valls from the Balearic Islands whom the Spanish inquisition sued for being a Marrano. In a word, this book is both antisemitic and anti-Zionist.

Yet it remains extremely discreet about where it comes from. That it emanates from the far right must be inferred from subtle clues. For example, Valls is accused of having been a supporter of Palestine, which a far-left book would rather have applauded. Another clue is that the book is printed by a little-known publisher (Facta) and is copyrighted under a cryptic acronym (EFHS) and also published without any author's name. By contrast, books produced by the far left would come with famous publishers or with their own dedicated publishing houses, and they would certainly not be anonymous. On the contrary, their authors, who often aspire to stardom, would proudly display their identity. This difference in visibility tells us of the perceived weakness of the far right, which in 2014 was still caught in a "spiral of silence." The latter term originates in Elizabeth Noelle-Neuman, *The Spiral of Silence, Public Opinion—Our Social Skin* (Chicago: University of Chicago Press, 1980).

2. Daniel Dayan, "Les médias dans la mêlée—Media et terrorisme," *Ina Global* (Ina, Paris), May 2015.

3. See also Michael Walzer's contributions to this discussion in "Antizionism and Antisemitism," *Dissent Magazine*, fall 2019, https://www.dissentmagazine.org/article/anti-zionism-and-anti-semitism, which is a translation of his original article in French, "Antisemitime et Antisionisme," which appeared in *Esprit*, no. 458, October 2019, https://esprit.presse.fr/article/michael-walzer/antisionisme-et-antisemitisme-42328.

4. Danny Trom, cited in Jean Birnbaum, "L'Expulsion Silencieuse," *Le Monde*, March 1, 2019, 3 (in the section *Monde de livres*).

5. Trom, cited in Birnbaum, "L'Expulsion Silencieuse," 3. This impotence gives a new relevance to Franz Neumann's warning that the dangers posed by the state-as-leviathan are balanced by those of a host of antistatist organizations that Neumann described by the name of another biblical monster, Behemoth, as articulated in Franz Neumann, *Behemoth: The Structure and Practice of National Socialism* (New York: Oxford University Press, 1942).

6. Emmanuel Brenner (with contributions by Alain Finkielkraut, Georges Bensoussan, et al.), *Les Territoires Perdus de la République* (Paris: Pluriel, 2002).

7. Jean-Claude Milner, cited in Birnbaum, "L'Expulsion Silencieuse," 3.

8. Trom, cited in Birnbaum, "L'Expulsion Silencieuse," 3.

9. This sense of betrayal was expressed by a former student of mine in a book called *What Happened to My Friends?* See Brigitte Stora, *Que sont mes amis devenus? Charlie et tous les autres* (Paris: Bord-de-l'eau, 2016).

10. Milner, cited in Birnbaum, "L'Expulsion Silencieuse," 3.

11. *The Death of Klinghoffer*, an opera composed by John Adams, directed by Peter Sellars, and with a libretto by Alice Goodman, premiered in 1991 at Théâtre de la Monnaie, Brussels, and at Opera de Lyon.

12. Sellars, Goodman, and Adams have frequently elaborated on these points in various statements on a range of media. Some of their most eloquent articulations, including the quotations I have used here, can be found in two papers that strongly support them: Robert Fink, "Klinghoffer in Brooklyn Heights," *Cambridge Opera Journal* 17, no. 2 (2005): 173–213; and Katherine Ames, "Opera as a Source of Healing," *Newsweek*, March 31, 1991.

13. Anonymous hostage, "Hypercacher, le recit d'un otage," *Le Monde*, January 18, 2015, 6.

14. Deborah Lipstadt, "Jeremey Corbyn's Ironically Ahistorical Anti-Semitism," *The Atlantic*, August 28, 2018, https://www.theatlantic.com/ideas/archive/2018/08/jeremy-corbyn-jews/568792/.

15. Jean François Lyotard, *The Differend: Phrases in Dispute* (Minneapolis: University of Minnesota Press, 1988).

16. Sam Knight, "Jeremy Corbyn's Antisemitism Crisis," *New Yorker*, August 12, 2018, https://www.newyorker.com/news/letter-from-the-uk/jeremy-corbyns-anti-semitism-crisis.

17. Sandor Ferenczi, "The Confusion of Tongues between the Adults and the Child," *International Journal of Psychoanalysis* 30 (1949): 225–30.

18. Emmanuel Todd, *Qui est Charlie? Sociologie d'une crise religieuse* (Paris: Éditions du Seuil, 2015).

19. Emmanuel Todd, cited in Birnbaum, "L'Expulsion Silencieuse," 3.

20. Françoise Cotta and Gilles Antonowicz, "Gang des barbares," *Le Monde*, July 12, 2009, https://www.lemonde.fr/idees/article/2009/07/13/gang-des-barbares-par-gilles-antonowicz-et-francoise-cotta_1218282_3232.html.

21. In the same vein, the lawyer of Benjamin Weller—a convert to Islam who was Alain Finkielkraut's assailant—insisted in an interview on the French TV channel FR3 that "the words of Mr. Weller have nothing to do with antisemitism." Here are the words in question: "Bloody Zionist! . . . Cursed be your race! France is ours! France is ours! Bloody racist! Hate monger! You will die! You'll go to hell! God will punish you! The creator will punish you! You shit! You Zionist!"

22. Marc Weitzmann, *Un Temps pour Haïr* (Paris: Grasset, 2018).

23. Paul Zawadzki, "Some Epistemological Issues in the Public Debate on Contemporary Antisemitism in France," *Contemporary Jewry* 37, no. 2 (2017), 295–308.

24. Michel Goldberg, *L'antisémitisme en toute liberté* (Paris: Le bord de l'eau, 2014). This work comprises a comprehensive anthology of essays on the scandal of La Rochelle and incorporates Michel Goldberg's own account.

25. Guy Konopnicki, "Antisémitisme sur scène à La Rochelle," in *Marianne* (June 6, 2013); also published in *Etudes du Crif* 25 (October 2013).

26. Goldberg, *L'antisémitisme*.

27. Goldberg, *L'antisémitisme*.

28. Eric Noel's counterattack is a wonderful example of what I would call "denial by syllogism," a genre that includes all statements that start with such words as "How could I be antisemitic since . . . ?" The syllogism offered by Noel is, "How could I be antisemitic since I am virtuous?"

Another example of denial by syllogism is provided by Jeremy Corbyn's entourage: "To Corbyn's supporters, the idea that he is hostile to Jewish people is a low attack and an absurdity. Anti-racism and inclusiveness are organizing principles of Corbyn's politics, so the notion that he could be anti-Semitic—or could allow prejudice to go unchecked—is a kind of logical fallacy." Knight, "Jeremy Corbyn's Antisemitism Crisis."

Anti-Zionism also relies on an extreme form of denial by syllogism. This is the holier-than-thou or "more-Jewish-than-thou" approach (discussed among others by Michael Walzer and Gil Ribak). This form of anti-Zionism starts by proclaiming a restrictive definition of what is meant by "Judaism" (an essentialized rabbinic tradition, or an equally essentialized "diasporeity"). Zionism is then condemned in the name of Judaism for "betraying" the brandished essence.

29. George-Elia Sarfati, "Une pièce de théâtre antisémite à La Rochelle," in *Etudes du Crif* 25, ed. Marc Knobel, October 2013, 27ff.

30. This is the point of the beautiful commentary offered by Deborah Baum on Saul Bellow's *Mr. Sammler's Planet* (New York: Penguin Books, 1970) in her own book *Feeling Jewish (a Book for Just About Anyone)* (New Haven, CT: Yale University Press, 2018), 86–117.

31. By its very wording, the notion of "political correctness" conflates *being in the wrong* (being morally or politically bad) with *being wrong* (being factually mistaken). Such a conflation results in transforming political/moral evaluation into a form of knowledge.

32. Axel Honneth, *The Struggle for Recognition: The Moral Grammar of Social Conflicts* (Oxford: Polity, 1995).

33. Daniel Dayan, *La Terreur Spectacle: Terrorisme et Television* (Louvain: DeBoek, 2007).

34. An "Übermensch" of victimization, the super-Other is a persona whose sufferings are not measurably higher than most but who is perceived as more significant and therefore given fuller visibility. In today's culture of victimization, the identity of super-Others may vary as a function of compassion trends—what I would call an "agenda setting" of compassion.

35. Levinas is cited in Alain Finkielkraut, ed., *Ce Que Peut la Littérature* (Paris: Stock, Les Essais, 2006). As with most texts from the French, the translation is mine.

36. This chapter has discussed the construction of blindness to antisemitism in France, but it does not claim that such a construction is left unchallenged. It acknowledges the existence of many lucid voices as well as the unambiguous position of the present government.

Concerning the existence of an Islamist antisemitism, sometimes legalistically minded, sometimes turned toward violent action, I should also stress that Muslims in France are far from unanimous in supporting it. In fact, many Muslim writers and intellectuals are on the front line when it comes to condemning it, often at great personal risk.

DANIEL DAYAN, a French cultural sociologist, film theorist, and semiotician, is Professor Emeritus at Centre National de la Recherche Scientifique, Paris, where he has held appointments in political communication, political anthropology, and media sociology. He is a fellow of the Marcel Mauss Institute. A graduate of the Sorbonne, EHESS, and Stanford University, Dayan studied comparative literature under René Etiemble, anthropology under Jean Rouch and Albert Memmi, and semiotics under Roland Barthes. Dayan has been a fellow of the European Science Foundation and a resident of the Rockefeller Foundation (Bellagio). He was a visiting professor in film and media theory at the universities of Bergen, Geneva, Jerusalem, Oslo, Pennsylvania, Stanford, Tel Aviv, and Southern California, as well as at New York's New School and at Sciences Po in Paris. Dayan received the ICA Fellows Award (2010) for his contribution to media anthropology. His work is available in thirteen languages.

10

Legislating and Distorting the History of the Holocaust
The Polish Case

Jan Grabowski

IT WILL COME AS NO SURPRISE THAT MY chapter focuses on Poland. That is not because Poland is the worst offender when it comes to Holocaust distortion (although Polish national narrative scores high in this competition) but because during recent decades I have been exposed most often to the various representations and demonstrations of the Polish brand of historical revisionism. Through the lens of Polish memory battles, one can attempt to track, analyze, and reflect on the main trends and challenges facing Holocaust research, education, and commemoration now and in the future. These issues, which still seem to be a distant cloud on the North American intellectual horizon, in Central and Eastern Europe have become immediate and often career-ending threats to our colleagues. The main themes that I touch on are applicable, in varying degrees, to other European countries, and they find eerie, strange, and unexpected echoes on the western side of the Atlantic, too.

Scene from the Past

This photograph, yellowed with age, which miraculously survived occupation and years in hiding, depicts a well-dressed woman and a boy in a scout's uniform. Both are smiling. An enlargement of the picture would show a Star of David on the boy's uniform, the uniform of the Jewish scouts, the Ha-shomer Ha-tsair. Judging by the deep shadows cast on the ground, the photo was taken on a beautiful, sunny day. The image projects a sense of peace and security. The woman on the left is my grandmother, Roma Abrahamer, painter, sculptor, and artist. The young scout next to her is my father, Ryszard Abrahamer, son of Joshua. This idyllic photo was taken in Kraków on one of the last days of August 1939, a moment before the Abrahamers' world, and the world of 3.5 million Polish Jews, collapsed.

Why present this particular photograph? First, the study of the Holocaust is and should remain focused on the fates of individual victims, to the extent possible. Lost in theory, we scholars often forget who the victims were. Second, we are rarely aware of the fragility of our own condition and the instability of our circumstances. Third, we need to remember that the signs of impending disaster are visible, hard to overlook. Naturally inclined toward complacency, we tend to disregard them. In November 2016, shortly before his death, my father called me from his Warsaw apartment. At the time, I was working as a visiting fellow in the United States Holocaust Memorial Museum archives in Washington and was thus somewhat detached from the tidal waves of political change that were then sweeping my native Poland. During our brief conversation, my father said, "Son, the shadows of the past are coming back. It is 1938 and 1939 all over again. I hear the same language; I see the same images. . . . The fascists, they are back!" His words still ring in my ears, as if they were spoken just yesterday.

The Polish Context

The Polish general elections of 2015 brought to power a right-wing, nationalistic party named PiS (the acronym in Polish stands for Prawo i Sprawiedliwość, or Law and Justice). Since then, the nationalists have been dismantling the fundamental components of Poland's democratic system, focusing much of their attention on destroying the independence of the judiciary. However, their obsession with the defense of the so-called "good name of the Polish nation" made the discipline of history one of the most internationally visible areas of confrontation. Holocaust studies, Holocaust research, and Holocaust education quickly became the very heart of this struggle over the past. This became particularly obvious in the context of the infamous Polish "Holocaust Law" of 2018, which stipulated prison terms of up to three years for independent and independently minded scholars and educators who dared to suggest that the "Polish nation was in any way complicit in the Holocaust."

On the eve of the next elections, scheduled for early October 2019, PiS published its political platform. In addition to reinforcing its allegiance to

Figure 10.1. Roma and Ryszard Abrahamer, August 1939, Kraków.

the Catholic Church and to defending Polish families against gays, lesbians, immigrants, political correctness, and the ill-defined but very threatening "ideology of gender," PiS promised to pay more attention to the world of academia. The manifesto states, "The only criteria which can shape scientific and academic pursuits are those based on merit and ethics." This affirmation was, however, conditional. The party platform read, "In justified cases science can also be shaped by *raison d'état*." The French expression *raison d'état* translates poorly into the English language; usually, it is rendered as "reason of state." It belongs to a group of expressions that seem, due to the complexities of history, to find much more traction in continental Europe than they do across the English Channel and on the other side of the Atlantic. A similar expression is the German term *Rechtsstaat*, or state based on the rule of law. In English, it sounds descriptive and innocuous. But the German term has deeper meaning than the simple translation would suggest. *Rechtsstaat* subsumes the existence of its antithesis; it exists in opposition to the painful reminder of a state based on lawlessness and fear, an all-too-well-known scenario in and around Germany.

Raison d'état also means more than the simple translation would indicate. It is a compelling and overriding principle that allows rulers who pursue the ill-defined or undefined "benefit of the state" to disregard or suppress the ideas and people seen as hostile—or simply insufficiently supportive—of the goals of the *Volksgemeinschaft*, or politically construed and ethnically defined national community. In October 2019, the Polish deputy prime minister, Jaroslaw Gowin, declared openly that the history of the Holocaust would be the very field in which the Polish raison d'état would have a special role to play. According to the prime minister, the study of Jewish-Polish relations during the Shoah is the best example of an area where raison d'état should trump independent research. In other words, as commentators summarized it without much subtlety, "We, the government, can write about the Jews any way we want."[1] It is obvious that the Polish authorities want to write the history of the Holocaust on their own terms, not on Jewish or Western terms, as the nationalists in Poland imply. The problem is, of course, not limited to one country. The challenges facing Holocaust research, commemoration, and education in Poland are echoed in Ukraine, Lithuania, Latvia, Hungary, Romania, Russia—and the list goes on.

The New Fear: Holocaust Deflection, Distortion, and Negationism

Pure Holocaust denial is today very much a fringe phenomenon. Disturbing and appalling as it is, the categorical denial that European Jews were exterminated by the Nazis banishes its disciples (denial of the Shoah may be likened to a bizarre cult) to a reservation that is visited by few and respected by none. Unfortunately, much more insidious, dangerous, and popular are the more recent forms of Holocaust denial: distortion of the Holocaust, and labeled more specifically, Holocaust deflection and Holocaust de-Judaization.

To begin, I provide two definitions of the challenges ahead. According to Manfred Gerstenfeld, "Holocaust deflection entails admitting that the Holocaust happened while denying the complicity or various types of participation of countries, specific groups or individuals, despite ample evidence to the contrary. Major examples of deflection occur in those countries where, during the war, Germans were helped by important segments of the local populations in the despoliation, deportation and killing of the Jews."[2] Efraim Zuroff of the Israeli Wiesenthal Center, expanding on the same issue, mentioned several frequently recurring factors in deflection attempts by Eastern European countries. Their main characteristics are "the attribution of Holocaust crimes entirely to German and Austrian Nazis (as opposed to locals); the exaggeration of the number of, and scope of, the assistance provided by local Righteous Gentiles; and attempts to claim that the only local participants in Holocaust crimes were criminals or totally peripheral elements of society."[3]

The Righteous Gentile Revolution: Deflecting the Holocaust

On March 24 each year, Poles celebrate and commemorate other Poles. To be more specific, they commemorate and celebrate Poles who rescued Jews under the German occupation. In 2019, the date was declared an official "National Day of Commemoration of Poles Who Helped the Jews under the German Occupation." On this national day celebrating virtue, the Polish prime minister Mateusz Morawiecki paid tribute to a Polish family killed by the Germans for trying to help Jews. The event took place in the village of Sadowne, located in Węgrów county, located some fifty miles northeast of Warsaw. During his visit to the village, Morawiecki declared, "The inhabitants of Węgrów county passed the exam of compassion with flying colors. Contrary to various slanders which are being published," the prime minister continued, "numerous sources testify to the great and positive role of the Poles during World War II."[4]

The commemoration of the Righteous Poles in this location was initiated by the Pilecki Institute, one of the many institutions of memory control created or funded by the right-wing nationalists in power in Warsaw.

There are 314 counties in Poland that the Polish prime minister could have visited to commemorate Poles who saved Jews under the Nazi occupation. It happens, however, that Węgrów county is precisely the county that I described in detail in *Night without End*, a two-volume, eighteen-hundred-page research work published in Polish in April 2018 that I coedited with Barbara Engelking, a study of Jewish survival strategies in nine selected counties of occupied Poland.[5] My own chapter dealt with Węgrów county, which the Polish prime minister chose to visit, a rural area best known to scholars of the Shoah as home to the Treblinka extermination camp. Our studies made note of the widespread betrayal of Jews by their Polish neighbors. We described the stages and elements of the German genocidal plan, but we also could not avoid including descriptions of Poles' involvement in the robbery, betrayal, and murder of their Jewish neighbors.

It is possible, although unlikely, that Prime Minister Morawiecki's visit to Węgrów was a complete coincidence. I doubt it, however. My skepticism is strengthened by the fact that a few days later Deputy Prime Minister Glinski also paid a visit to Węgrów and voiced exactly the same message, that the Poles of Węgrów "passed the wartime exam of compassion with flying colors" and that they helped save the Jews.

Well, one might ask, what is wrong with the prime minister commemorating brave people who gave their lives in order to save dying Jews? Unfortunately, it is not the Righteous who are being celebrated. Missing is the context without which one is unable to understand why helping Jews was so difficult and so deadly. In order to stress the courage, humanity, and sacrifice of the Poles who helped Jews in Sadowne, the Polish prime minister might have taken a page from the testimony of Adam Starkopf, a Polish Jew who spent a year and a half in that village. It should be added that the village of Sadowne is located next to the Warsaw-Łochów-Małkinia railway line, which, in 1942–43, carried hundreds of thousands of Jews to their deaths at the gas chambers of Treblinka.

Starkopf, blessed with "good Aryan looks," remained "on the surface" and (using a doctored ID) worked as a clerk in the local sawmill, pretending to be a Pole. In his memoir, he wrote, "The Christmas season of 1942–43 in Poland was not one of peace and good will. One cold night, early in January1943, . . . Pela and I were already sound asleep when we were awakened by the rattle of a passing railroad train followed by bursts of machine-gun fire. We could hear the train grind to a halt. I went to the window." Soon, neighbors came knocking on Starkopf's door and shared the news:

"Didn't you hear the commotion outside?! Some Jews just escaped from a train and the Germans started to shoot at them! They must have hit quite a few. Just think—all these Jews lying on the ground, ready for the taking! It's a windfall! We can go out, pick them up, and turn them over to the Gestapo. We'll take their clothes, clean out their pockets, and on top of that we'll get a reward from the Germans for bringing them in. Come on! Everybody else in the village is going, too, so we'd better hurry! Otherwise there'll be no Jews left for us to catch! . . ." Minutes later we could hear moans and screams outside as the wounded Jews were dragged through the snow to barns and stables. The chase went on all night long.[6]

It is precisely this context that allows us to appreciate the bravery of the few who decided to offer help to the dying Jews. The Righteous were not only confronting the Nazi terror—most of all, they had to confront their own neighbors, the hostility and antisemitism of their own community. They had to deal with the fact that it was not permitted to hide Jews and that the risk of denunciation was ever present. It is that very context that is unpalatable to the Polish nationalists. Without this context, however, the celebrations of Polish virtue turn into a sad farce. Moreover, they become an exercise in Holocaust distortion and Holocaust denial. "The inhabitants of Węgrów county passed the exam of compassion with flying colors," said Morawiecki. Adam Starkopf might have disagreed. But Starkopf is dead, and, as many nationalists will argue today, his is a Jewish testimony, after all. The negation of Jewish Holocaust testimony is well underway in today's Poland.

One does not need to leave the territory of the one small county that the Polish prime minister visited in March 2019 in order to find other representations of the triumphant Polish Holocaust narrative. September 22 marks the tragic anniversary of the liquidation of several ghettos in the Węgrów area. On that day in 1942, ten thousand Jews from Węgrów, twelve thousand Jews from Sokolow, and one thousand Jews from Stoczek, altogether twenty-three thousand people, were driven to cattle wagons and delivered to the nearby extermination camp at Treblinka. In the course of these tragic hours, the three small towns witnessed scenes of ultimate horror, with at least two thousand Jews killed in the streets of the ghettos. In all cases, Polish policemen, firefighters, and so-called bystanders or gawkers took an active part in rounding up, beating, robbing, and murdering their Jewish neighbors.

On September 22, 2019, the Pilecki Institute decided to commemorate these tragic events. In a village nearby, the employees of the institute unveiled a statue of a Pole who had died saving Jews. This occurred on a day that should commemorate Jewish suffering and not Polish bravery. Apart from the question of Holocaust denial and distortion, there is also an issue of simple human shame and decency, or in this case, the lack of them. Celebrating Polish virtue instead of commemorating Jewish suffering has become, however, de rigueur, a rule rather than an exception. However bizarre and unlikely it might seem to us, removing Jews from the Holocaust is a process that is well underway. And once Jews have been removed from the historical scene, it can easily be peopled with courageous and selfless gentiles. The Holocaust thus becomes a tragic and distant event that, most importantly, enabled Poles, Ukrainians, Hungarians, and so many other nationalities to claim unprecedented levels of moral excellence and empathy.

The removal of Jews from the history of the Holocaust can acquire different forms. Just a day after the Pilecki Institute's foray into the field of Holocaust distortion, the Polish Institute of National Remembrance (IPN), a huge institution of memory control, employing hundreds of historians and weaponized by the Polish state with a budget of hundreds of millions of dollars, convened a conference entitled "History, Education, Memory." The workshop was held at the site of the Bełżec extermination camp, in the small local museum. Bełżec is the third-largest Jewish cemetery in the world, a place of death for close to five hundred thousand victims killed in the gas chambers between March 1942 and June 1943. The day-long session featured only four papers. The first one dealt with the communist (read: Jewish) collaboration with the Soviets in eastern Poland in 1939–41. The second paper was devoted to Righteous Poles who saved the Jews, the third discussed the ways in which Polish authorities tried to alert the indifferent Western allies to the ongoing genocide, and the fourth focused on the issue of memory and commemoration of war among the local population. It takes a degree of something—courage? insouciance? mockery? contempt for the victims?—to hold a conference at the site of the Bełżec extermination camp and not mention the Jews.

The Conquest of Space

The unending celebration of national virtue and the gradual removal of Jews from the historical narrative go hand in hand with the appropriation of symbols and the conquest of the very few symbolic spaces on Polish territory that, until recently, belonged to the victims of the Holocaust. A recent example of the "Righteous defense" appropriating space devoted previously to victims of the Shoah can be observed in the immediate vicinity of the impressive Museum of the History of Polish Jews. The museum, which opened in 2014, was erected at the center of what had been the Warsaw Ghetto, the site of suffering and death of close to half a million Polish Jews. Today, the museum is surrounded by a firewall of visible representations of Polish virtue. In front of the museum, visitors encounter a monument honoring Righteous Pole Jan Karski, a courageous courier of the Polish underground who delivered to the West a firsthand account of the Holocaust. Next to it, along the southern wall of the museum, an alley is dedicated to Righteous Pole Irena Sendler, a courageous Polish woman who "saved 2,500 Jewish children," as some would believe. On the north side of the museum, a large monument dedicated to "Jews grateful to Righteous Poles who saved them" has been erected. A ten-minute walk from the museum is the "Park of the Righteous," which opened in 2014. These commemorative plaques, monuments, signs, and sculptures may be called *memory patches*; they are intended to cover the wounds, not to heal them. They convey that celebrating one's own virtue is insufficient. For maximum impact, the celebration must be appropriately located, and the memory patches applied, where the voices of Jewish victims are still heard, often to the discomfort of bystanders.

The Polish town of Kielce and the house at Planty 7 stand in history as places of infamy and symbols of vicious, murderous prejudice—an example of the "ritual murder" legend leading to a very real, and not a ritual, murder. It is here that on July 4, 1946, a Polish mob, enraged by the blood libel (tales of Christian children being drained of blood by Jews), murdered forty Holocaust survivors. It was the most recent and bloodiest pogrom in European history. In 2018, however, the scene of the murder received, as did the former Warsaw Ghetto, its own memory patch. The square in front of the notorious house at Planty 7 (from which the Jewish victims were dragged out and later murdered) now bears the name of Irena Sendler—the brave Polish woman who helped save hundreds of Jewish children from the Warsaw Ghetto. Once again, Kielce is a large city, and Sendler had no relation to it (her activity was limited to Warsaw), but the memory patch had to be strategically located, not in a place where it would make historical sense or where it would simply be in good taste but rather directly over the festering wound.

The Uncertain Future of Survivors' Testimony

Holocaust scholars and educators today are worried about the future of survivor testimony. Meetings, articles, and conferences are devoted to this very topic. The underlying question suggests possible challenges ahead. Can we preserve the value of Jewish testimony about the Holocaust once the generation of survivors is no longer with us? In order to preserve the memory, we have at our disposal powerful educational tools, such as the Shoah Foundation's Visual History Archive with the testimonies of fifty-five thousand survivors; we have museums and exhibitions and formidable archival collections; and we have programs and strategies. Most recently, with the help of advanced technology, museums have acquired interactive survivor testimonies, which many hope will have greater appeal for the younger generation. Can we, the self-appointed custodians of the memory of six million dead, feel confident that our mission has been accomplished? Rather not, I fear.

From my perch overlooking the peaceful landscape of Eastern Poland, let me offer you a glimpse of things to come. On May 30, 2018, a month after the publication of the previously mentioned eighteen-hundred-page, two-volume study, *Głos Siedlecki* (The voice of Siedlce), the main newspaper in Eastern Poland—a mainstay, middle-of-the-road publication, unlikely to become a tribune for fascists and right-wing zealots—carried a sensational story. Splashed across its front page was the following headline: "The Last Jew from Węgrów Lied!" The "lying Last Jew" referred to Szraga Fajwel Bielawski, a Holocaust survivor, enterprising merchant, self-made man, and brave fellow from Węgrów. In his harrowing book, he described in detail the liquidation action in the Węgrów Ghetto. There were the Germans and their Ukrainian helpers, wrote Bielawski, and there were the Poles, the Polish police, the firefighters, the "gawkers," and the neighbors. All of them were deadly, sometimes more deadly than the Germans. Bielawski's book describes, among many other things, the massive scale of the local Polish population's complicity in the destruction of the Jewish community of his hometown.

Local Polish historians, working hand in hand with local politicians, including the deputy leader of the Polish Senate and a member of the ruling populist Law and Justice Party, attempted to "defuse" and delegitimize the testimony of the Jewish survivor. How was that done? An inspection of the attic in which Bielawski is thought to have sought refuge during the liquidation of the ghetto reveals that it looks different today from the way it was described by the author. If Bielawski lied about his hideout, argue the local historians, he would have lied about other things, including the descriptions of Polish participation in the Holocaust. And why would a Jew lie about Poles? The newspapers' readers are not given any answers, but no

Figure 10.2. *The Voice of Siedlce* front page: "The Last Jew from Węgrów Lied!"

answers are really necessary. Readers already know the answer. It is, as my father said, 1938 and 1939 all over again. The fact that Bielawski's testimony is corroborated by multiple other Jewish and Polish sources seems to be of no importance to the triumphant Polish discourse of 2018. As for the Jewish survivor himself, he passed away many years ago and can no longer defend his own record and dignity.

Writing about the history of the Holocaust in Poland, a historian must anticipate a degree of hostility. Today, it is a part of the job. An attempt to delegitimize Jewish testimony regarding the Holocaust was, however, an unexpected phenomenon. Similar attempts were made by Polish courts right after the war to dismiss "unwelcome" Jewish testimonies, which placed part of the blame for the extermination on the shoulders of the local Polish population. "The Jew could not have seen the events under discussion from his hideout," Polish judges and lawyers argued in the late 1940s. The same awful logic and the same appalling reasoning seem to gain ground today, three generations later, with the blessing of Polish politicians. We know how important and how reliable the recollections engraved in the minds of survivors are. This knowledge, it seems, is being increasingly ignored, confronted, ridiculed, and rejected in Poland today.

During my last criminal trial in Poland, in 2016, when I fought off accusations of "having slandered the good name of the Polish nation," the lawyers queried me at length about my alleged predilection for Jewish survivor testimony. "But why do you base your account on Jewish testimony, after all?" I was asked. "Where is the Polish testimony? Do you have Polish witnesses to corroborate your account?" I have been asked repeatedly by the former deputy minister of justice of the Polish republic, who represented far right-wing Polish nationalists at the time. The far-reaching consequences of this line of questioning are not difficult for a Holocaust scholar to imagine.

The Polish "Holocaust Law"

The memory battles surrounding the Holocaust acquired, in Poland, a powerful momentum. In their pursuit of national myths, the ruling nationalists released forces that they were unable (and quite likely unwilling) to control. And so, during the so-called March of Independence in November 2017, sixty thousand Poles took to the streets of Warsaw in a demonstration co-organized by two neofascist organizations. It is of little importance whether all, few, or some of the participants shared the extremists' ideology. What matters is that they chose to take part in a march organized by the fascists.

It is within such a climate and such a political context that the authorities in Warsaw decided to move ahead with a new law "to defend the good name of the Polish nation." Certain of public support and contemptuous of the voice of international public opinion, they rammed the bill through the Parliament in February 2018.

To quote the new Polish Holocaust Law (Article 55 a.1), "Whoever claims, publicly and contrary to the facts, that the Polish Nation or the Republic of Poland is responsible or co-responsible for Nazi crimes committed by the Third Reich . . . or for other felonies that constitute crimes against peace, humanity, or war crimes, . . . shall be liable to a fine or imprisonment for up to 3 years. The sentence shall be made public."

One should not be deluded by the words "contrary to the facts" included in the new legislation, because it would be up to the police and the prosecutors to establish, henceforth, what are the facts and what can be said and written. How should one understand the real meaning of the new Polish legislation? What hides between the lines of the ambiguously worded paragraphs? This is the junction where Holocaust envy meets Holocaust distortion, which itself is a form of Holocaust denial. A memo sent out by the Polish Ministry of Foreign Affairs allows us to better understand the true intent of the Polish legal minds responsible for Article 55. In order to help historians avoid costly mistakes, the Polish Ministry of Foreign Affairs established a long list of "false memory codes," or expressions that "falsify the role of Poland during WWII" and that need to be reported to the nearest Polish diplomat for further action. Diplomats are involved because Article 55 was meant to have a global reach. As Zbigniew Ziobro, the Polish minister of justice (responsible for the recent destruction of the independence of the Polish judicial system), said, "Today, the Polish government has taken an important step to create more powerful tools which will allow us to better defend our rights, to defend the historical truth, but also to better defend the good name of the Polish nation, without distinction as to where in the world an act of slander of our nation or falsification of our history occurs."[7]

Sadly, and not by chance, the list of wrong memory codes that have to be expunged from historical narrative includes mostly expressions linked to the Holocaust. On this long List, one finds, among others, "Polish genocide," "Polish war crimes," "Polish mass murders," "Polish internment camps," "Polish work camps" (!), and, most importantly, "Polish participation in the Holocaust." The intensity of the international outcry that followed the introduction of the Polish Holocaust Law must have come as an unpleasant surprise to the authorities. It was, however, too late for any immediate changes—the new law was very popular with Law and Justice (PiS) voters and not unpopular with those who favor the opposition. Attacks from abroad were thus initially discounted as a foreign assault on "national history" and an "abuse of the honor of the Polish Nation."[8] The state-run TV and radio explained the protests against the new law as a vicious attack on Poland perpetrated by vaguely defined "Jewish-German interests."[9]

The "Antipolonism" Ploy

On June 27, 2018, Polish lawmakers, bowing to tremendous pressure from abroad, passed changes to the disputed Holocaust speech law, removing criminal provisions for attributing Nazi crimes to Poles. Once again, the changes were voted on at a breakneck pace. The law was rushed through without debate, without arguments being heard or questions asked. Barely out of the Parliament, the changes were signed into law by the obedient president, and on the same day, the Polish and Israeli prime ministers issued a joint declaration to indicate that the crisis was over and that business should return to normal. The joint declaration was not a simple admission of previous follies. It was another element in the ongoing "memory war" raging in Poland with the Holocaust as its stage. The joint declaration noted "heroic acts of numerous Poles, especially the Righteous Among the Nations, who risked their lives to save Jewish people." It also stressed the good offices of the Polish people and Polish government in exile in rescuing the Polish Jews, and, in a strange twist, it introduced a new term: *antipolonism*, placing it on an equal footing with antisemitism. Those who are unfamiliar with the darker corners of the internet, dusty spaces to which Polish nationalists and right-wing conspiracy theorists were, until recently, largely limited, should know that the term *antipolonism* presupposes the existence of a dark conspiracy whose names are many—Jews, Germans, Russians, and other evil forces that scheme to malign the good name of the Polish nation. During the recent meeting of the ruling Law and Justice (PiS) Party, Mateusz Morawiecki, the Polish prime minister, gave a speech to party members. In addition to many half-truths and outright lies, he went on to say, "Now, after a few months, I can say that Israel talks about history using our terms." This, unfortunately, seems to be true, at least as far as "official" Israel (Benyamin Netanyahu and his supporters) is concerned. Netanyahu's cozying up to the authoritarian regimes in Warsaw and Budapest can no longer be denied. According to Yehuda Bauer, the dean of Israeli Holocaust historians, Netanyahu's participation in the joint declaration amounted to nothing less than an act of treason to the memory of the six million Jewish victims of the Shoah: "It's a betrayal of the memory of the Holocaust and the interest of the Jewish people. And the reason for it is entirely pragmatic: the diplomatic, political, and economic ties between the Israeli government and the government of Poland."[10]

A few days later, Yad Vashem published an important, principled, and forceful statement that showed the joint Polish-Israeli governmental declaration on the Polish Holocaust Law for what it was: a disingenuous and heavy-handed attempt to distort the history of the Shoah. Israeli politicians seemed to be looking for badly needed political allies, while the Polish nationalists seemed to be looking for a way back to the diplomatic mainstream from which they were expelled during the controversy over the law. Historical truth seems to have been the victim.

It important to note that, with the notable exception of Israeli scholar Dina Porat, no historian of the Holocaust endorsed the Polish-Israeli declaration. The pernicious echoes of the declaration are, however, proliferating. Independent scholars have already been attacked by the Polish authorities and accused of "anti-Polish racism," whatever that might mean. In February 2019, the Polish prime minister, Morawiecki, made repeated references to "racist antipolonism," directing his remarks at the members of the Israeli government.[11] While international pressure managed to get Poland to annul the criminal sanctions threatening researchers, scholars, educators, and journalists, the controversial law still stipulates fines for individuals who accuse the "Polish Nation or the Republic of Poland" of having been complicit in the Holocaust. More importantly, it introduces into the legal arena the undefined, vague, and highly subjective concept of "the good name of the Polish nation" and gives NGOs and state institutions tools with which they can initiate civil legal action and harassment of those who cross the lines of the "historical warfare." The end of criminal charges is, of course, not a sign that Polish authorities have changed their minds about the past—quite to the contrary.

On June 27, 2018, the day the law was decriminalized, Morawiecki stated in the Parliament, "Those who claim that the Polish nation, or the Polish state, bears responsibility for the crimes of WWII, should—of course—be in prison. But we have to act bearing in mind international realities and that is why we take them into account." Not prone to subtlety, and using tough, military language, Morawiecki continued,

> Today an American or a German publisher will think twice before he publishes an article where "Polish concentration camps" are mentioned. He will face a threat of civil litigation and 100 million euros in fines. These provisions

remain in the law. We strengthened our ability to defend our rights. We are not retreating. This slight correction [the decriminalization] will only strengthen our positions. Over the last few months we were able to raise the consciousness of our partners. This [joint declaration] shows that our legislation was a step in the right direction. Our historical consciousness looks better today, and thanks to this legislation.[12]

One could continue quoting the jingoistic declarations of Polish politicians, but one thing is certain: the militant, threatening discourse and tone in matters of history, and most specifically in matters of Holocaust history, are now trademarks of the Polish political scene. For the nationalists in power, the legal, illegal, and semilegal instruments deployed to shore up and defend the myths of national innocence, to reaffirm their own ethos of victims of history who always held high moral ground, are not a marginal, fringe, after-hours pursuit. This theme, this area, is precisely what makes them who they are—it constitutes the core of their beliefs and, more importantly, the core beliefs of the electorate. One of the most pernicious aspects of the new "history laws" is that they are very popular because, in most cases, they reinforce what the vast majority believe and want to continue to believe. Until 1989, in Eastern Europe, communists tried to impose their own historical narrative. They were largely unsuccessful because they were selling merchandise that no one wanted to buy. Nationalists today offer a product that is not only palatable to but even desired by their audience. Who does not want to be told that one's forefathers, one's nation, or one's tribe held high moral ground throughout history and always found themselves on the side of justice and freedom? To quote George Orwell's *1984*, "The best books . . . are those that tell you what you already know."

Conclusion

As one can see, the level of tension and intensity associated with the study of the Holocaust did not diminish with time. Quite to the contrary, an opposite phenomenon seems to be taking place: the history battles acquire additional urgency and pitch the further we get from the historical event itself. During the last few decades, the Holocaust has become the universal benchmark of evil. The universality of the concept made it, in turn, a powerful beacon for various political and historical groups that would like to use the Holocaust to further their own causes. This ongoing assault on the history and memory of the Shoah is now being sponsored by state institutions, and attacks on independent scholars, teachers, and educators have become commonplace. Can this be related to the Holocaust becoming just one more tragic event of the past? Can it be that the void left by the generation of survivors is being filled with a different, often very hostile narrative? Can this phenomenon be related to the global rise of tribalism and populism? To all these causes together? These are just some of the questions with which we will have to struggle in the years to come.

Notes

1. See Adam Leszczynski, "PiS o nauce: 'ma być kształtowana przez rację stanu'. Gowin: to oznacza pisanie o Żydach tak, jak chcemy," OKO.press, September 18, 2019, https://oko.press/pis-o-nauce-racje-stanu-gowin/.
2. Manfred Gerstenfeld, *The Abuse of Holocaust Memory. Distortions and Responses* (Jerusalem: Jerusalem Center for Public Affairs, 2009), 22–23.
3. Efraim Zuroff, "Eastern Europe: Anti-Semitism in the Wake of Holocaust-Related Issues," *Jewish Political Studies Review* 17, nos. 1–2 (Spring 2005): 72.
4. Norbert Nowotnik and Aleksander Główczewski, "Premier w Sadownem złożył hołd Polakom ratującym Żydów w czasie wojny," Dzieje.pl, March 24, 2019, https://dzieje.pl/aktualnosci/premier-w-sadownem-zlozyl-hold-polakom-ratujacym-zydow-w-czasie-wojny.
5. Jan Grabowski and Barbara Engelking, eds., *Dalej jest noc: Losy Zydow w wybranych powiatach okupowanej Polski* [Night without end: The fate of Jews in selected counties of occupied Poland] (Warsaw: Polish Center for Holocaust Research, 2018).
6. Adam Starkopf, *Will to Live: One Family's Story of Surviving the Holocaust* (Albany: State University of New York Press, 1995), 158–60.
7. "Ustawa chroniąca dobre imię Polski uchwalona," gov.pl, January 26, 2018, https://www.gov.pl/web/sprawiedliwosc/ustawa-chroniaca-dobre-imie-polski-uchwalona.
8. "Ambasada Izraela zarzuca TVP Info antysemityzm—TVP przeprasza za błąd w omówieniu wywiadu Anny Azari," Wirtualnemedia.pl, February 3, 2018, https://www.wirtualnemedia.pl/artykul/ambasada-izraela-zarzuca-tvp-info-antysemityzm-fake-news-laczacy-nowelizacje-ustawy-o-ipn-z-reprywatyzacja.
9. "Prezes IPN Jarosław Szarek w TVP Polonia o nowelizacji ustawy o IPN," IPN, accessed April 1, 2020, https://ipn.gov.pl/pl/aktualnosci/46533,Prezes-IPN-Jaroslaw-Szarek-w-TVP-Polonia-o-nowelizacji-ustawy-o-IPN.html.
10. Yehuda Bauer, "Israel's Stupid, Ignorant and Amoral Betrayal of the Truth on Polish Involvement in the Holocaust," *Haaretz*, July 4, 2018, https://www.haaretz.com/opinion/.premium-okay-so-the-poles-didn-t-murder-jews-1.6242474.
11. He remarked, for instance, "It is sad that Antipolonism is the official stand of the Israeli government." Ofer Aderet, "Polish Prime Minister to Haaretz: Tens of Thousands of Poles Aided Jews. We Won't Give in to Lies," *Haaretz*, February 22, 2019, https://www.haaretz.com/world-news/europe/.premium-polish-pm-tens-of-thousands-of-poles-aided-the-jews-we-won-t-give-in-to-lies-1.6958388.
12. Morawiecki's comments following the signing of the joint Polish-Israeli declaration can be found in "Wspólna deklaracja Polski i Izraela. Netanjahu: Termin 'polskie obozy śmierci' jest nieprawdziwy. Morawiecki: Prawda o Polsce jest dobra," wPolityce.pl, June 27, 2018, https://wpolityce.pl/polityka/401535-premier-netanjahu-nie-bylo-polskich-obozow-smierci.

JAN GRABOWSKI is Professor of History of the Holocaust at the University of Ottawa and has been an invited professor at universities in France, Israel, Poland, and the United States. Professor Grabowski's book *Hunt for the Jews: Betrayal and Murder in German-Occupied Poland* (Indiana University Press) won the Yad Vashem International Book Prize in 2014. In 2016–17, Grabowski was the Ina Levine Senior Invitational Scholar in the Jack, Joseph and Morton Mandel Center for Advanced Holocaust Studies at the United States Holocaust Memorial Museum in Washington, DC. In 2018, he published a two-volume study (edited and authored with B. Engelking) in Polish: *Dalej jest noc* [Night without end: The fate of Jews in selected counties of occupied Poland]. An English edition is forthcoming. In March 2020, Grabowski published (in Poland) his most recent book, *Na Posterunku* [On duty: The involvement of Polish "blue" and criminal police in the Holocaust], forthcoming in English. In 2020, Professor Grabowski was appointed a Distinguished Fellow at the Institut für Zeitgeschichte in Munich, Germany.

11

The Changing Faces of European Antisemitism—the Hungarian Case
Attitudes toward Jews in Viktor Orbán's Semiauthoritarian Regime

János Gadó

AT THE END OF JULY 2019, ZSOLT BAYER, a progovernment journalist and close friend of Prime Minister Viktor Orbán, famous for his aggressive and vulgar tone, wrote an open letter in the government-controlled daily *Magyar Nemzet*.[1] Bayer reproached the French ambassador in Budapest for a French court ruling: in Paris, psychiatrists had concluded that the suspect of a 2017 Paris slaying of a Jewish woman was not fit to stand trial.

Bayer's task was clear: he wanted to demonstrate that antisemitism was out of hand in France and that the "manually controlled, vile, rotten, lying and dishonest press remains silent." Meanwhile, in Hungary, Bayer concluded, "Jewish culture is blossoming as never before . . . Jews are living in a maximum of safety, and there are simply no anti-Semitic attacks or atrocities."

Bayer's offensive style has been well known for many years. His fame had reached the American Congress, where the Bipartisan Taskforce for Combating Anti-Semitism protested[2] against him getting a government award.[3]

As we can guess, Bayer's pro-Jewish stance is pretty much a new trend. For many years, he spread the most vicious hatred of Jews. In one of his most infamous commentaries, he labeled a foreign Jew who criticized the Hungarian government as "stinking excrement" and recommended the methods of the 1919 white terror to eliminate him.[4]

This very same Bayer was now demanding, in the same aggressive tone, that the murderer of the French Jewish Sarah Halimi be tried and sentenced. A journalist inciting the murder of Jews has turned—in a short period—into the protector of the (French) Jews. Bayer's volte-face has since been duplicated by most of the right-wing media. It's worth asking the question: What has happened in Hungary in the past couple of years?

The Orbán Regime, the Progressive West, and the Jews

The Orbán regime's current stance toward the Jews is a reversed image of progressive Western attitudes. Progressive Western public opinion and media are often pro-Palestinian and highly critical of Israel. The Orbán government has been firmly pro-Israeli over the past couple of years and seems pretty uninterested in listening to Palestinian grievances. Hungarian representatives (just like their Polish, Czech, and Slovak colleagues) don't rush to condemn Israel in various UN bodies, often obstructing the adoption of a unified European position critical of Israel.[5]

In progressive Western public opinion and the media, Holocaust consciousness is crucial. Progressive politicians bow their heads to the victims of the Holocaust and basically acknowledge their respective nations' responsibility for the massacre of European Jewry. In Orbán's Hungary, the memory of the Holocaust is also important, but it is not supposed to trump the grievances of the Hungarian nation in the past or in the present. Hungarian politicians bow their heads to the victims of the Holocaust but won't acknowledge their nation's responsibility in the tragedy of Hungarian Jewry. (In official messages to the Jewish community, they tend to admit the "responsibility of the Hungarian state."[6])

The progressive West leaves behind the traditional twentieth-century religious, national worldview, espouses twenty-first-century multiculturalism, and regards the respect of the Other as the core of its policy. This policy is supposed to be a safe haven for Jews, who once—as the ultimate Others—were victims of the vilest persecutions.

Unlike in the progressive West, in Hungary the Other (usually the "migrants") is often the bad guy. It is considered suspicious, strange, and frightening; it is someone insensitive to the values of Western Christian (sometimes "Judeo-Christian") civilization; it is someone who does not respect women and hates Jews.

In Orbán's Hungary, the traditional early twentieth-century Christian, nationalistic worldview is still alive and valid, but—unlike in the 1930s, when it was heavily antisemitic—it is now said (by the government) to be a safe haven for the Jews, who in the multicultural West are harassed and persecuted by a coalition of Muslim immigrants and far-left local politicians. Only a strong nation-state like Hungary is able to protect the gates of Europe, which otherwise could not resist the hordes of anti-Zionist and antisemitic immigrants, who represent a lethal danger for the Jews. At least, this is what the Hungarian government argues.[7]

Progressive Western liberal political culture regards the Orbán government as antidemocratic and antisemitic at the same time. The government is accused of pursuing the twentieth-century old-school antisemitism. But in the traditionalist political culture of the Orbán government, it is the progressive West that should be accused of antisemitism. More precisely, the West is accused of pursuing the twenty-first-century new-school antisemitism, often referred to as anti-Zionism.

In the progressive West, the good Jew is one who espouses multiculturalism and keeps his or her distance from the traditional notions of Jewish nation and religion. In contemporary traditional-minded central Europe, the good Jew is someone who espouses the long-established ideas of nation and religion and rejects multiculturalism. To put it very bluntly, in western Europe multicultural Jews are the good guys, and Zionist Jews are the bad guys; in central-eastern Europe multicultural Jews are the bad guys, and Zionist Jews are the good guys (provided that these good guys do not strongly oppose the Holocaust discourse of the government).

The Orbán regime's policy in this respect is closest to that of the modernized Western far-right parties, such as the Rassemblement National of Marine Le Pen and the German AfD. One crucial difference is worth mentioning: Western far-right political parties often strive to limit Jewish (and Muslim) religious practices such as circumcision and ritual slaughter. The Orbán government acts the opposite way: it encourages Jewish religious practice and promotes kosher slaughtering, such as the building of a brand-new meat factory that exports kosher products to western Europe and Israel.[8]

Fragmented Antisemitism

As I have discussed above, in our time a new, fragmented version of antisemitism has emerged, and opposing political parties or movements accuse each other of various kinds of antisemitism. Progressive multiculturalists blame the antisemitic conspiracy theories of eastern European nationalists, while the nationalists blame the anti-Israeli obsession of the progressives. Each party has its beloved kind of Jew and its Jewish bogeyman.

From 1919 to 1945, the far-right, racist, fascist, Nazi version of Jew hatred dominated the Western world. From 1950 to 1989, it was the far-left communist version that prevailed. After 1989 (especially after 2000), Jew hatred strongly adapted to multiculturalism.

A deep analysis of this crucial change is absolutely required. It should include the process of upward mobility—the great majority in the Western societies lives at the middle-class level. They have too much to lose; there are no desperate millions who are ready to turn the whole society upside down in search of immediate salvation. The social reservoir of would-be totalitarian movements has been largely exhausted. Twenty-first-century Western political culture values democracy, abhors fascism, and has reached a rather high level of Holocaust consciousness. These are not the conditions in which a full-fledged antisemitism would take root and spread. One of the last genuine fascist parties of our time, the Hungarian Jobbik, turned under our noses into a modern nationalist antiestablishment party, rejected its former Jew hatred, and ended up sending Rosh Hashanah greetings to the Jewish community.[9]

In contrast, the deep crisis of Islam and the very strong feeling of deprivation overwhelming tens of millions in the Arab/Islamic world give these masses a tremendous impetus to seek immediate salvation. Islamism is a totalitarian ideology that—like fascism and communism in twentieth-century Europe—offers a simple and comprehensive explanation for Islam's (and the world's) contemporary crisis. In this vision, rotten, godless Western democracies and their false values are at the core of all the ills that haunt the Islamic world. The main culprits of these rotten democracies are of course the Jews, whose illegitimate state is a burning wound in Islam's heartland. Thus, the hatred of Israel (anti-Zionism) and the hatred of Jews (antisemitism) are equally present in contemporary Islamism, as is traditional, religious Jew hatred ("Jews are the sons of apes and pigs").

Contemporary Europe's fragmented antisemitism pales in comparison to Islamic hatred of Jews. In terms of aggression and hatred, industrialized, post-Holocaust twenty-first-century Europe just cannot compete with the Islamic world.[10] This is one of the reasons why Western far-right parties feel compelled to give up a great part of their antisemitism. The other reason is of course the threat of Islam itself, which is much more of a "clear and imminent danger" than Jews. Islam can easily be interpreted as a real threat for those who insist on protecting Europe from its enemies. For them, Israel is an ideal ally—a strong nation-state based on traditional religious values and still a modern twenty-first-century country. This is the process that basically changed the French National Front, the Austrian Freedom Party, and the Hungarian Jobbik Party. This is why Orbán's antidemocratic Fidesz Party (and similar parties in central and eastern Europe) are great allies of Israel. Emphasizing the friendship with Israel is also helpful in demonstrating their pro-Jewish stance and thus suppressing the memories of antisemitism in the past, which these parties would like to shake off for good.

In contrast, the political correctness of the modern European left obliges them to see Islamic masses as the oppressed ones and espouse their cause, their anti-Zionism included. Yet as protectors of the oppressed, they are also more likely to recognize the Holocaust guilt of their nation.

This is how European Jew hatred fell into pieces and different political camps picked up the different pieces. There is no longer any point in asking whether this or that person, politician, or party is antisemitic. You had better ask what mélange of philo- and antisemitism he, she, or it promotes. This is the early twenty-first-century image of Jews in the Western world.

Old models no longer work. In 1969, the Soviet Union was antidemocratic, antisemitic, and anti-Zionist. From a Jewish perspective, it was on the wrong side, no doubt. In 2019, the Swedish government is progressive, democratic, and rather anti-Zionist, while the Hungarian government is reactionary, rather antidemocratic, and pro-Zionist. Which government, which country, is on the right side, and which one is on the wrong side from a Jewish point of view?

Democratic and open European societies—which have a sizable Muslim minority—sometimes offer less safety to Jews than do the more repressive regimes of central and eastern Europe, which keep their gates closed to immigrants. In the past couple of years, it has been much riskier for a religious Jew to walk in the streets of Berlin than in the streets of Budapest.[11] The Orbán regime's policy toward the Jews should be understood against this background.

Hungary, Democracy, Self-Reflection

In the glorious year of 1989, the nations of the Eastern Bloc secured themselves the right to build up the same democratic institutions that had been long established in the Western part of Europe. Operating democratic institutions is a challenge and requires a high degree of political maturity. By establishing and maintaining the freedom of elections, the freedom of association, and the freedom of enterprise, the new democracies provided proof of this maturity.

However, by this time Western democracies had achieved a higher level of maturity—the culture of self-reflection was gaining ground. This kind of maturity proved to be too much of a challenge for the new democracies. They stopped at this point, hesitated, and started to retreat.

Self-reflection and soul-searching are not unknown in this part of the world. However, over the past ten to fifteen years, this culture has been marginalized in many of these countries; it became a tolerated minority opinion while unreflecting nationalism prevailed. The latter became a semiofficial opinion, cultivated by newly established "scientific" institutions.

Hungary and Poland are the best-known examples of this kind of restoration. Holocaust research has been an established discipline in these countries for quite a long time—but its results proved rather frightening and distressing for the nationalist mind. Collaboration or indifference toward the Jews in these countries during the Holocaust was much more common than selfless help. The glorified nation, allegedly a victim, proved to be very different.[12] This disappointing picture is simply intolerable for the new ultranationalist right that has come to power in these countries.

Countering this unfavorable image became imperative for the new right, which took serious measures to promote the traditional image of the nation. The best-known example is the infamous Polish law that makes it an offence "to attribute Nazi crimes to the Polish nation or state."[13] This is tantamount to legally restraining free speech and historical research.

In Hungary, the government has established new pseudoscientific institutions to promote the government agenda in the realm of social sciences, history, and letters. The undeclared mission of the Veritas Institute (established in 2013) is to whitewash the record of the authoritarian and antisemitic Miklós Horthy regime (1920–44), which is regarded by many nationalists as a political/ideological predecessor of the current government.[14]

This is a very strange political game. Orbán, who (in a conversation with Bernard-Henri Lévy) boasts of having excellent relations with Jews, says the following in the same interview: "I, Viktor Orbán, would be the first to praise Regent Horthy."[15]

Why praise Horthy, who was a self-declared antisemite, an ally of Hitler, whom the Hungarian Jews despise and abhor? Why doesn't Orbán try to find a nationalist but not antisemitic politician as his role model?

The reason is that Horthy was a nationalist, anti-liberal politician who referred to Christianity all the time—and Orbán is doing the same. Horthy, as a regent, could not be removed from his position, which is probably also not against Orbán's liking. Furthermore, it was Horthy (with Hitler on his side) who managed to get back much of those territories that Hungary lost as a consequence of the Treaty of Trianon in 1920. This treaty, which deprived Hungary of almost 70 percent of its territories, is still an open wound for most Hungarians. Over the main entrance of the Hungarian Parliament's building, the Hungarian flag flies on the left side. On the right side, however, there is no EU flag, as there used to be before 2010 (when Orbán came to power). What can be seen now is the Szekler's flag—an ethnic Hungarian group living in today's Romania. This is a clear sign of keeping past national grievances high on the agenda. In Orbán's world, all these aspects together prevail over Horthy's antisemitism and his responsibility for the Hungarian Jews' tragic fate.

For Hungarian Jews and the Hungarian left, this remains unacceptable. Therefore, Horthy's role in the destruction of the Hungarian Jews remains the subject of embittered debates in Hungary. Horthy remained in his position during the fateful months of May, June, and July 1944, when 435,000 Hungarian Jews were deported to Auschwitz. On June 26—after the Allied landing in Normandy, after being warned by President Roosevelt, Pope Pius XII, and Gustaf V, king of Sweden—Horthy decided to stop the deportations. (It took him several days to implement his decision.) Most Hungarian Jews, who regard him as a war criminal, argue that this is proof that he could have stopped the deportations much earlier. But many nationalist-minded Hungarians, for whom it is imperative to save Horthy's reputation, insist that he is the savior of the Budapest Jews. Hungarian Jews despise every attempt to whitewash Horthy and his regime. Concerning Horthy's (and the Hungarians') responsibility, there is not much common ground between the parties.[16]

With its ultranationalist policy, Orbán's Fidesz Party managed to take over the positions of the far-right Jobbik Party, which in the past four to five years ended up rejecting its fascist past. However, while taking over far-right positions, Fidesz managed to maintain its control of moderate-right positions as well.

Authoritarian Rule, Nationalized Antisemitism

This antidemocratic government curbs the freedom of speech; consequently, it curbs the freedom of antisemites as well. Using its excessive political power, it has managed to achieve dominant positions in the economy; using its economic power, it achieved a dominant role in the media.

All but one of the nationwide daily papers belong to loyal entrepreneurs. A huge government-run conglomerate dominates the market of radio and television stations. In the field of weekly papers and online news sites, the independent media still holds quite a strong position.

The government media is disciplined, aggressive, and keen to fight enemies at home and abroad. It regularly employs character assassination as a tool to overcome people deemed dangerous. Since the enemies are often depicted as foreigners, liberals, cosmopolites ("Brussels bureaucrats"), or orchestrated by a rich Jewish businessman (George Soros), one might guess some antisemitic motives in the government propaganda, especially when the Jewish banker's face was displayed on hundreds of billboards nationwide. However, Orbán has declared several times that the government has a policy of zero tolerance toward antisemitism.[17]

George Birnbaum, a committed Jew and a staunch supporter of Israel, one of the masterminds of the anti-Soros campaign, explained in an interview in January 2019, "When we planned the campaign, we never thought for a second about Soros being a Jew."[18] But in a conservative nationalist setting, Soros is the ideal scapegoat. He is a Jewish tycoon with a leftist agenda. In his person, the Jewish plutocrat and the Jewish revolutionary merge. As a Holocaust survivor, he can be easily accused of hating the Hungarians because of his past.

Some people claim that respondents to a survey didn't connect Soros's name to Jews.[19] Nonetheless, it remains clear that a cosmopolitan, liberal speculator conspiring against Europe of the Christian nations cannot be anything other than a Jew.[20]

On the national holiday of March 15, 2018, a few days before the general elections, Orbán delivered a speech in which he stated the following: "We have to fight an enemy that is different from us. Not open but hiding; not straightforward but crafty; not honest but base; not national but international; does not believe in working but speculates with money; does not have its own homeland but feels it owns the whole world. It is not generous but vengeful and it attacks the heart, especially when the heart is red, white and green."[21] This is undoubtedly a Nazi-like characterization of the Jews made without mentioning them.

As a counterbalance, let us quote what Orbán told the French philosopher Bernard-Henri Lévy during their meeting in May 2019 in Budapest: "And when I, in turn, ask him, in front of the camera, if he might have a message for his former mentor (Soros), he responds not once, but twice: 'I wish him good health and good luck.'"[22] This is proof that Orbán is a real "polyglot"—he speaks the language of hatred and the language of tolerance as well, depending on the audience he is speaking to.

Orbán Feels Entitled to Declare Who Is an Antisemite

These seemingly contradictory declarations can be synthesized as follows: The Orbán government has nationalized the issue of antisemitism. It has grown self-confident to the point of trying to define who is an antisemite and who is a Jew. (Remember, in our postmodern Europe, antisemites can also accuse others of antisemitism.)

Orbán's message is basically this: those on his right (such as the infamous although repentant Jobbik Party) are incorrigible Nazis, while those on his left are irresponsible politicians who—willingly or not—support the cosmopolite left-liberal camp and open the gates of Europe to mass Islamic immigration, which is a lethal danger to Jews. In his interpretation, therefore, Hungary is a safe haven for Jews, where left- and right-wing extremism is equally kept at bay.

A Certain Species of Antisemitism

George Soros, as the ultimate puppet master, and his left-liberal disciples—foreign and Hungarian—fit the good old image of the antinational, antireligious, liberal-cosmopolite Jewish conspiracy quite well. It should be emphasized again, though, that during all this hate campaign no direct allusions were made to Soros's Jewish background. What is more, the government's spokespersons vehemently rejected any allusions of this kind,[23] stating that a politician's Jewish origin cannot be an issue.

However, this image of the hostile Jew is well defined and can be quite well distinguished from other sorts of Jew hatred, such as religious anti-Judaism or postmodern anti-Zionism. Over the past couple of years, Orbán and his subordinates could be seen time and again in the company of ultra-orthodox Jews. Moreover, he—just like other leading politicians of the Visegrád countries—is a dedicated ally of the current Israeli government, has friendly relations with Prime Minister Netanyahu, and keeps blocking unanimous "Israel-critical" moves of various EU bodies.

Orbán's New Europe and Its New Enemies

When Orbán came to power in 2010, the press was free, and so was the (far) right press, which blamed the Jews for all evils of the world. The infamous Hungarian-language Nazi website kuruc.info not only encouraged anti-Jewish hatred but also mobilized for violence by publishing names and addresses of people it branded as enemies.

Orbán took advantage of the far right when seizing power, but he later disciplined them as well. The mass migration of 2015 was his best chance, and he used it fully. This was the year when government propaganda reinterpreted the challenges of the world and migrants became danger number one, thus overshadowing everyone else. (Some Jews were relegated to the small group of puppet masters.) It was during this reinterpretation that Palestinians were turned from good guys into bad guys—from victims of the Jews into ordinary Arab Muslims and potential migrants.

Not surprisingly, Hungarian right-wing nationalists had previously been pro-Palestinian, since the Palestinians were regarded as the victims of the Jews. In 2014, the Jobbik Party demonstrated together with the Palestinians in Budapest.[24]

After 2015, however, the Palestinians—as Arabs and Muslims of the third world—were silently relegated to the group of potential migrants, whose millions were just getting ready to flood the old continent. Hungarian government media stopped emphasizing Palestinian victimhood and Israeli guilt. In 2019, when Palestinians demonstrated again in Budapest, calling for the boycott of the Eurovision song contest in Tel Aviv, they remained alone; the Hungarian far right could not be seen with them, and the government media remained uninterested.[25]

This shift reinforced the earlier message: those threatened by the Muslims can be our allies. If you are not a liberal, cosmopolite, promigrant Jew but a traditionalist, nationalist Jew, you can be on our side. It was a clear proposal as to how the Jewish issue could be solved—declaring who is on the right side and who is on the wrong side. This was a clear scheme for a "new alliance."

Unfortunately for Orbán, most Hungarian Jews are liberal cosmopolites; they are mostly not interested in religion, abhor Hungarian nationalism, and are distrustful of Jewish nationalism too. They probably will not heed Orbán's message. The official representative body of the Hungarian Jews (Mazsihisz), however, must be more careful, since 80 percent of its revenues come from government resources. The chairman of Mazsihisz, András Heisler, stood up defiantly against Orbán's infamous anti-Soros campaign and urged him in no uncertain terms to stop it (to no avail). Somewhat later, Heisler also opined that it is awkward for Jews to live in an atmosphere of constant search for enemies. Encouraged by this, some civil groups invited Mazsihisz to take part in the resulting protest actions.

Politely but resolutely, Mazsihisz declined: "We cannot take on the role of opposition parties," Heisler explained.[26]

This is not the attitude of the other important Jewish religious denomination, the so-called United Hungarian Israelite Faith Community (EMIH) established by Chabad's Hungarian branch and led by Rabbi Slomó Köves. Köves cooperates more closely with the government and offers it direct support when necessary. This was the case when Köves stated that the anti-Soros campaign had no antisemitic overtones.[27] Köves has major projects that enjoy generous government funding, such as the building of a kosher meat factory, which exports kosher products to western Europe and Israel.[28]

The Orbán Government and the Memory of the Holocaust

Orbán's immense self-confidence motivates him to try to resolve the issue of Holocaust remembrance for good. The essence of his "solution" is this: the Hungarians recognize—mostly for the international and the Jewish public—the immensity and uniqueness of the Holocaust; in exchange, the Jews stop accusing Hungarians of Nazi collaboration concerning the crimes committed during this time. Admitting a certain amount of Hungarian responsibility, however, should be tolerable. As Gergely Gulyás, minister of the Prime Minister's Office, declared on the occasion of International Holocaust Memorial Day in 2019, "The Hungarian state bears responsibility for not protecting its citizens during the Holocaust; there is no collective guilt, but there is state responsibility."[29] Otherwise, the message that Orbán likes to transmit is that Hungarians and Jews share a common fate in good times and bad.

In order to convey this message, a new Holocaust memorial site was planned by the government: the notorious "House of Fates." This is not the first Holocaust memorial center in Budapest. The first one was the Holocaust Memorial and Documentation Center, inaugurated in 2005 by a previous, socialist government. However, this institution emphasized Hungarian responsibility for the Holocaust; therefore, it did not fit the Orbán government's narrative. The House of Fates was to be located in a smaller railway station building, out of service by this time. By 2015, only the reconstruction of the building had been completed, because a vigorous protest by local and foreign Jewish organizations prevented the implementation of the exhibition they wished to realize. Protesting Jewish organizations demanded to see the stage of the exhibition, a request the organizers would not deliver on. Respectable institutions such as the Yad Vashem expressed their criticism, which resulted in a deadlock. This lasted some three years until the reelected government made another effort to accomplish the project. They decided to involve a Jewish partner: Rabbi Slomó Köves and his community, EMIH. In September 2018, Rabbi Köves held a press conference together with Mária Schmidt, the regime's official historian. Köves stressed that the exhibition would be opened in 2019 and that emphasis should be given to "universal moral conclusions"—which in Jewish circles was interpreted as avoiding the question of Hungarian responsibility.[30]

As could be expected, a new wave of protests followed. Köves received heavy blows from liberal Jewish circles, and the deadlock remained. However, Köves is not the kind of man who gives up after a first failure. He took it as a challenge to produce a Holocaust discourse that would be acceptable to Hungarian Jews and Hungarian nationalists alike. If he succeeded, he would be the master of the Holocaust discourse and the master of Hungarian Jewish history as well.

Mission impossible, one could say, since for most Jews, Hungarians were perpetrators during World War II, while for most nationalist-minded Hungarians, they were heroes and victims. If you try to reconcile both perspectives, you may end up with an empty set.

Still, Köves set out to complete the new memorial. He recruited a new team with historians and other experts and had a new draft plan created, which was presented to the experts of the International Holocaust Remembrance Alliance (IHRA) on June 10. The IHRA forum was carefully supportive; it did not approve the project, but it appointed a team of experts to follow subsequent developments.[31] Köves is visibly being very careful; he is keen to gather strong professional and political support before going public with the concept of the exhibition.

The names of Hungarian experts working on the project have not been officially disclosed. Eight names, however, could be seen for a while during Köves's PowerPoint presentation to IHRA members. Szombat, a Jewish website, published the names in its report on the event.[32] *Magyar Narancs*, an independent weekly, famous for its investigative journalism, tracked down these listed experts.[33] Out of the eight, only two confirmed their involvement.

In their search for experts willing to support the House of Fates project, EMIH leaders also approached historians at the Institute for Hungarian Jewish History. The newly established institute operates under EMIH's auspices and is attached to the Milton Friedman University in Budapest, an academic institution newly acquired by the EMIH network. Yet four of the six historians—working at EMIH's own institute!—declined to comment on the project.³⁴ All this is a rather clear sign of renowned Hungarian historians lacking confidence. Mazsihisz is keeping its distance, too.³⁵

Orbán is probably also aware of the huge importance of this game. He gave fairly extensive room for maneuver to Köves, who went as far as to exclude Mária Schmidt, the official historian of the government, from the project. At least, this is what Köves said—only to be refuted the next day by Minister Gulyás.³⁶

Orbán has managed to subjugate many segments of the nongovernmental sphere (the Hungarian Academy of Sciences included), and he is successfully spreading his ideology across broad segments of society. Yet submitting the memory of the Holocaust to his version of history seems to be too much of a challenge. (The same is true for most of the countries of central and eastern Europe.) Orbán would not acknowledge that he had lost—which leaves the most crucial issue between him and the Hungarian Jews unresolved.

Conclusion

From a Jewish perspective, Orbán's record is very controversial:

- He is building up an "illiberal" society, which means centralizing power, reducing civil liberties, eliminating checks and balances, and trying to dominate the arts and sciences. This atmosphere is generally depressing for Jews.
- He has repeatedly referred to Admiral Miklós Horthy—the nationalistic, authoritarian, and antisemitic regent of Hungary between 1920 and 1944—as a worthy politician (although he admits that Horthy's last years, including the alliance with Hitler with all its tragic consequences, are unacceptable).
- He is protecting and financially subsidizing the Jewish community—which leaves the community politically and financially dependent.
- He is desperately struggling to reconcile his nationalistic Horthy nostalgia with the memory of the Holocaust and to elaborate a Holocaust narrative that leaves the Hungarian national self-esteem unharmed.
- He is blaming George Soros, a Jewish billionaire philanthropist, and "Brussels bureaucrats" for the ills of Hungary and Europe—although he insists that Soros's Jewish background has no role in his vilification.
- He is loudly and proudly declaring zero tolerance of antisemitism—an antisemitism of his own definition.
- He is whipping up a xenophobic atmosphere in which non-European Muslims (immigrants) are depicted as a lethal danger for Hungary

and Europe. He is blaming Soros and liberals for pushing mass immigration. Since the beginning of the anti-immigrant campaign, public anger has been focused on migrants, and antisemitic violence has practically stopped.
- He is praising Israel for its democratic achievements in a hostile Middle East, and he is building strong ties with the Jewish state. Hungary—along with other central European countries—votes more or less regularly against anti-Israeli decisions in various EU bodies. The government-run media stopped blaming Israel for Palestinian suffering and for Middle East troubles.
- His ministers and state secretaries can be seen time and again in the company of spectacularly orthodox Jews. Since orthodox Jewish figures with hat, side locks, and so on are generally used in antisemitic cartoons, this gesture is obviously intended to express the governments' philo-Semitism.
- He is recycling certain elements of the old-school twentieth-century antisemitism while eliminating others. This provides an opportunity for Western democratic leaders to blame him of antisemitism.
- Meanwhile, he is keeping the new-school twenty-first-century antisemitism far from Hungary. The carrier of this new antisemitism is the civil society (universities, unions, civil rights movements, etc.). By suffocating civil society, he also suffocates the new antisemitism, which uses the civil rights language to achieve its goals. This gives him in turn an opportunity to blame Western democracies for antisemitism.

Some may conclude that these turbulent political changes brought along deep changes in people's minds as well. However, a recent survey reveals the opposite: people's minds have remained pretty much unchanged.[37] According to this survey, antisemitic attitudes of the Hungarian public have not changed in most dimensions; only the proportion of Holocaust deniers keeps growing.

The old joke is still valid: "In our village, there is no antisemitism, but there is a demand for it."

Notes

1. Zsolt Bayer, "Tényleg mindenkinek elment az esze?" [Everyone has gone mad, indeed?], *Magyar Nemzet*, July 23, 2019, https://magyarnemzet.hu/velemeny/tenyleg-mindenkinek-elment-az-esze-7141334/.

2. US House of Representatives, Committee on Foreign Affairs, "Bipartisan Taskforce Introduces Legislation Focusing on European Anti-Semitism" (press release, October 7,

2016), https://foreignaffairs.house.gov/2016/10/bipartisan-taskforce-introduces-legislation-focusing-european-anti-semitism.

3. In 2016, Bayer was awarded the Hungarian Knight's Cross of Merit. In the following few weeks, more than seventy people protested by returning their awards to the government. "Bayer Botrány: Már 70 felett a lovagkeresztet visszaadók száma" [Bayer scandal: More than seventy people returned their Knight's Cross], Népszava, August 23, 2016, https://nepszava.hu/1103778_bayer-botrany-mar-70-felett-a-lovagkeresztet-visszaadok-szama.

4. "Bayer Zsolt: Ugyanaz a bűz" [Bayer Zsolt: The same stench again], *Magyar Hírlap*, January 4, 2011. (The website has since been deleted.) Bayer lamented that "Cohen, Cohn-Bendit, and Schiff could not all be buried up to their neck in earth in the forest of Orgovány." (The village of Orgovány was the site of the white terror in 1919, following a short-lived communist rule.)

5. Joanna Dyduch, "The Visegrád Group's Policy towards Israel," Stiftung Wissenschaft und Politik, December 2018, https://www.swp-berlin.org/en/publication/the-visegrad-groups-policy-towards-israel/.

6. Gulyás: "A magyar állam is közreműködött a holokauszt borzalmaiban" [Gulyás: "The Hungarian state was a partner in the horrors of the Holocaust"], MTI (Hungarian Telegraphic Office), magyarnarancs.hu, January 27, 2020, https://magyarnarancs.hu/belpol/gulyas-a-magyar-allam-is-kozremukodott-a-holokauszt-borzalmaiban-235433. Gergely Gulyás is the minister of chancellery for Viktor Orbán.

7. "Contemporary Europe is suffering from migration and terrorism; these tendencies should be countered. Modern anti-Semitism has developed aggressive forms in Europe. In our time anti-Semitism is on the rise in Western-Europe, while it is declining in Central-Eastern Europe. In Hungary anti-Semitism is not tolerated" (Orbán's words during a press conference in Jerusalem, MTI (Hungarian Telegraphic Office). "Orbán Viktor: Több kérdésben egyetértés van Netanjahuval" [Viktor Orbán: On quite a few questions I agree with Netanyahu], Origo, July 19, 2018, https://www.origo.hu/nagyvilag/20180719-orban-viktor-izrael-benjamin-netanjahu.html.

8. MTI (Hungarian Telegraphic Office), "Kóser vágóhidat adtak át Csengelén" [Kosher butchery opens up in Csengele], 168ora, July 5, 2017, https://168ora.hu/itthon/koser-vagohidat-adtak-at-csengelen-5256.

9. Lili Bayer, "Far Right Party's Hanukkah Greeting to Hungarian Jews Sets Off a Firestorm," *The Forward*, January 10, 2017, https://forward.com/news/359540/far-right-partys-hanukkah-greeting-to-hungarian-jews-sets-off-a-firestorm/.

10. "The Muslim fundamentalists—like the Nazis before and during the Shoah—rant against the 'anonymous powers' of globalization and the plutocratic West (symbolized by the World Trade Center and the city of New York) as fiercely as they battered the citadels of Soviet Communism in Afghanistan more than a decade ago. Like their totalitarian predecessors they (falsely) claim to speak for frustrated, underprivileged and impoverished masses betrayed by more traditional Arab and Muslim ruling elites and ruthlessly exploited by international capitalism. To the radical Muslims, 'Jewish' New York as much as the Zionist State of Israel, is the incarnation of satanic evil, just as Wall Street embodied the General Headquarters of corporate wickedness and cosmopolitan Jewry to the Nazis and other pre-war fascist true believers." Robert S. Wistrich, "Islamic Judeophobia: An Existential Threat," in *Muhammad's Monsters*, ed. David Bukay (Green Forest, AR: Balfour Books, 2004), 195–219. According to the ADL Global 100 survey, the percentage of those harboring antisemitic feelings in western Europe is 24 percent, in Eastern Europe it is 34 percent, and in the overwhelmingly Islamic Middle East and North Africa it is 75 percent. (The highest figure, 93 percent, was recorded in the Palestinian territories of the West Bank and Gaza.)

ADL's Global 100 is the first global survey of attitudes and opinions toward Jews in over one hundred countries around the world, conducted by the Anti-Defamation League in 2013–14 (https://global100.adl.org/).

11. In 2018, 1,083 antisemitic incidents were reported in Berlin. In 2017, the figure was 951. *Antisemitische Vorfälle 2018: Ein Bericht der Recherche- und Informationsstelle Antisemitismus Berlin* (RIAS), 2019, https://report-antisemitism.de/documents/2019-04-17_rias-be_Annual_Antisemitische-Vorfaelle-2018.pdf, 4. In 2018, thirty-two antisemitic incidents were reported in all of Hungary. In 2017, this figure was thirty-seven. *Antiszemita gyűlölet-bűncselekmények és incidensek Magyarországon 2018. éves rövid jelentés Tett és Védelem Alapítvány* [Anti-Semitic hate-crimes and incidents in Hungary, 2018, a short report], ed. Krisztián Nádasi, Dr. Kristóf Bodó, Gábor Bodó, and Gábor Tóth, Action and Protection Foundation, 2019, https://tev.hu/wp-content/uploads/2019/04/TEV_2018eves-rovid_72dpi.pdf, 4.

12. The classical example is probably Jan Gross's epic book *Neighbors: The Destruction of the Jewish Community in Jedwabne, Poland* (London: Penguin, 2002). Poles, who love to regard themselves as "the Christ of the Nations," were confronted with the fact that the Polish population had massacred the local Jews of a small town.

13. Edna Friedberg, "The Truth about Poland's Role in the Holocaust: A New Law Endangers an Honest Reckoning with a Complex Past," *The Atlantic*, February 6, 2018, https://www.theatlantic.com/international/archive/2018/02/poland-holocaust-death-camps/552455/.

14. "The Veritas Institute's Legends and Myths about the Hungarian Holocaust," *Hungarian Spectrum*, July 2, 2016, https://hungarianspectrum.org/2016/07/02/the-veritas-institutes-legends-and-myths-about-the-hungarian-holocaust/.

15. Bernard-Henri Lévy, "How an Anti-totalitarian Militant Discovered Ultranationalism: After 30 Years, I Spoke with Viktor Orbán Again," *The Atlantic*, May 13, 2019, https://www.theatlantic.com/ideas/archive/2019/05/bernard-henri-levy-interviews-viktor-orban/589102/.

16. Robert Philpot, "Hungary Has Not Yet Shaken Off Its Nazi Past: The Continuing Legacy of Miklós Horthy," *Jewish Chronicle*, March 28, 2017, https://www.thejc.com/news/world/hungary-has-not-yet-shaken-off-its-nazi-past-1.435170.

17. "Hungary Attacks Soros, EU Commission Chief in Anti-immigration Campaign," *Times of Israel*, February 19, 2019, https://www.timesofisrael.com/hungary-attacks-soros-eu-commission-chief-in-anti-immigration-campaign/.

18. Hannes Grassegger, "The Unbelievable Story of the Plot against George Soros," BuzzFeed News, January 20, 2019, https://www.buzzfeednews.com/article/hnsgrassegger/george-soros-conspiracy-finkelstein-birnbaum-orban-netanyahu.

19. Szalai KálmánX, "Rosszul beszélünk a holokausztról" [We don't speak correctly about the Holocaust], Neokohn, July 12, 2019, https://neokohn.hu/2019/07/12/szalai-kalman-rosszul-beszelunk-a-holokausztrol/. Kálmán Szalai, chairman of the Action and Protection Foundation, refers to a survey in which on hearing the codeword *Jew*, only 1 percent of the respondents connected it to George Soros, while on hearing the codeword *Soros*, only 2 percent connected it to the Jews.

20. "And when people mention the word Soros, they don't even have to say Jewish, it's understated." Emily Burack, "Howard Jacobson on His New Novel, British Anti-Semitism and Calling Himself the 'Jewish Jane Austen,'" Jewish Telegraphic Agency, September 12, 2019, https://www.jta.org/2019/09/12/culture/howard-jacobson-on-his-new-novel-british-anti-semitism-and-calling-himself-the-jewish-jane-austen.

21. Shaun Walker, "Hungarian Leader Says Europe Is Now 'under Invasion' by Migrants," *Guardian*, March 15, 2018, https://www.theguardian.com/world/2018/mar/15/hungarian-leader-says-europe-is-now-under-invasion-by-migrants.

22. Lévy, "How an Anti-totalitarian Militant Discovered Ultranationalism."

23. Kovács Zoltán, "A kormány sosem hivatkozik Soros zsidó gyökereire" [The government never refers to Soros's Jewish background], 24.hu, November 24, 2018, https://24.hu/kulfold/2018/11/24/kovacs-zoltan-soros-gyorgy-antiszemitizmus/.

24. "'Vesszen Izrael' a Jobbik és palesztinok tüntettek Budapesten" ["Down with Israel!" Jobbik and Palestinians demonstrated in Budapest], Szombat, July 16, 2014, https://www.szombat.org/hirek-lapszemle/vesszen-izrael-a-jobbik-es-palesztinok-tuntettek-budapesten.

25. "'Bojkottáld az Eurovíziót Izraelben'—palesztin tüntetés a bazilikánál" ["Boycott Eurovision in Israel"—Palestinian demonstration at downtown church], Szombat, May 17, 2019, https://www.szombat.org/politika/bojkottald-az-euroviziot-izraelben-palesztin-tuntetes-a-bazilikanal.

26. András Heisler, "Kritika és partnerség: A kormány és a Mazsihisz" [Criticism and Partnership: the government and the Mazsihisz], Szombat.org, June 8, 2018, https://www.szombat.org/politika/kritika-es-partnerseg-a-kormany-es-a-mazsihisz.

27. Cnaan Liphshiz, "Hungarian Government Denies Ending Anti-Soros Campaign Early," Jewish Telegraphic Agency, July 12, 2017, https://www.jta.org/2017/07/12/global/hungarian-government-denies-ending-anti-soros-campaign-early. See also Grassegger, "Unbelievable Story."

28. MTI (Hungarian Telegraphic Office), "Kóser vágóhidat adtak át Csengelén."

29. Pál Dániel Rényi, "Gulyás Gergely: A magyar államot felelősség terheli, amiért nem védte meg állampolgárait a holokauszt idején" [The Hungarian State bears responsibility for not protecting its citizens during the Holocaust], 444.hu, January 27, 2019, https://444.hu/2019/01/27/gulyas-gergely-a-magyar-allamot-felelosseg-terheli-amiert-nem-vedte-meg-allampolgarait-a-holokauszt-idejen.

30. "Jövőre megnyílik a Sorsok Háza—az EMIH a kormány zsidó partnere" [House of Fates will open next year—EMIH is the government's Jewish partner], Szombat, September 7, 2018, https://www.szombat.org/politika/jovore-megnyilik-a-sorsok-haza-az-emih-a-kormany-zsido-partnere.

31. "IHRA Chair's Statement on House of Fates, Budapest," International Holocaust Remembrance Alliance, June 11, 2019, https://holocaustremembrance.com/statements/ihra-chairs-statement-house-fates-budapest.

32. "Bemutatta a Sorsok Háza új koncepcióját az EMIH" [EMIH presented the new project for the House of Fates], Szombat, June 4, 2019, https://www.szombat.org/politika/bemutatta-a-sorsok-haza-uj-koncepciojat-az-emih.

33. "Keller-Alánt Ákos: Változó felállás a Sorsok Háza projektnél—Új arcok, régi gondoki" [House of Fates: New faces, old troubles], *Magyar Narancs*, June 20, 2019, https://magyarnarancs.hu/belpol/uj-arcok-regi-gondok-120704.

34. János Gadó, "Akik nem kívánták véleményezni a Sorsok Háza koncepcióját" [Those who declined to comment on the House of Fates project], Szombat, July 11, 2019, https://www.szombat.org/politika/akik-nem-kivantak-velemenyezni-a-sorsok-haza-koncepciojat.

35. For a more detailed background on the House of Fates, see János Gadó, "The Splendour and the Misery of the House of Fates," Cultures of History Forum, August 15, 2019, https://www.cultures-of-history.uni-jena.de/debates/hungary/the-splendour-and-the-misery-of-the-house-of-fates/.

36. "Sorsok Háza: A kormány mégis számít Schmidt Máriára?" [House of Fates: Is the government still counting on Mária Schmidt?], Szombat, June 5, 2019, https://www.szombat.org/hirek-lapszemle/sorsok-haza-a-kormany-megis-szamit-schmidt-mariara.

37. TEV, *Hann Endre—Róna Dániel: Antiszemita előítéletesség a mai magyar társadalomban. Reprezentatív felmérés 2018* [Antisemitic prejudices in contemporary Hungarian

society: A representative survey], 2019, https://tev.hu/wp-content/uploads/2019/07/TEV_Antiszemitizmus2018-Median_72dpiKE%CC%81SZ.pdf.

JÁNOS GADÓ is a sociologist and has been editor of *Szombat*, an independent Hungarian Jewish magazine and website, since 1992. He has written extensively on the situation of Jews in Hungary, on internal Jewish community affairs, and—since the outbreak of the Al Aqsa Intifada—on aspects of the new antisemitism. Since 2010, he has focused on the Hungarian Jews' struggle to find a place and purpose in the new, illiberal regime of Viktor Orbán.

12

Contradiction as Program
The German AfD between the Rejection of the Memory of the Holocaust and a Self-Proclaimed Political Home for Jews

Marc Grimm

THE FEDERAL REPUBLIC OF GERMANY WAS A STABLE, tripartite system between 1957 and 1980 consisting of the Christian conservative sister parties CDU and CSU, the social democratic SPD, and the liberal FDP. Between 1983 and 2013, only two other parties made it into the Bundestag: the Green Party in 1983 and the Socialist PDS (today die Linke) after reunification. In the elections between 1965 and 1983, the Conservatives and the Social Democrats together gained over 85 percent of the general vote. In the 2017 elections, this number was at 53.4 percent. Currently, Angela Merkel is serving as chancellor for the fourth time since 2005. Merkel's decline in voter support was accompanied by the rise of the Alternative für Deutschland (AfD, Alternative for Germany), which gained support by strictly opposing the government's integration politics. After the foundation of the AfD in early 2013, the party nearly made it into the national parliament later that year, gaining 4.7 percent and only slightly missing the 5 percent threshold. The party then was successful in all state elections and made it into the national parliament in 2017, gaining 12.7 percent of votes. The rise of the AfD to the status of a relevant political player in Germany (and in the European Parliament) is a challenge for Germany's democracy as the party expands the spectrum of politics to the right, taking a position far from CDU and CSU. The party functions as an enabler of racism and antisemitism. It tries to use the vulnerable situation of German Jews to argue against immigration, especially of Muslims. It also disseminates conspiracy theories of the type that motivated Stephan Balliet, the shooter who tried to kill Jews in a synagogue in Halle in October 2019.

This chapter deals with antisemitic tropes that the party ventilates and that align the party with the worldwide radical right. It then turns to the party's distortion of German politics of remembrance of the Holocaust and finally addresses the AfD's utilization of pro-Israeli statements for its political gain.

The Radicalization of the AfD

Since its founding in February 2013, the AfD has become increasingly radicalized. This development began with the party's success in the 2014 state elections in the eastern German states of Saxony, Thuringia, and Brandenburg. In these elections, the state associations followed the party line on economic questions, but in terms of sociopolitical issues, they focused on questions of culture and identity (*Kulturkampf*) and demanded the withdrawal of social liberalization measures and antidiscrimination policies. The AfD achieved election successes (9.7, 10.6, and 12.2 percent), which are noteworthy in that they indicate that the internal success of the right wing of the party and of the AfD as a whole cannot be interpreted only as a reaction to Germany's refugee policy since 2015. With the founding of the party wing Der Flügel (the Wing) and the Erfurt Resolution in March 2015, the *völkisch* members of the AfD united to initiate a reorientation of the AfD.[1] Björn Höcke, state chairman of the party in Thuringia,[2] has been officially leading Der Flügel from the beginning, and he is the informal leader of the party's right wing. The Flügel's efforts reached their first climax when the cofounder of the party, Bernd Lucke, and several hundred members of the national-liberal wing left the party in 2015. Der Flügel views the AfD not as a party in the parliamentary sense but "as a movement of our people against the social experiments of the last decades (gender mainstreaming, multiculturalism, educational arbitrariness, etc.), as a resistance movement against the further erosion of sovereignty and the identity of Germany, as a party that has the courage to tell the truth and to speak freely."[3] The reference to "movements" can be understood as a tribute to Hitler's NSDAP, which also understood itself as a *Bewegungspartei*, a movement resisting the established parties in the German Reichstag. In spring 2015, the AfD fell to a survey low of 4 percent of Germans saying they would vote for the party in the coming national elections.[4] At the same time, the refugee policy of the federal government divided public opinion and produced a demand for a fundamental opposition to precisely that policy. The AfD used this opportunity to switch their main focus from bailout payments for Greece (which had already become an outdated topic) to the issue of migration, agitating for the alleged defense of Germany and Europe and the denigration of refugees in general and Muslim refugees especially.

The fact that since 2015 the AfD has focused on the themes of migration and Islam does not imply that antisemitism has become obsolete as a central element of right-wing ideology. It remained to be seen how the young party would react to antisemitic incidents within its own ranks. Parties reflect attitudes of the people, and therefore it comes as no surprise that they have antisemitic members, given the spread of antisemitic attitudes in German society.[5] However, political parties not only reflect social conditions but also directly impact those conditions. It is therefore of central importance how parties deal with the antisemitism of their members. Is antisemitism recognized as a problem within the party, is it condemned by office holders in the party, and do members have to reckon with consequences if necessary? Additionally, there is the question of to what extent party members promote antisemitism with their policies and demands (on the internet, in speeches, and in programmatic writings) and in the form of memes, GIFs, and cartoons shared on the internet.

In this chapter, I examine the AfD's politics of remembrance of the Holocaust. I then discuss the antisemitic content of the social images that are used by leading politicians of the AfD. Finally, I assess the positive references to Israel and Judaism.

Politics of Memory and Holocaust Remembrance with the AfD

Six years after the founding of the AfD, it can be concluded that it is the only party represented in the Bundestag to reject the consensus on remembrance politics, which gives a central role to the recognition of Germany as the perpetrator of the murder of European Jews. As early as 2014, the state election program of the AfD in Saxony called for a "revaluation and reweighting of history education," which would give pupils a positive feeling of identification with the German nation.[6] Similarly, the 2016 election program demanded a turning away from a "one-sided concentration" on the "unfortunate years of our history," as the Nazi era and the Holocaust are euphemistically called.[7] This position was adopted by the federal party in May 2016. In the AfD Basic Program, the chapter "Culture, Language and Identity" reads, "The current focus of the German remembrance culture on the time of National Socialism is to be broken and recast in favor of an extended view of history, which also encompasses the positive aspects of German history that allow for a positive identification."[8]

With these demands for a renunciation of the established culture of remembrance, revisionist political positions and attitudes that were pushed out of the public sphere were revived. For decades, for Germans, the murder of European Jews by the Germans seemed to make a positive reference to their own nation impossible. Starting with Federal President Richard von Weizsäcker's 1985 speech on the fortieth anniversary of the end of World War II, national pride and responsibility were given a new frame. The Germans, so the new narrative goes, can be proud not despite Auschwitz but because they have come to terms with it. Hence, no longer does Auschwitz stand in opposition to the "positive aspects of German history," but coming to terms with it has become another source of national pride for the Germans. However, although these new memory politics allow Germans to identify positively with their nation, the AfD rejects it. They do so because they reject the notion of being proud of the new, multicultural Germany that confronts its past. Instead, the party aims at restoring a form of national pride with a different agenda. Alexander Gauland, cochairman of the party since September 2017 and cowhip of the party in the Bundestag, argued repeatedly and most blatantly in his speech at the Kyffhäuser Treffen (a yearly gathering of Der Flügel) that "if the French are rightly proud of their emperor and the Britons of Nelson and Churchill, we have the right to be proud of the achievements of the German soldiers in two world wars."[9] It is the consensus among historians that the Wehrmacht and other combat soldiers led a war of annihilation in the East and executed or backed the extermination of millions of ideological enemies of National Socialist Germany, including six million Jews. Gauland's comparison breaks taboos in order to restore political validity to positions that were forced out of the political realm with great effort and by means of a process that took decades.

The glorification of German soldiers goes hand in hand with the claim that only the victims of the Holocaust are remembered in Germany. This has been a popular trope of revisionists for a long time despite the fact that it is a legend. There is no case reported in which a family was kept from commemorating their family members who served as soldiers in World War II. Yet it is not the kind of commemoration that the AfD takes offense at but rather Germany's official politics of remembrance. The assertion that no events other than the Holocaust are being commemorated is false. This is evident both on public holidays (e.g., Memorial Day) and in the hundreds of monuments in German towns and villages commemorating, for example, German refugees from Eastern European countries and the German soldiers killed in action in both world wars. However, it is characteristic for the rejection of the established remembrance politics to falsely claim that no other events except the Holocaust, and therefore only murdered Jews, are commemorated.

The AfD is pushing for a change in Holocaust memory politics that, in their view, should make it possible again to be "proud of the achievements of German soldiers in two world wars," as Gauland put it. The memory of the Holocaust is thus a disruptive factor. Following the demand that Germany needs a 180-degree turn in memory politics, Höcke states that a culture of remembrance is needed "which above all, and first and foremost, brings us into contact with the great achievements of our ancestors." Höcke claims that it was Allied policy in World War II to "destroy us with stumps and stalks, to root out our roots. And together with the systematic re-education that began after 1945, this was almost achieved."[10] This conspiracy theory in the form of victim-perpetrator reversal, in which the Germans become the victims of an annihilation policy by the Allied forces, is widespread within the AfD and represents yet another form of secondary antisemitism that denies the true Holocaust victims their singular status as such. Dealing with the past, according to Höcke with reference to Franz Josef Strauß, paralyzes the German *Volk*.[11] This political narrative of remembrance is supported by large parts of the party, which is also indicated by how the AfD commemorates the international Holocaust Memorial Day. While all the parties represented in the Bundestag commemorated the event on January 27, 2017, the AfD kept quiet. It may therefore come as a surprise at first glance that a number of AfD MPs posted on Facebook on July 20, 2017, to commemorate the attempt of the German Wehrmacht officer Claus Schenk Graf von Stauffenberg to assassinate Adolf Hitler. It is especially interesting to look more closely at the post of Beatrix von Storch. Storch is the granddaughter of Lutz Graf Schwerin von Krosigk, who was minister of finance in Adolf Hitler's cabinet from the time of Hitler's appointment as chancellor until his death. She is also the AfD's coordinator for combating antisemitism.

In a detailed analysis, Monika Hübscher, a historian focusing on antisemitism on social media, shows that the videos and memes posted by Storch coalesce into a narrative. Storch implies in a video that the AfD is a resistance movement against the current German federal government, just as Stauffenberg was resisting against the dictatorial regime of National Socialism. What is central here is that Storch's narrative makes no reference to other resistance movements; even reference to the victims of National Socialism is completely absent.[12] Storch takes Stauffenberg out of this National Socialist context and embeds him in the "history of the German tradition of freedom." Her reference points are not Auschwitz and National Socialist racial ideology but "the liberal revolution of 1848, the workers' revolt in the GDR of 1953, and the liberal revolution of 1989."[13] Storch notes in particular that the resistance had risked a "rebellion of conscience"[14] in order to then point out lessons for the present: "Never again may we blindly follow a political leadership and place the state above our conscience."[15] Relating Stauffenberg to the AfD's politics serves to equate National Socialism with the current German government and to place the AfD in the tradition of the German freedom movement. This false comparison adds another stone to the mosaic that constitutes the AfD's perception of German history.

Despite many examples that illustrate that the AfD is opposing Germany's remembrance politics in order to focus on the more positive aspects of German history, recent events have shown that the AfD is testing different options for how to make the topic relevant. While the AfD did not react to Holocaust Memorial Day 2017, the events surrounding this Europe-wide Memorial Day in 2019 created a big stir. During a speech on January 27, 2019, in the Bavarian Parliament by Charlotte Knobloch, a leading figure of the Jewish community in Germany and currently commissioner for Holocaust memory for the Jewish World Congress, the AfD faction left the plenary hall almost unanimously when Knobloch stated that the AfD stood for hatred and exclusion.[16] While this may not be surprising, keeping in mind the AfD's remembrance politics and political demands mentioned above, this time the AfD chose to react differently—it avoided stressing revisionist positions and instead stressed the importance of commemoration of the murder of European Jews. Stefan Möller, parliamentary director of the AfD in the Parliament of Thuringia, stated, "Over the years we have shown that sincere remembrance of the victims of National Socialism without instrumentalizing them at the same time, is an important concern for us."[17] Those proclamations went hand in hand with accusations against the established parties that stressed that they were instrumentalizing the commemoration of the Holocaust for the political purpose of excluding the AfD.[18] This accusation was first phrased by the party association Juden in der AfD (JAfD, Jews in the AfD), which was formed in October 2018. The JAfD strongly criticized Knobloch for her speech in the Bavarian Parliament: "The entire AfD is deeply shocked by the enormously unscrupulous behavior of Charlotte Knobloch, who, and let me say it directly, !! trampled on the countless graves of dead Jews in the name of today's mainstream agenda! . . . At the same time you [Charlotte Knobloch] have DIRECTLY supported the policy of Islamic, Islamist and Islamofascist immigration by the governing parties."[19] The non-Jewish members of the AfD couldn't have made such a statement against a prominent Jew, but the Jewish members could. The statement was then shared on the internet by (non-Jewish) parliamentarians of the AfD and was supposed to show that members of the Bavarian parliamentary group were right to walk out during Knobloch's speech. It remains to be seen whether this type of communication will prevail, in which the JAfD accuses established Jewish associations and other parties of instrumentalizing commemoration, and then the AfD echoes these accusations. At present, it is clear that the limits of what can be said in public shifted again during the debate over Knobloch's speech in the Bavarian Landtag. A glance at the discussions, which took place primarily on Facebook, shows that a position is now being taken against an official representative of the Jewish community with malice, vehemence, and language that indicates that resentment against Jews is increasingly communicated directly and without detours. Since the speech in the Bavarian state parliament, Knobloch said at the request of the daily newspaper *Augsburger Allgemeine*, "almost every minute, threats and insults reach me by e-mail and telephone."[20]

Given the attitudes of its followers, it is only logical for the AfD to seek to implement the policies it has already prepared in its parliamentary work. In January 2017, the parliamentary group of the AfD in Baden-Wuerttemberg (led by the party cochair Jörg Meuthen) tabled a motion in the Budget Committee to withdraw financial support from a memorial site in Gurs, France, to which Jews and other Nazi victims were deported and held captive. The AfD also demanded that young people should no longer receive funding for trips to memorial sites but rather undertake journeys "to important sites of German history,"[21] making it clear that the AfD does not consider Holocaust memorial sites important to German history. Furthermore, the underlying idea that Germans focus only on the Holocaust and ignore positive aspects of German history and culture disregards the transformation of German memorial politics as it has developed in the Berlin republic, in which national pride is based on Germany's coming to terms with the National Socialist past.

The ideological fragments described, such as the rejection of established politics of remembrance, the idealization of German soldiers of two world wars, and the verbal attacks against members of the Jewish community who speak out against these politics, are coalescing into a right-wing extremist mindset. For the time being, the AfD is changing the public discourse. Their long-term goals are to change the public culture of remembrance and to correct school curricula.

Antisemitic Imagery

In addition to its openly expressed antisemitism, it is important to focus on how the AfD "promotes an antisemitic view of the world with its ideology and political positionings."[22] The question arises with regard not only to the AfD but to all worldviews and political convictions. The issue has two aspects: What makes antisemitism attractive for people as a pattern of thought? What sociopsychological benefits do antisemites derive from their convictions? In addition, to what extent do figures of thought, metaphors, and images of society in the collective pictorial memory have antisemitic connotations and thus evoke antisemitism? For example, there are antisemitic codes such as the image of the "power of the US East Coast" that stress the stereotypical image of the rich, influential Jew without explicitly talking about Jews. In the case of the AfD, however, the analysis is somewhat more complicated because the metaphors and images in question are not codes that deliberately seek to circumvent explicit antisemitism and represent a form of insider communication typical of the extreme right-wing scene. Rather, the social images transported by AfD representatives are historically linked to antisemitic topoi. The prejudices and stereotypes mobilized by the AfD "do not stand unconnected next to each other. Rather, they are integrated through a worldview that reduces the blame for the various phenomena fought to the work of concrete actors and groups of actors."[23] Part of this twisted worldview is that the federal government, its security authorities, politicians of the so-called *Systemparteien* (parties that represent the established political system), political dissenters who are defamed as being naive, the media who are denounced for spreading fake news, and other entities are accused of betraying the German people and German interests. The crystallizing point of various right-wing populist counternarratives, which are also popular in the AfD, is the conspiracy that the actors mentioned above deliberately betray the German people. Two examples illustrate how Gauland and Höcke, the leaders of party right, use antisemitic ciphers without explicitly referring to Jews.

In a much-discussed guest article in the *Frankfurter Allgemeine Zeitung* entitled "Why Populism?"[24] Gauland drew the picture of a "global" or "globalist class" "sitting in internationally active companies, in organizations such as the UN, in the media, start-ups, universities, NGOs, foundations, in political parties and their apparatuses, and because it controls the information it sets the pace culturally and politically."²⁵ Gauland's main criticism is "that this new elite is weakly tied to their respective homelands. In a detached parallel society they feel like citizens of the world. The rain that falls in their home countries does not wet them."²⁶ Bodo Kahmann, a political scientist who focuses on antisemitism and the German radical right, convincingly argues that Gauland is above all concerned with sharpening and confirming images of an enemy, a tactic that the political right was already cultivating during the Weimar Republic: "With his assertion of the existence of an urban, global and therefore homeless cultural elite [Gauland] stresses the connection between urbanity and rootlessness. Naturally the corresponding antisemitic connotations are also supplied with this equation."²⁷ Since the time of the German Empire, according to Kahmann, the antisemitic image of the Jew has stood for rootlessness and urbanity in *völkisch* thought. Gauland spreads motifs and images that are traditionally intertwined with antisemitism. What is striking in this context is that right-wing populists like to speak supposedly uncomfortable truths. If one takes a closer look at these supposed truths, they are stereotypes and simple explanatory schemes. The question of social inequality is understood by the AfD and in right-wing populism in the broader sense as a conflict either between Germans and immigrants or between the elite and the middle class. It is noteworthy that these images fall on fertile ground, even though Germany emerged politically and economically strengthened from the world financial crisis of 2007–8.²⁸ Economic development alone is therefore not sufficient to explain the increase in resentment and the attractiveness of images of society that are closely connected to antisemitic notions.

While Gauland stresses images that are closely connected with antisemitism, the following example sheds light on the popular narrative of the "great replacement." The replacement conspiracy theory has become a crystallization point for right-wing extremists worldwide. It originates from the French intellectual Renaud Camus. The core idea is that the migration movements of past years are in fact not migration movements but conspiracies of Western governments controlled by the Jews, who bring migrants to their countries in order to exchange the (white, non-Jewish) population with (Muslim, nonwhite) immigrants. While the nonwhite, Muslim immigrants are considered a threat to the cultural life of white people, they are not considered to be capable of organizing such an enterprise; rather, it is the Jews who are considered to be in charge of this master plan. The great replacement conspiracy theory combines racist and antisemitic images. In Germany, members of the AfD have contributed a great deal to popularizing this conspiracy, online as well as offline.

At a rally in Gera in Thuringia in 2015, Höcke made the following statement:

> I no longer believe in coincidences in connection with the so-called refugee crisis. I do not believe that it is a coincidence that the list of countries of origin of asylum seekers or transit countries and the list of countries in which interventions, interventions by the Western community of values have taken place in recent years and decades are remarkably similar. These countries are Kosovo, Syria, Iraq, Libya, and Afghanistan. Here in these countries, the Western community of values of freedom, human rights and democracy has intervened. The result was that these countries have been destabilized. I don't want to nurture conspiracy theories, but there are some conspiracy theories that contain a core of truth. And so I have the dull assumption that the flows of refugees that are now flowing into our country and into Europe, that these flows of refugees are perhaps being used as a weapon of migration in order to achieve something that can be called the destabilization of Europe, dear friends. And the role played by Mrs. Merkel, who is still claiming to this day that the right of asylum must not have an upper limit, can only be presumed. But in my opinion, there are actually only two possibilities: The first possibility is that Mrs. Merkel has lost her mind. And the second possibility is—that is so unbelievable, if it were, but it is in fact a realistic possibility in my eyes—the second possibility is she was privy to a grand, grand geopolitical plan and she is willingly implementing that plan.[29]

In Höcke's narrative, the German chancellor is privy to a plan, meaning that the plan is not her own and that she has people by her side who are influencing her. Those people act in secret, pull the strings in the background, and have great geopolitical plans with the ultimate goal of destabilizing Europe. Again, this image is connected to a stock of old and culturally transmitted images that are deeply intertwined with antisemitic tropes. Just as the vast majority of Germans know which animal has eaten Little Red Riding Hood and have a clear mental image of this animal in mind, so the images of those people who are evoked by Höcke's narrative are not arbitrary. Those acting in the background do not have to be named. The audience understands who is meant. Höcke's conspiracy narrative is as absurd as it is powerful. The idea that there is a secret plan perpetrated by Western governments to replace the populations with migrants is widespread within German right-wing populism and among leading politicians of the AfD.[30] In order for the replacement narrative to be at least consistent in itself, it must be assumed that there is a homogenous people that can be replaced by a foreign group.

The idea of a population exchange is therefore essentially racist and irrational. Migration is an old phenomenon; migration movements can be explained by taking a number of factors into account. Höcke, however, does not consider the obvious factors, such as war, poverty, and the prospect of a better life, to explain migration; instead, he explains migration as a process (the replacement of the population) that is controlled by a group that acts behind the scenes and that is powerful enough to force its will on the German chancellor.

As parliamentary democracy is designed to negotiate different interests, rational dialogue is indispensable for it. Conspiracy theories willingly ignore facts and therefore do not allow for rational dialogue; they make the rational dialogue that is constitutive of parliamentary democracy impossible. In addition, it is easy to see that the great replacement narrative serves a specific purpose: by turning migrants into colonizers who are weaponized by Jews with the aim of destabilizing Western countries, not only is the rejection of migration morally justified but so too are acts of terror and violence against those two groups portrayed as self-defense. It is essential for the analysis of antisemitism to bear in mind that people act on both words and emotions. The replacement narrative addresses ideas of belonging and community that are charged and highly emotional, and the narrative also identifies who and what threatens those ideas. Therefore, the replacement narrative has become one of the most influential narratives of the radical right wing in Europe and the United States.

Participants in the march of the alt-right in Charlottesville alluded to the replacement narrative when they chanted the slogan "Jews will not replace us." For the shooter who killed eleven Jews in the Tree of Life Synagogue in Pittsburgh, the replacement narrative supposedly orchestrated by Jews represented both the motivation and the legitimation of his actions. According to his self-image, he murdered Jews as he identified them behind the "migrant caravan" that made its way from Honduras to the US border.[31] The shooter who tried to enter the synagogue in Halle on Yom Kippur in 2019 also justified the decision to murder Jews by appealing to the narrative: "So why, you may ask, did I choose this target. It's the nearest location with a high population of Jews, simple as that. . . . I originally planned to storm a mosque or an antifa 'culture' center, which are way less defended, but even killing 100 golems won't make a difference, when on a single day more than that are shipped to Europe. The only way to win is to cut off the head of ZOG, which are the kikes. If I fail and die but kill a single Jew, it was worth it."[32]

A few hours after the assault on the synagogue and the killing of a woman on the street and a man who was hiding in a Döner Kebab fast-food place, Höcke wrote on Facebook, "It was with great dismay that I learned of the terrorist attack in Halle. My thoughts are with the relatives of the victims of this completely delusional crime. What kind of people do these things to other people?" One of many answers to Höcke's question is that there are people who believe in the same conspiracy theory that Höcke spreads and who act on it.

If we take a step back now and reconsider the images offered by Gauland and Höcke for the interpretation of social conditions, we may identify similarities. Gauland and Höcke offer rather trivial patterns of interpretation that do not adequately describe social reality. Their simplistic interpretations are designed in such a way that social relations are not understood as protracted and mediated processes but rather are personalized and are allegedly the undesirable creations of an uprooted cultural elite (Gauland) or of geopolitical conspirators acting in secret (Höcke). It is worth considering the criticism of antisemitism formulated by representatives of the Frankfurt School, in particular the sociopsychological aspects contained therein. Theodor W. Adorno and others have described stereotyping and personalization as complementary ideologies in their studies of the authoritarian personality. Stereotyping, so the argument goes, disables the subject's ability to openly experience the world because every perception of reality only confirms what is projected into the world beforehand.[33] Reality then is not accessible to the subject, and the world of stereotypes becomes a self-referential system. Complementary to this is personalization. Stereotyping and personalization are reluctant and at the same time complementary forms of inverted perception. They create order in chaos and calm amid a world that is perceived as increasingly confusing, cold, and impersonal. In the conspiracy thinking of right-wing populism and images as evoked by Gauland and Höcke, the confusion and abstractness are personalized. As discussed above, the groups and individuals that are described as powerful, uprooted, and distant from ordinary people and as acting in the background are not arbitrary but closely associated with images of Jewish power and influence. Such conspiracy narratives can be found on the internet, "for the most part close to antisemitic content, . . . either embedded in it or directly linked to it."[34] Personalizing understandings of society are often associated with antisemitism because the image of the Jew is a centuries-old trope present in the European collective memory that is highly stereotyped and may unite the most contradictory projections.

Pro-Israelism and Anti-antisemitism

Against the backdrop of the antisemitically connoted images that the AfD disseminates and its programmatic call for a change in the politics and culture of remembrance, the positive references to Judaism and Israel put forward by leading representatives of the AfD must come as a surprise. However, pro-Israeli and anti-antisemitic expressions are not a new phenomenon in European right-wing radical parties but have become increasingly central to the agitation of these parties in recent years. Already in the 1990s and more extensively after 9/11, the importance of rapprochement with Israel and the Jewish population grew to the extent that they intensified efforts to cut historical and ideological ties with fascism and National Socialism and to step out of Germany's political isolation. This strategy includes expressions of solidarity with the Jewish state, to which is attributed the role of a frontline state in the historical struggle of the Christian-Jewish West against Islam. The second element is a condemnation of Islamic antisemitism, which, in addition to the antisemitism of left-wing anti-imperialist groups, is the only form of antisemitism that is seen as problematic by the AfD. It is, however, not hard to see that the proclamations of standing with Israel serve the purpose of legitimizing the AfD's political positions.

From 2015, then cochairwoman Frauke Petry and her husband, Marcus Pretzell, had begun to position themselves in interviews as against antisemitism and anti-Zionism and as pro-Israel.[35] In an interview by the YouTube channel Jung und Naiv with Petry, it becomes clear in which context this positive reference is embedded: "In the field of security policy Israel has shown that despite massive hostilities from the Islamic world, it has been able to maintain this state for decades. And this can only be achieved with a militant democracy. People like to talk about it in Germany, but then Germany opens the borders to immigrants, you can imagine what would happen if Israel stopped carrying out border controls: the country would be finished within weeks."[36] Petry makes Israel's ever-fragile security a bargaining chip for her political struggle against immigration. Comparing the German and Israeli security situations serves to justify Petry's own anti-immigration position through the positive reference to the Jewish state and thus immunizes it against criticism. The same goes for German patriotism, which Petry praises not directly but again by relating it to national pride in Israel. In an interview for Israeli television in 2016, Petry complained that "in general in Israel people have fewer problems to identify with their own country and their own people—this is Germany's biggest problem."[37]

The AfD's criticism of antisemitism among Muslims is often as instrumental as the reference to the Jewish state. In his speech to the Bundestag in April 2018 on the seventieth anniversary of the founding of Israel, Gauland said, "But for us this also means that Israel's securing of its existence begins at the Brandenburg Gate. Those who burn the Star of David and attack Jews who wear Kippas have abused the right to hospitality in this country and thus forfeited it. Antisemitism must not become the collateral damage of a false refugee and immigration policy."[38] This is one of many examples that show that Gauland's criticism of antisemitism is directed exclusively toward antisemitism among Muslims. This serves the AfD primarily as the moral justification for an anti-immigration and nationalist politics. Pretzell, former chairman of the AfD parliamentary group in North Rhine-Westphalia and member of the European Parliament, most clearly expressed the connection among anti-immigration politics, pro-Israelism, and antisemitism. Pretzell's much-quoted statement in a speech in Koblenz in January 2017 reads, "Israel is our future in the way we deal with Islam."[39] Some understood that as a commitment to Israel. Nevertheless, the sentence shows quite clearly that Israel is again being instrumentalized and is mentioned only to legitimize a hardhanded policy toward Muslims. Pretzell's image of Israel is projective and misleading. He paints a distorted picture of the position of the Muslim minority and how Islam is dealt with in Israeli society.[40] For example, Israel allows Jewish as well as non-Jewish minorities such as Arabs, Druze, and Haredim to have their own school systems. Thus, there are Arabic schools and curricula for the Muslim minority in the country in which the pupils are taught in Arabic. Pretzell certainly did not have this in mind, because cultural-religious autonomy structures of this kind do not go together with the AfD's understanding of the German nation as a homogeneous ethnic community and of minorities as subordinate to it. Pretzell's image of Israel moves close to the image of Israel held by anti-imperialist leftists who regard Israel as a racist state—with the difference that Pretzell celebrates Israel for its supposedly tough treatment of Islam.

For the AfD, positive references to Israel and Judaism are associated with the hope of immunizing its own political position against criticism. In addition, this is meant to serve as a credible distancing from the right and to make the party eligible for voters in the political center. This political option has become obsolete with the resignations of Petry and Pretzell but is also no longer needed. The functional equivalent of pro-Israelism as represented by Petry and Pretzell is the JAfD, which caused strong opposition from over forty Jewish associations, such as the Central Council of Jews in

Germany, the Orthodox Rabbinical Conference, and the Jewish Women's Federation.[41] The declaration entitled "AfD—No Alternative for Jews"[42] is formulated in a very sharp tone and condemns the AfD for trying to play Jews against Muslims. It ends with a strong statement: "We do not allow ourselves to be instrumentalized by the AfD. . . . [T]he AfD is a racist and anti-Semitic party!"[43]

Almost simultaneously with the founding of the JAfD, the weekly magazine *Der Spiegel* published an interview with Knobloch in which she compared the rise of the AfD and the NSDAP. She said that the AfD should be called a "Nazi party" and its program could be summed up with the words "Jews out."[44] Thereupon Jörg Meuthen, who is chairing the party with Gauland, accused Knobloch of using hate speech against the AfD and stated that "more and more Jews in Germany recognize by whom they are really threatened: by no means from the ranks of our liberal-conservative and at the same time patriotic alternative to Merkel's policies of which she claims they have no alternative. No, they are endangered precisely because of Merkel's supposedly non-alternative politics of unlimited Muslim mass immigration. . . . Mrs. Knobloch, WE are those who uncompromisingly stand up for the freedom of our Jewish fellow citizens and their protection against imported, Muslim anti-Semitism. Judaism belongs to Germany, Islam does not."[45]

While almost the entire party and the AfD party leadership focus exclusively on imported antisemitism, the JAfD takes note of antisemitism within the party. Wolfgang Fuhl, cofounder of the JAfD and former member of the board of directors of the Central Council of Jews in Germany, said in an interview, "Of course there is antisemitism in society, and there is also antisemitism in the AfD as there is antisemitism in every other party."[46] When asked what worries the Jews in Germany, Fuhl stated, "The biggest worry at the moment is the antisemitism imported by Merkel. All murdered Jews in Europe in this millennium . . . were murdered by Muslims; this is a formative, negative experience that burns itself into the collective Jewish memory just as much as the Holocaust."[47] Fuhl's arguments fit into the scope of narratives of the AfD. The criticism of antisemitism among Muslim migrants is supposed to prove that the AfD is the only party that opposes imported antisemitism. There is no doubt that Muslim antisemitism is a pressing problem, and various empirical studies show that antisemitism is more pronounced among Muslims than among comparative groups.[48] Criticism of antisemitism among Muslims, however, stands in open contradiction to the absence of criticism of antisemitism within the

AfD. As Gideon Botsch and Christoph Kopke aptly put it, "anti-Semitism is addressed as a problem arising from immigration—and thus externalized in its causes and manifestations."⁴⁹

Conclusion

The disputes with and about the AfD have changed the political discourse, not only in terms of the tone of the communication but also in terms of legitimate political goals and means. The AfD makes the political demand for an ethnically homogenous people socially acceptable, where the memory of the Holocaust is repressed in favor of pride for the actions of German soldiers in two world wars. The fact that these demands not only fuel existing resentments in German society but also make the use of violence conceivable as a legitimate means of political conflict is confirmed by surveys. Among respondents with a right-wing populist orientation, the approval of and willingness to use violence as a form of political confrontation is clearly more strongly endorsed than the social average.⁵⁰ This posturing of self-empowerment corresponds with the resistance narratives that are circulated on the political right, which additionally questions the state's monopoly on the use of force. Moreover, the support for right-wing extremist statements is much more strongly pronounced among AfD sympathizers. In the 2016 opinion study "Gespaltene Mitte—Feindselige Zustände," the approval of advocacy of a right-wing dictatorship is indicated by approval of the following statement: "In the national interest, under certain circumstances a dictatorship is the better form of government." Self-identified supporters of the social-democratic SPD agreed to this statement by 1.4 percent and supporters of Angela Merkel's CDU/CSU by 2.6 percent. In strong contrast, supporters of the AfD agreed by 20.8 percent.⁵¹ According to Andreas Zick, director of the Institute for Interdisciplinary Research of Conflict and Violence at Bielefeld University, who conducted the study, "One group is particularly striking in the study. Among the respondents who sympathize with the AfD, xenophobic prejudices and prejudices directed against Roma and Muslims as well as pejorative opinions towards asylum seekers, refugees, and the unemployed find majority support; more than 50 percent of those who would vote for the AfD share hostile and right-wing opinions, more than 80 percent share attitudes that are typical for the New Right."⁵² Additionally, research shows that the party is also attractive to antisemites. The results of a survey commissioned by Germany's leading conservative daily, *Frankfurter Allgemeine Zeitung*, and conducted by the Allensbach Institute show "that the judgments on Jews among the supporters of the AfD are significantly more negative than among the supporters of all other parties."[53] The approval of the statement that "Jews have too much influence in the world" fluctuates between 16 percent (supporters of the SPD) and 20 percent (supporters of the socialist Die Linke): "Only the supporters of the AfD were completely out of line; 55 percent said that Jews had too much influence in the world. A deep chasm separates the AfD from the other parties."[54]

Notes

1. The Erfurt Resolution was written by Götz Kubitschek, a pioneer of the New Right in Germany. The resolution aimed at bundling the party's *völkisch* members into one party wing and turning the party into a *Bewegungspartei*—a term that was applied to Adolf Hitlers NSDAP and that is supposed to express that the AfD, unlike other parties, does not adhere to the usual conventions of established parties but makes contact with the people and with grassroots movements such as Pegida.

2. In the 2019 state election in Thuringia, the AfD more than doubled its result and gained 23.4 percent of the popular vote.

3. "Die 'Erfurter Resolution'—Wortlaut und Erstunterzeichner," Der Flügel, March 14, 2015, https://web.archive.org/web/20160105210808/https://www.derfluegel.de/2015/03/14/die-erfurter-resolution-wortlaut-und-erstunterzeichner/.

4. "AfD verliert massiv an Zustimmung," Zeit, July 12, 2015, https://www.zeit.de/politik/deutschland/2015-07/afd-umfrage-petry.

5. Andreas Zick, Küpper Beate, and Berghan Wilhelm, eds., *Verlorene Mitte—Feindselige Zustände: Rechtsextreme Einstellungen in Deutschland 2018/19* (Bonn: Dietz, 2019).

6. AfD Sachsen, "Wahlprogramm 2014. Langfassung," 2014, https://archiv.afd-fraktion-sachsen.de/audiowahlprogramm.html?file=files/afd/fraktion-sachsen/downloads/Wahlprogramm/AfD_Programm_Lang.pdf.

7. AfD Sachsen-Anhalt 2016, "Die Stimme der Bürger—unser Programm," Wahlprogramm zur Landtagswahl, March 13, 2016, http://ltw16.sachsen-anhalt-waehlt.de/fileadmin/LTW2016/Wahlprogramme/wahlprogramm_afd.pdf.

8. "Programm für Deutschland," AfD, 2016, https://www.afd.de/grundsatzprogramm, 48.

9. "Germany Should Be Proud of Its WW2 Soldiers, Far-Right Candidate Says," Reuters, September 14, 2017, https://www.reuters.com/article/us-germany-election-afd/germany-should-be-proud-of-its-ww2-soldiers-far-right-candidate-says-idUSKCN1BP2SS.

10. The translation here is mine. Original: "Man wollte uns mit Stumpf und Stiel zu vernichten, man wollte unsere Wurzeln roden. Und zusammen mit der dann nach 1945 begonnenen systematischen Umerziehung hat man das auch fast geschafft." Björn Höcke, "Rede bei den Dresdner Gesprächen," *Der Tagesspiegel*, July 17, 2019, https://www.tagesspiegel.de/politik/hoecke-rede-im-wortlaut-gemuetszustand-eines-total-besiegten-volkes/19273518.html.

11. Höcke, "Rede bei den Dresdner Gesprächen."

12. Beatrix von Storch, "Attentat vom 20. Juli 1944: Kampf gegen die NS-Diktatur," Facebook video, July 20, 2017, https://www.facebook.com/BeatrixVonStorch/videos/1660299040678201.

See also Monika Hübscher, "The AfD's Attitude towards National Socialism, the Holocaust and Antisemitism: A Facebook Analysis" (master's thesis, Haifa University, 2017), 54.

13. Storch, "Attentat."
14. Storch.
15. Storch.
16. Isabel Bernstein, "AfD verlässt Plenum während Holocaust-Gedenkrede," *Süddeutsche Zeitung*, January 23, 2019, https://www.sueddeutsche.de/bayern/afd-landtag-gedenkveranstaltung-opfer-nationalsozialismus-knobloch-1.4299382.
17. Stefan Möller, "Parlamentarischer Geschäftsführer der AfD im Thüringer Landtag," Facebook, January 24, 2019, https://facebook.com/story.php?story_fbid=2493400354008696&id=969753549706725.
18. The AfD refers to other established parties as *Systemparteien* or *Altparteien*, parties that represent the old and defeated system.
19. Original: "Die gesamte Bundesvereinigung ist zutiefst erschüttert über das enorm skrupellose Verhalten der Charlotte Knobloch, die, und lasst es mich ganz direkt sagen, !! Auf den unzähligen Gräbern der toten Juden im Namen der heutigen Mainstream Agenda herumtrampelt!! . . . Gleichzeitig haben Sie (gemeint ist Charlotte Knobloch—Anm.—MG) die Politik der islamischen, islamistischen und islamofaschistischen Einwanderung durch die Regierungsparteien DIREKT unterstützt." For more on Jews in the AfD, see JAfD, "Liebe Freunde, liebe Kolleginnen und Kollegen, was sich im Bayrischen Landtag abspielte - dafür finden wir keine Worte," Facebook, January 23, 2019, https://www.facebook.com/JudenindernAfD/posts/450723222424914?__tn__=K-R.
20. "Charlotte Knobloch wird nach AfD-Eklat im Landtag bedroht," *Augsburger Allgemeine*, January 24, 2019, https://www.augsburger-allgemeine.de/bayern/Charlotte-Knobloch-wird-nach-AfD-Eklat-im-Landtag-bedroht-id53279456.html.
21. See Rüdiger Soldt, "AfD will Geld für NS-Gedenkstätte streichen," *Frankfurter Allgemeine Zeitung*, January 23, 2017, https://www.faz.net/aktuell/politik/inland/joerg-meuthen-von-afd-ist-gegen-gelder-fuer-ns-gedenkstaette-14726516.html.
22. Stephan Grigat, "Von Österreich lernen: Die FPÖ als Vorbild der AfD und Antisemitismuskritik in Zeiten islamistischer Mobilmachung," in *AfD und FPÖ: Antisemitismus, völkischer Nationalismus und Geschlechterbilder*, trans. Stephan Grigat (Baden-Baden: Nomos Verlagsgesellschaft, 2017), 17.
23. Christoph Kopke and Gideon Botsch, "Antisemitismus ohne Antisemiten?," in *Wut—Verachtung—Abwertung: Rechtspopulismus in Deutschland*, trans. Ralf Melzer and Dietmar Molthagen (Bonn: J. H. W. Dietz, 2015), 189–94.
24. Alexander Gauland, "Warum muss es Populismus sein?," *Frankfurter Allgemeine Zeitung*, July 6, 2019.
25. Gauland, "Warum muss es Populismus sein?"
26. Gauland.
27. Bodo Kahmann, "Sin City: Die Großstadt ist das Feindbild alter und neuer Nazis," *konkret* 1 (2019): 36–37.
28. According to the Halle Institute for Economic Research, the lower interest rates saved the tax authorities around €100 billion, and the export surplus also grew in 2013 compared with the previous year. The trend has continued. In 2018, the unemployment rate fell below 5 percent, its lowest level since German reunification. From a political point of view, too, the second decade of the new millennium stands for Germany's rise as Europe's hegemonic power.
29. "Björn Höcke (AfD) in Gera am 30.10.2015—Flüchtlingsströme als Migrationswaffe," Armando Di Baja, video, 29:01, October 31, 2015, https://www.youtube.com/watch?v=HjWo8Bmy2_k.
30. Among others, Gauland supports the idea. See "Populismus und Demokratie—Dr. Alexander Gauland beim IfS," kanal schnellroda, video, 42:20, January 23, 2019, https://

www.youtube.com/watch?v=zMsR4grTlsQ. See also Floris Biskamp, ": Rechter Ideologe und schlechter Soziologe: Alexander Gaulands Rede über Populismus und Demokratie gelesen als Theorie, Ideologie und politische Herausforderung," February 11, 2019, http://blog.florisbiskamp.com/2019/02/11/rechter-ideologe-und-schlechter-soziologe-alexander-gaulands-rede-ueber-populismus-und-demokratie-gelesen-als-theorie-ideologie-und-politische-herausforderung/?fbclid=IwAR3C9ptSbFaqi8UzypwiQ7wKv6SDvPWwDYu1_kS9oBlPN_7dP1CE46gzHuo.

31. See Ben Collins, "Pittsburgh Synagogue Shooting Suspect Threatened Jewish Groups, Pushed Migrant Caravan Conspiracies," NBC News, October 27, 2018, https://www.nbcnews.com/news/crime-courts/pittsburgh-synagogue-shooting-suspect-threatened-jewish-groups-pushed-migrant-caravan-n925256.

32. Excerpts from Stephen Balliet's attack plan can be read at https://rotter.net/User_files/forum/5da0d8907359051e.pdf. *ZOG* (Zionist Occupied Government) is a phrase used by antisemites. It is a modern version of the idea that Jews hold the real power behind the scenes.

33. Theodor W. Adorno, *Studien zum autoritären Charakter* (Frankfurt am Main: Suhrkamp, 1973), 189ff.

34. Kopke and Botsch, "Antisemitismus ohne Antisemiten?," 193.

35. Pretzell was state chairman of the AfD in North Rhine-Westphalia between 2014 and 2017 and was also a member of the European Parliament between 2014 and 2019.

36. "Jung & naiv interviewt Frauke Petry," Ruhrkultour, June 28, 2016, http://ruhrkultour.de/jung-naiv-interviewt-frauke-petry-afd/.

37. "Frauke Petry im Interview," interview for Israeli television, kan11 (an Israeli news channel), video, 7:31, November 27, 2016, https://www.youtube.com/watch?v=l9_F8njF6C4.

38. Alexander Gauland, "29. Sitzung des Bundestages," Deutscher Bundestag, April 26, 2018, http://dipbt.bundestag.de/dip21/btp/19/19029.pdf#P.2623.

39. Grigat, "Von Österreich lernen," 15.

40. Grigat, 15.

41. At the time the declaration was published, it was supported by seventeen Jewish organizations.

42. Keine Alternative für Juden, *Gemeinsame Erklärung gegen die AfD*, July 12, 2019, https://www.zentralratderjuden.de/fileadmin/user_upload/pdfs/Gemeinsame_Erklaerung_gegen_die_AfD_.pdf.

43. Keine Alternative für Juden, *Gemeinsame Erklärung gegen die AfD*. The declaration reads:

> The AfD is a party in which Jewish hatred and relativization to the extent of denial of the Shoah have a home. The AfD is anti-democratic, inhuman, and in large part right-wing radical. A mere look at the events in Chemnitz should be enough to recognize on whose side the AfD is. There, AfD representatives marched side by side with neo-Nazis, hooligans, and Pegida supporters. They were not afraid to take to the streets with people who showed the Hitler salute. A Jewish restaurant in Chemnitz was attacked in of this climate of hatred and ethnic thinking.... The AfD is becoming increasingly radical and is not afraid to rewrite history.

At the same time, the declaration continues, Gauland is "proud of the achievements of German soldiers in two world wars.... The AfD is agitating outright against Muslims and other minorities in Germany. The AfD tries to portray 'the Muslims' as enemies of the Western world or 'the Jews'. Muslims are not the enemies of the Jews! The enemies of all democrats in this country are extremists, whether out of right-wing extremist, left-wing radical or radical Muslim sentiment."

44. Christoph Schult and Veit Medick, "Spiegel-Gespräch mit Charlotte Knobloch—'So schlimm wie heute war es noch nie,'" *Der Spiegel*, October 5, 2018, http://www.spiegel.de/plus

/charlotte-knobloch-so-schlimm-wie-heute-war-es-noch-nie-a-00000000-0002-0001-0000-000159786767.

45. Jörg Meuthen, "Nein, Frau Knobloch—Wir sind keine 'Nazi-Partei,'" *Michael Mannheimer Blog*, October 9, 2018, https://michael-mannheimer.net/2018/10/11/joerg-meuthen-afd-zum-nazivorwurf-der-praesidentin-des-zentralrats-der-juden-deutschlands-frau-knobloch-es-reicht/.

46. Alexander Wendt, "Sonst werden wir den Marsch durch die Institutionen antreten," *Publico*, October 6, 2018, https://www.publicomag.com/2018/10/sonst-werden-wir-den-marsch-durch-die-institutionen-antreten/.

47. Wendt, "Sonst werden wir den Marsch durch die Institutionen antreten."

48. Jürgen Mansel and Victoria Spaiser, *Soziale Beziehungen, Konfliktpotentiale und Vorurteile im Kontext von Erfahrungen verweigerter Teilhabe und Anerkennung bei Jugendlichen mit und ohne Migrationshintergrund* (Bielefeld: Beltz Juventa, 2010); Günther Jikeli, "Muslimischer Antisemitismus in Europa," in *Antisemitismus im 21. Jahrhundert: Virulenz einer alten Feindschaft in Zeiten von Islamismus und Terror*, trans. Marc Grimm and Bodo Kahmann (Oldenburg: Walter de Gruyter, 2018), 113–33.

49. Kopke and Botsch, "Antisemitismus ohne Antisemiten?," 188.

50. Zick et al., *Verlorene Mitte—Feindselige Zustände*, 122.

51. Zick et al., 137.

52. Zick et al., 210.

53. Thomas Petersen, "Wie antisemitisch ist Deutschland," *Frankfurter Allgemeine Zeitung*, June 19, 2018.

54. Petersen, "Wie antisemitisch ist Deutschland."

MARC GRIMM is a senior researcher at the Centre for Prevention and Intervention in Childhood and Adolescence at Bielefeld University in Germany. He studied political science and sociology in Augsburg (Germany), Vienna (Austria), and Vancouver (Canada) and worked as a Holocaust educator at the Max Mannheimer Study Center in Dachau for five years. A scholarship fellow at the University of Geneva and an Erasmus fellow at Haifa University, he has published on aesthetics, German philosophy, right-wing radicalism, antisemitism, and Holocaust education. His most recent publications are a monograph about the research on right-wing extremism in Germany and the anthology *Antisemitismus im 21. Jahrhundert: Virulenz einer alten Feindschaft in Zeiten von Islamismus und Terror* (DeGruyter, 2018), which includes articles by Alvin Rosenfeld, Matthias Küntzel, Dina Porat, and others.

13

A "Serious Attack on Jewish Life"
Antisemitic Stereotypes in the Public Debate about Ritual Male Circumcision in Germany in 2012

Dana Ionescu

AT PRESENT, MEDIA, POLITICS, AND ACADEMIA ARE DEEPLY engaged in discussing whether antisemitism is on the rise in Germany and whether it has become more visible or may even possess a new quality. Jews are insulted, threatened, and physically attacked in public spaces, at school, and at work.[1] The widespread character of antisemitism is also shown by a study published in December 2018 by the European Union Agency for Fundamental Rights. Forty-one percent of the Jews interviewed who live in Germany stated that they had been confronted with insulting or threatening antisemitic statements within the previous twelve months.[2] Out of fear of harassment and exclusion, some Jews hide their cultural-religious affiliation even when among colleagues or friends. Amid these developments, there erupted in Germany the controversy, on which this chapter is centered, over the ritual circumcision of male infants and boys.

On March 3, 2019, at 3:44 p.m., a Jewish young adult living in Germany wrote on his Twitter account, "I am on the way to a circumcision in my hometown synagogue," and added a yellow smiley.[3] Less than three hours later, at 6:19 p.m., he communicated on Twitter, "Thank you to the antisemite who brought a criminal charge against me because I participated in a Bris! Am Israel Chai."[4] Within those three intervening hours, the police had paid a visit to this individual's mother.[5] The criminal accusation that caused the police to act was put forward by an anticircumcision activist who did not accept the German law that allows ritual circumcision.[6]

The incident shows that German anticircumcision activists are still actively fighting against ritual male circumcision, although circumcision has been allowed in Germany since December 2012 without parents having to state any specific reasons.[7] Some of these anticircumcision activists yearn for a return to the situation that was in place immediately after the Cologne court ruling in May 2012, when ritual circumcision was illegal. Such activists want a ban to be reinstated and consistently try to win support for this position via various blogs, internet forums, and resolutions, and on the street.[8] The controversy and its effects are not yet in the past, as the above tweet makes clear.

Already, before this incident, during the controversy over the ritual circumcision of male infants and boys in 2012, circumcision opponents had reported on three rabbis—Yitshak Ehrenberg, David Goldberg, and Yehuda Teichtal—who exercised the practice in Germany.[9] In so doing, they gave weight to their demand for a ban. For Goldberg himself the reported offense was "an expression of antisemitism,"[10] but the opponents claimed that they respected Jewish traditions and did not act out of antisemitic feelings.[11] The newspaper *Jüdische Allgemeine* reported that for the first time in the history of the federal republic of Germany, a rabbi had been charged because he had carried out his religious duties.[12]

The Cologne Court Ruling and Anticircumcision Protagonists in Germany

On May 7, 2012, the regional court in Cologne announced that ritual male circumcision was a criminal act. It was no longer a parent's right to decide regarding their son's circumcision. The judge argued that "a religiously motivated circumcision of the foreskin of a male infant is bodily harm even if carried out with the consent of the child's parents."[13] A circumcision, he maintained, is not socially acceptable in German society; it constitutes an "unreasonable" injury of physical integrity, a permanent and irreparable change, and therefore runs "contrary to the interest of the child,"[14] as three law professors also argued in several articles published in scientific journals in 2008 and 2009.[15]

The Cologne case was initiated after Muslim parents had brought their four-year-old boy to a hospital. The boy had suffered complications following a circumcision conducted by another doctor.[16] After the court ruling became public, it became clear that it would affect not only Muslims but also Jews, since the religious and cultural practice of circumcision is important in both communities in Germany.[17]

Numerous representatives of the Jewish community and other individuals both in Germany and abroad strongly criticized the court judgment. It was unprecedented and dramatically intervened "in the right of self-determination of religious communities" by prohibiting a central identity-forming practice.[18] Many Jews in Germany felt that the judgment and the controversy threatened their existence as Jews. Charlotte Knobloch, president of the Jewish Community of Munich and Upper Bavaria, asked in the *Süddeutsche Zeitung*, "Do you still want us Jews?"[19] She asked whether those who reject foreskin circumcision, including the "countless know-it-alls from medicine, jurisprudence, psychology or politics, are even aware that they . . . are challenging the already tiny Jewish existence in Germany."[20] Rabbi Pinchas Goldschmidt, chairman of the Conference of European Rabbis, declared even more emphatically that the ban was "perhaps the most serious attack on Jewish life in Europe since the Holocaust."[21]

A survey published in 2014, conducted by the European Union Agency for Fundamental Rights, showed that despite their wide diversity, the majority of Jews in Europe say that circumcision is very important to their self-identification.[22] Moreover, 71 percent of survey respondents stated that a ban on circumcision "would be a very big or fairly big problem for them."[23] The agency consulted 5,847 Jews in eight European member states, including Germany, France, and Great Britain.[24] A second survey, on discrimination and hate crime against Jews in the EU, which encompassed almost 16,500 individuals who identified themselves as Jewish, showed even higher results: 74 percent of the respondents said that for them the prohibition of circumcision would be a problem.[25] Two other minor surveys produced similar results. Political scientist Kerem Öktem points out that the German debate "shocked many Jewish respondents"[26] and that in its wake "some voiced serious concerns about the future of Jewish life in Germany."[27] Social psychologist Andreas Zick has emphasized that, as an effect of that debate, some Jews no longer feel themselves to be a normally integrated part of society.[28]

Although the controversy over male circumcision has deeply impacted the majority of German Jews, research on antisemitism to date has left the topic largely unstudied. Only a dozen academic articles and essays that focus on antisemitism[29] or exclusion[30] in a broader sense have been published in relation to the debate since 2012. This absence of research stands in stark contrast to the serious impact it is having on Jews as a whole.

In this chapter, I offer critical analysis of anticircumcision arguments and elaborate on the underlying concepts of "the Jewish" and "Jews," as well as on complex entanglements of preexisting antisemitic stereotypes.[31] The goal of this investigation is to explore the question of how many anticircumcision activists argue not only against the ritual but also against Jews (and Muslims), for whom circumcision is important. I therefore analyze the mainstream media, including nationwide newspapers and online comments left by these papers' readers. The forum for this debate has largely been newspapers and online commentaries. I aim to discuss how antisemitic stereotypes can be voiced either implicitly and indirectly or explicitly.[32]

My opening claim concerns the reasons underlying the rejection of circumcision, as these are especially important to any analysis and interpretation of anticircumcision arguments. Anticircumcision activists, primarily non-Jews (and, it goes without saying, non-Muslims), have voiced not only criticism of the practice but also antisemitic and racist resentments. My argument here demonstrates that the jumble of expressions of anticircumcision sentiment can be decoded into discursive notions or stereotypes. I present the four of these that have become most dominant.[33]

My second contention in this chapter is that the abovementioned discursive notions in the public debate in Germany belie many "classic" and traditional anti-Jewish stereotypes. Jews were conceptualized as backward and unscrupulous, as child abusers, as Others, and as a group possessing special undue power.[34]

My third claim is that anticircumcision actors share some similar ideas but also maintain some divergent conceptions regarding Jews and Muslims as collectives.[35] Because they are talking about circumcision, which is important for many Jews and Muslims in Germany, it is possible to compare and contrast specific expressions directed against Jews with those directed against Muslims. Both the similar and different attributions created by the anticircumcision movement are of vital importance, since antisemitic and racist stereotypes can simultaneously differ from and resemble each other in rhetoric.

In Germany, anticircumcision protagonists are in fact a quite heterogeneous group. Various scholars assert that circumcision has been and can be criticized "for a variety of reasons."[36] For instance, Aryeh Tuchman, associate director of the Anti-Defamation League, argues, "Because circumcision is perhaps the oldest Jewish ritual, however, and is intrinsic to Jewish notions of self-identity, Jews have often interpreted opposition to circumcision as antisemitism. But motivations for the maligning or prohibition of circumcision are complex and may arise from antisemitism, general xenophobia, or the simple clash of cultural sensibilities, including changing attitudes toward the human body and sexuality."[37] If we share Tuchman's perspective and give weight to the variety of motivations held by anticircumcision activists, in order to distinguish among them, we need to look closely at their specific explanations and reasons for rejecting circumcision. In this context, it is important to differentiate between criticisms of and opposition to ritual circumcision, where the latter aspires to a circumcision ban.

The majority of protagonists in Germany are non-Jews and non-Muslims.[38] They reject only the cultural-religious practice and demand a ban on it because they differentiate fundamentally between ritual and medical reasons (with a healing intervention) for circumcision. Three important professions represented among anticircumcision activists are doctors, psychologists, and lawyers. They form an interdisciplinary scientific network—holding conferences together; publishing common resolutions, open letters, and articles in scientific journals; and writing guest commentaries in daily newspapers or participating in interviews.[39] The movement is predominantly male and works in respected professional positions. In addition, the movement includes civic social groups such as children's rights groups and organizations of circumcised males whose members are also neither Jews nor Muslims. They aspire to a circumcision ban.

The majority of comment writers are an elusive group because almost anybody can write an online comment. The rejection of circumcision is widespread in German society. Two opinion polls, published in daily newspapers in 2012, show that a majority of the German population voices opposition to ritual circumcision and welcomes the Cologne court ruling (56%).[40] Seventy percent of the population thinks that the law allowing circumcision is bad legislation.[41]

How Images of Jews Are Condensed into Antisemitic Stereotypes

The Stereotype of "Law-Breaking" Jews (and Muslims)

The public debate that followed the regional court ruling described above reached its crescendo between June and December 2012. By the time the German federal government enacted paragraph 1631d of the German Civil Code, which protects circumcision as a religious practice, almost every national newspaper had reported not only on the Cologne court decision but also about the ritual itself. Participants in the debate agreed that in principle various fundamental rights had to be mediated and balanced one with another. Anticircumcision activists placed great emphasis on a hierarchy of rights. They argued that religious parents who choose to circumcise violate their son's fundamental right of physical integrity and that in this scenario the son's right should be afforded priority over the parents' right. This notion was expressed implicitly and indirectly as well as explicitly. In an article published in the well-known and widespread left-liberal daily newspaper *Süddeutsche Zeitung*, editor Markus C. Schulte von Drach argued that in Germany there exists not only the fundamental right of physical integrity but also that of freedom of religion, which implies that "people can hold on to their faith and can perform rituals without fear of sanctions."[42] The sentence directly after this statement in his argument reads, "as long as they do not violate any laws."[43] By this, Schulte von Drach clearly refers to those who, in his view, would exercise their religious freedoms at the expense of the national and international consensus of human rights. The sentence is suggestive because it implies that Jewish and Muslim parents who want to circumcise their sons and those acting as circumcisers violate German and European law. At this point, Schulte von Drach does not name Jews and Muslims explicitly but rather leaves readers to draw this conclusion on their own.

Part of Schulte von Drach's argumentation involves a description of baptism or religious education as practiced in German schools. He judges these Christian practices unproblematic in comparison to foreskin circumcision because in them, no one suffers. Christian rituals, he asserts, do not leave "early childhood traumas" and "physical change."[44] Afterward, he contends, "Religious circumcision is a sacrifice that parents do not bring to their God, but which they force on their child before they can defend themselves against it. And the fact that a tradition is 4000 years old speaks above all for one thing: it comes from a society that cannot be compared to ours—and in which probably very few of us wish to live."[45] Given that he condemns foreskin circumcision as an inhumane, uncivilized, and backward tradition that goes back four thousand years, this part of the text shows that Schulte von Drach focuses especially on Jews.

In another article published in the *Frankfurter Allgemeine Zeitung*, a well-known and actively circulating conservative newspaper, editor Georg Paul Hefty claims that it is very important to limit parents' decisions: "A culture or religion, which has the regular bodily injury of minors in its program," is in "permanent conflict with essential constitutional goals of a free and secular state."[46] However, the author's discourse remains abstract and vague—except in one case, he consistently writes "culture" and "religion" but does not explicitly say Jews and Muslims. Similarly, editor Heide Oestreich argues in the well-known leftist *Tageszeitung* that in the case of foreskin circumcision, "religious minorities in Germany"—she means Jews and Muslims equally—"negate a fundamental human right."[47]

However, these oversimplifying accusations lodged by opponents of circumcision are incorrect, because ritual circumcision was not regulated by German law before the regional court's ruling in 2012. It was largely undisputed by the German legal practice and by lawyers on the basis "that parents have the right to allow a religious, or even a differently motivated, circumcision of their sons."[48] After the court ruling in May, Chancellor Angela Merkel's spokesman declared in July 2012 at the government's press conference that freedom of religion is of great value and has to be possible in Germany: "To everyone in the federal government it was absolutely clear," he said, "that we want Jewish and we want Muslim religious life in Germany."[49] In August 2012, the German Ethics Council held a public meeting and recommended unanimously that the federal government had to create "legal and technical standards for circumcision."[50] Later on, in December 2012, the German parliament allowed circumcision by law—the government enacted paragraph 1631d of the Civil Code, which protects circumcision without explaining parents' reasons. The paragraph in question states that the surgery (in general, but also as a cultural-religious practice) has to take place "according to the standards of the medical profession."[51] In the roll-call vote, 434 members of parliament voted in favor of the paragraph, 100 voted against, and 46 abstained.[52] Those members who voted against the law came from across all the parties represented in parliament, though most of them were from the Linkspartei, the Social Democratic Party (SPD), and the Green Party (Bündnis 90/Die Grünen).[53] The paragraph had become necessary because a juridical clarification was no longer possible. The doctor in the Cologne case carried out the circumcision correctly in accordance with medical practice.[54] The court decided that it could not have been expected of him to know that circumcision was illegal. It had been done for so long that it seemed legal, even though this no longer was the case. On this basis, the doctor was acquitted and could not fight against the ruling since the legal recourse to do so had de facto been excluded.

The motif we are dealing with here includes the accusation that Jews and Muslims, or "religious groups" in the author's sometimes vague terminology, justify their religious practices contrary to secular law and rationality. In the *Frankfurter Allgemeine Zeitung*, editor Jürgen Kaube argues that for the sake of "the child's welfare," religious communities should give up "traditions," "habits," and "customs," which are not collective fundamental rights, if it would protect the individual's (in this case, the boy's) fundamental right to physical integrity.[55]

Anticircumcision activists argue that Jews and Muslims refer to God or to religion, which is socially and politically superfluous and backward.[56] They shorten and simplify a complex constitutional discourse. The question of circumcision does not concern conflicting fundamental rights (the child's physical integrity or the parents' religious freedom and right of care and custody) but rather concerns the mediation of the relative positions of the two sets of rights. Both positions—the son's and the parents'—must be balanced with one another, because in principle no fundamental right can repeal another. That is why lawyers argue that parents must protect and ensure the rights of the son or rather the children until they grow up.[57] There is no fundamental right that protects a son from religious parents because "negative religious freedom"—as part of religious freedom—is directed against the German state and not against the parents.[58] Moreover, the adult son may decide not to be religious even if he is circumcised. Regardless, it is a challenge to reconcile fundamental rights and presumably different legal interests protected by the German constitution (*Grundgesetz*).

The question of balancing these rights has also been outlined differently. More explicitly, in a demonizing way, journalist and author Tilman Jens wrote in his book *Original Sin and the Depravation of the Rule of Law* that "Jews and Muslims are legally allowed to break the law on bodily integrity due to circumcision."[59] Countless online comments argue along these lines. In other comments, anticircumcision actors write that Jews are "criminals"[60] or that they have "committed a crime against humanity with foreskin circumcision."[61] Beyond that, it is said that "of course the Brit Mila is torture"[62] and that "the Jew ... must in this context be perceived not only as a perpetrator, but as a criminal, as a criminal against humanity."[63] The author of these comments—which are directed primarily against Jews—is a very active blogger on the blog *Forced Circumcision* (Zwangsbeschneidung .de) who also sends letters to the Jewish Museum in Berlin.[64] He is also responsible for bringing the criminal charge mentioned in this chapter's introduction.[65]

As we can see here, some facets of the discussions described above create, with their focus on circumcision, the image of German Jews as criminals. Antisemites use cultural and religious practices and traditions to label Jews as strangers, enemies, and scapegoats.[66] This is an old antisemitic stereotype that goes back to the nineteenth century. Particularly at the beginning of the twentieth century in Germany, it made its way into scientific statistics and into manuals for lawyers and administrative officials and was incorporated into criminology. Lawyer Erich Wulffen wrote in 1921 about a "specific crime" of the Jews and asserted that they are more criminal than Christians. Jews were viewed as a danger to German non-Jewish society.[67] In 1896, because the stereotype of the law-breaking Jew was widespread, the Committee for the Defense against Anti-Semitic Assaults in Berlin published a paper with the title "The Criminality of the Jews in Germany." The committee wanted to demonstrate to a broad public audience that in "relationship to the total population" in the German Reich, Jews were not more criminal or more frequently sentenced to prison or fined.[68] The Association for the Defense against Anti-Semitism acted similarly and in 1920 published a "Defense-ABC," which was aimed at "effectively countering" the most widespread antisemitic accusations.[69] There is an entry on the "criminality of the Jews," which shows that "there is no specifically Jewish criminality in criminology."[70]

By deploying the stereotype of "law-breaking" Jews and Muslims, anticircumcision activists stigmatize and devalue the decision of religious Jews and Muslims who circumcise their sons. Within this paradigm, the stereotype of a "damaged" and "traumatized" male body is viewed as an argumentative basis on which to call for a complete ban on circumcision.

The Stereotype of a "Damaged" and "Traumatized" Jewish Infant and Male

In the course of the public debate, many anticircumcision activists have insisted that ritual circumcision in general is basically something harmful, constituting a "bodily injury,"[71] "painful damage,"[72] "permanent genital damage,"[73] or "mutilations of infants."[74] This argument is indispensable to the anticircumcision cause. Pediatrician Volker von Loewenich summarizes, "The procedure is not completely free of complications, and the repeatedly claimed advantages have never been proven. The procedure is mutilating."[75] The opponents of circumcision deny that it has any health or hygienic benefits. Criminal lawyer Rolf Dietrich Herzberg contends that circumcision is a retrograde "mutilation of people" and "bloody injury" that takes place under the guise of religious tradition.[76] Holm Putzke, one of the most important non-Jewish opponents of ritual circumcision in contemporary Germany and also criminal lawyer, says, "The circumciser causes a (pathological) state that deviates adversely from the normal state of the bodily functions."⁷⁷

This perspective has been widespread for several centuries. Historians Sander L. Gilman and Klaus Hödl in particular analyze former rejections of cultural-religious circumcision and the antisemitic pathologization of the Jewish body.⁷⁸ In various lectures and publications since the 1980s, Gilman has dealt intensively and comprehensively with literary, sexual-scientific, ethnological, anthropological, medical, and psychological discourses of the eighteenth, nineteenth, and twentieth centuries and their specific constructions of the Jewish body. His methodological approach is discourse-analytical and psychoanalytical. He examines the contradictory assumptions that Jews have been "fundamentally *visible* in the European diaspora" (since they "look quite different") and "fundamentally *invisible*" at the same time.⁷⁹ Strictly speaking, stereotypes of the Jewish body have concerned the male Jewish body. This is why, in addition to antisemitic fantasies about the nose, skin color, and physiognomy of the Jew, those about the "Jewish penis" have played an important role.⁸⁰ The male Jewish body has been characterized by the ambivalence of looking exactly the same as everyone else and simultaneously differing in some profound sense. On the basis of medical and psychological sources, Gilman argues that from the nineteenth century to the present day, Jews have been regarded as impaired, damaged, and incomplete due to circumcision.⁸¹ The alleged "pathological nature of the Jews" and the notion of "Jewish otherness" can be seen most clearly from the perspective of the gentiles through foreskin circumcision.⁸² The "construction of the Jewish body in the West is absolutely linked to the underlying ideology of anti-Semitism, to the view that the Jew is inherently different."⁸³

Furthermore, with a stronger perspective on the present, anthropologist Eric Kline Silverman shows several anti-Jewish topoi on the basis of European and American historical and contemporary sources against circumcision.⁸⁴ The contemporary sources are "mainstream figures, publications, and websites" published mainly in the 1990s.⁸⁵ He characterizes "the portrayal of the Jew in this debate" as heavily affected by anti-Judaism.⁸⁶ These images were created by physicians, lawyers, activists, and academics, who have been the "central participants in this movement" in the United States.⁸⁷ Silverman's study is relevant because he analyzes several motifs, including the image of the Jewish male body as damaged. In addition, he reads this "anti-circumcision movement as a forum for expressing deep anxieties over almost everything but the foreskin—anxieties about masculinity, motherhood, sexuality, the medicalization of birth, state power, *and* the insidious influence of the Jews."[88]

In another formulation, anticircumcision activists speak about the circumcised being traumatized. In particular, doctor and psychoanalyst Matthias Franz argues in the *Frankfurter Allgemeine Zeitung* and in the *Tageszeitung* that "the removal of the foreskin in infancy or childhood indicates a trauma."[89] Ritual circumcision alone, in his characterization, can be placed in the framework of "the experience of parental violence," and he suggests that because of circumcision Jews (and Muslims) are not sensitive and cannot feel empathy for their sons.[90] Psychoanalyst Wolfgang Schmidbauer announces more generally in the *Süddeutsche Zeitung* that "no thoughtful and empathetic person will approve of infants having a part of their body cut off and possibly having to live with their sexual functions being impaired."[91] Like Schmidbauer, other anticircumcision protagonists talk about the sexuality of circumcised men.[92]

Sexual Fantasies and the Stereotypes of "Sexual Assault" and "Castration"

In the essay "Circumcision and German Law," published in a legal journal in 2008 and republished in 2012, criminal lawyer and psychoanalyst Günter Jerouschek describes the "classical Jewish ritual" as follows:

> The "Mohel" [Hebrew for the circumciser], stiffens the penis of the newborn with thumb and index finger and pulls the foreskin in front of the glans with tweezers along the length to be cut. The foreskin is then cut vertically with a knife just above the tweezers. With a long and filed thumbnail, the remaining foreskin hanging from the tip of the penis is then torn off. The thumbnail has been replaced by scissors or surgical instruments since the end of the 19th century. Traditionally, the Mohel taking the bleeding penis in his mouth, sucking the blood, then turning to take mouthfuls of wine from a goblet and spitting this wine on the infant's wound. Here, too, more aseptic methods have become established.[93]

Jerouschek does not testify to having observed a ritual circumcision himself but rather summarizes the extensive descriptions given by circumcision opponent David L. Gollaher.[94] Gollaher in turn refers to the alleged observations of the anthropologist Felix Bryk that were published in *Circumcision in Man and Woman* in 1934.[95] However, Bryk also had never been present at any ritual circumcision but took the description of the ceremony from the "Anthropological Studies" of the gynecologist and anthropologist Hermann Heinrich Ploss, which appeared for the first time in 1876.[96] Ploss had written in detail about ritual circumcision in the book *The Child in the Custom of the Tribes*.[97] Ploss at least testifies that he himself had been present at a Jewish circumcision ceremony.[98]

In contrast to Jerouschek's description, Ploss's text is much more detailed and mostly technical. It begins with the mohel blessing and praying for the infant in the operating room. Then Ploss describes exactly how the mohel holds the knife and how he makes the precise cut on which part of the foreskin. Only after this can the section of text quoted by Jerouschek be found.[99] Jerouschek distorts and depicts the Jewish practice as unhygienic, backward, traditional, painful, homoerotic, and pedophilic. No contextualization is offered indicating that there is no single way in which the "Jewish ritual" is performed.

During the circumcision controversy in 2012, the question of the potential effects of a foreskin circumcision on male sexuality or sexual pleasure was repeatedly raised and discussed in German daily newspapers. This question has also been a focus of medical research. On the one hand, there are medical studies that support a negative influence on the sexuality of the men interviewed (e.g., reduced sensitivity). On the other hand, there are also medical studies that describe "the opposite effect" and "an improved sexual satisfaction of the men and the interviewed partners" through circumcision.[100] The results of medical studies on the sexuality of circumcised men are very inconsistent and even contradictory.[101]

Anticircumcision activists, however, almost exclusively describe the sexuality of circumcised persons as "negatively influenced."[102] The circumcised person is described as sexually restricted and impaired because the "most sensitive part of the genital organ" is cut off.[103] This idea of a sexual loss of feeling through circumcision is associated by many activists not only with circumcised Jews and Muslims but with all circumcised men.[104]

In addition, anticircumcision activists connect ritual circumcision with "sexual abuse,"[105] a "sexual experience of violence,"[106] and a "sexual trauma."[107] The terms are mostly not further explained and defined but rather seem to stand for themselves. Psychoanalyst Matthias Franz in particular uses this description. In July 2012, the *Frankfurter Allgemeine Zeitung* published an open letter entitled "Freedom of Religion Cannot Be a Carte Blanche for Violence" that had been initiated by Franz. More than 740 experts, including doctors, lawyers, and psychologists, signed the open letter, which was sent to the German chancellor, federal minister, and members of parliament. The letter can be understood as an act of political mobilization through which opponents of circumcision tried to influence the lawmaking process of the German parliament that led to paragraph 1631d of the Civil Code. It argues that in German society a remarkable attitude dominates that denies empathy toward infants and boys, "who suffer greatly from genital circumcision."[108] The letter states, rather directly but without naming precisely whom it has in view, that "in this context freedom of religion cannot be a carte blanche for the use of (sexual) violence against boys who are incapable of consent."[109] If "sexual" here means "related to sexuality," then logically the sexuality of Jews and Muslims undergoing circumcision is implied. However, in Germany the collocation "sexual violence" can also mean more generally "to abuse someone sexually." In this second case, the act is classified as "sexual violence" because the perpetrator's aspiration or intention is the satisfaction of his sexual needs or satisfaction. In other words, the violence becomes "sexual" due to the nature of the perpetrator's feelings. It is precisely this ambiguous associative space that Franz and the other signatories of the letter open up when they describe ritual circumcisions as "(sexual) violence." Other anticircumcision activists explicitly write in online commentaries and internet blogs about ritual circumcision as "child abuse."[110] This point of view is reinforced and then related to the *Metzitza*, which we have already encountered in Jerouschek's earlier quoted description of Jewish ritual circumcision. The *Metzitza* designates that stage of the Jewish circumcision ritual when the circumciser removes "blood from the circumcision wound."[111]

On the blog *Forced Circumcision*, an active blogger and online comment writer states the following with regard to the ritual circumcision of Jewish infants: "Here everyone knows that the child is at risk of infection with the added risk of brain damage and death, and yet everything is done to ensure that these rabbis can still suck on the 'skinned' penis following genital mutilation."[112] Online comments such as this one particularly show that some anticircumcision activists imbue the circumcision ceremony with the obsessive notion that the mohel enjoys sexual perversion and homosexual pleasure or has a pedophilic motivation in carrying out the circumcision. Thus, the cultural-religious practice is reinterpreted as a perverse and pedophilic act.

In this and many other online comments, anticircumcision actors express antisemitic sentiments. In a forty-page-long essay entitled "The Jewish Circumcision," general medical practitioner Wolff Geisler alleges that Jews are more prone to certain diseases due to ritual circumcision and furthermore accuses them of spreading these diseases. In his view, circumcision causes numerous diseases including "cancer" and "brain damage"[113] and also leads to the spread of HIV, as HIV is bound "to Jewish persons."[114] In this antisemitic conspiracy theory, the ritual circumcision of Jewish infants threatens the physical integrity and health of German society and even of whole parts of the world. In order to clarify the "truth" of Jewish circumcision, Geisler sent his texts to various daily newspapers and to the Central Council of Jews and the Central Council of Muslims in Germany as well as to the Federal Medical Association, because in his mind media, politics, and religion were all too silent on the subject.[115]

In another formulation, anticircumcision activists consider the practice as "irreversible [literally, in German, "never again reparable"] mutilation"[116] and in a classifying and dramatizing manner as "partial bodily amputation"[117] or "castration."[118] The circumcision opponent and medical historian David L. Gollaher has emphasized that castration fears already existed in the Greek-Roman culture of antiquity.[119] The mockery by gentiles of Jewish circumcision resulted partly from a confusion between circumcision and castration. For most non-Jews, there was no difference between the foreskin and the penis; moreover, they had no idea as to exactly which operation was carried out on Jewish newborns.[120] From the perspective of gentiles, circumcision therefore belonged to the "secrets of a foreign religion" and became the subject of many misunderstandings and rumors.[121] At the beginning of the twentieth century, psychoanalyst Sigmund Freud had already taken for granted that antisemitism and castration anxiety were unconsciously connected.[122] In his early reflections on the "roots of antisemitism," he pointed out that even young gentile boys equated circumcision and castration and hated the Jews for it. According to Freud, antisemitism is a "disease of the uncircumcised"[123] that is "caused by the presence of the intact penis and the fear of castration."[124] In the psychoanalytic perspective, the penis is a phallic symbol associated with strength, power, and potency. The castration fantasy, in contrast, expresses the fear of disempowerment, weakness, and feminization. However, in the public debate, Jews in particular have been associated not only with "deficient masculinity" but also with power.[125]

The Stereotype of "Powerful Jews" and Their "Enormous Pressure" on German Politics

In the public debate in Germany, anticircumcision activists have often proclaimed the narrative of an enormous pressure being exerted on politics by Jews. In national newspapers, journalists have denounced members of the

Bundestag and the federal government for making a "senseless" and hurried political decision. In an open letter published in the *Frankfurter Allgemeine Zeitung*, more than 740 signatories warn against passing a rushed new law, which they present as a "snapshot," without thorough preparation of the law.[126]

The widely circulated newspaper *Süddeutsche Zeitung* reported that the members of parliament tried to stop the debate with "a legal trick."[127] In the article "Appointed Circumcision Law," Schulte von Drach claims that politicians tried to hide away the tricky question of circumcision. He alleges that since the beginning of the debate, parliament "has aspired to legalize the ritual."[128] Grievous bodily harm, he asserts, has been made a "permitted practice." "The devout" and "religious people" are allowed "special privileges."[129] If in an enlightened and modern society, circumcision possibly contravenes fundamental rights, he argues, then "religious people have to question their rituals."[130]

However, in another newspaper article in the *Tageszeitung*, Christoph Zimmermann argues more explicitly: "It is rare that legislation has been enacted so quickly. Only four months after the decision of the regional court in Cologne, the draft legislation was already available. The reason: every conflict with the Jewish community should be avoided."[131] Here it is worth emphasizing that neither the Muslim community nor Muslim representatives and their political-cultural interests were mentioned in the article. Neither seems to be viewed as a significant actor in the conflict.

Some article readers take on the perspectives presented in newspapers and harshly criticize politicians. In online comments, it is frequently argued that democracy in Germany is in danger because the will of the people is largely being ignored. Moreover, the blatant accusation is made that "the Central Council of Jews in Germany and extremely orthodox Rabbis order a law" and the federal government creates it.[132] The subnarrative here is of course that the Central Council of Jews in Germany enjoys excessive power that directs German politics. This is an old antisemitic stereotype of the Jew as an influential power-grabber.[133] Countless online comments in this vein are almost identical in wording.

By the same contention, however, there are some comments that argue that Muslims react acceptably and have had a quite obviously different tone. In the right-wing and conspiracy-theory newspaper *Compact*, the journalist Ken Jebsen argued in 2012, "Muslims have joined in the protest against the judgment, that is true, but in a quite obviously different tone, with completely different attitude towards the German legislator. The fact is: if a German court makes a landmark decision on bodily harm, Israel will succeed in making an exception for itself. No other country would intervene in the Federal Republic and neither has any done so."[134] But if we take a look at the declarations of the Central Council of Jews and some Muslim associations in Germany, we find that they are nearly identical. The Council of Jews condemned the decision as "an unprecedented and dramatic intrusion on the self-determination of religious communities."[135] The Coordinating Council of Muslims condemned the court ruling as "massive interference in religious freedom."[136] The Council of Muslims denounced the ruling as a "blatant and impermissible intrusion into the right of religious communities to self-determination and in parental rights."[137] Several Jewish and Muslim NGOs and associations called on the German parliament to pass legislation protecting circumcision as a religious practice.

The fact that all formal procedures during the legislative process were observed, including the three readings in the plenum of the German Bundestag, has been disregarded by many anticircumcision activists. Moreover, they ignore the fact that ritual foreskin circumcisions were extensively debated both in the German Bundestag and in the public sphere.

We can see here that anticircumcision activists accuse both Jews and Muslims of the same thing—being members of premodern religious communities. But they also denounce Jews and Muslims in different ways, as we can see when we encounter the classic stereotype of omnipotent Jewish power. It might be argued that antisemitic attributions differ from racist ones because Jews in particular are imagined as almighty and undemocratic in contrast to the very different perception of Muslims. In this way, anticircumcision activists appoint a special status to Jews. They believe in the existence of a sinister Jewish lobby that has more political privileges than any other organization. According to opinion polls in Germany, the stereotype of "Jewish power" is widespread among the population in Germany. Thus, not only in 2018 but also in past years, roughly 10 percent of the population agreed with the statement (responding "fully" or "predominantly") that "even today the influence of Jews is too high."[138] This is a conspiracy ideology that fulfills the need for a simple "pattern for explaining the world" with clearly designated positions of guilt.[139]

Conclusion

My analysis demonstrates how closely statements that merely express criticism of cultural-religious circumcisions are interwoven with those that have an antisemitic undertone. Nonantisemitic expressions are mixed with antisemitic rejections of ritual circumcision. The dynamics of the debate can be summarized as follows. In articles and guest commentaries in daily newspapers such as the *Frankfurter Allgemeine Zeitung*, the *Süddeutsche Zeitung*, and the *Tageszeitung*, journalists who are critical of circumcision and opponents of circumcision tend to express themselves moderately and implicitly. Nevertheless, their discourse shows that they imagine Jews as a homogeneous group, and recognition of all diversity is therefore excluded. With their articles and guest commentaries, however, anticircumcision protagonists create discursive conditions to which "antisemitic fragments" can be connected and which make antisemitic readings possible. This becomes clear in the corresponding online comments and contributions on blogs.[140]

Some facets of anticircumcision attitudes can be understood as a renewed form of antireligious intolerance against Jews (and Muslims) and as a mode of expression of today's antisemitism. If we look only at the antisemitic expressions in the debate, an image of the Jews that fixates on circumcision emerges, depicting Jewish ritual circumcision and circumcisers as "foreign," "committing a crime against humanity," "brutal," "cruel," "mutilating," "without empathy," "castrating," "damaging sexuality," "dominating German politics," and "exploiting the Holocaust." To be in opposition to cultural-religious circumcision is a form of communication that is gaining acceptance as politically correct and therefore able to be openly articulated. This is a major problem and challenge for the future. The ritual has become a new reference point for the public indictment of Jews. On the basis of circumcision, Jews are portrayed as the Other, as strangers, and as atavistic and brutal.[141] The debate is a new occasion for expressing antisemitism in the public sphere "justly" and "legitimately." The new event expands the spectrum of reference points for antisemitic statements. Thereby, Jewish culture and religion have been brought back into focus for antisemites. Although the large-scale controversy has ended among the general public, opponents of ritual circumcision are not as silent as the Twitter post in this chapter's introduction would seem to show.

Moreover, the debate is a good example of a politically overarching antisemitism. Not only right-wing extremists, radicalized Muslims, and left-wing actors are bearers of antisemitism; the so-called center of society is also and especially involved.

However, actors in the debate often indict the ritual in question, the circumcision itself. Therefore, the act itself is the alleged subject of criticism, rather than the religious community or concrete people. They say that circumcision is an "archaic genital trauma," a "cruel act," or a "bloody ritual."

In newspaper articles in particular, no one is explicitly blamed by journalists. They often write that "circumcision is a trauma" and only infrequently that "Jews traumatize their sons." Or they say, "circumcision is a bloody ritual," in place of "Jews practice a bloody ritual." But readers are easily able to draw the conclusions that follow from the condemnation of circumcision. This dynamic shows that antisemitism can develop through interaction. Antisemitism is outsourced from many articles to be concluded and ultimately completed and realized by media consumers.

Notes

1. See Daniel Poensgen and Benjamin Steinitz, "Alltagsprägende Erfahrung," in *Antisemitismus nach 9/11: Ereignisse, Debatten, Kontroversen*, ed. Samuel Salzborn (Baden-Baden: Nomos, 2019), 19–22; see also Verein für Demokratische Kultur in Berlin e.V. (VDK) and Recherche- und Informationsstelle Antisemitismus Berlin (RIAS), *Antisemitische Vorfälle Januar bis Juni 2018: Ein Bericht der Recherche- und Informationsstelle Antisemitismus Berlin* (Berlin: RIAS 2018), 4–5.

2. See European Union Agency for Fundamental Rights, *Experiences and Perceptions of Antisemitism: Second Survey on Discrimination and Hate Crime against Jews in the EU* (Luxembourg: Publications Office of the European Union, 2018), 46.

3. Felix E. Czosnowski, "Bin auf dem Weg zu einer Beschneidung in meiner Heimatsynagoge," Twitter, March 3, 2019, https://twitter.com/czossi/status/1102172795222589440.

4. Felix E. Czosnowski, "Danke an den Antisemiten, der mich wegen der Teilnahme an einer Bris angezeigt hat! Am Isroel Chai!," Twitter, March 3, 2019, https://twitter.com/czossi/status/1102212003123380224. *Bris* is the shortened form for the Hebrew *brit milah* or *mila*, sometimes also *Bris Milah*. "Am Israel Chai" means "the Jewish people live."

5. Felix E. Czosnowski, "Man merke wenn man etwas von Beschneidung und Synagoge twittert kann es passieren dass man von der uniformierten Staatsmacht Besuch bekommt ohne dass diese Ahnung von der aktuellen Rechtslage hat," Twitter, March 3, 2019, https://twitter.com/czossi/status/1102263426473254912.

6. Steffen Wasmund, "Ich darf Sie beruhigen. Nicht ein Antisemit hat die Anzeige erstattet, sondern ich," Twitter, March 3, 2019, https://twitter.com/Steffen_Wasmund/status/1102278618754048004.

7. See Federal Law Sheet (Bundesgesetzblatt), *Gesetz über den Umfang der Personensorge bei einer Beschneidung des männlichen Kindes* (Bonn: Bundesanzeiger, 2012), 2749–50.

8. See "Worldwide Day of Genital Autonomy," IntactiWiki, last updated February 2, 2021, https://de.intactiwiki.org/index.php/Worldwide_Day_of_Genital_Autonomy.

9. See Detlef David Kauschke, "Schädlicher Ritus," *Jüdische Allgemeine*, August 22, 2012, http://www.juedische-allgemeine.de/article/view/id/13829; Detlef David Kauschke, "Erneut Strafanzeige gegen Rabbiner," *Jüdische Allgemeine*, August 30, 2012, http://www.juedische-allgemeine.de/article/view/id/13894.

10. David Goldberg, quoted in Kauschke, "Schädlicher Ritus."

11. Sebastian Guevara Kamm, quoted in Kauschke, "Schädlicher Ritus"; cf. Christian Bahls, "Warum ich den orthodoxen Rabbiner Yehuda Teichtal für die Beschneidung seines

Sohnes anzeige," MOGiS e.V., March 23, 2013, https://mogis.info/blog/circumcision-mendel-teichtal-de.

12. See "Anzeige wegen Beschneidung," *Jüdische Allgemeine*, August 21, 2012, https://www.juedische-allgemeine.de/politik/anzeige-wegen-beschneidung/.

13. Regional court of Cologne (Landgericht Köln), "Urteil des Landgerichts Köln zu Beschneidung," openJur, May 7, 2012, http://openjur.de/u/433915.html.

14. Regional court of Cologne, "Urteil des Landgerichts Köln zu Beschneidung."

15. See Holm Putzke, "Die strafrechtliche Relevanz der Beschneidung von Knaben," in *Strafrecht zwischen System und Telos*, ed. Holm Putzke, Bernhard Hardtung, Tatjana Hörnle, Reinhard Merkel, Jörg Scheinfeld, Horst Schlehofer, and Jürgen Seier (Tübingen: Mohr Siebeck, 2008), 680, 704–6; Günter Jerouschek, "Beschneidung und das deutsche Recht: Historische, medizinische, psychologische und juristische Aspekte," *Neue Zeitschrift für Strafrecht* 6 (2008): 314–16; Rolf Dietrich Herzberg, "Rechtliche Probleme der rituellen Beschneidung," *Juristenzeitung* 7 (2009): 332–34.

16. See Yassin Musharbash, "Die Operation war einwandfrei," *Zeit*, July 12, 2012, http://www.zeit.de/2012/29/Beschneidung/komplettansicht; Jost Müller-Neuhof, "Religiöse Beschneidung: Chronik einer beispiellosen Debatte," *Tagesspiegel*, August 28, 2012, http://www.tagesspiegel.de/politik/religioese-beschneidung-chronik-einer-beispiellosen-debatte/7018904.html.

17. See Antje Yael Deusel, *Mein Bund, den ihr bewahren sollt* (Freiburg: Herder, 2012), 11; Alfred Bodenheimer, *Haut ab! Die Juden in der Beschneidungsdebatte* (Göttingen: Wallstein, 2012), 29; Felicitas Heimann-Jelinek and Cilly Kugelmann, *Haut ab! Haltungen zur rituellen Beschneidung* (Göttingen: Wallstein, 2014), 9; Nadeem Elyas, "Ist die Knaben-Beschneidung überhaupt Pflicht im Islam?," islam.de, July 21, 2012, http://islam.de/20776; cf. Benjamin Jokisch, "Islamische Knabenbeschneidung in Deutschland: Rechtliche Perspektiven im Spannungsfeld von Scharia und Grundgesetz," in *Beschneidung: Das Zeichen des Bundes in der Kritik*, ed. Johannes Heil and Stephan J. Kramer (Berlin: Metropol, 2012), 161–63.

18. "Zum Urteil des Kölner Landgerichts zur Beschneidung von Jungen," Central Council of Jews in Germany (Zentralrat der Juden in Deutschland), June 26, 2012, https://www.zentralratderjuden.de/aktuelle-meldung/artikel/news/zum-urteil-des-koelner-landgerichts-zur-beschneidung-von-jungen/.

19. Charlotte Knobloch, "Wollt ihr uns Juden noch?," *Süddeutsche Zeitung*, September 25, 2012, http://www.sueddeutsche.de/politik/beschneidungen-in-deutschland-wollt-ihr-uns-judennoch-1.1459038.

20. Knobloch, "Wollt ihr uns Juden noch?"

21. Pinchas Goldschmidt, quoted in Stephen Evans, "German Circumcision Ban: Is It a Parent's Right to Choose?," BBC News, July 13, 2012, http://www.bbc.com/news/magazine-18793842.

22. See European Union Agency for Fundamental Rights, *Discrimination and Hate Crime against Jews in EU Member States: Experiences and Perceptions of Antisemitism* (Luxembourg: Publications Office of the European Union, 2014), 64.

23. European Union Agency for Fundamental Rights, *Discrimination*, 63.

24. European Union Agency for Fundamental Rights, 3.

25. See European Union Agency for Fundamental Rights, *Experiences*, 71.

26. Kerem Öktem, *Signale aus der Mehrheitsgesellschaft: Auswirkungen der Beschneidungsdebatte und staatlicher Überwachung islamischer Organisationen auf Identitätsbildung und Integration in Deutschland* (Oxford: European Studies Centre, 2013), xi.

27. Öktem, *Signale aus der Mehrheitsgesellschaft*.

28. See Andreas Zick, Andreas Hövermann, Silke Jensen, and Julia Bernstein, *Jüdische Perspektiven auf Antisemitismus in Deutschland: Ein Studienbericht für den Expertenrat Antisemitismus* (Bielefeld: Institut für interdisziplinäre Konflikt- und Gewaltforschung, 2017), 45, 50–51, 59–60, 80.

29. See Bodenheimer, *Haut ab!*; Heiner Bielefeldt, "Der Kampf um die Beschneidung: Das Kölner Urteil und die Religionsfreiheit," *Blätter für deutsche und internationale Politik* 9 (2012): 63–71; Zülfukar Çetin, Heinz-Jürgen Voß, and Salih Alexander Wolter, *Interventionen gegen die deutsche "Beschneidungsdebatte"* (Münster: edition assemblage, 2012); Johannes Heil and Stephan J. Kramer, ed., *Beschneidung: Das Zeichen des Bundes in der Kritik. Zur Debatte um das Kölner Urteil* (Berlin: Metropol, 2012); Matthias Küntzel, "Kontaminiertes Terrain," *Perlentaucher*, August 8, 2012, https://www.perlentaucher.de/essay/kontaminiertes-terrain.html; Öktem, *Signale aus der Mehrheitsgesellschaft*; Yigal Blumenberg and Wolfgang Hegener, *Die "unheimliche Beschneidung. Aufklärung und die Wiederkehr des Verdrängten"* (Frankfurt am Main: Brandes und Apsel, 2013), 11–30; Vanessa Rau, "Vehementer Säkularismus als Antisemitismus?," *Aus Politik und Zeitgeschichte* 28–30 (2014): 31–38; Heimann-Jelinek and Kugelmann, *Haut ab!*; Unabhängiger Expertenkreis Antisemitismus, *Bericht des Unabhängigen Expertenkreises Antisemitismus*, Drucksache 18/11970, April 7, 2017, http://dip21.bundestag.de/dip21/btd/18/119/1811970.pdf, 245; Monika Schwarz-Friesel, *Antisemitismus 2.0 und die Netzkultur des Hasses. Ergebnisse der DFG-geförderten Langzeitstudie "Antisemitismus im www"* (Berlin: Technische Universität Berlin, 2018); Sander L. Gilman, "The Case of Circumcision: Diaspora Judaism as a Model for Islam?," in *Antisemitism and Islamophobia in Europe: A Shared Story?*, ed. James Renton and Ben Gidley (London: Palgrave Macmillan, 2017), 143–64; Dana Ionescu, *Judenbilder in der deutschen Beschneidungskontroverse* (Baden-Baden: Nomos, 2018).

30. See Gökçe Yurdakul, "Jews, Muslims and the Ritual Male Circumcision Debate: Religious Diversity and Social Inclusion in Germany," *Social Inclusion* 2 (2016): 77–86; Schirin Amir-Moazami, "Investigating the Secular Body: The Politics of the Male Circumcision Debate in Germany," *ReOrient* 2 (2016): 147–70.

31. Following the sociologist Helen Fein, I understand antisemitism "as a persisting latent structure of hostile beliefs toward *Jews as a collectivity* manifested in *individuals* as attitudes, and in *culture* as myth, ideology, folklore, and imagery, and in *actions*—social or legal discrimination, political mobilization against the Jews, and collective or state violence—which results in and/or is designed to distance, displace, or destroy Jews as Jews." Helen Fein, "Dimensions of Antisemitism: Attitudes, Collective Accusations, and Actions," in *The Persisting Question: Sociological Perspectives and Social Contexts of Modern Antisemitism*, ed. Helen Fein (Berlin: De Gruyter, 1987), 67; emphasis in the original.

32. Indirect means recognizable from the conclusions that can be drawn and from knowledge of the context; see Monika Schwarz-Friesel and Jehuda Reinharz, *Inside the Antisemitic Mind: The Language of Jew-Hatred in Contemporary Germany* (Waltham, MA: Brandeis University Press, 2017), 2.

33. In my PhD dissertation, I analyze more extensive images of Jews and Judaism that condense into antisemitic stereotypes, including circumcision as marginalized "genital mutilation," thousands of defenseless children, religious parents as "hurtful" and "cruel," the "lesson of the Nazi Era" does not allow ritual circumcision, allied Jews criticize circumcision, and analogies to cruel traditions (Ionescu, *Judenbilder*, 145–388). Thus, within each image, a course from criticism to condensed antisemitic stereotypes can be traced.

34. See Schwarz-Friesel, *Antisemitismus 2.0*, 21.

35. Some stereotypes are also directed against Muslims, but in my chapter, I focus on stereotypes against Jews.

36. Aryeh Tuchman, "Circumcision," in *Antisemitism: A Historical Encyclopedia of Prejudice and Persecution*, vol. 1, A–K, ed. Richard S. Levy (Santa Barbara, CA: ABC-CLIO, 2005), 128. See also Robin Judd, *Contested Rituals: Circumcision, Kosher Butchering, and Jewish Political Life in Germany, 1843–1933* (London: Cornell University Press, 2007), 246–48.

37. Tuchman, "Circumcision," 128.

38. Whereas in the US an inner-Jewish critical discussion about rejections of ritual male circumcision exists in the public, this is not the case in Germany. In the US, many circumcision opponents identify themselves as Jewish. They have published essays and books since the 1950s; see Leonard B. Glick, "'Something Less than Joyful': Jewish Americans and the Circumcision Dilemma," in *Flesh and Blood: Perspectives on the Problem of Circumcision in Contemporary Society*, ed. George C. Denniston, Frederick Mansfield Hodges, and Marilyn Fayre Milos (Boston: Springer US, 2004), 143–44; Ronald Goldman, "The Growing Jewish Circumcision Debate: A Psychosocial Critique," in Denniston et al., *Flesh and Blood*, 171. In contrast, in contemporary Germany, only a few anticircumcision activists talk about being Jewish (for example, Victor S. Schonfeld and Jonathan Enosch), and they barely publish anything. This is a huge difference between the public debates about the ritual in Germany and in the US.

39. See the resolution against ritual circumcision of boys, German Society for Psychosomatic Medicine and Medical Psychotherapy (Deutsche Gesellschaft für Psychosomatische Medizin und Ärztliche Psychotherapie), *Jungenbeschneidung in Deutschland—Abschlussforderungen*, 2017, http://www.jungenbeschneidung.de/material/Abschlussforderungen.pdf; "Ärzte kritisieren Beschneidungsgesetz," *Spiegel Online*, December 11, 2017, http://www.spiegel.de/gesundheit/diagnose/beschneidung-aerzteorganisationen-kritisieren-gesetz-a-1182714.html.

40. See "Mehrheit der Deutschen gegen Beschneidungen," *Die Welt*, June 30, 2012, https://www.welt.de/aktuell/article107612156/Mehrheit-der-Deutschen-gegen-Beschneidungen.html.

41. See "Mehrheit der Deutschen gegen Beschneidungsgesetz," *Spiegel Online*, December 22, 2012, http://www.spiegel.de/politik/deutschland/studie-mehrheit-der-deutschen-gegen-beschneidungsgesetz-a-874473.html.

42. Markus C. Schulte von Drach, "Fragwürdige Beschneidung der Religionsfreiheit," *Süddeutsche Zeitung*, June 28, 2012, http://www.sueddeutsche.de/panorama/umstrittenes-koelner-urteil-pro-fragwuerdige-beschneidung-der-religionsfreiheit-1.1394792.

43. Schulte von Drach, "Fragwürdige Beschneidung der Religionsfreiheit."

44. Schulte von Drach.

45. Schulte von Drach.

46. Georg Paul Hefty, "Strafbare Beschneidung," *Frankfurter Allgemeine Zeitung*, June 28, 2012, http://www.faz.net/aktuell/politik/inland/nach-dem-koelner-urteil-strafbare-beschneidung-11802626.html.

47. Heide Oestreich, "Männer kennen keinen Schmerz," *Tageszeitung*, July 23, 2012, http://www.taz.de/!5088376/.

48. Jens Haustein, "Erziehungsrecht versus Unversehrtheit: Politische und rechtliche Voraussetzungen der Beschneidungsdebatte," in *Säkulare Selbstbestimmung versus religiöse Fremdbestimmung? Zur Kritik an der öffentlichen Debatte um das Beschneidungsritual*, ed. Michael Wermke (Leipzig: Evang. Verl.-Anst., 2014), 13–26.

49. Steffen Seibert, "Transcript of the Government Press Conference," Bundesregierung, July 13, 2012, https://www.bundesregierung.de/ContentArchiv/DE/Archiv17/Mitschrift/Pressekonferenzen/2012/07/2012-07-13-regpk.html.

50. "Pressemitteilung: Ethikrat empfiehlt rechtliche und fachliche Standards für die Beschneidung," Deutscher Ethikrat, August 23, 2012, https://www.ethikrat.org/mitteilungen/2012/ethikrat-empfiehlt-rechtliche-und-fachliche-standards-fuer-die-beschneidung/.

51. Bürgerliches Gesetzbuch (BGB) § 1631d Beschneidung des männlichen Kindes [Circumcision of the male child], accessed July 25, 2019, https://www.gesetze-im-internet.de/bgb/__1631d.html.

52. See German parliament (Deutscher Bundestag), Stenographic Report, parliament meeting 213, December 12, 2012, issue 17/213, http://dipbt.bundestag.de/dip21/btp/17/17213.pdf.

53. Deutscher Bundestag, Stenographic Report.

54. See Regional court of Cologne, "Urteil des Landgerichts Köln zu Beschneidung," 4.

55. Jürgen Kaube, "Das Wohl des Kindes," *Frankfurter Allgemeine Zeitung*, June 28, 2012, http://www.faz.net/aktuell/feuilleton/debatten/urteil-zur-beschneidung-das-wohl-des-kindes-11801160.html.

56. Rau, "Vehementer Säkularismus," 32, 37.

57. Michael Germann, "Die grundrechtliche Freiheit zur religiös motivierten Beschneidung," in Heil and Kramer, *Beschneidung*, 89.

58. See Bielefeldt, "Der Kampf um die Beschneidung," 68.

59. Tilman Jens, *Der Sündenfall des Rechtsstaats: Eine Streitschrift zum neuen Religionskampf. Aus gegebenem Anlass* (Gütersloh: Gütersloher Verl.-Haus, 2013), 34.

60. See Birgitta vom Lehn, "Unterschätztes Trauma-Risiko," *Frankfurter Rundschau*, July 18, 2012, http://www.fr.de/wissen/beschneidungen-unterschaetztes-trauma-risiko-a-826239; Reiner Moysich, "Verbrechen gegen die Mitmenschlichkeit!," December 13, 2012, comment on "Bundestag billigt Gesetz zur Beschneidung," *Frankfurter Allgemeine Zeitung*, December 12, 2012, http://www.faz.net/aktuell/politik/inland/abschliessende-debatte-bundestag-billigt-gesetz-zur-beschneidung-11991251.html; rofelix, "Die amputation von äusserst lust- und reizfähigem gewebe . . . ist ohne jegliche frage ein verbrechen," July 20, 2012, comment on "Missbrauch der Vorhaut," *Tageszeitung*, July 18, 2012, https://taz.de/!5088755/.

61. "Pressemeldungen zur Beschneidung ohne speziellere Zuordnung 2014," Zwangsbeschneidung.de, accessed July 25, 2019, http://www.zwangsbeschneidung.de/presse-2014.html.

62. "Jüdische Presse und Stimmen zur Beschneidung und andere menschenrechtlich relevante Fundstellen mit Bezug zur jüdischen Religion," Zwangsbeschneidung.de, accessed July 25, 2019, http://www.zwangsbeschneidung.de/juedische-presse.html.

63. Zwangsbeschneidung.de, "Pressemeldungen zur Beschneidung 2014."

64. "Pressemeldungen zur Beschneidung ohne speziellere Zuordnung 2015," Zwangsbeschneidung.de, accessed July 25, 2019, http://www.zwangsbeschneidung.de/presse-2015.html.

65. Wasmund, "Ich darf Sie beruhigen."

66. See Wolfgang Benz, *Die Protokolle der Weisen von Zion: Die Legende von der jüdischen Weltverschwörung* (München: Beck, 2007), 20.

67. Erich Wulffen, *Der Sexualverbrecher: Ein Handbuch für Juristen, Verwaltungsbeamte und Ärzte* (Berlin: Langenscheidt, 1921), 301.

68. Comite zur Abwehr antisemitischer Angriffe, ed., *Die Kriminalität der Juden in Deutschland* (Berlin: Cronbach, 1896), viii.

69. Verein zur Abwehr des Antisemitismus, ed., *Abwehr-ABC* (Berlin: Möller und Borel, 1920), 2.

70. Verein zur Abwehr des Antisemitismus, *Abwehr-ABC*, 69.

71. Jasper von Altenbockum, "Ein Verbot wäre unverhältnismäßig," *Frankfurter Allgemeine Zeitung*, July 16, 2012, http://www.faz.net/aktuell/politik/harte-bretter/beschneidung-pro-und-contraein-verbot-waere-unverhaeltnismaessig-11819799.html; Oestreich, "Männer kennen keinen Schmerz."

72. Sonja Süss and Philip Eppelsheim, "Auch die Seele leidet," *Frankfurter Allgemeine Zeitung*, July 21, 2012, http://www.faz.net/aktuell/politik/inland/beschneidungsdebatte-auch-die-seele-leidet-11827698.html.

73. Matthias Franz, "Offener Brief zur Beschneidung: Religionsfreiheit kann kein Freibrief für Gewalt sein," *Frankfurter Allgemeine Zeitung*, July 21, 2012, http://www.faz.net/aktuell/politik/inland/offener-brief-zur-beschneidung-religionsfreiheit-kann-kein-freibrief-fuergewalt-sein-11827590.html.

74. Guillermo Acassuso, "Dem Kommentar kann man nur zustimmen," June 27, 2012, comment on Georg Paul Hefty, "Credo des Rechtsstaates," *Frankfurter Allgemeine Zeitung*, June 27, 2012, http://www.faz.net/aktuell/politik/inland/beschneidungs-urteil-credo-des-rechtsstaates-11800115.html.

75. Volker von Loewenich, "Medizinische Aspekte der rituellen Genitalbeschneidung nicht einwilligungsfähiger Jungen," in *Die Beschneidung von Jungen: Ein trauriges Vermächtnis*, ed. Matthias Franz (Göttingen: Vandenhoeck und Ruprecht, 2014), 77.

76. Rolf Dietrich Herzberg, "Religionsfreiheit und Kindeswohl: Wann ist die Körperverletzung durch Zirkumzision gerechtfertigt?," *Zeitschrift für Internationale Strafrechtsdogmatik* 7–8 (2010): 475.

77. Putzke, "Die strafrechtliche Relevanz der Beschneidung," 681.

78. See Sander L. Gilman, *Freud, Identität und Geschlecht* (Frankfurt am Main: S. Fischer, 1994), 12, 87, 101; Sander L. Gilman, "Der jüdische Körper: Gedanken zum physischen Anderssein der Juden," in *Die Macht der Bilder: Antisemitische Vorurteile und Mythen*, ed. Jüdisches Museum Wien (Wien: Picus, 1995), 168–79; Sander L. Gilman, "Zwölftes Bild: Der 'jüdische Körper,'" in *Antisemitismus: Vorurteile und Mythen*, ed. Julius H. Schoeps and Joachim Schlör (Frankfurt am Main: Zweitausendeins, 1997), 167–79; Sander L. Gilman, "Gesundheit, Krankheit und Glaube: Der Streit um die Beschneidung," in *Haut ab! Haltungen zur rituellen Beschneidung*, ed. Felicitas Heimann-Jelinek and Cilly Kugelmann (Göttingen: Wallstein, 2014), 119–26; Klaus Hödl, *Die Pathologisierung des jüdischen Körpers: Antisemitismus, Geschlecht und Medizin im Fin de Siècle* (Wien: Picus, 1997); Klaus Hödl, "Die deutschsprachige Beschneidungsdebatte im 19. Jahrhundert," *Aschkenas—Zeitschrift für Geschichte und Kultur der Juden* 1 (2003): 189–209.

79. Gilman, "Zwölftes Bild," 167; emphasis in the original.

80. Gilman.

81. See Gilman, *Freud, Identität und Geschlecht*, 12, 87, 101.

82. Gilman, 86.

83. Sander L. Gilman, "The Jewish Body: A Foot-note," in *People of the Body: Jews and Judaism from an Embodied Perspective*, ed. Howard Eilberg-Schwartz (Albany: State University of New York Press, 1992), 223.

84. See Eric Kline Silverman, *From Abraham to America: A History of Jewish Circumcision* (Lanham, MD: Rowman and Littlefield, 2006), 213.

85. Silverman, *From Abraham to America*, 237.

86. Silverman, 213.

87. See Silverman, xxvi.

88. Silverman, 214; emphasis in the original.

89. Matthias Franz, "Ritual, Trauma, Kindeswohl," *Frankfurter Allgemeine Zeitung*, July 8, 2012, http://www.faz.net/aktuell/politik/die-gegenwart/beschneidung-ritual-trauma-kindeswohl-11813995.html; Matthias Franz, "Es ist ein genitales Trauma," interview by Heide Oestreich, *Tageszeitung*, July 25, 2012, http://www.taz.de/!5088276/.

90. Franz, "Ritual, Trauma, Kindeswohl."

91. Wolfgang Schmidbauer, "Beschneidung ist nicht harmlos," *Süddeutsche Zeitung*, July 4, 2012, http://www.sueddeutsche.de/wissen/nach-dem-koelner-urteil-beschneidung-ist-nicht-harmlos-1.1401049.

92. For the sexual connotation of antisemitism, see Stephen Wilson, *Ideology and Experience: Antisemitism in France at the Time of the Dreyfus Affair* (Rutherford, NJ: Fairleigh Dickinson University Press, 1982), 584.

93. Jerouschek, "Beschneidung und das deutsche Recht," 315.

94. See David L. Gollaher, *Circumcision: A History of the World's Most Controversial Surgery* (New York: Basic Books, 2000), 25–26.

95. See Gollaher, *Circumcision*, 215; David L. Gollaher, *Das verletzte Geschlecht: Die Geschichte der Beschneidung* (Berlin: Aufbau, 2002), 42–43.

96. See Felix Bryk, *Circumcision in Man and Woman: Its History, Psychology and Ethnology* (New York: American Ethnological, 1934), 47.

97. See Hermann Heinrich Ploss, *Das Kind in Brauch und Sitte der Völker* (Leipzig: Th. Grieben's, 1884), 342–46.

98. Ploss, *Das Kind in Brauch und Sitte der Völker*, 348–49.

99. Ploss, 350.

100. Manuel Ritter and Jan Schabbeck, "Die Zirkumzision im Spannungsfeld zwischen Religionsfreiheit und dem Recht auf körperliche Unversehrtheit," *Aktuelle Dermatologie* 4 (2014): 134.

101. See Heinz-Jürgen Voß, "Beschneidung bei Jungen," in *Sexualität von Männern: Dritter Deutscher Männergesundheitsbericht*, ed. Stiftung Männergesundheit (Gießen: Psychosozial, 2017), 113–26.

102. Süss and Eppelsheim, "Auch die Seele leidet."

103. Rolf Dietrich Herzberg, "Die Beschneidung gesetzlich gestatten?," *Zeitschrift für Internationale Strafrechtsdogmatik* 10 (2012): 489.

104. Jerouschek, "Beschneidung und das deutsche Recht," 314–15.

105. Rainer Schweitzer, "Herr Bujtor," December 13, 2012, comment on "Bundestag billigt Gesetz zur Beschneidung," *Frankfurter Allgemeine Zeitung*, December 12, 2012, http://www.faz.net/aktuell/politik/inland/abschliessende-debatte-bundestag-billigt-gesetz-zur-beschneidung-11991251.html.

106. Matthias Franz, "Götterspeise—Vom Kindesopfer zur Beschneidung und zurück," in *Das Kindesopfer, eine Grundlage unserer Kultur*, ed. Mathias Hirsch (Gießen: Psychosozial, 2006), 128.

107. Franz, "Götterspeise."

108. Franz, "Offener Brief zur Beschneidung."

109. Franz, "Offener Brief zur Beschneidung."

110. Hanns J. Baum, "Oh Herr wirf Hirn hernieder!," July 18, 2012, comment on Reinhard Müller, "Grenzen in Gottesfragen," *Frankfurter Allgemeine Zeitung*, July 17, 2012, http://www.faz.net/aktuell/politik/inland/beschneidungsdebatte-grenzen-in-gottesfragen-11823530.html.

111. Robert Jütte, *Leib und Leben im Judentum* (Berlin: Jüdischer im Suhrkamp, 2016), 246.

112. Zwangsbeschneidung.de, "Pressemeldungen zur Beschneidung 2015."

113. Wolff Geisler, *Die jüdische Beschneidung*, Zwangsbeschneidung.de, 2015, http://www.zwangsbeschneidung.de/archiv/dr-geisler-die-juedische-beschneidung.pdf, 2.

114. Geisler, *Die jüdische Beschneidung*, 21.

115. Wolff Geisler, *Der Zweck der jüdischen Beschneidung*, 2012, http://www.luebeck-kunterbunt.de/Judentum/Die_juedische_Beschneidung.pdf, 6.

116. Helga Zießler, "Als absoluter Gegner dieses barbarischen Rituals habe ich mich bereits 'geoutet,'" July 23, 2012, comment on Süss and Eppelsheim, "Auch die Seele leidet,"

Frankfurter Allgemeine Zeitung, July 21, 2012, https://www.faz.net/aktuell/politik/inland /beschneidungsdebatte-auch-die-seele-leidet-11827698.html.

117. Zwangsbeschneidung.de, "Pressemeldungen zur Beschneidung 2015."

118. Phillip Stolze, "Was passiert eigentlich," July 23, 2012, comment on "Ein klassischer Wertekonflikt," *Frankfurter Allgemeine Zeitung*, July 21, 2012, https://www.faz.net/aktuell /politik/inland/im-gespraech-fritz-kuhn-ein-klassischer-wertekonflikt-11827712.html.

119. Gollaher, *Das verletzte Geschlecht*, 29.

120. See Gollaher, 30.

121. Gollaher.

122. See Wolfgang Hegener, "Sigmund Freud," in *Handbuch des Antisemitismus, Band 2 Personen, 1., A–K*, ed. Wolfgang Benz (Berlin: De Gruyter Saur, 2009), 249–52; cf. Samuel Salzborn, *Antisemitismus als negative Leitidee der Moderne: Sozialwissenschaftliche Theorien im Vergleich* (Frankfurt am Main: Campus, 2010), 37, 331.

123. Freud, quoted in Gilman, *Freud, Identität und Geschlecht*, 129.

124. Gilman, *Freud, Identität und Geschlecht*, 130.

125. Klaus Hödl, "Masculinity," in *Antisemitism: A Historical Encyclopedia of Prejudice and Persecution*, vol. 1, *A–K*, ed. Richard S. Levy (Santa Barbara, CA: ABC-CLIO, 2005), 448.

126. Franz, "Offener Brief zur Beschneidung."

127. Markus C. Schulte von Drach, "Beschneidungsrecht wie bestellt," *Süddeutsche Zeitung*, September 27, 2012, http://www.sueddeutsche.de/wissen/gesetzentwurf-des -bundesjustizministeriums-beschneidungsrecht-fuer-alle-1.1480166.

128. Schulte von Drach, "Beschneidungsrecht wie bestellt."

129. Schulte von Drach.

130. Schulte von Drach.

131. Christoph Zimmermann, "Genderbending für den Penis," *Tageszeitung*, October 29, 2012, http://www.taz.de/Beschneidungsdebatte/!5080711/.

132. Murat Atalan, "Demokratie in Deutschland: Die Meinung der Mehrheit wird ignoriert; Lobbys diktieren Gesetze," July 15, 2012, comment on Thomas Gutschker, "Kinderschutz," *Frankfurter Allgemeine Zeitung*, July 15, 2012, http://www.faz.net/aktuell/politik /urteil-zu-beschneidungen-kinderschutz-11820503.html.

133. Schwarz-Friesel and Reinharz, *Inside the Antisemitic Mind*, 41.

134. Ken Jebsen, "Alles Antisemiten—außer Mutti," *Compact* 11 (2012): 32.

135. Central Council of Jews in Germany, "Zum Urteil des Kölner Landgerichts."

136. Quoted in Association of Islamic Cultural Centres (Verband der Islamischen Kulturzentren), "KRM: Kölner Beschneidungsverbot ist ein massiver Eingriff in die Religionsfreiheit," VIKZ, 2012, http://vikz.de/index.php/pressemitteilungen/items/krm-koelner -beschneidungsverbot-ist-ein-massiver-eingriff-in-die-religionsfreiheit.html.

137. "Pressemitteilung des ZMD zum sogenannten 'Beschneidungsurteil,'" Central Council of Muslims in Germany (Zentralrat der Muslime in Deutschland), June 27, 2012, http:// zentralrat.de/20584.php.

138. Oliver Decker, Johannes Kiess, Julia Schuler, Barbara Handke, and Elmar Brähler, "Die Leipziger Autoritarismus-Studie 2018: Methoden, Ergebnisse und Langzeitverlauf," in *Flucht ins Autoritäre: Rechtsextreme Dynamiken in der Mitte der Gesellschaft*, ed. Oliver Decker and Elmar Brähler (Gießen: Psychosozial, 2018), 73, 78. See also Werner Bergmann and Anna Verena Münch, "Antisemitismus in Deutschland 1996 und 2006: Ein Vergleich," in *Jahrbuch für Antisemitismusforschung*, vol. 21, ed. Stefanie Schüler-Springorum (Berlin: Metropol, 2012), 328; Oliver Decker, Johannes Kiess, and Elmar Brähler, "Antisemitische Ressentiments in Deutschland: Verbreitung und Ursachen," in *Flucht ins Autoritäre: Rechtsextreme Dynamiken in der Mitte der Gesellschaft*, ed. Oliver Decker and Elmar Brähler (Gießen: Psychosozial, 2018), 193.

139. Albert Scherr and Barbara Schäuble, "*Ich habe nichts gegen Juden, aber . . .* " *Ausgangsbedingungen und Perspektiven gesellschaftspolitischer Bildungsarbeit gegen Antisemitismus* (Berlin: Amadeu Antonio Stiftung, Ratzlow Druck Berlin, 2007), 15.

140. Scherr and Schäuble, *Ich habe nichts gegen Juden, aber*, 13.

141. Schwarz-Friesel and Reinharz, *Inside the Antisemitic Mind*, 320, 1.

DANA IONESCU is currently a research associate and lecturer in the Gender Studies Program at Göttingen University. She received her PhD in political science at Technical University of Berlin in 2018; her dissertation examines public debates about ritual male circumcision in contemporary Germany. Her research and teaching focus on intersections of antisemitism and gender as well as on current antifeminist articulations in Germany. Her publications on antisemitism include *Judenbilder in der deutschen Beschneidungskontroverse* (Stereotypical images of the Jews in the controversy surrounding ritual circumcision in Germany, 2018), the coedited volume *Antisemitismus in deutschen Parteien* (Antisemitism in German political parties, 2014), and several articles.

14

What Role Does Antisemitism Play in Jeremy Corbyn's Labour Party?

Dave Rich

SINCE EARLY 2016, ANTISEMITISM HAS BECOME A NATIONAL political issue in the United Kingdom. This is a completely new experience for British Jews, who comprise around three hundred thousand people in a country of sixty-six million; two-thirds of British Jews live in either London or Manchester. Most people in the United Kingdom do not know any Jews and either never think about Jews or feel generally favorable toward them. Opinion polls consistently show that the general British population is one of the least antisemitic publics on Earth in comparison with other countries. An analysis by the Institute for Jewish Policy Research of surveys by the Pew Research Center between 1991 and 2014 and by the Anti-Defamation League between 2009 and 2014 found that both datasets showed the UK to stand alongside the United States as a country in which antisemitic attitudes were among the lowest of any countries polled.[1] Most British people, according to one recent poll, do not even know what the word *antisemitism* means.[2] And yet, that word has been on the front pages of British newspapers, it has led nightly news broadcasts, and it has been the subject of debates and arguments in Parliament—all because of Jeremy Corbyn's Labour Party.

Before delving into why this is the case and what role it plays in Corbyn's wider politics, some explanation of who Jeremy Corbyn is and how he came to be the leader of the Labour Party is necessary. The Labour Party was historically the party that British Jews voted for and that stood up for them against antisemitism. For much of the twentieth century, while the Conservatives were the party of the golf clubs, law firms, and city banks that did not want to allow Jews in through the door, Labour saw Jews as their national constituency. This began to change in the 1980s under Margaret Thatcher, who appreciated and admired the entrepreneurialism of British Jews, many of whom were making the shift from an immigrant working class to the professional middle class. Jewish voting patterns in Britain have not remained as loyal to Labour as they have to the Democrats on the other side of the Atlantic. Still, until recently, there was a genuine affection for the Labour Party among British Jews, particularly under the leadership of former Labour prime ministers Tony Blair and Gordon Brown.

Corbyn, unlike his predecessors, does not really come from a Labour tradition at all. He is a typical product of the radical 1960s New Left—the left that grew up in postwar prosperity; that cut its political teeth campaigning against nuclear weapons, apartheid, and the Vietnam War; that benefited from the novelty of mass higher education, although Corbyn was not intellectually capable of taking advantage of that particular privilege; that views Western colonialism as a historic crime of equal or greater magnitude than the Holocaust and sees American-led imperialism as its modern expression; and that sees Israel as a settler state created through ethnic cleansing, the last great colonial wrong that is still waiting to be put right. Corbyn became a member of Parliament in 1983 and used his platform to promote his favorite far-left causes. In the 1980s, he was best known for his support for the IRA during its terrorist campaigns—famously, in 1984 he invited two convicted IRA terrorists to meet him in Parliament two weeks after an IRA bomb killed five people at the Conservative Party conference in Brighton. At the same time, Corbyn was also an avowed anti-Zionist. When he became a member of Parliament in 1983, he was already a sponsor of a small group called the Labour Movement Campaign for Palestine that pledged to "eradicate Zionism" from the Labour Party, campaigned for Labour to cut ties with its Israeli sister party, and called for a single secular democratic state of Palestine to replace Israel. In 1985, Corbyn wrote in its newsletter that the Labour Movement Campaign for Palestine was "the only campaign rooted in the Labour Movement whose platform really tackles the important issues" in relation to Palestine and that "its activities ought to be supported by every Labour Party member."[3] There were other pro-Palestinian campaign groups in and around the Labour Party in the 1980s, but Corbyn, as he does on so many issues, gravitated toward the one with the most extreme rhetoric and the most radical platform.

When the Labour government of Tony Blair joined forces with the United States to invade Afghanistan in 2001 after the 9/11 terrorist attacks, and then, even worse, to attack Iraq in 2003, Corbyn was one of the leaders of the campaign against those wars. The Iraq War and the campaign against it are the foundational myth of Corbynism. The war was the product, so the myth goes, of a right-wing Labour leadership in thrall to American power, dazzled by free-market economics, damned by its support for Israel's efforts to suppress the second Palestinian intifada that was raging at that time, and funded by private donors, many of them Jewish. Corbyn became chair of the Stop the War Coalition, an antiwar campaign that was run by veterans of Britain's small Communist and Trotskyist parties, was allied with UK-based Islamists from the Muslim Brotherhood, and attracted the temporary support of huge numbers of ordinary members of the public due to the unpopularity of the war in Iraq. The Stop the War Coalition was quite happy to work with supporters of Islamist terrorist organizations, meeting representatives of Hamas, Hizballah, and others at conferences in the Middle East and demonstrating alongside supporters of those groups in the United Kingdom. The coalition endorsed statements supporting the right of Palestinians and Iraqis to resist occupation by "military struggle"—meaning, at that time, the killing of British troops in Iraq—and rejected "the legitimacy of the racist Zionist entity."[4] Corbyn is not the only leader of the Stop the War Coalition to make the jump from that campaign into the leadership of the Labour Party. One of his closest advisors in the Labour leader's office is Andrew Murray, who is a lifelong communist, was on the central committee of the Communist Party of Britain before going to work for Corbyn, and, like Corbyn, was for some years the chair of the Stop the War Coalition.

For this part of the left—Corbyn's left—Western power is at the root of all the world's problems, and violent resistance against Western power is always legitimate, because those powers hoard power and wealth and use it to oppress and subjugate other nations. In 2004, Corbyn wrote that "the wars of the 21st century are crude fights for oil or power and emanate from glittering boardrooms in Western capitals," while conflicts in Iraq and Palestine show "all that is wrong with the world's power structures."[5] In trying to understand the politics of Corbyn and his close associates, it is essential to understand that for them, everything comes down to the illegitimacy of Western power and the nexus of that power with capitalism and globalization. This original sin means that the West—usually America, Britain, or Israel—is to blame for whatever happens to others and also for whatever suffering comes back their way. The sentiments behind these views are widespread on the British left: according to one poll in March 2018,

68 percent of Labour Party members think that the United States is a force for bad in the world, and just 16 percent think it is a force for good, while only 50 percent think the United Kingdom is a force for good.[6]

Corbyn's closest adviser in the Labour Party is Seumas Milne, a longstanding journalist at the *Guardian* who left that newspaper to work for Corbyn shortly after he became leader. He is also a veteran of Britain's Stalinist fringe. Milne is best summed up by the column he wrote in the *Guardian* on September 13, 2001, two days after 9/11, in which he lamented that "nearly two days after the horrific suicide attacks on civilian workers in New York and Washington, it has become painfully clear that most Americans simply don't get it . . . any glimmer of recognition of . . . why the United States is hated with such bitterness, not only in Arab and Muslim countries, but across the developing world—seems almost entirely absent." Milne provided his answer: it is America's "record of unabashed national egotism and arrogance" that explains it.[7] Had Corbyn become prime minister, the so-called special relationship between Britain and the United States would no longer have applied—and this would have been the case whoever was in the White House. Corbyn, for example, has previously called for NATO to be dismantled, believing it to be a vehicle for Western military expansion that provoked the Cold War and the war in Ukraine. He was extremely reluctant to condemn President Assad for chemical attacks on Syrian civilians and did his best to avoid blaming Putin for the attempted murder of a Russian defector and his daughter in Britain last year. When it comes to foreign policy, Corbyn's first question has always been, What would America do? And then he does the opposite.

Corbyn's rise to the Labour Party leadership in 2015 should be seen as part of a wider populist surge that overturned political assumptions in many Western nations. The center ground has dropped out of British politics just as it has in several countries, but rather than the old, tired, established parties being replaced by insurgent newcomers, they have instead been whittled out from the inside by a combination of smart organizing and large-scale recruitment of new members. Corbyn's leadership campaign in 2015 harvested the membership lists and email contacts of the Stop the War Coalition, the Palestine Solidarity Campaign, and several other far-left campaign groups to persuade people to join Labour, solely for the purpose of electing Corbyn leader. Many of Labour's new members are young idealists who can see that they are likely to be less well off than their parents, with huge student debts, no chance of buying a home, and precarious job prospects, and were attracted by the promise of an alternative future. But many were returnees, former members of the Labour Party who had left in the 1980s when Labour was last the subject of a concerted—but failed—attempt by the hard left to take it over, or in the 1990s and 2000s when Tony Blair moved Labour to the center ground and won three elections as a result. These "retreads"—older, resentful, usually male, often with a history in one of the far left's smaller Trotskyist or Marxist groupings—are responsible for much of the antisemitism and a wider culture of bullying that has taken root across the party. Leftists of this generation imbibed their view of Israel and Zionism from the vast reservoir of Soviet antisemitic anti-Zionism. All the same allegations of Zionist conspiracies, Jewish disloyalty, fascist Israel, purges of Jewish party members for alleged disloyalty, the idea that claims of antisemitism are usually false, the framework of understanding the Israeli-Palestinian conflict through the slogan of "Zionism equals racism"—these are all commonplace in today's Labour Party, just as they were in the Soviet antisemitic canon.

There are many examples of Corbyn's own antisemitic record that have come to light in recent years, but four in particular, taken in combination, illustrate the complementary parts of Corbyn's hostile attitudes toward Israel, Zionism, and, I would argue, Jews. The first was in 2009, when Corbyn invited representatives of Hamas and Hizballah to speak at a meeting of the Stop the War Coalition in the British Parliament. He explained that he did it because Hamas, in his view, is "an organisation that is dedicated towards the good of the Palestinian people and bringing about long-term peace and social justice and political justice in the whole region" and should not be "labelled as a terrorist organisation."[8] This is significant because he did not just say that Hamas has a right to resist Israeli occupation, that it represents the oppressed, or that it forms the government in Gaza, so it is important to hear what it has to say—by claiming that Hamas is dedicated to "social justice and political justice," he aligned himself, and progressive politics in general, directly with its values and program. This opens a wide door to antisemitism, the justification of anti-Jewish terrorism, and the radicalization of left-wing attitudes to the Israeli-Palestinian conflict.

The second example came in 2012, when an American graffiti artist, Mear One, painted a large antisemitic mural on a wall in East London, an area known for impressive and imaginative street art. This mural represented a visual conspiracy theory about global inequality. It showed six old, white men, obviously wealthy, playing Monopoly on a board that rested on the backs of darker-skinned, crouching, faceless people. Above them was an eye in a pyramid, a symbol commonly associated by conspiracy theorists with the Illuminati, Freemasons, or other secret societies. Behind them was a scene of industrial dystopia, depicting machinery and chimneys belching fiery smoke into the atmosphere. A protestor stood to the side, clenched fist aloft, holding a placard that read, "The New World Order is the Enemy of Humanity." Not only was this an obvious conspiracy piece, but some of the men sitting around the table—the bad guys—looked like Jewish caricatures complete with big noses. The artist clarified that the banker figures were a mixture of "Jewish and white Anglos" but insisted that it was a critique of "class and privilege," not of Jews.[9] Despite his denials, the mural caused a huge fuss locally. It was denounced as antisemitic by political figures on all sides in Tower Hamlets as well as by people from the Jewish community, and it was subsequently removed. Mear One protested with a post on Facebook complaining that his mural was going to be painted over, and Corbyn posted a comment sympathizing with him. He even compared him to Diego Rivera, whose 1930s painting *Man at the Crossroads*, commissioned for Rockefeller Center in New York, was allegedly destroyed because it featured a picture of Lenin. When Corbyn was challenged on this last year, he first tried to justify his support for the mural on the grounds of free expression and then said he had not noticed it was antisemitic. Corbyn may well be telling the truth when he says he did not see any antisemitism in the mural. The fact that the depictions of some of the bankers in the mural were antisemitic—that the image of a Jewish banker with a big nose exploiting workers to get rich is itself an antisemitic caricature—completely eluded him. A charitable view is that he missed it because in his understanding of racism, it is impossible for rich, powerful white men to be victims of racism; it is the dark-skinned, downtrodden workers off of whose backs those bankers were making money who are the true victims. A less charitable view is that he did not spot the antisemitic stereotypes in the mural because he believed in them himself.

This latter explanation is more compelling in the light of Corbyn's endorsement of a book by John Hobson, a radical English writer whose theory of imperialism at the beginning of the twentieth century has carried great influence in left-wing thinking on the subject. In his 1902 book, *Imperialism: A Study*, Hobson argued that the European urge to conquer new lands in Africa and Asia in the decades before 1900 was, in fact, an urge to conquer new markets in which the great finance houses of Europe could invest the surplus wealth they had accumulated by repressing wages in Europe itself. These imperialist adventures were, for Hobson, driven directly by these banks, whose owners also manipulated the media to encourage popular support for their project. And who, according to Hobson, ran these finance houses? They were "controlled . . . chiefly by men of a single and peculiar race, who have behind them many centuries of financial experience" and "are in a unique position to manipulate the policy of nations." Furthermore, Hobson wrote, "Does anyone seriously suppose that a great war could be undertaken by any European state, or a great State loan subscribed, if the house of Rothschild and its connections sets their face against it?" Nor was this Hobson's only antisemitic work—his previous writings about both Jewish immigrants in London and Jewish involvement in the Boer War were riddled with anti-Jewish expressions. This did not prevent Corbyn from writing a glowing foreword to a new edition of *Imperialism* in 2011. "What is brilliant," Corbyn wrote in his foreword, was Hobson's "analysis of the pressures that were hard at work in pushing for a vast national effort, in grabbing new outposts of Empire on distant islands and shores." He went on, "Hobson's railing against the commercial interests that fuel the role of the popular press with tales of imperial might, that then lead on to racist caricatures of African and Asian peoples, was both correct and prescient." Yet Hobson clearly identified these "commercial interests" as being run by "men of a single and peculiar race"—in other words, by Jews. The old antisemitic stereotype of rapacious Jewish capitalism, relatively common in left-wing thinking during Hobson's time, is central to the theory that Corbyn praises as "correct and prescient." Corbyn did not mention this at all, yet he did criticize the racist language that Hobson used to describe African and Asian people. Again, either Corbyn missed the references to Jews entirely, or—more plausibly—he simply thought that Hobson was right.[10]

The final piece of this jigsaw is provided by a speech Corbyn gave in 2013 at a pro-Palestinian meeting in the UK. One of the Palestinian speakers at the meeting had been challenged by two pro-Israel activists in the audience, and Corbyn came to his defense. "Zionists," he said, "have two problems. One is that they don't want to study history, and secondly, having lived in this country for a very long time, probably all their lives, don't understand English irony either." As many people (including many on the left) pointed out, the implication of Corbyn's words is that English-born "Zionists" have failed to acquire the characteristics of indigenous English men and women—a construction that makes sense only if those English "Zionists" are descended from immigrant families. In other words, when Corbyn said "Zionists," he meant Jews.[11]

There are many other examples of antisemitic statements and actions by Corbyn, but these four bring together the main strands of thinking on his part of the left: the anti-imperialist identification with violent antisemitic movements that wish to eradicate the Jewish state, because those movements are perceived to be fighting against Western power; a conspiratorial association of Jews with capitalism, banking, and financial exploitation—what has become commonly known as the "socialism of fools"; and an older, very English type of antisemitism that will never accept Jews as fully part of the club.

Underpinning all of this is the increased presence of conspiracy theories as part of the discourse of mainstream politics and politicians. This is not something that afflicts only the United Kingdom or only the left, but it plays an important role in explaining why antisemitism has taken root in the Labour Party. When Corbyn was first running for the Labour leadership in August 2015, an opinion poll found that 28 percent of his supporters believed that the world is controlled by a secretive elite, compared to 13 percent of the general population.[12] Another poll in August 2016 found that 35 percent of Corbyn supporters even thought that some Labour MPs had been secretly planted in the party by the Conservatives to undermine the Labour left.[13] The antisemitic discourse in Labour-supporting social media is riddled with conspiracy theories. ISIS is run by Mossad (it stands for "Israeli Secret Intelligence Service," apparently). Jihadist terrorism in Europe and school shootings in America are Israeli "false flags." Zionist lobbyists have infiltrated Labour and are using Israeli money to manipulate its workings. The Rothschild Bank is behind all the wars in the world—in the United Kingdom, Google searches for conspiracy theories about the Rothschilds have gone up by 39 percent in the past three years. And of course, the notion that stories about antisemitism in the Labour Party are all part of a smear campaign by an alliance of Zionists, Tories, and Blairites to prevent a socialist government from coming to power is, itself, a conspiracy theory with antisemitic implications.

This goes right to the top: Jeremy Corbyn himself wrote in 2009 that "once again the Israeli tail wags the US dog," as a way of explaining why Israel is allowed to build more settlements.[14] In 2012, after an attack by jihadists on Egyptian soldiers in Sinai, he speculated on Iranian TV that "the hand of Israel" may have been behind the attacks.[15] The same year, he agreed with another interviewer that Israel might create a "false flag event" in order to trigger a war with Iran.[16] Corbyn has a weakness for conspiracy theories, and people with a weakness for conspiracy theories also often have a weakness for antisemitism. But then, the Labour Party's entire economic and political analysis under Corbyn is framed as a conspiracy, in which a global banking elite runs a rigged system to the detriment of all good working people. Launching Labour's 2017 general election campaign, Corbyn claimed that "a cosy cartel" has been allowed "to rig the system in favour of a few powerful and wealthy individuals and corporations. It is a rigged system set up by the wealth extractors, for the wealth extractors." The election, he claimed, was simply "the establishment versus the people."[17] Elsewhere he has spoken of "a failed economic system rigged for the wealthy and the corporate elite."[18] He used similar rhetoric throughout Labour's 2019 general election campaign. When Corbyn and his allies blame poverty, inequality, and racism on the greed of a faceless "global elite," they may or may not mean Jews, but there is no doubt that it excites antisemites. One of the most important but least asked questions for the Labour Party is why so many antisemites and conspiracy cranks have thought that Corbyn's Labour is the party for them.

This kind of left populism, just like its right-wing cousin, sees the media as very much part of a rigged system. In his speech at a Labour Party conference last year, Corbyn claimed that in Britain, "a free press has far too often meant the freedom to spread lies and half-truths, and to smear the powerless, not take on the powerful." He then addressed party members directly: "You challenge their propaganda of privilege by using the mass media of the 21st century: social media."[19] The twist is that Corbyn's supporters use social media to attack and harass opponents, including journalists who criticize Corbyn himself, and they have a particular animus for the BBC. Corbyn is not universally opposed to establishment or government-linked media—he has previously recommended Russia Today and Al-Jazeera as more objective and better-informed alternatives to the BBC and presented programs on Iran's Press TV for which he was paid around £20,000. But in Corbyn's worldview, Russia Today, Al-Jazeera, and Press TV are all part of the resistance to Western power, whereas the BBC is part of the rigged system through which that power maintains its global dominance.

Perhaps the best way to understand Corbyn's Labour Party, and therefore the role that antisemitism plays within it, is as a social movement rather than a formal party. Corbyn became leader due to an organizational surge from across the extra-parliamentary left. Many of those who voted him into office did not even join the party—under new rules, they could vote in Labour's leadership election by paying £3 to become a temporary supporter of the party rather than a full member. Similarly, much of Corbyn's emotional and rhetorical support, especially on social media, comes from people who tweet their Labour Party hashtags and emojis and join pro-Corbyn Facebook groups but are not actually Labour Party members. Of course, many have joined the party, and after nearly four years of churn, the membership is largely made up of people who have joined since Corbyn became leader; but you do not have to be a Labour Party member to feel that you are part of Corbyn's movement. As such, the issue of antisemitism acts to bind the disparate parts of this movement together and give them a common enemy to stand against. This is expressed in two ways: first, in the widespread and deeply held belief that allegations of antisemitism are part of a deliberate, malicious smear campaign to prevent Corbyn from taking power and ushering in a socialist utopia; and second, through extravagant support for Palestine. In March and April 2018, when Corbyn was under intense pressure over Labour's antisemitism and the Jewish community demonstrated outside Parliament, he and his closest allies made a point of tweeting repeated condemnation of the violence on Israel's border with Gaza. In September, after Labour had spent the summer under unrelenting pressure due to its stubborn reluctance to adopt the International Holocaust Remembrance Alliance's working definition of antisemitism, pro-Palestinian groups arranged for hundreds of delegates at Labour's annual conference to wave Palestinian flags on the conference floor. And had Jeremy Corbyn become prime minister in December 2019, he had pledged that one of the first acts of his government would have been to recognize the state of Palestine. This would have been a purely symbolic move, but that is the point: it would have signaled to Corbyn's supporters that they had won and that their Zionist, right-wing opponents—the wealthy elite who control the rigged system—had lost.

In the end, it was Corbyn's Labour that lost the 2019 general election, and this was no ordinary defeat. It was Labour's worst performance in a general election since 1935, a catastrophic loss built largely on the rejection of Corbyn by voters in Labour's traditional heartlands. Opinion polls repeatedly showed that Corbyn's personal ratings as a leader were astonishingly bad, and voters—in focus groups, opinion polls, and doorstep conversations with canvassers—repeatedly listed Labour's antisemitism among their reasons for disliking him. One of the most damaging moments for Corbyn during the campaign itself was when he was challenged to apologize to the Jewish community by Andrew Neil, the BBC's leading political interviewer, and refused to do so. After this defeat, the Labour Party now finds itself with a membership and activist base far to the left of most of the British electorate and a political program that has been comprehensively rejected. The fight now begins for the future of the party. Will it remain a vehicle for socialist utopianism and conspiracist anti-imperialism that acts as a magnet for antisemites, or will it revert to its social democratic moorings and in the process expunge the antisemitism that came to characterize its Corbynist years?

Notes

1. Jonathan Boyd and L. Daniel Staetsky, "Could It Happen Here? What Existing Data Tell Us about Contemporary Antisemitism in the UK," Institute for Jewish Policy Research, May 2015.
2. Rosa Doherty, "Exclusive: Fewer than Half of British Adults Know What 'Antisemitism' Means, Poll Reveals," *Jewish Chronicle*, March 14, 2019.
3. Jeremy Corbyn, *Labour Movement Campaign for Palestine Newsletter*, no. 2 (1985).
4. "2nd Cairo Declaration: With the Palestinian and Iraqi Resistance—against Capitalist Globalization and US Hegemony," Stop the War Coalition, December 14, 2003, http://www.mdsweb.jp/international/cairo_sec/cairo2_dec.html.
5. Jeremy Corbyn, "Liberation's 50-Year Struggle for Equality," *Morning Star*, May 26, 2004.
6. Sam Coates Sky, "Tonight as Jeremy Corbyn deals with the biggest fallout with his MPs since the election, we reveal the results of a Times/YouGov poll of Labour members," Twitter, March 30, 2018, https://twitter.com/SamCoatesSky/status/979833744122109955?s=20.
7. Seumas Milne, "They Can't See Why They Are Hated," *Guardian*, September 13, 2001.
8. Adrian Cousins, "Stop the War Coalition—Meet the Resistance—Jeremy Corbyn MP London 3 March 2009," YouTube video, March 30, 2009, https://www.youtube.com/watch?v=FQLKpY3NdeA.
9. Shane Croucher, "Mear One's Brick Lane Street Art: Is Mural Anti-Semitic?," *International Business Times*, October 4, 2012.
10. Daniel Finkelstein, "Corbyn's Praise for Deeply Antisemitic Book," *The Times*, April 30, 2019; David Feldman, "Jeremy Corbyn, 'Imperialism,' and Labour's Antisemitism Problem," *History Workshop*, June 12, 2019.
11. Jake Wallis Simons, "Exclusive: Jeremy Corbyn said British 'Zionists' Have 'No Sense of English Irony Despite Having Lived Here All Their Lives' and 'Need a Lesson', while Giving Speech alongside Islamic Extremists at a Conference Publicised by Hamas' Military Wing," *Daily Mail*, August 23, 2018, https://www.dailymail.co.uk/news/article-6087783/Jeremy-Corbyn-said-British-Zionists-no-sense-English-irony.html.
12. Freddie Sayers, "'You May Say That I'm a Dreamer': Inside the Mindset of Jeremy Corbyn's Supporters," YouGov, August 27, 2015, https://yougov.co.uk/news/2015/08/27/you-may-say-im-dreamer-inside-mindset-jeremy-corby/.
13. YouGov, *YouGov Survey Results*, August 25–29, 2016, https://d25d2506sfb94s.cloudfront.net/cumulus_uploads/document/pvxdr2lh73/InternalResults_160830_LabourSelectorate.pdf.
14. Dominic Kennedy, "Palestinian Lobby Group Paid for Corbyn to Meet Assad in Syria," *The Times*, October 29, 2016.
15. Jamie Doward, Toby Helm, and Jonah Ramchandan, "Second MP Investigated in Row over Labour's Antisemitism Code," *Observer*, July 29, 2018.
16. @TheGolem_, "EXCLUSIVE—In January 2012 @JeremyCorbyn gave an interview in Parliament to an antisemitic conspiracy theorist," Twitter, January 31, 2019, https://twitter.com/TheGolem_/status/1090995532603027456?s=20.

17. Labour Party, "Jeremy Corbyn First Speech of the 2017 General Election Campaign" (press statement, April 20, 2017), https://labour.org.uk/press/jeremy-corbyn-first-speech-of-the-2017-general/.

18. Jon Stone, "Corbyn Tells European Social Democrats: 'Reject Austerity and Neoliberalism or Voters Will Reject You,'" *Independent*, July 5, 2018.

19. Labour Party, "Jeremy Corbyn Speaking at Labour Party Conference Today" (press statement, September 26, 2018), https://labour.org.uk/press/jeremy-corbyn-speaking-labour-party-conference-today/.

DAVE RICH is Director of Policy at the Community Security Trust, a UK Jewish charity that advises and represents the UK Jewish community on matters relating to antisemitism, terrorism, and extremism. He is Associate Research Fellow at the Pears Institute for the Study of Antisemitism, Birkbeck, University of London, where he completed his PhD in 2015 on "Zionists and Anti-Zionists: Political Protest and Student Activism in Britain, 1968-1986." Dave is author of *The Left's Jewish Problem: Jeremy Corbyn, Israel and Antisemitism* (Biteback, 2016 and 2018) and writes about antisemitism, anti-Zionism, and extremism for newspapers and journals, including the *New York Times*, the *Guardian*, *Huffington Post*, *Ha'aretz*, *World Affairs Journal*, *Jewish Chronicle*, *Israel Journal of Foreign Affairs*, and *Forward*. His academic publications include chapters and articles on hate crime, Islamist extremism, the abuse of Holocaust memory, antisemitism on university campuses, and the UK campaign for Soviet Jewry. His latest publications include a chapter on "Walking a Mile in Asghar Bukhari's Shoes: Conspiracy Theories, Antisemitism and Extremism" in Campbell and Klaff, eds., *Unity and Diversity in Contemporary Antisemitism: The Bristol-Sheffield Hallam Colloquium on Contemporary Antisemitism* (Academic Studies Press, 2019) and a new introduction to a second edition of Hadassa Ben-Itto, *The Lie That Will Not Die: The Protocols of the Elders of Zion* (Vallentine Mitchell, 2020).

15

Antisemitism and the Left in the UK and the Global Significance of the Return of the "Jewish Question"

Philip Spencer

IN 2015, IN THE AFTERMATH OF A SECOND election defeat in a row, the British Labour Party experienced a major convulsion. It elected a hitherto marginal figure, Jeremy Corbyn, as its leader. This was presented by Corbyn and his supporters as a move to the radical left, a claim that has been largely taken as self-evident, although it is by no means the case. Much depends on what is meant by the radical left, which has taken several different forms over time, not least in relation to the question of antisemitism.[1] It is true that in breaking with the supposedly self-defeating compromises of his predecessors, Corbyn and his supporters have claimed to be pursuing a much more egalitarian domestic agenda than his predecessors pursued. One of the triggers for his unexpected initial victory was his opposition to the unwillingness of the Labour Party's interim leadership to oppose the Conservative government's efforts to make cuts in welfare. Of much greater significance in this context, however, has been his foreign policy agenda, which breaks in fundamental respects with the traditional stance of every British government (Labour or Conservative) since World War II.

In fact, the foreign policy question proved to be much more instrumental than his domestic policy agenda in his unexpected success. Corbyn was for some time the chair of the Stop the War movement in Britain, which succeeded in mobilizing very large numbers (of young people especially) in protest against Britain's involvement in the Iraq War. During the campaign to elect a new leader, Stop the War furnished Corbyn with an extensive social-media-based list of potential supporters and an experienced organizing capacity. Aided by the decision of the departing leader, Ed Miliband, to allow anyone to vote for a new leader upon payment of the somewhat derisory sum of £3 (even if they were not members of the party), Corbyn was able to use this support base to sweep to victory, as his new supporters numerically overwhelmed existing and traditional Labour Party members.

The interceding years have seen Corbyn and his allies tighten their grip on the party. First defeating a rather inept attempt by the overwhelming majority of MPs to replace him as leader, he and his allies have taken hold of key decision-making bodies and have intimidated the large majority of MPs from mounting any further challenge, not least by threatening them with deselection, which would mean they could not stand again for the party in a forthcoming election. It might seem surprising that they have been able to accomplish all this with such ease, given the fact that nearly all opinion polls have consistently shown Corbyn to be deeply unpopular in the country as a whole. However, this was also the case before the last election, called in 2017 by the then Conservative prime minister, who had confidently expected the Labour Party to be decimated. Instead, the Conservative Party lost its overall majority, although it was still able to continue in government. Corbyn and his allies indeed claimed the election result as a victory even though the Labour Party had actually lost, on the grounds that it had not been beaten by anything like as much as had been anticipated. The fact that the party had increased its share of the vote and number of seats—although how much any of this had to do with Corbyn himself is still unclear, considering that large numbers of Labour MPs who were successfully elected did their best to avoid mentioning him in their campaigns—was taken by Corbyn and his supporters as evidence that the tide was now running in their direction, despite the best efforts of what was portrayed as a sustained campaign of disinformation and smearing of Corbyn by the "mainstream media."

Labour and Britain's Jews

The consequences of this transformation of the Labour Party for Britain's small Jewish population are the subject of considerable debate, as the question of antisemitism has now become a major issue in British politics. For a very long time, the majority of Jews in Britain have identified strongly with the Labour Party. For the first time in both their history and that of the party, that loyalty is very seriously in doubt. The large majority of Jews now harbor grave concerns about the party's commitment to their security and welfare. Opinion polls as well as recent elections at local, national, and European levels show a sharp and sustained drop in the traditional Jewish vote for Labour. In an unprecedented move, in the summer of 2018, the three leading organizations representing Britain's Jews called a demonstration outside Parliament to protest on the basis of evidence of growing antisemitism within the party and of the leadership's (at best) failure to deal with it and (at worst) tacit encouragement of such attitudes and behavior.[2] The action was unprecedented in part because there is a long-standing tradition among Anglo-Jewry of keeping a very low profile, grounded in a fear that being visible will attract antisemitism. Only in recent years, with the more general rise of identity politics, has a younger generation felt confident enough to challenge what they see as a rather hidebound approach, which is grounded in an acceptance that, for all the much-lauded traditions of toleration in the UK, a uniquely British form of antisemitism continues to lurk beneath the surface.[3] It is highly unlikely, however, that the critics of this traditional approach foresaw that it would change because of antisemitism on the left, let alone that some on the left would go so far (as we shall see below) as to embrace some of that specifically British antisemitism.

A number of prominent Labour MPs (not all of them Jewish but including the chair of the Jewish Labour Movement) resigned from the party over this issue, having personally experienced sustained antisemitic abuse from fellow party members on social media as well as at meetings.[4] Little was done to stem the tide, as can be seen from a profoundly disturbing program shown on the BBC in the summer of the following year that revealed both an extraordinarily high level of antisemitism in the Labour Party and the leadership's persistent failure to do anything serious about it.[5] This was accompanied by something even more shocking: the referral of the party to the Equality and Human Rights Commission (a body actually set up by the Labour Party when it had last been in government) on the grounds that it was suspected of being an institutionally racist organization.[6] The only other party to have been so referred to the commission in the past has been the far-right British National Party. The charge of institutional racism, it should be stressed, is not a light one. The term was developed in the UK after a major inquiry (what became known as the Macpherson Report) into the prevalence and persistence of racism in the police force. In the now widely accepted definition adopted by that report, *institutional racism* refers to the "collective failure of an organization to provide an appropriate and professional service to people because of their colour, culture, or ethnic origin." One of the most important features of this definition is that it recognizes that organizations do not need to be full of overt and obvious racists for a racist culture to develop, because racism goes beyond this and can be "seen or detected in processes, attitudes, and behaviour which amount to discrimination through unwitting prejudice, ignorance, thoughtlessness and racist stereotyping."[7] That the Labour Party, a party of the left and one that in the eyes of its members and voters ought to be leading the fight against racism, should now be being investigated for this is, by any measure, a stunning development.

Local and Conjectural Explanations

All of this has come about in the few years since Corbyn became leader of the party. How and why this has happened has a lot to do with the background and core beliefs of the new leader, as well as with his most committed supporters, some of which can be explained in specifically local and conjunctural terms.[8]

In his many years as a marginal figure in the Labour Party (he was first elected as an MP in the 1980s and, before he himself began to demand loyalty from his MPs, voted against the party on more than five hundred occasions in Parliament), Corbyn devoted himself to foreign policy questions. His approach to this area was grounded in the visceral anti-imperialism that has formed the common sense of a major part of the radical left since the 1960s. The mobilizational capacity of such a worldview has waxed and waned over the years but received a very major boost in the UK with the Iraq War, which was imagined by many to be the early twenty-first-century version of the Vietnam War, in opposition to which many young people of an earlier generation had been radicalized. In the UK, there was of course one signal difference between the Vietnam and Iraq Wars: Britain stayed out of the first but entered the second. This made it possible to appeal to a much wider audience in the UK in the second case. The success of Stop the War in the UK context is therefore a particularly local and conjunctural factor in explaining the rise of Corbyn.

So too is a not so widely recognized aspect of his particular trajectory, which has to do with the relationship between the Labour Party and forces positioned to the left of it. Corbyn himself occupied a slightly unusual position in this anti-imperialist radical leftist world in the UK. Most of those radicalized the first time around (that is, in the anti–Vietnam War moment) were originally not in the Labour Party but outside it. That Corbyn was inside the party did not, however, expose him to general opprobrium. Rather, he was used as a convenient resource by extra-parliamentary activists. They could use him, for example, whenever they needed to be able to host meetings in a range of venues (including Parliament) or more generally when they needed to promote an image of themselves as politically significant, reaching further than they could otherwise claim into the mainstream. This is not a wholly trivial matter for Corbyn on a personal level. Occupying such a figurehead position over a long period would not have made it particularly desirable for Corbyn (or anyone in that privileged position) to engage in any rethinking or any questioning of fundamental axioms or articles of faith, since that would have imperiled both his image and his attractiveness. (Another way of putting it, more psychoanalytically, is that it would maximize any potential narcissism, which can often play an important role in the development of an individual's or collective's antisemitism.)[9]

Over time (for a host of reasons we do not have space to go into here), the extra-parliamentary movement in the UK declined, and more and more people found their way back into the Labour Party, faute de mieux. They then often left in disgust at the supposedly rightward drift of the Labour Party under Tony Blair, even though the latter did actually win three elections in a row whereas his successors have now lost the same number. When an opportunity arose—via the mobilizational capacities of Stop the War, in which they had joined forces with a new generation—to get rid of the so-called Blairites, many flooded back in to support him.[10]

Anti-imperialism and Anti-Zionism

A central component of the shared worldview of this coalition of old and young has been a common view of Israel, which also possesses an important local and conjunctural aspect. On much of the left in the UK (perhaps more so than elsewhere in the West), Israel has long been seen, especially since the Six-Day War, as a vital outpost of Western imperialism in the Middle East, serving the interests of its American masters and their closely allied British subordinates (or, in some versions, dictating those very interests), and as a settler-colonial society based on an inherently racist ideology (which is how Zionism is understood). Solidarity with any group or state that resists Western imperialism and Israel in particular is a sine qua non from this perspective. A significant element of specifically British guilt is invoked here, inasmuch as Britain was the occupying imperial state until just before the state of Israel was created in 1948. A particular responsibility for the original catastrophe that befell the Palestinians that year therefore supposedly lies with the British, who legitimized Zionist aspirations in the Balfour Declaration and both allowed and presided over the "fatal" rise in Jewish immigration to the region thereafter. The fact that Britain blocked Jewish immigration from Nazi persecution and then did not in fact vote for the creation of the state of Israel at the decisive UN assembly does not appear to be widely known by or even believable to the younger group who have been inducted into this worldview by their elders.

If some Palestinians in the UK or their supporters, individually or in groups, indulge from time to time in antisemitic rhetoric, that is understood to be at best unfortunate but is still more generally condoned. After all, if Israel is a Jewish state, and if it is understood that Israel is inherently racist and oppressive, it is only natural that those resisting it will see Jews generally as their enemy.[11]

Others have argued, particularly in the UK, that the extent of antisemitism in this context is deliberately exaggerated, if not manufactured by Zionists, in order to deflect and dismiss legitimate criticism of Israel.[12] Those who see Israel through this prism, the explanation goes, by definition cannot be called antisemitic because antiracism is a core part of the same worldview that makes them anti-Zionists in the first place. The charge of antisemitism is, from this perspective, an act of bad faith, dishonest and malign in both intent and effect. From this perspective, antisemitism is not so much understandable or condonable as nonexistent or irrelevant.

In any case, it is argued that antisemitism itself is no longer a significant form of racism because Jews are no longer oppressed. Just as Israel has become a key part of the global power structure at the level of the international order, Jews (generally in the West but especially in the UK, though even more so in the US) are now viewed as "white," having been integrated to become an important part of the dominant group that oppresses and exploits others.[13] Those who experience racism in the UK are the heirs of those who suffered from the empire, immigrants from former colonies who were subject to continuing racism from the beginning, in their original homelands and when they came to the UK (as the recent scandal over Windrush confirms). But in public discourse, this has less and less to do with antisemitism, which was supposedly only significant in the UK when there was immigration from eastern Europe in the late nineteenth and early twentieth centuries. Jews then were subject to racist attacks, but from the far right, especially from homegrown fascists in the 1930s, when the left at the time supposedly heroically and single-handedly defended them. However, they have experienced significant social mobility since then, in ways that were and still are not possible for those of a visibly different color. To put it another way, there were contingent reasons for antisemitism in Britain that had nothing to do with the fundamental structure of racism in the UK, which is rooted in empire, colony, and slavery. Jews were not victims of this and indeed on some accounts were actually complicit in it at times.[14]

Antiracism and Antisemitism

To put it mildly, this is at best a somewhat selective and rather reductive way of thinking about and responding to racism and antisemitism. It is not just that this view has real difficulty in registering the complexity of antisemitism itself, either as a distinctive form of racism, which sees Jews, for example, as both demonic and superhuman on the one hand and subhuman on the other, or as something that is not only a form of racism since it has also had, for example, a strong religious component, which has by no means disappeared. It is also a way of thinking that, in asserting that antisemitism is no longer a significant form of racism in the modern world immediately after it had taken its most radical and genocidal form, systematically downplays what happened to Jews specifically in the Holocaust. It does so on the basis of a much more general understanding of Nazism as a form of racism that targeted many different groups and should be understood only in the context of a European white and colonialist ideology. In this framework, what happened to the Jews of Europe was, more or less, only what had already been done to victims of European colonialist ideology for centuries.[15]

To emphasize Jewish suffering, from this angle, is to downplay the sufferings of so many others. Instead, there is a pronounced tendency to see the Holocaust only in universalist terms. In its aftermath, by assuming that antisemitism almost magically disappeared once the Nazis had been defeated (though their defeat had little to do with a revulsion against their genocidal antisemitism), this way of thinking permits little attention to or empathy for the trauma that that catastrophe visited on the Jewish people and, especially, the need many Jews now understandably felt to have state of their own. On the contrary, since antisemitism was now seen to be definitely over with and finished, there was, from this perspective, no need for a state of Israel at all. In fact, the argument for a state of Israel could (again from this perspective) all too easily be turned on its head. Israel could be seen not as a response to Nazi racism but, quite perversely, as is its successor.

Zionism could itself be defined as a form of racism, with Jews now presented as the oppressors of non-Jews in Palestine as they built their own state on pure ethno-nationalist principles, just as the Nazis had sought to do.

The Return of the "Jewish Question"

One crucial corollary of such arguments is the fairly explicit implication that Jews are once again acting in bad faith (or worse). If Jews claim that antisemitism still exists or has returned, given that the Holocaust supposedly put an end to it once and for all, they must be making it up, lying, and doing so for malign purposes. This takes us into a very different dimension of the problem that can be framed only in local and conjunctural terms. It has to do with a way of thinking about Jews that is central to modern antisemitism and with the notion that there is something called the "Jewish question."[16]

At the root of this supposed "question" lies the idea that Jews are a problem, not just for the radical right but also for some on the left. For the former, Jewish emancipation was of course always seen as a fundamental mistake. Jews were typically seen from this quarter as inherently rotten, as a source of corruption and of decomposition, responsible for all that had gone wrong in the modern world politically, socially, and economically. For a significant section of the left, however, Jewish emancipation could also come to be viewed as a problem. This was not, of course, because emancipation had been granted in the first place but because Jews had supposedly not fulfilled their side of the emancipation bargain. Already during the Enlightenment, many progressives had presented emancipation not as a good in itself but as a cure for the supposed ills of Jewish life, which had been (again supposedly) caused by their exclusion from society. Emancipation, it was assumed, would allow Jews to behave better, to remedy their many faults. They would no longer remain a separate and distinct nation, keeping to themselves and loyal only to their fellow Jews; in fact, their claim to nationhood itself made no sense in the modern world, since (having been dispersed across the world for millennia) they lacked the supposedly core attributes of a modern nation—a common language, a common culture, or a shared territory. It was also assumed that they would no longer continue with their absurdly outdated practices and beliefs—Judaism being seen as a particularly backward religion even in comparison to Christianity and Islam, which were at least universalist doctrines. It was assumed that they would cease to complain obsessively about their maltreatment by others, exaggerating their misfortunes and demanding special treatment. And, perhaps above all, it was assumed that they would no longer practice and specialize in the worst forms of economic behavior as usurers and exploiters.

However, for some on the left, emancipation had not produced any of these necessary changes. Jews continued to want to maintain their separate identity. They had not fully assimilated and had not ceased (as the first emancipatory state in the French Revolution had explicitly demanded) to be a "nation within a nation" but rather had maintained their loyalties to each other, even across borders.[17] They had even developed their own claims to national self-determination in the form of Zionism. They continued to engage in special pleading, exaggerating their sufferings. And far from remedying their bad economic behavior, they had become some of the worst financiers, bankers, and speculators in the modern world, bankrolling and even controlling the policies of many states.

In the nineteenth century, a number of radicals had used arguments of this kind to pin the blame on Jews for the left's own failure to bring about desired changes in economy, society, and polity. They had come to argue that in these circumstances, antisemitism might be understandable, condonable, and even something socialists could themselves exploit to win mass support. If the masses first experienced and understood their exploitation at the hands of Jews, they could come to see that a radical change in social relations was necessary. They could begin by attacking Jews and then be persuaded to move on to attacking other capitalists, financiers, speculators, and the whole political order, which was in league with and supported them.[18] Although some socialists criticized this way of thinking about antisemitism, dubbing it the "socialism of fools," even this criticism to some extent remained trapped within the same frame of reference, since it could be taken to imply that antisemitism was still some kind of socialism, however foolish.[19]

The Holocaust did not fundamentally change this way of thinking for many on the left. Indeed, the reaction of Jews to the Holocaust could itself be fitted into this way of thinking without too much difficulty. In supposedly exaggerating their own suffering and willfully minimizing that of many other victims of the Nazis, Jews had engaged in monumental special pleading, successfully demanding their own nation-state based on the worst set of archaic principles, at the same time allocating citizenship there on the kinds of ethno-national principles that modern states had (supposedly) abandoned long ago. Now Jews were not just in league with or controlling other states from within or through their extensive transnational contacts; they were also (and worse still), in the form of this perverse new state of

Israel, in league with (if not in control of) those Western imperialist states, notably the United States, which were responsible for the world's major ills.

These arguments were by no means confined to the UK, even if they found particular purchase there for the reasons earlier identified. They were in fact most clearly developed in some ways in the Soviet Union, for many decades a source of inspiration for much of the left. Here, building on earlier antisemitic mobilizations by the regime, anti-Zionism assumed a particularly virulent form, especially after the Holocaust.[20] Having already massively downplayed the numbers of Jewish victims at the time,[21] it now suppressed all efforts to memorialize specifically Jewish suffering.[22] The Stalinist regime now went further, casting Jews as enemies of the people on the superficially contradictory grounds that they were Zionists and cosmopolitans, a charge made first against the Jewish Anti-Fascist Committee and then extended throughout the Soviet Union and the entire Communist bloc.[23] What connected both charges was that Jews were seen as disloyal, a nation (again) within a nation, owing loyalty not to the Soviet state but to each other, and (as Israel rejected Soviet advances) a key part of the ongoing Western conspiracy to destroy the supposedly socialist motherland. Posing as the defender of anticolonial movements struggling against Western domination, the Soviet Union simultaneously cast Israel as the enemy of progress beyond the Soviet Union itself.

This is of more than historic interest. Even though the Soviet Union no longer exists, and even if many on the left today would probably claim (if pressed) to have no particular liking for the Soviet model or regret at its passing, the arguments developed then and disseminated globally over quite a long time remain alive and well.[24] Very little has been added by contemporary anti-Zionists to this repertoire. Israel and the large majority of Jews worldwide who support its continued existence remain cast as the enemies of progress. The construction of Israel as the enemy of progress is the prime form taken by the "Jewish question" today. Jews have supposedly once again failed to live up to conditions of the emancipation offer, so egregiously that they have themselves apparently not learned the lessons of the Holocaust.

The Debate over Antisemitism and the Holocaust

This way of thinking about Jews and the Holocaust was bound sooner or later to cause a major crisis, because it struck at the very heart of what so many Jews feel about their Jewish identity after what remains (to date) the most radical genocidal project in history. This is not to say that Jewish identity is solely to be constructed in relation to the Holocaust. It can be argued that this is too negative a way of imagining identity. Nevertheless, the shadow of the Holocaust hangs heavily over the vast majority of Jews, and this shadow is not likely to disappear for a very long time, if ever. The Nazis, after all, sought not just to expel Jews from a given area (Germany or Europe) or to kill them within that limited space but to annihilate them entirely, to remove them from the world. This fundamentally changed the conditions of existence for Jews everywhere. It gave them an acute sense of vulnerability that even they had never had, despite their experience of waves of antisemitism in its many different forms over a very long span of time. That sense led to a radical political shift within the many different communities that make up the Jewish people and gave birth to the recognition by an overwhelming majority of Jews (left or right, secular or religious) that a state of their own was now an urgent necessity. To accuse Jews of not having learned the lessons of the Holocaust was to turn things entirely on their head.

In the summer of 2018, that crisis duly erupted in a major debate in and around the Labour Party over the meaning of the Holocaust, Holocaust denial, and how to recognize and respond to antisemitism after the event. Over a number of years, the International Holocaust Remembrance Alliance (IHRA), an intergovernmental body founded in 2000 during the Stockholm International Forum on the Holocaust, had endeavored to come up with a definition of antisemitism that could guide all those committed to combating it and preserving Holocaust memory. The IHRA is an alliance of thirty-one countries with a range of International Permanent Partners including UNESCO, the United Nations, the Council of Europe, the European Union Fundamental Rights Agency, the Organization for Security and Co-operation in Europe, and the Conference for Jewish Material Claims against Germany. Eventually, after considerable discussion and debate, the IHRA produced what UNESCO described as the "first ever inter-governmental agreement on a definition of Holocaust denial . . . [to] help researchers, educators and policy-makers identify and combat better antisemitism and manifestations of Holocaust denial."[25] The IHRA's antisemitism definition is used by many governments, and in the UK, it is used not just by the national government but by the Scottish Government, the Welsh Assembly, the Crown Prosecution Service, the National Union of Students, and 124 local authorities, including scores of Labour-held local councils such as Haringey and Greater Manchester.

The definition itself appears in two parts: a paragraph that says antisemitism may be expressed as hatred toward Jews and then a series of examples (eleven in all), which include but "are not limited to these." They include crucially the following:

- Accusing the Jews as a people, or Israel as a state, of inventing or exaggerating the Holocaust.
- Accusing Jewish citizens of being more loyal to Israel, or to the alleged priorities of Jews worldwide, than to the interests of their own nations.
- Denying the Jewish people their right to self-determination, e.g., by claiming that the existence of a state of Israel is a racist endeavour.
- Drawing comparisons of contemporary Israeli policy to that of the Nazis.

At the same time, the document specifically says that "criticism of Israel similar to that levelled against any other country cannot be regarded as anti-Semitic."

Under Corbyn, the Labour Party initially tried to rewrite the Israel-related points and especially wanted to remove the charge that it is antisemitic to argue that a state of Israel (not just the existing state but *any* such state) is per se a racist endeavor. This would have constituted far more than an objection to the policies of any Israeli government at any moment in time; it was an objection to the idea that there could ever be such a state.

To understand this objection and its widespread ramifications, we need to place it precisely within the framework of a "Jewish question." Corbyn and his supporters operate entirely within this frame of reference. They think that Jews do exaggerate the Holocaust and engage in special pleading for malign, self-interested purposes; that Jews place a particularist loyalty to Israel above the interests not just of their own nations (and that the interests of the former necessarily run counter to the interests of the latter) but of humanity itself (conceived of as the world of legitimate nations); that the very idea that there can be a Jewish nation is outdated and reactionary because it rests on ethnic or racist assumptions, which the rest of the world (supposedly) has outgrown (and so Jews are once again clinging to an outdated set of beliefs and customs); and that it is then quite reasonable to compare the Israeli state to the Nazis and to see Zionism as the worst kind of racism, an ideology that has led to the appalling crime of apartheid (now designated as a crime against humanity in international law) and even to genocide.

The latter charge would seem to be a reasonably clear case of Holocaust inversion inasmuch as it effectively turns the victims of genocide into perpetrators.[26] It also strays dangerously close to Holocaust denial in that it projects onto Jews what actually pertains to those who seek to destroy them. This kind of projection is always an essential part of the genocidal process, since perpetrators always justify what they are doing with the mendacious claim that they are acting in self-defense.[27] In the case of the conflict between the Israelis and the Palestinians, in any case, it is clear that if there exists any genocidal intent, it is to be found not on the Israeli side but among some of the most powerful and vociferous supporters of the Palestinians. Hamas and Hizballah (and behind the latter, the Iranian regime) have made no secret of their desire to destroy Israel, to wipe it off the face of the earth, an ambition that is inherently genocidal.

One of the major concerns that the overwhelming majority of Jews in the UK have regarding Corbyn, of course, is that he has so repeatedly associated himself with movements and individuals who (without any effort to hide their antisemitism) have made such genocidal threats.[28] He has steadfastly refused to disassociate himself from them, claiming disingenuously that his only concern is with promoting peace in the region, a particularly hollow claim given their ambitions and his failure ever to meet with anyone on the Israeli side.

This association with overt antisemites of course undermines Corbyn's claim that he and his followers cannot possibly be antisemitic because they are on the left. But the absurdity of this claim needs to be thought about from at least two angles. From one angle, it shows that they have only the most superficial understanding of antisemitism, that for them it only ever appears anymore in Nazi regalia. The complexity of antisemitism—the way it mutates over time, taking different forms, exhibiting both continuities and discontinuities, as each new generation of antisemites reworks old themes and tropes, adds new ones, and recombines these elements within a new framework—is simply beyond them. It should be noted that this reworking was also true for Nazi antisemitism, which is the only kind taken seriously by Corbyn and his supporters. Their spuriously universalist insistence, however, that Nazi antisemitism was only a form of the imperialist racism that affected other victims equally (if not more), as we have seen, deliberately downplays its radically genocidal ambitions with regard to Jews specifically. It also fails to recognize how, in integrating old themes and tropes within a racist framework, Nazi antisemitism was able to mobilize so many religious antisemites in their genocidal project.[29] So, even in terms of understanding the one form of antisemitism they supposedly can recognize, Corbyn and his supporters' comprehension is problematic and deficient.

From another angle, it also involves a significant degree of self-deception, which has serious political consequences. A frequently voiced assertion is that Corbyn and his supporters themselves cannot possibly be antisemitic because they are on the left, a claim that is sometimes rather bizarrely expressed in the claim that Corbyn himself "does not have an antisemitic bone in his body," though where any such bone might be found is something of a mystery. This assertion not only flies in the face of the historical record, which we have only touched on here, but more importantly obscures the way in which, in the contemporary moment, this section of the left repeatedly borrows and recirculates the very same antisemitic ideas, images, and assertions from the very far right that they claim to oppose. In Corbyn's own case (and he is far from alone in this), there have been at least two startling such instances. One occurred when he defended an overtly antisemitic mural in East London, which (in classic far-right fashion) depicted Jews as bloodsucking, hook-nosed bankers controlling the world; another was when he openly deployed a classic British antisemitic trope that Jews not only had no understanding of history but were not really British, even if they had lived here for a long time, because they did not understand English irony.[30]

These are not in any way mere unfortunate accidents or simple errors made by an individual unaware of the provenance of the ideas, images, and assertions on which Corbyn periodically alights. It is not just that this is by no means the first time that borrowing of this kind has happened.[31] There is at stake a much more profound issue: that both the far right and this section of the left, even though they may begin from different premises, share the assumption that there is a Jewish question (that is, a Jewish problem) in the first place.

Conclusion

How widely shared that assumption may be now across the political spectrum is, at the time of this writing, not wholly clear, but it does not seem likely that the Jewish question has returned to haunt British politics alone. Perhaps it is too early to conclude that we are in the throes of witnessing the reemergence of antisemitism as the "cultural code" of our times, as Shulamit Volkov so persuasively argued was the case in Europe in the late nineteenth and early twentieth centuries (although if it is again such a code, it is likely to apply far more widely).[32] But that we can even begin to think of drawing such parallels is surely ominous enough and cause for some serious reflection, which needs to go beyond the consideration of and response to local and conjunctural factors (though, to repeat, these are certainly very important). We need to place this alarming development within a wider context, that of assumptions about Jews that may be shared across the political spectrum and that, even after the Holocaust, cast Jews as the cause of society's most significant ills and discontents, and not just in this one particular British national space.

This returns us to a point made at the beginning of this chapter concerning the left, that Corbyn and his supporters represent only a particular section of the left and that their claim to be *the* radical left should not be taken at face value. Their defective way of responding to antisemitism can and needs to be challenged by recourse to a very different tradition of thinking and responding, which has always existed on the left. That tradition may be traced back, in fact, to Marx himself but also certainly since the Holocaust to those on the left who, precisely in opposition to the wholly inadequate understanding of the Holocaust encountered here, took that catastrophe extremely seriously. Far from seeing Jews as responsible for all the ills of society and far from believing that there was any kind of Jewish question, they thought exactly the opposite.[33]

There never has been a Jewish question at all. What there has been and what there is again, on both the far right and part of the left, is an antisemitism question. Rather than Jews being the problem, antisemitism itself is (as it always has been) the primary indicator of all that is wrong with society. Nowhere was this clearer than in the Holocaust, the moment at which a major attempt was made not only to annihilate the Jewish people but also in the process to refashion humanity itself. Humanity is, after all inherently diverse. The removal of Jews and of this inherent diversity (through the most radical genocide yet attempted) would have changed our understanding of humanity itself. Put simply, humanity would no longer be what it was. The Holocaust was thus an assault, at one and the same time, on Jews and on humanity.

The refusal of Corbyn and his supporters to take the Holocaust seriously therefore reveals something that is, in the end, about even more than their (at best) inability to deal with antisemitism in their own ranks and (at worst) their condoning, collusion, facilitation, and encouragement of the world's "longest hatred." It reveals something profoundly problematic about their politics in a wider sense. For antisemitism is always about more than the Jews, though it is of course always about Jews. It is about our basic respect for and commitment to each other as fellow members of a diverse humanity. Those who attack or cannot defend Jews cannot, at the most fundamental level, be said to have that respect or to have made that commitment. In the end, it is this absence of fundamental human values that gives what has been happening on the left in the UK in the last few years the importance it has, an importance that is of far more than local or conjunctural significance.

Notes

1. For a discussion of alternative approaches on the left to the question of antisemitism, see Robert Fine and Philip Spencer, *Antisemitism and the Left: On the Return of the Jewish Question* (Manchester: Manchester University Press, 2017).

2. Greg Heffer, "Hundreds of Anti-Semitism Protesters Gather to Tell Jeremy Corbyn 'Enough Is Enough,'" Sky News, March 26, 2018, https://news.sky.com/story/hundreds-of-anti-semitism-protesters-gather-to-tell-jeremy-corbyn-enough-is-enough-11305208.

3. For a comprehensive survey of the history and distinguishing features of British antisemitism (which persisted through centuries in which there were no Jews at all in the UK), see Anthony Julius, *Trials of the Diaspora* (Oxford: Oxford University Press, 2010). Julius focuses on England, but the form of antisemitism he diagnoses was shared across the UK.

4. John Johnston, "Read the FULL Resignation Statements as Labour MPs Quit to Form 'The Independent Group,'" PoliticsHome, February 18, 2019, https://www.politicshome.com/news/uk/political-parties/labour-party/news/101916/read-full-resignation-statements-labour-mps-quit.

5. Daniel Sugarman, "The BBC Panorama Programme on Antisemitism Showed Us What Real Labour Heroes Look Like," *Jewish Chronicle*, July 11, 2019, https://www.thejc.com/comment/opinion/the-bbc-panorama-programme-on-antisemitism-showed-us-what-real-labour-heroes-look-like-1.486375.

6. "Investigation Opened into the Labour Party Following Complaints about Antisemitism," Equality and Human Rights Commission, May 28, 2019, https://www.equalityhumanrights.com/en/our-work/news/investigation-opened-labour-party-following-complaints-about-antisemitism.

7. The whole report can be found here: William Macpherson, *The Stephen Lawrence Inquiry*, February 1999, https://assets.publishing.service.gov.uk/government/uploads/system/uploads/attachment_data/file/277111/4262.pdf.

8. The most compelling explanation along these lines can be found in Dave Rich, *The Left's Jewish Problem: Jeremy Corbyn, Israel and Antisemitism* (London: Biteback, 2016). My argument here should not be read as an alternative but as a complement to Rich's carefully argued and well-documented analysis.

9. From their different perspectives, both Jean-Paul Sartre (in his *Antisemite and Jew*) and Theodor W. Adorno and Max Horkheimer (in the last chapter of their *Dialectic of Enlightenment*) pointed to the importance of this factor.

10. The suffix *-ite* always denotes something pejorative, as in the case of those identified in an earlier period as "Trotskyite" when those so labeled always called themselves Trotskyist.

11. I leave aside for the moment the debate recently triggered by moves in Israel to foreground this. It is not easy to understand why this assertion, per se, is such a problem. As a haven for Jews in a world of nation-states, Israel has always been a Jewish state. The issue is

not so much whether or not it is a Jewish state as it is what rights non-Jews should or can have within a Jewish state.

12. This wholly disingenuous argument has been thoroughly discredited by David Hirsh in his *Contemporary Left Antisemitism* (London: Routledge, 2018). Hirsh calls this the "Livingstone formulation" because it was so repeatedly advocated by the former Labour mayor of London, who was eventually revealed to be an overt antisemite when he claimed that Hitler and the Zionists were in fundamental agreement.

13. One can find this argument for the US in Karen Brodkin, *How Jews Became White Folks and What That Says about Race in America* (New Brunswick, NJ: Rutgers University Press, 1998). A devastating critique of this argument, which, among other things, exposes the racism that underpins it, can be found in Balázs Berkovits, "Critical Whiteness Studies and the 'Jewish Problem,'" *Zeitschrift für kritische Sozialtheorie und Philosophie* 5, no. 1 (2018): 86–102.

14. This was one of the more shocking claims made by the Labour activist Jacqui Walker, for which she was (eventually and after endless and still-ongoing protests) expelled from the Labour Party, as one of the remarkably few antisemites against whom some disciplinary action has been taken. See Jessica Elgot, "Labour Expels Jackie Walker for Leaked Antisemitism Remarks," *Guardian*, March 27, 2019, https://www.theguardian.com/politics/2019/mar/27/labour-expels-jackie-walker-for-leaked-antisemitism-comments.

15. This argument was most famously made by Aimé Césaire when he claimed that Europeans "tolerated Nazism before it was inflicted upon them, that they absolved it, shut their eyes to it, legitimised it, because, until then, it had been applied only to non-European peoples." Aimé Césaire, *Discourse on Colonialism* (New York: Monthly Review, 2000), 36.

16. For a detailed analysis of this way of thinking about Jews on the left, see Fine and Spencer, *Antisemitism and the Left*.

17. When in 1789 Clermont-Tonnerre argued that Jews should be given full civil and political rights, he insisted that "we must refuse everything to the Jews as a nation and accord everything to Jews as individuals. . . . It is repugnant to have in the state an association of non-citizens and a nation within the nation." Cited in Lynn Hunt, *Inventing Human Rights: A History* (New York: W. W. Norton, 2008), 158.

18. In 1923, one of the leaders of the German Communist Party encouraged Nazi students "to crush the Jewish capitalists, and hang them from the lamp posts," and then go on to hang other capitalists too. Cited in Davis William Daycock, "The KPD and the NSDAP: A Study of the Relationship between Political Extremes in Weimar Germany, 1923–1933" (PhD diss., London School of Economics, 1980).

19. This formulation is often attributed to August Bebel, the leader of the German Social Democratic party for many years, but the term actually originated not with him but with an Austrian liberal, Ferdinand Kronawetter. See Jack Jacobs, *On Socialists and 'the Jewish Question' after Marx* (New York: New York University Press, 1992), chap. 2, "Eduard Bernstein: After All. A German Jew." Bebel was himself not entirely happy with the use of the term *socialism* in this context. See his interview with Hermann Bahr in 1894, a translation of which may be found here: http://libcom.org/library/anti-semitism-international-interview-hermann-bahr-interviews-august-bebel.

20. Antisemitism had also been a feature of the Moscow trials of the late 1930s, where it formed a crucial subtext, and even before, in the context of actions taken against Trotsky in the 1920s. See Vadim Rogovin, *1937: Stalin's Year of Terror* (Sheffield: Mehring, 1998), 154. On the antisemitic aspect of the campaign against Trotsky in the 1920s, see Bernard Wasserstein, *On the Eve: The Jews of Europe before the Second World War* (New York: Simon and Schuster, 2012), 64.

21. The Soviet authorities maintained a systematic and sustained silence about what the Nazis were doing to the Jews. For example, the first report that fifty-two thousand Jews had been murdered at Babi Yar was revised down to a figure of one thousand. Arno Lustiger, *Stalin and the Jews: The Red Book—the Tragedy of the Jewish Anti-Fascist Committee and the Soviet Jews* (New York: Enigma, 2003), 106.

22. The Soviet Extraordinary State Commission to Investigate German-Fascist Crimes was given specific instructions to avoid stating that the victims of massacres had been Jews. The major documentary account by Ilya Ehrenburg and Vassily Grossman, *The Black Book: The Nazi Crime against the Jewish People*, was withdrawn in late 1947 from publication on the grounds that it contained "grave political errors," and all copies were destroyed along with the typeset. See Zvi Gitelman, "Politics and the Historiography of the Holocaust in the Soviet Union," in *Bitter Legacy: Confronting the Holocaust in the USSR*, ed. Zvi Gitelman (Bloomington: Indiana University Press, 1997), 19.

23. See Joshua Rubenstein and Vladimir P. Naumov, *Stalin's Secret Pogrom: The Postwar Inquisition of the Jewish Anti-Fascist Committee* (New Haven, CT: Yale University Press, 2001). The most explicit use of this charge in the show trials in eastern Europe was made in the Slansky trial in Czechoslovakia, the largest of all, where of the fourteen defendants singled out, eleven were Jews. See Tomas Snigeon, *Vanished History: The Holocaust in Czech and Slovak Political Culture* (Oxford: Berghahn, 2014), 61.

24. This is not the case, however, for two of Corbyn's closest advisers, Seamus Milne and Andrew Murray (the latter having played a key role in the Stop the War Campaign). Both still assert that the demise of the Soviet Union was a major setback for the left. This is not entirely surprising, as they were both longtime members of tiny and extremely sectarian communist grouplets and joined the Labour Party only when Corbyn became leader. That they are so close to Corbyn and so influential has been cited as one of the reasons for many MPs being so unhappy with his leadership (and not just over this question).

25. UNESCO Media Services, "First Intergovernmental Agreement on a Definition of Holocaust Denial Adopted," unesco.org, December 13, 2013, http://www.unesco.org/new/en/media-services/single-view/news/first_intergovernmental_agreement_on_a_definition_of_holocau/.

26. Alvin Rosenfeld, *The End of the Holocaust* (Bloomington: Indiana University Press, 2011); Georges Bensoussan, *L'Histoire Confisquée de la Destruction des Juifs d'Europe* (Paris: PUF, 2016).

27. For a fuller discussion of the question of denial, and especially its effects on survivors, see Philip Spencer, "Genocide Scholars and Legislating to Outlaw the Denial of Genocide," *Genocide Prevention Now*, no. 12 (2012).

28. These include, to give only one example, Raeed Salah, a pro-Palestinian activist who has zealously promoted the blood libel but was enthusiastically invited to tea in Parliament by Corbyn. For a list of several of these associations, see James Bloodworth, "Why Is No One Asking about Jeremy Corbyn's Worrying Connections?," *Guardian*, August 13, 2015, https://www.theguardian.com/commentisfree/2015/aug/13/jeremy-corbyn-labour-leadership-foreign-policy-antisemitism.

29. As Uriel Tal has carefully explained, Nazism both drew on Christian antisemitism in various ways and (as a pseudoreligion itself) attacked Christianity as a Jewish product while also drawing on pagan roots for both purposes. See "Religious and Anti-religious Roots of Modern Anti-Semitism," in *Religion, Politics and Ideology in the Third Reich* (London: Routledge, 2004).

30. Heather Stewart, "Corbyn in Antisemitism Row after Backing Artist behind 'Offensive' Mural," *Guardian*, March 23, 2018, https://www.theguardian.com/politics/2018/mar/23

/corbyn-criticised-after-backing-artist-behind-antisemitic-mural; David Hirsh, "Corbyn to Zionists: Even if You've Lived Here All Your Life, You Don't Get the English," *Times of Israel*, August 23, 2018, https://blogs.timesofisrael.com/corbyn-to-zionists-even-if-you-lived-here-all-your-life-you-dont-get-the-english/.

31. On the overlap, for example, between communist and Nazi propaganda in the early 1930s, see Timothy J. Brown, *Weimar Radicals* (New York: Berghahn Books, 2009).
One of the most telling examples Brown provides from this period is of communists producing leaflets, clearly drawing on Nazi propaganda, which depicted Hitler himself as in league with Jewish capitalists.

32. Volkov herself has suggested that we might well need to think this is the case. See her "Readjusting Cultural Codes: Reflections on Anti-Semitism and Anti-Zionism," *Journal of Israeli History* 25, no.1 (2009): 51–62. Her original argument can be found in Shulamit Volkov, "Antisemitism as a Cultural Code: Reflections on the History and Historiography of Anti-Semitism," in "Imperial Germany," *Leo Baeck Institute Yearbook* 23, no. 1 (1978): 25–46.

33. For a whole range of thinkers on the left, from Marx onward, who embody this tradition, see Fine and Spencer, *Antisemitism and the Left*.

PHILIP SPENCER is Emeritus Professor of Holocaust and Genocide Studies at Kingston University and Visiting Professor in Politics at Birkbeck College, London, where he is also an associate of the Pears Institute for the Study of Antisemitism. He is author of *Antisemitism and the Left: The Return of the Jewish Question* (Manchester University Press, 2017, with the late Robert Fine), *Genocide since 1945* (Routledge, 2012), *Nationalism—a Critical Introduction* (Sage, 2002, with Howard Wollman), and *Nations and Nationalism* (Edinburgh University Press, 2006, with Howard Wollman).

16

Rethinking the Role of Religion in the Arab-Israeli Conflict and Its Reflection on Arab Antisemitic Discourse

Esther Webman

SPEAKING ON NOVEMBER 16, 2018, AT A MEMORIAL for Nur Baraka, a militant who had died in a confrontation with Israeli forces just few days earlier, Hamas leader Yahya Sinwar invoked several religious symbols: Jerusalem, jihad (holy war), martyrdom, and the Islamic heroic heritage. He did so with the aim of preserving Hamas's national, patriotic image, which had reportedly been damaged by its indirect contacts with Israel. Such contacts were perceived as compromising the martyrs' blood for dollars and fuel and turning the Palestinian issue from a national to a humanitarian issue.[1] Sinwar invoked historic episodes from the Koran to demonstrate continuity between past and present militancy. One episode was the al-Badr battle (624), which ended with the victory of Muhammad's Muslim minority over the infidel Quraysh tribe, yet another warning to Israel that despite its numerical inferiority Hamas would emerge triumphant. Moreover, Sinwar was warning dissenting factions not to hinder Hamas from pursuing its struggle against Israel. The other episode he cited was the destruction of the Temple of the Children of Israel as a punishment for their sins, alluding to the forthcoming punishment of the Jews and encouraging his listeners that the day will come when they will liberate al-Aqsa.[2]

Sinwar's speech is neither exceptional nor unique. It reflects the kind of pseudotheological polemics that gradually developed since the 1920s and that served as a tool of mobilization against Zionism and the Jews. This polemics created a vocabulary and a reservoir of historical precedents to communicate messages, to interpret the present, and to draw encouragement from the historical Islamic heritage. Abundant examples appear in numerous works.[3]

This chapter explores the role of religion in the Arab-Israeli conflict and its reflection in Arab antisemitic discourse. It is a part of an ongoing project exploring references to the Jews in the Arab press, particularly the Palestinian, Egyptian, and Islamist as well as the nationalist press during major landmarks in the conflict's history, from the Arab Wailing Wall riots in 1929 to US president Donald Trump's recognition of Jerusalem as the capital of Israel in December 2017.[4] This qualitative research seeks to establish how and since when Islam has been utilized to exacerbate the Arab-Israeli conflict and Islamize it, how these attempts impacted the emergence of the new Islamic antisemitic discourse, and to what extent these Islamization efforts achieved their goals.

A basic premise of this study is that antisemitism in the Arab and Muslim world is a religious, cultural, social, and political construct of the contemporary era in the wake of the conflict and the rise of Arab nationalism and Islamism. Another premise is that it comprises religious anti-Judaic and Judeophobic themes as well as imported Christian European antisemitic themes. Hence, it is both a continuation of the past and a modern phenomenon, which creates a new authentic brand of antisemitism that can be termed Islamic new antisemitism. There is a great confusion about the terms used to define antisemitism in the Arab and Muslim worlds—anti-Jewishness, Jew hatred, anti-Judaism, Judeophobia, Islamic antisemitism, Muslim antisemitism, Islamist antisemitism, Islamic anti-Zionism, and so on.[5] Using the term *Islamic new antisemitism* refines the understanding of the phenomenon and avoids the pitfall of essentialism in the search for the roots of antisemitism in the Arab world, common in certain works that claim that it is "an inherent part of the Islamic culture."[6] It clearly applies to the old religious-based Judeophobia, which encompasses the denigration of Judaism, defamation of the Jewish character, discrimination against Jews, and efforts at their destruction; and to the new imported Western themes, encompassing perceptions of Jews as an omnipotent, subversive power seeking to control the world, contrary to Islamic culture, which perceives Jews as meek and cowardly.[7] This approach also corresponds with the periodization and characterization suggested by Douglas Pratt "to reflect the historical variants and developments of the relationship between Islam and Judaism": the early Islamic era with its originating paradigms of the

Muslim-Jewish encounter, the medieval period with the application of the historic-legal paradigms or the dhimmi regulations, the modern era with the emerging contemporary-negative paradigms, and recent years, which witness a cautious change of attitudes toward the Jews—the prospective-positive paradigms, based on acceptance and affirmation.[8]

A major contention of this study is that Islam has played a crucial role in the conflict since its very early stages, and it was naturally so because of its centrality in the identity and consciousness of Muslims and non-Muslims alike. Most writers about the conflict acknowledged the role of religion, but they considered it secondary to the role of the secular, nationalist discourse until the 1967 war, claiming that the conflict underwent an Islamization process with the surge of political Islam in the aftermath of this war.[9] However, it seems that from the very beginning of the conflict Islam was utilized to fan the conflict and mobilize domestic, Arab, and Muslim support for the Palestinian cause. As Ralph Coury, who examined Malay Muslim and non-Muslim national identity, contended, Islam often served to articulate the nationalism of groups "in contexts of confessional and national-ethnic conflict."[10] Moreover, as Jonathan Gribetz showed in his study of Muslim-Jewish relations in the late years of the Ottoman Empire, "the intellectuals of this period often thought of one another and interpreted one another's actions in terms of two central categories: religion and race."[11] Religion was central to the empire's relationship with its diverse populations and continued to be central during the Mandate period. As Palestinian scholar Musa Budeiri further elaborated, "the overt articulation of goals and policies was expressed in terms of Islam. Indeed, it could not be otherwise. No other ideological idiom would have been familiar or comprehensible to the rural inhabitants of the country, who constituted a majority and to whom the idea of nation and national interest was totally alien."[12] Furthermore, Islam is perceived as faith (*din*) and state (*dawla*), and even the modern concept of nationalism that emerged in the Arab world in the last quarter of the nineteenth century was infused with religion. The rise of Islamist movements exacerbated the attempts to Islamize the conflict and reinforced themes that already existed.

Another contention of this study is that the involvement of religion in the conflict had a decisive impact on the rise of antisemitism in Arab and Muslim societies and on its character. Since the Islamization of the conflict was seen by scholars as derived mainly from the surge of Islamist movements, they also assumed that the state-sponsored antisemitism of the 1950s and 1960s was inculcated from above, whereas Islamist antisemitism emerged from below, and as such it appears to be more deeply rooted than simple manipulation by a state.[13] But it seems that Islamist antisemitism was also inculcated from above with the efforts of the Palestinian leadership to conceptualize the conflict in religious terms from the 1920s onward. Both nationalist and Islamist discourses on the Jews drew anti-Jewish themes from Islamic sources, albeit from different standpoints and in different degrees. Islamist ideology combined the historical religious aspects of its perception of the conflict with national and social aspects including imported Western themes in its Judeophobic discourse, and nationalist discourse combined religious themes with its secular, national and territorial arguments, also infused with Western antisemitic tropes.[14]

This chapter is composed of two major parts that highlight the role of religion as a rallying force for action on the one hand and for the creation of discourse on the other hand. Accordingly, the first part deals with the patterns of the mobilization efforts since the early stages of the conflict to rally support for the Palestinian cause, and the second focuses on the conceptualization of the conflict in Judeophobic terms. The chapter does not discuss the Western antisemitic themes seamlessly incorporated in the new Islamic antisemitism, but it would claim that nevertheless they are much more pervasive in the Arab discourse than the Islamic ones despite the constant efforts of Islamization.[15]

Patterns of Mobilization

From 1918 on, conceded specialist in modern Islamic thought Suha Taji-Farouki, "the leadership of the Palestinian nationalist movement drew on Islamic arguments and sentiment in mobilizing popular support around specific threats in the struggle against the Jewish National Home and the British Mandate."[16] The Wailing Wall crisis of 1929, considered by Israeli historian Hillel Cohen as the "year zero of the Jewish-Arab conflict,"[17] was indeed the first important case of the use of Islam by the Palestinian leadership at the time, and as American scholar Nels Johnson contended, "it was the result of several years' campaign to make the world, and Palestinians, aware of a threat to the Muslim Holy Places."[18] The Wailing Wall is the most sacred site in Judaism, but it is also the Western boundary of the Haram al-Sharif, the Muslim sacred precinct that includes the al-Aqsa Mosque and the Dome of the Rock.[19] It is also where the Prophet tied the *Buraq*, the animal on which he rode during the Night of Ascension to Heaven (*Mi'raj*). The incidents began on a holy day—the Day of Atonement, September

24, 1928, when Jewish worshippers at the Wall set up screens to partition men from women. The Arabs considered the screens to be an abrogation of the status quo, and after they complained to the British authorities, the screens were removed. The Supreme Muslim Council aggravated the tension by harassing Jewish worshippers and by an active campaign to raise Palestinian consciousness of the perceived danger that Jews posed to the al-Aqsa Mosque. Since its establishment in 1922, the Supreme Muslim Council challenged the Jews' right of access to the Wall with ritual paraphernalia (screens, benches, and so forth), arguing that "the Wall was part of a *waqf* endowment and therefore Muslim property."[20] The riots reached their peak in summer 1929 and spread to other locations, including Hebron and Jaffa.[21] The council turned sanctified places into political symbols and infused politics into religious festivals during these events and the 1936–39 Arab revolt.[22]

In October 1928, the Committee for the Defense of Al-Buraq Al-Sharif (the mosque at the south end of the Western Wall), set up and inspired by the Grand Mufti Hajj Amin al-Husayni, issued a declaration addressed to all Muslims, stressing that it was incumbent on all Muslims to confront the aggression against their holy places "and make their 400 million voices a single voice, raised in defense of Al-Buraq Al-Sharif, which is part of the blessed Mosque of Al-Aqsa."[23] In a somewhat different interpretation, Ilan Pappé plays down the importance of Islam in this document, claiming that it was present "in the background and marginal," and it was not the insult to religion that was defended but the social and political rights of Muslim believers.[24] Nevertheless, the events of 1929 had a strong pan-Islamic impact, and Husayni exploited them to raise international Muslim interest in Palestine. In 1931, he convened in Jerusalem an Islamic Congress in defense of Jerusalem, attended by eminent scholars from all over the Muslim world, including the renowned Islamic thinker Muhammad Rashid Rida.[25] Following the lead of this congress, the Organization of the Islamic Conference (OIC), an international organization of over fifty Muslim states, was formed in 1969 after an arson attack by a Christian Australian on August 21 at the al-Aqsa Mosque. Although representing heads of states and not religious scholars, the OIC established a permanent committee on the Jerusalem issue and defined its goals as safeguarding the interests and securing the progress and well-being of their peoples and of all Muslims in the world.[26]

In 1934, with the increase in Jewish immigration due to the persecution of German Jews and the rise in land purchases, Husayni issued a fatwa that forbade the sale of land to Zionists or their agents. He defined the sale of land to Jews as *kufr* (apostasy) and treachery toward God and his Messenger. He also portrayed the Jews as seeking "'the extinction of the light of Islam and the Arabs from the holy land', which had been granted to the Palestinians as a divine trust (*amana*)."[27] Another fatwa reinforcing Husayni's ban on land sales conveying the same urgency was issued in January 1935 at the first conference of Palestinian 'ulama' in Jerusalem.[28] From then on, similar fatwas were repeatedly issued prohibiting the sale of lands, calling for jihad, and forbidding peace or normalization with Israel.[29] In April 1948, al-Azhar scholars issued a declaration on the duty to fight in Palestine and defined the war as jihad,[30] and a year after the 1967 war, the al-Azhar Academy of Islamic Research held a conference whose rulings further consolidated the rejection of the Jewish state in religious terms.[31] The rise of Islamist movements in the wake of the swift Israeli victory in the war and the blow dealt to the dominant pan-Arab political and ideological order gave another impetus to the exploitation of religion and the theologization of the conflict.

Several patterns of mobilization could be traced since the first violent confrontations between Arabs and Jews in the 1920s:

- Organizing demonstrations, processions, and riots, especially on the occasion of religious Muslim and Jewish festivities and in locations with religious significance, such as Jerusalem and Hebron
- Issuing fatwas (religious edicts) banning the sale of lands to Jews, forbidding concession of any part of Palestine, and since the 1980s justifying suicide attacks against Israeli targets
- Calling for jihad and glorifying martyrdom
- Convening conferences for the mobilization of the Muslim world
- Constructing the myth of Palestine as a sacred Muslim land and highlighting the importance of Jerusalem and the al-Aqsa Mosque in Islam
- Spreading rumors and incitement by political and religious leaders

The Palestinians continued to employ these measures in the first intifada in 1987–92, in the second intifada in 2000–4, and in subsequent encounters between the Palestinians and Israel. They were particularly evident in the activities of Hamas and Hizballah.

Both Hamas and Hizballah perceived the Arab-Israeli conflict as the epitome of an inherently irreconcilable struggle between Jews and Muslims, between Judaism and Islam. It was not a national or territorial conflict but a historical, religious, cultural, and existential conflict between truth and falsehood, Hamas's charter maintained. The only way to confront this struggle was through Islam and by means of jihad, until victory or martyrdom.[32] Both movements used what historian Bernard Wasserstein called "the calendar of communal riot" for popular mobilization.[33] This calendar included the following:

- Islamic holidays such as 'Id al-Adha (the feast of sacrifices concluding the hajj), the month of Ramadan, and the 'Ashura, commemorating Imam Husayn's martyrdom, which became a symbol of Shiite oppression and later Shiite activism for Hizballah
- Historic events such as the Battle of Badr
- Landmarks in the Arab-Israeli conflict—the Balfour Declaration, the Six-Day War of 1967, the Land Day of March 30,[34] and the first day of the first intifada[35]
- Memorial Days of the martyrs (*shuhada'*) killed during military operations
- Jerusalem Day, a commemorative holiday fixed on the last Friday of Ramadan by Ayatollah Ruhallah Khomeini in 1980, a year after he seized power in Iran[36]

All these were occasions for demonstrations, processions, riots, and commercial strikes. Throughout the Mandate period, concedes Budeiri, Islam served to shape an ideology of resistance: "The slogans and rallying cries of the anti-occupation movement have shown an increasing tendency since the 1980s to couch themselves in an Islamic mode," he argues, adding that "the practice of holding demonstrations after Friday prayers when people are congregating at mosques, the use of mosques as social support networks, their use as relatively safe havens and to carry out teaching when schools are closed and later as centers for the distribution of food and money, all tended to reinforce the view that political commitment is an extension of religious belief." However, he added, "religion was the medium not the message. . . . It is not that the Palestinians betrayed an early fundamentalist bias or possessed a doctrinal bent, but their struggle against Jewish colonization was perceived in religious terms and this was their only recognizable *Weltanschauung*."[37]

During the first intifada, leaflets conveyed general instructions to the population. They were also a platform for Hamas and the Fatah United National Committee to voice their respective ideologies and political positions.[38] Another tool of indoctrination and mobilization, especially after the 1967 war, was the educational system. The curriculum and the schoolbooks underpinned the perception of the conflict, Israel, and the Jews in religious terms.[39]

While the first intifada witnessed the canonization of civic resistance, the second intifada (al-Aqsa) witnessed the sanctification of suicide acts: "The suicide phenomenon emerged in the heat of a struggle for independence by a society in which Islamic symbols of heroism and sacrifice were inherent national elements," explained expert in Islamic movements Meir Hatina.[40] Palestinian suicide attacks became a religious ritual, and their perpetrators were perceived as martyrs (*shuhada'*).

The second intifada, also known as Al-Aqsa Intifada, broke out at the end of September 2000, after the visit of the then Israeli opposition leader, Ariel Sharon, to the Temple Mount. This intifada brought about an unprecedented wave of incitement and antisemitic manifestations in the Arab world and worldwide, including among Muslim communities in the West. It highlighted the religious dimension of the Arab-Israeli conflict and blurred the lines between the nationalist and Islamist discourses. In view of the importance Muslims attached to al-Aqsa, it was no surprise that this symbolic sacred Islamic site had the capacity to spark off such an aggressive Muslim reaction.

Besides the popular demonstrations and the violence, the intifada brought with it a wave of radicalized anti-Israeli and antisemitic rhetoric. Friday sermons at mosques throughout the Arab world were dominated by angry denunciations of Israeli brutality and calls for jihad, which was presented as a religious duty incumbent on all Muslims. In an interview with CNN, Shaykh Omar 'Abd al-Rahman, the spiritual leader of the Egyptian Islamic militant group al-Jama'a al-Islamiyya, imprisoned in the US for his involvement in the bombing of the New York Trade Center in 1993, said, "Jihad is now a duty for the entire *umma* until Palestine and al-Aqsa mosque are liberated and Jews are either pushed into their graves or back where they came from." Hamas leaders described Jews as "enemies of humanity" and "monsters in the shape of human beings" and reiterated that "Israel is a foreign body, imposed by force and will be eliminated by force."[41]

But these calls to action remained unheeded. The Islamists who generally succeeded in inculcating their perception of the struggle against Israel and the Jews among more moderate and secularist Arab circles failed to mobilize them for an all-out war of jihad. Public anger was mainly vented in demonstrations and a barrage of articles, caricatures, and TV programs invoking the blood libel, Nazi-era terminology and symbols, Holocaust denial, and *The Protocols of the Elders of Zion*. References to the Islamic scriptures were confined to Islamist media outlets and websites, with the depiction of al-Aqsa strangled by the Israeli occupation as one of the few religiously laden themes.

The Temple Mount and Jerusalem remained a major bone of contention and a fertile ground for conflict between the Palestinians and Israeli security forces. In mid-July 2017, disturbances erupted after the assassination of two Israeli police border guards at the exit from the Temple Mount by three Israeli Arabs from Umm al-Fahm. In response, Israeli authorities closed the compound to worshippers to facilitate the investigation of the incident and placed metal detectors at the entrance of the premises. These measures sparked protests and incitement in the Arab and Muslim worlds against what was interpreted as an Israeli attempt to change the status quo at the Temple Mount and as a further step in Israel's efforts to cleanse Palestine of its Palestinian inhabitants, take control of the Mount according to a "grand plan" to destroy the al-Aqsa Mosque, and build the Third Temple.[42]

Shaykh Kamal Khatib, deputy head of the northern branch of the Islamic Movement in Israel, in a televised interview to Al Jazeera TV on July 16, 2017, accused the Israeli government of injecting chemical substances with a long-term impact in the al-Aqsa Mosque to bring about its destruction. An Egyptian professor at al-Azhar, Ahmad Karima, called on the Muslim world to wage an armed jihad against the Jews, whom she described as aggressors, thieves, and slayers of prophets during an interview to the Palestinian Authority's official TV channel on July 20. Imams in Friday sermons, such as Egyptian-born 'Amr Shahin at the Islamic Center of Davis in California, called on July 14 and 21 to "liberate al-Aqsa Mosque from the filth of the Jews" and "turn Jerusalem into a graveyard for the Jews." On July 21, Shaykh Mahmud Harmush of the California-based Islamic Center of Riverside also called for the annihilation of the Jews and accused them of plotting not only to capture and destroy al-Aqsa but also to capture Mecca and Medina. After negotiations with King Abdallah of Jordan (who serves as the guardian of the holy sites in Jerusalem) and al-Aqsa leaders, the metal detectors were removed, and the previous entrance regulations were reinstated.[43] After three weeks of clashes around the Mount and across the West Bank, especially on Fridays, defined as "days of rage," the protests and demonstrations subsided.

Simultaneously, Arab commentators, such as Jihad al-Khazin in *al-Hayat* on July 22 and 28, 2017, denied any Jewish connection to Jerusalem despite Israel's efforts to find archeological proof to support its "lies" throughout its seventy-year history. On July 26, 'Ali Muhsin Hamid posted an article in the Egyptian daily *al-Ahram* titled "Jerusalem Was Never and Will Never Be Jewish." If the Israeli claims of Jewish connection were true, he asserted, the true Jewish inhabitants needed to be of Palestinian origin and not Russians, Indians, Americans, Ethiopians, and so on.

Similar reactions were triggered a few months later by President Trump's recognition of Jerusalem as the capital of Israel on December 6, 2017. In mid-December, Turkey's president, Recep Tayyip Erdogan, who aspires to represent the whole Muslim world, convened an extraordinary summit of the OIC in Istanbul, in which the participants reiterated the significance of Jerusalem for Islam and their support for the Palestinian struggle and resolved to cooperate and take action against Trump's decision. On December 12, Shaykh al-Azhar Ahmad al-Tayyib, the highest religious authority in the Sunni world, convened a council of al-Azhar scholars, which, according to London-based *al-Quds al-'Arabi*, on December 13, rejected Trump's declaration and defined it as "an injustice with no historical or legal foundations." The public protests encompassed most Arab and Muslim capitals, and calls encouraging a third intifada and jihad against Israel were voiced by Muslim preachers in Arab countries and in mosques of Muslim communities worldwide.

Again, it was Jewish history and the so-called Israeli and Zionist "invented myths" that preoccupied Arab writers and commentators, denying any Jewish ties to Palestine in general and to Jerusalem in particular. "There is no such thing as Israel or Tel Aviv," announced Kuwaiti politician Muhammad al-Mulla in an interview with Kuwaiti TV on December 12, adding that "Jerusalem is Arab and Islamic. Jerusalem is the city of Islam.... It will return to the Arab and Islamic nation." Trump adopted "the Zionist narrative," claimed Palestinian columnist 'Umar Hilmi al-Ghul in the Palestinian *al-Hayat al-Jadida* on December 9: "It is not our goal to examine the falsification of history and Trump's ignorance," he wrote. If Trump wants to learn the truth, he should read what Israeli archeologists wrote after "searching for the past 70 years for one archeological remnant proving the [presence] of a third temple [there were only two] or connecting the Jews to Palestine in general." Similarly, Hamas leader Muhammad Nazzal accused the Zionists of falsifying biblical remnants in the Lebanese *al-Akhbar* on December 13, claiming as well that Israeli archeological scholars, such as Israel Finkelstein and David Ussishkin, "failed to provide important proof that the city [Jerusalem] was inhabited [by Jews] in the 10th Century BC."

In this debate there was a tacit agreement among all Palestinian factions, Hamas, the Muslim Brothers in Jordan, and the Palestinian Authority's (PA's) representatives on the perception of Trump's declaration as a new and worse Balfour Declaration. Hamas leader Isma'il Haniyya described Trump's statement as even more dangerous than the Balfour Declaration at a rally on December 14 marking the thirty-year anniversary of the founding of Hamas. Fatah leaders and the PA considered it a "second Balfour Declaration," whereas journalist 'Abdelilah Belqaziz in the United Arab Emirates daily *al-Khalij* of December 18 described it as "the first bitter fruit" of the so-called "Arab Spring" and a severe crime, exceeding "Balfour's crime which is exactly one century old." Trump was even compared to Adolf Hitler. Ahmad Qadidi, a Tunisian politician and former ambassador to Qatar, published an article in the Qatari daily *al-Sharq* on December 14 describing the American move as "a final solution to the Palestinian problem," likening it to Hitler's final solution for the Jewish problem—a move in which he "did not succeed." On the same day, the Palestinian Fatah movement's social media posted in its hashtag "Hands Off Alquds" Trump's picture on top of Hitler's picture, with an English title: "I can't see the difference. Can you?"[44]

The Protocols of the Elders of Zion were also invoked in an article by Yasir 'Abdullah on December 19 in the Palestinian Ma'an News Agency. After describing the document and its goals, he claimed that Jerusalem was in danger and that the US was "a tool for the execution of the Zionist plots throughout the Arab world." Therefore, he suggested counteracting them by drafting the "Protocols of the Elders of Palestine/Arabs" for dealing with Arab weaknesses and inter-Palestinian rifts and enabling them in the next one hundred years "to retrieve the lands and restore Arab pride."[45]

However, there were a few voices, such as former PA minister Ziyad Abu Ziyad and the Saudi prince Turki al-Faysal, who advocated leveraging the declaration for the recognition of East Jerusalem as the capital of the Palestinian state.[46] The head of the Middle East Research Institute in Jedda, 'Abd al-Hamid Hakim, in a televised interview on al-Hurra TV on December 15, also expressed his support for Trump's declaration and recognized Jewish history and links to the city: "We must recognize and understand that Jerusalem is a religious symbol for the Jews. It is sacred [to them] as are Mecca and al-Madina to the Muslims." Hamid added that "the Arab mind must clear itself from the legacies of Nasserism and political Islam, both Sunni and Shi'i, which instilled a culture of hatred [toward] the Jews and denied their historical right to the region."[47]

Conceptualization of the Conflict in Judeophobic Terms

Alongside the mobilization efforts, there were attempts to conceptualize the conflict and justify it in national and religious terms. Aiming basically at undermining Zionist claims over Palestine and delegitimizing the state of Israel, historians, religious scholars, preachers, and journalists became obsessively preoccupied with the Jews, resulting in a vast body of scholarly and popular works on the following subjects:[48]

- Jewish history and its links to Palestine
- The roots of contemporary Jews and their relation to the Children of Israel
- The encounter between Muslims and Jews in the early days of Islam, according to the Koran and Islamic tradition
- The age-old Jewish hostility toward Islam and Muslims
- The alleged misconceptions and falsifications of the Torah by the Jews
- The Torah and the Talmud as the sources of Jewish mentality
- The Jews' inherent evil traits and behavior

According to historian Boris Havel, the Mufti of Jerusalem Hajj Amin Husayni was the first prominent Arab leader and cleric who based his anti-Jewish incitement on the early Islamic texts, but he also allegedly memorized the whole text of *The Protocols of the Elders of Zion* and combined it in his speeches with other political and religious arguments, depending on the audience.[49] Husayni interpreted Zionism as only the most recent of the "supposed age-old Jewish hostility not only to the Palestinians or Arabs as modern national groups but also to the religion of Islam." His lasting accomplishment, according to historian Jeffrey Herf, was "to fuse secular Arab anti-Zionism with the Islamist and thus theologically inspired hatred of the Jews and Judaism."[50] The propaganda he disseminated in Arabic through millions of leaflets and radio programs during World War II from Germany, where he found refuge in November 1941, was replete with Islamic anti-Jewish themes.[51]

This portrayal of the Jews led to the inevitable conclusion, which is part and parcel of the Islamists' ideology, that the conflict between Jews and Muslims is irreconcilable and the destruction of Israel is not only destined according to the Koran but also imperative in order to save humanity and civilization.[52] Jews were depicted as meek, cowardly, and doomed to misery and humiliation, on the one hand,[53] and as warmongers and traitors who betrayed their prophets and even killed them on the other hand.[54] They were stubborn, corrupt, and arrogant, as they consider themselves the "Chosen People," looking condescendingly and hatefully at other peoples.[55] They were violators of agreements, bloodsuckers, "descendants of apes and pigs" (based on a number of Koranic verses that state that some Jews were turned into apes and pigs by God, as a punishment for violating the Sabbath), disseminators of corruption on Earth, and "enemies of God and humanity."⁵⁶

The polemics against the Jews and the Children of Israel in the Koran "[serve] as a basis for the negative reconstruction of the Jewish character" and provide "an explanation for the Zionist successes, the offence in Palestine, and the political and economic Jewish domination in other parts of the world," explained Taji-Farouki.⁵⁷ The Jews' characteristics have remained constant since they were described in the Koran. As Israeli scholar S. Abraham asserted, "The Jew is unrepentant in his war against Muhammad, and whether cooperating with infidels against the Prophet's mission, or whether clothed in the rags of a miser engaged in usury, or whether in an Israeli officer's uniform, he has not changed and will not change. He will always be a swindler, a miser, despicable and arrogant, a person who subverts justice, morality and humanity."⁵⁸

During the 1990s, the Islamic media were a central platform for the polemics against the Jews. Hamas's monthly *Filastin al-Muslima*, Hizballah's *al-'Ahd* (replaced by *al-'Ahd al-Intiqad*), Jordanian weekly *al-Sabil*, and defunct Egyptian biweekly *al-Sha'b* dealt excessively with the so-called cultural-religious assault—the alleged endeavor of Jews to destroy religions and moral values. *Filastin al-Muslima* published, for example, a ten-part article entitled "This Is How the Prophet Spoke of the Jews," dwelling on the Jews' hostility to Islam since the time of Muhammad, their evil behavior, the wrath of God directed at them, the punishments inflicted on them, and the danger they pose.⁵⁹ In another series of articles analyzing the encounter of Muhammad with the Jews of Medina, the author Muhsin 'Abd al-Hamid, a Baghdad University professor, repeated the claims that Jews had betrayed him, rejected him, and plotted against him and against the new religion. The Prophet warned in the Koran that the "Jews are the most hostile to the believers," although he was lenient toward them since they were considered the People of the Book.⁶⁰

The Jews "exhibited pride and arrogance, not only because they rejected the new prophet's advances towards them and insisted on retaining their former allegiance," explained expert in Islamic religious thought Ronald Nettler, "but also, it seems, because they did so as an organized community insisting on maintaining their communal integrity. . . . This Jewish pride and arrogance—which in Qur'anic terms means their remaining independently Jewish—is what impelled them to resist the truth of Islam and to continue in the way of their perverted truth. This is, according to Islam, probably the single most outstanding feature of the Jews. This is the characteristic that makes them objectionable in a particularly Jewish way, a trait which, though suppressed by the force of Islamic rule, still retains its treacherous qualities."[61]

Salah al-Khalidi's book *Qur'anic Facts on the Palestinian Case*, published in *Filastin al-Muslima* in seven parts in 1991, drew particular attention and interest.[62] The book focuses on two major issues: proving the Palestinian right to Palestine and dismissing the Jewish right to the same territory, and providing a detailed description of the future of the Jews, who, as Livnat Holtzman and Eliezer Schlossberg summarized in their discussion of the book, "are quickly marching towards their death, destruction, and slaughter."[63] It is a soul-searching attempt to analyze the position of the Arab nation in view of the new crucial phase in its struggle with the Jews. The "Protocols of the Satans of Zion" are featured as the source of all evil and corruption in the world. The author claims that the Arabs are living in an era of "Jewish hegemony" but that this phase is ephemeral and doomed to end, and he prays to live to witness the promised destruction of the Jews by Islam. The book is particularly significant in discussing the Muslim-Jewish polemic because it clearly demonstrates the utilization of religious polemics for political gain.[64] Numerous books and articles reflecting the content and spirit of this book have been published and exhibited at Arab international book fairs.[65]

The Islamist media outlets did not resort only to Islamic sources to portray Jewish evil intention and deeds. In many cases, they combined religious and national arguments or Islamic Judeophobia with imported Western antisemitic tropes. An example of such a combination was a two-part article on Jewish corruption.[66] 'Abd al-Hamid purported to prove that Jews exploited the femininity of women throughout their history as a means to gain dominance and serve their interests. As proof, he cited the case of Queen Esther, who was used as a ploy by her uncle to reach power and get rid of the Jews' enemies. In more modern times, he claimed, the Jews exploited the crucial historical moment of transformation from feudalism to capitalism in order to dominate the industrial movement and then carefully planned how to drive the Christians away from their religion and damage their moral values. Worship of gold substituted the worship of God. New nonreligious social organizations based on man's bestiality were set up. This led to the final separation of religion from society and the complete domination of the Jews over modern civilization. Under the banner of equal rights and progress, Jewish conspiracies, aimed at demolishing man's civility, created the female revolution. The new state of permissibility and feminine challenge to man were manifested in various ways, brought about the dissemination of diseases, and shattered family life in the West. The Jews were behind all the revolutions in order to achieve full political, economic, and social domination. Now the planning centers of international Judaism and the Masonic societies were targeting Muslim women in an attempt to shake the moral values of Muslim society, as they had in the West.

Similar themes were published by the Jordanian Islamic weekly *al-Sabil*. 'Abd al-Mun'im Abu Zanat, a Jordanian Islamist and former member of parliament, wrote in the weekly's regular column Contemplations on the Qur'an a series that focused on "the danger of the Jews," their betrayal of God and his messengers, and their sins and crimes. The Koranic verses were used as a preface by the author for the delegitimization of Israel, "the evil cancerous state." Israel was said to be established by lies on the basis of the distorted Torah and the Talmud, which is tightly woven with threads of hatred. He described the Jews' worship of money and their use of it in plotting their conspiracies against their adversaries and in the shaping of their mental, social, economic, political, and military cohesion. In conclusion, Zanat urged the Arabs to uproot the Jewish-Zionist cancerous state before it exploded in the body of humanity.[67]

Polemics like this, found in scholarly works as well as in newspapers, television channels, and other media outlets, differ from the traditional Islamic polemics, as Holtzman and Schlossberg show in their study:

- It is a one-sided polemic. The author presents his arguments, but they do not receive any serious response and are not debated.
- It is found in the popular print media, whereas in the past it was a formal genre written in the form of chapters of books against various religions.
- It is conducted by politicians, publicists, and representatives of Islamic movements, whereas in the past the debaters were primarily members of the religious establishment, as well as philosophers and intellectuals.
- Contemporary debaters challenge, attack, cite, and quote the Talmud, whereas in the past Muslim polemicists attacked, cited, and quoted the Old Testament scriptures.
- The modern polemic is not exclusively religious but includes antisemitic themes adopted from the Western classical and racist vocabulary.
- Modern religious polemics generally serve political purposes and use holy Muslim scriptures to negate the Other rather than proving the superiority of the Islamic religion.[68]

Moreover, it seems that the modern polemics do not shy from inventing tradition and defying Islamic scriptures. The designation of Palestine as a religious endowment, or waqf, is a modern invention, aimed at preventing any concession of any part of the land in any future agreement with Israel. Similarly, jihad was traditionally perceived as an obligation on Muslims (*fard kifaya*) from which the majority are absolved, but jihad in Palestine turned into a personal duty incumbent on every Muslim (*fard 'ayn*). The denial of Jewish roots also contradicts Islamic scriptures. It gradually developed in response to the establishment of the state of Israel. Early attempts to challenge Zionists' claims to Palestine by Muslim scholars did not deny Jewish historical roots and links to Jerusalem. Rashid Rida opposed Zionism because it threatened to dislodge Muslims and Christians from Palestine and to replace the al-Aqsa Mosque with a new Jewish temple. He developed a strong antipathy toward Zionism that verged on antisemitism, but he could not dismiss revelation. Therefore, he drew unfavorable references from Koranic texts to portray Jews as hypocritical, treacherous, and hostile to Muslims. He also resorted to more contemporary themes, accusing them of responsibility for all subversive movements and ideologies that led to the weakening of the Ottoman Empire, adopting the spirit and the letter of *The Protocols of the Elders of Zion* without explicitly naming them.[69]

Muslim scholars and intellectuals were aware of the discrepancy between the claim that today's Jews are not the descendants of the Children of Israel and the insistence on the inherent negative traits of the Jews, and they addressed it as Rivka Yadlin showed in her study. The way to support the notion of continuity in character and still deny the Jews' ancestral connection to the Bible's Israelites is to explain the continuity in behavioral terms: "One might legitimately view the character of the Jews as a fixed phenomenon since their behavior today fits their description in the Qur'an. Jewish behavior, although its methods and means may change, remains the same in contemporary and ancient history. Continuity, therefore, is not biological but rather ideational and moral."[70]

Conclusion

Preliminary findings of this research show that both the mobilization efforts and the conceptualization of the conflict in religious terms failed despite the intensified exploitation of Islam in the conflict since its very beginnings. During the period between the two world wars, the Arab press was extensively preoccupied with the issue of the Jews, especially in view of the rising antisemitism in Europe and the immigration to Palestine, and exhibited a wide and diversified range of attitudes. Most articles were informative and did not obsessively deal with the inherent corrupted character of the Jews. Although Islamic sources were already used to provide justification for the delegitimization of Zionism and were welded with Western antisemitic tropes, the Islamist discourse acknowledged Jewish history and the Jewish link to the land of Israel—Palestine. An abrupt change in attitude occurred with the establishment of the state of Israel, bringing to the fore a more monolithic discourse, which strives to deny Jewish historical roots in Palestine and challenge the nationhood of the Jews.

In their discussion of the role of religion in interstate or interethnic conflicts worldwide, Hillel Frisch and Shmuel Sandler argue that however infused they are with religious substance, these conflicts remain essentially national or state centered. They claim that "while religion expresses prominent primordial values, the points of contention continue to be territorially centered and the dominant discourse, especially in the international arena, is usually more nationalist or statist than religious and theocratic." Referring to the al-Aqsa intifada, they reinforce the findings of this chapter, showing "that even though religious claims and symbols were important on both sides, they were consistently eclipsed by nationalist or realist discourses, claims, and symbols."[71] Basically, this is true also of the antisemitic discourse. Despite the Judeophobic content in the incitement against Israel, Zionism, and the Jews, the most popular recurring antisemitic themes derive from classical Christian and Western vocabulary, especially conspiracy theories, the blood libel, Nazi imagery, and Holocaust denial, which are not the focus of this chapter. These themes are more prominent in Arab discourse due to their universality, pervasiveness, and persistence. Even the antisemitic nature of many Islamic radical movements, asserted Olivier Roy, "has more to do with a Western and secular anti-Semitism than with the theological anti-Judaism of Islam. . . . Radical Muslims (and many moderate conservatives or even left-wing Arab secularists) quote the Protocols of the Elders of Zion or Holocaust-denial European authors such as Irving and Garaudy more than medieval Muslim theologians."[72]

An unpublished study of radical Islam conducted in the framework of a project on "Religious Actors in Conflict Areas" examined the British Muslim Brotherhood to establish to what extent radical Islam's animosity to Israel derived from classic Islam, an indigenous component, and what had been the role of other, modern and exogenous, components. Using computerized text mining to survey twenty thousand articles on the Muslim

Brotherhood website ikhwanweb.com, the study discovered that Jews and Israel had been associated foremost with the Arab-Israeli conflict (42 percent of the occurrences), followed by modern European antisemitism (33 percent), and classical Islam comes only in third place (less than 25 percent). An indigenous factor—namely, the classical heritage—contributes less than European antisemitism, and that is in the discourse of an Islamist movement. The findings suggest that there is a wide gap, perhaps unconscious, between ideology and practice, and they correlate with the conclusion that the most common antisemitic themes even among Islamists are not necessarily those based on Islamic sources.[73]

Another finding is that there is continuity in the pattern of Islamic mobilization, which started with the first Arab riots of the 1920s—the terms, symbols, and days of action. However, it seems that in the wake of the Arab revolutions of 2011 and the increasing aversion of Arab societies to Islamist ideology and practice (and as a result of regional and global strategic changes), there is a growing trend, albeit slow, of revisiting the attitudes toward and presentation of Israel and the Jews. A perusal of Hamas's mouthpiece *Filastin al-Muslima* in 2011–12 also shows that the obsessive preoccupation with the Jews in the Koran and with the early Muslim encounter with the Jews, which typified the issues of the 1990s, diminished significantly. Moreover, despite the surge of religiosity at various levels of Arab societies, there is a gap between rhetoric and praxis. While the volume of virulence and aggressiveness of the rhetoric against Jews continues unabated, especially in times of crises and confrontations between Israel and the Palestinians, the religiously based mobilization attempts failed to achieve their goals, and the Palestinians found themselves again and again alone in their struggle with Israel.

Notes

1. Due to the grave humanitarian conditions in Gaza, in 2018 Qatar transferred millions of dollars to Hamas to enable it to pay salaries to its employees, with Israeli consent.

2. Ronit Marzen, "To Carefully Listen to Sinwar," *Haaretz*, November 19, 2018. See also "Summary of Events in the Gaza Strip Border," Meir Amit Intelligence and Terrorism Information Center, November 19, 2018, https://www.terrorism-info.org.il/en/summary-events-gaza-strip-border/.

3. See, for example, Livnat Holtzman and Eliezer Schlossberg, "Fundamentals of the Modern Muslim-Jewish Polemic," in *Islamic Attitudes to Israel*, ed. Ephraim Karsh and P. R. Kumaraswamy (London: Routledge, 2008), 13–28; Meir Litvak, "The Islamization of the Palestinian-Israeli Conflict: The Case of Hamas," *Middle Eastern Studies* 34, no. 1 (January 1998): 148–63; Rivka Yadlin, *An Arrogant Oppressive Spirit: Anti-Zionism as Anti-Judaism in*

Egypt (Oxford: Pergamon Press for the Vidal Sassoon International Center for the Study of Antisemitism, 1989), 41–62.

4. The landmarks are the 1929 riots, the period between the two world wars and the 1936–39 Arab revolt, 1948 in the wake of the establishment of the state of Israel, the Tripartite War of 1956, the 1967 war, the first intifada, the second intifada, and the Arab Spring.

5. For a comprehensive discussion of this topic, see Daniel J. Schroeter, "'Islamic Anti-Semitism' in Historical Discourse," AHR Roundtable, *American Historical Review* 123, no. 4 (October 2018): 1172–89.

6. Raphael Israeli, "The New Muslim Anti-Semitism: Exploring Novel Avenues of Hatred," *Jewish Political Studies Review* 17, nos. 3–4 (Fall 2005), http://www.jcpa.org/phas/phas-israeli-f05.htm.

7. See Jonathan Judaken, "Rethinking Anti-Semitism: Introduction," AHR Roundtable, *American Historical Review* 123, no. 4 (October 2018): 1131–32.

8. Douglas Pratt, "Muslim-Jewish Relations: Some Islamic Paradigms," *Islam and Christian-Muslim Relations* 21, no. 1 (January 2010): 11–21.

9. See, for example, Litvak, "Islamization of the Palestinian-Israeli Conflict"; Emmanuel Sivan, "The Islamist Challenge," paper presented at "Facing Tomorrow: The Israeli Presidential Conference, 2008" (Jerusalem, Jewish People Policy Planning Institute, 2008).

10. Ralph M. Coury, "Nationalism and Culture in the Arab and Islamic Worlds: A Critique of Modern Scholarship," in *Islamic Thought in the Twentieth Century*, ed. Suha Taji-Farouki and Basheer M. Nafi (London: I. B. Tauris, 2004), 130.

11. Jonathan Marc Gribetz, *Defining Neighbors: Religion, Race, and the Early Zionist-Arab Encounter* (Princeton, NJ: Princeton University Press, 2014), 3.

12. Musa Budeiri, "The Palestinians: Tensions between Nationalist and Religious Identities," in *Rethinking Nationalism in the Arab Middle East*, ed. James Jankowski and Israel Gershoni (New York: Columbia University Press, 1997), 196.

13. Yehoshafat Harkabi, *Arab Attitudes towards Israel* (Jerusalem: John Wiley and Sons, 1974), 263–70.

14. 'Abd al-Fattah El-Awaisi, "The Conceptual Approach of the Egyptian Muslim Brothers towards the Palestine Question, 1928–1949," *Journal of Islamic Studies* 2, no. 2 (1991): 226, 234–44.

15. For a discussion of this issue, see, for example, Esther Webman, "Arab Antisemitic Discourse: Importation, Internalisation, and Recycling," in *The Medieval Roots of Antisemitism: Continuities and Discontinuities from the Middle Ages to the Present Day*, ed. Jonathan Adams and Cordelia Hess (New York: Routledge, 2018), 161–80; Esther Webman, "From the Damascus Blood Libel to the 'Arab Spring': The Evolution of Arab Antisemitism," *Antisemitism Studies* 1, no. 1 (Spring 2017): 157–206.

16. Suha Taji-Farouki, "Thinking on the Jews," in *Islamic Thought in the Twentieth Century*, ed. Suha Taji-Farouki and Basheer M. Nafi (London: I. B. Tauris, 2004), 321–22.

17. Hillel Cohen, *Year Zero of the Jewish-Arab Conflict* [in Hebrew] (Jerusalem: Keter Books, 2013). See also Maurice Samuel, *What Happened in Palestine: The Events of August, 1929, Their Background and Their Significance* (Boston: Stratford, 1929).

18. Nels Johnson, *Islam and the Politics of Meaning in Palestinian Nationalism* (London: Kegan Paul International, 1982), 24.

19. Hillel Cohen, "The Temple Mount/Al-Aqsa in Zionist and Palestinian National Consciousness: A Comparative View," *Israel Studies Review* 32, no. 1 (Summer 2017): 1–19.

20. Johnson, *Islam and the Politics of Meaning*, 25.

21. For further details, see Y. Porath, *The Palestine Arab National Movement: From Riots to Rebellion*, vol. 2, *1929–1939* (London: Frank Cass, 1977); Cohen, *Year Zero*.

22. M. Kupferschmidt, "Islam on the Defensive: The Supreme Muslim Council's Role in Mandatory Palestine," in *Studies in Islamic Societies: Contributions in Memory of Gabriel Baer*, ed. Gabriel R. Warburg and Gad G. Gilbar (Haifa: Haifa University Press, 1984), 175–206.

23. Johnson, *Islam and the Politics of Meaning*, 28; Kupferschmidt, "Islam on the Defensive," 191–92.

24. Ilan Pappé, "Understanding the Enemy: A Comparative Analysis of Palestinian Islamist and Nationalist Leaflets, 1920s–1980s," in *Muslim-Jewish Encounters: Intellectual Traditions and Modern Politics*, ed. Ronald L. Nettler and Suha Taji-Farouki (Amsterdam: Harwood Academic, 1998), 94.

25. On the 1931 Islamic Congress, see Martin Kramer, *Islam Assembled: The Advent of the Muslim Congresses* (New York: Columbia University Press, 1986), 123–41.

26. Beverly Milton-Edwards, "Political Islam and the Palestinian-Israeli Conflict," in *Islamic Attitudes to Israel*, ed. Ephraim Karsh and P. R. Kumaraswamy (London: Routledge, 2008), 78.

27. Taji-Farouki, "Thinking on the Jews," 322; Kupferschmidt, "Islam on the Defensive," 195.

28. Kupferschmidt, "Islam on the Defensive," 196–97; Jordanian Awqaf Department, *Fatwa of Muslim 'ulama' Prohibiting the Concession of Any Part of Palestine* [in Arabic] (Amman: Dar al-Furqan, 1990), 65–69.

29. For a collection of fatwas from the mid-1930s to 1990, see Jordanian Awqaf Department, *Fatwa of Muslim 'ulama'*.

30. James Jankowski, "Zionism and the Jews in Egyptian Nationalist Opinion, 1920–1939," in *Egypt and Palestine: A Millennium of Association (868–1948)*, ed. Amnon Cohen and Gabriel Baer (Jerusalem: Ben Zvi Institute for the Study of Jewish Communities in the East and St. Martin's Press, 1984), 320; Yitzhak Reiter, *War, Peace and International Relations in Islam: Muslim Scholars on Peace Accords with Israel* (Brighton: Sussex Academic, 2011), 79–80, 175–76; Benny Morris, "1948 as Jihad," in *The Yale Papers: Antisemitism in Comparative Perspective*, ed. Charles Asher Small (New York: ISGAP, 2015), 397–405.

31. D. F. Green, *Arab Theologians on Jews and Israel: Extracts from the Proceedings of the Fourth Conference of the Academy of Islamic Research* (Geneva: Editions de l'Avenir, 1971). For a critical discussion of the impact of this conference, see Schroeter, "'Islamic Anti-Semitism' in Historical Discourse."

32. Muhammad Maqdsi, "Charter of the Islamic Resistance Movement (Hamas) of Palestine," *Journal of Palestine Studies* 22, no. 4 (Summer 1993): 122–34; Andrea Nüsse, "The Ideology of Hamas: Palestinian Islamic Fundamentalist Thought on the Jews, Israel and Islam," in *Studies in Muslim-Jewish Relations*, ed. Ronald L. Nettler (Chur: Harwood Academic, 1993), 97–126; "The Charter Open Letter Addressed by Hizballah to the Downtrodden in Lebanon and in the World," as translated in Augustus Norton, *Amal and the Shi'a Struggle for the Soul of Lebanon* (Austin: University of Texas Press, 1987), 169; Martin Kramer, *The Moral Logic of Hizballah* (Tel Aviv: Dayan Center for Middle Eastern and African Studies, 1987).

33. Bernard Wassertein, "Patterns of Communal Conflict in Palestine," in *Essential Papers on Zionism*, ed. Jehuda Reinharz and Anita Shapira (New York: New York University Press, 1996), 671–88; Kupferschmidt, "Islam on the Defensive."

34. The Land Day of March 30 is a day marking the confrontations between Israeli authorities and striking Israeli Arabs over land expropriation in 1976.

35. December 9, 1987, was the first day of the uprisings in Gaza.

36. Esther Webman, *Anti-Semitic Motifs in the Ideology of Hizballah and Hamas* (Tel Aviv: Project for the Study of Anti-Semitism, 1994).

37. Budeiri, "Palestinians," 201.

38. Shaul Mishal and Reuven Aharoni, *Stones Are Not All: The Intifada and the Leaflets as a Weapon* [in Hebrew] (Tel Aviv: Hakibutz Hameuhad, 1989).

39. See for example, Chelsi Mueller, "The Educational Philosophy and Curriculum of the Palestinian Nationalist Movement: From Arab Palestine to Arab-Islamic Palestine," *Middle Eastern Studies* 48, no. 3 (2012): 345–62; Arnon Groiss, *Israel, Jews and the Conflict in Palestinian Authority Schoolbooks*, Meir Amit Intelligence and Terrorism Information Center, December 18, 2018, https://www.terrorism-info.org.il/app/uploads/2018/12/E_311_18.pdf.

40. Meir Hatina, "The 'Ulama' and the Cult of Death in Palestine," in *Islamic Attitudes to Israel*, ed. Ephraim Karsh and P. R. Kumaraswamy (London: Routledge, 2008), 33.

41. Esther Webman, "Al-Aqsa Intifada and 11 September: Fertile Ground for Arab Antisemitism," in *Antisemitism Worldwide 2001/2*, ed. Dina Porat and Roni Stauber (Tel Aviv: Stephen Roth Institute for the Study of Contemporary Antisemitism and Racism, 2003), 37–59.

42. "Temple Mount Crisis: A Timeline of Israeli-Palestinian Conflict's Latest Chapter," *Haaretz*, July 24, 2017, https://www.haaretz.com/israel-news/temple-mount-crisis-a-timeline-1.5434035.

43. Jordan has been recognized by Israel as the guardian of the holy places in Jerusalem since 1967, after its defeat in the war and retreat from the West Bank.

44. "Violent Incitement against Trump on Fatah Social Media Accounts," MEMRI, Special Dispatch No. 7239, December 19, 2017, https://www.memri.org/reports/violent-incitement-against-trump-fatah-social-media-accounts-comparisons-hitler-execution.

45. Yasir 'Abdullah, "Jerusalem between the Protocols of the Elders of the Arabs and the Liberation Strategies," Ma'an News Agency, December 19, 2017, https://www.maannews.net/Content.aspx?id=933590.

46. "Saudi Prince Turki Al-Faisal in Open Letter to Trump," MEMRI, Special Dispatch No. 7225, December 13, 2017, https://www.memri.org/reports/turki-faisal-open-letter-to-trump.

47. "Saudi Researcher Abdelhameed Hakeem: Jerusalem as Israeli Capital with Palestinian Management of Islamic Holy Places Is a Framework for Peace; Arabs Must Change Anti-Jewish Mentality," MemriTV, Clip No. 6324, December 15, 2017, https://www.memri.org/tv/saudi-researcher-jerusalem-is-capital-of-israel-opportunity-for-peace.

48. See, for example, Sulayman Naji, *Al-Mufsidun fi al-ard aw jara'im al-yahud al-siyasiyya wal-ijtimaʿiyya ʿabr al-ta'rikh* [The downtrodden on Earth or the Jews' political and social crimes through history] (Damascus, 1966); cAbduh al-Rajih, *Al-Shakhsiyya al-isra'iliyya* [The Israeli personality] (Cairo, 1969); Sayyid Qutb, *Ma'rakatuna ma'a al-Yahud* [Our struggle with the Jews] (Cairo: Dar Al-Shuruq, 2001); Muhammad Sayyid Tantawi, *Banu Isra'il fi al-Qur'an wal-sunna* [The Children of Israel in the Qur'an and the Sunna] (Cairo: Zahra' lil-I'lam al-'Arabi, 1986–87).

49. Boris Havel, "Haj Amin al-Husseini: Herald of Religious Anti-Judaism in the Contemporary Islamic World," *Journal of the Middle East and Africa* 5 (2014): 221–43. See also Gilbert Achcar, *The Arabs and the Holocaust: The Arab-Israeli War of Narratives* (London: Saqi, 2010), 128–53; Matthias Küntzel, *Jihad and Jew-Hatred: Islamism, Nazism and the Roots of 9/11* (New York: Telos, 2007), 31–34.

50. Jeffrey Herf, "Netanyahu, Husseini, and the Historians," Middle East Forum, October 22, 2015, http://www.meforum.org/5576/husseini-hitler.

51. Jeffrey Herf, *Nazi Propaganda for the Arab World* (New Haven, CT: Yale University Press, 2009); Küntzel, *Jihad and Jew-Hatred*, 34–43; Matthias Küntzel, "Islamic Antisemitism: Its Genesis, Meaning, and Effects," *Antisemitism Studies* 2, no. 2 (October 2018): 238–47.

52. For a discussion of the inevitable destruction of the Jews, see Esther Webman, "Redeeming Humanity from the Evil of the Jews—Islamist Rationalization of Antisemitism," in *Comprehending and Confronting Antisemitism: A Multi-Faceted Approach*, ed. Armin Lange, Kerstin Mayerhofer, Dina Porat, and Lawrence H. Schiffman (Berlin: DeGruyter, 2019), pp. 165–91.

53. 'Ali Muhammad Hasan, letter to the editor, *al-Risala*, October 15, 1945, 1132.

54. 'Ali Muhammad Hasan, "Qissat bani Isra'il fi al-qur'an al-karim" [The story of the Children of Israel in the venerable Koran], *al-Risala*, November 19, 1945, 1265–66.

55. 'Abd al-Ghaffar al-Jayyar, *Filastin lil-'arab* [Palestine for the Arabs] (Cairo, 1947), 78–80.

56. Litvak, "Islamization of the Israeli-Arab Conflict," 150–52; Webman, *Anti-Semitic Motifs*, 1–16; Menahem Milson, "What Is Arab Antisemitism?," MEMRI, Special Report No. 26, February 27, 2004, https://www.memri.org/reports/what-arab-antisemitism.

57. Suha Taji-Farouki, "A Contemporary Construction of the Jews in the Qur'an: A Review of Muhammad Sayyid Tantawi's *Banu Isra'il fi al-Qur'an wa al-Sunna* and 'Afif 'Abd al-Fattah Tabbara's *al-Yahud fi al-Qur'an*," in *Muslim-Jewish Encounters: Intellectual Tradition and Modern Politics*, ed. Ron Nettler and Suha Taji-Farouki (Oxford: Harwood Academic, 1998), 15.

58. S. Abraham, "The Jew and the Israeli in Modern Arabic Literature," *Jerusalem Quarterly* 2 (Winter 1974): 135.

59. Ibrahim al-'Ali, "This Is How the Prophet Spoke of the Jews: The Early Enmity of the Jews to Islam," *Filastin al-Muslima*, January–October 1996.

60. Muhsin 'Abd al-Hamid, "The Position of Judaism towards Islam and the Muslims," *Filastin al-Muslima*, March–May 1996.

61. Ronald L. Nettler, *Islam and the Minorities. Background to the Arab-Israeli Conflict* (Jerusalem: Israel Academic Committee on the Middle East, 1979), 7.

62. Salah 'Abd al-Fattah al-Khalidi, *Qur'anic Facts on the Palestinian Case* (London: Filastin al-Muslima Publishing House, 1991), *Filastin al-Muslima*, March–October 1995. The book can be accessed on several Arab internet sites.

63. Holtzman and Schlossberg, "Fundamentals of the Polemic," 17.

64. Holtzman and Schlossberg, 16.

65. See for example, Tantawi, *Banu Isra'il fi al-Qur'an wal-sunna*.

66. Muhsin 'Abd al-Hamid, "This Is How the Jews Planned to Spread Corruption in the Muslim World: The Jews and Sexual Permissiveness," *Filastin al-Muslima*, June–July 1995.

67. 'Abd al-Mun'im Abu Zanat, "The Divine Assurances on the Extinction of the So-Called Israel," *al-Sabil*, September 17, 24; October 1, 8, 1996.

68. Holtzman and Schlossberg, "Fundamentals of the Polemic," 14–15.

69. Gribetz, *Defining Neighbors*, 168–69; Sylvia G. Haim, "Islamic Anti-Zionism," *Jewish Quarterly* 31, no. 2 (1984): 49.

70. Yadlin, *Arrogant Oppressive Spirit*, 47.

71. Hillel Frisch and Shmuel Sandler, "Religion, State, and the International System in the Israeli-Palestinian Conflict," *International Political Science Review* 25, no. 1 (2004): 77.

72. Olivier Roy, *Globalised Islam: The Search for a New Ummah* (London: Hurst, 2004), 49.

73. Emmanuel Sivan and Eldad J. Pardo, "GIF Annual Scientific Progress Report: Opinion Mining in Religious Studies" (unpublished manuscript, 2012).

ESTHER WEBMAN is a senior research fellow at the Dayan Center for Middle Eastern Studies at Tel Aviv University and the academic advisor of the Program for the Study of Jews from Arab Lands. Her research is focused on Arab discourse analysis, mainly Arab antisemitism and Arab perceptions of the Holocaust. She has published extensively on these topics and has participated in numerous conferences. Her book *From Empathy to Denial: Arab Responses to the Holocaust*, authored with Meir Litvak, won the Washington Institute for Near East Policy's Gold Book Prize in 2010 and was published in Hebrew in 2015. She is editor of *The Global Impact of a Myth: The Protocols of the Elders of Zion* (2011) and the Arabic version of *Antisemitism: The Generic Hatred*, published in 2017.

17

Can the European Institutions Combat Antisemitism Effectively?

Michael Whine

EUROPEAN INSTITUTIONS HAVE MADE GREAT PROGRESS IN PROTECTING Jewish communities from antisemitism and anti-Jewish terrorism in recent years with agreements that commit them to action and with assisting states to implement the agreements. And yet diverse reports show a worsening situation with antisemitic incidents and Jewish fears rising.

I've written elsewhere about the historical and political processes involved in recognizing the development of contemporary antisemitism and acting to combat it, so I list here only some important highlights in this process before examining the implementation and effectiveness of such action.[1] What has become apparent over the past twenty years, however, is that the declarations and resolutions the institutions have agreed on will exist only as expressions of concern and good intentions and nothing more, unless they are followed by political pressure and practical assistance to implement them.

It is also important at the outset to note that the European Union (EU) assumed responsibility only for the area of justice and home affairs, in which the task of combating antisemitism falls, under the terms of the 2007 Lisbon Treaty, which came into force in 2009. Although the EU legislates at a continental level, the exercise of internal security and justice matters falls to the member states.[2]

Successive reports in recent years by the European institutions (the EU, the European Parliament, the European Commission and its agencies, the Council of Europe and its agencies, and the Organization for Security and

Co-operation Office for Democratic Institutions and Human Rights) have noted that their capacities to analyze and combat racism in general, and antisemitism in particular, have been improving but that they continue to be constrained by several important factors. These include the lack of a legal framework, no agreed-upon definition of contemporary antisemitism that law enforcement agencies could use to investigate and measure the problem, lack of adequate and comparable data, and member states' lack of understanding and expertise to combat the problem. Additionally, the recent economic and migration crises and the electoral successes of right-wing populists in some states have resulted in a refocus of attention by political leaders. These are the issues I explore below.

Recognizing the Issues

Mounting antisemitism in Europe from 2000 forced Jewish bodies to demand that both their governments and the European intergovernmental institutions take action. The first institution to do so was the European Monitoring Centre on Racism and Xenophobia (EUMC), an EU agency established to analyze the rise in racism and xenophobia and the successor to the short-lived EU Commission on Racism and Xenophobia, whose founding chairman had been Jean Kahn, the president of the Conseil Representatif des Institutions Juives de France (CRIF) and of the European Jewish Congress. In its first report, *Manifestations of Antisemitism in the EU 2002–2003*, the EUMC noted that contemporary antisemitism was coming from new and different directions and that a working definition of antisemitism was needed to enable criminal justice agencies and human rights agencies to monitor and record it.[3]

However, the reluctance of the EU to take meaningful action at that stage led American Jewish organizations to seek assistance from the Organization for Security and Co-operation in Europe (OSCE), which in 2003 convened a high-level meeting on antisemitism in Vienna.[4] This meeting did not give the agency any mandate for action, but a second conference was organized in Berlin in 2004 at which participating states undertook to enact specific laws to combat hate crimes, encourage victims to report these crimes, and facilitate training for law enforcement and criminal justice officials.[5] Subsequent conferences in Cordoba, Bucharest, and Astana expanded these agreements to include the publication of official data on antisemitic incidents as well as education on antisemitism and the Holocaust.[6]

Thereafter, the EU began to focus more effectively on combating racism and hate crime; the chronology of these European efforts is briefly examined below. The Lisbon Treaty on European Union, which established the European Community (EC) and which a further ten countries joined after 2004, had required member states to promote legislation against "social exclusion and discrimination" and to ensure "social justice and protection." States applying for membership in the union were now required to transpose into domestic legislation the EU *acquis communautaire* or body of laws and agreements, including those that dealt directly or indirectly with combating antisemitism.[7]

The 1950 European Convention on Human Rights, the 1992 Maastricht Treaty on European Union, the 2000 Charter of Fundamental Rights, and the 2007 Treaty on the Functioning of the EU established the primary laws of the EU, but it is the secondary laws that are of particular relevance in combating antisemitism. In 2008, the EU passed the Framework Decision on combating racism and xenophobia, which required member states to establish a minimum legal level of criminal incitement based on racial and religious grounds, as well as for denial or gross trivialization of genocide, including of the Holocaust.[8] Thereafter, the 2012 Victims Directive established minimum standards on the rights, support, and protection of victims of crime. It did not reference antisemitism specifically, but the protection afforded to Jews was thereby strengthened, as the needs and rights of victims of crime were made the focus of the criminal justice process.[9] EU member states were required to transpose both directives into domestic legislation, and the legal protection against antisemitic crime was further strengthened by two other developments.

First, member states were required to transpose the 2003 Additional Protocol on Cyberhate to the Council of Europe Cybercrime Convention, which required them to adopt criminal laws against racist- and xenophobic-motivated threats and insults and the denial of genocide (including the Holocaust) committed through computer systems.[10]

Second, the case law of the European Court of Human Rights (ECtHR) has upheld relevant judgments by national courts, including one that requires states to "unmask" any racist motive behind hate crime, as well as several landmark judgments on antisemitic incitement and Holocaust denial. Council of Europe states are required to take notice of the court's judgments and to reflect them in their own judicial decisions.[11]

In 2010, the EC disseminated an action plan to all the European institutions for implementing the Stockholm Programme of priorities to advance

Europe's work on freedom, security, and justice by strengthening its mechanisms, including the 2008 Framework Decision. It noted that criminal law "is a relatively novel area of EU action" but that the Lisbon Treaty had set out a clear legal framework and that member states' judicial systems should no longer impede progress in these areas.[12]

In 2013, the European Parliament (EP) adopted a resolution urging states to take action against hate crime and to promote antidiscrimination policies, and in 2014 it adopted a substantial resolution on fundamental rights noting the requirements of the European Convention on Human Rights, ECtHR judgments, and the European Social Charter—the latter laid out human rights and freedoms within the EU and established a supervisory mechanism guaranteeing their respect.[13] It condemned antisemitic violence and other forms of racist violence, which it noted had reached "alarming levels." It furthermore called for coordinated and comprehensive action to combat hate crime, to make hate crime data visible so that progress could be monitored, and for the EC to launch infringement proceedings against those states that had failed to implement the 2008 Framework Decision.

In 2017, the EP adopted another resolution on combating antisemitism, which called, inter alia, for the adoption of the working definition of antisemitism in order to uphold law enforcement and judicial action, the enhancement of Jewish communities' security, assistance for the coordinator on combating antisemitism, the appointment of national coordinators to combat antisemitism, improved data collection, and the establishment of cross-party parliamentary groups to strengthen support across the political spectrum.[14] The December 2018 EU Council Declaration on antisemitism marks the most recent reminder to member states of their obligations and provides a summary of the above EU agreements.[15]

The Parliamentary Assembly of the Council of Europe, a body of parliamentarians appointed by their national legislatures (unlike the EP, whose members are directly elected by constituents in the member states), passed two resolutions on antisemitism: the first in 2007, on combating antisemitism in Europe, and another in 2016, which called for comprehensive legislation against all forms of hate crime, prosecution of public figures who incite antisemitism, improved data collection, improved education, improved security for Jewish communities, and recognition of the role that civil society can play in combating antisemitism.[16] Additionally, the 2000 Stockholm Declaration committed signatory states to commemorate the Holocaust, and in 2016 the Council of Europe human rights commissioner issued a call for member states to remember and commemorate the Holocaust as a human rights imperative.[17] These all strengthened political efforts to institute Holocaust commemoration and counter Holocaust denial.

In 2014, the OSCE Office for Democratic Institutions and Human Rights (ODIHR) held a conference in Berlin to review the progress made in the intervening ten years since the first Berlin conference.[18] The debates there were reflected in the OSCE Ministerial Council declaration, issued in Basel in December 2014 and in the aftermath of terrorist attacks against Jewish institutions in Belgium, France, and Denmark. They expressed concern and called on participating states and ODIHR to improve their responses by exchanging best practices, improving data collection, and increasing collaboration with civil society.[19]

Addressing the Data Gap on Antisemitism

Although the European Union Agency for Fundamental Rights (FRA) had dropped the EUMC working definition of antisemitism some years earlier, it was still necessary to provide one for criminal justice and human rights agencies. European states were still dramatically underrecording antisemitic incidents, and it was apparent that the failure to define the problem of mutating antisemitism and identify the changing directions from which it was emerging had led to an underappreciation of its seriousness by the European institutions.[20] Finally, the International Holocaust Remembrance Alliance (IHRA), the Berlin-headquartered intergovernmental agency devoted to commemorating the Holocaust, which also promotes the Stockholm Declaration on the Holocaust, adopted the working definition in 2016, albeit with reordered examples, alongside its working definition of Holocaust denial.[21] These definitions address, inter alia, the issue of criticism of Israel or Zionism serving as a mask for antisemitism and belittlement of the scale of the Holocaust. The definition was subsequently adopted by the EP, the EC, and an increasing number of member states and their criminal justice agencies.[22]

The FRA, the EUMC successor agency, conducts research on discrimination and racist victimization of minority groups via the European Union Minorities and Discrimination Surveys in combination with other surveys designed to address the gaps in official hate crime reporting. In 2013, the FRA published its first major research report on antisemitism, *Discrimination and Hate Crime against Jews in EU Member States: Experiences and Perceptions of Antisemitism*. The results indicated that Jews perceived antisemitism to be rising, that they were increasingly fearful of being victims, and that they were losing confidence in their police and governments to do anything about it.[23]

Sixty-six percent of the respondents considered antisemitism to be a problem, ahead of other concerns such as general crime levels, immigration, and the state of health services. Forty-six percent were concerned about being verbally insulted or harassed on the street, and 33 percent worried about being physically attacked. In the twelve months preceding the survey, over 20 percent had experienced an incident or incidents involving verbal insult, harassment, or a physical attack because they were Jewish. Almost half of all respondents worried about becoming a victim of antisemitic verbal insult or harassment in the following twelve months. Among the most alarming findings were that 82 percent did not report the most serious incident that they had personally experienced to any authority or organization and that 57 percent did not do so because they believed nothing would change as a result. The survey did show, however, that victims of antisemitism were more likely to report to the Jewish security organizations than to official bodies.[24]

The FRA noted that "the lack of robust and comparable data on the situation of antisemitism in the EU, however, is such that policy actors across the EU can often only base their decisions on patchy evidence which limits their capacity to counter antisemitism effectively."[25] The survey covered seven EU states, which contained 90 percent of the EU Jewish population. At that time, only thirteen of the twenty-eight member states collected official data on antisemitic incidents reported to the police or processed through criminal justice systems. And of those, only Finland, the Netherlands, Sweden, and the UK operated comprehensive data collection mechanisms.

The FRA published a second survey, *Experiences and Perceptions of Antisemitism*, in December 2018, which covered five additional states and which demonstrated a deteriorating situation.[26] Eighty-seven percent of respondents now reported that antisemitism had increased in their country, and 85 percent believed it to be a serious problem. Seventy-three percent believed it to be most problematic on the internet, while the same percentage believed it to be problematic in public spaces. Twenty-eight percent had personally experienced antisemitic harassment at least once in the preceding twelve months, while 37 percent of those carrying or wearing items that identified them as Jewish were subjected to more harassment. Forty-seven percent worried about being subjected to verbal insults or harassment, and

40 percent worried about being attacked. On this occasion, 54 percent positively assessed their national government's efforts to ensure the security needs of the Jewish community, but 70 percent believed that their government failed to combat antisemitism effectively.[27]

The survey report explained that Jews face so much antisemitic abuse that some of the abuse appears trivial; for this reason, 79 percent did not report serious incidents to the police or other organizations, and 48 percent of victims believed nothing would change if they did so. The report additionally noted that the range of perpetrators is widening. Thirty-one percent of victims could not identify the perpetrators, but 30 percent of perpetrators were identified as extremist Muslims, 21 percent as those holding left-wing political views, and 13 percent as those holding far-right political views. Importantly, the report noted that several states still had not transposed the 2008 Framework Decision into domestic law.[28] On this occasion, the FRA director observed that "the findings make for a sobering read. They underscore that antisemitism remains pervasive across the EU—and has, in many ways, become disturbingly normalised."[29]

Coming to Grips with Antisemitism

In 2013, the FRA organized a major EU conference on hate crime in Vilnius, which focused on themes that it believed the European institutions and member states needed to address more effectively. These included gathering evidence on the extent of hate crime, improving the underreporting of hate crime, filling in the gaps in monitoring hate crime, enacting legal instruments to combat hate crime, improving victim support services, instituting effective investigatory and prosecution practices, addressing the discriminatory aspects of hate crime, human rights education and remembrance, capacity-building for law enforcement and criminal justice systems, and addressing the challenges posed by cyberhate.[30] Shortly after, the highest European authority, the Council of the EU, disseminated the conference conclusions together with a request to all parties (member states as well as EC and EU agencies) to increase their efforts to facilitate the exchange of best practices, improve data collection, and fund research into hate crime.[31] In the following years, the EU slowly implemented most of the recommendations.

Notwithstanding the foregoing, it had become apparent that high-level personal interventions were also needed to convey the agencies' decisions to European states and to assist in their implementation. In 2005, the OSCE appointed its first Personal Representative of the Chairman in Office on Combating Antisemitism, whose task would be to observe and report back on participating states' progress in applying decisions made to combat antisemitism. This represented the first effective external scrutiny of the decisions made by the organization.[32]

In 2015, the EC appointed a coordinator for combating antisemitism with a mandate to liaise with Jewish communities and organizations, bring their concerns directly to the EU's leadership, advance EU action on antisemitism, and build coalitions with international, national, and local institutions as well as civil society actors.[33] The work of these appointees has proved vital in drawing the states' attention to their shortcomings and in offering assistance to improve them.

Again, at the wider European level, the 2009 OSCE Ministerial Declaration set in motion a system for measuring antisemitic incidents, training for police and prosecutors, and education on Jews, Jewish history, and the Holocaust.[34] This became particularly relevant for those states still dealing with the legacy of Soviet rule, which were now required to make substantial adjustments to their human rights laws, educational curricula, and law enforcement training. However, financial constraints have meant that the educational materials were not disseminated as widely as intended.

Other OSCE initiatives included continuing programs to train criminal justice agencies to identify, record, and prosecute hate crime, including antisemitic hate crime.[35] In recent years, the series of devastating terrorist attacks against Jewish institutions in Brussels, Paris, and Copenhagen made it obvious that yet more determined action was required. The December 2014 OSCE Basel Ministerial Council Declaration therefore called on participating states to investigate and prosecute acts of violence motivated by antisemitism, promote and facilitate interfaith and intercultural contacts, offer states best practices for countering antisemitism, assist official data collection efforts on antisemitic incidents, and include civil society in this work.[36]

Focused training for police and prosecutors had been instituted by the OSCE in its Training against Hate Crimes for Law Enforcement (TAHCLE) and Prosecutors and Hate Crimes Training (PAHCT) courses, which are designed to raise the standards and knowledge base of European criminal justice agencies' primary responders to hate crime.[37] The OSCE ODIHR also instituted annual expert-level meetings of National Points of Contact on Hate Crimes to promote exchange of best practices among European law enforcement personnel.[38]

In 2016, the OSCE announced the Words into Action project, comprising three components: security, education, and coalition building. The first element in the program offered tools and resources to better equip governments to assist Jewish communities with their security, and it includes a practical security guide drafted by police officers and Jewish community security experts as well as an online platform for reporting anti-Jewish crimes and hate speech.

The OSCE has promoted workshops for police, security services, and Jewish communities using the security guide as a manual. The education element provides guidance on educational syllabus development as well as a set of guidelines produced and published together with UNESCO, whose Holocaust and antidiscrimination education programs have been developed over recent years. The third element, coalition building, aims to foster the formation of networks among individuals and civil society organizations to promote tolerance.[39] In September 2019, the important Words into Action program was given the funding to continue into 2020.

In 2014, the EC launched the EU High Level Group on combating racism, xenophobia, and other forms of intolerance, as well as a subgroup to "take appropriate measures to expedite the reporting of hate crimes by victims and where possible associations supporting them, including measures to build trust in police and other state institutions."[40] The 2013 Vilnius conference had recommended improving the recording and identification process for collecting hate crime data under the guidance of the FRA, and the subgroup was established to advise on improving data comparability and collection processes. In November 2018, the FRA reported that only eleven states reported official data on antisemitic crimes, although it missed at least one, as the UK delivered its report too late for publication.[41]

The FRA and ODIHR routinely commented and continue to regret that approximately half their member states fail to collect data on hate crime, that when they do so it is not disaggregated, and that it may be of reported incidents, prosecutions, or convictions so that any analysis or policy formulation is therefore frustrated by the lack of comparable data. The subgroup includes membership from all the relevant agencies, and although it was due to function only for an initial period of two years to improve coordination and data exchange between them, it remains in operation.

The inability of states to confront the data issue was further compounded by tardy application of the decisions that had been agreed on at the wider level. Unifying legislation and practice built up over centuries by independent nation-states is a slow process. Changes were needed to constitutions as well as national laws, at a time when the states also had other preoccupations. Bringing former Soviet Bloc states into the EU and the wider Council of Europe required substantial legislative and political changes. Democratic governance replaced Communism, which had itself replaced Nazism or fascism, and central and eastern states therefore lacked experience in dealing with the many new challenges. Their criminal justice agencies had to learn to protect populations' human rights rather than the government itself, and a profound catch-up process was therefore required. In western Europe, states faced the disparate challenges of ever-closer political union, slowing global trade and development, adverse reactions to the loss of cultural and political identities, massive inward migration, and the subsequent move to right-wing populism to address voters' concerns and expectations.

However, spreading best practices has proven useful. Fortunately, several of the agreements advocate this approach and are prepared to fund such projects. Appointing national leaders or commissioners who can span government activities and government-level inquiries to drive European and states' policies forward are demonstrating their value. Finally, the December 2018 European Council Declaration references many of the aforementioned decisions, including the 2008 and 2012 directives, which established European legislation; the work of the EU High Level Group; the EP adoption of the IHRA working definition of antisemitism; the June 2017 EP Resolution; and calls on member states to reinforce the protection of Jewish communities. Importantly, it "invites" them to provide for the financing and implementation of the security measures for the communities and their institutions, participate in ongoing training of law enforcement and criminal justice agencies, and involve civil society expertise, and it tellingly recommends a long-term approach to confronting the problem of antisemitism.[42]

Confronting the Problems

A major hurdle that the European institutions had to confront at the beginning of the twenty-first century was the renewed growth of toxic antisemitism, which was coming from new and different directions. The antisemitism of the church and the extreme right was now augmented by that from the extreme left, from extreme forms of Islam, and indeed from some elements within general populations. Recognizing these new sources and confronting them adequately or honestly has been a difficult process.

It has become apparent from the FRA and ODIHR reports and other surveys not only that antisemitism and antisemitic violence follow tension between Israel and the Palestinians but also that antisemitism in one form or another has become normalized, and there has been a continued and dramatic rise without any stimulus from the Middle East. Before the turn of the twenty-first century, European institutions had been unwilling to accept the inevitable conclusions of their earlier surveys and indeed had sought to hide these conclusions, for any admission that European institutions would blame one section of the community, which itself was also suffering from racism and discrimination, undermined the very purpose and ethos of European postwar institutions. These failures have now been addressed by highlighting the shifting directions from which contemporary antisemitism comes, and FRA annual reports on antisemitism now identify the ideologies of perpetrators.

A second hurdle was the lack of a practical definition of antisemitism that would explain how antisemitism is manifested and why it appears and that would be useful for law enforcement and criminal justice agencies who are charged with investigating and recording hate crime to acceptable and consistent common standards. The definition had to be easily understood by first responders (that is, police officers and prosecutors) rather than be a definition for academics, if it was to be used. It was also important that it be used for guidance rather than as a legal instrument, which would have required changes in each member state's laws. The 2008 Framework Decision had already provided the European basic law, albeit one designed to provide only a common minimum legal standard for all states.

Adopting the working definition therefore became important, but adoption by itself is of no practical benefit unless it is employed at a local level by the criminal justice agencies. Some European states are now exploring how they can follow the UK's lead, where it has been adopted by the police, prosecution services, and judiciary as policy guidance and where central government is keen that all local authorities adopt and use it.[43]

A third hurdle has been the application of European agreements at the national level and reconciling them with well-established national laws. This has required constitutional changes in many states at a time when those states have many other and more pressing priorities.

Abandoning laws that have been enacted for a national context and adopting new supranational laws is not an easy process, but it has been a requirement for accession states to the EU to transpose the common legislation. Again, amending legislation itself is only half the task—this has to be followed by assistance in training police, prosecutors, and the judiciary to accept and use the legislation, which takes time. The overlapping responsibilities of the European institutions has presented another set of barriers to combating antisemitism. It takes time to adopt a common approach and to delineate responsibilities and the allocation of tasks, which is also complicated by the different and overlapping membership of the institutions—the EU numbers twenty-eight member states, the Council of Europe numbers forty-eight states, and the OSCE contains fifty-seven states. Competing projects and responsibilities need to be resolved to make it possible to work effectively in concert.

States will respond to a crisis or a serious problem that affects them all (as antisemitism has become), but inevitably and necessarily their attention drifts, loses momentum, and moves on to other matters in due course; concomitantly, agreements may get put aside or ignored after the initial enthusiasm and publicity unless there are mechanisms to maintain focus. Failing to apply decisions and agreements arrived at collectively has therefore been another barrier to combating antisemitism, as it has been to combating all forms of racism. Only by effective and continuing follow-up and by holding states to account can the European institutions effectively combat antisemitism. As far as applying the secondary legislation is concerned, the 2014 EP resolution on fundamental rights in the European Union allowed the EC to launch infringement proceedings against member states that failed to implement the 2008 Framework Decision.

Given its history, longevity, and origins, combating antisemitism has to be reliant on more than narrow, short-term programs. Continuing and focused attention spanning multiple fields of legislation and law enforcement, as well as education about Jews and the Holocaust, the consequences of racism, and the place of Jews in European society, is needed. The uniqueness of antisemitism demands that it be tackled as a separate phenomenon and not just folded into other antiracism programs. European antiracism programs fail to recognize the emergence of left-wing or Islamist antisemitism, yet these are the very areas that increasingly disturb Jews in Europe.[44]

The possibility that the Words into Action program might be absorbed into existing initiatives to combat racism and other forms of hatred threatens a retreat from the advice and experience of police, Jewish security, and education experts who advised on its content. Another valuable exercise has been the Facing Facts and Facing All the Facts projects, funded by the EC and others, which trained civil society and more recently police officers to monitor and record hate crimes (including antisemitism) to criminal justice standards, but these may also terminate when funding ceases.[45]

Conclusions

The European institutions are aware that the agreements they have signed with member states are not being applied (or have not been applied) effectively, and that mechanisms are needed to assist states to transpose them and to improve their performance. Member states and the European institutions believed initially that antisemitism should be fought within the framework of general antiracism programs, but it has now become clear that a focus on the specificities and uniqueness of antisemitism would be more effective. This is not to argue that there is any hierarchy of hate or that antisemitism stands apart from racism, but that its unique characteristics of religious, political, racist, and cultural hatred, as well as its longevity, require a separate focus and programs at the point of delivery.

The barriers to effective action include the data deficit, lack of legislation, and lack of definition, which have masked the growth of antisemitism and the directions from which it was emerging. The EU High Level Group now assists states and their law enforcement agencies in addressing these areas, while the FRA carries out surveys to provide information from the victims.

That many Jews had no faith in their law enforcement agencies' abilities or capacity to protect them shocked the institutions and pushed them to create more effective enforcement mechanisms. It is clear that the European institutions have made strenuous efforts in the right direction, reluctantly and slowly but with increasing confidence and expertise. These efforts have been assisted by recognizing that best practices need to be spread and that civil society expertise needs to be employed, particularly for those states that have demonstrated lack of understanding and capacity.

Ultimately, however, the political will and leadership shown by member states will determine whether the institutions are able to combat antisemitism effectively. In the current European climate, with the growth of antimigrant and right-wing populism in some EU states as well as financial limitations, many states conclude they have more urgent considerations.

Notes

1. Michael Whine, "Combating Antisemitism in Europe," *Israel Journal of Foreign Affairs* 8, no. 1 (2015): 81–94, https://www.tandfonline.com/doi/abs/10.1080/23739770.2014.11446629; Michael Whine, "Can the European Agencies Combat Antisemitism Effectively?," *Israel Journal of Foreign Affairs* 12, no. 1 (2018): 371–81, https://www.tandfonline.com/doi/abs/10.1080/23739770.2017.1424697?journalCode=rifa20.

2. "Treaty of Lisbon amending the Treaty on European Union and the Treaty establishing the European Community," Title 5, *Official Journal of the European Union*, Lisbon, December 13, 2007, https://eur-lex.europa.eu/legal-content/EN/TXT/?uri=celex%3A12007L%2FTXT.

3. European Union Monitoring Centre, *Manifestations of Antisemitism in the EU 2002–2003*, Vienna, 2003, https://fra.europa.eu/en/publication/2010/manifestations-antisemitism-eu-2002-2003.

4. "Anti-Semitism Conference 2003," Organization for Security and Co-operation in Europe, Vienna, June 20, 2003, https://www.osce.org/node/65986.

5. Bulgarian Chairmanship, Chairman-in-Office, "Berlin Declaration," Organization for Security and Co-operation in Europe, April 29, 2004, https://www.osce.org/cio/31432?download=true.

6. Slovenian Chairmanship, Chairman-in-Office, "Cordoba Declaration," Organization for Security and Co-operation in Europe, CIO.GAL/76/Rev.2, June 9, 2005, https://www.osce.org/cio/15548?download=true; Chairman-in-Office, "Bucharest Declaration," Organization for Security and Co-operation in Europe, CIO.GAL/89/07, June 7, 2007, https://www.osce.org/cio/25598?download=true; Chairperson-in-Office, "Astana Declaration," Organization for Security and Co-operation in Europe, CIO.GAL/111/10, June 30, 2010, https://www.osce.org/cio/68972?download=true.

7. Jens-Peter Bonde, ed., *The Lisbon Treaty: The Readable Version*, Foundation for EU Democracy, December 1, 2009, https://www.worldcat.org/title/lisbon-treaty-the-readable-version/oclc/951588221.

8. "Council Framework Decision 2008/913/JHA of 28 November 2008 on Combating Certain Forms and Expressions of Racism and Xenophobia by Means of Criminal Law," *Official Journal of the European Union*, https://eur-lex.europa.eu/legal-content/EN/TXT/HTML/?uri=CELEX:32008F0913&from=EN.

9. "Directive 2012/29/EU of the European Parliament and of the Council of 25 October 2012 Establishing Minimum Standards on the Rights, Support and Protection of Victims of Crime, and Replacing Council Framework Decision 2001/220/JHA," *Official Journal of the European Union*, https://eur-lex.europa.eu/legal-content/EN/TXT/PDF/?uri=CELEX:32012L0029&from=en.

10. "Additional Protocol to the Convention on Cybercrime, Concerning the Criminalization of Acts of a Racist and Xenophobic Nature Committed through Computer Systems," Council of Europe, Strasbourg, September 2003, https://www.coe.int/en/web/conventions/full-list/-/conventions/rms/090000168008160f.

11. "Hate Speech," European Court of Human Rights, Strasbourg, January 2019, https://www.echr.coe.int/Documents/FS_Hate_speech_ENG.pdf.

12. See "Action Plan Implementing the Stockholm Programme," European Commission, COM(2020) 171 final, Brussels, April 20, 2010, https://ec.europa.eu/anti-trafficking/sites/default/files/com_2010_171_action_plan_implementing_stockholm_programme_en_1.pdf, 5.

13. "Strengthening the Fight against Racism, Xenophobia and Hate Crime," European Parliament, Resolution 2013/2543, March 14, 2013, http://www.europarl.europa.eu/sides/getDoc.do?pubRef=-//EP//NONSGML+TA+P7-TA-2013-0090+0+DOC+PDF+V0//EN; "Fundamental Rights in the European Union," European Parliament, Resolution A7-0051/2014, February 27, 2014, http://www.europarl.europa.eu/sides/getDoc.do?pubRef=-//EP//NONSGML+TA+P7-TA-2014-0173+0+DOC+PDF+V0//EN, paras. 59, 60, 61.

14. "Combating Anti-Semitism," European Parliament, 2017/2692(RSP), June 1, 2017, http://www.europarl.europa.eu/doceo/document/TA-8-2017-0243_EN.html?redirect.

15. "Council Declaration on the Fight against Antisemitism and the Development of a Common Security Approach to Better Protect Jewish Communities and Institutions in Europe," Council of the European Union, Brussels, December 6, 2018, http://data.consilium.europa.eu/doc/document/ST-15213-2018-INIT/en/pdf.

16. "Combating Anti-Semitism in Europe," Parliamentary Assembly, Council of Europe, Resolution 1563 (2007), Strasbourg, 2007, http://www.assembly.coe.int/nw/xml/XRef/Xref-DocDetails-EN.asp?FileID=17561&lang=EN; "Renewed Commitment in the Fight against

Antisemitism in Europe," Parliamentary Assembly, Council of Europe, Resolution 2106 (2016), 2016, http://assembly.coe.int/nw/xml/XRef/Xref-XML2HTML-en.asp?fileid=22716.

17. "Stockholm Declaration," International Holocaust Remembrance Alliance, January 2000, https://www.holocaustremembrance.com/stockholm-declaration; "Why Remembering the Holocaust Is a Human Rights Imperative," Human Rights Commissioner, Council of Europe, Strasbourg, 2016, https://www.coe.int/en/web/commissioner/-/why-remembering-the-holocaust-is-a-human-rights-imperative.

18. "10th Anniversary of the OSCE's Berlin Conference on Anti-Semitism," Swiss OSCE Chairmanship conclusions, Berlin, November 12–13, 2014, https://www.osce.org/odihr/126710?download=true.

19. "Declaration on Enhancing Efforts to Combat Anti-Semitism," Ministerial Council, Organization for Security and Co-operation in Europe, MC.DOC/8/14, Basel, 2014, https://www.osce.org/cio/130556?download=true. Moreover, the FRA continued to note the need for a definition in several of its annual reports on antisemitism.

20. See, for example, "Antisemitism: Overview of antisemitic incidents recorded in the European Union 2009–2019," European Union Agency for Fundamental Rights, September 10, 2020, https://fra.europa.eu/en/publication/2020/antisemitism-overview-2009-2019.

21. "Working Definitions and Charters—Policy Guidance from IHRA Experts," International Holocaust Remembrance Alliance, accessed March 12, 2021, https://www.holocaustremembrance.com/working-definitions-and-charters.

22. See Michael Whine, "Applying the Working Definition of Antisemitism," *Justice*, no. 61 (Autumn 2018): 9–16, http://intjewishlawyers.org/justice/no61/#8.

23. See European Union Agency for Fundamental Rights, *Discrimination and Hate Crime against Jews in the EU Member States: Experiences and Perceptions of Antisemitism*, Vienna, 2013, https://fra.europa.eu/en/publication/2013/discrimination-and-hate-crime-against-jews-eu-member-states-experiences-and, pp. 56–58.

24. FRA, *Discrimination and Hate Crime*, 12–13.

25. FRA, 7.

26. European Union Agency for Fundamental Rights, *Experiences and Perceptions of Antisemitism—Second Survey on Discrimination and Hate Crime against Jews in the EU*, Vienna, 2018, https://fra.europa.eu/en/publication/2018/2nd-survey-discrimination-hate-crime-against-jews.

27. FRA, *Experiences and Perceptions of Antisemitism*, 7.

28. FRA, 11–13.

29. FRA, 3.

30. "Combating Hate Crime in the EU," Fundamental Rights Conference 2013, FRA, Vilnius, November 12–13, 2013, https://fra.europa.eu/sites/default/files/frc2013-conclusions_en.pdf.

31. "Council Conclusions on Combating Hate Crime in the European Union," Council of the European Union, Brussels, December 5–6, 2013, https://www.consilium.europa.eu/uedocs/cms_data/docs/pressdata/en/jha/139949.pdf.

32. "OSCE Chair Appoints Three Personal Representatives to Promote Tolerance and Non-discrimination," OSCE, Sofia, December 23, 2004, https://www.osce.org/cio/57094.

33. "Commission Appoints Coordinators on Antisemitism and Anti-Muslim Hatred," Migration and Home Affairs, EC, December 1, 2015, https://ec.europa.eu/home-affairs/what-is-new/news/news/2015/20151201_2_en.

34. "Decision No.9/09: Combating Hate Crimes," Ministerial Council, OSCE, MC.DEC/9/09, Athens, December 2, 2009, https://www.osce.org/cio/40695?download=true.

35. OSCE ODIHR, *Training against Hate Crimes for Law Enforcement*, 2012, https://www.osce.org/odihr/tahcle?download=true.

36. "Declaration on Enhancing Efforts to Combat Anti-Semitism," Twenty-First Meeting of the Ministerial Council, OSCE, MC.DC/8/14, Basel, December 4–5, 2014, https://www.osce.org/mc/158436?download=true.

37. OSCE ODIHR, *Training against Hate Crimes*; OSCE ODIHR, *Prosecutors and Hate Crimes Training*, 2014, https://www.osce.org/odihr/pahct?download=true.

38. See, for example, "Meeting of National Points of Contact on Combating Hate Crime," OSCE ODIHR, June 16–17, 2008, https://www.osce.org/odihr/61541; "National Contact Points on Combating Hate Crime Meet in Warsaw," OSCE ODIHR, November 16, 2010, https://www.osce.org/odihr/74635.

39. OSCE ODIHR, *Words into Action to Address Anti-Semitism*, September 28, 2016, Shttps://www.osce.org/odihr/269756?download=true.

40. "Terms of Reference," Working Party on Improved Reporting and Recording of Hate Crime in the EU, Inaugural Meeting Report, Rome, November 4, 2014, https://fra.europa.eu/sites/default/files/fra_uploads/annes_1_terms_of_reference_wphc_rome.tor.pdf.

41. See "Antisemitism—Overview of Data Available in the European Union 2007–2017," European Union Agency for Fundamental Rights, November 2018, https://fra.europa.eu/en/publication/2018/antisemitism-overview-2007-2017, 16.

42. FRA, "Antisemitism—Overview," 7–10, "Council Declaration on the Fight against Antisemitism."

43. William Eichler, "Councils Urged to Adopt Working Definition of Antisemitism," LocalGov, September 16, 2019, https:///www.localgov.co.uk/Councils-urged-to-adopt-working-definition-of-antisemitism-/48152.

44. For recent studies of left-wing and Muslim antisemitism, see David Hirsh, *Contemporary Left Antisemitism* (London: Routledge, 2017); Dave Rich, *The Left's Jewish Problem: Jeremy Corbyn, Israel and Anti-Semitism*, updated ed. (London: Biteback, 2018); Guenther Jikeli, *European Muslim Antisemitism: Why Young Urban Males Say They Don't Like Jews* (Bloomington: Indiana University Press, 2015).

45. Facing Facts, 2019, https://www.facingfacts.eu/.

MICHAEL WHINE is Government and International Affairs Director at the Community Security Trust, an agency of the UK Jewish Community, for which he has worked since 1986. He is also the UK member of ECRI, a standing commission of the Council of Europe that advises member states on human rights and inspects their compliance with the European Convention on Human Rights. He was recently appointed Senior Consultant to the World Jewish Congress. Additionally, he is a member of the UK Government Hate Crime Independent Advisory Group and the Crown Prosecution Service Hate Crime Scrutiny Panel. He was formerly Lay Advisor to the Counter Terrorism Division of the Crown Prosecution Service.

INDEX

Note: Page numbers in italics refer to illustrations.

'Abd al-Hamid, Muhsin, 356, 357
Abdallah, King of Jordan, 352
'Abd al-Rahman, Omar, 351
'Abdullah, Yasir, 354
Abraham, S., 356
Abrahamer, Roma, 232, 233
Abrahamer, Ryszard, 232, 233
academic anti-Zionism, 75
Action Française movement, 97
Adams, John, 216, 228n12
Additional Protocol on Cyberhate to the Council of Europe Cybercrime Convention (2003), 369
Adelson, Sheldon, 121
Adorno, Theodor W., 75, 278
African Americans: and Black Lives Matter (BLM), 117, 119; and Black nationalism, 151; and "Ferguson to Palestine" slogan/sentiment, 119, 122, 125, 164; and intolerance model of combating discrimination, 200; and white nationalism, 146
Agamben, Giorgio, 90
al-Aqsa Mosque, 344, 347, 348, 349, 351, 352, 359
Al-Awda—the Palestine Right to Return Coalition, 124
al-Azhar Academy of Islamic Research, 349
Al-Buraq Al-Sharif, 348
alt-lite movement, 161–62, 168–70, 177
alt-right movement: about, 160–61; ADL on, 146; attacks on Jews / Jewish interests, 169–70; and Evola, 100; and "Fourteen Words," 169; and freedom of speech, 168; and ideological purity, 175–76, 177; provocateurs of, 166, 176; transgression embraced by, 168–69; transmission of messages by, 173; and Trump, 170–71; and truth in campus politics, 174

AMCHA Initiative, 142
America First philosophy, 137, 146. *See also* nationalism/nationalists
American Israel Public Affairs Committee (AIPAC), 117, 122
American Jewish Committee (AJC), 58, 122
Anglin, Andrew, 172
Annan, Kofi, 53
Anti-Defamation League (ADL): on Al-Awda, 124; on alt-right, 146; on campus antisemitism, 142, 159, 178n2; and circumcision controversy, 290–91; Global 100 survey of, 1, 263n10; on Jewish Voice for Peace, 113, 114, 123; as Jewish Voice for Peace's target, 122, 123; on low rates of antisemitism in the UK, 313; on white supremacists on college campuses, 160; on Yiannopoulos, 169
"antipolonism" in Poland, 244–46, 247n11
Antisemite and Jew (Sartre), 21
Anti-Semitism Awareness Act (AAA), 11, 186, 187–88
Anti-Semitism in America (Dinnerstein), 178n1
"Anti-Semitism in America" (survey), 159
"Anti-Semitism in the UK" (House of Commons Select Committee on Home Affairs), 9
"Antisemitism on the College Campus: Perceptions and Reality" (Saxe, Sasson, Wright, and Hecht), 141–42
"Anti-Zionism, Antisemitism, and the Dynamics of Delegitimization" (2016), ix, x, xi
anti-Zionists / anti-Zionism: academic anti-Zionism, 75; among progressives / political left, 214, 251; antisemitism's relationship with, 145–46, 148; on college/university campuses, 142–43, 147–48,

383

anti-Zionists / anti-Zionism (*Cont.*)
189, 200; of Corbyn and Labour Party, 44, 314, 317, 319, 330–31; and *Death of Klinghoffer*, 216–17; and downplaying of Jewish suffering, 334; and evil Jews tropes, 148; as form of denial by syllogism, 229n28; in France, 214; and intolerance model of combating antisemitism, 200; of Islamism, 252, 355; of Muslim scholars, 359; and Nazi equivalence, 32; and power tropes, 148; predicated on illegitimacy of Zionist enterprise, 44; propaganda of, 25; of public intellectuals, 24; of Swedish government, 253; and Title VI protections, 186; and virtuous antisemitism, 226. *See also* Jewish Voice for Peace

Antonowicz, Gilles, 220–21

apartheid state in Israel, myth of: attempts to associate Israel with, 24, 35, 36; and BDS movement, 47, 48; and campus antisemitism, 163; and definition of antisemitism by IHRA, 14; and HRW's campaigns, 56; and Kairos Palestine document, 64n5; and language used to deny self-determination, 58; and Veracini, 89

"Appointed Circumcision Law" (Schulte von Drach), 301

Arab-Israeli conflict, 344–61; and Arab press, 359–60; and ban on land sales to Zionists, 349; and colonial-settler characterization of Israel, 162; conceptualized in Judeophobic terms, 354–59, 360; and intifada, first (1987–92), 349, 350–51; and intifada, second (2000–4), 349, 350, 360; Islam as medium for, 350; and Islamic new antisemitism, 345–46; and Jerusalem, 345, 348–49, 352–55, 359; landmarks in history of, 345, 362n4; mobilization efforts of Palestinians, 347–54, 361; as perceived by Hamas and Hizballah, 349–50; radicalized rhetoric of, 351; and references to the Jews in Arab press, 345; role of Islam in rise of Arab antisemitism, 346–47; suicide acts in, 351; and tension at Temple Mount, 352; and Trump on Jerusalem as capital of Israel, 345, 353–54; and Wailing Wall crisis (1929), 345, 347–48. *See also* Palestinian conflict

Arab-Israeli War (1967), 85, 89, 350
Arktos Media, 100–101, 102, 103, 105
Asaf, Rose, 176–77
Assad, Bashar al-, 316
assimilation of Jews, 76–77, 333
Association for the Defense against Anti-Semitism, 295
Atzmon, Gilad, 117
Auschwitz death camp, 255, 270
Austrian Freedom Party, 253
authoritarianism, rise of, 2
authoritarian personalities, 278
authority, intellectual/moral, 220

Badawi, Khulood, 59–60, 69n101
Bakan, Abigail, 80–81, 93n15
Balfour Declaration, 330, 350, 353–54
Balliet, Stephan, 268, 285n32
Bannon, Steve, 96, 102, 105, 106, 112n77. *See also* Traditionalism
Baraka, Nur, 344
Barghouti, Omar, 116
Barhoum, Nadia, 56
Barkat, Nir, 168
Basel Ministerial Council Declaration, OSCE, 374
Bashi, Sari, 56, 57
Bauer, Yehuda, 59, 244–45
Baum, Deborah, 225–26
Bayer, Zsolt, 249–50, 263nn3–4
BBC, 321, 327
BDS movement. *See* boycotts, divestment, and sanctions (BDS) movements
Bebel, August, 341n19
Belgium, assaults on Jews in, 1
belief state, antisemitism as, 20–22, 28
Belqaziz, 'Abdelilah, 354
Bennett, Andrew Mark, 115
Berger, Luciana, 37–38
Berkeley Free Speech Movement, 167
Berkovits, Balázs, 75–92
Berlin, Germany, x
Bernstein, Robert, 49, 52
Beyda, Rachel, 143
Bielawski, Szraga Fajwel, 240, 242
bigotry, Israel accused of, 59–60
"Birds of a Feather" (Elia), 63
Birnbaum, George, 256
birthright program, 120–22

blacklist published by UNHRC, 57
Black Lives Matter (BLM), 117, 119
Black nationalism, 151
Blair, Tony, 314–15, 317, 329
Blitt, Robert, 50
Bloc Identitaire movement, 146
blood libel myths/accusations: and antisemitism on the right, 117; and definition of antisemitism by IHRA, 12, 46; as demonizing rhetoric, 193; and Islamists, 351; and Kielce murders, 239; Nazis' reliance on, 30; and Noel's *The Role of Your Children in the World's Economic Recovery*, 225; promoted by Corbyn's associates, 342n28; Puar's allegations of, 174
body, stereotypes of the Jewish, 296–97
Bolton, Kerry, 105
Borns Jewish Studies Program at Indiana University, xii
Botsch, Gideon, 282
Bowers, Robert, 137
boycotts, divestment, and sanctions (BDS) movements: applying IHRA definition to, 47–48, 49; on college/university campuses, 37, 138, 141, 142–43, 147, 148–49, 154, 162; and colonial-settler characterization of Israel, 162; Dweik/Asaf's involvement in, 177; exceptionalism and eliminationism demonstrated by, 26; goals of, 23; HRW as leader in, 55–58; and HRW's use of symbols/images, 61–62; identified as antisemitism in Germany, 48, 58; and Jewish Voice for Peace, 113, 115, 117, 119; and language used to deny self-determination, 59; left's support of, 23, 25; and "one-state solution," 162
Braham, Philippe, 218
Brandeis University, 121, 141, 144, 166
Breitbart News, 96, 106, 169
British National Party, 327
Brodkin, Karen, 76–77
Brody, Reed, 52
Bronfman, Charles, 121
Brown, Gordon, 314
Brown, Michael, 125
Brown University, 148
Bruce, Lenny, 167
Bryk, Felix, 297

Budeiri, Musa, 346, 350
Busbridge, Rachel, 91

Campus Free Speech Protection Act, 203
Camus, Renaud, 275
Casey, Bob, 11
Césaire, Aimé, 341n15
Chabloz, Alison, 34
Chakrabati, Shami, 39
Charlie Hebdo massacre, 218–19, 220
Charlottesville, Virginia, "Unite the Right" rally in, 105, 137, 161, 164–65, 277
Charter of Fundamental Rights (2000), 369
Chemerinsky, Erwin, 188
Cheyette, Bryan, 78, 92
The Child in the Custom of the Tribes (Ploss), 298
child molestation, 219
Christianity/Christians: and BDS activism of Jewish Voice for Peace, 117–18; Dugin's rejection of Western, 104; in Israel, 25; and Jewish ritual circumcision, 292; and Traditionalism, 103
circumcision, ritual, 287–304; anticircumcision activism in Germany, 287–88, 289–90; and anti-Jewish stereotypes, 290; and balance of rights of parents and child, 294; court rulings on, in Germany, 288–89, 291, 293; and "damaged"/"traumatized" victim stereotype, 295–97, 303–4; descriptions of procedure, 297–98; and disease-vulnerability myth, 299–300; and freedom of religion, 292, 293, 294, 298; German attitudes on, 291; and Hungary's Orbán regime, 251; and "law-breaking" stereotype, 291–95, 303; legislation on, in Germany, 301–2; motivations behind objections to, 290–91; and "powerful Jews" / "political pressure" stereotype, 300–302, 303; and psychoanalytic perspective of Freud, 300; and "sexual assault" / "castration" stereotypes, 297–300, 303
"Circumcision and German Law" (Jerouschek), 297
Circumcision in Man and Woman (Bryk), 297
City College of New York, 173

386 | Index

City University of New York, 143, 166–67
Civil Rights Act, Title VI (1964), 185–86, 188–89, 195–97
Civil Service Commission (US), 46
Claims Conference, 45
Clermont-Tonnerre, Stanislas de, 341n17
Clinton, Chelsea, 176–77
Coalition for Combating Antisemitism, 11
Codreanu, Cornelius, 99–100, 101, 108n20
Cohen, Hillel, 347
Cohen, Yohan, 218
Cohen Center for Modern Jewish studies at Brandis University, 121
college and university campuses, 137–54, 158–78, 185–204; Anti-Defamation League on antisemitism on, 142, 159; anti-Zionism on, 142–43, 147–48, 189; and BDS movement, 37, 138, 141, 142–43, 147, 148–49, 154, 162; and campus politics, 173; consequences of antisemitism on, 149–51; "Deadly Exchange" campaign of JVP on, 123; and freedom of speech, 150, 159, 165, 167, 168, 173, 187, 188–89, 203; and *Higher Ground* report by UCI, 153, 154; hostility toward Israel/Jews on, 141–43, 144, 159; HRW's campaigns on, 56; identification of antisemitism on, 143–44, 147–49, 153; and "intersectionality," 149, 164; intolerance model of combating antisemitism on, 197–204, *199*; Jewish students seen as "white"/"privileged," 149, 161, 163, 189; left-wing antisemitism on, 138, 144–45, 146, 150, 162–67; and Nazi equivalence, 35; new antisemitism on, 44; off-campus sources of antisemitism, 145, 149; and "Principles against Intolerance" by UC Regents, 139, 143, 151–52; and reports of overblown antisemitism, 144, 155n12; resolutions condemning antisemitism in, 143; responses of leadership to antisemitism on, 139, 143–44, 150–51; rhetoric spreading on, ix; right-wing antisemitism on, 138, 144–45, 146–47, 149, 160–62; rise in antisemitism on, 138, 158, 159, 185; and scholars who support Israel, 175; and study-abroad programs in Israel, 116; and Title VI protections, 185–86, 188–89, 195–97, 204; white supremacism on, 160, 172

Collier, David, 126
colonialism, accusing Israel of, 14, 24, 48, 58
colonial-settler state, Israel as: and academic field of colonial-settler studies, 78, 81–82, 86–91; and BDS movement, 162; and decolonization goal, 85, 88, 90, 91; and definition of antisemitism by IHRA, 14; distinction between colonialism and settler colonialism, 87–88; failure to demonstrate status of, 90–91; and legitimacy challenges against Israel, 82; and Palestinian conflict, 87, 88–89; and political antisemitism, 24, 25; prevalence of idea, 82; progressive critique of, 162; and violence, 88; and whiteness of Jews, 79; and Zionism, 81–86
Columbia University, 150
Committee for Accuracy in Middle East Reporting in America (CAMERA), 114
Committee for Open Debate on the Holocaust, 173
Committee for the Defense of Al-Buraq Al-Sharif, 348
Committee on the Exercise of the Inalienable Rights of the Palestinian People (CEIRPP), 47
Communications Act 2003, Section 127, 34
Community Security Trust, 33
Compact, 301
conceptual model of antisemitism, 194–95, *195*
conferences addressing antisemitism, ix, x, xi–xii
Conseil Representatif des Institutions Juives de France (CRIF), 368
conservatives. *See* political right / conservatives
conspiracy myths: and antisemitic intent, 30–31; control myth/stereotype, 22, 39, 139–40; and Corbyn and Labour Party, 320–21; and definition of antisemitism by IHRA, 28, 46, 193; Dugin as proponent of, 105; the "great replacement," 275–78; Islamist media on, 357–58; and Mear One's "New World Order" mural, 317–18; and new antisemitism, 44, 140; and purity tests of far right, 175; reappearance in right-wing antisemitism, 146–47; and Traditionalism, 107; and Trump, 170. *See also* blood libel myths/accusations

"Contending with Antisemitism in a Rapidly Changing Political Climate" (2019), x, xi, xii–xiii, xiv, 2–3
control myth/stereotype, 22, 39, 139–40
Conway, David, 39–40
Coordinating Council of Muslims, 302
Corbyn, Jeremy, 313–23; anti-Zionism of, 44, 314, 317, 319; association with antisemitic movements/individuals, 337; background of, 314, 328–29; and conspiracy theories, 320–21; and definition of antisemitism by IHRA, 10, 39; denial of antisemitism, 219, 229n28, 338; election of, 321–22, 325, 326; foreign policy agenda of, 316, 325–26, 328; Griffin's support of, 37; and Hobson's *Imperialism*, 318–19; and Holocaust, 339; on illegitimacy of Western power, 315–16; and Iraq War, 315; and Jewish citizens of Britain, 40; and Mear One's "New World Order" mural, 317–18, 338; on media/press, 321; support for Palestine, 314, 315, 317, 319, 322; and Tree of Life Synagogue shootings in Pittsburgh, 219
Cornell University, 148, 151
Cotler, Irwin, xii, 45
Cotta, Françoise, 220–21
Coughlin, Charles, 146
Coulibaly, Amedy, 217–18
Council of Europe, 46, 367, 369, 370–71, 376, 378
Counter-Currents website, 101
Coury, Ralph, 346
Crenshaw, Kimberlé, 164
Crime and Disorder Act (1998), 33
crimes, underreporting of antisemitic, 373
Criminal Justice Act (2003), 33–34
The Crisis of the Modern World (Guénon), 97
critical whiteness studies, 76–79
Crown Prosecution Service, 32, 33

Daily Stormer, 172
Dann, Naomi, 115
Dartmouth College, 150
data gap on antisemitism, 371–73
Davis v. Monroe County Board of Education, 201
Dayan, Daniel, 211–27
"Deadly Exchange" campaign of JVP, 122–23, 127, 131n44
The Death of Klinghoffer (opera), 216–17

De Benoist, Alain, 102, 103, 109n39
"Deciphering the New Antisemitism" (2014), x, xi
defamation: and definition of antisemitism by IHRA, 49; distinguishing legitimate criticism from, 28; freedom of speech vs., 28–40; and political antisemitism, 27
"Defense-ABC" (Association for the Defense against Anti-Semitism), 295
Defense for Children International–Palestine, 116
defensive antisemitism, 211, 212, 216
The Definition of Anti-Semitism (Marcus), 189–90
definition of antisemitism by IHRA, 9–40, 44–63; adaptations of, 11–12; adoption of, 11, 46, 335–36, 371, 376; alleged defects of, 10; as attempt to silence criticism of Israel, 17–18, 19, 48, 49; background of, 45–47; and BDS movement, 47–48, 49, 55–58; and belief vs. emotions driven antisemitism, 20–22, 28; and campus antisemitism, 159; coherence of, 27; and conceptual model of antisemitism, 194–95, *195*; conceptual shortcomings of, 19–20; and Corbyn's Labour Party, 9–10, 17, 39–40, 319, 336; criticisms of, 48–49, 187–89; definition in full, 186–87; on "dehumanizing, demonizing" content, 192–94, *195*, 196; and EUMC definition, 11; examples offered in, 10, 12, 14, 27, 28, 190, 191, 195; freedom of speech arguments against, 10, 15–18, 187, 188–89; and HRW's double standards applied to Israel, 50–55; and HRW's leadership of BDS movement, 55–58; and HRW's use of symbols/images, 60–62; and Human Rights Watch case study, 49–50; and intention, 9, 15, 30–31, 33, 35, 194, *195*; internal structure and logic of, 190–94; and language used to deny self-determination, 58–60; on "mendacious" argumentation, 192, 194, *195*; objection to definition as legal tool, 10, 13–15; old/new antisemitism represented in, 46; pro-Palestinian advocates' rejection of, 187; rethinking, 189–95; on "stereotypical" themes, 193–94, *195*
dehumanizing and demonizing language, 58, 59, 192–94, *195*, 196, 198
"delegitimating" Israel, 27

De Maistre, Joseph, 97
Democratic Party, 160, 170
denied antisemitism, 211, 212, 216–18
Denying the Holocaust: The Growing Assault on Truth and Memory (Lipstadt), 32
Department of Palestinian Affairs (DPA), 47
Der Flügel (the Wing), 268
Der Stürmer, 29, 30, 31
Dieudonné (comedian), 218
Dinnerstein, Leonard, 178n1
discrimination: Israel accused of, 60; and Title VI protections of Civil Rights Act (1964), 185, 186, 188–89, 196–97
Discrimination and Hate Crime against Jews in EU Member States: Experiences and Perceptions of Antisemitism (2013), 371–72
Dome of the Rock, 347
double standards applied to Israel, 12, 46, 49, 50–55, 192
Dream Defenders, 119
Dugin, Aleksandr, 96, 102–5, 106
Duke, David, 105
Duke University Press, 174
Durban Conference (UN, 2001), xi, 47, 52–53, 56, 58, 59
Dweik, Leen, 176–77

Eastern Europe, 215, 263n10
Edelstein, Juli, ix
Ehrenberg, Yitshak, 288
Elia, Nada, 63
Eliade, Mircea, 99–100, 108n20, 108n23
eliminationism, 22, 26, 198
Elman, Miriam F., 113–28
emancipation of the Jews, 332–33
EMIH (Köves's community), 260–61
emotional disposition, antisemitism as, 20–22, 28, 29, 30
Engelking, Barbara, 236
Epstein, Benjamin R., 178n2
Epstein, Hedy, 125
Equality Act 2010, 16, 34, 35
Equality and Human Rights Commission, 327
Equal Protection Clause of the Fourteenth Amendment, 198–99
equivocal antisemitism, 212, 216, 218–19

Erdogan, Recep Tayyip, 353
Erfurt Resolution (2015), 268, 283n1
esotericism, 98–99
"An Establishment Conservative's Guide to the Alt-Right" (Yiannopoulos), 169
Eurasianist theory, 102–3
European Commission, 367
European Community (EC), 369–70, 371, 374, 375, 378
European Convention on Human Rights (1950): Article 10, 16, 17, 29, 31, 37; establishment of EU's laws, 369; and European Parliament, 370
European Council Declaration (2018), 376
European Court of Human Rights (ECtHR), 16, 36, 369
European Institute for the Study of Contemporary Antisemitism (EISCA), 32
European institutions' fight against antisemitism, 367–79; action taken by institutions, 368–71; addressing data gap on antisemitism, 371–73, 379; constraints on institutions' capacities, 368; and definition of antisemitism, 368, 370, 371, 376, 377, 379; and enforcement considerations, 373, 374, 376, 377, 378, 379; implementation of decisions, 373–76; legislation supporting, 367, 369, 370, 375–76, 377–78, 379; and renewed growth of toxic antisemitism, 376
European Jewish Congress, 368
European Jews, 214–15. *See also specific countries*
European Parliament (EP), 367, 370, 371, 376, 378
European Social Charter, 370
European Union (EU), 367, 369, 378
European Union Agency for Fundamental Rights, 289
European Union Commission on Racism and Xenophobia, 368–71
European Union Council Declaration (2018), 370
European Union High Level Group, 375, 376, 379
European Union Minorities and Discrimination Surveys, 371

European Union Monitoring Centre on Racism and Xenophobia (EUMC), 11, 46, 368, 371
evil, attempts to associate Israel with, 24, 27, 148
Evola, Julius, 96, 98–102, 104, 105, 106
exceptionalism, 22, 26
Experiences and Perceptions of Antisemitism (2018), 372–73
extremist movements, democratic values under threat from, 2

Facebook, 171
Facing Facts / Facing All the Facts projects, 378
Farrakhan, Louis, 123, 165, 180n23, 193
fascism: and AfD of Germany, 279; defined, 106; and Eliade, 100; and Evola, 99, 100; NWSA statement on, 165; in Poland, 232, 242–43; resurgence of, 232; and Traditionalism, 106
Faurisson, Robert, 101
Faysal, Turk al-, 354
Federal Bureau of Investigation (FBI), 1
Fein, Helen, 306n31
Feinstein, Dianne, 172
feminism, 166
Ferenczi, Sandor, 219
"Ferguson to Palestine" slogan/sentiment, 119, 122, 125, 164
Fidesz Party, 253, 255
Fielding, Henry, 27
FIFA (Fédération Internationale de Football Association), 58
Filastin al-Muslima, 356, 357, 361
financial crisis of 2007–8, 275
Finkelstein, Israel, 353
Finkielkraut, Alain, 220, 228n21
First Amendment rights, 188, 189, 198–99, 201, 203, 204
First Palestinian Conference for the Boycott of Israel, 47–48
Fitzpatrick, Catherine, 50
Five Ts of campus antisemitism, 167–78; *Taharanut*/purity, 158–59, 175–77; Transgression, 158, 167–70; Transmission, 158, 171–73; Trump, 158, 170–71; Truth, 158, 173–75
Fofana, Yousouf, 221

Forced Circumcision blog, 294, 299
Ford, Henry, 146
Foreman, Jonathan, 50–52, 61
Forman, Ira, xi–xii
Forster, Arnold, 178n2
Foundation for Individual Rights in Education (FIRE), 206n20
The Foundations of Geopolitics: Russia's Geopolitical Future (Dugin), 103
Fourteenth Amendment, Equal Protection Clause of, 198–99
"Fourteen Words," 169
The Fourth Political Theory (Dugin), 103
fragmentation of antisemitism, 251–53
Framework Decision (2008), 369, 370, 373, 377
France, 211–27; and affirmative antisemitism, 211; assaults on Jews in, 1; Bayer's criticisms of antisemitism in, 249, 250; betrayal of Jews in, 215; blindness to antisemitism in, 212, 217, 222–24, 229n36; and *Charlie Hebdo* massacre, 218–19, 220; coordinating antisemitisms, 213; and *Death of Klinghoffer* opera, 216–17; and defensive antisemitism, 211, 212, 216; denied antisemitism in, 211, 212, 216–18; economic crisis in, xiv; equivocal antisemitism in, 212, 216, 218–19; identification of antisemitism in, 212; Islamist antisemitism in, 213, 229n36; language/cultural contributions of Jews in, 214; magisterial (or spectatorial) antisemitism in, 212, 219–24; resurgence of antisemitism in, 212, 214–15; violence against Jews in, 217–18, 219–20, 223; virtuous antisemitism in, 212, 224–27; visibility of Jews in, 213–14; "yellow vest" movement in, 214–15
Frank, Anne, 34
Frank, Otto, 34
Frankfurter Allgemeine Zeitung, 292–94, 297, 298, 301, 303
Frankfurt School, 62
Franz, Matthias, 297, 298, 299
Fraser v. University and College Union, 34, 35
Freedom House, 51–52
freedom of religion, 292, 293, 294, 298
"Freedom of Religion Cannot Be a Carte Blanche for Violence" (open letter), 298–99

freedom of speech: and alt-lite movement, 161, 168–69; on college/university campuses, 150, 159, 165, 167, 168, 173, 187, 188–89, 203; defamation vs., 28–40; definition of antisemitism as threat to, 10, 15–18, 187, 188–89; in Hungary, 255; and intolerance model of combating antisemitism, 201, 203; right and alt-right's championing of, 168; and silencing/suppression of nonprogressive voices, 167, 168; and Title VI protections of Civil Rights Act (1964), 188–89; and virtuous antisemitism, 224–25

Free Speech on Campus (Chemerinsky and Gillman), 188

Free Speech on Israel, 13

French National Front, 253

Freud, Sigmund, 98, 300

Friends of Sabeel North America (FOSNA), 118

Frisch, Hillel, 360

Fudge, Shelley Cohen, 118

Fuhl, Wolfgang, 281

Fundamental Rights Agency (FRA), 11, 45, 46, 371–73, 376–77

Gadó, János, 249–62

Garlasco, Marc, 53–54

Gauchet, Marcel, 224

Gauland, Alexander, 270, 271, 274–75, 278, 280, 284n30, 285n43

Gaza: Gaza Beach incident (2006), 53–54; as "genocide," 62; HRW's accusations of war crimes in, 55, 56; and HRW's double standards, 51–52, 55; and HRW's use of symbols/images, 61; and language used to deny self-determination, 60; rate of antisemitism in, 263n10; Said's on Israel's occupation of, 24; UN Human Rights Council report on, 18

Geisler, Wolff, 299–300

Generation Identitaire, 146

genocide: denialism, 12, 16; equation of Holocaust with Palestinian conflict, 62; and Framework Decision (2008), 369; "structural genocide" term of Wolfe, 90. *See also* Holocaust

German AfD (Alternative für Deutschland), 267–83; antisemitic imagery of, 274–78; antisemitic members of, 267; conspiracy theories disseminated by, 267–68; and Der Flügel (the Wing), 268; as enabler of racism and antisemitism, 267; and Erfurt Resolution (2015), 268; goals of, 274; and Holocaust remembrance, 267–74; immigration policy of, 267, 269, 279; impact on political discourse, 282–83; Jewish people in (JAfD), 272–73, 281; and Muslim antisemitism, 279–81; and Muslim minority, 267, 269, 275, 279, 281, 285n43; and politics of memory, 269–74; pro-Israel stance of, 279–82; radicalization of, 268–69; and replacement conspiracy theory, 275–78; rise of, 267; and state election results, 268, 269, 283n2

Germany, 287–304; assaults on Jews in, 1; and BDS movement, 48, 58; and Central Council of Jews, 280–81, 300, 301, 302; immigration policy in, xiv, 281; and Merkel, xiv, 267, 276, 281, 282, 293; politics of remembrance in, 269–73; refugee policy of, 268–69; rise of antisemitism in, 287; stability of political system in, 267. *See also* circumcision, ritual; German AfD (Alternative für Deutschland)

Gerstenfeld, Manfred, 235

"Gespaltene Mitte—Feindselige Zustände" (opinion study), 282

Gillman, Howard, 152, 153, 188

Gilman, Sander L., 296

Glick, David, 118

Glinski, Piotr, 236

Głos Siedlecki, 240, 241

Goebbels, Joseph, 24

Goetschel, Willi, 78

Gold, Ariel, 118

Goldberg, David (German rabbi), 288

Goldberg, David Theo (racism scholar), 79–80, 81

Goldberg, Michel, 224–25

Goldschmidt, Pinchas, 289

Goldstone, Richard, 18–19, 54, 61

Goldstone Report, 18–19, 54–55

Gollaher, David L., 297, 300

Goodman, Alice, 216, 228n12

Gould, Rebecca Ruth, 10, 16, 17–18, 31

Gowin, Jaroslaw, 234

Grabowski, Jan, 231–47

"great replacement" conspiracy theory, 275–78

Greenblatt, Jonathan, 142
Gribetz, Jonathan, 346
Griffin, Nick, 37
Griffith, Roger, 106
Grimm, Marc, 267–83
Guénon, René, 96, 97–99, 100, 101, 104, 106
Gulyás, Gergely, 259
Gumilev, Lev, 104

Hagler, Graylan S., 117
Haifa University, 151
Hakim, 'Abd al-Hamid, 354
Halimi, Ilan, 220–21
Halimi, Sarah, 221–22, 249, 250
Halle synagogue attack (2019), 268, 277–78
Hamas: and Arab-Israeli conflict, 344, 349–50, 351, 353; and Corbyn, 317; on "cultural-religious assault" of Jews, 356; goals of, 23; and Goldstone Report, 18, 19; mobilization efforts by, 349–50; and Qatar's financial support, 361n1; slowly changing attitudes in, 361; spikes in antisemitism during clashes with, 33; and Stop the War Coalition, 315, 317
Hamid, 'Ali Muhsin, 352
Haniyya, Isma'il, 353–54
Haram al-Sharif, 347
harassment standard of US Supreme Court, 201, 203, 204
Harmush, Shaykh Mahmud, 352
Harpon, Mickael, 223
Harrison, Bernard, 48, 49
Hate Crime Operational Guidance, 33
hate crimes: and definition of antisemitism, 377; European Community's measures to address, 374; European Parliament's resolution on, 370; lack of data on, 373, 375–76; legislation on, 32; and OSCE initiatives, 374–75; rising incidence of, 1; underreporting of, 373; and Vilnius conference (2013), 373, 375
hate groups, 171–72, 213
Hatina, Meir, 351
hatred of Jews: adapted to multiculturalism, 252; among far left / far right, 252; as a belief state, 20–22, 28; and definition of antisemitism, 13–15, 20, 188, 190; and intolerance model of combating antisemitism, *199*; Islamic, 252; Jewish Voice for Peace's dissemination of, 123

Havel, Boris, 355
Haynes, Douglas E., 153
Hefty, Georg Paul, 292–93
Heimbach, Matthew, 105–6
Heisler, András, 258–59
Herf, Jeffrey, 355
Herzberg, Rolf Dietrich, 295
Higher Ground: The Alignment of UCI's Policies, Principles, and Programs with the UC Regents' Principles against Intolerance, 153, 154
high holidays, Jewish, 118–20
Hillel (organization), 127–28
Himmler, Heinrich, 100
Hirsh, David, 48, 89, 150, 341n12
Hirsi Ali, Ayaan, 166
"History, Education, Memory" conference, 238
Hitler, Adolf, 100, 206n25, 268, 271
Hizballah, 18, 23, 54, 315, 317, 349–50
Hobson, John, 318–19
Höcke, Björn, 268, 271, 276–77, 278
Hödl, Klaus, 296
Holocaust: accusations of inventing/exaggerating, 12, 187, 192, 333, 336; and campus antisemitism, 163, 173; commemoration of, in European states, 371; comparing Palestinian conflict to, 14, 62; and Corbyn's Labour Party, 335, 336, 339; and culture of self-reflection, 254; and definition of antisemitism by IHRA, 192, 371; deflection of, in Poland, 235–38; denialism, 12, 32–33, 147, 171, 172, 173, 234–35, 243, 262, 336–37; distortion of, in Poland, 237, 238; equivalence, 32–33; fate of survivors' testimony in Poland, 239–42; fates of individual victims in, 232; and Framework Decision (2008) of the EU, 369; and German AfD, 267–74; and Hungary's Orbán regime, 250, 259–61; ignorance of younger generations regarding, xiii; impact of, 335, 339; inversion, 147, 336; Israel as "compensation" for, 26; and Jewish identity, 335; Poland's "Holocaust Law" (2018), 232, 242–46, 254; revisionism, 34; rise in jokes about, 149; and supersessionist thinking, 78–79; trivialization of, 34; Wolfe's relativizing of, 90

Holocaust Memorial Day, international, 271–73
Holtzman, Livnat, 357, 358
Horthy, Miklós, 254–55, 261
House of Commons, UK, 9–10. *See also* Labour Party (UK)
How Jews Became White Folks (Brodkin), 76–77
Hübscher, Monika, 271
human rights, language of, used in accusations against Jews, 45
Human Rights Council (UNHRC), 47
Human Rights Watch (HRW): about, 49–50; and BDS movement, 55–58; as case study, 49–50, 63, 66n37; double standards applied to Israel by, 50–55; and Goldstone's nomination, 54; and language used to deny self-determination, 59–60; and Permanent Agenda Item 7 of UNHRC, 67n57; "stolen land" references of, 58, 60, 62; use of antisemitic symbols and images, 60–62
Hume, David, 20
Hungary, 249–62; antisemitic attitudes in, 262; antisemitic incidents in, 264n11; and Bayer's criticisms of antisemitism in France, 249, 250; extremists kept at bay in, 257; freedom of speech in, 255; Holocaust denialism in, 262; Holocaust remembrance in, 250, 259–61; and Horthy, 254–55, 261; and House of Fates, 259–60; Jobbik Party of, 252, 253, 255, 257, 258; and Kuruc.info Nazi website, 257–58; and mass migration of 2015, 258; nationalists in, 254, 258, 260; the "Other" in, 250; and Palestinians, 258; press/media in, 255–56, 257, 258; progressive West compared to Orbán regime in, 250–51; pro-Zionist stance of, 253; self-reflection in, 254; and Soros, 256–57, 258, 259, 261, 262; traditionalist political culture of Orbán regime in, 250–51; and Treaty of Trianon (1920), 255
Hunt, Jeremy, 48
Husayni, Amin al-, 348–49, 355

identitarians, 146
Identity Evropa, 149
identity politics, 164
ideological purity, 175–77
If Americans Knew (IAK), 124
IfNotNow (INN), 121, 131n44
immigrants and refugees: and antimigrant sentiments, 379; and antisemitism on the right, 147; Germany's AfD's position on, 267, 269, 279; and Merkel, xiv, 281; and replacement conspiracy theory, 275–78; and white nationalism, 146
Imperialism: A Study (Hobson), 318–19
Independent Group (TIG), 38
Independent Jewish Voices, 13
Indiana University, Bloomington, ix
Indiana University Press, x
inexistentialism, 224
Institute for Hungarian Jewish History, 260
Institute for Jewish Policy Research, 35, 313
Institute for the Study of Contemporary Antisemitism, ix–xi, xii, 2–3
institutional racism, 327–28
International Criminal Court, 45, 53
International Holocaust Remembrance Alliance (IHRA), 45, 186, 260, 335, 371. *See also* definition of antisemitism by IHRA
International Jewish Anti-Zionist Network, 62
International Solidarity Movement (ISM), 121, 130n21
internet, antisemitism on, 32, 34, 372
"intersectionality" on college campuses, 149, 164
intolerance model of combating antisemitism on college campuses, 197–204, 199
Ionescu, Dana, 287–304
Iran, 23
Iraq, 276
Iraq War, 315, 325–26, 328
Iron Guard, 149
ISIS, 174
Islam and Muslims: and al-Aqsa Mosque, 344, 347, 348, 349, 351, 352, 359; anti-Zionism of, 252, 355; and calendar of communal riot, 350; and circumcision controversy, 288, 290–95, 297, 298–300, 301–2, 303; fatwas of, 348–49; and German AfD, 267, 269, 275, 279–81, 285n43; and Islamic new antisemitism, 345–46;

Islamism's threat to democratic values, 2; Islamophobia, 119, 222; and Jerusalem, 349; and jihad, 344, 350, 351, 352, 353, 359; Muslim antisemitism in France, 213, 229n36; and Muslim migrants/refugees, 258, 262, 267, 269, 275, 281; and nationalism in Arab world, 346, 347; and New Zealand mosque massacre, 176–77; and Orbán, 258, 261–62; and Ottoman Empire, 346; and progressives / political left, 165–66, 253; and replacement conspiracy theory, 275–78; rise of Islamism, 349; as source of antisemitic abuse in EU, 373, 376; suicide acts of, 351; terms for antisemitism of, 345; and violence against Jews, 213

Israel: and AfD of Germany, 279–82; attempts to associate evil with, 24; and Balfour Declaration, 330, 350, 353–54; and birthright program, 120–22; and Britain, 330; creation of state, 330; criticisms of, nonantisemitic, 18–19, 36, 49; criticisms "silenced" by definition of antisemitism, 9–10, 17–18, 19, 48, 49; criticism vs. defamation of Israel, 27, 28–40, 49; demonization of, 58, 59; as diverse, multicultural society, 25; double standards applied to, 12, 46, 49, 50–55, 192; as the "enemy of progress," 334; foundation of state, 25; and Goldstone Report, 18–19; holding Jews accountable for actions of, 12; and HRW's use of symbols/images, 60–62; Jews accused of giving priority to, 12; left's animosity toward, 37–38, 176; legitimacy challenged, 14, 23, 27–28; Nazi comparisons to policies of, 12, 15, 36, 40, 46, 47, 62–63; and Nazi equivalence, 24, 34; and Nazi racism, 331–32; new antisemitism's focus on, 44, 45, 140, 145; and Orbán regime in Hungary, 250, 257, 262; and peace in Middle East, 25; police exchange programs with US, 123; and political antisemitism, 22–27; and right-wing politics, 170–71, 252–53, 279; and Six Day War (1967), 85, 89, 350; "stolen land" references, 58, 60, 62; study-abroad programs in, 149, 151; as target of antisemitism, 11, 12, 14; Trump on Jerusalem as capital of, 345, 353–54; and United States, 28, 334; "war crimes" of, 48, 53–55, 56; and Western imperialism, 329; as "white" colony, 79–81. *See also* colonial-settler state, Israel as

Israel and Settler Society (Veracini), 89

Israel Defense Forces (IDF): diversity in, 25; and Jenin refugee camp, 53; Muslim Arab Israelis in, 25; SJP students' hostility toward Reservists, 154; as target of Human Rights Watch, 50, 53, 54, 56, 60, 61

Israel Studies (journal), 82

Italy, assaults on Jews in, 1

Jacobs, Jill, 123
Jeffries, Leonard, 173
Jenin refugee camp, 53
Jens, Tilman, 294
Jerouschek, Günter, 297, 298, 299
Jerusalem: and Arab-Israeli conflict, 345, 348–49, 352–55, 359; and early Muslim scholars, 359; Jordan's role as guardian of, 352, 364n43; recognized as Israel's capital by Trump, 345, 353–54
"Jerusalem Was Never and Will Never Be Jewish" (Hamid), 352
Jesus (biblical), 193
Jewish Anti-Fascist Committee, 334
Jewish Community Relations Council, 128
Jewish Federations of North America, 121, 128
Jewish Institute for National Security Affairs (JINSA), 122
Jewish Labour Movement, 327
"Jewish question," 78, 81, 332–34, 336, 338, 339
Jewish Voice for Peace (JVP), 113–28; activism of, 116–20; Anti-Defamation League on, 113, 114, 123; *On Antisemitism*, 115–16; anti-Zionist rhetoric of, 114–16; and BDS movement, 113, 115, 117, 119; campaign targeting Birthright, 120–22; "Deadly Exchange" campaign of, 122–23, 127, 131n44; extremist ties of, 113, 116, 130n21; identity theft of Jewish heritage, 118–20; influence of, 114; presence on college campuses, 116–17; and Protestant churches, 117–18; radical rhetoric of, 113–14; resisting, 126–28; silencing of nonprogressive voices, 167; and Weir collaboration, 123–26

Jewish World Congress, 272
Jews for Justice for Palestine, 13
Jews Indigenous to the Middle East and North Africa (JIMENA), 127
Jikeli, Guenther, xii
Jobbik Party of Hungary, 252, 253, 255, 257, 258
Johnson, Alan, 146
Johnson, Daniel, 1
Johnson, Nels, 347
Johnson, Paul, 29
Jones, Alex, 174
Jordan, 352, 358, 364n43
Juden in der AfD (JAfD, Jews in the AfD), 272–73, 281
Judeophobia, 345
Jüdische Allgemeine, 288
Julius, Anthony, 44

Kahmann, Bodo, 275
Kahn, Jean, 368
Kairos Palestine document (2009), 44, 64n5
Karega, Joy, 117, 174
Karima, Ahmad, 352
Karski, Jan, 239
Katz, Rebekah, 141
Katz, Talia, 150–51
Kaube, Jürgen, 293–94
Kavanaugh, Brett, 147, 172
Kelman, Ari Y., 144, 155n12
Kerem Navot, 58
Khalidi, Salah al-, 357
Khatib, Shaykh Kamal, 352
Khazin, Jihad al-, 352
"kikes" slur, 149
Kill All Normies (Nagle), 168–69
Kimmerling, Baruch, 86
Ki-Moon, Ban, 54
Klaff, Lesley, 48, 49
Klinghoffer, Leon, 216–17, 228n12
Knobloch, Charlotte, 272, 289
Knoll, Mireille, 220, 222
Kohn, Daniel, 63
Kopke, Christoph, 282
kosher slaughtering, 251, 259
Kosovo, 276
Köves, Slomó, 259, 260
Kronawetter, Ferdinand, 341n19
Krosigk, Lutz Graf Schwerin von, 271

Labour Movement Campaign for Palestine, 314
Labour Party (UK): anti-imperialism of, 329; and anti-Zionism, 44, 314, 317, 330–31; and conspiracy theories, 320–21; and definition of antisemitism by IHRA, 9–10, 17, 39–40, 319, 336; and election of 2015, 325; and election of 2017, 326; and election of 2019, 322; and Holocaust, 335, 336, 339; and Human Rights Watch's tactics, 62; and institutional racism charges, 327–28; Jewish population's identification with, 326–27; members' perceptions of the US, 316; and new antisemitism, 44; prevalence of antisemitism in, 327–28; as social movement, 321; young idealist members of, 316–17. *See also* Corbyn, Jeremy
Landau, Susan, 126
language used to deny self-determination, 58–60
Laruelle, Marlene, 102–3
Law and Justice (PiS) Party in Poland, 232, 234, 240, 244
"law-breaking" stereotype, 291–95, 303
Lebanon War, 54, 60–61
legitimacy challenges against Israel: and BDS movement, 23, 48; and colonial-settler characterization of Israel, 82, 87; and definition of antisemitism by IHRA, 14, 27–28; and HRW's use of symbols/images, 61; and language used to deny self-determination, 59; and new antisemitism, 44, 45
Leicht, Lotte, 62
Le Monde, 221
Levi, Sylvain, 97
Lévy, Bernard-Henri, 145, 254, 256–57
Lewis, Bernard, 29
liberalism, 103, 107. *See also* political left / progressives
Libya, 276
Lindbergh, Charles, 146–47
Lipstadt, Deborah, 32–33, 62
Lisbon Treaty (2007), 369, 370
Livingstone formulation, 48, 341n12
Loewenich, Volker von, 295
Lorber, Ben, 121
Lucke, Bernd, 268

Maastricht Treaty on European Union (1992), 369
Macpherson Report, 15, 31, 327
magisterial (or spectatorial) antisemitism, 212, 219–24
Magyar Narancs, 260
Magyar Nemzet, 249
Maizels, Linda, 158–78
Malicious Communications Act (1998), 34
Mallory, Tamika, 123
Manifestations of Antisemitism in the EU 2002–2003, 368
Marcus, Kenneth L., 45, 186, 187, 189–90
Maritain, Jacques, 97
Martin, Tony, 173
Marttila Communications Group, 159
Marx, Karl, 120, 339
Massad, Joseph, 89
"A Matter of Civil Rights" (Whitson), 59
May, Gary, 151
Mazsihisz, 258–59, 261
McGowan Davis, Mary, 18
McRobbie, Michael, ix
Mear One's "New World Order" mural, 317–18, 338
Medina, 352
Meir, Lucy, 56
Memmi, Sartre, 141, 144
Men among the Ruins (Evola), 102
Mercer, Rebekah, 106
Merkel, Angela, xiv, 267, 276, 281, 282, 293
Middle East: Israel as "threat" to peace in, 25; rate of antisemitism in, 263n10. *See also* Arab-Israeli conflict
Mihoub, Yacine, 222
Miliband, Ed, 326
Milne, Seumas, 316, 342n24
Milner, Jean Claude, 215
Milton Friedman University in Budapest, 260
Möller, Stefan, 272
money, myth of Jewish control of, 22
Moore, Roy, 112n77
Morawiecki, Mateusz, 235, 236, 237, 244, 245–46, 247n12
Morgan, John, 101
Morris, Benny, 86
Moshe, Shiri, 118
Mossad, 174, 320

Movement for Black Lives, 164
Muhammad, Elijah, 180n23
Muhammad, Prophet, 356
Mulla, Muhammad al-, 353
multiculturalism, 250, 251, 252
Muravchik, Joshua, 120
Murray, Andrew, 315, 342n24
Muslim Brotherhood, 315, 360–61
Muslim Brothers in Jordan, 353
Muslim Student Union (MSU), 166
Mussolini, Benito, 100
Mutti, Claudio, 101, 102

Nagle, Angela, 168–69
nationalism/nationalists: America First philosophy, 137, 146; in Arab world, 346; Dugin's advocacy of, 104; and Horthy, 254–55; in Hungary, 254, 258, 260; in Poland, 232, 234, 235–36, 237, 242, 244, 245–46; rise of, 2
National Points of Contact on Hate Crimes, 374
National Rasmea Defense Committee, 118
National Socialist Legion, 146, 149
National Women's Studies Association (NWSA), 164–65
Nation of Islam (NOI), 165, 180n23, 193
Native Americans, 127
nativism, rise of, 2
NATO (North Atlantic Treaty Organization), 316
Nazis / National Socialism: and AfD of Germany, 271–72, 279; antisemitism of, 29–30, 100, 337; and antisemitism on the right, 146; comparing Israeli policy to, 12, 15, 24, 36, 40, 46, 47, 62–63, 118; and definition of antisemitism, 187; as form of racism, 331–32; and fundamental changes of Holocaust, 335; and German remembrance culture, 269, 270, 272, 273; and Goldberg on whiteness of Jews, 79–80; and Heimbach, 106; Hungarian-language website of, 257–58; ignorance of younger generations regarding, xiii; and Nazi equivalence, 27, 32, 34, 35, 37; neo-Nazis, 146, 172; and Poland's "Holocaust Law" (2018), 243; recruitment on college campuses, 149; and Stauffenberg, 271–72; and swastikas, 35, 37, 142, 143, 146, 151, 173

Nazzal, Muhammad, 353
Neil, Andrew, 322
Neiwert, David, 174
Nelson, Cary, 174
neo-Nazis, 146, 172
neoreactionaries, 146
Netanyahu, Benjamin: and Adelson, 121; and authoritarian regimes in Warsaw and Budapest, 244–45; depicted in anti-Zionist propaganda, 35; and Human Rights Watch, 58; JVP's criticisms of, 119, 127; and Orbán, 257; and Trump, 170
Netherlands, assaults on Jews in, 1
Nettler, Ronald, 356
Neumann, Franz, 228n5
new antisemitism: attributes of, 140; and definition of antisemitism by IHRA, 48, 66n37; emergence of, 44; ideology of, 45; Islamic new antisemitism, 345; Israel as focus of, 44, 45, 145, 147; left-wing sources of, 145, 146; and Orbán regime in Hungary, 262; overlap with "old" antisemitism, 44, 46; violence associated with, 45
The New Anti-Semitism (Forster and Epstein), 178n2
"New Right" movement, 102, 103, 254, 282, 283n1
"New World Order" mural (Mear One), 317–18, 338
New York City, assaults on Jews in, 1
New York Trade Center bombing (1993), 351
New York University, 148, 149, 150, 176–77
New Zealand mosque massacre, 176–77
NGOs (nongovernmental organizations), 47, 63
Night without End (Grabowski and Engelking, eds.), 236
1984 (Orwell), 246
Noel, Eric, 224, 225, 229n28
normalization of antisemitism, xiii, 80, 113, 377
North Africa, 263n10
NY Committee for Justice in Palestine, 118

Obama, Barack, 54, 170
Oberlin College, 163–64, 174
"Occupation Inc." (HRW report), 57
Odeh, Rasmea, 116, 118

Oestreich, Heide, 293
Öktem, Kerem, 289
Oliver, Melvin, 151
Olmert, Ehud, 168
Omar, Ilhan, 160, 176–77
On Antisemitism (Jewish Voice for Peace), 115–16
online antisemitism, 32, 34, 372
Orbán, Viktor: and Bayer, 249; controversial record of, 261–62; and Fidesz Party, 253, 255; and Holocaust remembrance, 259, 261; and Horthy, 254–55, 261; and Israel, 257, 262; and left- and right-wing extremists, 257; and Muslim/Arab migrants, 258, 261–62; and Soros, 256–57, 258, 259, 261, 262
Oren, Michael, 166, 168
Organization for Security and Cooperation in Europe (OSCE), 11, 367–68, 371, 373–75, 378
Organization of the Islamic Conference (OIC), 348
Oriental Metaphysics (Guénon), 97
Original Sin and the Depravation of the Rule of Law (Jens), 294
Orwell, George, 246
OSCE Office for Democratic Institutions and Human Rights (OSCE/ODIHR), 45, 371, 374, 376
Other, Jewish people as, 22, 214, 226, 303
Ottoman Empire, 346, 359

Palestine Return Centre, 13
Palestine Solidarity Campaign, 13, 316
Palestinian Authority (PA), 19, 353
Palestinian conflict: analogized to plight of African Americans, 119, 122, 125, 164; and BDS movement, 162, 164; and Black nationalist thought, 151; and campus antisemitism, 163; and church-based NGOs, 44; and colonial-settler characterization of Israel, 87, 88–89; conceptualized in religious terms, 347; and definition of antisemitism by IHRA, 187; equation of Holocaust with, 14, 62; examples of antisemitism related to, 14; "extrajudicial killings" in the West Bank, 122; framed as whites vs. people of color, 151, 162; and genocidal intent of

Palestinians, 337; and "one-state solution," 162; progressive critique of, 162; and progressive West vs. Hungary's Orbán regime, 250–51; transmission of messages about, 172. *See also* Arab-Israeli conflict

Palestinians: and blacklist published by UNHRC, 57; considered people of color, 151, 162; Corbyn's support for, 314, 315, 317, 319, 322; and Goldberg on whiteness of Jews, 79–80; Klinghoffer's murder by terrorists, 216–17; and Orbán regime in Hungary, 258; as racial "other," 81; and "right of return," 59

Palestinian territories: partition plan for, 83–84; rate of antisemitism in, 263n10; as sacred Muslim land (myth), 349

Pan-Afrikan Student Union, 172–73

Pappé, Ilan, 86, 88–89, 348

Paris kosher supermarket, massacre in, 217–18

Parliamentary Assembly of the Council of Europe, 370

pathologization of the Jewish body, 296

Pearl, Daniel, ix

Pearl, Judea, ix

Penslar, Derek, 92n8

people of color: and alt-lite movement, 161; and critical whiteness studies, 76; and Jewish Voice for Peace, 122, 127; Palestinians seen as, 151, 162; progressives' support for, 161

perennial philosophy. *See* Traditionalism

Petry, Frauke, 279, 280

Pettibone, Brittany, 105

Pew Research Center, 313

Phillips, N. A., 34–35

Picciolini, Christian, 105

Pilecki Institute, 235, 237, 238

Piterberg, Gabriel, 82, 83–84

Ploss, Hermann Heinrich, 297–98

The Plot against America (Roth), 147

Poland, 231–47; and "antipolonism," 244–46, 247n11; assaults on Jews in, 1; Auschwitz death camp, 255, 270; conference held at Bełżec extermination camp, 238; criminal trial of author in, 242; fate of survivors' testimony in, 239–42; *Głos Siedlecki* newspaper in, 240, *241*; "Holocaust Law" (2018), 232, 242–46, 254; and Kielce murders, 239; Law and Justice (PiS) Party, 232, 234, 240, 244; March of Independence (2017), 242–43; memory patches in, 239; museum in Warsaw Ghetto of, 239; nationalists in, 232, 234, 235–36, 237, 242, 244, 245–46; prevalence of antisemitism in, 1; resurgence of fascism in, 232, 242–43; Righteous Poles and deflection of Holocaust, 235–38, 239; Treblinka extermination camp, 236, 237; Węgrów county, 235–37, 240, *241*

polarization of contemporary political climate, xiv, 177, 185

police, underreporting of antisemitic crimes to, 373

Polish Institute of National Remembrance (IPN), 238

political antisemitism, 21–27, 28, 39–40

political correctness, 225–26, 229n31, 253

political left / progressives: animosity toward Israel/Jews, 37–38, 176, 252; anti-Zionism among, 214, 251; blind spot to antisemitism, 165; on college/university campuses, 138, 144–45, 150, 162–67; defamation of Israel by, 37–38; democratic values under threat from, 2; and Hungary's Orbán regime, 250–51; and ideological purity, 176–77; and Islam, 253; and the "Jewish question," 332–34, 336, 338; and multiculturalism, 250, 251, 252; and new antisemitism, 145, 146; and political correctness, 253; radicalization of, 328–29; rise in antisemitism among, 215; roots of, in Soviet anti-Western propaganda, 126; silencing/suppression of nonprogressive voices, 167, 168; as source of antisemitic abuse in EU, 373, 376; swastikas employed by, 173; transgression eschewed by, 167–70; transmission of messages of, 172–73; and Trump, 170; and truth in campus politics, 173–75. *See also* boycotts, divestment, and sanctions (BDS) movements; Labour Party (UK)

political right / conservatives: alternative facts of, 173–74; alt-lite movement, 161–62, 168–70, 177; books produced by, 227n1; on college/university campuses, 138, 144–45, 146–47, 149; countering unfavorable Holocaust history by, 254; democratic

political right / conservatives (Cont.)
  values under threat from, 2; and freedom of speech, 168; hatred of Jews among far right, 252; and Hungary's Orbán regime, 251; and ideological purity, 175–76, 177; and Israel, 170–71, 252–53, 279; "New Right" movement, 102, 103, 254, 282, 283n1; provocateurs of, 176; and replacement conspiracy theory, 275–78; as source of antisemitic abuse in EU, 373, 376; support of hard left's antisemitism, 37; swastikas employed by, 173; and Traditionalism, 106–7; transgression embraced by, 167–70; transmission of messages of, 171–72, 173; and Trump, 170–71; and truth in campus politics, 173–75; "Unite the Right" rally in Charlottesville, 105, 137, 161, 164–65; willingness to use violence, 282. See also alt-right movement
political speech, legal protection of, 36
Popular Front for the Liberation of Palestine (PFLP), 116
populism, rise of, 2, 316, 379
Porat, Dina, 245
Portrait of a Jew (Memmi), 141
postcolonialism, 78
Postone, Moishe, 224
Poway synagogue shooting, 1, 62
power of Jewish people, myth of: and alternative facts of contemporary right, 174; and antisemitism on the right, 146–47; and anti-Zionism, 148; and campus antisemitism, 142; and circumcision controversy, 300–302; and Judeophobia, 345; and new antisemitism, 139–40
Pratt, Douglas, 345
Pretzell, Marcus, 279, 280
Price, Vincent E., 151
"Principles against Intolerance" by UC Regents, 139, 143, 151–52
The Promise and the Obstacle, the Radical Left and the Jewish Problem (Trom), 78
Prosecutors and Hate Crimes Training (PAHCT), 374
Protestant churches, 117–18, 162
Protocols of the Elders of Zion: and Arab-Israeli conflict, 351, 354, 355, 359, 360; distributed at Durban Conference, 52; Evola's foreword for new edition of, 100; and Human Rights Watch's tactics, 62; and Jewish Voice for Peace's tactics, 122; and Noel's *The Role of Your Children in the World's Economic Recovery*, 225
psychoanalytic perspective on antisemitism, 300
Puar, Jasbir, 117, 174
"Public Law and the State of Israel" (conference), 38
Public Order Act 1986, 32, 33
public safety as justification for antisemitism, 38
purity/*Taharanut* (Five Ts of campus antisemitism), 158–59, 175–77
Putin, Vladimir, 96, 102, 103
Putzke, Holm, 295

Qadid, Ahmad, 354
Quayson, Ato, 78
Qui Est Charlie? (Todd), 220
Qur'anic Facts on the Palestinian Case (Khalidi), 357

R. (E) v. Governing Body of JFS, 34–35
"race realists," 146
racism: antisemitism as related to, 330–32; attempts to associate Israel with, 24, 27, 36; institutional racism, 327–28; and language used to deny self-determination, 58, 59, 60
Raheb, Mitri, 117
Rajkovic, Nikolas M., 50
The Reign of Quantity and the Signs of the Times (Guénon), 98
Religion after Religion (Wasserstrom), 108n23
"Religious Actors in Conflict Areas," 360–61
replacement conspiracy theory, 275–78
replacement theology (also known as supersessionism), 44, 61, 78–79
Republican Party, 160
"Resurgent Antisemitism—a Global Perspective" (2011), x, xi
revisionism, historical, 2, 34
Revolt against the Modern World (Evola), 97, 99–100
Ribak, Gil, 229n28

Rida, Muhammad Rashid, 348
Rida, Rashid, 359
The Right to Maim (Puar), 174
Robertson, Geoffrey, 10, 13–15, 16, 17, 28–29, 30, 31, 32–33, 35, 36, 37
Rodinson, Maxime, 86
The Role of Your Children in the World's Economic Recovery (play), 224–25
Rose, Jaqueline, 24
Rosenfeld, Alvin H., ix, xii, 1–5, 116
Rosenthal, Hannah, xi–xii
Rosh Hashanah, 119
Rossman-Benjamin, Tammi, 185–204
Roth, Kenneth, 50, 51–52, 56–58, 59, 60, 61, 62–63
Roth, Philip, 147
Rothschilds family, 174, 320
Roy, Olivier, 360

Saada, François Michel, 218
Sabeel Ecumenical Liberation Theology Center, 44, 118
Sacks, Jonathan, 145
Sahl, Mort, 167
Said, Edward, 24, 86
Salah, Raeed, 342n28
Samidoun, 116
San Diego State University, 143
Sandler, Shmuel, 360
Sandy Hook massacre, 174
San Francisco State University, 150
Sarsour, Linda, 116, 166–67
Sartre, Jean-Paul, 21
Sasson, Theodore, 141
Saxe, Leonard, 141
Sayegh, Faez, 86
Schaefer, Peter, 58
Schlossberg, Eliezer, 357, 358
Schmidbauer, Wolfgang, 297
Schmidt, Mária, 260
Schnurbein, Katharina von, xii
Scholem, Gershom, 104
Schraub, David, 126
Schulte von Drach, Markus, 292, 301
Schumer, Chuck, 172
Scott, Tim, 11
The Secret Relationship between Blacks and Jews (Martin), 173

Sedgwick, Mark, 97, 99, 106
Sedley, Sir Stephen, 10, 16, 17, 18, 28–29, 31
self-determination of Jewish people, denying, 12, 46, 47, 58–60, 171
Sellars, Peter, 216, 228n12
Sendler, Irena, 239
"Separate and Unequal" (HRW), 59
separatism, 332, 333
"Sephardic and Mizrachi Communal Response to Jewish Voice for Peace" (2019 statement), 127
September 11, 2001, terrorist attacks, 174, 316
Settler Colonial Studies, 87, 88, 91
Shafir, Gershon, 82, 83–86
Shahin, 'Amr, 352
Shakir, Omar S., 56, 57–58, 60
Sharansky, Natan, 28
Sharon, Ariel, 351
Sherrell, Isabel Storch, 163–64
Shire, Emily, 116
Shoah Foundation's Visual History Archive, 240
Silverman, Eric Kline, 296
Sinwar, Yahya, 344
Six Day War (1967), 85, 89, 350
Sklar, Jonathan, 219
Skorzeny, Otto, 100
Snelson, A. M., 34, 35–36
socialists/socialism, 320, 322, 333, 334
social media, 171, 213, 321
social science, activist, 75–76
Soros, George, 256–57, 258, 259, 261, 262, 264nn19–20
Southern, Lauren, 105
Southern Poverty Law Center, 146
Southgate, Troy, 101–2, 109n36
Soviet Union, 253, 334, 342nn21–22, 342n24, 374
Spencer, Philip, 325–40
Spencer, Richard, 100, 105, 115, 160, 170–71
Squirrel Hill shootings in Pittsburgh (2018), 150
Stanford University, 143, 144
Starkopf, Adam, 236–37
Stauffenberg, Claus Schenk Graf von, 271–72
Steinberg, Gerald M., 44–63
Steinhardt, Michael, 121

stereotypes of Jewish people, 287–304; and affirmative antisemitism, 211; and circumcision controversy, 290; of economic behaviors, 333; and function of stereotyping, 278; of the Jewish body, 296–97; and Jewish Voice for Peace, 113; "law-breaking" stereotype, 291–95, 303; and Mear One's "New World Order" mural, 317–18, 338; on money, 22; and new antisemitism, 45; and "powerful Jews" / "political pressure" stereotype, 300–302. *See also* power of Jewish people, myth of
Stern, Kenneth S., 171
Sternhell, Zeev, 82, 83
Stockholm Declaration, 370
Stockholm International Forum on the Holocaust, 45
Stockholm Programme, 369–70
"stolen land" theme, 58, 60, 62
Stony Brook University, 176
Stop the War Coalition/movement (UK), 315, 316, 317, 325–26, 328, 329
Storch, Beatrix von, 271–72
Stork, Joel, 50, 56
Strauß, Franz Josef, 271
Strawson, John, 82
Stroehlein, Andrew, 62
"structural genocide" term of Wolfe, 90
Students for Justice in Palestine (SJP), 141, 150, 152, 154, 167, 176, 177
Studies in Antisemitism journal, x
study-abroad programs in Israel, 116, 149, 151
Süddeutsche Zeitung, 289, 292, 297, 301, 303
"super-Others," 226, 229n34
supersessionism (also known as replacement theology), 44, 61, 78–79
Supreme Muslim Council, 348
Surasky, Cecilie, 114–15
Swarthmore College, 148
swastikas, 35, 37, 142, 143, 146, 151, 173
Swedish government, 253
SWR Worldwide, 159
syllogism, denial by, 229n28
symbols/images associated with antisemitism, 12, 44, 46. *See also specific symbols, including* swastikas
Synthesis of the Doctrine of Race (Evola), 100
Syria, 276

Szekler ethnic group, 255
Szombat (website), 260

Tageszeitung, 293, 297, 301, 303
Taglit-Birthright Israel, 120–22
Taharanut/purity (Five Ts of campus antisemitism), 158–59, 175–77
Taji-Farouki, Suha, 347, 356
Tal, Uriel, 342n29
Tapia, Blanca, 11
Tayyib, al-Azhar Ahmad al-, 353
technology's role in transmission of antisemitism, 171
Teichtal, Yehuda, 288
Temple, destruction of the, 344
Temple Mount in Jerusalem, 352
tenets of antisemitism, 140–41
terrorist attacks against Jewish institutions, 374
Thatcher, Margaret, 314
theocratic extremism, rise of, 2
Title VI protections of Civil Rights Act (1964), 185–86, 188–89, 195–97, 199, 200, 201, 204
Tlaib, Rashida, 160
Todd, Emmanuel, 220
Tomlinson, Hugh, 10, 13–15, 17, 20, 28, 29, 31, 33
Traditionalism (Perennial Philosophy), 96–107; allure of, to right-wing movement, 107; and Bannon, 96, 102, 105, 106, 112n77; defined, 97; and Dugin, 96, 102–5, 106; and Evola, 96, 98–102, 104, 105, 106; and fascism, 106; and Guénon, 96, 97–99, 100, 101, 104, 106
Traditionalist Workers Party, 105
Training against Hate Crimes for Law Enforcement (TAHCLE), 374
Transgression (Five Ts of campus antisemitism), 158, 167–70
Transmission (Five Ts of campus antisemitism), 158, 171–73
Traore, Kobili, 221–22
Treaty of Trianon (1920), 255
Treaty on the Functioning of the EU (2007), 369
Treblinka extermination camp, 236, 237
Tree of Life Synagogue shootings in Pittsburgh, 1, 62, 137, 151, 219, 277

Trom, Danny, 78, 214, 215
Trump (Five Ts of campus antisemitism), 158, 170–71
Trump, Donald: and alt-right, 160, 170–71; anti-Trump rallies of JVP, 119; on Jerusalem as capital of Israel, 345, 353–54; and Netanyahu, 170
Truth (Five Ts of campus antisemitism), 158, 173–75
Tuchman, Aryeh, 290–91
Tufts University, 172

Ukraine, 1, 103
Umarji, Sheikh Osman, 166
Umm al-Fahm, 352
Understanding the "Nazi Card" (EISCA, 2009), 32
UNESCO, 45, 375
UNGA Resolution (1975), 58
UNICEF, 47
United Hungarian Israelite Faith Community (EMIH), 259
United Kingdom (UK), 325–40; assaults on Jews in, 1; and BBC, 321, 327; and Brexit, xiv; Jewish voting patterns in, 314, 326–27; and Mear One's "New World Order" mural, 317–18, 338; prevalence of antisemitism in, 313, 330; and racism as related to antisemitism, 330–32. *See also* Corbyn, Jeremy; Labour Party (UK)
United Nations (UN): and definition of antisemitism by IHRA, 45, 47, 63; Durban Conference (UN, 2001), xi, 47, 52–53, 56, 58, 59; harassment of Israel, 46–47; "Zionism is racism" resolution (1975), 47
United Nations Commission of Investigation (COI), 61
United Nations Durban Conference, 47
United Nations Human Rights Council (UNHRC): and accusations of human rights violations by Israel, 45; blacklist published by, 57; and HRW's accusations of war crimes, 53–55; and Permanent Agenda Item 7, 67n57; report on Gaza campaign (2008–9), 18; and working definition of antisemitism, 47
United Nations Office of the High Commissioner of Human Rights, 65n23

United Nations Relief and Works Agency (UNRWA), 47
United States: acculturation/assimilation of Jews in, 76–77, 80; assaults on Jews in, 1; circumcision controversy in, 307n38; Dugin on, 103, 104; hate crimes in, 1; and Israel, 28, 334; Labour Party members' perceptions of, 316; police exchange programs with Israel, 123; police shootings of African Americans in, 122; political polarization in, xiv, 177, 185; racial tensions in, 119, 122, 125, 137
United States Academic and Cultural Boycott of Israel, 116
United States Commission on Civil Rights, 11
United States Committee on the Academic and Cultural Boycott of Israel, 149
United States Congress, 160
United States Department of Education's Office of Civil Rights (OCR), 185–88, 190, 195, 197, 201
United States Department of State, 11, 39, 46, 186, 206n20
United States Holocaust Memorial Museum, 62, 232
United States Supreme Court, 140, 201, 203, 204
Universal Declaration of Human Rights, 49
University of California, Berkeley, 143
University of California, Davis, 142–43, 151, 154
University of California, Irvine, 152–53, 154, 166
University of California, Los Angeles, 142, 154, 176
University of California, Riverside, 154
University of California, San Diego, 188
University of California, Santa Barbara, 143, 148
University of California, Santa Cruz, 143
University of California Regents, 139, 143, 151–52
University of Illinois, 150
University of La Rochelle, 224
University of Michigan, 151
University of Minnesota, 146
University of Southampton, 38
University of Tennessee, Knoxville, 151

Un temps pour Haïr (Weitzmann), 221–22
Ussishkin, David, 353

Valls, Manuel, 227n1
Vanguard America, 149
Van Zile, Dexter, 114
Vashem, Yad, 245
vengeance theme, 60–62
Vennesson, Pascal, 50
Veracini, Lorenzo, 87, 88
Veritas Institute, 254
victimization, 226, 229n34
Victims Directive (2012), 369
Vilkomerson, Rebecca, 115, 124, 125
Vilnius conference (2013), 373, 375
violence against Jews: and conceptual model of antisemitism, *195*; Crystal Night, 206n25; and definition of antisemitism by IHRA, 191; in France, 217–18, 219–20, 223; increases in incidents of, ix, xiii; language condoning/inciting, 191; and motivations of violent actors, 223; and new antisemitism, 45; by radical Islamists, 213; terrorist attacks, 374; and Title VI protections of Civil Rights Act (1964), 196–97; unreported/underreported, 1, 373; and visibility of Jews in France, 213–14. *See also* Holocaust
virtuous antisemitism, 212, 224–27
visibility of Jews in France, 213–14
Volkov, Shulamit, 338, 343n32

Wailing Wall crisis (1929), 345, 347–48
Walker, Jacqui, 341n14
Waltzer, Kenneth, 126, 137–54
Walzer, Michael, 229n28
war, attempts to associate Israel with, 24
"war crimes" of Israel, 48, 53–55, 56
Ward, Eric K., 146, 160–61
Warsaw Ghetto of Poland, 239
Wasserstein, Bernard, 350
Wasserstrom, Steven, 108n23
Weber, Max, 91
Webman, Esther, 344–61
Weir, Alison, 123–26
Weitzman, Mark, 96–107
Weitzmann, Marc, 221–22
Weizsäcker, Richard von, 270
Welby, Justin, 206n29

Weller, Benjamin, 228n21
Wellesley College, 173
West Bank, 24, 121, 122, 263n10
western Europe, antisemitism in, 263n10
Whine, Michael, 367–79
"white identity" and the alt-right, 160
white nationalism/nationalists: about, 160–61; and alt-lite movement, 161; and alt-right, 160; antisemitism at core of, 146; rise of, xi; and Spencer's claim as "white Zionist," 170–71; and "Unite the Right" rally in Charlottesville, 161
"whiteness" of Jews, perceived, 76–81, 125, 163–64
white supremacism/supremacists, 62–63; and alt-lite movement, 161; and alt-right, 160; and Jewish Voice for Peace, 114–15; NWSA statement on, 165; off-campus sources of, 172; propaganda of, 137, 172; recruitment on college campuses, 149; rise of, xi; and "Unite the Right" rally in Charlottesville, 161
Whitson, Sarah Leah, 50, 56, 57, 58, 59, 60, 62
"Why Populism?" (Gauland), 274–75
Wiesel, Elie, 34
Wistrich, Robert, 32, 46–47, 145, 206n25, 263n10
Wolfe, Patrick, 88, 90
Women's March for the Nation of Islam, 165
Words into Action project, 375, 378
World War II, ignorance of younger generations regarding, xiii
Wulffen, Erich, 295

X, Malcolm, 172–73

Yadlin, Rivka, 359
Yad Vashem, 259–60
Yakira, Elhanan, 23
"yellow vest" movement in France, 214–15
Yiannopoulos, Milo, 169, 176
Yom Kippur, 119

Zanat, 'Abd al-Mun'im Abu, 358
Zawadzki, Paul, 223
Zeid Ra'ad Al Hussein, 57
Zeskind, Leonard, 174
Zick, Andreas, 282, 289

Zimmermann, Christoph, 301
Ziobro, Zbigniew, 243
Zionism: and Al-Awda, 124; and alt-right, 170–71; and ban on land sales to Zionists, 349; British Jews self-identifying as Zionists, 35; and campus antisemitism, 176; and colonial-settler characterization of Israel, 81–86; Elia's comparison of fascism to, 63; and feminism, 166; and Hungary's Orbán regime, 251; and Jewish Voice for Peace, 113; progressive critique of, 168; and right-wing politics, 170–71; Weir's criticisms of, 124
Zionist Occupied Government (ZOG), 174
Ziyad, Ziyad Abu, 354
Zuroff, Efraim, 235

Alvin H. Rosenfeld holds the Irving M. Glazer Chair in Jewish Studies at Indiana University and serves as Founding Director of the university's Institute for the Study of Contemporary Antisemitism. Previously, he created and for thirty years directed Indiana University's Borns Jewish Studies Program. He is author of numerous books and articles on the Holocaust, antisemitism, and Jewish literature, including *A Double Dying: Reflections on Holocaust Literature*, *Imagining Hitler*, and *The End of the Holocaust*. He is editor of *Resurgent Antisemitism: Global Perspectives*, *Deciphering the New Antisemitism*, and *Anti-Zionism and Antisemitism: The Dynamics of Delegitimization*, among other works. In 2018, Indiana University awarded him the President's Medal, the university's highest award, in recognition of his many distinguished contributions to scholarship and leadership.

www.ingramcontent.com/pod-product-compliance
Lightning Source LLC
Chambersburg PA
CBHW030516230426
43665CB00010B/635